To Shirley,

With much love
+ best wishes,

Nick

April 1996

Technology and Industrial Progress

To my parents
and my sisters

Technology and Industrial Progress

The Foundations of Economic Growth

G.N. von Tunzelmann
Reader in the Economics of Science and Technology
Science Policy Research Unit
University of Sussex

Edward Elgar
Aldershot, UK – Brookfield, US

Published by
Edward Elgar Publishing Limited
Gower House
Croft Road
Aldershot
Hants GU11 3HR
UK

Edward Elgar Publishing Company
Old Post Road
Brookfield
Vermont 05036
US

British Library Cataloguing in Publication Data

Tunzelmann, G.N. Von
Technology and Industrial Progress:
Foundations of Economic Growth
I. Title
338.064

Library of Congress Cataloguing in Publication Data

Von Tunzelmann, G.N.
Technology and industrial progress: the foundations of economic growth / G.N. von Tunzelmann.
Includes bibliographical references and indexes.
1. Economic growth. 2. Technological innovations—Economic aspects. 3. Industrialization. I. Title.
HD82.V62 1995
338'.064—dc20 95–10745
CIP

ISBN 1 85898 174 3

Printed and bound in Great Britain by
Hartnolls Limited, Bodmin, Cornwall

Contents

Tables and Figures

Tables

Figures

Abbreviations

(NB: Some of these acronyms have changed over time. The form given is as in the text.)

ABB	Asea Brown Boveri (Sweden/Switzerland) (1987--)
AC	Alternating Current
AEC	Atomic Energy Commission (USA) (1946-1973)
AEG	Allgemeine Elektrizitäts Gesellschaft (Germany) (1887--)
AIC	Advanced Industrial Country
APEC	Asia-Pacific Economic Co-operation (1989--)
AT&T	American Telephone and Telegraph (USA) (1885/1900--)
BASF	Badische Anilin- und Soda-Fabrik (Germany) (1861--)
BBC	British Broadcasting Corporation (UK) (1922--)
BNDE	Banco Nacional de Desenvolvimento Econômico (National Bank for Economic Development) (Brazil) (1952--)
BP	British Petroleum (UK) (1954--) (previously Anglo-Iranian)
CAD	Computer-Aided Design
CAM	Computer-Aided Manufacture
CAPES	Conselho de Aperfeiçoamento de Pessoal do Ensino Superior (Council for the Perfection of Human Resources at University Level) (Brazil)
CEO	Chief Executive Officer
CIM	Computer-Integrated Manufacturing
CIMA	Chartered Institute of Management Accountants
CMEA	Council of Mutual Economic Assistance (East Europe) (1949--)
CNC	Computer Numerical Control
CNPq	Conselho Nacional de [Pesquisa] Desenvolvimento Cientifico e Tecnologico (National Council for [Research] Scientific and Technological Development (Brazil)
COCOM	Co-Ordinating Committee for Multilateral Export Controls (1949--)
CONICET	(National Council for Science and Technology) (Argentina) (1958--)
CPE	Centrally Planned Economy

CREES	Centre for Research in East European Studies (University of Birmingham, UK)
DC	Direct Current
DNC	Direct Numerical Control
DoD	Department of Defense (USA)
DRAM	Dynamic Random Access Memory
DSIR	Department of Scientific and Industrial Research (UK) (1916--)
DWT	Dead-Weight Tonnage
ECLA	Economic Commission for Latin America (1948--)
EEC	European Economic Community (1957--)
ERSO	Electronic Research and Service Organization (Taiwan) (1973--)
FDI	Foreign Direct Investment
FINEP	Financiadora de Estudos e Projetos (Agency for Financing Studies and Projects) (Brazil) (1973--)
FL	Foreign Licensing
FMS	Flexible Manufacturing System
FSU	Former Soviet Union
FTC	Fair Trade Commission (Japan) (1947--)
FTC	Federal Trade Commission (USA) (1914--)
FYP	Five-Year Plan
GATT	General Agreement on Tariffs and Trade (1948--)
GDP	Gross Domestic Product
GM	General Motors (USA) (1908--)
GNE	Gross National Expenditure
GNP	Gross National Product
HHI	Hyundai Heavy Industries
HQ	Headquarters
IBJ	Industrial Bank of Japan (Japan) (1900--)
IBM	International Business Machines (USA) (1924--)
IC	Integrated Circuit (1962--)
ICI	Imperial Chemical Industries (UK) (1926--)
ICOT	Institute for New Generation Computer Technology (Japan) (1982--)
ICT	Information and Communication Technology
IMF	International Monetary Fund (1946--)
IPR	Intellectual Property Right
ISI	Import-Substituting Industrialization
IT	Information Technology
ITC	Indigenous technological capability
JDB	Japan Development Bank (Japan) (1951--)
JIT	Just-in-Time

JV	Joint Venture
JVC	Victor Company of Japan (Japan) (1927--)
KAIST	Korean Advanced Institute of Science and Technology (S. Korea) (1980--)
LF	Large Firm
LIC	Less-Industrialized Country
LSI	Large-Scale Integration
MAN	Maschinenfabrik Augsburg-Nürnberg (Germany)
MCC	Microelectronics and Computer Technologies Corporation (USA) (1982--)
MEG	Modern Economic Growth
MERIT	Maastricht Economic Research Institute on Innovation and Technology (University of Limburg, Netherlands) (1988--)
MES	Minimum Efficient Scale
MIT	Massachusetts Institute of Technology (USA) (1861--)
MITI	Ministry of International Trade and Industry (Japan) (1949--)
MNC	Multinational Company
MTBF	Mean Time Between Failures
NAFTA	North American Free Trade Agreement (1993--)
NASA	National Aeronautics and Space Agency (USA) (1958--)
NCMT	Numerically Controlled Machine Tool
NEC	Nippon Electric Company (Japan) (1899--)
NIC	Newly Industrializing Country
NIESR	National Institute of Economic and Social Research (UK)
NIH	Not Invented Here
NSI	National System of Innovation
NTBF	New Technology-Based Firm
OCC	Organic Composition of Capital (Marx)
ODM	Own Design and Manufacture
OECD	Organization for Economic Co-operation and Development (1961--)
OEEC	Organization for European Economic Co-operation (1948-1961)
OEM	Original Equipment Manufacturer
POSCO	Pohang Iron and Steel Company (S. Korea) (1968--)
QSE	Qualified Scientists and Engineers
R&D	Research and Development
RA	Research Association
RCA	Radio Corporation of America (USA) (1919--)
ROI	Rate of Return on Investment
S&T	Science and Technology
SIC	Standard Industrial Classification

SMF	Small and Medium-sized Firm
SPRU	Science Policy Research Unit (University of Sussex, UK) (1966--)
TFP	Total Factor Productivity
TQC	Total Quality Control
UNESCO	United Nations Economic, Social and Cultural Organization (1946--)
VLSI	Very Large-Scale Integration

Preface

This is intended as the first of a series of surveys of the long-term role of technology. Later works are intended to cover more exhaustively the technologies themselves, the role of government, and the roles of labour and capital.

Specific thanks for assistance with the text are owed to Steve Broadberry, John Cantwell, Carol Dyhouse, James Foreman-Peck, Les Hannah, Joel Mokyr, Slavo Radosevic, and especially Keith Pavitt, plus the exceptional help of the two anonymous referees appointed by Edward Elgar; all of whom read and commented upon parts or all of earlier drafts of the typescript. Remaining infelicities are my own fault. More general intellectual debts are acknowledged throughout the text in the usual manner, but it is only right to mention here those who have profoundly influenced my somewhat tortuous academic career. In the field of economics I could mention, among many others: Bert Brownlie, Michael Hudson, Frank Tay, Peter Hampton, Joe Stiglitz, and all the department at the University of Canterbury; Peter Hammond, Jim Mirrlees, Peter Sinclair, Roger Witcomb and many others at Nuffield College, Oxford; Tony Atkinson, Aubrey Silberston, Mervyn King, John Llewellyn and the students at St John's College, Cambridge. In economic history the debts are larger and geographically broader, including (in roughly chronological order) Graham Miller, Charlie Kindleberger, Bob Fogel, Peter Temin, Paul David, Jeff Williamson, Max Hartwell, Robin Matthews, Gary Hawke, John Tyce, Hrothgar (Sir John) Habakkuk, Don McCloskey, Peter Mathias, Stan Engerman, Nate Rosenberg, Roderick Floud, Charles Feinstein, Brian Mitchell, Phyllis Deane, Doug North, Donald Coleman, Nick Crafts, Jane Humphries, Patrick O'Brien, Joel Mokyr, and Maxine Berg. And in my most recent reincarnation in innovation studies I could not overlook Chris Freeman, Stan Metcalfe, Dick Nelson, Keith Pavitt, Margaret Sharp, Pari Patel, Slavo Radosevic, Mike Hobday, Martin Bell, William Walker, Bö Carlsson, Öve Granstrand, Jan Fagerberg, Keith Smith, Tine Bruland, Bent Dalum, Bengt-Åke Lundvall, Luc Soete, Bart Verspagen, François Chesnais, Marc Willinger, Patrick Llerena, and almost too many to mention in Italy (not least Fabio Arcangeli, Daniele Archibugi, Fiorenza Belussi, Roberto Camagni, Mario Cimoli, Giovanni Dosi, Massimo Egidi, Franco

Malerba, Luigi Marengo, Enrico Santarelli, Roberto Scazzieri, Roberto Simonetti, Sepi Tattara, and Salvo Torrisi). The lecture series organized for me at the Università di Padova in 1988 by Eugenio Benedetti and Arrigo Opocher effectively launched the work that has led to this book; my only regret after a marvellously hospitable stay in Padua is that my response has taken so long. What has succeeded in getting it together is the lecture series I have shared with Keith Pavitt at SPRU in the autumn terms of 1992 to 1994. It is to all my colleagues in SPRU and above all to my doctoral and masters students, who have taught me and forced me to think about so much, that my deepest intellectual debts are owed. I am also greatly indebted to other participants in networks (like EUNETIC) which have multiplied the perspectives from which I have been required to assess industrialization and technological progress, and in similar fashion to my co-editors on *Industrial and Corporate Change*: David Teece, Nathan Rosenberg, Giovanni Dosi and Giulio Sapelli.

These have to be set alongside the huge debts incurred on the social side. Carol, Alex, and Eugénie have become accustomed over the past year or more to my disappearing to the computer whenever opportunity allowed, and often when their own needs of time and academic study were just as great. The book is, however, dedicated to an earlier generation of domestic debts – my parents, Maurice and Valerie, and my sisters, Adrienne and Catherine. In addition to their tolerance of any egoistical work obsession, which must have been all too frequent, they were also instrumental – along with their spouses Peter and Alan – in setting up discussions with the New Zealand Treasury and the Ministry of Research, Science and Technology (MORST) in September 1992, at the time of my parents' golden wedding, which were decisive in orienting me towards policy issues. The research agenda suggested by these discussions will take me much longer to fulfil.

The task of preparing the camera-ready version of the typescript – which turned into many versions – fell to my secretary, Janet French, who among a myriad of other talents has the idiosyncratic ability to decipher my own handwriting to me. The frequent rewrites were met by her unfailing good humour. Finally, my warmest thanks to all the staff at Edward Elgar, including David Clark, Dymphna Evans, Julie Leppard, Hilary Quinn and Edward himself, for getting the typescript into publication.

Nick von Tunzelmann
Brighton 1995

1. Introduction

The guiding aim of this work is to synthesize and interpret the patterns of industrialization past and present. I have termed this 'industrial progress', not out of any Panglossian view that industrialization is always for the best – a view which I most certainly do not share. Technology and industry have not uncommonly led to disastrous social outcomes. The book instead concentrates on the causes and nature of industrialization, rather than its consequences.

Despite extensive scholarship and an immense amount of accumulated practical experience, not many generalizations have yet emerged about the nature of industrialization, beyond the patently obvious. One important reason for this is that the findings have been too scattered among studies of particular technologies, particular industries, or particular countries, with the result that their broader implications have not been grasped outside. To generalize from them involves interpreting them first, which is a major object of the book. A work of synthesis such as this must depend heavily on the insights of the studies thus consulted, and I am ruefully aware of the much greater number of studies (especially those not in the English language) which I have overlooked. I cannot pass without acknowledging inspiration to those who have earlier trodden this path of comparative studies of industrialization, including Joel Mokyr (1990), Michael Best (1990), William Lazonick (1991) and a number of pan-European studies noted in Chapter 5 of this book.

Although the book is in large part synthesis, it also provides a more personal interpretation of the varying experiences countries have had with industrial progress. This interpretation comes from an amalgam of my own backgrounds, first theoretically in economics, later empirically in history (especially quantitative economic history or 'cliometrics'), and most recently in the mixed theoretical–empirical arena of innovation studies. Its motivation comes from a deep disenchantment I have felt with the way growth and development, and the role of technology in that development, have been traditionally accounted for, either theoretically or empirically. There are hopeful signs that this situation is beginning to change at least at a theoretical level.[1] Two such developments are particularly relevant here: one is the effort now being undertaken by the theoretical literature to *endogenize* technological change (e.g. in the 'new growth theory'); the second is the emphasis on *varieties* of experience (e.g. in 'evolutionary theory'). But even this literature is still short on 'stylized facts', and the very nature of these welcome theoretical advances makes such a lack at the empirical end ever more serious.

This book cannot, of course, claim to be a complete account of either technology or industrialization. It says relatively little about the technologies themselves, as it is addressed to how they relate to their wider context. Instead it concentrates on the role of *firms* and their contributions to the industrial progress of *countries*. A complete picture of industrialization would require more attention to elements such as government policy formation, or banking, or trade unions – elements which here remain as essentially exogenous to individual firms, though they deserve study at full length in subsequent work.

The remainder of this chapter aims to establish the methodological and analytical framework of the book. Those readers who are not concerned with such a credo, or who are unfamiliar with the economic jargon, can skip to Chapter 2.

I: THE ROLE OF FIRMS

The main objective of this book is thus to develop the micro-foundations of macro-level growth and development behaviour. These micro-foundations are sought at the level of the *firm* or enterprise, rather than at the level of the *industry*.[2] This emphasis on the firm follows both more classical thinking (outlined in Chapter 2 below) and recent views emerging from the 'evolutionary' school of economists – the basic reason for it here being that it is at the level of the firm that decision-making normally takes place.[3]

To see this, we have to begin by defining the role of the firm. Why do firms exist? Coase won the Nobel Prize in economics in 1991 for his

1 See, for example, the recent work surveyed in Fagerberg *et al.* 1994.

2 The industry level is used in the somewhat similar-looking approach of Porter (1990) and his 'diamond'. Porter comes from the older 'Structure–Conduct–Performance' school of industrial economics, in which industry structure is the main determinant of firm behaviour. He now accepts that industry structure can be changed by firm performance as well as the reverse, but continues to regard the (product-defined) industry as the primary issue.

3 An illuminating survey of current schools of thought in industrial economics is given by Teece *et al.* 1990.

attempt to ask and resolve this seemingly innocuous question.[4] In the argument of Oliver Williamson, who has explored this notion farthest, firms exist because (managerial) 'hierarchies' are often cheaper ways of achieving certain outcomes than relying on markets. Specifically, hierarchies will be adopted when they (rather than markets) minimize the 'governance costs' of particular sets of business operations. Following Coase, these costs can be divided into 'transaction costs' when they arise between firms and 'management costs' when they occur within firms. Governance takes the form of a hierarchy in order to curb 'opportunism', i.e. the temptation that Williamson perceives as endemic in human nature to mistrust and deceive. He accepts that trust and reputation are important in business, but contends that his approach is 'not vitiated' by this[5] – this is disingenuous. The notion of decision-making through hierarchies creates additional problems when we turn to the variety of experiences of industrialization in later chapters of this book, but these are ignored for the moment. The Coase–Williamson view is essentially a modified neoclassical one in which the solution which minimizes the static costs, internal and external to the firm, will be adopted. The approach is often used to clarify the decision as to whether to 'make or buy', i.e. produce a good within a firm or purchase it from another producer; but this involves considering costs of production (for making) as well as governance.

In the transaction–cost approach, all cost structures are assumed to be knowable in principle (there is no real 'learning' in this approach, though there is sequential decision-making[6]), and the information that needs to be acquired is finite, though probably beyond the bounds of an individual decision-maker to know it all.[7] Production issues are in effect taken as givens, and all too often it is supposed that production costs differ little between firms and are exogenous, so that governance costs become the main issue.[8] In practice, cases can readily be found in which changes in production (greater specialization, etc.) bring about new sets of transaction costs or management costs. In this fashion it is possible to make the transaction–costs view of the firm more dynamic;[9] but the interpretation of firms offered in this book represents a more radical departure from such norms.

---

4 Cf. Williamson and Winter 1993.

5 Williamson 1975, p. 108; see also his discussion of Japanese firms in Williamson 1985, pp. 120–23.

6 Williamson refers frequently to learning by doing, but usually to compare the situation before and after, i.e. as a comparative static device rather than as a learning process.

7 Fransman 1994.

8 Demsetz, in Williamson and Winter 1993.

9 See Langlois 1992; Nooteboom 1992; and p. 266 below.

The point that no individual can know all that he/she needs to be informed about ('bounded rationality') is accepted here, but the present views lean towards recent 'evolutionary' opinion which favours learning-based notions of production and distribution behaviour, in which the relevant information is unbounded. By way of their learning processes firms accumulate 'knowledge' that is specific to them, and usually tacit.[10] This accumulation of production knowledge (knowhow) leads to a dynamic rather than static view of economic decision-making. It is the production process rather than the transaction which is central to the present analysis. Production is thought of as being *anterior to* exchange activity. By comparison, in the transaction–costs view, exchange is usually regarded as anterior to production, e.g. through drawing up 'contracts' for employment and the like, or through firms responding adaptively to market changes.[11] In practice, production may well be influenced by changes in exchange relationships (rising prices, etc.), so that in a properly dynamic model the causation will run in both directions. For example, the standard economics of technology tends to take factor prices such as wages as 'givens', for instance through high wages creating incentives for labour-saving technological change. Here I begin with the opposite view, of seeing high wages more as the *outcome* of high levels of technical efficiency in production, rather like the classical economists' notion of an 'economy of high wages'. But the full classical model of the 'circular flow', outlined at the beginning of the next chapter, demonstrates that each affects the other: high wages are both a cause and a consequence of high productive efficiency, so that a complete analysis would consider these mutual interactions. In this manner, we shall see how, for countries like South Korea studied in Chapter 11, rapidly rising productive efficiency has led to higher wages, which have squeezed profit margins in labour-intensive activities and thus created pressures for further gains in efficiency.

II: PRODUCTION, KNOWLEDGE AND INFORMATION

The 'production first' emphasis in this book carries the implication that the major influence upon production is the knowledge base accumulated over time by the producing unit, i.e. the firm.[12] Knowledge in this sense is the cumulation of learning processes, studied at greater length in Chapter 2, which can result from either past production experience or the acquisition

---

10 Dosi *et al.* 1988. Williamson (1975) calls this 'language limits'.

11 Lazonick 1991, p. 214.

12 Hohenberg 1967, ch. 3; Freeman 1982, p. 4.

of new information by study etc. In contrast to the traditional economic view which equates information with knowledge,[13] we here regard them as essentially different – information represents the sum total of 'messages' generated in the world at large, and is in principle marketable;[14] whereas knowledge is generally not marketable, being embodied in the very various learning processes of different individuals or firms (of course, this knowledge can be used to generate further information, which may indeed be marketable).[15]

In this sense, we can give a different answer to why it is that firms exist, because in the first place they are knowledge-accumulating institutions. Limitations on the ability of individuals to accumulate knowledge – and even more, to utilize that knowledge in actual production – thus help explain why firms emerge. What the firm is able to learn from the myriad of messages flying around the world will depend crucially on the amount of knowledge it has already accumulated. A scientific paper on, say, a new advance in biotechnological processes for producing insulin will mean much more to an enterprise which already undertakes such production than to one in a different industry. Thus the value of particular items of information to a particular firm depends upon its existing knowledge base – contrary to what one might at first imagine, the more the firm already knows of related kinds, the higher the value the message is likely to have. Rosenberg quotes Boswell's *Life of Johnson*: 'Knowledge is of two kinds. We know a subject ourselves, or we know where we can find information upon it'.[16] Knowledge and information are not so much identical as strongly complementary.

In accumulating production knowledge, the firm generally has an advantage over an individual. This is more than just a question of the greater scale on which a firm operates. The knowledge required for production (and subsequent exchange) is such as to involve a *transformation* in existing knowledge bases. Production capabilities are wider than technical capabilities.[17] On the one side, the firm may be able to access information on a range of technologies relevant to its production circumstances. On the other side, it may be able to obtain a certain amount

---

13 Williamson coins the term 'information impactedness' to describe both information asymmetries and tacit knowledge.

14 In reality, as Arrow (1962a) showed, pricing information in a market usually raises substantial problems, e.g. because of 'opportunism'.

15 Such sales of information can generate increasing returns, because the supplier's own stock of knowledge is not directly depleted by them, cf. the discussion of 'new growth theory' in Chapter 3 below.

16 Rosenberg 1994, p. 12; also Penrose 1959/1980, pp. 53–4. Note also the conclusions of Gibbons and Johnston (1974) regarding the benefits of university education.

17 Scazzieri 1993, p. 8.

of market information about demands for, or competing supplies of, its product(s). Both of these may be used to augment its own knowledge base about technologies and products. What occurs within firms is a transformation of the knowledge about technology into the knowledge about products. This is their unique contribution to production. At one extreme, scientific knowledge develops according to the ways in which scientific disciplines are organized – physics, chemistry, biology, etc. At the other extreme, products are arrayed according to product market structures – types of computers, buildings, clothing, etc., sold to consumers. Between the two extremes, production processes pull together certain items of disciplinary-based knowledge (which may come from more than one field) in ways appropriate to the particular product – the components required for a computer and how they function, the materials for a building or item of clothing and their properties, and so on. Even if the firm simply imitates other firms in all information relating to products, it must still have knowledge of how the components are suitably assembled into a marketable computer (etc.), and this is included in the knowledge translation element being emphasized here.

In contrast, markets may be very efficient for conveying and economizing upon certain types of information, as advocates such as Hayek (1945) have argued. The informational content of prices, however, is probably more limited than Hayek implied, and above all it is information that they convey *rather than* knowledge. Moreover, to fulfil the objectives that Hayek sees prices as doing requires that market prices are associated one-to-one with particular quantities. Production knowledge, on the contrary, gains much of its uniqueness and possible competitive strength from the idiosyncratically *different* ways in which individual firms convert technological knowhow into product knowhow. Whereas the transaction–costs view emphasizes transfers of products (goods and services),[18] this perspective considers transfers of knowledge. The transaction–costs view assumes that the alternative to such internal knowledge flows is to transact through markets, which may be more expensive but in principle feasible. The view here is that such feasibility is rather uncommon. Transaction-cost interpretations of knowledge flows between as well as within companies, which place greatest emphasis on 'opportunism' (i.e. distrust), at present strike one as exceedingly unsatisfactory.

18 Chandler 1990, p. 17.

III: A DEMAND/SUPPLY SCHEMA – TECHNOLOGIES AND PRODUCTS

It follows that knowledge of the technology alone is not sufficient to produce the products in an efficient way. The most obvious way of demonstrating this is to point out that most individual products involve a range of technologies – think of a domestic appliance or a motor vehicle. Conversely, many technologies are applicable to a range of products (more will be made of this in Chapter 8). To characterize the individual firm, we must consider the forces which account for its range of both technologies and products. Table 1.1 attempts a schema that is based on the age-old economic issues of demand and supply. Unlike the orthodox economist's model, which concentrates on the demand for and supply of products, there is a parallel format for the technologies. It has to be said that the patterns in regard to technologies are much less clearly drawn in the literature than they are for products, so there is scope for some disagreement about where the particular aspects should be located. Whether we see the influences on technological change as being demand-led or supply-led – or some combination of the two – rests rather substantially on the classifications to demand or supply adopted here. It is important to stress that the viewpoint being taken is that of the individual firm.

Table 1.1: Domestic demand and supply from the viewpoint of the firm

	TECHNOLOGIES		*PRODUCTS*
DEMAND	Firm Size, Scale and Scope Derived Product Demand	←	Market Size Income Distribution, Tastes, Prices
SUPPLY (Exogenous)	Focusing Devices Induced Innovation S&T Breakthroughs	←	Factor Prices
SUPPLY (Endogenous)	Technological Accumulation	→	Costs of Production

The demand for the firm's products follows immediately from the standard demand function of conventional economics, resting on market size, income distribution, relative prices and consumer tastes. All are assumed to be outside its control (exogenous), except the price of the firm's own product(s). The latter can be affected by the firm's costs of production, shown as one of the determinants of product supply conditions. Product supply is also affected by the costs of inputs, which are also regarded in the mean time as beyond the firm's own control. That is, in economics jargon, the firm is assumed to be a price-taker in markets for the factors of production.

Now let us examine the somewhat more complex pattern for technologies. Corresponding to the market–size determinant of product demand is a firm–size determinant of technology demand. This has been given particular attention in the literature on diffusion.[19] Size, assessed as level of output or investment of the firm, ought to be distinguished from 'scale' – the number of *processes* utilized or the intensity of use of those processes – and 'scope' – the number of *products* produced.[20] Scale and scope can both be increased without *necessarily* increasing firm size, and all three have strong implications for technology demand. However, 'demand-pull' of the kind normally supposed in the innovation literature follows indirectly from market demands for the products.[21] This is represented in the table as a 'derived demand' for technologies, arising out of their connection with the associated products. Pure 'demand-pull' influences require that it is a burst of product demand *alone* which accounts for the innovations. In this book I dwell extensively on 'time-saving' technical changes, i.e. innovations that allow a firm to produce its products faster, which often are quite close to this ideal type of 'demand-pull'. Scale and scope are likely to be closely related to such time savings.[22]

But many innovations often thought of as having originated in 'demand-pull' have supply-side determinants as well. The kinds of influences which have been labelled as 'exogenous supply' in Table 1.1 are sometimes quirky and include many which Rosenberg termed 'focusing devices',[23] and many which other economic historians have called 'bottlenecks' or 'imbalances'. They can be thought of as more general instances of what the economics literature refers to as 'induced innovation'. The latter usually considers a narrower range of imbalances, arising out of input costs. Much the most common assertion made here is that technological change may be biased towards 'labour-saving' – note that, in the economics literature, this implies a *relative* saving of labour as compared with any other factor inputs such as

19 E.g. Davies 1979.
20 Corsi 1991, ch. 3; Morroni 1992; Scazzieri 1993, *passim.*
21 Mowery and Rosenberg 1979.
22 Scazzieri 1993, pp. 219–23.
23 Rosenberg 1976, ch. 6.

capital.[24] The cause of such relative labour-saving is presumed to come from high labour costs, and in so far as these in turn stem from high wage rates, they are exogenous to the individual firm here, since it is being seen as a price-taker in factor markets. We can think of the wage level as being set by the overall demand versus supply of labour in the country as a whole.

At the level of the individual firm, such 'exogenous supply' influences may arise in at least three ways. One is through an existing disequilibrium (bottleneck), which remains unresolved at least for the time being, for example a continuing shortage of a certain raw material. A second is through the occurrence of exogenous events, as in Rosenberg's 'focusing devices' of strikes or wars as causes of labour-saving. A third may be regarded as a 'counterfactual' or 'expectational' disequilibrium: an imbalance (which could lie in either the economic or the technical aspects) which does not exert itself just at present, but which would arise were demand to grow, and put pressure on those inputs whose supply was most difficult to expand.[25] This last type clearly requires a demand as well as a supply component among the determinants.

A more obvious 'exogenous supply' influence follows from innovational breakthroughs developed elsewhere in the country's Science and Technology (S&T) system, or for that matter in other countries. For the firm, this represents technological 'imitation'. However, the emerging consensus in the economics of innovation literature is that such imitation is by no means costless for the imitating firm, and often involves heavy outlays of money and effort.[26] Thus this 'exogenous' source of supply, like the others, is likely to require some commensurate internal undertaking by the firm.

The endogenous supply determinants of technologies are those which lie within the firm's control. These are the outcome of 'technological accumulation', which is taken to be the growth of the firm's idiosyncratic technological knowledge, and represent the firm's individual actions (serendipity) or responses to the above-mentioned demand and supply pressures. This is accumulated through learning of the kinds explained at greater length in the next chapter, and includes formal Research and Development (R&D) conducted by the firm, but also substantial learning through informal means. Such endogenously generated technological accumulation reduces the firm's production costs and thus the supply prices for its products in the market. In this sense, the costs of production on the right-hand size of Table 1.1, as product supply determinants, might be thought of as 'derived supply'.

---

24 See Stoneman 1983 and references therein; also Chapters 4 and 6 below.

25 E.g. Fellner 1961; cf. Chapter 3 below.

26 Teece 1977; Cohen and Levinthal 1989; Bell and Pavitt 1993.

The size of an individual firm is constrained by its ability to borrow funds externally and/or accumulate and reinvest profits internally. It is also limited by managerial competences, size of product markets, etc. Broadening the firm's scale and scope, i.e. diversifying its range of processes and products, will depend on the costs of enlarging the knowledge base relating to technologies, products, or their linkages (processes etc.), relative to those from increased specialization in the existing areas. For any of these reasons, firms may link to other firms rather than trying to do everything themselves. In either way, *systems* of innovation have evolved.

IV: SYSTEMS OF INNOVATION AND PRODUCTION

It is obvious that certain firms may actually be in a position to influence any or all of the sources of change which for simplification are here taken to be exogenous to them; for example, a particular firm may succeed in a production breakthrough in a biotechnology product which alters the basic scientific thinking in the subject. To make the subject analytically tractable, we have to distinguish between exogenous and endogenous elements, at least as a first approximation. The 'exogenous' factors, both technical and economic, thus comprise the 'techno-economic environment' within which individual firms are assumed to have to operate at any point of time. It will be supposed that changes in this environment occur only slowly, perhaps only in the course of a 'long wave' of the kind introduced in Chapter 3 below. For simplicity, the environment will be assumed to function (and change) at a national level. Thus the S&T system can be described as the 'National System of Innovation' or NSI.[27] However, this is not the only 'national system' that is relevant to us. We also need to consider the national system for finance, for the organization of production, and so on (see Chapter 2 below). The sum total of all of these can be described as the 'National System of Production'. This represents the 'techno-economic environment' in a particular country. Such a National System of Production provides the context for the ways in which individual firms within the country can develop.

The National System of Innovation, or the National System of Production, is far more than a set of constraints. The significant contribution of the recent NSI literature has been to emphasize the range of positive opportunities provided by differing NSI arrangements. From what has already been said, it follows that the NSI is influenced to a large extent by

27 Lundvall 1992; Nelson 1993.

what takes place within the country's firms as a whole. By endogenously changing their circumstances through technological accumulation, firms may ultimately alter the national system itself.

Even more important in this perspective is the structure of firms in the economy as a whole, and the relationships among them. Some firms supply other firms with capital goods or raw materials, and those other firms in turn may be suppliers to yet other firms, or to final consumers. The extent of *vertical integration* reflects how far these linkages are consolidated within a particular firm, so that they become in principle part of the same decision-making process. The NSI literature has chosen to emphasize links that are *not* consolidated in this manner but take place between firms.

In some of the economies studied in later chapters, these linkages between firms involve little more than 'arm's–length' market transactions: firms selling (say) intermediate goods to other firms do so on the basis of the price/performance characteristics of their product, and they are free to change their suppliers or purchasers if prices or performances are unsatisfactory. However, in many cases we shall find that, even when transactions of this kind take place between firms, the relationship is rather stronger than is embodied in just a set of price/performance characteristics. Information may pass between the two of greater complexity than simply encapsulated in prices, and – even more important for us – the process of accumulating knowledge by either or both may be strongly influenced by these ultra-market linkages. Such linkages are often referred to in the NSI literature as 'user–producer' links. The theoretical problem such linkages raise is that they do not conform precisely to the characteristics of either pure 'markets' or pure 'hierarchies' (organizations) in the senses defined above, but have certain strands of both.[28] Efforts to squash such relationships into the transaction–costs approach to markets vs. hierarchies have not met with great success. But from the perspective offered here, which concentrates upon firms and other institutions (including markets) as learning mechanisms, their existence seems quite natural.

Inter-firm linkages may also arise 'horizontally', i.e. at the same stage of processing, without necessarily developing into a horizontally integrated firm. There is mounting evidence to suggest that a great deal of interchange of information and knowledge is likely to occur, even in supposedly very

28 Lundvall (1992, ch. 3) therefore refers to them as 'organized markets'. Such markets are quite different from the 'organized markets' referred to by Alfred Marshall (1919, p. 256). The latter imply strong formal institutional arrangements, exemplified by, say, the Stock Market. Marshall shows that such markets require highly standardized products, subject to rapid price fluctuations. The situation here, where the arrangements are mostly informal, is the opposite – unstandardized commodities and fairly stable prices.

competitive economies.[29] Horizontal links of this kind may take place directly among the firms themselves or be mediated through an agency, such as an industry-based research association. The former (and sometimes both) are likely to be especially strong when geographically concentrated into a local district. Such linkages will be given further consideration in Chapters 7 and 8 below. For the moment, we can note their role in helping to constitute the NSI.

The development of such vertical and horizontal linkages for knowledge accumulation gives rise to a possibly more benign view of collaboration than emerges from the conventional industrial organization literature.[30] An important reason for this attitude is that the latter considers industries as being structured simply on the basis of identical or very similar products. The left-hand column of Table 1.1 is effectively ignored. Horizontal linkages for sharing technologies and processes such as are accounted for here carry different implications from those for sharing product markets.

V: PRODUCT AND PROCESS INNOVATION

The technology and innovation studies literature places considerable emphasis on distinguishing between product innovation and process innovation. Within a firm the distinction between the product sphere and the process sphere is apparent enough. Between firms, or in vertically integrated firms, the distinction is more ambiguous. A product innovation for an *upstream* industry (say a new type of electric motor produced by an electrical engineering firm) may become a process innovation when installed in the industry next *downstream* (say a factory using that motor to drive its equipment). We need to consider the whole production stream, and the range of horizontal and vertical linkages. In the specific chapters below, upstream/downstream process links are contrasted with backward/forward product links. The former are based on capital goods connections – thus for the textiles industry, the textile producer is linked upwards to the textile machinery manufacturer, who in turn links further up to the machine tool manufacturer, etc. This is a quite distinct pattern from the backward/forward linkages arising through the progressive processing of the product (raw material to yarn, to cloth, to finished item). Both are unfortunately usually described as vertical linkages. It emerges that countries (or industries) could simultaneously be experiencing greater

29 See for instance the study of US steel minimills by von Hippel 1989.

30 E.g. from the Structure–Conduct–Performance model, as in Porter 1990.

vertical integration (consolidation in particular firms) in the product chain and greater vertical *dis*-integration in the process chain.[31]

An implication of the stress on process as much as product change is that the former is likely to be more readily promoted by knowledge sharing, whereas the latter may well be better advanced by competition of the more orthodox kind. Processes, it will be recalled, embody the transformation of technological knowledge into product-related knowledge. The idiosyncratic, firm-specific nature of this transformation indicates why vertical linkages should gain – mutually – from collaboration, e.g. the machinery manufacturer learning what the textile producer needed by way of equipment performance at the same time as the latter learned what kinds of equipment the former could provide. However, much the same applies to horizontal links, between firms at similar stages of the production process – many of the examples von Hippel[32] observed among American steel mills consisted of exchanges of equipment and even of labour (firms were observed to train employees of a 'rival' firm). The assumption here is that each party has something to gain from reciprocity, even if only temporarily. If the processes involved constitute a wider technical or economic system, then little is likely to be lost, either, from such sharing and spillovers ('interactive learning'). Competition may be more appropriate between products intended for final consumers, or in cases where the new processes are effectively stand-alone, non-systemic products (for example, a more efficient delivery van). The diffusion of such product innovations would then rest on the spread of *information* in the strict sense, and might well be accelerated by market pressures. But even product-based industry arrangements could often benefit from a degree of collaboration, depending as will emerge in Chapter 8 on the particular context of circumstances. Where imitation and diffusion require the generation of *knowledge* at the firm level, collaboration could potentially benefit all participants, and even consumers. The explanation can be traced back to the respective learning mechanisms involved, on which more will be said in the next chapter. This is not to deny that such collaboration may sometimes become heavy-handed and against consumer interests.

A second, and overlapping, reason for trying to distinguish process from product innovation lies in the search for the basic causes of technological advance and the direction it takes. The issue has been raised via Table 1.1 above; here the product/process distinction is added as a way of disentangling the specified demand and supply issues. To examine this, we must first explain how the technologies on the left-hand side of the table evolve.

31 See Chapter 6 on the 19th-century USA.

32 Von Hippel 1988, ch. 6; 1989.

VI: PARADIGMS, HEURISTICS AND TRAJECTORIES

For the evolutionary school of economists of innovation, the kinds of technologies that are actually developed are much more narrowly circumscribed than the factors listed in the table might initially suggest.[33] Following Dosi (1982), the evolution of technologies can be described in terms of 'paradigms', 'heuristics' and 'trajectories'. There are many different ways in which such concepts have been defined. The notion of a 'technological paradigm' is akin to the 'scientific paradigm' advanced by T.S. Kuhn (1970) in his influential work, *The Structure of Scientific Revolutions*. The first edition of Kuhn's book (1962) had been alternatively criticized for having no definition of the paradigm concept or for having over twenty implicit definitions. In applying the concept to technology, the ground is even more hazardous, in that there is much less articulation of what things are being done and why they are being done in technology than in science. Dosi (1982) treats the technological paradigm as the general area of technology in which the search for innovation is conducted by a significant group of innovators, within a particular historical context. This appears very close to Kuhn's view (or views) for science. The concept thus has both an *artifactual* dimension (a particular field of technology, e.g. steam power) and a *cognitive* dimension. The latter is far more important in this particular study. It represents the '-ology' bit of 'technology', and is intended to describe the field looked to for solving technical 'puzzles' (the latter term also derives from Kuhn). For example, when problems arose in mining (flooding, lifting, etc.) during the British Industrial Revolution, steam power was the technical solution first looked into by the mine-owners or inventors. In other historical and technological contexts, other techniques for dealing with the problems of mining might be examined first, but at this time steam power was on hand and potentially flexible enough to meet the required range of puzzles. Thus the emphasis lies on steam power (or any other chosen paradigm) as an 'idea'.

The paradigm thus sets the technological domain within which technologies evolve. In that evolutionary process, particular 'heuristics' define the main guideposts. The concept of the heuristic comes from another seminal work of modern times in the philosophy of science: I. Lakatos's *The Methodology of Scientific Research Programmes*. According to Lakatos, 'The [research] programme consists of methodological rules: some tell us what paths of research to avoid (negative heuristic), and others what paths to pursue (positive heuristic)'.[34] Thus in technology, the

33 Nelson and Winter 1977; Dosi 1982.

34 Lakatos 1987, p. 47.

heuristics give rules of thumb about where to continue searching for solutions, and which other areas to avoid. Typically this involves the continued scaling (up or down) of the key performance characteristics.[35] To extend the example already given, in mining the problems intensified as mines were dug deeper and deeper, so the area for solution tended to be constructing *more powerful* steam engines. However, when steam power was later applied to manufacturing and to transportation (ships and railways), a different heuristic emerged: what was required was for the engine to be *more fuel-efficient*. Over time the technological paths diverged (engines for mining were mostly low-pressure engines, those for transportation high-pressure engines, etc.). Thus the positive heuristics establish the ways in which paradigms unfold, while the negative heuristics set the bounds to the paradigms, in defining areas that remain undeveloped, at least for the time being. It will be seen that the heuristics can alternatively be defined in terms of physical magnitudes (more powerful vs. more efficient engines, etc.) or of technical characteristics (low-pressure vs. high-pressure engines, etc.).

'Technological trajectories' at one level represent the precise set of solutions undertaken; hence if examining the fuel efficiency of engines one could measure 'lbs of coal consumed per horsepower per hour'.[36] In this sense, the trajectories are a specific subset of the technological fields defined by the paradigm and its heuristics, i.e. particular points or sequences of points within the possible range. In practice, however, they usually bring in wider sets of considerations as well. Particular values (points) may be chosen because of responding to broader economic or social pressures. For example, the country in question may face particular 'scarcities' of a factor of production such as labour, or it may practise a particular form of hierarchical control in its social organization. The technical outcome may well incorporate those constraints; for instance, a country deficient in coal may select a technique from the range of those which are technically feasible which especially reduces the pounds of coal consumed. Strictly speaking, we should perhaps talk in terms of 'techno-economic trajectories', etc.

Just as technologies can be thought of as being characterized by paradigms, heuristics and trajectories, so can the other major functions (organization etc.). Their analysis will constitute a major part of the empirical chapters of the book. Particular attention will be drawn to the *conjuncture* of technological and organizational or economic paradigms, which in the same manner ought to be referred to as techno-organizational or techno-economic systems. A technology has the power to become a

35 Sahal 1981, 1985.

36 This was indeed the orthodox measure used at this time, cf. von Tunzelmann 1978.

techno-economic system through its pervasive adoption and consequent repercussions throughout an economic system.[37]

VII: CONJUNCTURES AND COUNTRIES

The issue about conjuncture is important, because it implies some degree of specificity in time and place. This book supposes that there have been three major leading 'waves' of industrialization: the first beginning in the British Industrial Revolution was based on a conjuncture of technology and organization (machinery and the factory); the second which began in the United States in the later 19th century came from a conjuncture of organization and management; and the third originating in Japan in the second half of the 20th century followed from a conjuncture of organization and production processes. In other countries, there were variants on these themes (a longer survey will be undertaken in the Conclusion), but a main point of the book is the different structure of these successive patterns of industrialization. To understand industrialization thus requires a multi-dimensioned approach: the process of industrialization cannot be collapsed into a single dimension, as is done in orthodox economics.

The issue here, therefore, is the way in which these different functions come together at a particular time and place. This accounts for the primary emphasis being on the national or regional level. Although the evolution of particular technologies (etc.) is not examined at length in this book, and warrants a separate study, some generalizations can be briefly set out here.

Even with well-functioning markets, demand and supply may not lead immediately to equilibrium, as occurs in the standard general-equilibrium model of economic theory developed by Walras and others from the late 19th century (see introduction to Chapter 3 below). On the contrary, even if expectations are highly 'rational', it has been shown that, in the markets for foreign exchange for example, exchange rates may alternately overshoot and undershoot in responding to any given exogenous source of maladjustment.[38] The model of lagged adjustments leading to a variety of cycles, some converging towards 'equilibrium' but others not doing so, can be derived in a number of ways, and elsewhere I have described the model of Malthus which was laid out in terms of its disequilibrium properties.[39] The same paper shows that such disequilibria can have varying periodicities, depending on the particular source of (mal-)adjustment. In

37 Freeman 1994; cf. Andersen 1991.
38 Dornbusch 1976.
39 Von Tunzelmann 1991; cf. also Chapter 2 below.

particular, in the technological field, where as shown above progress is mainly dependent on an often rather sluggish process of knowledge accumulation, even a single disturbance may lead to a long interval of disequilibrium before any semblance of equilibrium is restored. Of course, long before this happens, it is likely that further disturbances will arise. In such fashion, and indeed in other ways as pointed out in Chapter 3, the system may 'self-organize' around a new point far away from the initial point of equilibrium, as in the manner formulated by modern theories of disequilibrium thermodynamics.[40] At least two significant implications are analysed in later empirical chapters. One is the 'long wave' phenomenon of sustained bursts of disequilibrium (introduced at a more theoretical level in Chapter 3), and the second is the different ways in which new 'National Systems of Production' (techno-economic systems) eventually emerged in different countries.

VIII: INDUSTRIAL EVOLUTION

Some industries allegedly follow a 'lifecycle', characterized in terms of both a 'product cycle' and a 'process cycle'.[41] The product cycle is depicted as beginning with a period of extensive product proliferation and product innovation, with growth demand-led, but as time goes on the variety of products contracts as 'dominant designs' emerge to lead the market. Eventually the product matures, and the rate of growth of demand may slow markedly. The early stage is marked by rapid new entry of swarming 'Schumpeterian' firms (see Chapter 3 below), each with their different designs, and with no standardization at all of processes. As greater numbers of particular emerging designs begin to be sold, the rate of process innovation climbs. This later increase of process innovation reinforces the extent of standardization of products from the supply side.[42] Thus the process cycle follows the product cycle with a lag. In terms of scale and scope, we can compare the situation in markets with that in firms. The lifecycle approach presumes that scope economies may be large in markets but generally small at first within firms; that is, there may be many different types of motor car (say) available to consumers, though each (small) producer builds only a handful of these types. Later the position may be reversed – a more restricted number of types but each (larger) producer supplying most of them. Scale economies, in the sense of number of

40 See e.g. Dosi *et al.* 1988.

41 Utterback and Abernathy 1975; Abernathy and Utterback 1978; Hayes and Wheelwright 1984; Utterback 1994.

42 Cf. Chapter 7 below.

processes, will initially be low in both markets and firms. As shown in Chapter 3, subsequent developments depend on whether the economies of scale are external or internal to firms.

This lifecycle approach has been applied with some success to a number of industries,[43] especially motor vehicles, though attempts to ratify it in other industries have met with contradictory results. In services – and no doubt other industries which are dependent upon 'specialized suppliers'[44] – it is suggested that a 'reverse product cycle' occurs, with the suppliers initiating change via new techniques adopted by the users.[45] The latter is, of course, a reflection of the upstream-product vs. downstream-process link already described. The main issue from the viewpoint of this book is the distinction and interaction between product and process changes in industries over time. The 'dominant design' concept of standardization in the course of the product cycle is of considerable importance here, as the equivalent in the product dimension to the notion of trajectories in the technological dimension.

In general, though, the more eclectic position of emphasizing certain differences in patterns of technology and industry evolution is adopted in this book, rather than overall uniformity as implied by unique lifecycles. Pavitt (1984) has shown that much can be learnt from breaking industry up into four or five categories – known in his most recent assessment as 'supplier-dominated' (e.g. many branches of traditional manufacture), 'scale-intensive' (e.g. bulk materials like steel), 'information-intensive' (e.g. financial services), 'science-based' (e.g. electronics), and 'specialised-supplier' (e.g. instruments or software). He goes on to show that these are typified not only by different sectors of the economy, but also by different sizes of firms, different types of users, different sources and directions of technological accumulation, different strategic managerial tasks, etc.

IX: ORGANIZATIONAL EVOLUTION

The rise and decline of particular industries also carries implications for their organizational structures. The technology–product linkages within firms have tended to become more complex (e.g. Chapter 6 below). Manufacturing firms have moved – though more erratically than is sometimes supposed – from being simple-technology, single-product, single-plant, towards being multi-technology, multi-product, multi-site. The

43 Summarized in Utterback 1994.
44 The term comes from Pavitt 1984, see below.
45 Barras 1986, 1990.

diversification of technologies and products has imposed its own strains, however. Firms have sometimes over-extended themselves, especially when the S&T environment has changed rapidly and left them weakened against newer and more specialized competitors. Firms thus have to weigh the synergistic advantages of greater diversification against the burdens imposed by 'bounded rationality' (i.e. limited ability to process ever-broadening information).

Shifts in industry patterns have also influenced firm size, as partly implied in the Pavitt taxonomy just described ('scale-intensive' industries, etc.). The shift about a century ago from lighter consumer-oriented industries, such as textiles, towards heavier industries more oriented to capital and intermediate goods, such as metallurgy or chemicals, had evident effects on economies of scale. The emergence of powerful large and diversified firms in turn influenced the demand for further technological change, along lines suggested by Table 1.1 above. However, the 'specialised-suppliers' and some 'science-based' industries in Pavitt's taxonomy did not necessarily shift towards more hierarchical and complex administrations.

Recently, Miller *et al.* (1995) have drawn attention to 'complex systems', such as telecommunications exchanges, heavy electrical equipment, nuclear power plants, large vehicles (ships, aircraft, etc.), military systems, and their own study of flight simulators. In these, no 'dominant design' may emerge, and the industry – being design-intensive and software-intensive – continues to be dominated by user–producer relationships rather than standardizing via markets. Such 'complex systems' can be thought of as highly diversified in both scale and scope, and revolve around product linkages. In this they differ from those discussed by Rosenberg,[46] who uses the term to describe non-customized production involving a very long sequence of individual processes, i.e. process linkages. This distinction is similar to Marx's between heterogeneous and serial production.[47] Serial production, which is diversified in scale along the process sequence but less so in scope, has been dominated in recent times by the Japanese 'system of manufactures', as in Chapter 10 below. Both heterogeneous and serial production have grown over time.

In terms of locations, most attention in recent years has been drawn to siting production in several countries, i.e. to 'globalization' and the role of multinational companies (MNCs). Most economic analysis is concerned with the exchange of products, whereas here the question instead is one of setting up production and innovation facilities abroad. Patel and Pavitt (1991) have queried the extent to which innovation has become globalized, in the sense of how much R&D the MNCs conduct outside their home

46 .Rosenberg 1994, pp. 123–5.

47 Marx 1887/1965, pp. 342–50; Scazzieri 1993, p. 58.

country. While doubting the extent of globalization in technologies, Patel points out that it was most marked in a somewhat miscellaneous range of new and older industries, such as pharmaceuticals and building materials. This is attributed to the degree of differentiation across countries in the relevant *product* markets – where such product differentiation was high, as in these examples, a greater proportion of technological development was entrusted to those foreign countries themselves.[48] Recent surveys conclude that the pull influences from host countries have to be seen alongside the push influences of home countries,[49] and as in Table 1.1 this means assessing both technologies and products. The general pattern of evolution, spelt out in greater detail in Chapters 7 and 8 below, has been one of first exporting products, later (often much later) exporting production facilities, and later still exporting facilities for technological development. The reason for the lag in regard to technologies lies chiefly in the extent of 'interactive learning' required for technological development, as described earlier in relation to NSIs. Thus it remains appropriate, even today, to think of technological systems as being predominantly nationally based, whereas product systems have long been extensively 'globalized'.

X: IMPLICATIONS FOR ECONOMIC GROWTH

For simplicity, I have made the conventional economics assumption here, that firms are individually too small to have any detectable impact on markets for the basic factors of production, such as the land, labour and capital highlighted in Chapter 2. Rather than influencing average wage levels (etc.), which are assumed to be set by demand and supply conditions operating at the macro level, I shall argue that dynamic firms aimed mainly to change what they could control more effectively. The successful firms backed and often advanced those technologies and processes that had the highest growth potential.

Though internal change within a particular firm is critical, external sources of knowledge concerning technologies and products are bound to have major impacts upon it. On the supply side, new technologies originate in advances in more basic science and technology ('know-why'), which may come at the national level or may incorporate spillovers from scientific and technological breakthroughs in other countries. On the demand side, new demand structures may emerge (e.g. through changes in income distribution), as might new taste patterns (e.g. from increased environmental

48 Patel 1995; see also Granstrand *et al.* 1992, ch. 9.

49 Pearce 1993, ch. 2 and Apps.

concern), for reasons largely beyond the individual firm's control, and to which firms may be more or less successful at responding.

Industries can be regarded as those firms which undertake (fairly) similar activities. More specifically, having defined firms as agents for transforming technologies into products, we can define industries as activities with a certain limited range of technologies *associated with* a limited range of products (this resembles the von Neumann 'activity analysis' approach in economics[50]). In this sense, they define the areas in which external sources of technological and product change are most likely to be found by individual firms. In practice, orthodox listings of industries such as the Standard Industrial Classification (SIC) are actually hotch-potches of technologies and products. Some industries like biotechnology have a relatively high degree of relatedness in terms of technologies, others like health-care have higher degrees of relatedness in terms of products. Ideally, a matrix relationship between technologies and products might be developed, in which industries could be located as clusters, but no standard system as yet has emerged. As mentioned already, the larger firms have become multi-technology, multi-product firms (see especially Chapters 6–8 below). Such firms could span several industries or even sectors according to the conventional definitions, a common example being a large manufacturing firm that also undertakes services (e.g. IBM, General Electric, etc.). Thus in practice there is no simple subdivision of an industry into firms, or converse grouping of firms into industries.

Equally, neither firms nor industries can nowadays readily be grouped into economies. It is well known that many multinational companies (MNCs) are larger in size than small and even small–medium-sized countries, and their innovational activities may be on a much larger scale. Their operations have become so widespread (cf. Chapters 7–8) that the scope for the exercise of industrial or other policies by many governments is becoming severely curtailed.

XI: THE ROLE OF GOVERNMENTS

With the emphasis on the viewpoint of the firm and on the micro foundations of economic growth, in this study governments are also taken to be exogenous so far as the firms are concerned. Needless to say, this is one of the many simplifications that one would not wish to defend very far. Indeed, it will emerge in Chapter 10 that the successes of Japanese industrial policy postwar, such as they were, rested on mutual interaction

50 Cf. Hicks 1973, ch. 1; Gomulka 1990, ch. 1.

between business and government. Governments are important here for being a (or sometimes the) major influence on the general climate of business opinion – the set of institutions and ideologies referred to in the underlying schema introduced in Chapter 2. They can also have fundamental impacts on macro-level entities which are here taken to be exogenous to individual firms – on the national S&T system (National System of Innovation), on the national financial system, and on aggregate demand. However, if the book were to be written from a macro and policy-oriented standpoint, it would look very different.

As a result, the discussions of government policies at the end of each empirical chapter below are intended to summarize some of the effects and implications for industrialization, rather than being full-scale analyses of the governmental process. The latter will have to await another study, in which national systems of organization can play a bigger part.

XII: STRUCTURE OF THE BOOK

With its focus borne in mind, the structure of the book is straightforward. The next two chapters deal with major currents in previous thinking on these subjects, primarily by economists. Chapter 2 studies the classical economists, while Chapter 3 focuses on 20th-century thought, in more selective fashion.

The remaining chapters contain the main historical and empirical content, arranged in approximately chronological fashion. In each chapter, I shall follow a roughly similar pattern, of commencing with some brief remarks about macroeconomic performance, before descending to the micro level and using a taxonomy introduced in the next chapter, then lastly coming back to consider the role of government policy and the nature of its impact on the industrialization effort. In this vein, Chapter 4 studies the British Industrial Revolution from the middle of the 18th century, which I argue was the first occasion on which technological development came to be viewed as the norm rather than as the exception. Chapter 5 considers the spread of industrialization to Continental Europe in the 19th century. This continued the British pattern in a number of ways, but placed differing emphases on technology or products, and through attempts to catch up took finance and organization in quite different directions from those found in the UK. Chapter 6 briefly mentions the subsequent British 'decline' (in relative terms) before tackling the so-called 'Second Industrial Revolution' emerging in the USA in the last third of the 19th Century, which, although roughly contemporaneous with the developments in Continental Europe, had an entirely different momentum. The next two chapters describe 20th-century developments in the Advanced Industrial Countries (AICs) – Chapter 7 takes the story from about the 1930s to the 1970s in a period of massive expansion, while Chapter 8 sets out the intensifying problems of such patterns from the late 1960s or early 1970s. These chapters concentrate mainly on capitalist countries and on the USA as the world's acknowledged industrial leader, at least during the earlier period. Chapter 9 considers instead the socialist economy of the USSR, up to the point at which state socialism disintegrated at the end of the 1980s. Despite the different political regimes, these countries had many similarities in industrialization with what was happening in the West: the most glaring difference was of course the virtual absence of a product or market dimension. In Chapter 10 the attention shifts to the rapidly expanding Japanese industrialization process, and attempts to show how this more adequately coped with the ills coming to prevail in the western AICs, even though partly by force of circumstance rather than by design. Chapter 11 studies the Newly Industrializing Countries (NICs) as the most recent examples of apparently successful industrialization. More precisely, it compares the relative success of industrialization in two East Asian countries (South Korea and Taiwan) and the possible determinants, with two rather less successful Latin American countries (Brazil and Argentina). Finally, the Conclusion summarizes the different patterns of industrial evolution in each particular national environment and draws more general implications.

2. Classical Theories of Economic Growth and Structure

This chapter goes back to the origins of modern thinking about industrial progress, by reconsidering the contribution of economists and 'political economy' from the late 18th to the mid–19th centuries. These were the years of the first great wave of industrialization, studied in Chapter 4 below. The analysis here makes no pretension to being an adequate account of the economics of these classical writers – comparison with an orthodox history of economic thought such as Blaug (1962) quickly reveals many differences. Rather, the chapter seeks to tease out of their broader works what they had to say about the main theme of this book, namely the micro foundations of growth and change at the national (macro) level. Particular emphasis is given to seeking the causes and effects of technology. For these reasons, the chapter gives more attention to heterodox political economists such as Malthus and Marx than economists normally do. I do not intend to claim that their work is thus better than those whom I treat more sketchily, such as Ricardo; merely that they have more to say in the way of original contributions to my main topics. In this and the next chapter (on more recent thought) I shall avoid belabouring the weaknesses of each main thinker, and place most emphasis on what seem to me to be their constructive contributions.

I. THE 'CIRCULAR FLOW'

In his great work, published in 1776, Adam Smith set out the agenda for classical political economy, beginning with his title: *An Inquiry into the Nature and Causes of the Wealth of Nations*. Building on the work of his immediate predecessors, especially the French Physiocrats, he considered the structure of an economy along lines resembling those set out in Figure 2.1. From those predecessors he took the notion of the economy as a circular flow of interactions, but instead of their emphasis on flows of goods between sectors, Smith stressed the nature of production within each sector, and thus was led to envisaging the economic system as one of

Figure 2.1: The circular flow of classical political economy

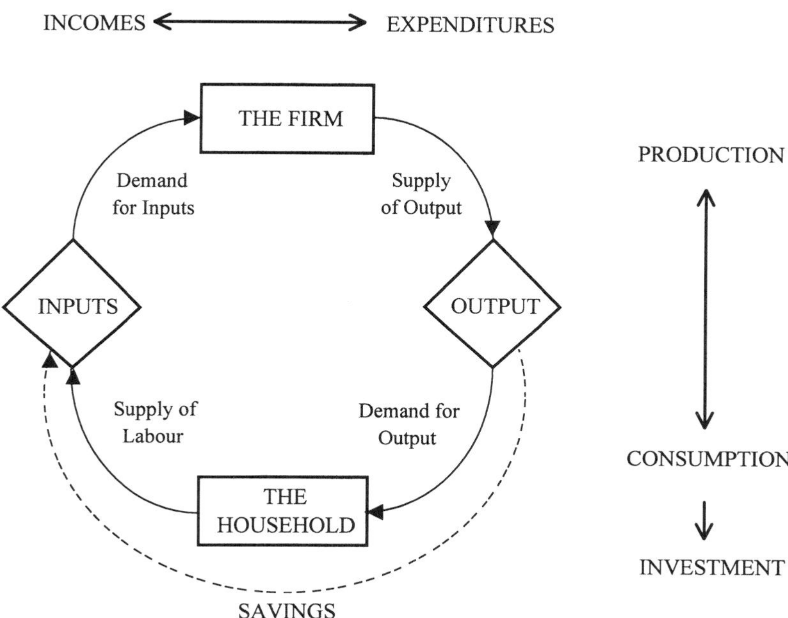

interactions between inputs and outputs. The arrows of the figure provide a simplified sketch of what was involved, in a schema of demand and supply for the inputs and outputs.

The *Wealth of Nations* includes the first recognizably modern – in some respects, very modern – portrayal of the inputs into production, known nowadays to economists as the 'factors of production': land, labour and capital.

A. Land

Land was treated by the classical economists as, to all intents and purposes, fixed in supply – they were thinking of conditions in Western Europe and above all in the sea-girt British Isles rather than on, say, the unfolding prairies of North America. Although land was seen as the source of the basic essentials of life, it was not given the pre-eminence that it had earlier been by the Physiocrats. From the beginning of the 19th Century, land was assumed to be subject to 'diminishing returns', such that adding further and further increments of the other inputs to the fixed supply of land would yield smaller and smaller increments of output.

B. Labour

Labour was instead regarded as the source of the 'value' of output. Precisely how the quantity of labour employed related to the value of goods and services produced was a question of major dispute among the classical economists from Smith onwards. For the moment, it is sufficient to note that the amount of *productive* labour employed was regarded as a rough index of output capacity. As a very first approximation, we can assume that even this productive labour was unskilled.

C. Capital

Capital was inherently the least self-evident of the inputs, and where Smith's contributions to clarifying the nature of the factors of production were greatest.

(a) Again as a very first approximation, it was simplest to regard all capital as being *working capital,* or the materials and other resources that labour needed to work with to produce saleable output, such as the yarns and fuels required to produce clothing. Such working capital could be thought of either as a 'flow', in the form of items required for working up by labour while production took place, or as a 'stock', in the form of accumulations of such materials prior to production, work-in-progress during production, and inventories of output as yet unsold. To increase productive employment and output, such working capital should have to be increased in equal measure. The classical economists, however, focused less on the physical quantity of materials than on the financial resources allowing the employment of the associated amount of productive labour.

(b) With the advance of industrialization, *fixed capital* became increasingly important relative to working capital (see Chapter 4). Fixed capital took two main forms: plant, i.e. buildings and similar structures, and equipment, i.e. machinery and similar (transport equipment, etc.). Nowadays most economists instinctively think of capital first and foremost as fixed capital, but for the classical economists of two centuries ago, the notion of fixed capital raised considerable problems for valuing output by way of the labour employed in its production, so their models generally assumed that fixed capital behaved like seed (working capital) in agriculture, with a fixed period for turnover (one year exactly in the case of seed).[1] On reflection, it is obvious that there will be very different periods of turnover according to the type of fixed capital – for equipment it might average 5 to 10 years, for plant maybe 50 years. As we shall see below, the shift of emphasis to regarding capital as predominantly fixed came later, with the work of writers like Karl Marx.

(c) But Smith was ahead of his time in the extended consideration he gave to *human capital*, i.e. the investments in building up human competences for production via education and training. Although often sarcastic about educational institutions like Oxford University, he did not underestimate the value of the accumulation of knowledge. However, as we shall see shortly, he also saw that skills arose from practical on-the-job experience, as well as from formal learning.

The 'holy trinity' of classical factors of production – land, labour and capital – was associated in Smith's great work with different types of factor payments. Land was rewarded in the form of rents, labour through wages, and capital through interest and profits. These differed not just trivially in the terminology and levels observed, but fundamentally in the market structures and attendant institutions through which they came about. Relationships between input levels and their rewards were crucial for determining the incentives to growth in any industrializing society. In Figure 2.1, the factor payments – 'incomes' – can be thought of as relating to the left-hand side of the diagram, while 'expenditures' appear on the right-hand side. The flow of payments for both outputs and inputs can be represented by arrows pointing in the reverse direction to those of the figure, for example from the Household to Output as payment for consumption, from the Firm to Input for the factor payments like wages.

The ratio of outputs to inputs is referred to as 'productivity'. Economists and economic historians concerned with growth often aggregate both outputs and inputs, and describe this ratio of aggregate output to aggregate input as 'Total Factor Productivity' (TFP). However, productivity is often considered to be the ratio of output to just the labour input – strictly, 'labour productivity'. There are several reasons for this simplification, for example the classical one (that labour is the source of value), the welfare one (that this measures the potential for individual income-earning), and quite often

1 Marx 1919, chs 7–11.

the data one (that figures on labour inputs are easier to obtain than some other inputs).

The classification of outputs, on the right-hand side of Figure 2.1, also posed certain problems. The simplest procedure was to classify according to product type, and to distinguish between agriculture and manufacturing. Many modern interpretations of classical theory preserve such a product-based (sectoral) dichotomy, but the classical economists themselves often adopted a different dichotomy – between productive and unproductive labour.[2] This meant more than useful vs. useless labour – primitive societies often employed higher proportions of their labour usefully than did advanced ones.[3] Being 'productive' related to process rather than to product: productive labourers worked with capital in a relatively efficient way to produce worthwhile output, while unproductive labourers formed a succubus dissipating the wealth created by their productive counterparts. Retainers and others in domestic services were a major component of unproductive labour.[4]

Finally, it will be noted that the conversion of inputs into outputs flows through the 'black box' of the firm, as illustrated in the top half of Figure 2.1. The firm demands inputs like labour, as shown by the inward-pointing arrow, in order to produce and supply output, as shown by the outward-pointing one. The bulk of this chapter will be devoted to analysing the flow of resources through this particular 'black box'. The lower half of the diagram shows the output being demanded by a second black box, the household, for consumption purposes. The consumption of necessities and other desirable products permits the household to supply labour inputs to production, to continue the 'circular flow', as in Marx's model of 'simple reproduction'. The nature of this second black box, the household, will not be appraised at length in this book. It is the foundation of the study of demography, and also followed principally from the work of the classical economists (especially Smith and Malthus). The chapters to follow do, however, pay considerable attention to 'intermediate demand', arising out of the demands of user industries for capital goods produced by upstream industries.

---

2 Smith 1776/1976, p. 10; Mill 1844, ch. 3; Mill 1848, bk. I, chs 3–4.
3 Smith, *loc. cit.*
4 *Ibid.*, pp. 330, 420, 675; cf. Lewis 1954, p. 142.

II. GROWTH AND STRUCTURAL CHANGE IN THE CLASSICAL MODEL

To analyse growth and change in such a model, we can usefully begin by conjecturing what was needed to keep the economy ticking over without any such growth. Evidently the amounts that needed to be invested, and thus saved in order to invest, would equal the consumption of capital during the period in question. The simplest example to illustrate, and the one so favoured by the classical economists, is that of seed (working capital) in arable agriculture. Only a fairly small proportion of the crop needs to be retained by the farmer (i.e. saved) in order to grow the same level of crop output next year. This proportion is the amount of capital consumed in preserving the level of output at the status quo. Thus although in this example there has to be some gross savings, invested in working capital formation, the amount of net capital formation is zero – all of the gross savings are consumed in the production of next year's crop at this year's level.

It is clear that a relatively small reduction in present consumption can give rise to a considerable increase in next year's production. For example, if 10 per cent of the crop needs to be saved as seed in order to produce the same total output next year, a further 1 per cent decline in present consumption may generate a 9 per cent increase in next year's production by being saved and invested in growing next year's crop. The example, which of course assumes that suitable land is available, etc., makes it clear that the amount of growth that will ensue depends upon the productivity of the investment, in this case in seed.

Thus growth can come about in the first instance from diverting output from consumption to savings. Through this means, the 'circular flow' was transformed into what Marx later called a 'spiral flow'. This is indicated by the direct dashed line leading from output back to inputs, obviating consumption in households. It was this view that led some economists in the 19th Century to regard capital formation as 'abstinence' – the greater the immediate sacrifice of consumption, the greater the potential payoff in longer-run production, and hence longer-run consumption.

For the classical economists, such capital formation permitted a greater quantity of productive labour to be employed. The increase of working capital allowed more to be paid out as wages. This additional employment would ideally come from recruiting hitherto unproductive workers, but alternatively from increasing the total labour supply, i.e. by population growth. Most of the classical economists feared that higher wage payments would encourage a higher population, through demographic mechanisms such as those suggested by Malthus (although, contrary to popular impression, Malthus did not argue that higher wages would *necessarily* raise population). If so, the economy could fall into a 'Malthusian trap'.

The second way in which growth could arise in this model of a circular flow was through improving the efficiency of transforming inputs into outputs, i.e. through increasing the productivity of the inputs. 'Technical progress' is often seen as little more than this, but the figure, simple as it is, shows that to understand efficiency gains we must understand what happens within the 'black box' of firms. For instance, the justly celebrated opening pages of the *Wealth of Nations* adopted the division of labour to explain such increases in efficiency. But because the issues lie within the 'black box', there has been no consensus among economists or others about the appropriate way to analyse the relationship between output and inputs – if there are any lessons that can be generalized, they probably lie beyond the domain of conventional economics. The classical economists further supposed that technical progress itself would not be likely to lead to population growth, so that incomes could rise per capita as well as in aggregate.

For structural change there needs to be a shift in the composition of either inputs or outputs (or both). On the inputs side, the most obvious possibility is of a rise in capital relative to labour. If working capital bore a one-to-one relationship to labour and employment, this increase would have to come through a shift to fixed or human capital. From what was shown above, it is evident that the main issue is the productivity of the various forms of capital. The assessment is, however, complicated by the fact that the payoff to fixed capital is likely to come only in the medium to long term, and that to human capital only in the very long term. Moreover, the investments may not be readily separable – investments in fixed capital may require or be required by investments in human capital, etc.

Alternatively, structural change may derive from changes in the pattern of outputs, notably sectoral outputs. As implied above, it comes from moving from unproductive to productive employments. With the inclusion of 'diminishing returns' into models such as that of Ricardo, agriculture had come to be identified by many with unproductive labour, so that growth came from moving labour out of agriculture and into manufacturing. Shifts of employment and output from agriculture to manufacturing output, and perhaps later to services, had been perspicaciously considered by the 17th-century author of *Political Arithmetick,* Sir William Petty.[5] However, some emphasized different *products* (agricultural, manufactured), and others

5 See Clark 1940/1960, p. 492.

different *productivities.*[6] Mill was adamant that a sectoral (product) classification of work was of limited insight.[7] With some modification, this is the general line argued in the present book – that it is productivities and technologies which are of greatest concern here. In the long term, it is likely that economic expansion will depend less on immediate (short-term) productivity gaps between sectors than on long-term differences in the possibilities offered for growth, i.e. which sectors had greatest potential for sustained productivity growth.

III. A MICROECONOMIC TAXONOMY

The most likely reasons for structural change come from the evolution of demand patterns as per capita incomes grow, on the one side, and from technological change in the broadest sense, on the other (supply) side. To interpret macro-level changes of such kinds, I shall throughout this book use a micro-level taxonomy, set out here in preliminary form in Figure 2.2. The presumption is that by analysing growth and change at the micro level, we may be in a better position to understand longer-term macroeconomic development. Figure 2.2 therefore prises apart the individual firm, which was shown to be the crucial 'black box' in Figure 2.1 above.

It was noted in Chapter 1 that knowledge of the technology *per se* is not sufficient to produce the products in an efficient way. This is most apparent in multi-technology, multi-product firms, where a whole range of technologies may be required to produce each individual product, and conversely each technology may be utilized in a range of different products. To convert technological knowledge into product knowledge, as shown in Figure 2.2, requires first that the firm has an efficient set of production *processes* – when I refer later to organization and organizational capability, I shall usually be thinking of the organization of production in this sense.

To many, the most perplexing aspect of this taxonomy is the distinction between technologies and processes. This distinction is perhaps best illustrated by an example. Take two different motor cars – the Ford Escort and the Rolls Royce. The technologies they require are basically similar (principles of petroleum combustion, transmission systems, electronic monitoring, rubber moulding, etc.). The production processes are, however, entirely different, being for the most part automation and assembly line in the former case and craft methods in the latter. The organizational literature

6 Smith, with his Physiocratic forebears, was unwilling to accept that agricultural labour was less productive, and instead stressed capital formation for raising productivity regardless of sector (Smith 1776/1976, pp. 343, 363–7).

7 Mill 1848, bk. I, ch. 2.

Figure 2.2: A micro-level taxonomy for production in the firm

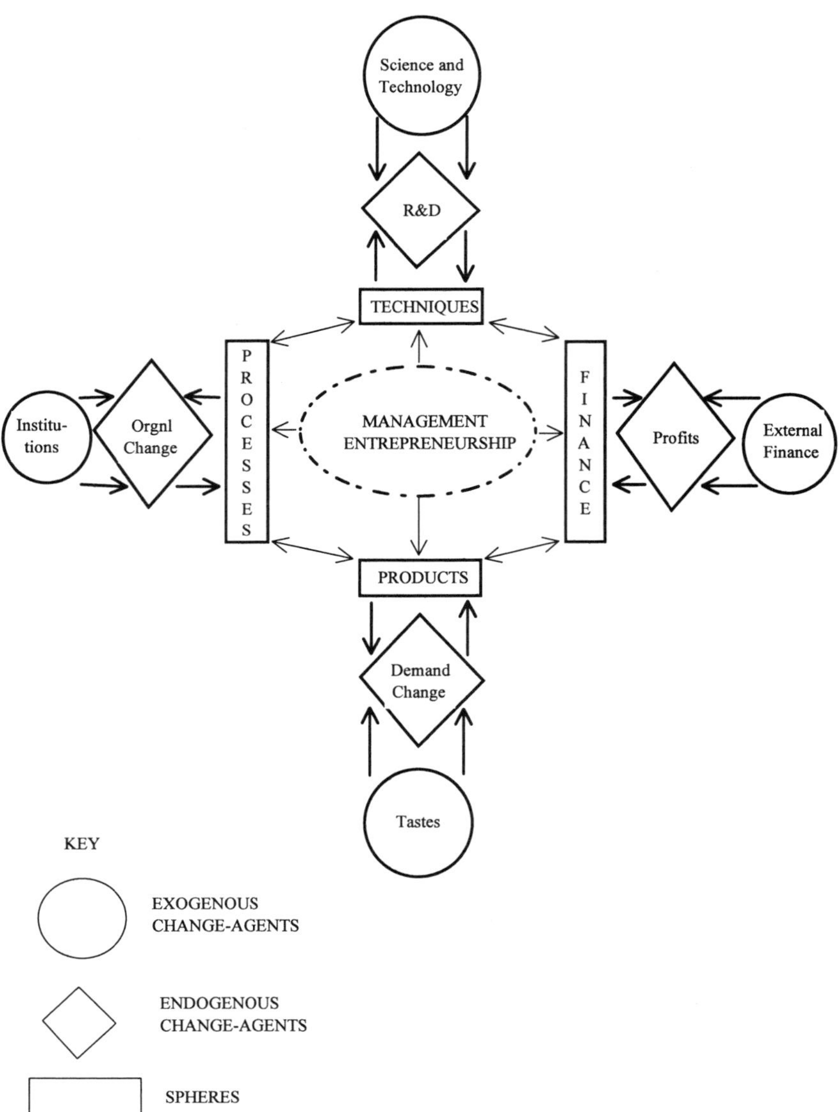

has focused mainly on what it calls 'labour process', i.e. the way in which the labour force is controlled so as to carry out the production. In this book I shall give greater attention to the corresponding notion here dubbed 'capital process', i.e. the way in which the fixed and working capital (plant and equipment, etc.) are organized for the same purpose.[8] It is perfectly true that the dividing line between technology and processes may often be somewhat fuzzy. What contributes to making it so is that, for complex processes such as building an automobile, parts of the processes will involve technologies of their own – for example the mechanical handling principles and motive equipment of a moving assembly line. Processes, it should be noted, are not just assembly – they are ways in which technological principles are realized in actual production.

Second, the operations of the firm need to be efficiently organized – these are represented in the *administrative* and *financial* capacities of the firm. They are exhibited in the range of processes used by the firm and the range of products it produces, i.e. its 'scale' and 'scope'. The ploughback of profits into the firm, as in the classical model above, enables expansion of the firm in depth (scale) or breadth (scope).

All firms, i.e. all institutions for production of goods or services, involve all four functions of technologies, processes, administration (finance), and products, as the spheres of the figure. The links between each of these spheres need to be suitably *managed,* in the interests of overall efficiency. Of course some firms make more of or do better at one or other area, and indeed in the analyses to follow it will emerge that the firms of particular countries perform better in differing characteristics. One reflection of this result is that 'management' tends to be oriented towards one or two particular spheres or links, but which spheres or links these are also differ across countries. That is, management is 'captured' by different functions, so that for some countries management will be considered primarily in relation to finance, in others primarily to processes (organization of production), etc. Management is thus primarily aimed at functional efficiency. *Entrepreneurship* is regarded as something beyond 'mere management', in which non-routine measures are taken to change the firm's behaviour in one or more such spheres. Entrepreneurship thus requires *strategic* efficiency, in the sense of Chandler (1962). A similar distinction is that of Lazonick – management aims at maximizing within a given set of constraints, while entrepreneurship involves changing some of those constraints, in order to achieve more in the long term.[9] This will be amplified in discussing Schumpeter's work in Chapter 3.

---

8 For a fuller exposition, see von Tunzelmann 1989; also Marx 1858/1973, pp. 691–5; 1887/1965, pp. 379–83.

9 Cf. Lazonick 1981a, 1983.

Details such as those just discussed will be reintroduced in the text as and when required – it is not necessary to belabour the description at this point. It is, however, useful to point out that each sphere is likely to take on unique values for each particular firm involved in the industry. Thus the function of technology will be demonstrated by particular technical choices made in each firm, which may vary from one firm to the next – for this reason, the precise set of choices for a particular firm is referred to as its 'techniques', and any change in the firm's choices is referred to as a 'technical change'. Similar arguments apply to the other three functions. Second, each sphere is associated with some endogenous source of change, such as technological learning (R&D, etc.) in the case of the techniques, and with some exogenous source of change, e.g. the science and technology (S&T) base in the case of the same function. The change-agents, endogenous and exogenous, are for the most part self-explanatory, but perhaps a little more should be said about the exogenous element in the organizational (processes) sphere. This is most conveniently referred to as 'institutions', using that term to connote the economic framework more generally,[10] rather than specific institutions such as (say) the banking system – thus it includes such things as the nature of competition. An alternative term for it would be 'ideology', were it not for the undertone of polemics in such a word – 'climate of opinion' is perhaps more appropriate, or 'spirit of a people' in the sense of Steuart,[11] or 'ethic' in the sense of Weber.[12]

Finally, it should be emphasized that each of the four spheres is intended to cover *all* of the activities in the firm – thus while technology might be delegated to a specific R&D laboratory or sales to a specific marketing department in particular firms, here I am considering all of the technologies, products, etc. that are in use in the firm, in all of its departments. This differs from the approach of, say, Stigler (1951), who also recommended a functional approach to the firm but assumed that the functions could be separated and later their individual cost curves aggregated into a total for the firm as a whole.

IV. MICRO DETERMINANTS: PROCESSES

To analyse the ingredients of growth and structural change, the technologies, processes, finance and products will mostly be discussed in

---

10 As also by Lewis 1955, ch. 3; Matthews 1986.

11 Steuart 1767, bk. I, ch. 2.

12 Weber 1927; see also Gerschenkron 1968, pp. 89–90 and Chapter 3 below.

that order, in the national studies to follow in Chapters 4 to 11. However, historically it all began differently, and with Adam Smith the first emphasis was placed upon processes, so in this chapter I shall do likewise.

Much the most widely read section of the *Wealth of Nations* is the opening few pages where Smith introduced the notion of the division of labour, which he sees as the main cause of productive labour.[13] He illustrated the concept by using the example (borrowed from the French Encyclopedists) of a factory for making pins. In the pin factory, 'One man draws out the wire, another straights it, a third cuts it, a fourth points it, a fifth grinds it at the top for receiving the head; to make the head requires two or three distinct operations; to put it on, is a peculiar business, to whiten the pins is another; it is even a trade by itself to put them into the paper; and the important business of making a pin is, in this manner, divided into about eighteen distinct operations'.[14]

As compared with production where one person undertook all of the tasks, the effect was to raise labour productivity dramatically:

> 'Each person [in a factory employing just ten people] might be considered as making four thousand eight hundred pins in a day. But if they had all wrought separately and independently, and without any of them having been educated to this peculiar business, they certainly could not each of them have made twenty, perhaps not one pin in a day; that is, certainly, not the two hundred and fortieth, perhaps not the four thousand eight hundredth part of what they are at present capable of performing, in consequence of a proper division and combination of their different operations.'[15]

It is evident how this relates to the notion of scale, defined as the number of processes undertaken and their throughput, introduced in Chapter 1.

The sources of these dramatic rises in productivity were spelt out by Smith in a sentence which has also been much quoted, though typically accepted with greater reservations than the rest of his argument:

> 'This great increase of the quantity of work which, in consequence of the division of labour, the same number of people are capable of performing, is owing to three different circumstances; first, to the increase of dexterity in every particular workman; secondly, to the saving of the time which is commonly lost in passing from one species of work to another; and lastly, to the invention of a great number of machines which facilitate and abridge labour, and enable one man to do the work of many.'[16]

---

13 Smith 1776/1976, p. 13.

14 *Ibid.*, p. 15.

15 *Idem.*

16 *Ibid.*, p. 17.

Specifically these amounted to the following.

(a) Improved worker dexterity from concentration upon one operation – Smith compares a blacksmith unaccustomed to nail-making, who might be able to make 800–1000 nails a day, with a teenage boy trained in nail-making, who could be capable of 2300 or more nails a day. However, the gains from concentration for any individual worker would soon tail off, and later in the *Wealth of Nations* he instead emphasized the boredom likely to come about from the routine repetition of the same tasks.[17]

(b) Smith's second gain, of saving time through not having to move between tasks, is also often regarded as one-off.[18] However, it opens up larger possibilities of time-saving gains from what is described in Chapter 4 as 'systemic co-ordination', and what are argued there to be the dominant technological characteristics of early British industrialization. More broadly, it extends to the dual character of 'labour process' and 'capital process' highlighted in this book, as exemplified in Henry Ford's moving assembly line (see Chapter 7 below).

(c) Most important were thus the dynamic effects flowing from the focus on processes, to technological advance via mechanization: 'A great part of the machines made use of in those manufactures in which labour is most subdivided, were originally the inventions of common workmen, who, being each of them employed in some very simple operation, naturally turned their thoughts towards finding out easier and readier methods of performing it'.[19]

(d) A fourth advantage was not defined by Smith but put forward in 1832 by Charles Babbage, celebrated today as the inventor of the mechanical computer. Babbage argued that the division of labour would allow slotting individual workers into vocations for which they were best fitted, particularly those most closely matching their skills, thus providing what he referred to as a mental division of labour. This fourth factor became famous (or notorious) as the foundation for 'scientific management' along Taylorist lines in the 20th Century (see Chapter 7). Equally important here is that the impact came through the relationship

17 *Ibid.*, p. 782; also Say 1821, bk. I, p. 86 and Marx 1887/1965, pp. 341, 362. Marshall (1919, pp. 353–4) quoted evidence from the Zeiss glass works that both could be true. From quite different evidence, Arrow in his seminal paper (1962b) on 'learning by doing' came to rather similar conclusions about the limited nature of gains from sheer repetition, cf. Bell and Scott-Kemmis 1985 and p. 73 below.

18 E.g. Mill 1848/1909, pp. 125–8.

19 Smith 1776/1976, p. 20.

between individual processes or skilled workers and the total throughput[20] – again this is often interpreted statically, but here is seen dynamically through 'systemic co-ordination'.

This division of labour required prior accumulation of capital, and its progressive development hinged upon continued capital formation, although the accumulation could perhaps be divided among different firms.[21] This in itself brought further pressures to improve machinery. Because division of labour could be taken further in manufacturing than in agriculture, greater growth possibilities ultimately came from the former,[22] even when productivity at a point of time was higher in the latter.

Smith believed that the principle established for production *within* a firm also could hold for production and exchange *among* firms. He emphasized that the division of labour did not result from any human planning: 'It is the necessary, though very slow and gradual consequence of a certain propensity in human nature which has in view no such extensive utility; the propensity to truck, barter, and exchange one thing for another'.[23] Thus every person going about their own particular business in their own self-interest generates the greater advantage of the nation as a whole. In another much-quoted sentence, Smith contends, 'It is not from the benevolence of the butcher, the brewer, or the baker, that we expect our dinner, but from their regard to their own interest. We address ourselves, not to their humanity but to their self-love, and never talk to them of our own necessities but of their advantages.'[24] Thus emerged what is often regarded as the fundamental theorem of economics, based on the notion that competition bred of individual self-interest secures maximum economic efficiency. This is normally known, from a phrase which Smith originally used in a different context, as the 'invisible hand' principle: that the independent decisions of vast numbers of producers and consumers in the economy, left unfettered to maximize their own interests in a competitive environment, would generate equilibrium in the macro-economy, at the highest level of welfare attainable. In terms of Figure 2.2, the development of production processes via the division of labour therefore stemmed from an ideology of the competitive market-place. How far Smith really believed in the efficacy of competition, and the policy implications, will be pursued below.

---

20 What Babbage (1832, pp. 172–3) termed the principle of 'multiples'.

21 Smith 1776/1976, pp. 276–7, 677; Say 1821, bk. I, pp. 85–6.

22 Smith 1776/1976, p. 676.

23 *Ibid.*, p. 25.

24 *Ibid.*, pp. 26–7.

V. TECHNOLOGIES

A. Causes of New Technologies

The preceding section has shown that, for Smith, technologies flowed from instituting production processes that gave rise to greater output per unit of time. New techniques thus came partly through the effects of workers' concentration on their chosen tasks, but this was not the only way in which the new technology evolved:

> 'All the improvements in machinery, however, have by no means been the invention of those who had the occasion to use the machines. Many improvements have been made by the ingenuity of the makers of the machines, when to make them became the business of a peculiar trade; and some by that of those who are called philosophers [scientists] or men of speculation, whose trade it is, not to do any thing, but to observe every thing; and who, upon that account, are often capable of combining together the powers of the most distant and dissimilar objects.'[25]

This quite remarkable sentence amalgamates the three main sources of what today is described as 'learning' in regard to new technologies. Innovation thus came through:

(a) 'learning by using', specifically by workers on particular machines with which they were entrusted, and depending on how free they were to reap the benefits;[26]

(b) 'learning by doing', through specialization in machine production;

(c) formal (scientific) learning.

Emphasis is therefore placed on specialization and on learning – a kind of specialization in knowhow, as in Babbage's 'mental division of labour'.[27] Such specialization was not just to achieve the maximum gain from existing opportunities but to open up new ones – a dynamic rather than a static specialization. Marx[28] argued that division of labour made it easier to impart the knowledge of each particular occupation to the next generation. In science, Smith saw the contribution as coming, not from deductive reasoning as one might expect, but from a more serendipitous process of making new connections and combinations. What may seem surprising here is that the 'Scientific Revolution' of the late 17th Century, which will be touched on in Chapter 4, was noted for its switch of emphasis towards

25 *Ibid.*, p. 21.
26 *Ibid.*, p. 684.
27 Say 1821, bk. I, ch. 8; Babbage 1832, ch. 19; Reid 1989.
28 Marx 1887/1965, pp. 339–40.

theory and deduction, while Smith a century later was still seeing the potential industrial contributions as more haphazard and inductive. Be that as it may, Smith's was still a more positive view of the role of science than his predecessors had allotted to it. In his edition of the *Wealth of Nations* (1776/1961), Cannan quoted Mandeville's *Fable of the Bees* of half a century earlier:

> 'They are very seldom the same sort of people, those that invent arts and improvements in them and those that inquire into the reason of things: this latter is most commonly practised by such as are idle and indolent, that are fond of retirement, hate business and take delight in speculation; whereas none succeed oftener in the first than active, stirring and laborious men, such as will put their hand to the plough, try experiments and give all their attention to what they are about.'[29]

The predominant view emerged that science – at best – could provide 'information' that was readily transmissible, whereas development in industry required application and the accumulation of 'knowledge' within the enterprise:

> 'It is worth while to remark, that the knowledge of the man of science, indispensable as it is to the development of industry, circulates with ease and rapidity from one nation to all the rest. And men of science have themselves an interest in its diffusion; for upon that diffusion they rest their hopes of fortune, and, what is more prized by them, of reputation too. For this reason, a nation, in which science is but little cultivated, may nevertheless carry its industry to a very great length, by taking advantage of the information derivable from abroad. But there is no way of dispensing with the other two operations of [technical progress in] industry, the art of applying the knowledge of man to the supply of his wants, and the skill of execution. These qualities are of advantage to none but their possessors; so that a country [powerfully benefits from being] well stocked with intelligent merchants, manufacturers, and agriculturists.'[30]

Similar views are still often espoused today.[31] We shall see in later chapters that, in practice, things were a little less clear-cut.

B. Consequences of New Technologies

After Smith, the main attention of the classical economists shifted from production to distribution, and from the causes of technological change (often then referred to as the 'arts of production') to its economic and social consequences. In particular, the notion of machines for 'facilitating and

29 Smith 1776/1961, p. 7n; 1776/1976, p. 21n.

30 Say 1821, bk. I, pp. 52–3.

31 E.g. Dasgupta and David 1987, and Chapter 3 below.

abridging labour' (to use Smith's phrase) led to anxieties about possible technological unemployment from introducing the machinery. The orthodox answer given was that any such ill effects could only be temporary.[32] David Ricardo (1817) focused mainly on substitution between (fixed) capital and labour *for a given level of technological knowledge*; thus analysing the problem as one of comparative statics, or in the manner described in this book – somewhat anachronistically in the case of Ricardo – as 'neoclassical'.[33] In particular, Ricardo stressed the effect that rising wages would have on encouraging a shift towards more labour-saving (capital-intensive) machinery. The greater fixed-capital intensity would increase the average period of production, i.e. the degree of 'roundaboutness' in production. In this view, labourers would not lose from mechanization, because it was their higher wages which had induced the substitution of capital for labour in the first place.

Ricardo's celebrated addition to the third edition of his *Principles of Political Economy and Taxation* (1821) – the chapter called 'On Machinery' – confused his followers by appearing, on the contrary, to accept that labourers were not being illogical in resisting new machinery. Ricardo here took the case of a new technique, embodied in a machine. As this involved some investment in fixed capital to install the new type of machine, the fund of working capital that could be used to employ workers (at fixed wage rates) would temporarily decline, through diversion into this fixed capital formation. Until the final goods appeared on the market in sufficient quantities to overcome this deficiency, workers would be without full employment. Hence Ricardo appeared to be accepting technological unemployment in the case of new and exogenously developed techniques, though not with induced substitution of capital for labour.

The belief of many classical economists that the economy would tend to stabilize itself – through the operation of the 'invisible hand' and its repercussions – implied that one or more 'compensation mechanisms' would offset the immediate labour-saving effect.[34] The major compensation mechanisms can be listed as follows:[35]

(a) via new investments (the after-effects of Ricardo's case, when the profits from innovation are eventually re-invested);

(b) via new machines (i.e. employment created in building the new equipment itself);

32 Steuart 1767, bk. I, ch. 19.

33 Schumpeter 1954, p. 473, referred to the fixing of assumptions pertaining to everything but the immediate objective as the 'Ricardian Vice'.

34 Cf. also Marx 1887/1965, pp. 438–47.

35 Taken from Vivarelli 1991; cf. Say 1821, bk. I, ch. 7, and bk. II, ch. 3.

(c) via decreasing wages (from the rise in unemployment, allowing some workers to be profitably re-employed at the now lower level of wages);

(d) via lower prices (encouraging expansion of consumer demand and thus output);

(e) via new products (product innovation creating new jobs).

Most thought these would operate in the fullness of time, if not necessarily immediately.[36] Vivarelli points out that there is in fact no guarantee that all – or indeed any – of these will operate in any given case, and each individually has serious limitations on its capacity to reabsorb those made technologically unemployed. Indeed J.-B. Say, who introduced 'Say's Law of Markets' that markets would tend to equilibrate,[37] later expressed doubts that the Law would hold good in circumstances of innovation.

Like many of the classical economists, Say felt more comfortable in drawing attention to the merits of saving time in both distribution and production, which he thought would be capital-saving rather than labour-saving:

> 'The activity of circulation is at the utmost pitch to which it can be carried with advantage, when the product passes into the hands of a new productive agent the instant it is fit to receive a new modification, and is ultimately handed over to the consumer, the instant it has received the last finish. All kind of activity and bustle not tending to this end, far from giving additional activity to circulation, is an impediment to the course of production, – an obstacle to circulation by all means to be avoided.
>
> 'With respect to the rapidity of production arising from the more skilful direction of industry, it is an increase of rapidity, not in circulation, but in productive energy. The advantage is analogous; it abridges the occupation of capital.'[38]

VI. MANAGEMENT AND LARGE FIRMS

Smith's conclusions regarding the 'invisible hand' depended on the existence of effective competition, which accounts for his use of such illustrations as butchers and bakers. However, monopolistic producers not facing competitive pressures could easily act so as to exploit the hapless consumers, and so defeat the proposition that the nation's welfare was maximized by the individual pursuit of private profit. Smith was deeply suspicious of large enterprises and industrial combinations: 'The whole

---

36 Mill 1848/1909, pp. 96–9, 744–5.

37 Say 1821, bk. I, ch. 15.

38 *Ibid.*, pp. 185–6; cf. the discussion of Marx below, p. 58.

book is directed against "the mean rapacity, the monopolizing spirit of merchants and manufacturers, who neither are, nor ought to be, the rulers of mankind"'.[39] The common impression that the *Wealth of Nations* is a licence for profiteering is misinformed. Joint-stock organization should, he thought, be limited to: (i) banking, (ii) insurance, (iii) infrastructural construction (e.g. canal-building), (iv) water supply.[40]

However, the emphasis on small-scale activity and anti-monopoly policy which he pursues so adamantly ran into possible contradictions. It had to be reconciled with having to rely on small firms to innovate. But we have already seen that innovation for Smith came principally through specialization and division of labour, which was likely to require at least medium-sized firms to set up.[41] The alternative of developing the division of labour between firms rather than within firms ran the risk of increased combination and anti-competitive behaviour. This potential for conflict between competition (for the invisible hand) and collaboration (for the division of labour) was never adequately resolved by Smith.[42]

Smith believed that co-operation within large joint-stock companies, such as the East India Company of his day, was disadvantageous. Managers entrusted with middle-ranking responsibilities would, he thought, act more in their own interests than those of the firm for which they worked. In this way, he was able to contend that, whatever the process advantages from increased division of labour might be, these would be swamped by increased managerial costs if firms grew too large – thus he could reassert the superiority of small and medium-sized firms (SMFs) even in a dynamic setting. Writing 60 to 70 years later, by which time the Industrial Revolution was well advanced, the political economists Nassau Senior and John Stuart Mill took different views. Senior (1836) argued that traditional activities, especially agriculture, were characterized by 'diminishing returns' of the kind enunciated by the likes of Malthus and Ricardo, so that extra inputs of capital and labour gave smaller additions to output. Manufacturing, on the other hand, he believed to be characterized by 'increasing returns', whereby output rose more than proportionately with inputs. Mill[43] also placed heavy emphasis on such static 'economies of size' (cheaper production from larger manufacturing firms), an inference which

39 Blaug 1962, p. 38, quoting Smith 1776/1976, p. 493, also pp. 145, 267, 471.

40 *Ibid.*, pp. 756–8.

41 Scazzieri 1993, ch. 3, shows that division of labour can be reconciled with SMFs only when the tasks are 'symmetric', i.e. allotted equal portions of total effort, a point implied by both Babbage and Marx. The pin factory in reality was not 'symmetric' in this sense, as the operation of heading the pins accounted for about half the total costs, cf. Dutton and Jones 1983.

42 Reid 1989, chs 4, 9.

43 Mill 1848, bk. I, ch. 9.

he drew somewhat inaccurately from Babbage's analysis of the division of labour,[44] but unlike Senior he was wary about elevating this observation into a law.[45] Mill instead placed at least as much emphasis on long-run *dynamic* increasing returns – the importance of innovation, education, etc., for permitting growth of output to outstrip the growth of inputs over a much longer time interval.[46] 'Improvement here must be understood in the wide sense, including not only new industrial inventions, or an extended use of those already known, but improvements in institutions, education, opinions, and human affairs generally, provided they tend, as almost all improvements do, to give new motives or new facilities to production.'[47] A transformation of the social system – the Institutions of my schema – was essential for innovation and large-scale production to benefit all classes of society.[48]

Mill[49] also took issue with Smith's views about the inefficiency of management in very large firms – what would nowadays be called high transaction costs and scope for opportunism. Mill himself worked for much of his life in the East India Company, and took a more charitable view. He accepted Smith's view that hired workers, including managers, worked less well than did owner-managers, especially in carrying out non-routine tasks and through ignoring the systemic nature of the larger firm. However, he thought such disadvantages could be offset by establishing appropriate incentives for hired managers, for example profit-sharing arrangements. He also stressed that people of high ability should be employed – hiring the cheapest was a false economy. This led him into one of the first discussions by an economist of the management of firms composed of a number of divisions or departments, and thus the issue of managing diversified enterprises. Less was said about the role of the entrepreneur at the top of the pyramid. Marx[50] likened it to the conductor of an orchestra, albeit a somewhat hostile one. Say[51] drew the sharpest contrast between capitalists and entrepreneurs, and saw the latter as I do, in the role of uniting a range of functions in the enterprise through possessing a range of personal abilities.

---

44 Scazzieri 1993, p. 48; Rosenberg 1994, p. 41.

45 Mill 1848/1909, p. 703.

46 *Ibid.*, bk. I, ch. 12, also bk. IV, 'Influence of the Progress of Society on Production and Distribution'.

47 *Ibid.*, p. 192.

48 *Ibid.*, bk. IV, ch. 7.

49 *Ibid.*, bk. I, ch. 9.

50 Marx 1887/1965, p. 331; 1909/1977, p. 383.

51 Say 1821, bk. II, ch. 7.

VII: DEMAND

A. Aggregate Demand – the 'Extent of the Market'

Since the division of labour depended upon buying and selling in markets, the extent of those markets determined how far specialization could be taken. 'When the market is very small, no person can have any encouragement to dedicate himself entirely to one employment'.[52] Smith conjectures the case of a nail-maker in a remote part of the Scottish Highlands, who, even if he supplied the whole of the local community, would not be able to find gainful employment for the whole year just from making nails.[53] In Smith's analysis, the extent of the market was widened:

(a) by cheaper external communications (Smith stressed water transportation[54]), that is to say by 'extensive' factors;

(b) by the dynamic effects of internal growth brought about by the successive division of labour, especially in manufacturing, that is to say by 'intensive' factors.

The latter is particularly significant, since it implies that Smith's well-known result that 'the division of labour is limited by the extent of the market' is more than the comparative static result it is sometimes made out to be – instead Smith is portraying a dynamic interaction whereby the enlargement of the market permits greater division of labour, which then further enlarges the market by way of the productivity gains, and so on.[55] Through the division of labour, an extraordinary complexity of input–output relations was built up.[56] Division of labour in production both prompted and required exchange.[57] Smith tended to believe that 'extensive' factors initiated this dynamic process,[58] and this was a reason for spending so much of the book advocating expansion of foreign trade, which could be more or less infinitely extended.[59]

B. Overseas Demand and Free Trade

Despite this, Smith opposed giving any preference to foreign trade over home trade, and it was in this context that he made his famous reference to

52 Smith 1776/1976, p. 31.
53 *Ibid.*, p. 32.
54 *Ibid.*, pp. 32–6.
55 Young 1928, p. 533; Corsi 1991, p. 24.
56 Smith 1776/1976, p. 23; Mill 1848/1909, pp. 29–30.
57 Smith 1776/1976, p. 37.
58 *Ibid.*, p. 34.
59 *Ibid.*, p. 374.

the 'invisible hand'.[60] He saw overseas trade as sometimes originating in supply shifts, such as the discovery of a new resource – this constituted a 'vent for surplus', and typified the opening up of colonies.[61] Though the main emphasis came to fall instead upon new demands from foreign markets, the more guarded, like Steuart,[62] argued that the demand boost would be once-for-all unless there were corresponding advances on the supply side. Either way, Smith[63] saw exports as contributing to the wealth of their nations, but in opposition to the 'Mercantile System' which governed much of British overseas trade at the time he was writing, he did not see the increase of export surpluses and the associated rising exchange rate and influx of 'treasure' as ends in themselves.[64] For the continued expansion of the circular flow, and also in the interests of consumers, imports ought to expand alongside exports – if foreign producers were cheaper, the country should 'buy', not 'make'. The accumulation of treasure and/or surplus of exports over imports was to him a misleading indication of the gains from trade.

Smith also rejected the political economy of the Mercantile System, both for the colony concerned and in terms of its monopolist structure, on the grounds set out above under the heading of Management ('the negligence, profusion, and malversation of their servants'[65]). Above all, he objected to the monopolies conferred on regulated or joint-stock companies like the East India Company, which he regarded as wholly opposed to the interests of both Indian peoples and European consumers.[66]

Thus Smith wanted freer trade through increased competition, and the abolition of many government tariffs and subsidies. However tariffs, he argued,[67] could be justified: (i) for defence purposes, (ii) if there were parallel duties on home goods for the domestic market, (iii) as retaliation for foreign tariffs, (iv) to prevent 'dumping'. In any case, the political opposition to removal would be too strong. 'To expect, indeed, that freedom of trade should ever be entirely restored in Great Britain is as absurd as to expect that an Oceana or Utopia should ever be established in it.'[68] Yet about three-quarters of a century later, by the time John Stuart Mill – paradoxically, as already mentioned, an erstwhile employee of the East

60 *Ibid.*, pp. 372, 455, 456.
61 *Ibid.*, pp. 446–7; Myint 1964.
62 Steuart 1767, bk. II, chs 9–12.
63 Smith 1776, bk. IV.
64 Mill 1848/1909, pp. 2–3; cf. Postlethwayt 1749.
65 Smith 1776/1976, p. 755.
66 *Ibid.*, pp. 91, 449, 635–41, 732–4, 840.
67 *Ibid.*, pp. 463–71.
68 *Ibid.*, p. 471.

India Company – had come to publish his *Principles,* such free trade effectively existed in the country.

The case for free trade appeared to be sealed by Ricardo's formalization of the 'theory of comparative advantage'. The basis for trade in Ricardo is often described as being rooted in technology differences between pairs of trading countries. However, this should be interpreted in terms of the meaning attached by orthodox economics to 'technology', effectively as an index of productivity,[69] rather than the everyday notion of technology more like that used in Chapter 1 above. International trade thus comes about because of differences in (labour) productivity. The theory of comparative advantage argues that, irrespective of absolute productivity differences between two trading partners, if there are two goods to be traded, the country will specialize in exporting the good in which it is less inefficient (i.e. where *relative* productivity is less disadvantageous). Both countries gain from such specialization, and again free trade appears to maximize the gains to be derived from international trade.

C. Demand Deficiency vs. Say's Law – the Composition of Demand

The invisible hand theorem is often construed in the light of 'Say's Law', that supply creates its own demand – this is because incomes earned on the left-hand side of Figure 2.1 must match the expenditures incurred on the right-hand side, as they represent the same quantities.[70] Say[71] believed that the converse view of demand creating supply was a licence to wasteful ostentation at the expense of economy. Savings appeared at first sight to provide an exception to the Law, since they looked like a 'leakage' out of the circular flow. However, the savings that 'disappeared' from the circle on the right-hand side of the diagram could be expected to reappear as investment expenditures (capital formation) among the inputs on the left-hand side, as in the dashed line, so again the two sides seemed to balance. As Smith – writing well before Say – put it, 'What is annually saved is as regularly consumed as what is annually spent, and nearly in the same time too; but it is consumed by a different set of people'.[72] There were two problems here. One was that the spending side might take much longer than one year, as in the case of fixed capital already encountered. The second was the disparity between savers and investors as different groups of people – this was the starting point for Keynesian macroeconomics a century and a half later, as described below in Chapter 3.

---

69 See above p. 30, and Chapter 3 below.
70 Cf. Say 1821, bk. I, chs 11, 15; Mill 1848, bk. I, ch. 5, and bk. III, ch. 14.
71 Say 1821, bk. III, chs 5–6.
72 Smith 1776/1976, pp. 337–8.

Much of Keynes's argument had in fact been made just a generation after Smith by the Rev. Robert Malthus (1820/1989), better known for his allegedly gloomy (in fact widely misinterpreted) views on population growth. Like Keynes much later, Malthus emphasized that demand and supply were the results of decisions by 'different sets of people' or institutions, though he spelled them out rather differently from Keynes. Supply factors reflected production decisions in manufacturing firms and on farms, and in the long-term supply could be raised by:

(a) accumulation of capital;
(b) fertility of soil;
(c) inventions to save labour.[73]

Demand, however, was determined by spending decisions of the various social classes, demarcated in Malthus's work as:

(a) landowners (upper classes), whose demand included many worthless and whimsical fripperies;
(b) labourers, demanding mainly necessities and with limited wants;
(c) middle classes, demanding the –conveniences and comforts of life'.

Imbalances between supply and demand could arise in the short run, for instance because supply (production) decisions typically had to be made well before demands were expressed through buying the products – in this case there could be 'gluts' or periods of depression. However, these would not be permanent. Here our chief interest lies in the longer-run imbalances, especially those surrounding the 'inventions to save labour'. In regard to technological unemployment, Malthus showed that whether the displaced labour would be reabsorbed or not depended on the demand factors, and in particular how suited were the innovations to the tastes of each social group and to the structure of society as a whole.

Malthus's methodology differs fundamentally from that of Ricardo, as he himself pointed out in their correspondence,[74] and it is this, I believe, which largely accounts for the frequent misunderstanding of his contribution.[75] In place of Ricardo's comparative statics he uses methods of comparative dynamics, to trace out the interactions between demand and supply over time. In this way, Malthus allowed for short-run disruptions to stability, e.g. from bad harvests or wars, but also for the long-run disruptions, as from the list of supply factors quoted above (capital accumulation, etc.). In particular, innovations could give rise to booms lasting anywhere from 20 to 100 years – what are termed 'long waves' in Chapter 3 here – so long as

73 Malthus 1820/1989, vol. 1, p. 413.
74 Keynes 1933/1973, pp. 97–8
75 Von Tunzelmann 1991.

demand factors supported the supply-enhancing innovations. With his concern for 'diminishing returns', Malthus was anxious about the possibility that consumer demand might become satiated by the existing range of goods, and hence advocated a focus on developing product as well as process innovations, to revitalize demand. In Chapter 8 below I shall refer to some modern theses concerning recent 'satiation of wants'.

VIII. IMPLICATIONS FOR GOVERNMENT POLICY

It is customary to see the classical economists as apostles of 'laissez-faire' and, associated with that, of free trade. Although Adam Smith was a vigorous opponent of arbitrary and irrational government regulations, these were normally contrasted with *good* regulations (not uncommonly those of his native Scotland), rather than with *no* regulations.[76] The legal system was the main device for preventing the powerful using market or other forces to harass the weak, unlike the political system which was likely to be dominated by the former.[77] I have already implied that Smith had serious doubts about absolute economic freedom for the private sector and its producers. Similarly he argued for the need to regulate banking: 'Such regulations may, no doubt, be considered in some respect a violation of natural liberty. But those exertions of natural liberty of a few individuals, which might endanger the security of a whole society, are, and ought to be, restrained by the laws of all governments; of the most free, as well as of the most despotical.'[78] Nor did he believe in eliminating the role of government in the economy.[79] Specifically, he defined positive roles for government in:

(a) defence;
(b) administering justice;
(c) undertaking public works where they were privately unprofitable;
(d) subsidizing mass education.

Adam Smith's name is often uttered by present-day politicians seeking to reduce participation by governments in these activities, especially the last two, but his great work offers scant support for such appeals. Virtually all of the classical economists, no matter how vehemently they voiced arguments for freedom and the invisible hand, spoke out explicitly in favour of greater government support for elementary education. This may not seem a great concession in our day, but it should be remembered that there was

76 E.g. Smith 1776/1976, pp. 135–59.
77 Say 1821, bk. I, pp. 196–9.
78 Smith 1776/1976, p. 324.
79 *Ibid.*, bk. V.

no substantial government support for elementary education in Britain until a number of decades after the classical era of political economy had passed.

As shown above, Smith supported freer trade (than he himself experienced in the so-called Age of Mercantilism), but not necessarily completely free trade. Here his successors generally went further than he, and were eventually to see it happen. Some, however, stood out against free trade, most conspicuously Malthus, on the grounds that cheap grain imports would undermine the basis of domestic demand. While this led many contemporaries to distrust him, the consequences of cheap imported grain in the last quarter of the 19th Century for Britain were not so far removed from what Malthus feared.

Non-British economists were less universally enamoured of free trade, though of course most countries had their advocates of it. In the United States, Alexander Hamilton, a signatory of the Declaration of Independence, led arguments for protectionism towards new manufacturing industries. In France, economists like Say[80] and philosophers like Saint-Simon, different as they were in other ways, accepted similar infringements of free trade. The German, Friedrich List, published letters while resident in the USA in 1827 in defence of the tariff system raised by that country against the British (see Chapter 6 below). Following his return to Germany, he published a series of works collected together in the English translation as *The National System of Political Economy* (1844). List attacked a heavily caricatured version of Adam Smith by arguing in favour of customs duties under certain circumstances, specifically in situations where nations were beginning to industrialize and their manufactures needed protection against the absolute advantage of British manufacturing – situations that both the USA and Germany were finding themselves in at this time. This 'infant industry' justification for manufacturing protection had been accepted even by pro-trade British economists.[81] However, List emphasized that such protection should only be temporary, that *internal* free trade (the German *Zollverein*) was extremely desirable, and that universal free trade was an ultimate ideal.[82] For our purposes, what is even more interesting about List was his continuing emphasis on nationality and the role of the nation-state. As his title suggests, this places him near the head of writers on national

80 Say 1821, bk. I, pp. 250–52.

81 E.g. Steuart 1767, bk. II, ch. 19; Smith 1776/1976, p. 458; Mill 1848/1909, p. 922; Marshall 1919, pp. 761–2.

82 List also rejected the case for protecting agriculture, contrary to the policy Bismarck was later to follow in Germany, and indeed argued that Britain would gain from repealing the Corn Laws, as it was to do a few years later. By contrast, Say (1821, bk. II, pp. 207–8) thought Britain was right to pursue self-sufficiency in corn.

systems of production and innovation, of the kind described in Chapter 1 above, as indeed Freeman[83] has argued.

Despite List's rhetoric, we should still place him in the classical pantheon of political economy. The position of another German emigrant, Karl Marx, is somewhat different.

IX: MARX ON TECHNOLOGY AND ORGANIZATION

Marx's analysis of industrialization can be a study in itself, as it indeed was in 'Second World' countries until recently. Although he is conventionally listed as the last of the great classical economists, separate attention will be devoted to him in this chapter. An obvious reason for doing so is his political heterodoxy, but at a different point on the political spectrum Malthus was also a heretic. The main reason is that, whereas the above writers generally envisaged technology and industrialization from just one perspective of the taxonomy in Figure 2.2, or one at a time, Marx gave substantial attention to all four spheres – technology, production, finance, and products – and developed their *interactions* through his dialectic method. The combinations of these spheres at particular points of time emerged as identifiably different 'stages' in his analysis of growth, and these stages are central to the interpretation of Marx offered here (see Table 2.1 on p. 55 below). In doing this, he happens to address many of the key questions of my subsequent discussion, of course often with different conclusions. Marx's macro-level spheres (the 'national systems' of Chapter 1 above) are built up from his micro-level analyses of capital accumulation and technical change, which is where I begin.

A. Value and Surplus Value

It has already been noted that classical political economy found the treatment of fixed capital very awkward for the 'circular flow'. Variations in the length of turnover of the fixed capital invalidated Ricardo's 'labour-embodied' theory of value and thus measure of output. Both Ricardo, in his later years, and Marx seem to have accepted that the root of the problem lay in the fact that the labour theory required consideration of both labour and *time,* but neither developed a satisfactory framework for the latter.[84] For Marx, time entered into the determination of *all* prices, not just interest.[85]

83 Freeman 1987, pp. 98–100.
84 Morishima 1973, ch. 13; I am indebted to Jonathan Fraenkel for this point.
85 Marx 1909/1977, p. 356.

Capitalistic competition brought about the *minimum* labour-time for production, through using up-to-date technology.[86]

Like Malthus, Marx presents a framework couched in terms of social class, but here defined from the side of production rather than consumption. Marx's (producer) classes consist of workers and capitalists. 'Value' was created by the processes of production, and thus by the technologies that entered into these. *Changes* in value brought about by technology etc. largely dictated *changes* in product prices.[87] Marx adapted the labour-embodied theory of value in an attempt to prove that all 'surplus value', i.e. the excess of sales receipts over variable costs, derived from labour employed and exploited by capitalists. The benefit that the latter therefore obtain from surplus value can be thought of as 'unpaid labour time'. The ratio of surplus value (or unpaid labour time) to wage payments (paid labour time) is defined as 'relative surplus-value'; when appropriated by a capitalist class, this measures the 'rate of exploitation' of labour.[88] 'Absolute surplus-value' is raised by lengthening the working day;[89] 'relative surplus-value' raised by technical progress (see below) or by reducing wage payments through exploiting docile female and child labour.[90]

B. 'Labour-saving' Technical Change

Along with a rise in the ratio of fixed to working capital under industrialization went a historical tendency under capitalism towards 'labour-saving' technical change. His argument here, which associates technological change with changes in 'relative surplus-value', has often been misinterpreted: 'It is sometimes said about machinery, therefore, that it *saves labour*; however, as Lauderdale correctly remarked, the mere *saving* of labour is not the characteristic thing. ... What is characteristic is the *saving* of necessary labour and the creating of *surplus* [unpaid] *labour*'.[91] 'Surplus labour' – labour devoted to producing surplus value – and 'surplus time' were for Marx interchangeable (because of the Ricardian value confusion just mentioned). 'Relative surplus-value' was thus increased by

---

86 Marx 1859, p. 57.

87 Marx 1909/1977, pp. 179, 206. Marx was notoriously unsuccessful in solving the 'transformation problem' of how values are translated into prices (*ibid.*, chs 9, 10). Personally I agree with authors who claim that there needs to be a relationship but it does not have to be one of strict proportionality (Morishima 1973, chs 4, 7; Desai 1974, chs. 11–12).

88 Foley 1986, p. 40.

89 Marx 1887, part III.

90 *Ibid.*, part IV.

91 Marx 1857/1973, p. 389. Emphasis in original.

trying to compel workers to work at a faster pace, i.e. 'intensifying' work.[92] But eventually the pressures on capitalists to raise relative 'surplus time' to the utmost had the effect of lowering workers' effective demand; so 'surplus-value' rose more slowly than technology and eventually caused the latter itself to slow down.[93] This dialectical interaction would in due course undermine capitalism itself, working through the 'law of the falling rate of profit'.[94]

Marx rejected what he saw as Smith's view that such pressures towards reductions in the necessary labour time came about from demand-led expansion through the extent of the market – instead they arose from the imperatives of industrial capitalism.[95] Intensification of work could be either labour saving (employing fewer workers for the same length of time) or time saving (employing the same number for a shorter period), and usually both.[96] Naturally in his more apocalyptic moments, Marx chose to stress the labour saving rather than the time saving. Part of the reason was that he linked time saving proper, i.e. declines in time required per unit of output, to declines in time worked; for example the number of hours needed to produce a certain type of machine fell with the number of hours worked per day. The latter he presumed directly helped to cause the former, as exemplified by the speed-up following the passage of the Ten Hours Act in Britain.[97] Reduced hours of work were vigorously resisted by individual capitalists, but came about through wider social pressures.[98] Even when it happened, the capitalist could fight back by 'intensifying' work.

Through a somewhat dubious extension of surplus labour time to imply surplus population, capitalism was seen as creating a 'reserve army' of the unemployed.[99] Marx thus explicitly rejected the 'neoclassical' argument that the cause of labour saving lay in some scarcity of labour[100] – machinery arrives where there is *too much* labour rather than *too little*.[101] He did

92 Von Tunzelmann 1981.

93 Marx 1857/1973, p. 422.

94 The status of this 'law' has been much criticized, and Marx himself admitted that it was a 'tendency' rather than a 'law' (Marx 1909, ch. 14).

95 Marx 1857/1973, pp. 688–9; Marx 1909/1977, pp. 261–2; cf. Lazonick 1990, p. 342.

96 *Ibid.*, p. 247; Marx 1859/1971, p. 37.

97 Marx 1887/1965, pp. 409–17; von Tunzelmann 1978, pp. 216–18.

98 It was only under socialism that reductions of time worked would become paramount. Cf. Marx 1909/1977, p. 820; and see below.

99 Howard and King 1985, pp. 197–9.

100 Marx 1909/1977, pp. 398, 702; Marx 1887/1965, p. 430n; Elster 1985, pp. 151–3; and cf. Chapter 3 below.

101 He noted that low wages could deter implementation of machinery, without necessarily deterring its invention: 'Hence nowhere do we find a more shameful squandering of human labour-power for the most despicable purposes than in England, the land of machinery' (Marx *op. cit.*, p. 394).

consider some political influences towards saving labour, especially the desire of capitalists to crush working-class revolts.[102] The rise in 'relative surplus-value' might have come through tougher supervision and discipline of the labour force in factories, or through reducing wage payments to a minimum, but Lazonick argues convincingly that in reality a faster workpace eventually required deals to be struck between capitalists and workers, in such forms as better work conditions, greater job security, or higher wages.[103] In any case, Marx's numerical examples instead suggest that he saw the saving of necessary labour as principally coming quite directly from the technical progress itself, raising the efficiency of *capital*. Overall, and without ever giving any really compelling argument, he appears to have believed that saving 'necessary labour' was simply the natural trajectory for technological change in the era he was describing.[104]

C. Centralization of Capital

With the rising proportion of fixed to working capital,[105] Marx believed there would be centralization of ownership of the capital in a decreasing number of hands. This centralization came about partly for technological reasons, associated with a rising 'minimum efficient scale' (MES) of production in Modern Industry, and partly through pressure from the credit system.[106] It might proceed violently through tooth-and-claw competition, or more peaceably through formation of joint-stock companies etc., as for the rapid construction of British and European railways (see Chapters 4 and 5 below).

His earlier view was that labour saving was intertwined with this emergence of larger firms exercising monopolistic powers or realizing economies of size[107] – time savings would be more likely than labour savings if labourers themselves owned the machinery.[108] Since centralized capital preferred to deal with fewer rather than more labourers, other things being equal, it thus helped foster the 'industrial reserve army' of the unemployed, competing for jobs with the labourers providing necessary labour. However, in volume II of *Capital* he argued that centralized capital was often responsible for time savings, aided and abetted by the

102 *Ibid.*, pp. 436–7; Marx 1859, p. 141; Bruland 1982; Elster 1985, p. 147.
103 Lazonick 1991, pp. 135–6.
104 Elster 1985, p. 153; cf. Marx 1909/1977, pp. 249–50.
105 Strictly speaking Marx focused on the 'organic composition of capital' (OCC), which was the equivalent viewed from the side of labour rather than of capital.
106 Marx 1887/1965, pp. 625–6; 1909, ch. 27.
107 E.g. Marx 1858/1973, pp. 704–5; Marx 1887/1965, pp. 324–5, 628, 635.
108 Marx 1858/1973, p. 768.

development of credit.[109] This could arise through labour co-operation (as in amassing huge 'navvy' labour forces to build railways) or through technical progress (enabling advanced equipment and machinery).

D. The Role of Capital Goods

Industry was seen by Marx as having slowly transformed from medieval 'Handicrafts' to 'Manufacture' in the early modern period (see Table 2.1). But by 'manufacture' Marx at this juncture meant the term in its literal Latin sense, i.e. making by hand. At this stage the tools and machines were the product of workmen, working together 'co-operatively' even if under a capitalist employer. Following Adam Smith, he saw mechanization as coming first through vertical disintegration via division of labour, and only later, under 'Modern Industry' proper, when 'all the sciences have been pressed into the service of capital', would it be the case that, 'Invention then becomes a business'.[110] This next stage of development led finally into 'machinofacture' in the 19th Century, in which machines were used to make machines – that is, involving machine tools, steam engines, etc.[111] This he thought of as the basic characteristic of Modern Industry in its latest stage, and conferred dynamic advantages of:

(a) permitting scale economies in the making of large machinery ('internal economies');

(b) permitting efficient utilization of by-products ('external economies');

(c) leading to increased efficiency in types of machinery (saving capital and time);

(d) having 'downstream' effects on using industries.[112]

However, Marx stressed that these gains were not purely mechanistic – they rested on a social combination of labour and capital, i.e. labour and capital process. Such co-operation, or the kind of team-work discussed by later writers,[113] was the basis for rapid learning by doing.[114] Learning by using came from the separation of the capital goods sector from consumer goods, as the two sectors mutually interacted. These 'internal' capital-saving and time-saving effects from the more efficient machinery were boosted by the 'external' provision of time-saving infrastructure, such as better communications (see p. 58 below).

---

109 Marx 1919/1967, pp. 229–30.
110 Marx 1858/1973, p. 704; MacKenzie 1984.
111 Rosenberg 1982, ch. 2.
112 Marx 1909, ch. 5.
113 E.g. Alchian and Demsetz 1972.
114 Marx 1909/1977, p. 104.

Table 2.1: A representation of Marx's historical stages

A. Technologies	B. Modes of Production	C. Capital	D. Product Relations
1. Pure Labour	Pre-Capitalist :Asiatic :Ancient Slavery :Feudalism	Usurer's	Subsistence :Simple Commodities
2. Handicrafts	Early Capitalism :Guilds		Generalized Commodities
3. Manufacture	:Merchant	Primitive Capitalist	Simple Reproduction
4. Modern Industry :Machinofacture	Bourgeois Capitalism	Relative Surplus-Value	Extended Reproduction
	(5. Socialism)		
	6. Communism		

E. Modes of Production

Just as techniques (which along with the factors or means of production Marx termed the 'forces of production') evolved in a sequence of stages – handicrafts, manufacture, machinofacture, etc. – so did the 'social relations of production'. In Marxist literature these latter types of stages are referred to as 'modes of production', and they are similar to what I called in Chapter 1 the 'national system of organization'.

The major pre-capitalist modes of production detailed by Marx (see Table 2.1) had in common an in-built resistance to technological change, i.e. to new forces of production. In England Marx detected a slow transition from feudalism to capitalism between the 14th and late 18th Centuries. The second half of this period of organizational change was also marked by the rise of 'manufactures' in terms of the technologies (forces of production).

This could come about in workshops specializing either in particular *products* (requiring a range of craft processes) or in particular *processes* (leading to process-related division of labour), with the latter involving greater pressure to save time.[115] The concentration of capital in large firms, and the recruitment of science into technology, bring about the stage of Modern Industry (where the machines themselves were the products of such workshops) and ultimately machinofacture (where machines were used to construct machinery). 'Simple tools; accumulation of tools; composite tools; setting in motion of a composite tool by a single hand engine, by man; setting in motion of these instruments by natural forces, machines; system of machines having one motor; system of machines having one automatic motor – this is the progress of machinery.'[116] Workshops and machinery were the *cause* of division of labour, for Marx.

Modern Industry was thereby associated with bourgeois capitalism. This spread across sectors by converting all labour into wage labour, and across countries through international competition.[117] Marx predicted that capitalism in turn would break down:

(a) when capitalist relations of production became inadequate for the most rapid advance of technology (the forces of production), i.e. not in the best interests of *employers* (e.g. 'over-production' of capital leading to excessive competition among capitalists);

(b) when capitalist relations became intolerable for its *workers* (e.g. 'over-production' of labourers or labour time), leading to revolution, and giving rise ultimately to communism.

The problems of generating demand ('realization') if labour saving was carried too far seem to be of these kinds: 'Beyond a certain point, the development of the powers of production becomes a barrier for capital. ... The growing incompatibility between the productive development of society and its hitherto existing relations of production expresses itself in bitter contradictions, crises, spasms.'[118]

One difficulty was that (a) and (b) might arise at different times or indeed be contradictory. Marx seems to have believed that revolutions would begin in more backward countries, for reason (b), but take hold properly only when they eventually spread to the most advanced countries, where reason (a) was presumed to be operating.

115 Marx 1887/1965, pp. 336–8, 345. This opens up Marx's distinction between heterogeneous production (the former case) and serial production (the latter), discussed above in Chapter 1.

116 Marx 1859, p. 117.

117 Marx 1858/1973, p. 730; Marx and Engels 1888/1967, p. 84.

118 Marx 1858/1973, p. 749; also Marx and Engels 1888/1967, p. 86.

The consequence of large-scale industry as a technological phenomenon was a new set of social relations in which capital process took over and labour was pushed to the side: 'the human being comes to relate more as watchman and regulator to the production process itself',[119] thus increasing his or her alienation. Science and skills are both transposed into the machine.[120] For Marx, capitalism was seen as both a *spur* to technical change, in encouraging the search for innovations and a *bridle* on it, in regard to the selection chosen to be introduced.[121] The stage reached by the technology and that reached by production organization would generally correspond, but at some point they will come into conflict with each other, and this conflict is deemed to set up pressures for change in both: 'From forms of development of the productive forces these relations turn into their fetters. Then begins an era of social revolution. The changes in the economic foundation lead sooner or later to the transformation of the whole immense superstructure.'[122]

Marx believed that communism would be superior to capitalism in terms of its *dynamic* advantages: the intensity of search for new techniques, the efficiency of selecting new techniques among those thrown up by the search, and the efficiency with which the selected techniques are used in production. 'This a priori belief that all good things go together is a major weakness of his social theory.'[123] In later chapters I shall examine the use made of conflict between technology and organization in some modern approaches to growth and fluctuation, and also the actual experience of 'Second World' communism.

F. Finance and Products

It was not for nothing that Marx's magnum opus was entitled *Capital*, in view of the attention he paid to defining and analysing that subject. As has already been hinted, his main interest for us, however, lies in the ways in which he relates the various spheres together. The same can be said of his analyses of capital and products, each of which also evolved through a sequence of stages, which overlapped but partially with the stages already outlined for technology and for organization.

The stages are approximated in Table 2.1 above; though it should be borne in mind that changes in the various spheres are not completely synchronous. This was not just a matter of historical accuracy but a

119 Marx 1858/1973, p. 705.
120 *Ibid.*, p. 715.
121 Elster 1985, pp. 261–2.
122 Marx 1859/1971, pp. 20–1; also Marx 1909/1977, pp. 883–4.
123 Elster 1985, p. 267.

requirement of his dialectical method; with stage changes occurring because of conflict with other spheres (e.g. when optimum technology and optimum organization become contradictory).

We have seen that the phase of 'relative surplus value' arose where there was pressure to innovate in order to shorten the time required to produce the goods necessary for the labourer's survival. While the duration of the *production process* itself was a matter of technology and organization,[124] the capitalist also had a powerful incentive to shorten the turnover time of his *capital*.[125] In particular, any period of time during which the capital was tied up after production but before the output was sold (the 'circulation time') brought no gain and some loss to the capitalist.[126] Unlike the shortening of necessary labour time in production, Marx did allow that circulation time could be shortened through an expansion of *demand*.[127] Here the agreement with Smith was close. The difficulty was that, under capitalism, Marx believed income distribution would worsen, so any expansion of markets had to be sought abroad.[128]

The turnover time for capital, which as previously noted was the key to value, was the sum of production time and circulation time.[129] Advance thus came from more rapid and/or less costly *production* on the supply side (e.g. recently through developments in science) and more rapid *marketing* for both demand and supply reasons which would lower the 'costs of circulation' (i.e. transaction costs).[130] Again the implication of time saving in Marx would appear to be saving capital rather than saving labour: 'The chief means of reducing the time of circulation is improved communications. The last fifty years have brought about a revolution in this field, comparable only with the industrial revolution of the latter half of the 18th Century ... the efficacy of the capital involved in it [world commerce] has been more than doubled or trebled.'[131] Thus Marx spoke of the 'annihilation of space by time'.[132]

The concerted pressure to cut labour time under capitalism would be eased under communism: 'In a future society, in which class antagonism will have ceased, in which there will no longer be any classes, use will no longer be determined by the *minimum* time of production; but the time of

124 *Ibid.*, p. 545; Marx 1919, ch. 12; Marx 1909/1977, pp. 70–71.

125 E.g. Marx 1858/1973, pp. 538–9, 617, 636–7, 663–7, 741; Marx 1919, chs 14–15; Marx 1909, chs 4, 16–18; Morgan and Sayer 1988, p. 18.

126 Marx 1909, pp. 624–5; Marx 1919/1967, p. 128.

127 Marx 1858/1973, p. 539; Marx 1919/1967, p. 320; Marx 1909/1977, pp. 244–5.

128 *Idem.*

129 Marx 1919, ch. 7.

130 Cf. *ibid.*, ch. 6.

131 Marx 1909/1977, p. 71; quoted by Rosenberg 1982, p. 46.

132 Marx 1858/1973, p. 539.

production devoted to an article will be determined by the degree of its utility'.[133] The role of product demand and quality could thus be suitably expressed; whereas under modern capitalism production had come to dominate consumption.[134] But innovation in Marx is about process innovation, not product innovation,[135] in keeping with the focus on producer rather than consumer classes. The stages of 'products' in Table 2.1 do not refer to kinds of products in the usual sense, but to varying conditions under which they are exchanged (for barter, money, etc.) – they are thus labelled 'product relations'.

Relations of power, above all economic power, dictated the ways in which the system of production came together. Under capitalism, 'It is now no longer the labourer that employs the means of production, but the means of production that employ the labourer'.[136] While Smith aimed to show that self-interest drove society as a whole to an optimum outcome, Marx stressed that it would render the labourers much worse off than under a more equitable social system.[137] Only under the forthcoming communism did he expect the role of political power to subside. It followed that politics – and conflict – played a much more prominent part than for many of his classical predecessors. As he so frequently reminded his readers, this did not mean that classical economists were apolitical, but that their politics were only occasionally made explicit. To describe their work collectively as 'political economy' seems entirely appropriate.

133 Marx 1859, p. 55.
134 *Ibid.*, p. 59.
135 Roemer 1981, p. 130.
136 Marx 1887/1965, p. 310.
137 Roemer 1988, p. 3.

3. Modern Analyses of Growth and Structural Change

> Earlier economists studied the world and knew it was round. Only their maps were flat. Too many later economists studied the maps and mistook them for the world. (Schmookler 1972[1])

From the last quarter of the 19th Century, the classical economics outlined in the previous chapter was usurped by 'neoclassical' schools of economists. In place of political economy, these brought new standards in terms of analytical rigour, based on a particular conception of Newtonian mechanics, an assumption of reversibility, and a presumption that models of exchange were appropriate for models of production.[2] What Lakatos (1987) might have described as the 'hard core' of this approach was the principle of maximization subject to constraints: thus consumers maximized their utilities subject to constraints of incomes, etc., while producers maximized profits subject to constraints of costs, etc. This gain in analytical rigour was achieved at a high price in terms of the concerns of this book. Economists' norms placed higher virtue on such simplicity than complexity,[3] at the cost of ignoring the multi-dimensionality of the real world (as in my Figure 2.2 above, simplified as much as that is). Concepts such as the 'division of labour' disappeared into the background. Major issues such as technology became part of the set of constraints, and ceased to be analysed for their own sakes. Not only did such theorization become artificial, in both its assumptions and its conclusions, it also lost any sense of *time* as part of the process of economic growth. Analysis was static, or more often 'comparative static' as earlier for Ricardo, i.e. making one parametric change and observing the consequences. It was supposed, at its crudest, that one could consider a period of time long enough for all the adjustments to (re-)establish maximization, without other events interrupting or contradicting the process. In Keynes's famous criticism: 'In the long run, we are all dead'. Thus the ability to analyse longer-run questions of *actual*

1 Schmookler 1972, p. 62.
2 Mirowski 1989.
3 Latsis, in Latsis 1976.

growth and development experience, and indeed shorter-run questions of fluctuations, became seriously impaired. For such reasons, this chapter will balance discussion of the landmark contributions in mainstream analysis with consideration of the more heterodox schools of economists. It will also dwell on the contributions of economic historians and others, for whom such general questions remained paramount. For reasons of space, the discussion will mostly be limited to the major figures, as in Chapter 2. Like the previous chapter, this one ends with a brief survey of more recent developments, in which some of the issues appear to be coalescing in a more productive way.

The chapter will concentrate on 20th century contributions to interpreting industrialization, paying most attention to theory and evidence about structural change in the Advanced Industrial Countries (AICs). As in Chapter 2, the aim is to 'accentuate the positive and (partially) eliminate the negative', by stressing the more constructive arguments. More recent theoretical and empirical work has tended to emphasize the spread of industrialization among well-advanced countries, and this will be reflected in the later sections of the chapter.

I: GROWTH AND STRUCTURAL CHANGE

A. The Neoclassical Approach

The neoclassical 'production function', introduced from the late 19th Century, related output directly to factor inputs, thus linking the far-right-hand side of the diagram used above to illustrate classical political economy (Figure 2.1, on p. 25) immediately to the far-left-hand side. The top (production) part of the diagram, in which the transformation of inputs into outputs involved specific choices of technologies, processes, financial arrangements and products within firms (cf. Figure 2.2, p. 32) was ignored, in the sense that such conditions were taken to be exogenous.[4] After giving the celebrated definition of economics as 'the science which studies human behaviour as a relationship between ends and scarce means which have alternative uses', Lionel Robbins argued that analysis of technology was inappropriate for economists.[5] 'Technology' in neoclassical economics thus really means productivity, and relates to the specific bundle of inputs. Notions such as 'high-tech' have no real meaning in this analysis, except in

4 For an enlightened neoclassicist's view that a theory of ideology is required, see North 1981.

5 Robbins 1932, pp. 16, 32–8; Corsi 1991, p. 48n. Interestingly, Robbins especially emphasized scarcity of time along with the 'means' (*op. cit.*, pp. 12–15).

so far as 'high-tech' methods might be more productive. The bottom part of the diagram (consumption) was collapsed into a formulation such as Say's Law (or its modification, Walras's Law), which drove the system to equilibrium.

This neoclassical approach permitted growth to come about endogenously through capital formation (i.e. specific input growth), in similar fashion to that aspect of the preceding classical approach. Alternatively, growth could come from exogenous factors, amongst which technology proper was included (technical progress altered the scaling factor relating output to the total package of inputs). Technology at the microeconomic level is seen as a 'one-off' event, permitting comparative static analysis of the situation before and after its impact. The inherent continuity of innovation which came with the Industrial Revolution is missing from this story.[6] As such, it is more applicable to 'myopic' circumstances in which a cost–benefit analysis can be conducted on each change separately, than to 'dynamic' circumstances where *failing* to undertake some change alters the whole nature of the firm's problem.[7] Nor has any satisfactory means yet been found for endogenizing technical progress in this model (see below, pp. 72–4). Structural change other than through capital formation was effectively ruled out of orthodox studies in the neoclassical framework, by assuming homogeneity of output (a 'one-product' industry or economy).

Major empirical studies in this framework, making use of an 'aggregate production function' (i.e. for the whole economy), however, produced striking results. It appeared that the growth component which could be endogenized, namely capital formation, explained only a small fraction of long-term productivity growth.[8] Most long-run growth thus had to be attributed to the scaling factor used for the production function, and this in turn was loosely ascribed to technical progress (it was pointed out that this 'residual' was in practice a variety of phenomena as well as technology in the strict sense). Thus the model intended to explain growth seemed to have little to say about the actual experience of growth – the main explanatory factor remained exogenous to it.

Without deserting the neoclassical model, two main emendations were attempted in the decade or so following the publication of these results. One was to alter the input composition so as to allow for changing quality as well as quantity of inputs: in particular, the capital input was adjusted to measure capital services more accurately.[9] While this seemed to be fairly successful in shrinking the residual, it did not overcome the basic

---

6 Veblen 1919/1961, p. 232; cf. Chapter 4 below.
7 Pavitt and Patel 1988.
8 Abramovitz 1956; Solow 1957.
9 Jorgenson and Griliches 1967.

deficiency. Technical progress (etc.) became buried within the capital services measure, which thus masked elements which continued to be exogenous.

The alternative was to accept the large contribution of the residual, but try to disaggregate it into components such as sectoral output shifts, economies of scale, human capital formation and technological progress more narrowly. Quantitative studies[10] seemed quite successful in cracking open the residual, but of course did nothing to resolve the theoretical shortcomings of the approach. There were also many objections to the precise ways in which these authors obtained their results – for instance, Denison[11] arbitrarily assumed that 60 per cent of American educational expenditures represented human capital formation.

These modifications therefore failed to rehabilitate the neoclassical approach to growth and development in the eyes of many critics. The results could indeed be used in conjunction with alternative theories and standpoints, which aimed at a more satisfying description of long-term growth and change.

B. Lewis and Development Economics

Sir Arthur Lewis[12] believed that his model of 'economic development with unlimited supplies of labour' represented an alternative to neoclassical models, and derived from the classical models discussed above in Chapter 2. His 1954 paper, one of the most important ever published in the economics of development, begins with the assertion, 'This essay is written in classical tradition, making the classical assumption, and asking the classical question'.[13] The heart of the development problem was to shift the economy's 'centre of gravity',[14] from unproductive to productive categories – in sectoral terms, to shift labour from agriculture to industry. The latter followed from Ricardo's notion of a stationary state that would ensue from lack of technical progress in agriculture; though it was not entirely obvious that agriculture should be 'unproductive', as Lewis was well aware. Indeed it is argued in this book that one can reasonably talk in terms of less productive and more productive *technologies*, but less assuredly about less productive and more productive *sectors*. The Lewis model argued that capital formation in industry was sufficient to achieve this shift towards more productive sectors, so long as the supply of labour to industry from

10 E.g. Denison 1962; Denison and Poullier 1967.
11 Denison 1962, p. 69.
12 Lewis 1954, 1958.
13 Lewis 1954, p. 139.
14 Fei and Ranis 1964.

the unproductive sector(s) was 'unlimited'.[15] However, in a closed economy, i.e. one with no foreign trade, problems would begin to arise once this condition no longer held; for then a transfer of labour out of agriculture would reduce agricultural output, or in classical terminology reduce the output of 'wage goods' on which basic subsistence depended, including the subsistence of those now to be employed in industry. Unless agriculture were also to be developed, this could bring the process of industrialization to a premature halt. However, if development proceeded successfully, agricultural wages would rise towards the levels of industrial wages, and according to Lewis one would enter a neoclassical world. Because of the need to make surplus agricultural labour 'productive' as rapidly as possible, Fei and Ranis (1964) argued that technical progress should be labour-intensive, as opposed to labour saving.

The main implications for this present study are: (i) the need for some degree of sectoral balance between sectors on the supply side; (ii) the desirability of labour-intensive rather than labour-saving technologies in early stages of development. The latter point might, however, raise additional problems. Because of general-equilibrium effects (for example on population growth), classical economists had been wary of advocating increased labour intensity.[16] Other development economists have queried whether the labour-intensive technologies would be adequate for raising productivity in the long term.[17]

C. Kuznets and 'Modern Economic Growth'

Simon Kuznets devoted the bulk of his long academic life to detailed empirical studies of economic growth and fluctuations. His method was one of collating observations across countries and through time, to permit large enough samples on which generalizations could be based ('stylized facts').[18]

Kuznets provided a lucid overview of his own work in his Nobel Lecture, which began with the sentence: 'A country's economic growth may be defined as a long-term rise in capacity to supply increasingly diverse economic goods to its population, this growing capacity based on advancing technology and the institutional and ideological adjustments that it

15 Mokyr (1976, ch. 4), shows that it is not necessary to assume strictly 'unlimited supplies of labour' to obtain the substantive results; and the model was used to advantage in Kindleberger (1967), an analysis of postwar Europe.

16 E.g. Steuart 1767, bk I, ch. 20; cf. p. 29 above.

17 E.g. Sen 1960.

18 These data are summarized in Kuznets (1971).

demands. All three components of the definition are important'.[19] This is therefore a macro-level version of the microeconomic taxonomy of Chapter 2 (implicitly subsuming the managerial/financial factors under the institutional). Kuznets then goes on to argue that advancing technology *per se* is only *permissive* and requires such institutional change ('social invention') for efficient use and further development. 'Epochal' innovations, which combine elements of the technological and institutional, are seen as having changed the course of economic development, including ushering in what he terms 'Modern Economic Growth' (hereafter MEG).[20]

From his enormous extent of empirical studies on national income, the following generalizations about structural change have been drawn, many of them of course predicted in earlier work by other authors.[21]

(a) High rates of growth of per capita product *and* population in the Advanced Industrial Countries (AICs).

(b) High growth rates of productivity (not just labour productivity).

(c) Low growth of *physical* capital per head except during early industrialization, so that little of the subsequent growth in efficiency came *directly* from capital.

(d) High rates of structural transformation of the economies, including:

- i a shift from agricultural to nonagricultural production, but with rising agricultural productivity;
- ii a more recent shift from manufacturing to services, though less consistent;
- iii associated shifts in the structure of employment;
- iv shifts from rents, dividends and interest towards corporate profits within the share of income going to capital, but perhaps a slight decline overall in the share of capital in favour of that of labour;
- v a shift from personal to impersonal organization of firms, and a rise in scale;
- vi shifts in the structure of consumption, including relative increases of government consumption and gross capital formation, though again relatively moderate, while changes in particular categories of private consumption (like food) were considerably less than expected;
- vii shifts between domestic and foreign supplies.

---

19 Kuznets 1973, p. 247; 1974, p. 165.

20 Cf. Kuznets 1964, 1966.

21 Based on Kuznets 1966, pp. 490–500; 1971, 1973.

(e) Changes in the structure and ideology of societies, including urbanization and secularization.

(f) Outward expansion of the AICs through the use of advanced technologies e.g. in transportation and communications, having the effect of globalizing economies.

(g) But only limited spread of MEG, with three-quarters of the world's population still falling far short of deriving its full advantages.

Kuznets showed that several of these factors were causally related, but he explicitly stopped short of any precise causal modelling. He had, however, asserted that trends in industrial structure were associated with 'technological necessities', on both supply and demand sides.[22] Technological progress was the 'necessary condition' for MEG – combined with capital formation, entrepreneurship, and adequate demand it became the 'sufficient condition'.[23] Finally, one may note that Kuznets's macroeconomic approach emphasized the role of national systems and the nation-state, as the level at which such interactions took place.

D. Hicks on Capital and Time

A contribution to the analysis of structural change that has perhaps been given less than its due is that of Hicks.[24] Hicks took over from Ricardo and from the Austrian economists of the late 19th Century the notion that MEG was associated with increasing 'roundaboutness' in production processes. This was reflected most obviously in the growth of industries dependent on huge capital investments, as in Chapters 5 and 6 below. But Hicks pursued the argument somewhat further, to suggest that fixed capital and processes arose in two stages: first, a stage of construction, which would have to be financed while no output was forthcoming; second, a stage of operation, which would have to cover the sacrifices made in the first period, as well as make its own profits.[25]

Hicks's work, and that of the Austrian school generally, does not fit easily into the neoclassical framework, because of implicitly or explicitly rejecting the notion of a timeless equilibrium. More precisely, they replace the orthodox neoclassical notion of 'Newtonian' time (essentially the result of solving differential equations) with an interpretation that has been described

22 Kuznets 1964, p. 45; 1965, p. 95; 1966, pp. 155–6.

23 Kuznets 1959, p. 32.

24 E.g. Hicks 1965, 1973.

25 Lewis (1955, p. 213), argues similarly; for an analysis more explicitly related to innovation, see Amendola and Gaffard 1988.

as one of 'real time'.[26] The latter evidently approaches more closely the notion of historical time used in this book. Hicks[27] described the transition from the old pre-machine situation to the new as a 'traverse', which would occur so long as technology was changing, or more generally when there was more than one capital good.

At an aggregate level, we shall in fact find that there was no simple chronology of construction period followed by operation period, because different investments and processes were being initiated at different times (see Chapter 5 below). Nevertheless, the Hicksian argument turns out to have considerable applicability to the kinds of issues discussed in the empirical chapters here. I shall also be examining the idea of 'roundaboutness', and in particular how its seemingly problematical consequences of delaying production were overcome.[28]

E. Rostow and Stage Theories of Growth

In Chapter 2 it was observed that Marx divided history into stages, and his periodization can now be compared with some other stage theories, as in Table 3.1. Adam Smith's stages,[29] later adapted by John Stuart Mill,[30] have proven difficult to relate to Smith's other theoretical concerns or indeed to historical fact – Smith's history is often described as 'conjectural', with any gaps in the empirical evidence being filled by his *a priori* reasoning. For obvious reasons, his stages have little to say about the evolution of the industrial era. Marx's list has also had to be extended in the light of later developments, most obviously the prolonged – perhaps infinitely prolonged – delay between bourgeois capitalism and its purported crisis. Lenin and others thus added to the list of modes of production later stages of capitalism (like Imperialism – the 'Highest Stage of Capitalism'),[31] and later stages of capital ('Finance Capital').

The American economist Walt Rostow offered a more optimistic interpretation of capitalism and its future, in his book, *The Stages of Economic Growth* (1960), pointedly subtitled *A Non-Communist Manifesto*. Rostow claimed to be drawing heavily on the empirical results of Kuznets. The nature of his successive stages is fairly apparent from their labels, as set out in the right-hand column of Table 3.1. Rostow's description of his stages rests mostly on the products sphere ('high mass consumption',

26 O'Driscoll and Rizzo 1985.
27 Hicks 1965, ch. 16; 1973, Part II.
28 See also Lazonick 1991, p. 128.
29 Outlined in Smith 1776/1976, pp. 689–95.
30 Mill, 1848/1909, pp. 9–20.
31 Lenin 1917.

Table 3.1: Some stage theories of growth

A: Smith/Mill (Sectoral Composition)	B: Marx (Modes of Production only)	C: Rostow (Sectoral Change)
1. Hunting		
2. Pasturage (nomadic)		
	1. Pre-capitalist	1. Traditional Society
3. Agriculture		
4. Manufactures	2. Early Capitalism	2. Preconditions for Take-off
5. Foreign Commerce	3. Bourgeois Capitalism	
		3. Take-off
		4. Drive to Maturity
	4. Socialism	
	5. Communism	5. Age of High Mass Consumption

Note: The horizontal alignment of stages (corresponding to successive historical periods) can only be approximate, given the different criteria employed. For a fuller exposition of Marx's stages, see Table 2.1.

etc.), and they are related to consumer criteria and sectoral characteristics rather than to producer criteria. Rostow argues that his stages are differentiated not by levels of prosperity (per-capita GNP) but in kind, and especially by the sectoral composition.[32] The particular sectors which brought about 'take-off' (etc.), however, varied considerably from country to country.[33] The perspective is one of a simple lifecycle, in which sectors rise then fall fairly regularly. His work has in general been treated sceptically by economic historians, but there has been some support for his notion that the 'take-off' stage in which industrialization first really takes hold involves the advance of just a very few 'leading sectors', for example cotton textiles and iron in the case of Britain. The take-off is also associated with developments in the capital/finance sphere, where Rostow contends that the rate of investment rises from 5 per cent or under of GNP to 10 per

32 Rostow 1960/1971, p. ix.

33 *Ibid.*, p. 57; cf. Chapter 5 below.

cent or over during the relatively short (about 30-year) span of the take-off, a proposition borrowed from the work of Lewis. Though foreign capital inflows may assist this (the railroad is regarded as 'historically the most powerful single initiator of take-offs'[34]), it was the domestic effort which was critical. The rise in investment was intended to include all aspects of innovation, especially the 'increasing returns' from the creation of new industries, but it also rose *because of* innovation.

Rostow then argues that the gains of these 'leading sectors' spread around the economy in the ensuing stage of the 'drive to maturity', through backward linkages, forward linkages and lateral linkages, with the latter reflecting the collateral developments in social and economic infrastructure.[35] These linkages are interpreted as arising through products and sectors rather than processes, and it is in this way that Rostow sees the leading sectors developing into interrelated complexes. Technological spillovers from more advanced countries allowed later developers to experience surges of very rapid sectoral growth as they sought to catch up.[36]

The final stage, the 'age of high mass consumption', is a misnomer, because different countries had in practice sought varying combinations of three outcomes: external pursuit of power and influence, internal egalitarian effort towards the welfare state, and mass consumption proper.[37]

One of the most interesting aspects of Rostow's analysis was the emphasis on the interconnections between economic and political or social events, e.g. the role of 'xenophobic nationalism' in the industrialization of some later-starters (see, for instance, Chapter 10 below on Japan). Again the results are somewhat inconclusive since such reactions might lead downwards rather than upwards, but Rostow's work in this area[38] has perhaps been treated more sympathetically than his analysis of economic development, not least because of the greater care taken with history. In the end, his analytical position is closer to Marx than he is willing to admit, emphasizing as he does stages and multiple interactions, even though his political conclusions are so overtly hostile to Marx.

Elster[39] divides stage models into three:

(a) models of unique development, with all nations going through the same stages in the same order, though not necessarily at the same times;

---

34 *Ibid.*, p. 55.
35 The terminology was derived from Hirschman 1958.
36 Rostow 1980, ch. 6.
37 Rostow 1960/1971, ch. 6.
38 Developed further in Rostow 1971.
39 Elster 1985, pp. 302–3.

(b) bloc-models of development, with the nations as a whole going through the specified stages, though each nation may not do so;

(c) torch-relay models of development – whichever country first arrives at a particular stage, another must lead into the next stage.

Rostow's model would seem to conform to (a), although he accepted that stage transitions might be aborted,[40] and Adam Smith's to (b). According to Elster,[41] Marx offers all three kinds of model at varying times, and ultimately Marx himself may not have had any single view about his stages – as illustrated, for example, in his inconclusive debate with Russian socialists over whether Russia had to go through capitalism first, before communism.[42] The implicit model in this book comes closest to (c), in so far as any stage model is involved. I would, however, agree most with Schumpeter, when he argued that rigid demarcation into stages was unwarranted by the historical evidence, but that it was reasonable to apply such concepts flexibly.[43] Like Marx one has to consider multiple dimensions, which in turn may give rise to indefiniteness in trying to identify any particular country as being in any one stage, and in specifying the source of any particular transition from one stage to the next. A stage theory proper requires that both of the latter be clarified rather than obscured.[44] Thus in contrast to stage theories, I personally would place greater stress on varieties of growth patterns and alternatives to them, as in the Gerschenkronian approach.

F. Gerschenkron and 'Economic Backwardness'

Alexander Gerschenkron[45] vigorously objected to unique models of evolution and to the determinism of stage theories. His basic argument was that development required certain 'prerequisites', but that in the absence of all the prerequisites in the later developing countries, substitutes could be found for them. Specifically:

1 The more backward the country, the more rapid will be its industrialization, i.e. the faster will be its rate of growth of industrial production.

---

40 Rostow 1963, p. xix.

41 Elster 1985, p. 304.

42 Marx and Engels 1888/1967, pp. 66–7; Nove 1969, p. 34; Rostow 1990, p. 145.

43 Schumpeter 1928, p. 362.

44 See e.g. Kuznets, in Rostow 1963, p. 24; Kuznets 1974, p. 212. The stage model of Porter (1990, ch. 10) is even weaker than this in its commitment.

45 Gerschenkron 1952, 1962.

2 The more backward the country, the greater will be its stress on producer (capital) goods as compared with consumer goods.
3 The more backward the country, the larger will be the typical scale of plant and firm, and the greater will be the emphasis on latest, up-to-date technology.
4 The more backward the country, the greater will be the pressure on the consumption levels of the population; consumption levels will be squeezed to promote a high rate of capital formation.
5 The more backward the country, the less will be the role of the agricultural sector as a market for industrial goods and as a source of rising productivity in its own right.
6 The more backward the country, the more active will be the role of special institutional factors – great banks as in Germany, the government ministry of finance as in Russia – in supplying capital and promoting industrialization.
7 The more backward the country, the more important will be ideologies of industrialization in the shaping of policies and events.[46]

In particular, Gerschenkron emphasized:

(a) the role of the state, especially in conditions of extreme backwardness;

(b) the role of financial institutions, especially the German type of bank ('universal bank') combining commercial and investment banking;

(c) the role of ideology, because the greater the degree of backwardness, the more entrenched anti-developmental forces (aristocracies, etc.) were likely to be.[47]

Again, these are straightforward to relate to the taxonomy introduced in Chapter 2, and specifically the determinants of growth treated as exogenous to the firm but endogenous to the country. In this respect, Gerschenkron can be interpreted as arguing that the nature and relative significance of the various determinants will change as time goes on and the gap between leaders and followers widens. There was no guarantee that substitutes would be found – as in Bulgaria, the opportunity for industrialization could be missed altogether.[48]

In regard to technology, Gerschenkron's view was that, contrary to popular opinion, low wages in the more backward countries did not mean that such labour was truly 'cheap' – creating a stable and disciplined labour force might be very costly.[49] This belief turns out to be one of the best supported generalizations in the chapters to follow below. Its implications

---

46 Sylla and Toniolo 1991/1992, p. 5; paraphrased mainly from Gerschenkron 1963, pp. 152–3, 353–4, and 1968, pp. 90–92.

47 Sylla and Toniolo 1991/1992, pp. 16–21.

48 Gerschenkron 1962, pp. 362–4; see also Harley, in Sylla and Toniolo, ch. 2.

49 Rosovsky 1966.

include his point that backward countries undertaking catch-up might benefit by defying apparent economic logic and instead investing in labour-saving technologies; although this is a point accepted with greater reservations hereafter.

A common criticism of Gerschenkron is that his explanation applied, if at all, only to the European countries of his detailed study. Later developers such as Japan did not necessarily take the role of the state, say, further still. Different patterns prevailed in very different environments, as it is the task of this book to establish. However, there may be some support for the view that one can group industrialization patterns in different 'modes' – the European mode, the American mode and the Japanese mode, for instance – and *within* each of these 'modes' something of a Gerschenkronian pattern exists, though not necessarily all his points. I shall return to this in the Conclusion.

II: TECHNOLOGY

A. Neoclassical Economics of Innovation

It has been noted that neoclassical economics did not have any theory of technology, although some of its most capable exponents had demonstrated just how important technical change (very broadly interpreted) seemed to be in economic growth. The problem is more serious than it is often considered. 'Technology' in this approach flowed from the concept of the production function, and was represented as the set of relationships between a collection of inputs and an output (product). Technology could advance exogenously from scientific progress, as discussed in the next sub-section, which would appear as a parametric shift in the overall ratio of output to inputs. Alternatively, technology could advance endogenously from inducements offered by the high costs of one particular input (cf. Table 1.1, p. 7). Neoclassical economics struggled to provide an explanation for the common observation, referred to in Chapter 1, that 'expensive' labour would lead to labour-saving technical change.[50] These often tortuous efforts failed to elicit any consensual support from most economists.[51]

Neoclassical economics instead, like Ricardo's early work, focuses on substitution between capital and labour: if the price of labour rises relative to that of capital (i.e. wages rise relative to interest rates), managers should

50 E.g. Kennedy 1964; Hahn and Matthews 1964; Samuelson 1965; von Weiszäcker 1966.

51 David 1975, ch. 1.

substitute capital for labour as it becomes relatively cheaper. This raises difficult empirical questions of distinguishing between factor substitution and genuine technological progress in practice.[52] Even more problematic is that it says nothing about innovation, and indeed explicitly assumes no change in technology – the substitution represents a move from one point of equilibrium (particular capital/labour ratio) to another which is supposed to be based on the same technology, hence it is a question of choosing particular techniques from a given technology. If we assume that all such changes have been made and that the system comes to rest at a new point of equilibrium, there is no reason to expect that innovation (change in the technology) should now be biased any further in this direction; because by definition, at the point of equilibrium all inputs are equally cheap (or dear). The arguments here are rather complex, but the outcome is that, to explain a labour-saving bias to innovation, the orthodox economist has to resort to some kind of tacked-on assumption. It may be, for instance, that expectations about future changes of input prices (e.g. expectations of rising wages in later years) guide entrepreneurs towards saving labour (etc.), or that expectations about future technological trends do so, but these have to remain unexplained in themselves.

In the orthodox neoclassical framework there is no learning of the kinds described in the previous chapter. One of the most distinguished of modern economists, Arrow,[53] inserted the notion of 'learning by doing' into economics, brought from a reading of the literature on psychology. The 'learning curve' or 'experience curve' indicated a time pattern of productivity growth in a particular activity. As briefly noted in Chapter 2, Arrow used the psychology and engineering literature to argue that learning from existing production set-ups would rapidly diminish as familiarity took over – continuing to learn required new situations and thus, for Arrow, new investments rather than simply more output.[54] One could imagine a production function which itself became a function of gross output or gross investment, but such a step towards endogenizing technology is rarely taken, probably because neoclassical economics prefers to work in terms of stable or parametric functions (the usual procedure instead is to add a simple time trend to the production function). Other forms of learning such as 'learning by using' are still more difficult to incorporate, because 'technologies' are so product-specific. In the framework suggested in this book, where technologies and products are conceptually distinguished, such difficulties abate.

52 Nelson and Winter 1974.

53 Arrow 1962b.

54 Bell and Scott-Kemmis 1985.

These deficiencies arose in turn from presuming that the role of the firm was a 'black box', passively implementing best-practice technology which came parametrically – 'like manna from heaven' in the stereotype[55] – presumably from the exogenous advance of the Science and Technology system. The notion of firms as the main generators of technical change was alien to this conception. 'Textbook firms have one goal, profit maximization; one strategy, price competition; and one organizational means, cost minimization.'[56] In Chapter 8 below we find that the firms which actually limited themselves to this particular mix of goal, strategy and means were ultimately doomed.

B. The Role of Science and Technology (S&T)

We can turn next to the determinant of technology which is regarded as exogenous to the firm, namely general progress in S&T. Kuznets had long seen the 'epochal' innovation underlying MEG as being, 'the emergence of modern science as the basis of advancing technology – a breakthrough in the evolution of science that produced a potential for technology far greater than existed previously'.[57] But the role of science had evidently risen later in the 19th century, and he was ambivalent about its relationship to early industrialization.[58] He accepted other findings that much technical progress was as 'a stream of relatively cheap changes and improvements whose cumulative effect is a drastic reduction in input of resources accompanied by increases in output', though even these were sustained by scientific advance.[59] He therefore cautioned against attributing too much to one particular innovation, favouring instead the consolidation of a stream into 'a large subcomplex' of interrelated inventions.[60]

The chain linkage between science and technology could reach far back into the realms of seemingly useless abstract science, and there might be long lags between the science and the resulting technology.[61] But existing science did not have all the answers, and Kuznets referred to a positive feedback that could 'permit the development of new efficient tools for scientific use and supply new data on the behavior of natural processes under the stress of modification in economic production'.[62] Part of the

55 Hahn and Matthews 1964.
56 Best 1990, p. 139.
57 Kuznets 1973, p. 249; 1974, p. 169.
58 Kuznets 1965, pp. 85–6; 1966, pp. 10–11.
59 Kuznets 1965, p. 34; 1989, p. 10.
60 Kuznets 1966, p. 471; 1979, pp. 65, 110.
61 Kuznets 1965, p. 84; 1971, pp. 330, 351; 1979, pp. 60, 64, 95.
62 Kuznets 1973, p. 250; 1974, p. 171; also 1979, pp. 83–6.

feedback could take the form of learning, and thus *induced* human capital formation.[63] In the historical discussion of Chapter 4 we shall see just how important such feedbacks were in practice. After his early work (1930), Kuznets gave no statistical measures of science or technology, or their linkages.

If technology and growth came from science, why was the whole world not developed? His reply was that the stocks of applied technical advances were responses to specific industrial needs, which would limit their usefulness for later industrializing countries. The less-industrialized countries (LICs) would require substantial modifications of material technologies, but still more of their institutional and ideological environments, i.e. their social and political structures and climates of opinion.[64] As noted below in discussing fluctuations, such interactions could well be disruptive.

At first sight, Rostow appears to be taking the same view as Kuznets: 'What distinguishes the world since the industrial revolution from the world before is the systematic, regular, and progressive application of science and technology to the production of goods and services'.[65] The contribution of technology was at first assigned to three arbitrarily given (historically derived) 'propensities': the propensity to develop fundamental science (physical and social), the propensity to apply science to economic ends, and the propensity to accept innovations, which were taken to be sectoral applications of the more general 'propensity to seek material advance'.[66] Later, Rostow's analysis of the relationship between science and technology in early industrialization became much more sceptical than the above quote implies,[67] and considerably more accurate than Kuznets's (see Chapter 4 below). In other respects, technology is assumed to respond to 'necessity' in the crude way so adeptly criticized by Mowery and Rosenberg (1979); subject only to a simple lifecycle of expansion and deceleration, which itself was also based on Kuznets's early work (1930). Through the latter cycle, first increasing returns and later diminishing returns induced technical progress. Rostow's own theory of cycles is outlined below.

The role of technology in Rostow's stages is to provide what he terms its 'analytic bone-structure', driving the economy forward not only within each stage but also from one stage to the next. Despite this central function, Rostow concentrates on the *product* linkages (including viewing machinery as a product), and says little about the nature of the relevant technologies

63 *Ibid.*, p. 93.
64 Kuznets 1966, p. 12; 1973, p. 256.
65 Rostow 1975, p. 2.
66 Rostow 1953/1960, chs 1–2.
67 Rostow 1975, ch. 4.

themselves.[68] Apart from the rather ambiguous role of science, there is no technological creativity in the model – the drive to technological maturity comes from a passive build-up of 'technological absorptive capacity' through education, etc., aimed at adopting a backlog of existing technologies.[69] In the light of the rationale of the firm introduced in Chapter 1 above, I would argue that this oversight is to his cost, and that the emergence of accepted technological or other heuristics in particular sectors provides a more convincing analytic bone-structure.

C. Schumpeter and 'New Combinations'

In many ways Joseph Schumpeter stands in a similar position in regard to 20th-century studies of industrialization as Marx does to the classical era. Schumpeter himself frequently acknowledged similarities between his position and that of Marx. Both long remained outside the mainstream of economic analysis, and in many respects still do so. The obvious differences were that Schumpeter preceded rather than succeeded the main body of work to which his analysis of capitalist development was relevant, and that the two came from very different points on the political spectrum (although both predicted the eventual demise of capitalism).

For Schumpeter, the economy in a situation of circular flow was in a state of 'normality' rather than 'abnormality'. A tendency to economic equilibrium prevailed, although in contrast to the classical circular flow outlined in the previous chapter, this did not mean that nothing was changing: 'The data may change, and everyone will act accordingly as soon as it is noticed. But everyone will cling as tightly as possible to habitual economic methods.'[70] Risk was also not completely absent, but there was no significant uncertainty. Such habitual behaviour was bred of long experience. These notions of routine have been important for more recent microeconomic analyses in the Schumpeterian spirit, e.g. by Nelson and Winter (1982). In this situation of the circular flow, Schumpeter believed that neoclassical economic analysis as outlined above should indeed apply. However, he considered that, unlike the image conveyed by neoclassical economics of optimization, the economy would probably *not* be operating

68 In part this may have resulted from Rostow's antipathy to Marx, and the latter's division between capital and consumption goods rather than product-based sectors. Rostow 1960/1971 (p. 239) quotes Marxian critiques which emphasize the distinction between the forces of production and the social relations, but does not seem to grasp them. Rostow 1990 (pp. 451–70, 546–53) summarizes his general views on what the role of technology ought to be.

69 *Ibid.*, p. 432.

70 Schumpeter 1911/1961, pp. 8–9.

at full technological capacity.[71] This was because the technological 'trajectories' (here to use the more recent phrase) that evolved were subject to routine incremental improvement, and might not have incorporated more radical advances – they were not necessarily the best that the economy might have chosen on the basis of existing technological knowledge.

Development, for Schumpeter, is the opposing state of 'abnormality'. It is characterized by 'dynamics' rather than by 'statics', and Schumpeter emphasized that in the cases of at least two of the sources of disturbance we need to go beyond simple exogeneity. The two factors that are most relevant for us are 'changes in technique and in productive organization'.[72] He explicitly drew parallels with Marx in this insistence on internal development rather than mere adaptation. In the *Theory of Economic Development*, Schumpeter identified the entrepreneur as the bearer of change, because the entrepreneur brings into being 'new combinations', meaning radically different patterns of production. He chose the wording 'new combinations' deliberately to emphasize putting things into economic operation rather than the initial discoveries. A dynamic discontinuity of such kind 'is that kind of change arising from within the system *which so displaces its equilibrium point that the new one cannot be reached from the old one by infinitesimal steps*. Add successively as many mail coaches as you please, you will never get a railway thereby.'[73] More precisely, these new combinations are listed as:

(1) The introduction of a new good – that is one with which consumers are not yet familiar – or of a new quality of a good.
(2) The introduction of a new method of production, that is one not yet tested by experience in the branch of manufacture concerned, which need by no means be founded upon a discovery scientifically new, and can also exist in a new way of handling a commodity commercially.
(3) The opening of a new market, that is a market into which the particular branch of manufacture of the country in question has not previously entered, whether or not this market has existed before.
(4) The conquest of a new source of supply of raw materials or half-manufactured goods, again irrespective of whether this source already exists or whether it has first to be created.
(5) The carrying out of the new organization of any industry, like the creation of a monopoly position (for example through trustification) or the breaking up of a monopoly position.[74]

---

71 *Ibid.*, pp. 12–15.
72 *Ibid.*, p. 60n.
73 *Ibid.*, p. 64n, author's italics.
74 *Ibid.*, p. 66.

In later works such as *Capitalism, Socialism and Democracy* (1943), Schumpeter emphasized that capitalism itself evolved, through a process he termed 'Creative Destruction'. Innovations, in the above sense of new combinations, 'incessantly revolutionize the economic structure *from within*, incessantly destroying the old one, incessantly creating a new one'.[75] Again, the point followed from Marx.[76] Such Creative Destruction was witnessed by his belief that innovations were typically – though not universally – characterized by New Plant, New Firms and New Men.[77] This radical institutional change permitted a change of what Schumpeter called economic 'Horizon'.[78]

It is clear that, for Schumpeter, a new combination did not mean just technological change – technology was just one among many ingredients of a radical discontinuity. Schumpeter's list indeed covers the full range of possibilities suggested by my taxonomy in Figure 2.2 (p. 32). We can thus proceed to considering the organizational sphere in 20th-century economic thinking; since processes have not been well defined in this literature the discussion will be combined with that on management.

III: ORGANIZATION AND MANAGEMENT

A. Schumpeter and Entrepreneurship

Schumpeter's earlier work has often stood accused of glorifying the 'heroic entrepreneur'. Although he was anxious to dispel this impression in later works, there seems considerable evidence to support the view that this early work was much influenced by the German philosopher, Friedrich Nietzsche, and the notion of the 'Superman'.[79] In the *Theory of Economic Development*,[80] he did stress that, 'new combinations are, as a rule, embodied ... in new firms which generally do not arise out of the old ones but start producing beside them; to keep to the example already chosen, in general it is not the owner of stage-coaches who build railways'. But on the following page of that work he noted that in large 'combines' (conglomerate or multidivisional firms) or in socialist economies, new combinations might take place internally within the existing unit, for example through setting up a new division. Whatever his early thinking,

75 Schumpeter 1943, p. 83.
76 *Ibid.*, p. 82.
77 Schumpeter 1939, pp. 94–5.
78 *Ibid.*, p. 99.
79 Santarelli and Pesciarelli 1990.
80 Schumpeter 1911/1961, p. 66.

Schumpeter's work is more often associated today with the focus he came to in his later work on large firms and monopolies, and their bureaucratic administration systems. Entrepreneurship could still emerge in large combines, but he stressed that it differed from Alfred Marshall's concept of 'mere management', because of the emphasis on bringing the kind of discontinuities associated with 'new combinations' into effective operation.

To this can be added several other key features of Schumpeter's notions of entrepreneurship and development:

(a) that entrepreneurship involved genuine uncertainty, not just some kind of (insurable) risk;

(b) that it involved 'leadership' though not necessarily charisma – its main requirement was to overcome the forces of habit to carry on simply repeating past practices, i.e. a change of 'paradigm' in the more recent terminology;[81]

(c) that it will require sustained support from the banking (credit) system, which in parallel fashion would have to supply 'abnormal credit' as opposed to 'normal credit' (here Schumpeter was thinking of something like modern-day venture capital).

B. Schumpeter and Large Firms

In Schumpeter's later works, he on the one hand rejected the view of some Marxists that monopoly proper was increasing, but on the other hand accepted that 'monopolistic competition' between large firms (i.e. oligopolistic competition) was rising. In his view, this derived from their inherent advantages for innovation:

> there are advantages which, though not strictly unattainable on the competitive level of enterprise, are as a matter of fact secured only on the monopoly level, for instance, because monopolization may increase the sphere of influence of the better, and decrease the sphere of influence of the inferior, brains, or because the monopoly enjoys a disproportionately higher financial standing.[82]

But in this concentration of R&D lay some of the seeds of eventual collapse. In such giant firms: 'innovation itself is being reduced to a routine. Technological progress is increasingly becoming the business of teams of trained specialists who turn out what is required and make it work in predictable ways'.[83]

---

81 *Ibid.*, p. 86; cf. Chapter 1 above.

82 Schumpeter 1943, p. 101; note that here monopoly means giant firms.

83 *Ibid.*, p. 132.

For Schumpeter, such routinization of R&D was one of the ingredients of bureaucratization and depersonalization in large firms that eventually would lead to something like socialism:

> [Capitalist enterprise will] break to pieces under the pressure of its own success. The perfectly bureaucratized giant industrial unit not only ousts the small or medium-sized firm and 'expropriates' its owners, but in the end it also ousts the entrepreneur and expropriates the bourgeoisie as a class. The true pacemakers of socialism were not the intellectuals or agitators who preached it but the Vanderbilts, Carnegies and Rockefellers.[84]

As he admitted,[85] this brought him back to a position akin to that of the Marxists, though from the opposite theoretical (and political!) standpoint. It may be noted that Alfred Marshall had earlier had similar anxieties.[86] These may be thought of as later equivalents of the negative aspects of the division of labour (association with routine) noted by Adam Smith, subsequently to be taken up by Arrow. Marshall drew less apocalyptic conclusions than did Schumpeter, by concluding that this routinization would continue to provide a role in creativity for SMFs.[87]

C. Marshall and Economies of Scale

Although Schumpeter makes use of the John Stuart Mill argument about higher-quality employees in large firms (p. 43 above), as seen in one of the above quotations, he does not refer explicitly to 'economies of scale' in R&D, which today is often identified as 'the' Schumpeterian hypothesis.[88] This latter argument was in fact put forward more directly by Alfred Marshall[89] than by Schumpeter, and can best be seen as part of his more general exegesis of 'economies of scale'.

Marshall today is primarily remembered as one of the founders of neoclassical economics, in particular for developing the 'partial equilibrium' approach to determining prices and quantities in his *Principles of Economics* (1890, especially Book V). The simplest exposition of such an approach assumes 'perfect competition', i.e. the existence of many competing producers, each individually too small to influence market prices. To illustrate the approach, Marshall devised the 'representative firm', drawn from considering such as the English cotton textile industry.

---

84 *Ibid.*, p. 134.
85 E.g. *ibid.*, p. 61.
86 Marshall 1919, pp. 242–3.
87 *Ibid.*, p. 249.
88 E.g. Fisher and Temin 1973.
89 Marshall 1919, pp. 172–3, 593–4.

However, he drew extensive attention to the existence of economies of scale, which the representative firm was assumed to have already gained. Marshall associated such scale economies with the passage of time, for in the long term there were few if any 'fixed costs', as plant and equipment, etc. could be varied.

Marshall distinguished 'internal' economies of scale, which arose within a firm through greater and greater division of labour, from 'external' scale economies. For a firm to be in equilibrium, according to Marshall, it must already have reaped its internal scale economies, otherwise it could always gain from further expansion. However, economies of scale external to firms, but internal to industries, were compatible with equilibrium among the firms. These external economies related to spillover gains among firms, where each could benefit from the others' presence. Examples included vertical linkages between firms, and localization economies e.g. through learning environments.[90] External economies were long considered something of a freak, but have recently been restored to an important place, through association with networks, 'flexible specialization', etc. (see Chapter 8 below). A major issue for Marshall was whether economies of scale are 'reversible' – to remain in a neoclassical world, they need to be in order that, if outputs were to decline again, costs would climb back to their initial levels. But the common sources of falling long-run costs such as technical progress are normally regarded as 'irreversible', and Marshall himself seems to have thought the same – in other words, the gains would not be lost if for some reason output later shrank back.[91] In this case, we have effectively moved out of a 'timeless' neoclassical world – something which, in fairness, Marshall long strove to do. Some major recent reappraisals of economies of scale in this light have been briefly noted above in Chapter 1.

Marshall's major later work, *Industry and Trade* (1919), like Schumpeter's, placed almost all of its emphasis on large firms and monopolistic environments. Formal analysis was eschewed, and Marshall instead discussed at length the contributions of technology, management, and marketing, placing much greater emphasis on the last-named than any other front-rank economist.

---

90 Marshall 1890/1961, pp. 267–77; 1919, pp. 286–7.

91 Blaug 1962, pp. 364–6.

IV: MARKETS AND PRODUCTS

A. Imperfect and Monopolistic Competition

Marshall's and Schumpeter's ideas about large firms were naturally extended by a variety of economists in the 1920s and 1930s to the analysis of imperfectly competitive firms, i.e. firms large enough to have an influence on the prices at which their products sold in markets. Lazonick[92] provides a lucid analysis of how the dynamic questions posed by Marshall got diverted into the static issue of compatibility between imperfect competition and market equilibrium. Pure monopolies, facing no competition, would thus find the maximum profit position by trading off higher output against lower prices per unit of output.

The more interesting case, however, was of firms individually large enough to affect their product prices, but not so large as to be able to act as pure monopolies. Typical of many 20th-century industries appeared to be the situation of oligopoly (literally, few sellers; in practice often around three to six); with the firms often locked in intense competition with one another. Such firms were likely to be large, but this would be in order to reduce external 'competitive uncertainty'[93] or exert external control, rather than for efficiency within the firm as sought from internal scale economies. Analysis, initially through concepts such as the 'kinked' demand curve,[94] and subsequently via game theory, set out the importance of leadership and retaliation in oligopolistic markets. The kinked demand curve view argued that oligopolistic firms were likely to avoid changing prices, because if one were to raise its price, its competitors would not, and it could lose much of its market. However, if one firm were to reduce its price, competitors would follow suit, a 'price war' would ensue, until stability eventually returned, either through agreed lower prices (in which case the consumer would benefit), or through knocking some of the competition out of the market. The rather unattractive prospects of price reductions so far as the producers were concerned thus tended to preserve stability for long periods. All these results seemed to accord with empirical observation (see Chapter 6 below).

An implication was that oligopolistic firms would try to compete either through trying to increase the loyalty of their customers to their products, e.g. through advertising and brand-names, or through reducing costs and raising product qualities, rather than through cutting prices as in conventional competition.

---

92 Lazonick 1991, ch. 5.
93 Freeman 1982, ch. 7.
94 Sweezy 1939.

> But in capitalist reality as distinguished from its textbook picture, it is not that kind of [static price] competition which counts but the competition from the new commodity, the new technology, the new source of supply, the new type of organization (the largest-scale unit of control for instance) – competition which commands a decisive cost or quality advantage and which strikes not at the margins of the profits and the outputs of existing firms but at their foundations and their very lives.[95]

The focus on cost reductions, the intensity of the competition, and the relatively small number of participants (hence lower costs of information transmission), all provided reasons why one might expect oligopolies to be in the forefront of technological progress, as in the Schumpeterian view stated earlier. The even more obvious reason, and probably Schumpeter's main one, was their possession of or access to adequate capital funds. However, the empirical evidence that oligopolies are in the vanguard of technology remains controversial, as already implied.

An alternative possibility is that the potential instability of oligopoly would set up forces driving the industrial structure towards monopoly, either through direct acquisitions, etc., or indirectly through cartels to achieve similar objectives. Price wars often ended in attempts to pool or cartelize. The issues are dealt with empirically in Chapters 5 and 6 below.

B. Economies of Scope

Economies of size arose simply from larger total output. As shown in Chapter 1, economies of scale in a stricter sense derived from having more processes or more intensive processes; the classic example is Henry Ford's assembly line, discussed in Chapters 6 to 8 below. As shown there, 20th-century firms have increasingly aimed at a greater and greater range of product variants, as well as (or sometimes instead of) a greater output of a particular product. The extent to which such diversification can bring gains through lower costs and/or higher profits is referred to as 'economies of scope'.

The usual presumption is that scope economies derive from synergies in one or more of the firm's spheres of activity (as defined in Figure 2.2). Thus they could come about through savings per unit in marketing or finance, out of selling or funding a larger range of products. In the neoclassical approach, where 'technology' refers to a combination of inputs to produce an output, economies of scope thus come from 'joint production', i.e. using the same inputs for more than one product. As true joint products are rather uncommon, it is often presumed in practice that the synergies lie in

---

95 Schumpeter 1943, p. 84.

technologies – the ability to use very similar technology to produce a different good. In the neoclassical formulation outlined above, it is by no means straightforward to analyse such technological scope economies, because the technologies themselves are not separately identified. Orthodox microeconomics uses the concept of 'cross-elasticities' to indicate how close one product is to another in terms of demands for them; but on the supply side, the framework can only show the extent to which one input can readily be substituted for another (the 'elasticity of substitution'), which may have little connection with the issue of turning the technology to use for producing other products. In the methodology introduced in Chapter 1, where technologies and products are initially distinguished, there is no such problem.

C. Income Distribution

As shown later in this book, the major cause of such proliferation of products inside firms was the expansion of demand in general, and especially its strengthening in the middle-income ranges. As follows from Malthus's class-based discussion of demand in Chapter 2 above, a highly unequal income distribution is likely to be associated with a polarization between luxury goods on the one hand and basic necessities on the other hand, whereas a more egalitarian distribution of income and wealth is likely to encourage demand for 'decencies'. The shift of demand towards consumer durables and the like, as illustrated in the empirical chapters hereafter, corresponds with this inference.

Kuznets included income distribution in his extensive empirical studies. He drew the conclusion that early industrialization was likely to be associated with an *increase* in income inequality.[96] Later, however, the pattern would reverse, so that the middle and final stages of industrialization were likely to bring increased equality.[97] This may have come about through the so-called 'trickle-down' effect, though experts are divided about how automatic trickle-down can be. Although there are some notable exceptions, for instance in Latin America (cf. Chapter 11 below), most writers have been willing to accept the Kuznets inverse-U curve, with first rising then falling inequality, as a 'stylized fact'. Partly because of the curve shape, Kuznets was less willing to commit himself to any opinion about whether greater or lesser inequality would be good for growth.

96 E.g. Kuznets 1965, pp. 142–75, 257–303.

97 Similar conclusions had been reached much earlier by Tocqueville in 1835, also later by Rostow 1978a, p. 64.

D. Keynes and Aggregate Demand

John Maynard Keynes deferred completely to Schumpeter so far as long-run issues were concerned.[98] For short-run analysis, however, he revolutionized the subject of economics, and in terms of economic policy-making his subsequent influence neared that of Adam Smith in the 18th Century. Keynes argued that the macro-economy is more than just the sum-total of intended behaviours at the micro level within. Each agent operating in his or her best interest may not necessarily be acting in the best interests of the economy. This flagrant denial of the invisible hand principle comes from separating the supply side from the demand side. Keynes rejected Say's Law on the grounds, adumbrated in Smith (see Chapter 2 above), that savers and investors are different people, with different motives. There is no reason why their *ex ante* plans to save or invest should be equal. However, as a matter of national income accounting, the aggregate level of savings and investment must be equal, *ex post*.

This leads into the most important part of Keynes's contribution. Given that intended (*ex ante*) savings do not equal intended investment, i.e. that intended aggregate supply does not equal intended aggregate demand, how is it that they are eventually equalized (*ex post*)? In that respect, his analysis was of the dynamic paths pursued by an economy in disequilibrium, and especially of the paths followed to bring the system back towards some kind of equilibrium. The problem was exacerbated by the fact that savings were dictated by supply considerations but investment by demand issues. If intended savings fell short of intended investment, there would result inflation that would raise actual savings to a level sufficient to cover the level of investments. Conversely, if intended investment was lower than intended savings, there would be a period of unemployment to allow ultimate equalization. In order to argue this, Keynes reversed the pattern of causation implied by Say's Law, that supply created its own demand – in his model, investment led savings rather than vice versa.

Keynes derived such results by effectively reversing the time-pattern of causation implied by Marshall's short run and long run, referred to above. In Marshallian (neoclassical) economics, prices react immediately, output only in the medium term, and capital for production decisions only in the long term. Keynes instead argued that some prices (notably wages as the price of labour) cannot react speedily, and the brunt of short-term response to some shock is necessarily taken up by changes in quantities and employment.[99] Moreover, the effect of unemployment in terms of reduced aggregate demand (lower incomes) will cause that unemployment to spiral

98 Keynes 1930/1971, pp. 85–6.
99 Leijonhufvud 1968.

upwards. Keynes, however, unduly simplified the demand determinants at this point by reducing product demand to the 'consumption function', instead of preserving the variety of consumption determinants found in his mentors such as Malthus.[100]

Keynes's personal influence helped dictate the course of postwar economic history through his direct contributions to the structure of international trade and payments (Chapter 7). His analysis of aggregate demand and supply for many years dominated economic policy, in a whole host of countries after the Second World War. In a way that he himself would probably not have desired, this led to arguments that put demand ahead of supply, while the real message was one of establishing paths that would keep them in balance.

E. Unbalanced vs. Balanced Growth

For present purposes, Keynes's main contribution, apart from his influence on government macroeconomic policy-making, was in asserting the independent role of demand in determining growth and fluctuations. Growth models based on Keynes, such as those of Harrod (1939) and Domar (1946), compared growth of demand with growth of supply, and showed that the two might be in conflict – indeed in the Harrod version, equilibrium sat on a 'knife-edge'. The role of demand-led growth also came in sectoral models, such as that of Kaldor (1966), who envisaged growth in non-manufacturing sectors as resulting from a boost to aggregate demand arising out of manufacturing expansion. For Less-Industrialized Countries (LICs), equivalent models of 'unbalanced growth' were suggested, for example, by Hirschman, who put forward the view that supply-side deficiencies could be overcome, '*provided, however, that economic development first raises its head*'.[101] Hirschman argued that Keynesian macroeconomic management was quite inadequate to achieve this. Schumpeter (1939) had argued for constructing infrastructure such as railways, and thus 'building ahead of demand' (see Chapter 6 below). Hirschman,[102] however, believed that the best strategy was to maximize backward plus forward linkages, and thus rejected both infrastructure and final consumer goods as avenues for rapid growth, plumping instead for intermediate manufactures like iron and steel, with large input/output connections. He considered that capital-intensive production at the firm level might well be justified in LICs, despite its apparent economic

---

100 Chapter 2 above; and Keynes 1933/1973, ch. 12, especially p. 98.

101 Hirschman 1958, p. 5, author's italics.

102 *Ibid.*, chs 5–6.

irrationality, if it brought machine pacing and process control.[103] To initiate unbalance might require an inflow of foreign capital.[104]

This 'unbalanced growth' notion was by way of a riposte to the concept of 'balanced growth' previously formulated by Nurkse[105] and others. Nurkse's view was that resources like capital were so scarce in LICs that their conservation and optimal use was essential. This was best achieved through developing sectors in accordance with 'income elasticities of demand', i.e. with consumer preferences as their incomes gradually rose. Too often the pattern in LICs had been one of producing in 'export enclaves' for the demands of AICs rather than indigenous needs, with the consequence of limiting technological and employment spillovers to the domestic economy. But Nurkse cautioned against the 'demonstration effect' of imitating luxury consumption in the AICs, if market forces were simply left to operate freely. 'Balanced growth' thus required active government intervention and usually planning for co-ordination, in order to reap the external economies from advancing on several fronts at once.

V: MODERN GROWTH THEORIES

A. Convergence or Divergence?: Empirical Evidence

To the extent that it was valid, Gerschenkron's argument about backwardness indicated that later developers would catch up the earlier leaders of industrialization, as a result of their more rapid growth spurts. A series of articles in major US economics and economic history journals in the later 1980s argued that the pattern of growth across countries could to some extent be accounted for by long-term 'convergence' of growth performances, especially in regard to labour productivity.

Baumol (1986) began by examining productivity in the AICs over the period 1870–1979, to show a strong negative correlation between 1870 productivity levels and subsequent growth performance – for example, Australia had the highest productivity level in 1870 but the slowest subsequent growth rate among the AICs he considered. This appeared to support notions such as Gerschenkron's about catching-up.

However, when Baumol considered a much wider range of countries over the briefer period for which reasonable data were available, a different picture emerged. Several bands of countries now appear:

---

[103] *Ibid.*, ch. 8.
[104] *Ibid.*, pp. 205–9.
[105] Nurkse 1953, 1961, ch. 10.

(a) the AICs, exhibiting convergence;

(b) the Centrally Planned Economies (CPEs), and certain others at intermediate levels of productivity, which showed no great extent of catching-up;

(c) the LICs, which actually showed indications of a widening 'divergence', not only from the AICs but even among the LICs themselves. This group was later split between Asian and African groups of countries.

Thus Baumol suggested that there were at best 'clubs' within which convergence operated, but without any guarantee of convergence between the clubs – moreover the lowest club did not show convergence within.

Baumol's results for the AICs were attacked, successfully, by De Long (1988), who showed that Baumol had been guilty of *ex post* selection of the AICs – had he chosen the countries with highest productivity in the *initial* year (1870) rather than in the *final* year (1979), as the hypothesis clearly requires, he would not have come up with a strong pattern of convergence even for the AICs. For example, the Latin American countries appeared low down in the list of highest-productivity countries as of 1870, but then grew very slowly,[106] ending up in club (b). Subsequent studies on much larger groups of countries over varying periods of time reinforce the view that convergence is, at best, geographically and economically limited.[107] Moreover, the measure adopted for convergence may matter – even for the relatively homogeneous European countries, different results emerge from using growth rates or growth levels.[108]

B. Convergence or Divergence?: Theoretical Justifications

1. Technological 'spillovers'

The empirical work of Baumol and many others coincided with an outburst of interest in the theory of economic growth. This partly reflected a growing concern within the USA about the increasing challenge it faced in its role as the world's technological and economic leader (see Chapter 8 below). Its theoretical orientation came more generally from a long-felt concern about the inadequacy of orthodox 'neoclassical' growth theory to account for much of the perceived causes of economic growth in AICs.[109] Thus most growth in practice seemed to come from unexplained, exogenous technical

---

106 Cf. Chapter 11 below.

107 E.g. Dowrick and Nguyen 1989; Dowrick 1992; Fagerberg *et al.* 1994.

108 Von Tunzelmann 1992b; Wolff (1994), however shows that the choice between labour productivity and total factor productivity (TFP) makes relatively little difference.

109 Abramovitz 1956; Solow 1957.

progress. Moreover, variations in observable data such as savings rates were shown in these formalizations to have no theoretical impact on variations in productivity growth rates (though they could influence productivity *levels*).

Although there were some forerunners, the main theoretical reaction to these implications came with the so-called 'new growth theory' from the mid-1980s. Many models were produced with a variety of assumptions, but common to many of them was a belief that technical progress could be endogenized and would yield 'increasing returns', i.e. dynamic economies of scale. Technology could be thought of as being composed partly of technological 'information', e.g. as blueprints, and partly of 'embodied' technological knowhow. The former information element could be interpreted through the notion of 'formal learning', and the latter knowhow element through 'learning by doing' and 'learning by using', to use the categories which were applied to Adam Smith in Chapter 2. Since the former was generic and could equally be relevant to all producers, it could be thought of as a 'public good' – its adoption reflected spillovers of technological information to those producers in the community at large. This public good or externality characteristic allowed the theorists to reconcile the existence of increasing returns with that of competitive market forces (traditional economic theory argued that they were mutually incompatible, and that increasing returns were likely to be captured by large firms).

At a national level, Baumol thus believed that technological spillovers from research originally undertaken in the USA allowed other AICs to catch up – they did not have to 'reinvent the wheel'. He saw this in terms of a post-Schumpeterian race between innovation (by the leader country) and imitation (by the followers). Second, he pointed to an 'investment effect', whereby trade and imitation would raise wages in the follower countries. Similar models combining innovation and cost effects and leading to innovation vs. imitation races have been developed by a range of writers, from a neoclassical standpoint[110] and also from an evolutionary standpoint[111] – indeed David Hume[112] long ago outlined a similar argument. They are often described nowadays as 'North/South models'.

Recently, Abramovitz has argued that such spillovers were less likely in earlier years of the 20th Century, because the technologies evolved in the leader country at that time – the USA – were inappropriate for followers; the advanced technologies being material-intensive and capital-intensive, which the followers were not.[113] Since the Second World War, there has

110 E.g. Krugman 1979; Dollar 1986.

111 E.g. Dosi 1984.

112 Hume 1752/1955, pp. 34, 203.

113 Abramovitz 1994; see Chapter 6 below.

been a greater 'technological congruence' between the technologies that have been developed by the leaders and what the immediate followers can feasibly adopt. In the prewar era many countries fell behind, whereas in the postwar period more of them caught up.

The argument underlying this book suggests that the amount that spills over as a 'free good' can be greatly overestimated, and that incorporation into the industries of recipient countries involves substantial advances of their own. The USA has remained more in command of some of the high-tech areas it pioneered than of a number of older industries, and where countries like Japan have overtaken it in certain sectors or technologies, this has rested on a massive indigenous effort in those new areas. As argued in Chapter 1 above, technological 'knowledge' involves much more than freely available technological 'information'.

2. Human capital formation

Other models within the general ambit of the 'new growth theory' put greater emphasis on human capital formation than on technology.[114] Such investment in education, etc., was seen as having similar public-good or externality effects to those noted above for technological information. For comparisons across countries, however, the argument needs to be remodelled along the lines suggested in the critique of spillover models in the previous paragraph. True, some countries benefited from having their graduates educated in the USA, e.g. Taiwan, but most of the increase in education had to be supplied indigenously. Nevertheless, empirical estimates for the extent of catching-up which have included an education variable have generally proved to explain growth performance rather well, although this relationship weakens when an investment variable is added since education and investment turn out to be highly correlated in their patterns. In Chapter 11 below, it is argued that education does indeed appear to have a significant role to play in differentiating some of the more successful late-developers from some of the less successful.

3. 'Social capabilities'

Abramovitz (1986) showed a more complex pattern than convergence, well captured by his title, 'Catching Up, Forging Ahead, and Falling Behind'. Convergence is limited by 'social capability': 'a country's potential for rapid growth is strong not when it is backward without qualification, but rather when it is technologically backward but socially advanced'.[115] Plausible as this sounded, the problem – as Abramovitz accepted – was to establish workable criteria for assessing 'social capabilities'. The most

---

114 E.g. Lucas 1988; Barro 1991.

115 Abramovitz 1986, p. 388.

obvious indicator was education, which implied an overlap with the human capital explanation, although Abramovitz was seeing education in its wider sociocultural context. In addition, he suggests factors such as organizational capacity as part of the social capabilities, but again quantitative criteria are difficult to obtain. Later chapters in this book will try to suggest not just social (institutional/ideological) but financial, market and similar factors that permitted some countries with technological backwardness to begin to catch up.

4. Spread vs. backwash effects

Kuznets considered that,

> the difficulty of making the institutional and ideological transformations needed to convert the new large potential of modern technology into economic growth in the relatively short period since the eighteenth century limited the spread of the system. Moreover, obstacles to such transformation were, and still are being, imposed on the less developed regions by the policies of the developed countries.[116]

In this sense, social capabilities were being held back not just by lack of application in the LICs but also by the international environment. Earlier, Myrdal and Hirschman[117] had argued that the effects of leader countries on followers could include the 'spread' or 'trickling down' of positive trade impacts, technological spillovers, etc., but could also give rise to a 'backwash' or 'polarization', in which the AICs suck the growth impetus out of the LICs. The AICs could grow cumulatively through 'virtuous circles', in which export performance fosters investment, investment fosters innovation, innovation fosters further exports, and so on. The 'technology gap' explanation of trade flows, as most often expressed nowadays by adherents of the evolutionary school of economics,[118] draws particular attention to the role of innovation in this 'virtuous circle'. Conversely, the LICs, initially suffering from weak trade situations, may experience 'vicious circles' of low investment, low innovation, low exports, etc. Such views are not new, although given further impetus by the development of scientific theories such as 'self-organizing systems' that tend to generate virtuous and vicious circles.[119]

---

[116] Kuznets 1973, p. 250; see also Kuznets 1966, chs 8–9.

[117] Myrdal 1957; Hirschman 1957; 1958, ch. 10.

[118] E.g. Dosi *et al.* 1990.

[119] Dosi *et al.* 1988. An early example of a backwash was Marx's famous alleged quotation from a Governor-General of India in 1834/35, that, in response to the take-off of the British cotton industry, 'The bones of the cotton-weavers are bleaching the plains of India' (Marx 1887/1965, p. 432).

One obvious conclusion is that industrialization patterns never exactly repeat themselves, inasmuch as later industrializers have also to contend with countries that are further advanced. Problems on the supply side might be exacerbated on the demand side, as elites in LICs copied the consumption patterns and life-styles of the AICs, through the 'demonstration effect' discussed above.

C. Policy Implications

The empirical and theoretical developments spelled out above brought renewed attention to the role of government policy in promoting growth and development. These views ranged from a cautious reassertion of a limited role for policy to full-scale assertions of autarky. These changes of emphasis were superimposed on the emerging economic orthodoxies of the 1980s, surveyed at greater length in Chapters 8 and 9 below. Of particular influence was the rising political predominance of ideologies asserting the superiority of the operations of free markets over government regulation and especially government planning. The consequent debate over the state's role in economic growth was thus being simultaneously pulled in two contradictory directions.

1. Market regulation

The mainstream of economic orthodoxy was perhaps best represented by neoclassical economists who implicitly combined two elements of classical economics described in the previous chapter – on the one hand, Ricardo's notion of 'comparative advantage', and on the other hand, Smith's limited domain for the role of the state. As stressed in Chapter 2, the latter did not mean unequivocally free markets. The role of the government in this view could well encompass the following:[120]

- i maintaining macroeconomic stability;
- ii providing physical infrastructure;
- iii supplying 'public goods' (education, law, defence, etc.);
- iv improving mobility in factor markets (labour, finance, technology, etc.);
- v eliminating distortions arising out of 'market failure';
- vi sometimes, redistribution to meet 'basic needs'.

While these could potentially justify a wide range of government strategies, in practice the mainstream neoclassical emphasis lay on reducing direct government intervention. This compromised their attitude towards income redistribution policies – whereas political economists like Myrdal

[120] Based on Wade 1990, p. 11.

could actively endorse the 'welfare state', for equity and also demand-side reasons, the neoclassical mainstream worried about the implied tax burdens, as supposed impositions on the supply side. Fundamentalists seem to believe in a 'divine right of markets', instead of seeing markets as institutions defined by their contexts. For the less dogmatic, the main role for the state was interpreted as providing a satisfactory environment for the operation of the economy, rather than undertaking that operation of the economy itself. Neoclassical economists in theory could pursue the 'market failure' argument for intervention, but most often were more perturbed about the possibilities of 'government failure'; usually to the point where, if there was any conflict, the 'failure' in markets was seen as the lesser of two evils.[121] In terms of the above theoretical categories, the neoclassical view might incorporate point (2) concerning human capital formation (as a public good) and some of point (3) for the development of social capabilities. Point (1) about technological spillovers could be met only so far as technology was interpreted as 'information' rather than as 'knowledge'. The emphasis on comparative advantage and on an 'outward orientation' implied a concentration only on the 'spread' effects of global growth, in regard to point (4).

2. State regulation

The more heterodox advocates of 'state regulation' spanned an even broader range of specific ideologies and policy standpoints. Without describing such a range in any detail, we can here lump together those who would believe that markets were not enough in the quest for economic development, and perhaps positively obstructive in many circumstances. Whereas the 'market regulation' view led in the direction of 'getting the prices right', this state regulation view might on occasions argue in favour of 'getting the prices wrong'.[122] In the context of the Japanese economy, studied in Chapter 10 below, it can be interpreted as the supremacy of 'competitive advantage' over 'comparative advantage'. 'Competitive advantage' involved a strategy for long-run economic development, in which it might well turn out that, for the catching-up countries, immediate comparative advantage (say in simpler technologies or lighter industries) would not provide the fastest route to advance. In regard to the theoretical point (4), adherents of such views would not necessarily dismiss the possible benefits of an 'outward orientation' – as we shall see in Chapter 11, the successful East Asian developers heavily emphasized export promotion, etc. However, they would have to weigh the beneficial 'spread' effects against the dangers of 'backwashes', and construct growth and trade

121 Schmitz and Cassiolato 1992, ch. 1.

122 Amsden 1989.

strategies accordingly. In regard to point (1), they would place great stress on the 'knowledge' as well as the 'information' view of technology, and would see the role of government reaching far down into the microeconomic level of the operations of individual firms.

This does not necessarily imply that governments should actually operate production (through nationalization, etc.), nor that there needed to be total government control via planning of the kind undertaken in the Eastern European economies of Chapter 9. The Japanese case analysed in Chapter 10 usually met the requirements for 'state regulation' without doing either to any significant extent. With this reservation, the 'state regulation' view has obvious affinities with the Gerschenkron approach to catching up, and has understandably been more popular in later rather than earlier developers.

3. Specific policy proposals

The theoretical underpinnings of modern growth theory translated variously into specific policy recommendations. These we have examined at somewhat greater length, with more extensive referencing, in Fagerberg *et al.* (1994, Introduction), and in the later chapters of this book. They can be summarized briefly as follows.

(a) *Controlling or promoting technology spillovers*. The Baumol (1986) emphasis on spillovers led to the uncomfortable policy implication that, for the USA to retain its lead, it somehow had to prevent its science and technology leaking abroad. Baumol himself rejected such policies, but the general notion received some popular and political support within the country. Indeed, the industrial leaders have for centuries tried to restrict the outflow of skilled personnel and advanced equipment. As already argued, this would seem to misread the evidence, and that 'spillovers' require intensive efforts of indigenization (see point (c) below). The catching-up countries equally have tried to promulgate technology spillovers, by 'importing' skilled labour and modern plant and equipment from the AICs, or by sending part of their own labour force abroad to observe and acquire best practices.

(b) *Indigenous socioeconomic policies*. The enhancement of 'social capabilities', following Abramovitz (1986), carried obvious implications for domestic progress in education and in organizational capacities. However, as we shall see in Chapter 11, in such fields the amount to be gained by copying foreign best-practice was even more limited than in the area of technology. Domestic institutional arrangements would have to be harnessed to a suitable set of development-oriented policies.

(c) *Indigenous technological accumulation.* Reliance simply on lower costs (such as low hourly wage rates) to provide competitiveness might enable some short-term success in certain areas of industrialization, but failed to meet the more fundamental characteristics of industrial technologies that had to do with their tacitness, cumulativeness and idiosyncrasy (cf. p. 4 above). For longer-run 'competitive advantage' there was little escape from the accumulation of indigenous technological capabilities, of the kinds elaborated upon in our later chapters. To foster such indigenous technological accumulation in the face of competition from more advanced countries might involve protectionist policies. The 'infant industry' arguments raised in the times of classical political economy – significantly by writers from catching-up countries – have been outlined in Chapter 2. A modern descendant is often referred to by its supporters as 'strategic trade theory'[123] and by its critics as 'neo-Mercantilism'. Evidently policies as well as patterns of economic development follow a kind of long historical cycle.

VI: MODERN THEORIES OF FLUCTUATIONS

A. Schumpeter and Business Cycles

In regard to fluctuations, Schumpeter began by asserting the variety of economic disturbances, and pointed out that they could originate on the demand side or equally on the supply side.[124] Accidents such as wars could also bring economic disturbance. But Schumpeter chose to lay particular stress on the jerky and discontinuous appearance of spurts of 'economic development', i.e. the new combinations, which '*appear, if at all, discontinuously in groups or swarms*'.[125] The upswing promulgated by the new combination and entrepreneurial demand is prolonged through generating a 'secondary wave' of general increase in purchasing power.[126] Conversely, the downswing comes from the failure of the older, eclipsed firms, and also from the process of digestion (diffusion) of the newer combinations. Despite the pain suffered by those adversely affected by the downswing, which would include those suffering from technological unemployment,[127] governments should not intervene to persevere with older

123 E.g. Krugman 1986.
124 Schumpeter 1911/1961, p. 219.
125 *Ibid.*, p. 223. Author's emphasis.
126 *Ibid.*, p. 226.
127 *Ibid.*, p. 250.

combinations and firms, since the downswing phase was just as important to longer-term economic growth as was the preceding upswing.

More detailed analysis of the business cycle was spelled out by way of a preface to extensive empirical work in his later study, *Business Cycles* (1939). This largely repeated his earlier views on the central role of innovation, though admitting that other factors (including random exogenous events) could play a large part in individual cycles:

> Technological change in the production of commodities already in use, the opening up of new markets or of new sources of supply, Taylorization of work, improved handling of materials, the setting up of new business organizations such as department stores – in short, any 'doing things differently' in the realm of economic life – all these are what we shall refer to by the term Innovation. It should be noticed at once that that concept is not synonymous with 'invention'.[128]

Because it was somewhat easier than actual innovating to copy the leaders, and also to apply their advances to other similar but not identical contexts, innovations were likely to be bunched (i) in time, and (ii) in particular industries.[129]

In this later model, developed in the aftermath of the Great Slump of the 1930s, the two-phase upswing/downswing (prosperity/recession) cycle could become a four-phase cycle, successively Prosperity, Recession, Depression and Recovery. The Recession of his earlier model could turn into a full-blown Depression as a result of some 'Vicious Spiral', e.g. a panic. In the earlier work, Schumpeter, while making manifest his animosity to government intervention in general, did allow government some role in counter-cyclical policy, e.g. postponing or bringing forward public works programmes, so long as the underlying dynamics of growth through cycles were not interfered with.[130] As a Depression on the scale of that of the 1930s clearly no longer provided the latent economic stimulus of a Recession, 'The case for government action in depression, especially government action of certain types, remains, independently of humanitarian considerations, incomparably stronger than it is in a recession'.[131]

The empirical analysis in his work led him to construct a multi-tiered system of cycles. In addition to the 'Juglar cycle' of 9–10 years which had underlain his previous model, and which is usually related to cycles in re-equipment, he drew attention to the short 'Kitchin cycle' of about three years (normally seen as being based on inventory rebuilding), and – most

128 Schumpeter 1939, p. 84.
129 *Ibid.*, pp. 100–101.
130 Schumpeter 1911/1961, p. 253.
131 Schumpeter 1939, p. 155.

importantly for us – the ‘Kondratiev cycle’ (Long Wave) of about 50 years. Schumpeter also mentioned other cycles, like Kuznets’s 25-year ‘long swing’ (cf. below), but thought these three met most of the needs to consider short, medium and long runs. The Kondratiev cycle was especially important because he considered it not to be linked to any one particular innovation, ‘but is the result of all industrial and commercial processes of that epoch’,[132] in other words a complete change in what below is described as the techno-economic system.

B. Long Swings and Long Waves

The literature on business cycles is too enormous to summarize here, but it is important to consider a branch of that literature that is particularly concerned with cycles of longer duration (periodicity). There has been considerable controversy over whether these cycles actually exist. The historical record of industrialization is too short to allow strong conclusions, and even with the meagre evidence we have, many have rejected the Kondratiev wave or preferred the Kuznets ‘long swing’.[133] Below I suggest a way of trying to interpret the long wave, at least qualitatively, which may perhaps resolve a few of the problems.

If such cycles exist, how do we explain them? Delbeke (1981) has shown that almost every input has been isolated and given special emphasis for its association with Kondratiev waves, as indeed Kondratiev (1984) himself had done. As already mentioned, Schumpeter focused on the association with innovations, albeit interpreting them in his broad sense of ‘new combinations’ only vestigially related (if at all) to inventions.[134] This has not prevented later scholars from trying to draw stronger links with quantitative data on inventions and innovations.[135] The major questions have been: (i) whether quantitative indicators of inventions or innovations have any validity (patents, discoveries, etc.); (ii) do the innovation upswings they hint at come as a result of depression (the ‘depression trigger’) or of incipient economic upswing? Because of the former problem, answers to the latter have had to be guarded – my personal inclination is towards Freeman’s view, that scientific breakthroughs occur randomly in

132 *Ibid.*, p. 168.

133 Kuznets 1940; 1965, pp. 317–78; Abramovitz 1961, 1968; Easterlin 1968; McCormick and Franks 1971; Solomou 1987. Kondratiev’s work was republished in 1984.

134 Kuznets in his early work (1930) also related his shorter swings to lifecycle movements in industry.

135 E.g. Mensch 1979; Kleinknecht 1981; van Duijn 1983; cf. Freeman *et al.* 1982, ch. 3.

time, but tend to be converted into commercialized innovations when demand conditions support them, i.e. at times of economic recovery. It has to be accepted, however, that questions of causality, timing, impact and recurrence have been inadequately addressed to date.[136]

Other inputs apart from innovations also have their advocates. Some post-Marxist scholars, notably Mandel (1978), argue that long-wave trends in capital accumulation, related to swings in profitability, are the key issue. Some non-Marxist writers, for example those in the tradition of 'systems dynamics', also give primary attention to capital formation.[137] Rostow,[138] an avowed anti-Marxist as we have seen, plumped instead for long waves in energy and raw materials supplies, though placing more emphasis on movements in *prices* than in quantities. Rather inconveniently, Marx himself had suggested a similar mechanism.[139] Reliance on prices forced Rostow[140] into arguing that the 1950s and 1960s represented a Kondratiev *downswing* (with falling agricultural and materials prices) and the 1970s an *upswing,* a perverse view which few were willing to share with him. Finally, patterns in employment have been emphasized, e.g. by Freeman who claims that upswings are periods of labour-intensity and employment expansion, while downswings are periods of labour saving and job redundancies.[141]

These do not need to be mutually exclusive arguments, although the interconnections may be complex. Schumpeter related price movements to innovations through their assumed association with credit-financed inflation. Rostow's price swings are claimed to depend in part on different gestation periods for different types of investment,[142] and partly through such investment, innovation and diffusion become aspects of the long wave.[143] With minor disagreements, he accepts Freeman *et al.* (1982) on the innovational content of long waves; though both demand-driven profitability (and thus prices) and materials shortages were seen as sparking off innovation.[144] The relationship with science-led innovation is left more obscure.

Freeman[145] has argued that long waves are characterized by distinctive 'techno-economic paradigms'. The central issue here is that what is

---

136 Rosenberg and Frischtak 1984.
137 E.g. Forrester 1971; see Chapter 8 below.
138 Rostow 1953/1960, ch. 6; 1978a; 1978b/19799.
139 Marx 1909, ch. 6; also Lewis 1978.
140 E.g. Rostow 1980, ch. 1.
141 Freeman *et al.* 1982, ch. 2.
142 Rostow 1953/1960, ch. 5; 1987, p. 84.
143 Rostow 1987.
144 *Ibid.*, pp. 81–90.
145 Freeman *et al.* 1982, ch. 4; Freeman and Perez 1988.

involved is more than a (new) technological paradigm – it also requires a new 'economic' paradigm, which I shall take to be the compound of organizational, financial and product-based changes of my taxonomy. With a new Kondratiev is associated a new techno-economic paradigm, with characteristics listed by Freeman as:

- i a new product mix;
- ii new trends in radical and incremental innovation;
- iii a wave of infrastructural investment;
- iv development of powerful large firms and innovative small firms;
- v new best practices in forms of organization;
- vi new profiles of labour skills;
- vii new 'national systems of innovation';
- viii new patterns of location of investment, nationally and internationally.

The mechanics of how all these things come together appear particularly complex, and this no doubt accounts for the profusion of theories tendered.

Freeman and Perez (1988) argue that a new technological paradigm may not immediately conform with the prevailing economic paradigm. Instead there is likely to be a period of 'mismatch', with the two contradicting rather than reinforcing each other. This has obvious undertones of the work of Schumpeter described above and of Marx in the previous chapter. Kuznets, too, drew attention to the 'dislocation effects' of innovation – obsolescence, unemployment and inequality – and suggested a possible cyclical pattern.[146]

MEG was likely to involve a 'controlled revolution'.[147] Thus such misalignments of technology and economy could have profound political and social forms of expression or consequences, as witnessed by Nazi Germany in the 1930s and early 1940s. In the Freeman–Perez approach, the upswing of the long wave represents the response to a period of mismatch, as the new techno-economic paradigm begins to gel.

In this book, I shall be adopting the long wave as a supplementary method of analysis, though accepting that its dynamics (if indeed such waves exist) may help to explain much about transitions between major phases of industrialization, for example in the ways suggested by Freeman and Perez. Such waves seem to arise initially at the micro level, in terms of technological innovations, new products, etc., and only after a considerable lapse of time come to be systemically integrated. The effects at the macro level of whole economies are thus postponed by the full length of a wave.

---

146 Kuznets 1974, pp. 182, 202–11.

147 Kuznets 1973, p. 252.

Thus the odd-numbered Kondratievs of the conventional datings[148] connote the industrial breakthroughs (British Industrial Revolution in the late 18th Century, American supremacy in the late 19th Century, East Asian take-off in the late 20th Century); while the even-numbered ones transmit those breakthroughs into growth rates of the relevant national economies and also their immediate international diffusion (Britain to Europe, etc.). This is also consistent with Rostow's suggestion of an average 60-year lag between his 'take-off' and his 'drive to maturity',[149] though my emphasis is on maturity in the same industries whereas Rostow envisages shifts to new sectors.

In this manner, we have at best witnessed only three 'super-cycles' in the experience of industrialization, on my reckoning. The remaining empirical chapters of this book will examine those three 'super-cycles' from their microeconomic stirrings through to the macroeconomic consequences, and on to their direct and indirect spillovers to their followers.

148 See for instance Freeman 1989.

149 Rostow 1960/1971, p. 60.

4. Britain in the Industrial Revolution

Time is the greatest innovatour (Francis Bacon 1625)

Each chapter to follow will have a common pattern, in order to show the extent to which the patterns of industrialization in different regions or periods paralleled or differed from the others. The chapter will normally begin with a brief discussion of growth experience in the light of the classical circular flow of Figure 2.1, i.e. by looking at data on inputs and (sectoral) outputs. This summary in no way pretends to reappraise standard views of individual countries: the purpose is simply to act as a backdrop for the ensuing micro-level discussion. Thereafter the discussion will move to the microeconomic taxonomy of Figure 2.2 and take technology, production, finance and products/demand in turn, with management aligned as deemed appropriate to the particular situation. This figure will be elaborated in Figure 4.1. Finally will follow a brief discussion of government policies germane to the macro or micro performances discussed.

I: GROWTH

A. Output and Productivity

Recent research has emphasized that growth in the early years of British industrialization was fairly slow, especially if measured in per-capita terms. Recent estimates by Crafts show *per-capita* national income growing annually at 0.3 per cent 1700–1760, under 0.2 per cent 1760–1800 (during the years usually specified as the 'take-off'), and just over 0.5 per cent, 1800–1830, before climbing to about 2 per cent p.a. 1830–70.[1] The annual growth rate of *total* industrial production was 0.7 per cent, 1.7 per cent, and

1 Mokyr 1993, p. 9.

Figure 4.1: Microeconomic Taxonomy, Excluding Linkages

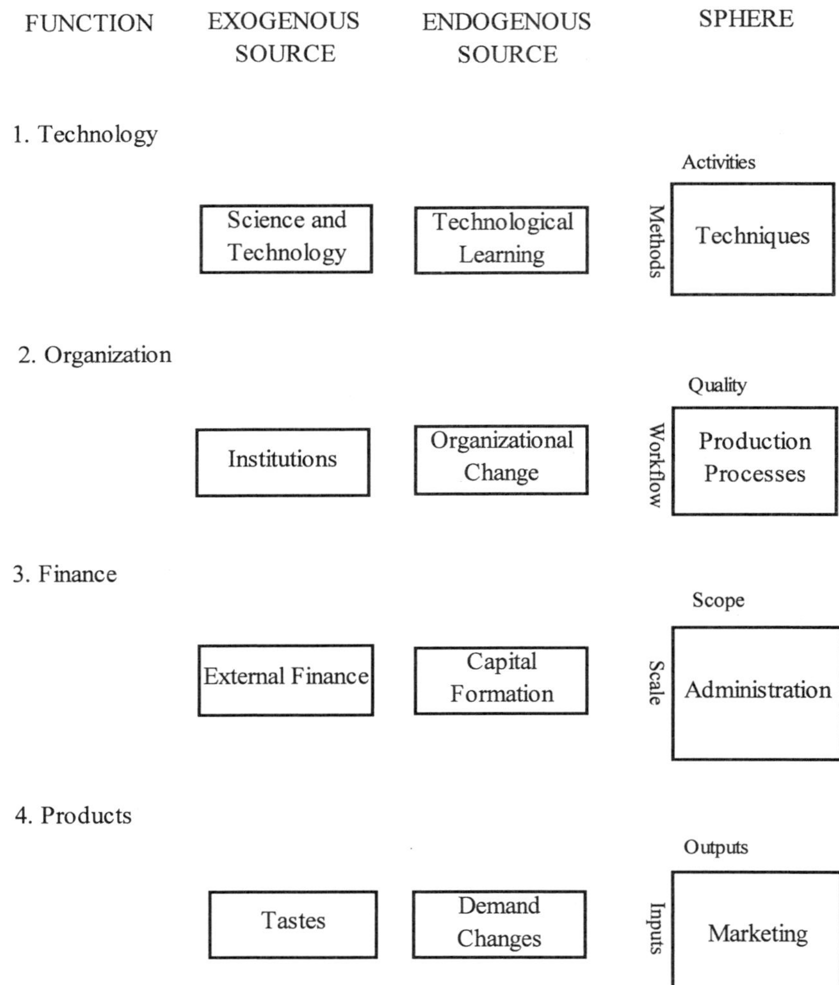

2.8 per cent, in the first three sub-periods,[2] while older data suggest about 3 per cent again in the final sub-period (1830–70).

Most attention has focused upon the per-capita results, and especially the contrast between slow growth in the 18th century and accelerating growth during the 19th century. The earlier data have inspired some to reject the applicability of the term 'Industrial Revolution'. It is perhaps more appropriate to conclude that macro data – here and elsewhere – can give guidance about micro-level transformations only when carefully interpreted. As Rostow and many others had pointed out, industrialization was at this time confined to a limited number of sectors that were still very small in relation to GNP (see p. 104 below), so that one would not expect any massive impact on the latter for a considerable period.[3] Landes (1993) stresses that the micro changes are just as persuasive evidence for 'Revolution' as macroeconomic growth – a view also taken in this book, as implied at the end of the last chapter. Even more persuasive is that observed acceleration in total industrial output after about 1760.

B. Inputs and Their Contributions

The disparity between per-capita growth and total output is, of course, largely explained by the concurrent rise in population, which was under way by the middle of the 18th century.[4] There has been a long-running debate on whether this population growth came about in 'Malthusian' fashion as a consequence of industrial expansion, or whether the opposite was the case, that industrial growth was a consequence of population growth (or both, or indeed neither). The consensus view now appears to be that population growth (which was fairly general, across Europe) and industrial growth originally developed separately, and related to each other by historical accident, but that in due course the two became interconnected (i.e. 'neither' followed by 'both').

Crafts[5] has computed that gross investment as a proportion of GDP rose from 4 per cent in 1700 to 10.8 per cent in 1840, remarkably like Rostow's much criticized assertion, although over a longer period of time than Rostow allowed.[6]

---

2 Crafts, in Floud and McCloskey 1994, p. 47 – these figures differ slightly from those on which the per-capita data are based.

3 *Ibid.*, pp. 11–14.

4 Wrigley and Schofield 1981.

5 Crafts, in Floud and McCloskey 1994, p. 45.

6 In Rostow 1978a, p. 383, the British 'take-off' has been re-dated to 1783–1830.

A 'growth-accounting' assessment of the contribution of the various inputs has been attempted by Crafts.[7] This suggests that the contribution of labour force growth to total income growth is slightly higher than that of capital formation during the central industrialization period, 1760–1830. Both are higher than the estimated contribution of the 'residual' – the miscellany of factors including technological progress, which are not estimated directly by this approach – after the onset of industrialization. It should be emphasized that the method of estimation is likely to give rise to errors that will be especially large in this residual item. The estimate also supports the simplification made by the classical economists, that land was effectively fixed in supply. The more significant micro-level repercussions of these macro trends will be argued in the rest of this chapter.

II: TECHNOLOGY

In discussing the various spheres of microeconomic change, it will be useful to elaborate on the figure used in Chapter 2 (Figure 2.2), as in Figure 4.1. In this form, the diagram does not specify any interrelationships between the spheres, but sets them out in the order discussed, with in each case the 'exogenous' influence in the left-hand box, the 'endogenous' change-factor in the middle box, and the sphere itself shown in the right-hand box. The elaboration consists of defining the axes of the latter. Each of them is regarded as a two-dimensional entity, reflecting varieties of input–output relationships. The 'inputs' (in a very broad sense for some of the spheres) are shown on the vertical axis and the 'outputs' on the horizontal. The exogenous and endogenous sources of change may affect either axis in particular cases, since there is no assumption of a 'linear' flow of causation.

A. Changes in Activities

The extent of direct impact of regular innovation was somewhat limited during the early years of the Industrial Revolution. A few new sectors have become famous, e.g. iron and cotton textiles – these were what Rostow[8] termed the 'leading sectors'. Mokyr (1994) lists the more dynamic sectors as textiles (especially cotton and worsteds), energy utilization (especially stationary steam power), metallurgy (especially iron) and 'miscellaneous', including a few branches of chemicals, gas-lighting, machine tools and pottery. By and large, the activities involved were in already established

7 Crafts and Harley 1992; Harley 1993, p. 198.
8 See p. 68 above.

industries, and if they involved new products, the latter were substitutes for existing items of consumption, rather than forging radically new sets of tastes.

The most significant aspect of the changes in activities was the shift towards manufacturing at large. As seen in Chapter 2, the later classical economists such as Nassau Senior depicted this as a shift from sectors like agriculture, characterized by relatively low productivity and 'diminishing returns', to manufacturing, where productivity was relatively high and there existed constant or even increasing returns. The superiority of manufacturing clearly did not come from the consumption side – its advantages lay in production. To understand why manufacturing had such characteristics, we need to examine the methods of production it used, the organization of its processes, and the scale on which those methods were used.

B. Changes in Methods

The Industrial Revolution witnessed the first sustained period of technological change: it was the era in which technological change became the norm rather than the exception.[9] Entrepreneurs setting up in new activities for the first time had to assume that others would soon be competing against them with even better techniques, and therefore they too had to consider undertaking continual improvement. In such an environment, they had to have principles for steadily improving their processes or products. In the dynamic sectors of manufacturing, it was 'the substitution of machines – rapid, regular, precise, tireless – for human skill and effort'.[10] Such cognitive understanding of how to go about technological improvement was referred to in Chapter 1 as a *technological paradigm*. Thus for the Industrial Revolution, and as we shall see for many years to follow, the prevailing paradigm in manufacturing was mechanization. The skills required were a 'new combination' of the competences of the pre-industrial era: especially millwrights, smiths and clock-makers. As mentioned in Chapter 1, the issue here is not the machinery as artifacts or as particular items of capital equipment, but the notion that machinery represented a standard solution to the technological problems faced by manufacturers in this era. By the later 19th century, as Veblen[11] put it, people had 'learned to think in the terms in which the technological processes act', and the latter meant the actions of the mechanical engineer.

9 Rostow 1963, p. 21.
10 Landes 1969, p. 41.
11 Veblen 1919/1961, p. 17.

This predominance of machinery can be compared with the second type of change listed by Landes: 'the substitution of inanimate for animate sources of power, in particular, the introduction of engines for converting heat into work, thereby opening to man a new and almost unlimited supply of energy'.[12] The steam engine, originally stationary and later (in the early 19th century) for locomotive purposes, was probably the greatest technological achievement of the early Industrial Revolution period. However, it was developed in the first instance for pumping, with the most important initial application being to pumping the water out of coal-mines as the latter were dug deeper. The application of stationary engines to driving machinery came later, and when it came it often represented such a minor technological advance in its own right that we have little or no record of its occurrence.[13] The early machinery was in fact originally developed for being driven by other sources of power, typically animate or water power. What the application of steam power to driving machinery did was to permit continued mechanization with little if any increase in power costs.[14] In the fullness of time there was innovative interaction between further developments of the steam engine and those of the machinery, but this was of little significance until late in the Industrial Revolution.

For the mining, however, the adoption of the steam engine was indeed the relevant technological paradigm, in that it represented the standard technological solution to the problems encountered by the mining industry, and it was the most important factor permitting rapid growth of coal production alongside a steady decline in the real price of coal.[15] Subsequent technological development of the steam engine, however, had to look elsewhere, to James Watt's celebrated engine of 1769, because coal-mines had no great incentive to improve the fuel efficiency of the engine, since they had large supplies of otherwise unsaleable small coal to hand. A major early application of the improved engine was to copper-mining in Cornwall where coal was rather more expensive,[16] and it was the 'compound' engine developed in Cornwall that was adopted in other European countries which suffered from inadequate supplies of coal.

Agriculture developed according to yet another paradigm. Here the most relevant technology was 'biological',[17] and was aimed at increasing the fertility of the soil, e.g. through use of fertilizer, new crops and crop

---

12 Landes *loc. cit.*; also Kuznets 1966, p. 10; 1974, pp. 193–4.

13 This argument was made correctly by Marx (1887/1965, p. 375), though subsequently overlooked.

14 Von Tunzelmann 1978, especially p. 160.

15 Flinn 1984, p. 308.

16 Von Tunzelmann 1978, ch. 9.

17 Cf. Hayami and Ruttan 1971, ch. 3.

rotations, selective breeding of animals, etc. Only around the middle of the 19th century did the technological paradigm for British agriculture begin shifting from a biological to a more mechanical one,[18] and even then much less avidly than in the USA. The reasons will be argued below.

C. Product and Process Innovation

In the 'early modern' period, say the 16th to early 18th Centuries, the predominant form of technical progress in activities such as textiles was 'product innovation' – in this case, the introduction of new types or grades of cloth. Among the most famous were the 'New Draperies' of the 17th century, which were cloths woven from the relatively new material called 'worsted' (i.e. long-staple wool), or mixtures of worsted with other yarns.

During the classic period of the Industrial Revolution, from the mid-18th to early 19th Centuries, the focus of attention switched instead to 'process innovations'. There had, of course, been process changes even in textiles (e.g. the spinning wheel or stocking frame) during the 'early modern' period, but these had been one-off advances. With the spread of the mechanization paradigm, process changes came to dominate during the Industrial Revolution. Hence arose the succession of major innovations about which every British schoolchild is supposed to be taught – flying shuttle, spinning jenny, water frame, cotton mule, etc.

Product innovation continued into these years,[19] but much of it required (or followed from) simultaneous process innovation, i.e. attendant changes in the machinery in order to spin the new yarns or weave the new fabrics. Without this link to process innovation (mechanization), contemporaries claimed that product innovation was often one step on the way to industrial decline, as for the older worsted industry of East Anglia.

Yet it is easy to exaggerate the difference between the pre-industrial era and industrialization in this respect. Sometimes product innovation led process innovation. The well-known (if frequently misinterpreted) case of the invention of coke-smelting of iron, at Coalbrookdale in 1709, resulted from specialization of the inventor, Abraham Darby, on one particular type of product which lent itself to being smelted by coke rather than charcoal.[20] Later developments in the printing of textile fabrics were also often examples of following from particular product innovations (in the nature of the fabrics). Moreover, as suggested in Chapter 1 above, product changes in upstream activities such as the building of steam engines became process innovations when harnessed to driving machinery in the downstream

18 Mill 1848/1909, pp. 108, 183–5, 716–17.

19 Griffiths *et al.* 1992.

20 Hyde 1977, ch. 2. The product concerned was known as thin-walled castings.

sectors – so, for example, the 'high-pressure' steam engine of the early 19th century was a product innovation for the engineering industry but a process innovation when adopted inside a textile mill.

It is conceivable that the switch from product-oriented towards process-oriented technological changes was associated with the advent of more adequate 'intellectual property rights' (IPRs). The early British patent system, as it emerged in the early 17th century, was aimed mainly at encouraging *imitation*, since at this stage the English were intent upon catching up foreign technological leaders such as Venice.[21] But by the mid-18th century, patents had become a form of protection for *invention*, and by this stage actively discouraged imitation, or at least required imitators to licence the patent and pay a fee (royalty). By the time of the Industrial Revolution, it was claimed to be much easier to be granted a patent on a new machine rather than a new product. Indeed, inventors of certain new cloths in the early 19th century tried to patent the tools used to produce them instead, because they stood little chance of securing a patent for the cloths themselves. Professional inventors concentrated on using the patenting system to develop machinery (see below, p. 118).

D. Demand Factors as Causes of Technological Change

Investigations of the causes of technological change have often tried to identify the primary source by contrasting 'demand-pull' influences with 'supply-push'. It might, for instance, be supposed that there ought to be some relationship between product innovation and demand-pull on the one hand, and between process innovation and supply-push on the other; in which case we might be tempted to deduce that the Industrial Revolution saw a shift from demand-pull to supply-push determinants of innovation. The two were, however, coupled in many instances. For example, the innovations in coal-mining during the Industrial Revolution can be said to have had a demand element: as the market demand for fuels rose, fuel prices would have risen substantially in the absence of any such innovations. A similar case can be made for the shift from wood to iron as a material, e.g. in machinery – shortages of wood would have become more serious as the pressure of industrial demand intensified. Yet in both cases the nature of the supply side is an equally important part of the story, via the cost pressures involved, so the two must be considered together.

An even more serious shortcoming of the demand-pull approach is that ascribing too much to 'rising demand' leaves us without a technological explanation for the Industrial Revolution. This is because, if it is being

---

21 MacLeod 1988, ch. 1.

argued that rising demand (from economic growth presumably) gave rise to innovation, then logically that rising demand or economic growth must precede the innovation, so we cannot on these grounds claim that innovations 'caused' growth and industrialization. Neither of these shortcomings proves that the demand-pull explanation is 'wrong' – indeed I would argue that much of it is valid as a description of the period. Lilley[22] charts data to suggest that the well-known technical breakthroughs in cotton came at the *end* of periods of output growth, though in a dynamic vein they could also be regarded as launching new periods of even more rapid growth some years later.

E. Supply Factors: Biases in Technological Change

Economists – and others – often favour explanations for technological change that see the advances as spurred by desires to 'save' on one or other particular type of input. Rather than thinking of changes in techniques as being designed to expand output from given inputs, as in the demand-pull case, this view tends to focus on reducing inputs for a given level of output. We have seen that the classical economists often supposed that technical change would save labour, but also that some like Say and Marx also found occasions on which capital rather than labour was saved. Many if not most innovations save both labour and capital (and perhaps other inputs) per unit of output – that is how they lead to lower costs and prices. The main question, however, is which input was saved to the greatest degree – was it indeed the case that labour inputs per unit of output were reduced faster than capital or other inputs, so that labour was indeed the factor most saved? If so, we would have a *prima facie* case that the observed changes in technology stemmed from a particular desire to save labour.

1. Saving labour

It seems self-evident that machines replaced human labour (per unit of output), and from this the inference often follows that mechanization was biased towards saving labour. However, in the sense just discussed of which input was saved most, it does not necessarily follow that machinery was on balance labour saving.

We certainly know of some machines that were explicitly aimed by their inventors at saving labour. Perhaps the best-known case, extensively analysed by Marx, was the 'self-acting' (semi-automated) version of the cotton mule, developed by the engineer Richard Roberts in patents of 1825 and 1830.[23] Roberts was commissioned by Lancashire textile bosses to

22 Lilley 1973, p. 195.
23 Catling 1970, ch. 4.

design a machine that would enable them to bypass the highly skilled mule-spinners, such as were required on the older 'common' mule – these mule-spinners were notorious for their high wage demands and proclivity to strike. Although Roberts's self-actor was a considerable technological feat – probably the most advanced piece of automation of its time – it was a long time before it dramatically changed employment patterns in cotton spinning. Its diffusion in textile mills was initially quite slow, and in any case some of the skilled spinners were able to retain and even strengthen their positions with the adoption of the self-actor.[24] If anything, the skills required of minding a self-actor were more demanding than those on a common mule.[25]

Even this represented an extreme case, and at most indicated conditions in the later years of the Industrial Revolution. The original hand mule (non-automated), invented by Crompton in 1779, had a quite different objective, which was to extend the role of labour, not to replace it. Crompton, who was a cotton worker himself, wanted the mules to be adopted in workers' cottages, not in factories, and tried to design them accordingly. Until the second quarter of the 19th century, this aim of using innovation for creating employment was frequently voiced.[26] It may be noted that, if the rapid early advances in cotton spinning, etc., did 'save' any labour, it was labour of the cheapest kind, namely that of females and children.[27]

In Ricardo's model of technological substitution (see p. 40 above), labour may be replaced by capital depending on rises in wages. Modern evidence, however, shows little rise in wages before the 1820s, i.e. over half a century after industrialization is normally supposed to have begun. There was therefore little incentive to save labour in this period in terms of offsetting real wage increases. Even without rising real wages, there were nevertheless periods in which labour shortages were recorded, most notably at times during the French Wars ('Napoleonic Wars'), when up to half a million men were drafted into the armed forces. Table 4.1 summarizes MacLeod's evaluation of the claims made by patentees for the principal economic effects of their patents, over the period 1660–1799. The first three items show that the stated aim of saving labour somewhat exceeded the combined aims of creating employment and improving working conditions, but closer analysis shows that half of the alleged labour saving came in the final decade of her study, the 1790s – the first years of the French Wars. With such exceptions, the supply of labour until the 1820s can be said to have

24 Lazonick 1979; 1990, ch. 3; Bruland 1982.

25 Catling 1970, ch. 5; Lazonick, *loc. cit.*

26 As implied in the discussion of technological unemployment in Chapter 2, however, the 'compensation' from extra output might not be sufficient.

27 For a range of contemporary opinions on labour saving, see Berg 1985, ch. 2.

Table 4.1: Patentees' stated aims of invention, 1660–1799

	AIM	NO. OF CASES				
		1660–1719	1720–1759	1760–1789	1790–1799	TOTAL
1	Create employment	22	19	2	0	43
2	Improve working conds.	5	5	12	9	31
3	Save labour	3	11	32	47	93
4	Save capital	89	136	251	214	690
5	Save time	11	10	52	43	116
6	Reduce prices	22	16	29	15	82
7	Improve quality	43	66	347	201	657
8	Import substitution	38	25	16	2	81
9	Government benefits	32	29	7	1	69
	Unspecified	339	315	1202	762	2618
	Total cases	604	632	1950	1294	4480

Source: Based on MacLeod 1988, Table 9.1. Two cases were allowed per patent. See text for further clarification.

been fairly 'elastic', i.e. available in reasonably large quantities at low and roughly constant real cost levels (real wages).

However, highly skilled labour could always prove something of a bottleneck for expansion, and it was here that some explicit attempts were made to replace such skilled labour with unskilled labour or machinery ('deskilling'), particularly during the Napoleonic Wars. The most famous episode was the outbreak of 'Luddism' – attacks on machinery – which is often equated with a general opposition to machinery, though in practice was mostly opposition to the replacement of skilled by unskilled labour. Such evidence as I have found supports the view that resistance to machinery was most often directed at the (capitalist) system within which it was to be introduced, rather than at the machinery *per se*,[28] i.e. at the social relations of production rather than the forces of production.

When real wages started to rise in more consistent fashion from the 1820s, there was a more sustained shift towards saving labour, such as for the self-acting mule. It has been shown above that this, too, was mainly intended to be deskilling, though in this it was none too successful.[29] Finally, it may be

---

28 Marx 1887/1965, p. 429; Braun and Senker 1982, ch. 4.
29 Lazonick 1979.

noted that major changes of *product* structure could be associated with saving labour, by way of consequence rather than cause – perhaps the best-known shift was from arable to pastoral agriculture in the Midlands.

2. Saving natural resources

As with labour, the primary goal in regard to natural resources was to replace inputs that were relatively scarce in supply with those that were potentially more plentiful, i.e. characterized by high 'elasticity' of supply. Traditional materials were not necessarily all that expensive, but if demand were to rise quickly they might become so. Thus the process of technological substitution replaced inputs like timber that were in inelastic supply with those like coal, once the technological problems of deep-mining coal had been sorted out via the steam engine. Note first that, as the coal/steam example shows, availability of resources does not mean their abundance underground (etc.), but the ability to extract and utilize them at relatively low cost – in other words, the definition of available resources makes sense only when related to existing levels of technology (see Chapter 6). In this sense, there is a 'feedback' relationship whereby technology helps dictate the choice of resources just as much as resources help dictate the choice of technologies.

Note second that the time scale is important here. Ultimately coal was a more 'exhaustible' resource than timber, since, given time and space (land availability), more timber could be grown to replace that used up. But with industrialization the time lag became too long and, even more importantly, the land was not readily available. Real coal prices trended downwards from the early 18th century, and in doing so encouraged widespread substitution of coal or coke for wood or charcoal. Eventually this fall in coal prices flattened out and subsequently reversed, and in doing so caused coal to become the fuel in need of replacement (by oil, etc.).

As the classical economists and their assumption of a fixed supply of land had implied, it was land that showed the greatest inelasticity of supply of the major inputs. It was this difference in the supply conditions which inspired the 'biological' nature of agricultural technology, as mentioned above (p. 106). The object of the new fertilizers, new crop rotations, etc., was to improve the yield of land, i.e. output per acre, and since land was effectively fixed in supply, this was a rational strategy. The alternative of a machine-based technology would have allowed the rural workforce to cultivate greater amounts of land,[30] but as there was little more land to be had, this would hardly have made sense. Alternatively the machine technology could have allowed the same amount of land to be worked by

30 Hayami and Ruttan *loc. cit.*

fewer workers, as indeed happened after 1850, but in the Industrial Revolution when rural labour was elastic in supply there was no strong reason to do this and a good reason – creating unemployment – not to do it.[31] Moreover, many such biological developments could be introduced on relatively small farms, without major reorganizations of ownership, etc.[32]

However, the land 'available' could be increased extensively rather than intensively, by making use of overseas trade and colonization. The fixed supply of land in Britain could be offset by the opening up of vast tracts of land in the New World to the white man and his agricultural technology. Most important at this stage was the rapid spread of cotton growing on slave plantations across the southern states of the USA. With massive expansion of supplies from systems based on cheap land, slave labour and some technology (e.g. the cotton 'gin'), the price of raw cotton to British textile manufacturers dropped sharply. In later years, there were to be similar effects of prairie wheat, Australian wool, minerals from mineral-rich countries, and so on. The policy implications are considered at the end of this chapter.

3. Saving capital

Capital-saving technologies are less frequently remarked upon than labour-saving technologies, perhaps because they are less obviously conspicuous. But, as the examples from Marx showed (see Chapter 2), they could play a significant role in practice. Adam Smith also drew attention to capital-saving innovation: 'all such improvements in mechanicks, as enable the same number of workmen to perform an equal quantity of work, with cheaper and simpler machinery than had been usual before, are always regarded as advantageous to every society'.[33] As economists such as Samuelson (1965) have stressed, it is easy to be misled by the outward appearance of the innovations. Thus steam engines look big and bulky, but may nevertheless be capital–saving by comparison with what they replaced, such as a team of horses.[34] There were many improvements making for 'cheaper and simpler machinery', including the substitution of iron for wood in making the machinery. Other advances permitted the major items of capital equipment to be used more productively: for example, in coastal shipping, minor advances in wharfside loading, steam tug handling, etc.,

31 In some areas, land-using product changes had to be introduced, as they were out-competed by the rising grain production of other areas favoured by the new crop rotations, and unemployment was the result – for the complex argument involved, see Jones 1965.

32 Milward and Saul 1973, p. 76.

33 Smith 1776/1976, p. 287, also p. 292.

34 Ashton 1955, pp. 110–11.

allowed the boats to make more journeys a year, even though the size of the boats barely altered.[35] Hicks[36] suggested that the cheapening of capital goods, resulting from the application of science to industry and from the adoption of machine tools, induced capital-saving innovation. In terms of his own neoclassically-based theories, he failed to distinguish between factor substitution and innovation proper. But if (as here) we regard that issue as misleading, there would appear to be a case worth further investigation.

MacLeod's estimate of claims of patentees to save capital is shown in row 4 of Table 4.1. It will be seen immediately that such claims outnumber those to save labour (row 3) by a factor of around seven (690 as compared with just 93), for the period 1660–1799. The capital-saving row appears to include savings on materials such as fuel, which has been treated separately above. We might also add those claiming to save time (row 5), i.e. another 116, to those saving capital, and further add to the disproportion. Stated claims of course should not be taken as too strong evidence of real intentions, much less of actual outcomes – there may have been good political reasons not to over-emphasize the saving of labour – but the results are still striking.

4. Saving time

In everyday language we speak fairly interchangeably about inventions which save labour and those which save time. Modern economists, however, have concentrated almost exclusively on the former, the major reason being that 'time' is not a factor of production in the same way as are labour, capital and natural resources. Along lines already suggested in discussing Marx, I thus draw a distinction in this book between time saving, namely completing a production task in shorter time, in theory with the same number of employees, and labour saving, involving no shortening of time but a reduced number of workers. In practice, of course, there were usually elements of both.

Writing in 1757, the mercantilist Malachy Postlethwayt (one of Marx's rare heroes), who believed that 'ingenuity' depended on the extent of domestic consumption (demand), asserted, 'We do not see any objection that can be made to the oeconomising of time', since labour could thus be made more productive while expanding employment.[37] Around the same time, Steuart argued that, 'The first thing to be known of any manufacture when it comes to be sold, is, how much of it a person can perform in a day, a week, a month, according to the nature of the work. ... Hence the reason

35 Ville 1986.

36 Hicks 1969, p. 153.

37 Postlethwayt 1757, vol. 2, p. 419; Berg 1985, p. 56.

why some people thrive by their industry, and others not; why some manufactures flourish in one place and not in another.'[38] The more rigorous John Stuart Mill later noted that, 'In manufactures and commerce, some of the most important improvements consist in economizing time; in making the return follow more speedily upon the labour and outlay'.[39]

Babbage was much more knowledgeable than most of these about manufacturing, and in his book *On the Economy of Machinery and Manufactures* he began with the sweeping remark: 'The advantages which are derived from machinery and manufactures seem to arise principally from three sources: *the addition which they make to human power. – The economy they produce of human time. – The conversion of substances apparently common and worthless into valuable products*.'[40] Within his next few pages it becomes clear that the first of these three relates mainly to the energy (steam-power) paradigm and the last to the chemicals paradigm, and on neither does he have a great deal more to say, whereas the theme of saving time becomes one of the main foci of the book. '*The economy of human time* is ... so extensive and important ... that we might, if we were inclined to generalize, embrace almost all of the advantages under this single head'.[41] He later makes it clear that he believes that time saving applies to what he calls the mental division of labour as well as the physical (see Chapter 2 above).

In agriculture, saving time availed little except at peak periods, because production was regulated by the seasons and the calendar year[42] – part of the reason why land saving was much more important. In manufacturing it was a different matter. In the cotton textile industry of the Industrial Revolution, there were often dramatic reductions in the time taken for particular processes, often by the adoption of *mechanical* processes based on rotary motion.[43] As Marshall pointed out, 'the easiest motions of the hand are backwards and forwards, the easiest motions of a machine are rotary. The rate of movement of the hand is limited; and therefore if it is to do much work, it must exert a considerable part of its small strength at each stroke. But ... a machine tool can be made to rotate at any speed, however great, provided it does not generate too much jar or too much heat.'[44] Thus inventors had to move from trying to base their advances on duplicating the

38 Steuart 1767/1966, p. 160.
39 Mill 1848/1909, p. 108.
40 Babbage 1832, p. 6, his italics.
41 *Ibid.*, p. 8. Our later discussion includes machine time as well as labour time.
42 Marx 1858/1973, pp. 602–3.
43 Von Tunzelmann 1995.
44 Marshall 1919, p. 210.

human being to new sets of principles based on circular motion.[45] Despite the primacy of mechanical advance, no reduction of time was greater than in the bleaching of cotton cloth, which was reduced from around eight months to eventually just a few hours, by adopting *chemical* processes for bleaching.[46] Analysis of mechanization in this period revealed the following types of gain:

(a) reduced *downtime*, as the improvement of machines made them more reliable – for example, improved power-looms were less liable to tear the fabric, and adopted mechanisms to stop the weaving quickly if did breakages occur;

(b) more obviously, increased *throughput*, i.e. faster processing during the actual production phase, most often by this adoption of rotary motion for mounting the key items of equipment (and subsequently rotating them faster);

(c) increased *machine co-ordination*, as different parts of the machines were better able to synchronize with one another, for example through relating the feeding-in and taking-out phases more closely to the principal processes;

(d) increased *system co-ordination*, as different processes were each speeded up in turn – for example, the faster spinning of cotton induced a speed-up of weaving and also finishing processes (bleaching, printing, etc.), and similarly in iron, with speed-up of the blast furnaces (smelting) inducing matching changes in the forge (for wrought iron), in rolling the products, etc.

Thus in the other main 'leading sector' of British industrialization, the iron industry, Cort's puddling and rolling processes are estimated to have raised the speed of throughput eventually by some 25 times.[47] This schema of methods of time saving will also be used in later chapters below, for the study of more recent change.

The significance of such time-saving changes is threefold. First, they represented a major way in which the 'paradigm' of mechanization could be explored. In the terminology introduced in Chapter 1 above, time saving was the 'heuristic' principle for guiding innovation, i.e. it provided a 'rule of thumb' whereby machines were initially introduced, and subsequently improved, in accordance with their ability to save time (as in the four ways noted above). Second, the principle was a technological rather than an economic one – this meant that the more narrowly economic concerns such as saving labour or capital came about in response to the technology changes rather than truly causing them. This does not signify that the

45 Marx 1887/1965, p. 486.
46 Cf. Marx 1919/1967, p. 243.
47 Harris 1988, p. 40.

economic aspects were unimportant – on the contrary, they helped to shape the precise 'trajectories' which technologies pursued, within the general ambit of the paradigm of mechanization and the (engineering) rule of thumb about saving time. Third, these time savings constituted a direct link between demand determinants (growth of markets, etc.) and the evolution of technology, by dint of their permitting the production of greater output per unit of time. As stated in regard to demand factors above, this still leaves the source(s) of the increased demand, and thus the ultimate 'cause' of industrialization, unexplained.[48]

F. Technological Learning

It is helpful to repeat the masterly summary of technological learning given in the opening pages of the *Wealth of Nations*: 'All the improvements in machinery, however, have by no means been the inventions of those who had occasion to use the machines. Many improvements have been made by the ingenuity of the makers of the machines, when to make them became the business of a peculiar trade; and some by that of those who are called philosophers [scientists] or men of speculation'.[49] Let us take these in turn, beginning with the second.

1. Learning by doing

Strictly speaking, learning by doing in this context refers to activities in producing capital goods, which may then have 'downstream' effects on user industries. Smith (and Marshall) refer rightly to the splitting off of the machine-making industry from user industries – what is described in Chapter 6 as 'vertical process disintegration'. Here I shall widen the term to include practical improvement in a variety of workshops, not all of which were necessarily split off from the user activity.[50]

Some of the most radical advances were first suggested by people from quite outside the industry concerned, e.g. Cartwright, inventor of the power-loom and the wool-combing machine, was a parson; Arkwright, inventor of the water-frame and improved cotton-carding machine, was originally a barber and wig-maker. Their very detachment might have allowed them to see things differently from those within the industry and accustomed to its

---

48 It may be noted that the *exchange* function of market expansion itself can be viewed as basically saving time – a view that Scazzieri attributes to the early economist, Sir James Steuart (1767). See Scazzieri 1993, p. 4; also Marx 1858/1973, p. 859.

49 Smith 1776/1976, p. 21.

50 The nature of such workshops has been studied at length by Berg (1985, chs 3, 11).

traditional routines.[51] However, the successful ones nearly always entered the industry in a very active way before their machines were widely adopted – Cartwright remained a parson and his machines failed commercially, whereas Arkwright set up in the cotton industry and amassed a fortune. New ideas were one thing, but commercial success required unremitting attention to detail and to improvement.

Veblen believed that industrial activity increased from around the beginning of the 18th century, and continued, 'But somewhere in the third quarter of the century the primacy among the habits of thought that made up the technological scheme may be said to have passed *from workmanship to engineering*',[52] though this arose gradually and insensibly out of handicraft traditions. Most of the *process* innovation that can be described as learning by doing probably came from owners of medium-sized workshops. Some of these, like Bessemer or Armstrong, became notable innovators in the middle 19th century, when in the above-mentioned sense the capital goods activities became more clearly separated from the user industries. Employees, even skilled employees, were less likely to be involved in such innovation, for the obvious reason of fear of making themselves technologically unemployed. The skilled workers were much more prominent in areas like the metal trades, where *product* innovation was more widespread, and fears of technological unemployment correspondingly reduced.

It is premature to talk about 'R&D' at this early stage of industrial development, but studies of early 19th-century patenting have shown that there were already signs of a recognizable, if still small, 'invention industry', consisting of people making some kind of a living out of concocting patentable inventions.[53] But only those who were also closely involved with actual production activities are still remembered today, like Joseph Bramah.

2. Learning by using

Adoption of the new machines could allow users to experiment with new products and new qualities of existing products. There were attempts to exert greater control over quality. In some areas, like textiles, schools of design were set up to try to make the design process more coherent and controllable. Opinions vary on the extent to which these could have been successful – beauty here is very much in the eye of the beholder, and not

---

51 See Porter 1990 for a more general assessment of the role of outsiders in modern industry.

52 Veblen 1915/1964, p. 117, my italics.

53 Dutton 1984, ch. 7.

everyone today approves of Victorian tastes – but there seems little reason to doubt a greater degree of standardization.

Recent research suggests a much more crucial role for users than just adaptation of machinery. MacLeod (1992) examines that part of the mechanical engineering industry responsible for developing production machinery, and finds a dominant role for users rather than producers in *process* innovation. Users made most of even the more radical innovations in this area, with producers contributing a larger share of the incremental innovations (the machine-maker Richard Roberts was the main exception to this rule). She finds that 19th-century modifications of patent law to encourage licensing (which was liberally extended to users) were significant in inspiring innovation among users. However, in steam engines and in machine tools, the machine-makers played a relatively much larger part. They were also more active in diffusion, not least to overseas markets (as we shall see in Chapter 5).

3. Formal (scientific) learning

It is traditional to equate modern science with the founding of the Royal Society in 1662. The 'Scientific Revolution' of which this formed a part is often seen as the forerunner of the Industrial Revolution, coming as it did approximately a century earlier. Rostow, for example, wrote in *How It All Began*:

> It is the central thesis of this book that the scientific revolution, in all its consequences, is the element in the equation of history that distinguishes early modern Europe from all previous periods of economic expansion. ... We know or sense that the scientific revolution irreversibly changed the way man thought and felt about himself and society, about the physical world, and about religion. The scientific revolution also related, *somehow*, to the coming of the first industrial revolution at the end of the eighteenth century.[54]

Kuznets and Lewis wrote in similar vein.[55] The difficulty is knowing what *precisely* was the role of the Scientific Revolution in relation to the Industrial Revolution, as Rostow indeed comes to confess when he looks in further detail at the question. Some believe that there were significant and direct carryovers from science to industry; most argue that such carryovers were surprisingly few for the following reasons.

(a) Science was ill-developed, despite the rush of new work, and in particular was concentrated in areas that as yet had no industrial application, e.g. astronomy, analytical mechanics, crystallography, magnetism, etc. Conversely, the needs of industry, e.g. for science-

54 Rostow 1975, pp. 132–3; my italics.

55 Kuznets 1973, etc. (see Chapter 3 above); Lewis 1955, ch. 4.

based metallurgy or bacteriology, were not to be met until much later.

(b) Most of the science actually picked up by industry was older in nature than the new science (based on deduction and experiment) associated with the Scientific Revolution. An example was the adoption of chlorine for bleaching, with the dramatic effects on time saving already noted – this followed from the observation of chemical properties rather than the newer deductive chemistry. Other examples are just myths, like the argument that James Watt got his ideas for improving the steam engine from Joseph Black and his theory of latent heat (Watt himself explicitly disowned this argument).

(c) Science was much further advanced in certain other countries, notably France (see Chapter 5 below). Even more awkward for the science-led hypothesis was its early predominance in the Middle East and Far East. France was also responsible for many radical inventions that the British were to exploit more fully,[56] but was unable to carry through industrialization until long after Britain.

(d) The line of causation at this time, if anything, may have been more often in the reverse direction, from technology or industry back to science. A celebrated case was the science of thermodynamics, which arose out of the practical experience of a French engineer, Sadi Carnot, that the compound steam engines he was supervising were behaving too efficiently to be explained by existing science.

Thus there was no substantial 'linear' flow from science to invention, of the kind perceived by the French economist Say.[57] Smith was probably nearer the mark in considering the contribution of science as coming from serendipitous 'new combinations'. Mill,[58] writing towards the end of the Industrial Revolution era, noted some such examples of fortuitous scientific spin-off, but believed that the results were normally too far detached from the original scientific work to have influenced industry. To this could be added that the source of such serendipity may have lain in the technology rather than in the science, as for thermodynamics. However, there were two significant ways in which the Scientific Revolution could plausibly have promoted innovation.

(e) At the heart of the Scientific Revolution was the development of 'scientific method', which involved repeated experimentation and empirical investigation in the process of

56 Mokyr 1990, ch. 10.
57 Say 1821, bk. I, ch. 6; Langlois 1986.
58 Mill 1848/1909, pp. 41–2.

advancing scientific theory. This trial-and-error check on theorizing via experimentation was picked up by 18th-century engineers like the great John Smeaton, and used to discriminate between, say, efficient and less efficient energy sources, or to compute the strength of buildings and bridges.

(f) Rostow, Price and others have also pointed out a more artifactual connection, in the development of scientific instruments for such experimentation.[59] Some could be used directly for industry, e.g. the thermometer, others were developed by industry itself to carry out its own testing programmes, e.g. the hygrometer and saccharometer for brewing.[60] The most important of these innovations in instruments were in horology (time-keeping), which grew out of the needs of commerce and grew into the needs of manufacturing.[61]

It was probably in these somewhat indirect ways that the mingling of scientists and industrialists in clubs and societies had its greatest effects. More broadly, there is considerable support for the view that the 'Scientific Revolution' encouraged people to see the world as potentially controllable. Schmookler[62] contended that the links between science and technology should be seen as psychological as much as mechanistic. In this respect, it worked through the Institutional rather than the Technological domain in my schema (Figure 4.1). Whatever the case, it does not seem necessary to explain why Britain was the first country to industrialize through any superiority of its science.

More broadly, it is generally agreed that levels of formal education at primary and secondary level in England were low (though possibly somewhat better in Scotland). What there was was entirely privately funded and operated. There is considerable debate over whether standards of education rose or fell during the Industrial Revolution – it would seem that there was little detectable change.[63] This has led some to claim that, at this level of industrial technology, formal education for workers was not required, since learning by doing etc. could proceed without it. It seems evident that the major negative consequences were stored up until after the Industrial Revolution period proper. However, the failure of educational improvement perhaps hastened a shift from worker-led innovation to a reliance on management or ownership to lead innovation, which in turn narrowed the scope for maintaining advance. It will be recalled from

59 Rostow 1975, p. 154; Price 1984.
60 Mathias 1959.
61 See below; also Landes 1983.
62 Schmookler 1966, p. 200.
63 See the summary by Mitch 1993.

Chapter 2 that most of the classical economists, despite their alleged laissez-faire principles, advocated state subsidization of education; but this did not come in England until the 1870s.

G. Diffusion

A more enlightened educational system might have speeded up the *diffusion* of new technologies. Receptivity to new methods and new products ought to be higher among a more educated labour force. In practice, the distinction between innovation and diffusion, which lies at the heart of many economic analyses of technological change, becomes difficult to draw. In taking a new process to a new product, modifications in that process will normally be required; but this strengthens rather than weakens the case for better training. The amount of learning required for – and obtained from – diffusion may be not far less than for innovation. As it was, the British capability for diffusion was, if anything, ahead of its capability for innovation. Mokyr[64] notes the adoption in Britain of French inventions such as the paper-making machine, chlorine bleaching, the Leblanc soda process, the Jacquard loom for fancy weaving, the wet-spinning process for flax, etc. Many of these required considerable attention before commercial success, and the British success lay in the *commercialization* of technologies. Porter[65] quotes the example of the early machine printing press, invented by a German (Koenig), who had to come to England for its machine design skills in order to convert his ideas into practical success. The firm he founded returned to Germany in 1818 and had much early difficulty in training its labour force up to existing English standards; but survived to become one of the world's leaders to this day in the printing press industry. It is alas unlikely that this would have happened had he stayed in England. To understand why Britain succeeded at this time in the commercialization of new technologies, and indeed why it failed later, we have to turn to the sphere of organization.

III: ORGANIZATIONAL CHANGE

A. The Rise of Capitalism

In the historical literature, it has been almost as common to identify the Industrial Revolution with the dominance of capitalism as with the rise of

---

64 Mokyr 1993, p. 18.
65 Porter 1990, p. 182.

industrialism. When Arnold Toynbee in 1884 delivered his lectures on the 'Industrial Revolution' and first popularized the term in Britain, he did so by stressing the ideological change it betokened rather than the technological one.[66] According to the classical model of Chapter 2, capital of some kind is always required for production of goods; what distinguishes 'capitalism' from previous eras was an economic and social system in which effective ownership and control of production is in the hands of those possessing substantial capital, i.e. the financial and/or managerial elites. That the period saw a concentration of capital in the hands of those responsible for production, together with their rising political authority, is generally accepted. This went with a shift away from the medieval 'moral economy' based on notions of just prices, etc., towards a fully functioning market economy.

It will be recalled that, according to Marx, capitalism preceded industrialization, in its earlier stage of merchant (or 'primitive') capital accumulation. Bourgeois capitalism proper required an association with industry and especially technological change (altering 'relative surplus-value'). Again, such a view seems widely accepted, though how this earlier capitalism became transformed into industrial capitalism has been considerably more controversial.

At the micro level, this phase of industrial capitalism was reflected in a particular type of ownership/management structure: one in which owners and managers were the same, ownership was personal rather than impersonal, and most often it was concentrated in one or a very few families in regard to each firm. Historians have thus described this period as one of 'personal' or 'proprietary' capitalism. Underlying it was the steady emergence, over a much longer period, of 'property rights' to owning fixed and floating assets, i.e. fixed and working capital ('property thefts' in the eyes of critics like Proudhon). The view popularized by contemporary philosophers like John Locke, down to present-day theorists of 'transaction costs', has been that stability came through the political triumph embodied in the 'Glorious Revolution' of 1688, though nowadays seen as having been spread over a much longer time period.[67] Typically this concentration of ownership of capital went with greater exercise of control over production, as most obviously seen in the coming of the factory system.

B. The Rise of the Factory

For manufacturing, the key organizational change was the rise of the factory. However, as with the rise of capitalism, one cannot exactly equate

66 Cannadine 1984; von Tunzelmann 1985.
67 North and Weingast 1989.

the rise of the factory with industrialism. Early capitalism rarely involved factories of any description. Only a small proportion of total employment occurred in factories even at the end of the Industrial Revolution as conventionally dated – it took a very long time for factories to dominate total production, though like technology they advanced more rapidly in certain sectors. It is not even very clear what exactly constituted a 'factory' in the earlier years of industrialization: some identified it with purpose-built plant and a centralized power source, but many that were commonly regarded as factories did not have these characteristics (e.g. Smith's pin factory). The considerable debate in the literature boils down to whether one interprets factories primarily in regard to their ideological role (association with capitalism) or alternatively in regard to their technological role (association with industrial equipment). Marx seemed to some to be casting his lot with the latter, in his remark that, 'The hand-mill gives you society with the feudal lord; the steam-mill, society with the industrial capitalist',[68] but it is obvious from context that Marx thought that the relationship between 'forces of production' and 'social relations of production' ran in both directions (see Chapter 2 above). For the moment I shall use the former definition, and return below to the link between organizational and technological change.

1. The factory and output

In many activities, like the textile industries, factories gradually supplanted production systems in which workers carried out production in their own homes, using their own or rented equipment. In the latter, known to many present-day historians as 'proto-industrialization' but more informatively known to contemporaries as the 'putting-out system', the capitalists normally owned the working capital, i.e. the goods at various stages of processing up until final sale to customers, while the quantities of fixed capital were very limited (and often owned by the workers). This suited the low availability of funds for fixed capital in the early stages of industrialization (see below, pp. 129–30), and established a production structure based on the division of labour *according to product*.[69] This permitted dynamic learning effects, arising out of the large degree of responsibility entrusted to the individual worker in his or her own home. The basic problems of the system had to do with the speed and quality of production. Workflow was lethargically slow, as the materials gradually went the rounds of the many processes conducted in homes that might be scattered over considerable distances. Quality of product could not be guaranteed because of the absence of direct supervision, and there was

---

68 Marx 1859, p. 92.

69 Von Tunzelmann 1993, p. 267.

much (sometimes apparently valid) suspicion that workers were often secretly embezzling the materials[70] – in other words, there was high temptation for the workers to act 'opportunistically'.[71]

Thus the factory emerged in such sectors as a mode of organization intended to remedy these two defects – to control workpace by Smith's strategy of reducing the gaps between each process, and to control the quality of work through direct supervision (overseers, etc.). In Figure 4.1, the axes of the organization sphere relate directly to these issues: quality and workflow. Division of labour by product in sectors such as textiles was replaced by division of labour *according to process*, which squared with the shift in innovational patterns noted above and brought in the central role of 'capital process'. However, as argued further in Chapter 5, there was no guarantee that 'proto-industrialization' would lead next into the factory system; sometimes it led to industrial decline. For success it had to be linked, sooner or later, to progressive technologies and organizational structures.[72] Industries which emerged from proto-industrialization were responsible for developing the key *trajectories* of technological change through learning by using, but needed to be related to the kinds of workshops which Marx described to develop the *heuristics*, through learning by doing in capital goods sectors.

2. The factory and labour

In a celebrated article, Marglin (1974) argued that, under capitalism, workers lost control of production in two stages. In pre-industrial manufacture, workers were part of a hierarchy, but in Marglin's view this was a linear hierarchy (masters – journeymen – apprentices), and individuals gradually moved up the hierarchy over their lifetime, with reasonable prospects of eventually becoming masters of the small firm. This was replaced in industrial Britain by a pyramidal hierarchy in which few (if any) advanced. The workers lost control first of *products* through the adoption of putting-out (workers were responsible for individual stages of production but not for the sale of the final product). With the later shift to the factory they lost control second of *processes*, as they became subject to the authority of overseers and the workpace set by machinery. According to Marx, the co-operation among workers which rose with early factories declined again in Modern Industry, as the 'capital process' interconnecting

70 Pollard 1965, p. 33.

71 Williamson 1985, ch. 9.

72 Speed-up characterized the garments industry from the 1860s, based on the sewing machine, but by way of 'sweated industry', usually in the worker's own home; cf. Lazonick 1990, p. 48.

machines supplanted the 'labour process' connecting labourers.[73] By 1864, the 48,000 pins per day produced by Adam Smith's ten workers co-operating in manufacture had been replaced by one woman tending four machines, able to produce about 600,000 a day.[74]

Marxist scholars, then, focus on two kinds of effects. First was worker 'alienation' from both products and processes, with attendant effects on boredom, social unrest, etc. Along with the development of rigidifying and pyramidal hierarchies, this led to social class divisions and might ultimately occasion worker-led revolutions. Second, the shift of control away from the worker and towards the machine itself (or its owners), with the machine setting the workpace and also the quality standards, allegedly downgraded workers to the role of automatons, 'deskilled' from their traditional vocations.[75] If this marched hand-in-hand with the speed-up of machinery, as Braverman argued, it is difficult to see how there could have been any result other than the progressive degradation of the labour force. Most scholars have been unwilling to regard the working classes as so powerless, and therefore see 'deskilling' as a simplification of what actually occurred, where in addition to the deskilling of many of the old handicrafts there was also the rise of a new 'labour aristocracy' based on new production skills associated with the machinery.[76] Lazonick[77] claims that management bought off conflict of the Marxian kind by subsequent development of what he describes as 'effort-saving' technologies, by compensation such as higher wages or better job security, and by leaving shopfloor processes in the hands of craftsmen and foremen; though some of these were long delayed.

3. The factory and management

There is a popular belief that the 19th century remained the era of the self-made man, so that the linear hierarchy still existed for those of ability. This was also a common view at the time, as advanced by writers like Samuel Smiles (though Smiles's views were much darker than often portrayed). Modern research, however, indicates that the view is largely fallacious, and that most entrepreneurs came not from the working class, nor even the lower middle class where the legend persists most strongly today, but from

73 Marx 1887/1965, pp. 420–21.

74 *Ibid.*, p. 460. The creation of factory discipline is expertly summarized by Pollard (1965, ch. 5); see also Clark 1994.

75 Braverman 1974, chs 3, 5, 9; cf. Marx 1887/1965, p. 423.

76 Marshall 1890/1961, pp. 255–6.

77 Lazonick 1979, 1990; 1991, ch. 8.

already fairly well-to-do middle-class backgrounds.[78] This in turn implies that social class differences were not greatly dismantled by industrialism.

As firms grew in size (which was by no means a steady process even in the 19th century), needs arose for greater delegation of responsibilities and thus for managerial hierarchies. With ownership still concentrated in the hands of top management, the typical British solution was – as just noted – the entrusting of process control to the foremen, overseers, etc., or even relying on the skilled labour itself (the new labour aristocracy), rather than building a proper managerial pyramid. Such delegation involved the need for development of formal managerial techniques such as accountancy,[79] but until appropriate managerial structures developed – which came very much later – these remained primitive.

C. Technological and Organizational Change

Capitalism in some guise undoubtedly preceded the Industrial Revolution, though it may itself have come about partly in response to earlier industrial developments, in the manner of the Marxian dialectical interaction. Whether the Industrial Revolution of 18th-century Britain would have come about at all, had capitalism not become the dominant ideology, is very difficult to answer. Many of the major technological breakthroughs in fields such as textiles were begun in traditional organizations, such as small workshops. We can, however, be fairly sure that the evolution of technology along the particular trajectories it pursued owed a considerable amount to the fact that this took place in a capitalist environment. The simplest way of doing this was to combine an expert in technology with one in marketing in a partnership, as in the celebrated pairing of Watt and Boulton for steam engines.[80] Control by the owners/managers/capitalists (rolled into one, as it were) was found to be most effective when exerted at specific locations (factories) where the plant, energy source and equipment were congregated. Thus the factory represented the paradigm for *organization* of manufacturing in similar fashion to the way that the machine represented the paradigm for *technology*. Debate continues about whether the Industrial Revolution was led by technological change or by organizational change[81] – there is some indication that it came into being for the organizational reasons but became sustained through the technological heuristics.

---

78 Honeyman 1982; Crouzet 1985. The definitive study of management recruitment, training and status, is once again that by Pollard (1965, ch. 4).

79 *Ibid.*, ch. 6.

80 Note however that Watt had to oversee Boulton on finance, cf. Roll 1930.

81 E.g. Landes 1986.

Moreover, the specific heuristics of developing machinery through speeding-up also interacted with the development of the factory system. Because it involved larger amounts of fixed capital, it was a matter of simple economics that the factory had to work faster than its predecessors such as putting-out, just to cover the extra capital costs; or else find ways of cutting costs elsewhere.[82] The control mechanisms instituted in factories, over workpace, quality, and so on, instead gave stronger motivation to raise speeds, and there is considerable surviving documentary evidence from the early innovator-capitalists to support this view.[83] The alternative of cutting labour costs slighted the still widespread needs for a competent labour force, especially for skills in working with machinery.

Furthermore, the higher levels of output of the factory system in principle allowed a reduction of machine (or worker) downtime in situations where, under the traditional domestic system, some of the equipment would have to have been left underutilized for part of the time – this was a direct consequence of the Smith–Babbage insights into the division of labour.[84] The faster production speeds themselves set up 'feedback' requirements for even better control mechanisms.[85] In such ways, the technological and organizational changes came to feed off each other in the course of the Industrial Revolution.

As already implied, the reverse side of this coin was the loss of control by workers over the production process, especially that by unskilled workers tending machinery. They were increasingly compelled to work at rates set by the machine and the economics of the factory. 'Clock time' replaced natural time.[86] In Chapter 2 above, it was seen how Marx described this process as the 'intensification' of labour, and regarded it as the principal source of rising 'relative surplus-value' under industrial capitalism. Though the average productivity of labour in physical terms (pounds of yarn spun or yards of cloth woven, etc.) rose sharply, rises in average wages were long postponed. Rises in wages could be held off, and labour costs cut, by increased employment of relatively defenceless women and children at low wage levels. But government legislation slowly restricted child labour and certain types of female labour (e.g. in mines), and later curbed hours of work. The combination of these regulatory changes to restrict 'exploitation' of labour with broader macroeconomic and demographic trends in the

82 Marx 1858/1973, pp. 777, 819–21.
83 Von Tunzelmann 1995.
84 Morroni 1992, p. 46.
85 Beniger 1986.
86 Thompson 1967; Berg 1985, p. 88.

labour market led to more sustained wage increases by the middle of the 19th century, supported by technological change.[87]

IV: FINANCE

A. The Financial System

Like the Scientific Revolution, what has been described as the 'Financial Revolution' long preceded the conventional dating of the Industrial Revolution. The 'Financial Revolution' is usually dated from the late 17th century, epitomized by events such as the founding of the Bank of England in 1694. It consisted primarily of the development of financial markets for dealing in government stocks and shares, also those of a few large operations. It was not directed towards manufacturing industry in any significant way, and suggestions of making such an extension were halted by the South Sea Bubble of 1720, which cast a long shadow over organized finance for commerce or industry. It did, however, prove possible to undertake limited financial operations for transport and similar infrastructural investments, like the Turnpike Trusts, or the 'Canal Mania' of the 1790s. Recent opinion has favoured a broader impact of new financial instruments (e.g. bills of exchange) and rising financial intermediaries (e.g. attorneys).[88]

Some of these needs, and those of manufacturing industry, were directly met by local banks, located much nearer to the new centres of industry (such as north-west England); these were called the 'country banks' as being outside the area defined as the monopoly of the Bank of England. However, what these were prepared to supply to English industry was mostly working capital funds, i.e. support for the circulating capital.[89] There were ways in which such working capital could be extended to the longer term,[90] but this need was met more commonly by more traditional sources such as large merchants, for the larger firms, or family and friends, for the greater number of small firms. In the move towards the factory system, what manufacturing industry required was provision of funding for fixed capital – fixed capital rose from about 30 per cent of national wealth in

87 Von Tunzelmann 1978, ch. 7.

88 Neal, in Floud and McCloskey 1994.

89 Pressnell 1956.

90 Cameron *et al.* 1967, ch. 2; Neal, *loc. cit.*

1760 to 50 per cent by 1830.[91] In Scotland, banks played a much more active industrial role, though still providing little fixed capital.[92]

B. 'Ploughback' and Fixed Capital

The way in which the new manufacturing entrepreneurs were thus compelled to fund fixed capital was to utilize the morsels of working capital from banks, merchants, other manufacturers, friends, etc., and delay them – hold up repayment until the new factory or machinery was purchased, installed and yielding additional output.[93] In this manner the new sales would generate revenue from which to repay what had been almost inadvertently lent to them. By so doing, the Ricardo gap between investment in fixed capital and the returns therefrom was kept as brief as possible. The system – or more exactly the lack of a system – for fixed capital provision put a premium on cheap plant and equipment that was quick to install and get operating, i.e. on the capital-saving and time-saving innovations noted above, reducing what Marx called the circulation period of capital.

C. Size of Firms

One effect of the limitations on fixed capital funding was to keep the size of firms fairly small. In the early 19th century, the layout of textile factories became standardized for a particular and rather small level of output, and production systems of this type were easily and widely replicated.[94] The largest textile factories at the beginning of the century had shrunk to medium size by mid-century, and there was thus regression towards a mean at the small–medium level.[95] Similarly, in the Birmingham metal trades, the medium-sized firm prevailed.[96] There was little 'horizontal integration' of industry, i.e. little in the way of combining firms through merger or acquisition, because of the weakness of management structures and especially the weakness of financial support for expansion. In the 'vertical' dimensions – in this case, along the supply chain of the raw material as it underwent successive processing – there was if anything a tendency towards disintegration,[97] with different factories and managers responsible

91 Feinstein 1978.
92 Smith 1776/1976, pp. 297–318; Cameron *et al.* 1967, ch. 3.
93 Pollard 1964; Crouzet 1972.
94 Chapman 1972.
95 Gatrell 1977.
96 Berg 1985, p. 292.
97 Taylor 1949; Temin 1988.

for, say, the weaving or finishing branches of the industry as opposed to the spinning. Different towns or sub-regions became specialized in one or other task, benefiting from external economies in what Marshall (1919) was later to describe as 'industrial districts' (see Chapter 8) – with the gains from specialization and learning exceeding the perceived gains from integration. In the Midlands metal-working industries, there was a similar highly localized pattern of specialization, based on local expertise in particular *products*.[98] This combination of technological, managerial and financial factors locked Britain into an industrial world dominated by SMF (small and medium-sized firm) enterprises, described by Marshall's phrase 'the representative firm'. Such firms constituted the theoretical basis of the perfectly competitive world of the orthodox neoclassical economic model, and in doing so also fulfilled Adam Smith's classical dream of the institutions for the operation of the 'invisible hand'.

V: PRODUCTS AND DEMAND

The role of demand has been examined at length above in connection with the impetus it provided to technological innovation. To recapitulate, the Industrial Revolution saw a shift of emphasis from product innovation (new types of goods) to process innovation. Nevertheless, the growth of demand appeared to play a significant role in the timing of innovation and had a direct impact on its nature (via time-saving technical improvements). That still leaves the source of the demand influences – and if the argument is correct, the timing of industrialization – relatively unexplained.

A. Social Class and Quality Innovation

Economists often include a variable related to income distribution as one of the determinants of demand. This can usefully be linked to Malthus's analysis of the composition of demand, as outlined in Chapter 2, where the emphasis was placed on social class as dictating consumption patterns. Many of the significant advances in consumer goods were responses to middle-class wants, dignified as 'the comforts and conveniences of life', often therefore known (following Smith) as 'decencies'. Veblen[99] unkindly described these 'mandatory' decencies of the British as 'physically superfluous and commonly aesthetically obnoxious'.

98 Berg 1985, ch. 12.
99 Veblen 1915/1964, p. 147.

The concept sometimes known as 'quality innovation' was significant here.[100] Economists typically draw demand and supply curves by relating prices or costs to *quantity* demanded or supplied, but a similar pair of schedules can be devised for *quality* demanded and supplied. Such a supply curve turns up sharply once high qualities are reached – in other words, any further increase in product quality can be achieved only through a substantial increase in costs of production.[101] This was in essence the story of the cotton mule, the most sophisticated machine developed for the textile industry during the Industrial Revolution. The advantages of the cotton mule were greatest in fine-quality yarns, where its use permitted the substitution of a relatively cheap yarn spun on machinery in Britain for a very expensive, hand-produced, imported product. Thus lower middle and upper working class consumers could afford clothing made from very fine yarns. Although the demand schedule for higher qualities will also rise, beyond some point few customers will be willing to pay for the great increase in production costs involved. Without innovations such as the mule, higher qualities will not be produced by machine methods. It will be noted that we have once again had to consider demand as linked with supply, rather than taking demand in isolation.

The mule was, however, something of an exception for its time. The more usual pattern during the Industrial Revolution was the introduction of machines first into the low grades, as for instance with the power-loom in the mechanization of textile weaving – essentially because the early machines were too crude in their mode of operation to cope with more delicate materials. The machines were then progressively scaled up to higher qualities as learning took place and their modes of operation steadily improved.

The general implication is that British industry was producing goods that were more standardized, predominantly in the medium-quality range. Commentators have often remarked upon the 'trickle-down' effect of consumption patterns, in products such as clothing or pottery (Wedgwood, etc.), from the well-to-do classes to their domestic servants or other urban dwellers. For the lower classes this implied a 'levelling-up' of tastes.[102] The major process changes in the relevant industries meant that such a rise in tastes could be satisfied from the consequential rapid decline of the price of those goods. The key to growth was the way in which product (design) changes were linked to this process efficiency.

---

100 Cf. Swann 1986.

101 Von Tunzelmann 1994.

102 Cf. Berg 1985, ch. 7.

B. Overseas Trade

Historians of international trade have argued for a 'Commercial Revolution' in water transportation from about the middle of the 17th century.[103] Sea transportation over long distances cheapened remarkably, mainly through organizational advances.[104] A certain amount also owed to the maritime supremacy of the Royal Navy, first achieved with the victory over the Dutch fleet at this time. The 'Commercial Revolution' paved the way for the wide extension of the market overseas on which Smith pinned his hopes for continued growth. Although Marx himself thought that merchants were likely to consolidate pre-industrial forms of organization, and that new technology and mode of production were required for the rise of modern capitalism,[105] the evidence suggests that the growth of the merchants supplied some of the finance for early industry, some of the entrepreneurs themselves, and above all an interconnected structure of marketing, including the promotion of new tastes.[106] The 'representative' British SMF could entrust marketing arrangements to the long-established merchant organizations (for internal as well as external trade), who could also supply it with raw materials, and thus became the customary end-point of the putting-out system. A few famous manufacturers developed their own marketing arrangements, but they were the exception rather than the rule. Although Smith railed against 'a nation of shopkeepers',[107] this integrative role of the merchant was the key to the 'First Industrial Revolution'. It was in this way that the disparate functions were brought together.[108] Technology was but a small part of this interlinkage, but it came through the needs of commerce for time-keeping driving on through both processes (clockwork) and products (time-pieces) into those of manufacturing industry.[109]

One view has it that Europe, including Britain, was able to industrialize on the basis of trading with the peripheral countries of the globe only at the expense of the latter, which were consigned to underdevelopment.[110] This view has much in common with the Myrdalian 'cumulative causation' model of vicious and virtuous circles outlined in Chapter 3. However, it has

---

103 Rostow 1975, ch. 3.

104 North 1968.

105 Marx 1909, ch. 20.

106 Steuart 1767, bk. II, ch. 5; Marx 1858/1973, p. 856.

107 Smith 1776/1976, p. 613; the phrase as applied to Britain was later made famous by Napoleon.

108 Price 1989.

109 Rosenberg and Birdzell 1986, pp. 148–50.

110 Wallerstein 1979; Goldfrank 1979.

not been widely accepted by historians.[111] An obvious difficulty is that the most aggressive imperialist powers in the early modern period were Spain and Portugal, but these long remained among the most underdeveloped countries of Europe.[112] Much depended on the ways in which trade was used domestically, and here Smith's arguments against crude mercantilism were especially relevant. Using trade to import hoards of precious metals, as practised by the Spanish and Portuguese, was no necessary path to prosperity.

Smith had an even more fundamental argument against colonial trade, which was the 'opportunity cost' one. Although Britain had gained something from her colonies, and the colonies themselves perhaps something more, both could have benefited more from trading competitively with other nations.[113] Moreover, Britain would have turned over its capital faster by concentrating more on trading with nearby Europe.[114] In other words, possession of colonies actually *slowed down* capital accumulation for industry. To the best of my knowledge, these propositions have not been formally tested.

British trade to distant countries originally sought luxury items to import into the country. As industrialization progressed, however, it ran progressively greater export surpluses, based on the cheap good-quality manufactures in which it had a world lead. Its problem increasingly became one of finding adequate imports rather than its early quest for adequate exports.[115] In part, imbalances were met by constructing multilateral in lieu of bilateral trade and payments systems, including the notorious Slave Triangle.[116] This was also a major factor underlying the urgent demands of manufacturers for repeal of the Corn Laws in the early 19th century.[117] Even so, it is doubtful whether we should regard this as 'export-led growth', because the initial superiority of the export items had to be established within the country. As Hume[118] put it, 'The encrease of domestic industry lays the foundation of foreign commerce'. Exports thus followed domestic technological and market success rather than preceding it.

---

111 O'Brien 1982a.
112 Smith 1776/1976, pp. 220, 256, 541, 609, 627.
113 *Ibid.*, pp. 594–600, 631.
114 *Ibid.*, pp. 600–604.
115 Hatton *et al.* 1983.
116 Williams 1944. There is a large literature on this issue.
117 Matthews 1954, ch. 6; von Tunzelmann 1967.
118 Hume 1758/1955, p. 79.

VI: GOVERNMENT POLICY

It has been shown that most of the 'exogenous' sources of growth for British firms had been revolutionized well before the Industrial Revolution itself (cf. Figure 4.1). There had been:

(a) a 'Scientific Revolution', conventionally dated to 1662;
(b) a 'Capitalist Revolution', conventionally dated to 1688;
(c) a 'Financial Revolution', conventionally dated to 1694; and
(d) a 'Commercial Revolution', conventionally dated to 1660.

There had also been, at the sectoral level, an 'Agricultural Revolution' of profound importance, again dating from about the middle of the 17th century.

Although the synchrony of dates seems striking, the direct link between any of these and the Industrial Revolution is far from straightforward, as the above discussion has tried to show. For all the individual advances, none by themselves would probably have launched industrialization without interacting with the others, and the leadership of one or more spheres; and in my interpretation the latter came from commerce and the role of the merchant. For example, it seems unlikely that, without the support of merchants and their needs for goods, property rights established via 'capitalism' would have been oriented towards *industrial* capital. This primacy of the merchant was emphasized at the time by Hume,[119] Steuart[120] and many others, including of course Adam Smith. The point can be made in another way, by looking at the implications for government policy.

A. Capitalism and Laissez-Faire

In the discussion of organizational change, it was noted that the rise of capitalism seems indisputably established, but whether this can be regarded as *laissez-faire* capitalism, in which governments withdraw from any exercise of control over the capitalists, is much more dubious. By such laissez-faire capitalism is meant an economic system in which capitalists are given virtually free rein to make use of the power that they derive from such ownership and control – in particular, the government imposes few if any restraints on their exercise of such power. The point is of considerable policy significance, for instance because it was this interpretation of 'Victorian values' which helped drive governments of the 1980s, most explicitly the Thatcher government in the UK, to 'roll back the frontiers of the state'. The implication was that such policies made Britain into the

---

119 Hume 1752/1955, pp. 52–4.
120 Steuart 1767, bk. II, ch. 3.

workshop of the world' in Victorian times and might lead to industrial renaissance in the present.

Some do indeed see the early Victorian period (early–mid 19th-century) as the heyday of free enterprise, guided by doctrines such as Jeremy Bentham's 'utilitarianism', i.e. 'the greatest good of the greatest number', in turn assumed to follow from Adam Smith's ethos of vigorous competition and freedom from arbitrary state regulation. However, one can put the opposite interpretation on the period by highlighting other aspects, including a surge in provision of services by local government (lighting, gas, water, etc.). While private enterprise may have been waxing in manufacturing, it was neatly offset by rising *public* enterprise in infrastructure.[121] In that sense, the Victorian model is a poor one for Thatcherism. Paradoxically enough, future historians may well see the Thatcher era in similar light, as being one of 're-regulation' rather than 'de-regulation' (see Chapter 8).

The most contested domain for governmental action was in regard to poverty. Malthus (1798) believed that the poor laws discouraged worker effort while adding excessively to employers' costs.[122] Much turns on whether the poor laws represented a subsidy to wages, thus raising labour costs, or a subsidy to incomes, thus raising demand.[123] There is reasonable evidence that the latter view is a more adequate description of the historical situation, and that Malthus would have been on stronger ground if he had given emphasis to the (positive) demand aspects, as he did throughout the rest of his economics writings. But in the era of utilitarianism after 1834, the 'New Poor Law' sided with Malthus's (mis-)interpretation.

B. Free Trade

The expansion of international trade benefited the British manufacturer through cheap imports, but had more controversial impacts on British agriculture. Some items like raw cotton were irrelevant to the latter, since they could not be grown successfully in the British Isles, but items like wheat and other grains or wool provided more or less direct competition. Policy debate in classical political economy, as noted in Chapter 2, became polarized around the existence of the 'Corn Laws', which were taken as being emblematic of a political and economic struggle between agriculture and manufacturing in the early 19th century. Manufacturing itself had delayed free trade for some years in areas where it felt most threatened[124] –

---

121 Jones 1988, p. 21.
122 Himmelfarb 1984; von Tunzelmann 1986.
123 McCloskey 1973b.
124 See Smith 1776/1976, bk. IV, ch. 8.

notably in the attempted prohibition of exports of 'artizans and machinery', i.e. exports of embodied skills and capital goods.

Yet in Chapter 2 it was mentioned that, by the end of the Industrial Revolution, free trade had gone far further than Adam Smith had ever foreseen. With the Repeal of the Corn Laws in 1846, Britain had effectively attained complete liberalization of trade. Recent economic historians have cast doubt on the boost to economic growth that free trade offered.[125] Though many such arguments rest upon a neoclassical approach which is not shared here, it seems quite likely that this result would hold good under more adequate evolutionary assumptions, as one has to set the gains for manufacturing against the losses incurred in other sectors such as agriculture. After a period of agricultural prosperity, the repeal paved the way for the 'Great Depression' in British agriculture a quarter of a century later. But the full reckoning of the gains from free trade still remains to be assessed.

The significance of free trade ran wider than the *economic* boost to British exports that free trade gave, for it included the *political* triumph of commerce, and of the manufacturing classes over the agricultural classes. In the 18th century and earlier, the primary arena of political conflict lay within agriculture, between its various classes (as were highlighted in debates over causes of the English Civil War in the mid 17th-century). With the sectoral shift towards manufacturing there arose this sectoral political debate. The manufacturers did not yet have it all their own way, and were forced to submit to legislation for shorter hours of work in the next few years, with the effects on time saving, etc., already considered. With the subsequent retreat of agriculture as the 19th century progressed, the crux of political debate shifted back to class conflict, this time between employers and workers within manufacturing. Commerce drifted away from its close links with manufacturing and embraced finance, to set up a divide with profound implications for subsequent British industrial 'decline', as set out in Chapter 6 below. Before examining that 'decline', I shall pursue the expansion of the British industrialization model in Continental Europe in Chapter 5.

---

125 E.g. McCloskey 1981, ch. 8.

5. European Industrialization, Late 18th to Early 20th Centuries

> Mechanization, which is making steady advances, disturbs and alarms us, and it gradually comes nearer and nearer like a storm controlled from without which is bound to come and hit us. ... We must take up these innovations ourselves. (Goethe 1800[1])

The diffusion of the 'British model' of industrialization across Continental Europe is the subject of this chapter. In the context of the theoretical chapters (1 to 3 above), the main issue is the extent to which the knowledge base being accumulated in Great Britain, as described in the preceding chapter, could 'spill over' to neighbouring countries in north-west Europe; or alternatively the extent to which those countries would have to accumulate their own technological and productive knowledge. We shall see that, though the basic industrial model remained British, it also developed its own national characteristics. Today the German ('Rhineland') model is regarded by some as having more in common with the 'Asian' model, which it helped inspire, than the 'Anglo-American' model.[2]

I: GROWTH

A. Regions, Nations and Internationalism

Reference to 'national systems of innovation' or of industry until well into the 19th century is premature. Nation-states of the kinds that are nowadays identified with such national systems were often just coming into existence. The most obvious examples were the fragmented political states that were later to unify into Germany, Switzerland and Italy. At the other extreme lay dynastic empires that spanned several nationalities, like the Habsburg Empire of Austria–Hungary, the Tsarist rule in Russia (including Poland), and the Turkish Empire (including the Balkans). Wars and political

1 *Wilhelm Meisters Wanderjahre*, quoted by Biucchi 1973, p. 633.
2 Albert 1993; see the discussion in Chapters 7 and 8 below.

alliances from Napoleon to Stalin introduced further changes, often somewhat haphazard in terms of their economic justification.

Economic unity was also long delayed.[3] Industry in the late 18th and early 19th Centuries was predominantly confined to a smallish number of rather circumscribed regions, several of which cut across national boundaries. Though some of these regions subsequently faded, like Normandy in France or Saxony in Germany, and a few new ones arose, like the German Ruhr, for the most part growth spurts intensified regional differences for a time. Thus Modern Economic Growth (MEG) in Kuznets's sense came to regions rather than to nations.[4] In Italy, even the ideologies of industrialization differed sharply among regions.[5] In cases like the Habsburg monarchy, nationalism involved *exacerbating* regional industrialization differences, with the object of achieving autarky.[6] As noted in Chapter 2 above, Friedrich List's notion of a national economy was intended to amalgamate economic unity (expressed in terms of free internal mobility of goods and factors of production) with political unity (expressed as protectionism externally until economic catch-up was achieved). The *Zollverein* formed by Prussia and the German states in 1834 thus used economic unification as a step towards political union, which came in 1870/71. The issue of free trade vs. protectionism is considered further in discussing government policies at the end of this chapter.

Nationalism intensified from 1870 to 1914, to culminate in the horrors of the First World War. The war itself saw governments as becoming decisive in many areas of their economies, thus if anything adding to the political pressures which had brought it about. The interwar period, and the depression years of the 1930s especially, were years of economic nationalism rampant, to the point of autarky. Only after a Second World War had been fought did a stronger internationalist spirit arise, with consequences for Europe noted in Chapter 8 below.

B. Lags in the 'Take-off'

Some countries appeared to undergo a 'take-off' of the Rostowian kind, such as Belgium after 1835, Germany after about 1850, Italy after 1890, and often with the rising investment ratio which Rostow predicted; but others grew more gradually, including France, the Netherlands, Denmark

3 Myrdal 1956, chs 3–4.

4 Pollard 1981, ch. 3; Harrison 1983 for Spain; Lee 1988 for Germany; Esposto 1992 for Italy.

5 Zamagni 1993, pp. 103–9.

6 Gross 1973, p. 242.

and Sweden.[7] The relatively early Belgian advance can be seen at least partly as a spin-off from British industrialization, but there is no other clear relationship between speed or timing of industrialization and the extent to which the process could have been 'imported' from Britain. The growth spurts, which also occurred sporadically in the steadier-growing economies, were normally associated with the emergence of a narrow range of 'leading sectors', though not necessarily the same sectors as found in the British case; for example, the German leading sectors consisted of coal, iron and engineering rather than textiles, similarly industries like cotton spinning failed to impart sustained growth in Tsarist Russia.[8] The leading sectors could play the kind of dynamic role which Rostow had in mind, through their backward and particularly their forward linkages (to user industries), but I argue that the linkages had to be substantially 'home-grown'.

C. Income and Output

Economic historians have made heroic attempts to construct or estimate national income of the countries of Europe over the past two centuries.[9] Controversy surrounds individual estimates of course, but the broad patterns are adequate for present purposes. It seems clear that there was no close relationship between levels of national income per capita before industrialization and the onset of industrialization and growth; for example, Italy according to Bairoch's figures was above the European average in 1830 but, even after two decades of rapid industrialization, 20 per cent below by 1913; Russian industry was about as advanced as German industry in the early 19th century.[10] Part of the reason for the lack of association lies in the varying regional differences within countries as noted above, but even regional income per capita was not closely correlated with growth. For example, Flanders in Belgium was one of the richest regions in western Europe before industrialization but (despite Belgium's early spurt) one of the poorest by 1914; even more mysterious is that early spurt in Belgium, then part of the 'United Provinces', as compared with stagnation in the previously wealthy north of that country (Holland etc.).[11] Industrialization itself was not always closely allied with economic growth, measured in terms of national income per capita. France long stood condemned by historians (not least French historians themselves) of lagging

7 For a sophisticated analysis of some time series, see Crafts *et al.*, in Sylla and Toniolo 1991.
8 Milward and Saul 1977, p. 403.
9 E.g. Bairoch 1976, 1982; Crafts 1983; Maddison 1983, 1991.
10 Milward and Saul 1977, p. 350.
11 Cf. Mokyr 1976.

in the industrialization stakes, but the evidence of growth rates controversially suggests no great gap behind Britain over the longer term.[12] Part of the reason in the case of France was the relatively slow growth of its population, which meant that national income could rise more slowly while still achieving respectable growth in incomes per capita; more important for us was the *nature* of French industrialization as outlined below.

The conclusion that scholars have reached is that some regions or countries which seemed poised for growth did not become early industrializers, and the factors responsible appear to lie in the Kuznets–Abramovitz category of differences in 'social capabilities'.[13] To this may be added the point just made, that we should perhaps modify our notions of 'industrialization' to accommodate the varieties of industrial experiences.

D. The British Model and Indigenous Efforts

Technological indicators like coal or iron output or steam horsepower per head show all Continental countries with a long lag behind Britain in the middle of the 19th century.[14] In dealing with technology, it is reasonable to view the initial situation as one of attempted catch-up. Pollard[15] argued that British technology was transferred whole, without serious adaptation, to the Continental countries, e.g. as steam engines, spinning mules, blast furnaces or railways – though often the sequence of adoption was different from Britain, and, one might add, the types of equipment favoured on the Continent differed from those most favoured in Britain itself. Local alternatives, Pollard considers, were little developed until the last quarter of the 19th century. Furthermore, he claims that processes as well as products were similar to those in Britain – what differed were the resources (in terms of such things as skills, employment systems, capital sources and entrepreneurial functions) and the environments (e.g. legal and social frameworks). Gerschenkron[16] similarly believed that the most modern techniques were transferred. Below I shall instead argue that different learning heuristics had begun to emerge for the processes and products well *before* the last quarter of the 19th century.[17]

Continental Europe was indeed already experiencing some industrial advance before the impact of the British Industrial Revolution. Sometimes

---

12 Roehl 1976; O'Brien and Keyder 1978.

13 Milward and Saul 1973, p. 250.

14 Pollard 1981, p. 108.

15 *Ibid.*, p. 86, also 1973, and in Dosi *et al.* 1992, pp. 47–9.

16 Gerschenkron 1962, pp. 8–10.

17 Cf. also Veblen 1915/1964, pp. 85–6.

direct confrontation with Britain was then avoided by developing industries where the new mechanical paradigm was less intrusive or overpowering in its impact on *processes* employed; for example, when the French cotton industry moved towards factory production by first focusing on printing and dyeing rather than the more mechanized branch of spinning. Equally, the industry might choose *products* where mechanized competition was less severe; for example the silk industry of Lyon, or the Swiss watch industry. Further implications are examined in the discussion of product vs. process innovation below. Even the later developing regions further east sometimes flourished best on the basis of indigenous breakthroughs, for example Robert's diffusion process for refining beet sugar in Bohemia 1864 (which helped create the Czech machinery industry e.g. Škoda), large-scale flour milling in Hungary, or lager brewing in Plzen.[18] Inescapable factors like climate and topography also enforced the creation of indigenous technologies, especially in agriculture.[19]

There was thus little escape from the need to develop heuristics to advance the technologies of a country in sustained fashion, whether directly imitating the British heuristics or alternatively going off at a tangent, and to develop capabilities at the firm level to exploit those heuristics – in particular, learning capabilities. Countries that looked much the same in developmental terms in the middle of the 19th century – for instance, the Scandinavian countries on the one hand and those of south-east Europe on the other – could look very different half a century later. The former had managed to develop successful industrial learning strategies, underpinned by social, educational and similar changes, while the latter had not. The study of learning behaviour below will argue that technological 'information', for instance knowledge embodied in machinery, accounted for less than the indigenous efforts by particular countries to develop their own associated knowledge bases.

E. Sectors and the Role of Demand

Industrialization was naturally linked to a rising share of manufacturing in national income, and labour productivity was higher in secondary industry than in agriculture. The evidence, however, also suggests the importance of some degree of balance across sectors. For instance, the average productivity of German agricultural workers rose 60–90 per cent in the second half of the 19th century, while that in industry and mining rose an estimated 123 per cent.[20] Conversely, those countries with stagnant primary

18 Milward and Saul 1977, pp. 308–10.
19 See also Cameron 1985; O'Brien 1986.
20 Milward and Saul 1977, p. 54.

sectors were likely to be dragged back in terms of their industrialization efforts, as for example in Spain and, for many years, Italy. Thus, though growth was led by industry, modernizers such as Cavour in Italy in the mid-19th century, or Witte in Russia and Xenopol in Romania late in the century, learnt to their cost that ignoring non-industrial sectors could well threaten their industrial strategies.[21] On the demand side, agriculture could contribute internally through its demand for manufactures or – as was more common in areas of unequal land distribution – through export revenues. Gerschenkron's belief that later industrializing countries would be more and more biased towards industry was at best true only in the short run.[22]

One of the 'backwash' effects of industrialization was to set up 'demonstration effects' for taste patterns of those regions yet to industrialize.[23] Such demonstration effects were probably adverse for industrialization, supporting innovations in luxury goods, the provision of railway and public utility layouts which favoured the rich, and so on.[24] Early 19th-century cities were predominantly political centres and also for the most part centres of conspicuous consumption – they were little involved in industrialization spurts until the advent of newer industries at the end of the century. Lowish regional or national consumption levels, stemming from low wages, did not seem to matter too much – Belgium and Germany, both with fairly low wage levels, were among the earliest Continental industrializers. Part of the reason was that low wages could also mean low costs on the supply side, as argued below. But income distributions did seem to matter considerably, and indeed Milward and Saul[25] regard this as the major conclusion of their earlier study of comparative European industrialization. The late industrializing countries of eastern Europe were characterized by extreme income inequalities. The Tocqueville–Kuznets inverse-U curve of early rises in inequality also seems supported by the evidence, e.g. for Sweden.[26]

Other countries faced advantages or disadvantages in demand for their products abroad, i.e. in international trade. A decline of foreign demand was not necessarily a bad thing – for example, when Belgium was cut off from French and then Dutch markets after 1818, it had to seek others, which it did through its industrialization effort. Except for smaller countries like Belgium, Switzerland and Finland, however, trade tended to lag behind

21 *Ibid.*, p. 536.

22 However, this need for 'balance' on the demand (sectoral) side did not have to imply a need for balance on the supply (technology) side (von Tunzelmann 1993).

23 Nurkse 1953.

24 Pollard 1981, pp. 212–13.

25 Milward and Saul 1973, p. 23.

26 Soltow 1989; see p. 84 above.

growth rather than acting as its 'engine'. Most often this was because development began with a phase of import substitution, often behind tariff barriers. With a few exceptions, such as Swiss textiles, industrial growth thus rested first on home-market demand rather than foreign demand – as just noted, the foreign demand in advanced countries was likely to be for primary products. For Germany, and later Austria and Italy, trade patterns were of the *Mittlerstellung* (intermediary) kind – importing manufactures including capital goods from advanced countries like Britain, and exporting their own manufactures to less advanced countries further east and south.[27]

As industrialization proceeded, most successful European countries raised their export surpluses of manufactures or semi-manufactures and their import surpluses of primary products.[28] But Pollard is quite right to stress that this was not simply a question of demand and products – it was becoming a matter of productive efficiency. Trade increasingly related to technology content, as in the 'technology gap' models.[29] Thus coal was a primary product, but in 19th-century terms it was a technology-based product, and was exported by the more advanced countries. Countries like Norway built growth on an expansion of processed primary products such as sawmilling timber. Danish reliance for growth on agricultural exports reflected the fact that, in Denmark by this time, agriculture (dairy products, bacon, etc.) was to be seen as producing *high-tech* products, rather than specifically *primary* products.[30] As Germany itself forged ahead in advanced industries, it engaged in interchanges of similar manufactured items with other advanced countries, as for instance in iron and steel, where the import/export pattern depended on quite specific technology and product advantages ('intra-trade'). Despite the political significance of trade with LICs such as south-east Europe, in economic terms the AICs were becoming one another's best customers.[31] For sustained growth, it was therefore the technological (supply) opportunities rather than product (demand) opportunities which ultimately counted (see also Chapter 11 below). Without strong domestic efforts to progress, the industrial products of more advanced countries could simply wipe out domestic manufactures, as happened for example to the Flemish linen industry after the 1830s, leaving the 'backwash' effects to swamp any 'spread' effects of international trade.

---

27 Pollard 1981, pp. 177, 226.

28 Milward and Saul 1977, p. 481.

29 Pollard 1981, pp. 174–5; see p. 91 above.

30 *Ibid.*, p. 235.

31 Landes 1969, p. 241.

F. Inputs and Supply Factors

This leads us into a consideration of the supply side, to examine the inputs into emerging industries and their costs.

1. Transportation

Transportation in pre-industrial Europe was often inordinately slow – at an extreme, Russian iron produced in the Urals often took two years to get to markets in St Petersburg.[32] As in Britain, and *pace* Adam Smith, access to water was normally the key to expanding trade internally or externally. Much was therefore spent by governments and private speculators on improving waterways and digging canals; hence for all its shortcomings, Russia had one of the most extensive waterway systems in Europe by 1830. But costs of construction were everywhere fairly high, and the coverage remained restricted for obvious topographical reasons. It is not surprising that the railway was seen throughout Europe as the harbinger of economic development. Some early industrializers like Belgium thus concentrated on rapid provision of a dense railway network; however, there were others in this category, notably Switzerland and Sweden, where the building of the railways came belatedly. Because imitation of British technology could be rapid where topography allowed, railway construction diffused across Europe much faster than did the growth of manufactures. Generally a pattern therefore emerges of railway construction behind other industrialization in Britain and north-west Europe, contemporaneous with industrialization in central Europe, and well ahead of industrialization in south and east Europe.[33] The middle case was likely to involve the closest interlinkages between railways and manufacturing expansion, both on the supply side e.g. through fostering market unification in Germany (and indeed its increasingly important role at the centre of the European economy), and on the demand side e.g. through 'backward linkages' to iron and engineering development. The later industrializers of south and east Europe, like Cavour in Italy after 1848, sought similar gains, but with much less success. Contrary to his wishes, the demands for inputs of iron or engineering flowed straight back to the industries of the then more advanced countries further north and west, and the same happened in Spain after its Railway Law of 1855.[34] In eastern Europe, lines were most often built for political rather than economic reasons, and long remained

32 Milward and Saul 1973, p. 90.

33 Pollard 1981, p. 130.

34 Tortella 1972; Nadal 1973, pp. 597–8; Milward and Saul 1977, pp. 244–5.

unprofitable.[35] As with international trade, railway provision alone did not guarantee industrial success – it all depended on what industry itself managed to accomplish.

2. Energy

British industrialization, as seen in the previous chapter, was based on cheap and abundant coal and later iron. This posed serious problems for the European countries that were employing British technology some decades later to achieve similar objectives. Belgium had the cheapest coal in Europe until the mid 19th-century, and was an early industrializer as we have seen, whereas many later industrializers, like Scandinavia, the Netherlands, Italy and Spain, had little coal to speak of. One is tempted to argue that the timing of industrialization depended on having the right resources in abundance. But the best coal resources relative to existing technologies were in Upper Silesia,[36] an area which failed to industrialize in these years. Conversely, other early industrializers like Switzerland had little coal (or iron), and France did not have much. Moreover, Belgium in fact exported much of its coal, and used water power rather than steam in manufacturing. To some extent the countries with limited resources could import them, as France did extensively from Belgium, and later countries did from Britain, but the main ingredients of success were to adapt to expensive fuels or to substitute for them (see the discussion of supply determinants of technology below). Even Belgium pioneered recovery of gas from blast furnaces, well ahead of Britain.[37] Later in the 19th century new deep-mining areas providing excellent coking coal were opened up, especially the Ruhr. Later still, eastern Europe opened up its oilfields, in Romania and especially the Baku region in southern Russia – in 1900, Russia produced as much as one-third of the world's oil, more than the United States.

Steam engines were first adopted in quantity in conditions similar to those met by early British engines – coal-mining areas requiring water to be pumped out, like the Borinage district in Belgium.[38] Elsewhere the coal could be replaced by alternative fuels. Water power could meet many industrial needs in areas like Switzerland and Alsace, and these regions became world leaders in developing water-power technologies such as turbines. However, there was little process-related integration between power source and machinery – turbines were designed by theorists and built

35 Pollard 1981, p. 209. The impact of railways on growth in particular countries is surveyed in O'Brien 1982b.

36 Pounds and Parker 1957, p. 216.

37 Mokyr 1976, p. 57.

38 Dhondt and Bruwier 1973, p. 333.

mostly to customer order.[39] Most important was thus the development of hydro-electricity towards the end of the 19th century, which led to a fusion with user technologies in ways noted below. It was on hydro power that the industrialization spurts of Sweden, Norway and Italy were largely founded,[40] while Denmark had a two-spurt pattern based first on steam power and later on electricity.[41] Less obvious in its causes, but equally dramatic in its effects, was the early German and French lead in the internal combustion engine.[42] It may be concluded that having the right energy resources helped sustain growth, but they did not initiate it, and their absence did not have to rule out industrialization in this era.[43] The classic example of where natural resource constraints could be overcome was Switzerland which, for all the jokes about the Swiss Navy, built world-class leadership in marine engineering.

3. Materials

Much the same could therefore be said about other materials, of which iron ore was the most important. Availability of iron ore allowed Sweden to produce about half of Europe's iron in the mid-18th century, but it did not at that stage link 'forward' into significant engineering or metal manufactures.[44] The opening up of the northern Swedish ore fields late in the 19th century led mainly to ore exports, especially to Germany. Similarly, Spanish ore from the Vizcaya (Basque) region was at this time principally exported to Britain, rather than being developed as iron or steel manufactures to supply Spanish railways. The iron ore of Lorraine, Luxembourg, Belgium and Germany was too high in phosphoric content to allow great use of Bessemer's process of 1856 for making steel, and the breakthrough in those countries came with the Gilchrist–Thomas process for 'basic' steel in 1878 (see below) – hence the resource content was very much defined by the availability of technologies to exploit it. Sometimes a resource plus technology could initiate an industry, as with the Belgian zinc industry, but it was the technological capability accruing from production which allowed this activity to continue when local resources expired.[45] Often the benefits of rich mineral resources largely passed to users abroad, as in Spain (not only in the iron, but also the lead mines of Andalusia, the

39 Constant 1983.

40 Pollard 1981, pp. 229–36; Zamagni 1993, p. 93.

41 Kœrgård 1990.

42 Milward and Saul 1973, p. 216.

43 Pollard 1981, pp. 77, 120–21; cf. Kindleberger 1964, ch. 2; Kenwood and Lougheed 1982, ch. 8.

44 Milward and Saul 1973, p. 472.

45 Cameron 1961, pp. 353–64; Milward and Saul 1977, p. 166.

copper mines of Rio Tinto, and the mercury of Almadén) – over 91 per cent of Spanish metal production was exported between 1881 and 1913, and much of the ownership was foreign.[46] Conversely industries could grow entirely on the basis of imported raw materials, most obviously in the case of the cotton industry which formed the entrée to industrialization for so many countries.

An important element in the departure of Continental technological heuristics from those in Britain lay in the quest for finding alternatives to materials that were unavailable or very expensive. The whole motif of the German organic chemicals industry, and indeed of much German innovation, was precisely to overcome deficiencies in materials (see below). Anxieties about materials supplies also helped drive expansionism, and thus contributed to bringing about the world wars.

4. Capital

Capital requirements were rising: when Britain was industrializing in the late 18th century, the capital required per worker was equivalent to about 4–5 months' wages, in the heyday of French industrialization around the middle of the 19th century this had risen to some 6–8 months' wages, but when the late industrializers like Hungary advanced at the end of the 19th century, the ratio had climbed to some 3.5 years.[47] In practice, the financing of a major part of the increased capital intensities of countries did not prove exceptionally problematic, in so far as this arose in the construction of railways and other social overhead capital ('infrastructure').[48] The powerful association between the rise of the stock market in Britain and the coming of the railways spread to the rest of Europe – these were fields for investment in which the financial world was well versed, and able to extend its expertise, not only to all parts of Europe, but all corners of the globe. There was in effect a single European market for capital for railway building in the second half of the 19th century.[49] The development of oil late in the century was even more dominated by foreign capital. The fact that countries like Belgium, France and later Austria moved quickly to the status of capital exporters suggests that the supply of capital at the macroeconomic level was not particularly deficient. Moreover, nominal interest rates fell to extremely low levels in the latter part of the 19th century. However, the international capital market was less acquainted with

46 Nadal 1973, p. 582.
47 Pollard 1981, p. 221.
48 Gerschenkron 1968, p. 103.
49 *Ibid.*, pp. 118–19.

investment in manufacturing industry.[50] Here domestic efforts again had to count for most, and here the pressures of capital shortages were more keenly felt, leading eventually to institutional changes of the kind surveyed in discussing Finance below. The formal capital market was thus highly segmented, and efforts to pool small savings, e.g. through co-operative credit institutions, were widely resorted to.[51]

Hicks's approach, set out briefly in Chapter 3, drew a distinction between the construction phase and operation phase of new investments. So far as *countries* were concerned, periods of railway construction might succeed, coincide with, or precede expansion of manufacturing, as shown above. The first-named group, of early industrializers, effectively financed their social overhead from the profits of earlier growth in industry; the middle group, like Germany, used government subsidies etc. to tide themselves over. The main problem arose for the last-named group, in the peripheral European countries, where there was no revenue forthcoming from operation of railways etc. for many years to come, with the result that the servicing of their foreign debts became onerous and further curtailed their efforts to catch up industrially.

5. Labour

In contrast to capital, there seemed at first sight to be little problem about supplies of labour. Wage rates were low, and in many locations very low, suggesting a surplus of labour of the Lewis kind. The so-called 'proto-industrialization' argument, introduced briefly in Chapter 4, contends that districts with surplus cheap labour, often associated with relatively infertile lands preventing much agricultural expansion or with marked seasonal variations in the demand for labour, were likely to develop rural industries at a very early stage, which could then perhaps become nuclei for subsequent industrialization proper.[52] The proposition, which clearly emphasizes cost factors rather than demand etc. as the major determinant of industrialization, has been highly controversial and spawned a large literature.[53] A serious difficulty with the argument is that in many cases such 'proto-industrialization' in fact failed to lead to Modern Economic Growth (MEG),[54] and may even have hampered its onset where the

---

50 Earlier industrializers, however, made little use of inward investment; Milward and Saul 1977, p. 492.

51 *Ibid.*, p. 519; Gerschenkron 1962, p. 85.

52 Mendels 1972; Mokyr 1976; Kriedte *et al.* 1981.

53 E.g. Coleman 1983; Clarkson 1985; Berg 1985, ch. 3, and 1991; Goodman and Honeyman 1988, chs 3, 5.

54 Pollard 1981, pp. 65–77, and 1991; Houston and Snell 1984; Berg 1985, ch. 5.

technological dynamics were lacking.[55] This seems to have been so when wages and demand continued to fall.[56] The emergence of industry proper in fact required the inculcation of industrial skills and learning behaviour, including technological heuristics – not least because high wages may have been a greater stimulus to mechanization. This appears to explain why, say, cotton spinning in Russia, which shifted to low-wage areas later in the 19th century, failed to impart a dynamic stimulus to industrialization, despite fairly rapid output growth. However, as the example of the Netherlands shows, high wages were no guarantee of dynamic success either.

II: TECHNOLOGY

A. New Industries

Within the shift towards manufacturing detailed above, there were significant changes over time as to which particular industries acted as 'leading sectors' for the impetus to industrialization. Early industrializers borrowed the British model most closely in relying upon textiles to underpin the take-off, especially in Switzerland and France. Germany a little later placed heavier dependence upon mining and metallurgical industries, but later in the 19th century also began to develop rapidly in chemicals. Chemicals, motor vehicles and electricity formed the core of a group often known as the 'new industries', which were to carry growth through into the second half of the 20th century, before beginning to give way to industries such as electronics as set out in Chapter 8 below.

There has been considerable debate over the definition and contribution of these 'new industries' which were introduced late in the 19th century. The problems arise partly because there is no explicit agreement about whether they should be approached primarily from the demand side or alternatively from the supply side.[57] The demand standpoints include emphases upon new products and qualities, new demand structures (such as mass markets), and new regional and trade patterns; while the supply aspects include emphases upon new technologies, new science, new forms of organization and management, new forms of competition, etc. Depending on which among these one wishes to uphold, one can get very different pictures of both the timing and the scale of industrial change. The demand side will be

55 G. Lewis 1991.
56 Medick 1976.
57 Von Tunzelmann 1982.

examined in Section VI below (pp. 178–9), while new technologies are discussed in this section and new organizations in the next.

Such changes in 'leading sectors' had direct implications for the growth bases of both new entrants into the industrialization stakes and their predecessors. New entrants could achieve take-off rates of surge through 'leapfrogging' fairly directly into the new activities – for example the growth rate of new industries like electricity, chemicals, light engineering and iron and steel in Italy between 1896 and 1908 was the highest of any country for which we have data,[58] although growth in some older industries like cotton (but using newer processes) was also rapid in the same period. For countries still undergoing their main push into industry, growth would have to depend on sustaining growth in previous-generation activities, simply because the newest industries were not yet large enough in terms of output to have a marked impact on overall growth – this was true, for example, for Germany up to 1914.[59] The earliest countries, like Britain and France, had been somewhat displaced by the changes of the mid-19th century, but now had the opportunity to return to the fray – an opportunity which France (e.g. in automobiles) seized somewhat earlier than Britain or Belgium.

There is no space here to describe particular industries and their performance at length, but some comments about where they were coming from and where they may have been going to are relevant to the general purpose of the chapter.

1. Textiles

Even if their traditional strengths lay in other fabrics, most countries sought to industrialize first through cotton. Machine methods for spinning flax were invented in France but taken up on a commercial scale in Britain,[60] to the point where many of the rather extensive European linen industries were practically driven out of business. In woollens and silks, the cost advantages of mechanization were much less overwhelming than in cotton, especially in countries where labour was comparatively cheap; which gave the catching-up countries greater leeway to survive mechanized competition from Britain, but also fewer opportunities to increase productivity from eventual mechanization. It should be noted, however, that many of these traditional textile industries faced problems in regard to organization and markets as well as technology.[61]

58 Milward and Saul 1977, p. 257; Pollard 1981, p. 231.
59 Milward and Saul 1977, p. 25.
60 Rimmer 1960, pp. 170–71.
61 Milward and Saul 1973, p. 397.

British machinery and skills in cotton spinning were so powerful by the standards of the time, that there was little chance of competing vigorously in this branch, even where wages were considerably lower than in Britain (Britain itself had been able to undercut much lower wages in fine cottons in India). Consequently, although the machinery for spinning was often rapidly adopted on the Continent, e.g. in Switzerland by 1801, in Alsace by 1802 and in Catalonia (Spain), it was in the weaving and finishing branches that the market opportunities were greater. In the more successful cases, the industry was sustained by persistent technical ingenuity, as in Switzerland, even though the initial level of mechanization was often lower. The Swiss used the learning base developed in cotton textiles to move forward on the one side into machinery and engineering for textile weaving and finishing (where they are still world leaders), and on the other side into dyestuffs and subsequently fine chemicals (where again they remain today close to the world frontier). The German cotton industry declined earlier than the Swiss, but also shifted in similar directions. The continued dependence of smaller countries like Norway on British machinery restricted their indigenization of the industry.[62] Thus the Rostow 'leading sectors' concept has to be extended to include, and perhaps concentrate upon, 'leading technologies', with forward linkages in processes as well as products. It is worth noting that there was much less coupling of cotton mechanization trajectories to those of steam power in Continental Europe than had happened in Britain from the 1790s, so that the 'development blocs' evolved in rather different fashion.

2. Iron and steel

Metal industries, which had somewhat lagged behind textiles in the UK in terms of contribution to GNP, were more important for some of the Continental countries. Nevertheless, their growth was restrained by problems of imitating the British-invented technologies, until new resource bases were found and/or new technologies to exploit local resources were developed. The smelting of iron by coke, first successfully achieved in England in 1709, proved awkward to use with local materials in Belgium from the 1830s. The high cost of coal relative to wood (charcoal) also delayed coke-smelting in Continental Europe, so charcoal smelting played a larger role until the second half of the 19th century, producing more expensive but higher quality pig iron, which better suited their markets. There is room for debate over whether demand or supply factors were more important causes of the delay (cf. Chapter 6 below), but what seems beyond dispute is that it did not come from lack of information.[63] Hence, just as

62 Bruland 1989, ch. 6.
63 Pounds and Parker 1957, pp. 240–41.

cotton reversed the British technological pattern by developing from weaving, so did iron by developing from refining. On the supply side, this can be attributed to the greater ore and fuel economies in refining and the lesser chemical problems from materials because of absence of direct contact during the refining process.[64]

The dynamic element in this industry was, however, moving on to steel from the mid-19th century, beginning with the Lohage–Bremme process for puddled steel in 1849. As noted above, the Bessemer converter of 1856 was very inflexible in terms of the ores with which it could be used, so the Continental industry continued to lag behind the British. The 'open hearth' furnace developed by C.W. Siemens in Britain and the Martin brothers in France, commercialized in 1864, was much more adaptable, since it allowed the use of scrap iron and also low-grade fuels,[65] but it was the Gilchrist–Thomas ('basic') process of 1878/79 allowing the use of phosphoric ores which really permitted rapid expansion. The counterpart was the utilization of excellent coking coal from the newly developed Ruhr district in western Germany. The electric arc furnace developed by Wilhelm Siemens in Germany in 1878 proved especially successful in areas where hydro-electricity could be supplied cheaply, such as Sweden and the French Alps.[66] Steel was important in terms of forward technological linkages to industries such as shipbuilding, and of forward product linkages to industries like electricity and construction (e.g. in Germany). On the other hand, demand from older activities like railways slowed down (e.g. in France), not only because railway growth was slowing, but also because steel rails lasted much longer than iron.

3. Mechanical engineering

In the successful large industrializers, the composition of mechanical engineering naturally followed the growth industries, by way of being upstream equipment suppliers. However, its own processes owed little to its predecessor in Britain. British tools and traditions were little used, though after the middle 19th century American machine tools became very important.[67] The Germans themselves came to dominate European machine tool manufacture in highly skilled branches, especially the newer lighter tools.[68] Smaller but still successful countries like Sweden found niches, often based on locally produced innovations, requiring world markets to overcome the limitations of small domestic demand. Likewise, the Swiss

64 Landes 1969, pp. 175–6.
65 Mokyr 1990, p. 118.
66 Pounds and Parker 1957, p. 179.
67 Milward and Saul 1973, pp. 211–12.
68 *Ibid.*, p. 213.

engineering industry developed a strong tradition of high-quality production and constant innovation.[69] To critics like visiting Americans they had, however, become too unspecialized and 'over-engineered'.

Thus while Continental mechanization often advanced initially through learning-by-using in industries like textiles, it drifted more and more into an emphasis on learning-by-doing in the mechanical engineering industry itself. The focus on machine and engine making is crucial to the story of Continental industrialization, and factors which promoted persistent learning in the sector are detailed below. The role of users shifted towards integrating this machinery with other new input technologies like electricals and chemicals.

4. Electrical engineering

The long establishment of steam power in such early industrializers as Britain and Belgium gave the incentive to those catching them to resort to different approaches, including electricity. Britain in fact continued to act as one of the leaders in the scientific base, through the work of people like James Clerk Maxwell and Oliver Lodge, and the Italian Marconi for one came to Britain to develop his inventions.[70] But there were also important scientific advances on the Continent, for example by Hertz in Germany and Tesla in Croatia, and the Continentals showed greater persistence in the commercialization and adoption of electrically-based discoveries, through innovative firms such as Siemens–Halske (1847) and AEG (1887) in Germany, Philips (1891) in the Netherlands, and Ganz (1878) in Hungary. Some of these firms led in diffusing electrical technology to other parts of Europe and the rest of the world, but in Europe they were also faced by American competition from the 1890s with companies like Thomson–Houston.

The obvious backward linkage into electrical power and distribution was pursued by firms like AEG and later by Siemens. It was the forward process-based links (lateral links in Rostow terminology) which were, however, particularly interesting. The advent of cheap hydro-electricity in later industrializing countries noted above formed the base for the advance of electro-chemical and electro-metallurgical industries – among the European innovations were the electrolysis of salt (England and Germany ca. 1890), the electric arc process for producing nitrogen (Norway 1903, leading to the foundation of Norsk Hydro), the electric furnace for steel (Siemens in Germany 1878), and the electrolytic process for producing aluminium (Héroult in France 1886).

---

69 *Ibid.*, p. 224.

70 Aitken 1976.

5. Motor vehicles

In the case of the internal combustion engine, the original technical breakthroughs were actually made in Continental Europe, in France and especially Germany (Otto, Diesel, Benz, Daimler etc.). This was not because of any great advantage in fuel supplies – the main factor was the development of mechanical engineering as described above. Early engines ran too slowly for practical use – the key advance for commercialization was thus Daimler's high-speed engine of 1886. Despite the head start which Germany achieved in the technology of the engine, it was in fact the French automobile industry which grew most rapidly in Europe up to 1914. This partly reflected a reverse catch-up, where the typical French inventor-entrepreneur suited the early style of the car industry, often (like Peugeot) using German licences and American machine tools.[71] It may also have reflected the fact that many early automobile manufacturers came from a background in building bicycles, again like Peugeot. The automobile industry in this form was originally basically an assembly activity, producing one-off customized cars, and was widely dispersed. Increasingly it standardized models in orthodox 'product cycle' fashion (cf. Chapter 1 above), but the location of component supplies came to dictate the location of major producers. The Italian industry seems to have had similar influences.[72] Thus industrial districts of the Marshall kind, based on vertical (user–producer) linkages, had developed around Paris, Turin, Stuttgart and several other cities by 1914. The rubber industry was boosted in France (e.g. Michelin), Italy (Pirelli), etc., and France had also become the biggest producer of aircraft in Europe by 1913.[73]

Through such linkages, the automobile industry went on in the 20th century to act as a dynamic development bloc, with complex forward and backward linkages, as indeed demonstrated by Rostow.[74] This story is taken further in Chapter 7 below.

6. Chemicals

The older heavy chemicals branch continued to dominate later in the 19th century in earlier industrializers like Belgium and France, developing new process technologies like the Solvay process (from Belgium) for making soda, with the main objectives of using cheaper materials and utilizing by-products.[75] Later industrializers like Germany were able to leapfrog more directly into these newer methods. The constantly expanding importance of

---

71 Milward and Saul 1977, p. 98.
72 Zamagni 1993, pp. 97–8.
73 Milward and Saul 1977, p. 100.
74 Rostow 1960/1971, App. A; 1978, App. C.
75 Hohenberg 1967.

chemicals as inputs to user industries allowed them to play greater roles in industrial (and agricultural) activity at large. Chemical processes were also brought into producing products where other methods had previously been employed, for example Sweden set up the world's first chemical pulp mill in 1872.

French and even German heavy chemicals, despite their success in developing new processes and economizing upon materials, did not keep pace with the British industry in the mid-19th century years.[76] Instead, the most interesting developments came in the rise of the organic chemicals and synthetics industries, led by Germany even though much of the raw material (coal tar) initially came from Britain – indeed from the 1880s up to the First World War, apart from some advance in neighbouring Switzerland, Germany had an effective monopoly. Again this had been preceded by some earlier scientific work in Britain and France, whose patents Germans had acquired. Origins in textile dyestuffs etc. have been mentioned above. Development in Germany to its leadership status came primarily from its unremitting commitment to scientific training and particularly to R&D in-house in the laboratories of private firms.[77] Strengths in synthetic dyes allowed Germany to move into medicinal drugs, photographic materials, artificial fibres, early plastics and new explosives. This high R&D intensity has led to the supposition that the chemicals industry can be described as an example of 'technology-push', but on closer scrutiny it appears that all the breakthroughs were specifically targeted at *known* markets.[78] Since the technology had to be provided as well, it seems that Freeman's erratic coupling model combining technology-push with demand-pull gives the best description.[79] Over time, the balance may, however, have shifted from demand-led to supply-led, as the industry moved from being a 'specialized supplier' to being 'science-based' and 'scale-intensive'.[80]

The combination of high-tech intensity and economic goal (substitution by synthetics) justifies describing this as a new techno-economic paradigm. The technology directly contributed to forging a new 'National System of Innovation' through creating national self-sufficiency.

7. Food processing

Other industries deserve equal attention, but, in the light of my point that technologies as well as products matter, special attention is merited by

76 Haber 1958, ch. 4.

77 Freeman 1982, p. 30; Liebenau 1987; see the discussion of R&D below.

78 In a few cases a different market had originally been targeted, as in Perkin's original synthesis of mauve in 1856, which arose out of a search for synthetic quinine.

79 Freeman 1982, p. 109; Walsh 1984.

80 Hohenberg 1967, p. 47; Pavitt 1984.

industries that processed primary products, such as the sawmilling of timber and milling of paper in Scandinavia, the manufacture of corks in Spain, and especially the various food-processing industries. These were the basis of growth in countries like Denmark (including brewing), but also of key significance in countries like Switzerland (condensed milk and dehydrated soups, e.g. Nestlé and Maggi) and the Netherlands (margarine and cocoa powder, etc.); also later in central and eastern Europe.[81] In Italy, these close links between agriculture and industry reflected social structure as well as technological factors.[82]

B. Process and Product Innovation

Activities like food processing relied extensively on improved technologies in agriculture, and these in turn were increasingly processes spun off from other industries. Artificial fertilizers like superphosphates came from the chemicals industry, also 'basic slag' as a waste-product of the Gilchrist–Thomas steel process. High-tech agriculture also became more mechanized, using the products of local engineering like the Laval cream separator (Sweden) in intensive activities like dairying, but mainly American machinery imports in extensive activities like grain harvesting.

Machine methods of course replaced labour to some extent. It has already been shown that hand methods could not compete against efficient British machinery in areas like cotton spinning, without wages falling below subsistence levels. Continental countries in early stages of industrialization thus sought growth through fields like textile weaving and finishing, where the economic advantages of the machine methods were not so compelling. Output and employment could expand sufficiently using hand methods, even if productivity grew more slowly than with fully mechanized operations. At the same time, stagnation still beckoned unless the hand methods themselves were improved, as for example the Swiss did in applying the Jacquard loom for weaving fancy cloths to silk, and going on to develop the broad-stitch and chain-stitch looms for fancy designs.[83] Steam-powered methods were slow to be adopted, unlike in the British cotton industry, for reasons already given – for instance, in Germany cotton machinery was not steam-powered until the 1840s in the Rhineland and 1850s in Bavaria and Saxony.[84] Moreover, the mechanical engineering

81 Berend and Ránki 1974, pp. 150–51.
82 Zamagni 1993, p. 83.
83 Milward and Saul 1973, pp. 457–8.
84 *Ibid.*, pp. 402–3.

industry itself, building such machines, was typically labour-intensive and often based on small firms.[85]

Use of machine tools permitted standardization, and obviated some the deficiencies in regard to skills in user (downstream) industries. For such reasons, Marshall[86] considered that, 'engineering has special claims to be regarded as the leading representative of modern industries'. But by the time he was writing, other upstream industries of the kinds noted above had joined mechanical engineering as important shapers of technological trajectories. He pointed out himself (footnoting Marx) that, 'Water power inaugurated the modern era',[87] and we have seen how the advent of cheap hydro-electricity late in the 19th century linked forward into electro-metallurgy, electro-chemistry, etc. A dramatic example was aluminium, whose price was over $500 per pound in the mid-1850s when first manufactured, and had dropped to just $0.30 by the 1890s.[88] Marshall[89] pointed out that the chemist's balance, too, was important for standardization. The fusion of chemical processes with other process technology has been mentioned above, e.g. the adoption of the sodium sulphate process in pulp-making in the 1890s, allowing the use of sawdust etc. The celebrated Haber–Bosch process for the synthesis of ammonia at BASF in 1914 ushered in the 20th-century chemical engineering industry, allying use of special steels etc. to the chemical processes. In general, it could be said that a greater *variety* of process technologies were arising out of the diverging technological paths, and permitting entry by countries with differing resource and skill complements.

Such variety in process innovation also permitted a greater range of products to be produced relatively efficiently. The industries that had progressed from artisanal (handicrafts) production to domestic production under 'proto-industrialization' were initially threatened by machine-produced items from advanced countries like Britain, and squeezed into higher-quality markets, like Swedish steel or Alsace cottons. In these niches, the successful eventually developed or applied machine-based methods, which secured their hold at the top end of the market – and often supplying the knowledge base for linking forward into advancing industries like engineering and chemicals, as seen above. The progress of mechanization was closely related to 'quality innovation' of the kind noted in Chapter 4, whereby machines were extended over time to producing finer

---

85 *Ibid.*, pp. 224–5.
86 Marshall 1919, p. 206.
87 *Ibid.*, p. 790.
88 Milward and Saul 1973, p. 232.
89 *Op. cit.*, p. 211.

and fancier items.[90] As in Britain, such quality innovation needed to be linked to progressive technological heuristics and to accommodating demand structures (the luxury glass industry of Bohemia which failed to innovate instead shrank).

C. Demand vs. Supply Determinants of Innovation

Product innovation was of course also partly steered from the demand side. The role of income distribution was noted in Section I above – the existence of luxury demand from high incomes in pre-industrial and industrializing Europe is normally considered to have been retrogressive, in dissuading producers from modernization of processes and organizations. Demands of the bourgeoisie, often more of a *haute bourgeoisie* than in Britain, however, are generally assumed to be more progressive. These not only influenced the top end of the product range for early industrial products like fine textiles, but also the emergence of new industries in fields such as automobiles, though export demand also mattered. It seems likely that the slow development of textiles in both Spain and Italy through most of the 19th century can be accounted for partly by the slow growth of consumer incomes,[91] but the close inter-coupling of demand and supply factors and inadequacies of data make it difficult to separate demand and supply influences.

Derived demands for capital goods are easier to unravel. The delayed introduction of processes such as coke-smelting of iron owed something to erratic demands as well as problems with the raw materials – coke-smelting for reasons of scale required full-time operation. Such more modern methods were rescued in north-west Europe by railway demand, but railways were unable to affix a modern iron sector in southern Europe. Population growth and density have been accorded a role in explaining innovation, but as noted previously the links are very unclear – population growth was at fairly similar rates across Europe, unlike innovation, and population growth without income growth in any case could accentuate demands for lower-quality and less innovative products. Demand alone did not necessarily generate technological change, as for instance it failed to do in housing.[92]

However, the growth of demand through both higher or more equally distributed incomes and population growth could feed directly into innovation through the kinds of 'time savings' stressed in Chapter 4. Speed in production to get one's grain quickly harvested and to market has been

90 Fohlen 1973, pp. 27, 66.
91 Milward and Saul 1977, p. 237.
92 Milward and Saul 1973, p. 245.

adjudged a more important reason for the adoption of threshing machines in agriculture than savings of relatively 'cheap' labour.[93] Interestingly, French railway engine-drivers were paid a bonus according to their fuel savings, whereas in Germany they received bonuses for arrival on time.[94] There were, however, both supply and demand factors restricting machinery speeds in Europe. In cotton spinning, for example, spindle speeds were reduced when power costs were higher, because otherwise the total power bill would become too large to bear.[95] Thus one finds that, as late as the 1890s, Alsace spindles ran a quarter slower than those in Lancashire, and downtime was greater.[96] Despite this, the Alsace process was more labour-intensive – around the 1830s, Alsace workers looked after only half the number of spindles as those in England, and earned only about half as much notwithstanding a longer working week. The offsetting gain came because 'the high cost of coal induced a great deal of technical expertise in designing the machinery so that coal consumption was considerably less than in Britain for the equivalent output of cloth'.[97] Emphasis on quality differences limited the gains from standardization, in textiles, metallurgy, etc., for both product and process reasons; for example, the open-hearth furnace (producing higher quality steel) was much slower in tap-to-tap time than the Bessemer converter.

Supply constraints from inadequate (limited or poor-quality) endowments of fuels and materials could delay industrialization, but it has been shown (in Section I above), that such problems could be overcome by new technologies to exploit them better, or by developing substitutes such as synthetics. The technological solutions weaned manufacturing in Continental Europe, especially Germany, away from the British model and its techno-economic paradigm focused on machinery adoption and learning-by-using. The high cost of capital and capital goods in most European countries in earlier years (except perhaps in Switzerland), arising out of the segmented capital market described above, the high cost of materials like iron, plus the tendency to 'over-engineer' the machinery that was produced, were all further deterrents to investment in mechanization. That capital market gradually recovered through local co-operatives, but this still meant for many a limitation to machinery of small scale such as sewing machines – often too small as exemplified by the boats of the Norwegian fishing fleet.[98] As already mentioned, there was often little alternative in catching

93 *Ibid.*, pp. 238–40.
94 *Ibid.*, p. 173.
95 Von Tunzelmann 1978, pp. 205–9.
96 Milward and Saul 1973, p. 177.
97 *Ibid.*, p. 319; von Tunzelmann 1978, pp. 276–81.
98 Milward and Saul 1973, p. 522.

up to adopting modern capital-intensive equipment regardless of its cost: 'Sometimes the technical choices were all bunched at the capital-intensive end, as in steel, with only minor adjustments possible in the handling of the metal but not in its actual processing. For the manufacture of interchangeable parts there was often no alternative machine technique, so exacting were the standards of accuracy required.'[99]

Equipment like sewing machines could be made profitable by sufficiently low labour costs.[100] Wages in north-west Europe rose from the relatively low levels noted above as productivity improved, but those in Germany were still only about three-quarters of those in England in 1908[101] – certainly Marshall considered German willingness to work long hours at comparatively low wages an important cause of their industrial success.[102] Low hourly or weekly wages by themselves were only part of the story, since they were evidently lower still in southern and eastern Europe. What mattered was the 'efficiency wage', i.e. adjusted for labour productivity, and this depended mainly on how successful the industry or country was at *learning* how to produce industrial goods with up-to-date technologies.

D. Learning and the Institutionalization of R&D

There is little evidence that lack of *information* hindered the catching-up process on the Continent. The flying shuttle of John Kay, who fled to France, was being set up there as early as 1747. France had its first spinning jenny in 1773, just four years after Britain, and mechanical spinning in 1778, while first installations of mechanical cotton spinning included Prussia in 1784, Spain in 1791, Russia in 1793 and Switzerland in 1794.[103] When news of the Gilchrist–Thomas process leaked out in 1879, potential German adopters raced one another to Middlesbrough to secure the licence.[104] The issue, I shall argue, was instead one of developing an appropriate *knowledge* base, which often had to differ from that in Britain because of local conditions.

From an early date, Continental industrialists had spent long periods in Britain discovering (by industrial espionage etc.) both technologies and production processes. Conversely, British innovators and workmen flowed to Europe in substantial numbers. There were laws from 1695 until 1843 trying to prevent the emigration of 'artizans and machinery', but these were

99 *Ibid.*, p. 175.
100 Gerschenkron 1962, pp. 127–8.
101 Marshall 1919, p. 853n.
102 *Ibid.*, p. 545.
103 Milward and Saul 1973, p. 190; Borchardt 1973, p. 76; Nadal 1973, p. 607.
104 Pounds and Parker 1957, p. 242; Landes 1969, p. 259.

(and still are) regarded as ineffectual – a nuisance at best.[105] The outflow of inventors and entrepreneurs was substantial, accredited with major responsibility for developing the Normandy cotton industry (John Holker), Alsace textile machinery (Richard Roberts), Belgian woollen and iron industries (John Cockerill), coke-smelting of iron in France and Silesia (William Wilkinson), Russian steel (John Hughes) and many others. The successful among these brought more knowledge than information, as locals had generally tried earlier to copy British practice. They were followed not only by the requisite machinery but by hordes of skilled British workmen to guide the operation of that machinery (which was predominantly of British design). 'There is no single important industry in any of the major continental regions that did not have British pioneers as entrepreneurs, mechanics, machine builders, skilled foremen and workmen, or suppliers of capital (and usually several of these combined) to set them going',[106] despite some significant local inventions. When links were severed, as during much of the French and Napoleonic Wars (1793/1815), the imitators fell behind. Even so, such extensive transplants of equipment and skills did not guarantee success, as Bruland (1989) shows in the most detailed study of attempted transfer, that of the Norwegian cotton industry, which ultimately failed despite prolonged effort. The delay to first adoption was usually quite short, but the delay to sustained local interest in the adopting region could be considerable, and then another delay typically occurred before the technology was locally assimilated.[107]

What seems to have been lacking was the 'tacit knowledge' required to operate familiar processes and equipment in unfamiliar surroundings – that is, the British innovators and skilled workmen were not necessarily aware of all the reasons why they had been successful in their home country.[108] Although modern science has revealed some of the reasons why they failed in different environments, this question of the tacitness of technological knowledge remains critical even today.[109] It is clear enough that copying alone was insufficient – success was more likely to accrue when the imitation was adjusted to local environments. French ironmaster Georges Dufaud stated, 'Generalities are nothing – everything is in the detail'.[110] French iron producers who visited Britain but clung to their small-scale charcoal-fired furnaces did better than large plants like Le Creusot that were

---

105 Pollard 1981, p. 144.
106 *Ibid.*, p. 145.
107 *Ibid.*, p. 147.
108 *Ibid.*, pp. 147–8.
109 E.g. Pavitt 1986; Senker 1995.
110 Quoted by Caron 1979, p. 155.

directly modelled on British equivalents.[111] Still more important as time went on was to initiate a distinctive pattern of indigenous technological development – the rapid advance of the Scandinavian countries later in the 19th century can be put down to such internal efforts.[112] Conversely, the stagnation of the Dutch economy for most of the period covered in this chapter can be put down to the failure to develop a sustained technological style.[113]

An important aspect of those internal efforts was the local development of machines to make machines (Marx's 'machinofacture'), based on mechanical and later electrical engineering. As seen above, these owed little to British examples, and the Continental countries, especially Germany, became major innovators – moreover, Germany steadily replaced Britain as the model for later developers to copy.[114] Constructing and operating machinery called for skills in the workforce as well as of innovators. Marshall[115] thus argued his case for external economies and the role of industrial districts, not only in generating knowledge among its residents, but also in attracting potentially able industrialists and workers from other parts.

Although machinery has often been seen as having substituted for skilled labour, its growing complexity in fact called for new kinds of skills. As seen in Chapter 4, France had an early lead in applicable science, but lagged in technology. By comparison with France's elitist educational system, headed by the École Polytechnique (1794/95), those of Germany and Sweden spanned the full range of requirements, with early moves to compulsory primary education, a more practical curriculum in secondary schools as in the 'Real schools', and the provision of abundant universities for pure science or tertiary education for applied science.[116] These were backed towards the end of the 19th century by formal vocational education within some of the large firms, like Borsig and MAN in the German engineering industry. Germany may have lagged behind France and Britain in scientific *theory* until the beginning of the 20th century, but from early days it forged ahead in the organization of science, e.g. in laboratories. Particular stress has been laid on the dissemination of technical training below the research level in the *Technische Hochschulen* (polytechnics, e.g. Prague 1806) and *Gewerbeschulen* (mechanics' institutes), set up by state

[111] Milward and Saul 1973, pp. 327–8.
[112] *Ibid.*, pp. 499, 512, 528.
[113] Cf. Mokyr 1976, pp. 89, 119.
[114] Bruland 1991, chs 13–14.
[115] Marshall 1919, p. 287.
[116] *Ibid.*, p. 357; Musgrave 1967, chs 3–7; Sandberg 1979.

and provincial government initiatives through the 19th century.[117] Many of their professors came from large firms, and in reverse some of their researchers set up innovative companies or technologies, like Linde and Diesel.[118] German engineers, however, long felt that they lacked the social status accorded to engineers in England or France.[119] Educational patterns were reflected in innovational patterns (the relationships no doubt being two-way): 'France affords the chief instance of a leadership based mainly on individual skill; and Germany of a leadership based mainly on trained ability and high organization.'[120] Such differences emerged in the contrasting successes in newer industries – the French performing better in the automobile industry in its earlier years (dominated by independent inventor-entrepreneurs), the Germans better in electrical engineering and especially organic chemicals.

Technical training for businessmen had been increasing in Germany since the 1840s, with engineers replacing managers especially around 1890, and with a large proportion of managers in any case having degrees in technical subjects. Industrial research laboratories were being founded from the 1850s, often closely linked to academia, and with leaders who often went on to head large firms.[121] In chemicals, the French led in appointing individual scientists to positions in companies, whence their early success; but the Germans led in setting up research teams and dividing up problems for teamwork, and instituting a division of labour in R&D.[122] Marshall[123] pointed out that the scientific work might be more pedestrian than in universities, but teamwork was vital especially in fields that straddled scientific borderlines. This helped companies to move quickly into new areas, like the shift from synthetic dyes to pharmaceuticals etc. by the German and Swiss organic chemicals industries.

Because of this *scope* of industrial research, as well as its scale, in-house R&D was thus likely to be located in large firms. Moreover, the growing complexity of industrial technologies through time added to the concentration in large firms.[124] This was of course the basic Schumpeterian point about R&D outlined in Chapter 3 above. While this led, as Schumpeter feared, to a certain amount of bureaucratization, it also helped

---

117 Manegold 1978; Keck, in Nelson 1993. High-tech in agriculture also was associated with educating the many rather than the few, as for instance in the rural Folk High Schools in Denmark.

118 Locke 1984, ch. 2.

119 Manegold 1978; Locke 1984, pp. 35–6, 80.

120 Marshall 1919, p. 106; cf. Landes 1969, p. 187.

121 Kocka 1980.

122 Marshall 1919, p. 134; Manegold 1978; Dornseifer and Kocka 1993.

123 Marshall 1919, p. 205.

124 *Ibid.*, pp. 172–3.

fund a long-term commitment to specific projects ('patient money', like the years spent by German firms developing synthetic indigo[125]). What has perhaps been less sufficiently stressed in the extensive literature on this subject is that German firms, growing up in an atmosphere of catching up, also drew freely on overseas advances and on their contacts with SMFs as sources of innovation.[126] Advances elsewhere were not seen as a substitute for in-house development but as a complement.

Incorporation into large firms also permitted rapid commercialization, as seen in the new drugs marketed by the bigger pharmaceutical companies, such as aspirin by Bayer in 1897 (backed by a massive advertising campaign). Industries less permeated by formal R&D laboratories relied even more on strengths other than technology: 'The heavy chemical industry was the triumph of the engineer and the salesman rather than of the chemist. It was also the triumph of the diplomat for after Solvay relatively little emphasis was given to further technological change but far more to organizing control over world markets.'[127] We should now turn, necessarily more sketchily, to those issues.

III: ORGANIZATION

A. Ideology

Feudalism and serfdom have conventionally been regarded as antithetic to industrialization and industrial capitalism. There was, however, no sharp break between precapitalist agriculture and capitalist industry in many countries of Europe, contrary to the Marxian stages.[128] Traditional aristocrats were often to be found engaging in exports from their estates. Indeed, the coming of industry was sometimes accompanied by an *increase* of serfdom rather than its dissolution.[129] The problems that serfdom raised for industrialization may initially have lain more on the demand side, via income distribution as already described, than on the side of supply. But Marx was surely right that some degree of capitalist ethos was required in 19th-century circumstances to advance industrialization very far. It is therefore not surprising that some economic historians, like Milward and Saul,[130] have granted as great a role to the French Revolution (political

125 Cf. Freeman 1982, p. 31.
126 Milward and Saul 1973, pp. 181, 231.
127 *Ibid.*, p. 228; this view is now thought to be somewhat overstated.
128 Milward and Saul 1977, p. 523.
129 Milward and Saul 1973, pp. 56, 67–8, 475; Pollard 1981, p. 200.
130 *Ibid.*, p. 250.

liberalism) as to the British Industrial Revolution (technology) in laying the foundations for development.

The French Revolution brought the bourgeoisie as a class to power in France, with political beliefs favouring individual property rights. Contrary to the thinking of economists then and now, this brought rather dubious benefits so far as economic growth of the country as a whole was concerned, much as it may have benefited the bourgeoisie themselves.[131] Arguably the bourgeoisie were in the mean time transformed more into rentiers than into industrialists.[132] The Revolution was unquestionably a telling blow struck against feudal power elsewhere in Europe, but it took until about the 1870s for the bourgeoisie as a class to dominate right across the Continent, at a time of rising nationalism.[133]

Despite the background in liberal thought, France actually entered a period of substantial industrial protectionism after 1815, when Napoleon's defeat exposed French industry to stern British competition. Protectionist tariffs, controlled prices and similar policies in early 19th-century France rang as strongly of mercantilism as of the Enlightenment and liberalism. True, the overall level of tariffs as a proportion of imports was often lower than in Britain, because of the large share of primary products in their imports.[134] And there was a much greater role for private initiative in industry than in the mercantilist state of Colbert's times in the 17th century, or than under the guilds and corporations which ran crafts and industries in many early modern towns. Yet the traditions of local community and paternalism engendered under the guilds were less radically swept away than in the UK. There are well-known accounts of would-be entrepreneurs fleeing the towns to escape the dead hand of corporations (in Britain also), but some areas where guilds continued to have some authority remained strong industrial centres well into modern times, e.g. Lyon silk and Alsace cotton.

The consequence was that capitalism was less individualist in most of Continental Europe than in Britain or the USA. The Co-operative movement in Britain after 1844 was aimed at workers and at *consumers*, i.e. distribution,[135] whereas co-operative functions like credit and marketing aimed primarily at *producers* were successfully established on the Continent. The most obvious examples arose in progressive agricultural regions, hampered by lack of access to credit in segmented capital markets, like the single-village co-ops of the type set up by Raiffeisen in Germany,

---

131 *Ibid.*, p. 262; Kemp 1971, ch. 5; Palmade 1972, pp. 70–74.
132 Kemp 1971, p. 109.
133 Landes 1969, pp. 129–30; Pollard 1981, pp. 219, 252.
134 Nye 1991.
135 Marshall 1919.

which were widely imitated.[136] The attitudes spread well outside agriculture, however, and Chandler[137] describes the whole ethos of German industry as one of 'co-operative capitalism'. This can be demonstrated internally within firms, in the evolution of paternalist workplace relations, and externally between firms, in the rise of inter-firm agreements like cartels, etc.[138] Socialism of course took the notion of co-operation in different directions (see Chapter 9).

B. Labour Process

Within firms, paternalist 'social relations of production' (to use Marx's term) derived partly from the medieval and early modern guilds just mentioned. In France, the domestic form of organization was often taken more or less wholesale into the early 'factories'.[139] Still more important, at least in central Europe, were traditions of government bureaucracy.[140] When Siemens moved from being an informal family concern to a large-scale operation through setting up its works at Siemensstadt in Berlin, about the only role model it could find was that of the Prussian state bureaucracy.[141] The founder of AEG, Emil Rathenau, had a more visionary impulse towards benevolent paternalism. Companies like BASF in chemicals provided libraries, schools, canteens, savings banks, housing, etc. – and these were not substitutes for state provision in Germany but complements to Bismarck's compulsory national social insurance schemes from 1881 for unemployment, sickness and old age.[142] Thus developed attempts to reconcile community and company (*Gemeinschaft und Gesellschaft*). Even more than in Britain, exploitation of labour was arguably more serious outside factories, in the so-called 'sweated' trades in large cities.

In similar vein, tendencies towards deskilling the labour force were less pronounced than in the UK or USA. Mechanization in general proceeded less rapidly on the Continent and production continued to be skill-intensive, with skilled labour being little more costly than unskilled across Europe.[143] There was at the same time rising emphasis on universal education – the latter came originally from desires for political or social control, but

136 Milward and Saul 1977, pp. 58, 232.
137 Chandler 1990, part IV.
138 See Section IV below.
139 Caron 1979, p. 137.
140 Significantly, the seminal study of bureaucracy was the work of the German sociologist, Max Weber. See Littler 1982 for an illuminating study of how such notions relate to subsequent views of 'labour process'.
141 Kocka 1981.
142 *Idem.*
143 Smith 1776/1976, p. 119.

increasingly became respected for its role in extending attitudes favourable to learning and vocational commitment. In France, where managers came from more elitist backgrounds, there was greater emphasis on hierarchy and status, and technical and supervisory staff retained considerable control over tradesmen in industries like shipbuilding.[144] Attempts to take this hierarchical attitude further and introduce assembly lines on the Fordist model in the larger car firms like Renault nevertheless failed for many years.[145]

C. Capital Process

The concern with technology and engineering in countries like Germany, Switzerland, France, and later Sweden, tended to give pride of place to quality rather than to quantity in the organization of production, at least by comparison with the British and American manufacturing sectors. We saw earlier that machinery on the Continent generally ran more slowly than in Britain, even when it was British-built, and we have just seen that the adoption of flow production (like assembly lines) connecting separate machine operations was somewhat tardy. Thus throughput rates tended to be slower than in the rival industrial countries, with a concentration in low-volume, high-value-added niches.[146] The drive to increased scale of operations later in the 19th century, e.g. in the German steel industry, was partly a response to these constraints – through greater process control and integration of operations, the disadvantages of product differentiation and fuel charges could be offset. For the control of production in French chemical firms, the traditional practice was allegedly putting a 'retired policeman' in charge![147]

On the other hand, the factory was by no means the only route to industrial progress. Small workshops and quasi-domestic systems continued to predominate in many regions, and were able to provide some dynamism through adopting small-scale technology like the sewing machine.[148] Large firms and small firms were often complements rather than substitutes, networked to undertake the variety of processes involved in producing a consumer good. There were marked differences in the role of large vs. small firms in different European countries, which appear to come from a number of factors, including those related to technology (energy source, R&D),

---

144 Lorenz 1984.

145 Fridenson 1978; Lévy-Leboyer 1980.

146 Chandler 1990, pp. 456–63; Dornseifer and Kocka 1993.

147 Hohenberg 1967, p. 92.

148 Sabel and Zeitlin 1985; Berg 1985, ch. 6; Goodman and Honeyman 1988, chs 3, 5.

product (sectoral patterns) and finance (provision of industrial capital). These issues are taken further in the next three sections of the chapter.

IV: MANAGEMENT

A. Entrepreneurship

The earlier part of the period surveyed in this chapter was dominated by 'heroic entrepreneurs' in the early Schumpeterian mode. The successful among them were likely to set up family dynasties to develop their corporate entities, like Siemens and Borsig in German engineering, or Sulzer and Brown in Swiss engineering.[149] The successful dynasties proved highly adaptable in the products they produced, like the Peugeots in France, who began in 1810 in steelworks, linked with a branch of the family in 1832 who had developed textiles since 1759, specialized in frames for umbrellas and crinolines in the mid-19th century, diversified into small steel goods and then bicycles after 1885, before coming to automobiles in 1889.[150] Although much has been made in the literature about differences in entrepreneurial quality, along the lines of the early Schumpeter, there is no convincing evidence that nations were differently endowed in such abilities.[151] Such views can too easily slide into the fallacy of *post hoc ergo propter hoc* (after this, therefore because of this). There is some evidence that particular minority groups were well represented among leading businessmen, but this seems to be always true, and there is no consistent pattern of ethnic or religious affiliation and regional growth.[152] The increasing persecution of ethnic minorities like the Jews for supposed industrial or financial success blighted progress in ways too well-known and horrific to have to stress.

The period later saw the rise of professional management, usually salaried, in the bureaucratized firms, taking over from the owner-entrepreneurs. German steel-masters like Krupp and Thyssen had come from the ranks of technicians, and senior management in Germany continued to be dominated by technical and engineering traditions. Reinvestment of profits and long-term technological advance continued to

149 C.E.L. Brown emigrated from Britain to work at Sulzer in 1851, his son set up Brown Boveri in 1891.

150 Kindleberger 1964, p. 120; Palmade 1972, pp. 97, 157, 205.

151 The best analysis is Kindleberger's comparison of France and Britain, *op. cit.*, chs 5–6.

152 Rostow 1960/1971, p. 51; Gerschenkron 1962, ch. 3.

be given high priority.[153] Obsession with technological standards was associated with taking long-term perspectives on investment and innovational decisions.[154] French management came from a more elitist educational system, as noted above – through time, notably around the 1890s, business came to be more acceptable as a career for this elite.[155]

B. Administration and Groups

Such traditions, including that of state bureaucracies in Germany, fostered a tendency to develop formal organizational structures at comparatively early times. Quite intricate administrative systems were sometimes developed (like the early adoption of the M-form structure to be described in Chapter 6 at Siemens in Germany and St-Gobain in France), often necessitated by the lack of specialization within firms.[156] These were, however, the exceptions rather than the rule. In France most of the largest firms as late as 1950 were still organized in large groups with one firm having large shareholdings ('participations') in various others with which it was associated. Control exercised through such groups was rather loose, being indirect rather than direct, and typically based on financial rather than production considerations. In such cases, with low co-ordination and rationalization, the managerial and administrative costs tended to be excessive, while the smaller number of holding companies that formed around core companies like St-Gobain on the contrary tended to be excessively centralized.[157] Their main justification was that by and large they avoided bankruptcy even during the troubled 1930s. After the Second World War there were several large mergers between such core-based holding companies, but rationalization into divisions in the manner described in the next chapter was often long postponed.

The diversified but rather inward-looking groups in France and companies in Germany were based on legal formats which differed somewhat from the Anglo-American archetypes. The Code of Commerce in France in 1808 (subsequently extended), and roughly parallel arrangements in Germany, provided legal protection – including anonymity and limited liability – for small and medium firms (SMFs) as well as large. Even the joint-stock forms (the *société anonyme* in France and the *Aktiengesellschaft* in Germany) allowed fairly tight internal control and little shift of decision-making to shareholders outside of their executive boards or groups. The

---

153 Kocka 1980.
154 Landes 1969, p. 354.
155 Lévy-Leboyer 1980.
156 Kocka 1980; Lévy-Leboyer 1980.
157 *Idem.*

Interessengemeinschaft (I.G.) in Germany represented a formal combine, in which the chief participants retained much of their autonomy.

C. Integration and Cartels

The characteristically unspecialized firms in Germany in the first half of the 19th century faced only moderate-sized markets. Some, but by no means all, grew later into diversified larger enterprises, with the vertical integration being based on the product rather than the process. The market factors in industries like metals and textiles which encouraged growth from refining, weaving, etc., meant that much of the integration developed 'backwards' up the product supply chain. By 1913, the typical European steelworks was a large integrated plant, conducting all operations from the blast furnace to manufacturing bars etc. In this manner external economies from by-products were internalized for use at another stage, and fuel saved from dispensing with reheating (the 'hot process'). Chemical companies also tended to develop as large interlinked blocs. Since large individual complexes came to dominate whole communities, e.g. Krupps at Essen in the Ruhr, such blocs also internalized control of valuable raw materials supplies.

An alternative to vertical integration was the formation of cartels, usually developed through *horizontal* links across firms.[158] Cartels began usually as arrangements to fix prices among firms, especially during the price declines of the so-called 'Great Depression' (1873–95). Later, as these seemed threatened by continuing over-supply of markets through inflated prices, they turned to fixing outputs of firms by quotas etc., but these also encouraged over-supply (to pre-empt larger quotas). As prices recovered around the turn of the century, many of the cartels developed joint marketing and distribution systems. The number of known cartels in Germany rose from just four in 1875 to 205 by 1896 and about 1500 by 1925 – in 1907 their members accounted for about one-quarter of total industrial output and by 1938 one-half.[159] Cartels were less necessary in industries which could appropriate markets in other ways – for example, in the case of organic chemicals through patent rights.[160] However, the costs of the R&D programmes responsible for those patents led them to pool patent rights and profits after 1904, with some market sharing to follow. Eventually the German 'Big Three' of Hoechst, BASF and Bayer, plus several others, were to merge into the giant I.G. Farben in 1925 (broken up for war crimes after the Second World War). Such multi-mergers

---

[158] Marshall 1919, p. 507.
[159] Kocka 1980.
[160] Marshall 1919, p. 570.

encouraged rivals, such as the formation of ICI in the UK in 1926 out of large chemicals firms like Brunner Mond and United Alkali,[161] and the merger of Rhône and Poulenc in the French chemicals industry in 1928.

A similar exercise of what Galbraith[162] describes as 'countervailing power' took place when horizontal consolidations into cartels encouraged other cartels to form in vertically linked industries. Thus in Germany the Westphalian coal cartel (1893) was matched by the steelworks cartel (1904), reckoned as the world's two largest on the eve of the First World War.[163] Attempts at 'general' cartels, i.e. cartels of cartels, usually proved less successful.[164] Cartels also developed internationally across Europe, e.g. in electrical engineering. Such cartels often arose to counteract dumping, i.e. selling abroad at prices below production costs, as in the first international rail cartel (between Britain, Belgium and Germany) in 1884.[165] An alternative here was for companies to set up branch plants abroad, often to get behind tariff barriers, or (especially in chemicals) to protect patent rights.[166] These were particularly common in the newer industries like electricals (two-thirds of Siemens's workforce were employed outside Germany as early as 1872), and were spurred on by the 'invasion' of American MNCs in such fields in the 1890s (Westinghouse, Thomson–Houston, International Western Electric, International Harvester, etc.). Alliances across national boundaries between companies in similar fields were also strong in these fields, e.g. between Siemens in Germany and Schneider in France (1898). Yet another alternative was for newer countries to enter joint ventures (JVs) with more experienced partners, for example the Italian steel industry pitted Ansaldo, allied with Schneider at Le Creusot, against Terni, allied with the British firm Vickers.[167]

There was a darker side to the cartels, for alliances between rival international cartels as well as within them were vulnerable. Lenin (1917) perceived in them the origins of the First World War, which he attributed to the struggle between international cartels for the re-division of colonies (formal or informal) in the hitherto non-industrial world, like the Balkans.

---

161 Reader 1970, vol. 1, ch. 19.
162 Galbraith 1952, ch. 8.
163 Marshall 1919, p. 522.
164 *Ibid.*, p. 560.
165 Milward and Saul 1977, p. 475.
166 Milward and Saul 1973, p. 183.
167 *Ibid.*, p. 194; Segreto 1985.

V: FINANCE

A. Firm Size

There was no monotonic trend towards domination of economies by ever larger firms. In France between 1906 and 1966 the shares of different firm-size groups (excluding the very small) in total employment were fairly stable.[168] The greatest inter-country differences were across industries. The sectoral pattern of large firms (LFs) in Germany, biased towards capital goods, differed from that in Britain, where consumer goods were well represented among the LFs.[169] The differences that were opening up between the various National Systems of Production were therefore observable in the importance accorded to LFs, but the continuing role of SMFs in the same sectors ought not to be overlooked.

Technological and process factors underlying the growth in firm sizes, like spreading R&D overheads or generating internal and external scale economies in production, have already been dealt with. The spread of electricity networks and of compact oil and electric motors benefited small firms as much as large,[170] for example in Denmark where SMFs were predominant. 'Specialized supplier' firms in areas like machinery and chemicals were likely to remain as relatively small units in most countries, despite the often high demands on knowledge.[171]

It remains to consider factors coming from the side of finance and marketing. Marshall in fact believed that most technical efficiency economies could be reaped by medium-sized firms – what drove large firms were the economies in marketing.[172] Technical efficiency would be expected to appear *within* a plant, but the LFs were typically becoming multi-plant firms.[173] Most interest has instead been directed at the financial factors, which could be linked to any or all of these just discussed. As with marketing, these were most evident in multi-plant firms, such as were emerging in France after 1815.[174] Economies of scale in Italy during its catching-up period came from the substantial contribution of banking and the state to industry – few *plants* were of large size, even in new industries.[175] Similarly, in late 19th-century Russia, where the state

---

168 Kindleberger 1964, p. 169; Caron 1979, pp. 277–81.
169 Kocka 1980; Chandler 1990, p. 394.
170 See also Chapter 6.
171 Hohenberg 1967, ch. 4.
172 Marshall 1890/1961, pp. 281–9; 1919, pp. 509. 511, 589.
173 *Ibid.*, p. 845; see also Kindleberger 1964, p. 164, and Chapter 7 below.
174 Palmade 1972, pp. 93–4.
175 Cafagna 1973, p. 319; Rossi and Toniolo 1992.

supplanted the role of banks in promoting industry, it concentrated on big firms.[176]

This is not to deny that the Minimum Efficient Scale (MES) for some newer activities was sometimes high. The sheer scale of operations required of the oil industry late in the 19th century – exploration (overseas), extraction, processing and distribution (pipelines and tankers) – required large-scale financing, whether from the state ('Royal Dutch' in the Netherlands obtained part of its funding from the Dutch royal family) or from large banks. The role of finance will be pursued further in a moment.

B. Diversification and Scope

It has also been noted that German firms were more diversified, often from the beginning, than their British counterparts. A diversification index constructed by Kocka (1980) showed a significant increase among the 100 largest firms, especially in primary metals, electrical and mechanical engineering, over the period for which data were satisfactory (1887–1907). German firms were smaller than American equivalents but nevertheless more diversified. This diversification came almost entirely from internal developments within the firm.[177] The disadvantage was that German firms lost product markets to Americans during the 'invasion' from the 1890s, especially in standardized goods.[178] French firms avoided diversification in this period, and instead new firms or new entrants usually advanced the new 'combinations', often rather successfully. The reason appears to lie partly in the different role of the engineer in France as compared with Germany – the German technician more thoroughly explored technical as well as market synergies.

C. Finance Capital

Early Belgian textile entrepreneurs followed the British pattern of relying mainly on ploughed-back profits for investment[179] – probably from necessity (banks were not forthcoming with funds) rather than choice. French entrepreneurs preferred to limit themselves whenever possible to internal growth, going no further afield than their tight family groups or local district connections.[180] German textile firms in the mid 19th century generally acted likewise, but the needs of firms in newer industries pushed

176 Gerschenkron 1962, p. 129.

177 Dornseifer and Kocka 1993.

178 Milward and Saul 1977, p. 40.

179 Mokyr 1976, pp. 39–40, 134.

180 Kemp 1971, pp. 183, 261–2; Milward and Saul 1973, p. 325; Caron 1979.

them into the arms of the bankers. After 1880, even medium-sized German chemical firms were using local banks to float share issues. The danger was that of losing control of the industrial firm to financiers. Under the joint-stock system, ownership and management became separated. Following Hilferding (1981/1910), Lenin (1917) dubbed the takeover of control by external finance, 'finance capitalism', and it formed the domestic counterpart to the external operations of MNCs in underdeveloped countries as outlined briefly above – together they constituted his theory of imperialism.

Investment banking is often regarded as having begun in Belgium in 1822, when Dutch banks of the United Provinces refused to lend to new Belgian industries. The Société Générale (full name significantly the 'Société Générale des Pays-bas pour favoriser l'industrie nationale') was then set up, though it was perhaps more like an 18th-century mercantilist institution than a 19th-century investment bank[181] (some would say it still is today). It was followed by the more speculative Banque de Belgique in 1835.[182] There were early attempts also in France, like the private Caisse Générale pour le Commerce in 1837, inspired by St-Simon. More spectacular was the establishment of the joint-stock Crédit Mobilier by the Péreire brothers (also St-Simonians) in 1852, mainly for investing in railway construction. This was supplemented by the Crédit Foncier, intended for long-term investment in agriculture, also in 1852. Neither in fact operated very effectively to launch new industrial developments, and they were arguably more important for their 'demonstration effect' to later industrializers than for industrialization in France.[183] Deposit banks like the Crédit Lyonnais (1863) borrowed their notion of mobilizing the full range of private savings, and included functions of long-term lending to industry, although they drew away after 1870. In Germany regional banks had long provided similar services: indeed the Crédit Foncier was modelled on long-term mortgage banks in Prussia and Saxony, which dated back to the 1760s and were extended after 1835. At a national level, investment in infrastructure and industry was taken up by the 'universal banks' combining commercial and investment functions.[184] Banks modelled on the Crédit Mobilier or German universal banks were set up shortly after in Austria

---

181 Milward and Saul 1973, p. 449.

182 Cameron *et al.* 1967, ch. 5, provides an excellent discussion of the Belgian banking system and industry.

183 See for example Japan in Chapter 10 below.

184 Schumpeter 1939, vol. 1, pp. 348–50; Gerschenkron 1962, pp. 13–14; Cameron *et al.* 1967, ch. 6; Sylla and Toniolo 1991, pp. 18–19, 51–2, 164–72, 181–4. The Prussian state was opposed to joint-stock banking, so the Darmstädter Bank set up just outside the border in 1853 as an offshoot of the Crédit Mobilier.

(Creditanstalt 1855), Bohemia (Böhmische Eskompte Bank 1863), Sweden (the Enskilda banks, following the Stockholms Enskilda Bank 1857), Denmark (Privatbank 1857), etc. When industrialization moved to southern Europe towards the end of the century, the German banking model moved too – Italy had the Banca Commerciale Italiana 1894 and the Credito Italiano 1895, both set up by German consortia, though also with important domestic influences.[185] Industry in later developing countries like Russia often depended heavily on foreign capital and banks.

The contribution that banks made to kick-starting growth can be disputed. Kocka,[186] basing himself on the German experience, has argued forcefully that the role of investment banks, like that of joint-stock companies, was less an indication of advance than further evidence of relative backwardness – it was thus a Gerschenkronian response to a lack of sources such as the merchant capital employed in production in the UK. Although Gerschenkron and others have given banks a starring role, most opinion now seems to favour the view that they followed rather than led (the most convincing evidence is for Sweden).[187] Joint-stock banks accounted for no more than about a quarter of bank credit in Germany, and their role in developing the organic chemicals industry was minor. Another view, advanced by similar sceptics, is that banks diverted too much investment into heavy industry.[188] Perhaps the cause of this was that the joint-stock banks concentrated mainly on large, already strong firms, and contributed significantly to company mergers and acquisitions.[189] In Austria, banks withdrew from industrial activities after a severe stock exchange crash in Vienna in 1873, just as industrialization was getting under way. In late developing areas like Serbia, joint-stock banks scarcely contributed to industry.[190] The role of other credit institutions such as co-operatives, savings banks, or private banking houses should be given greater stress for long-term finance, though the 'universal bank' in Germany after about 1870 to some extent united these functions.[191] In some countries there is stronger evidence of a leading role for the joint-stock banks, e.g. the importance of the Privatbank in Denmark for new company formation,[192] or of the German-type Italian banks in new industries, but this depended on adaptation to local circumstances.

---

185 Gerschenkron 1962, pp. 87–8 and 1968, p. 107; Milward and Saul 1977, p. 261.
186 Kocka 1980, p. 110.
187 Presented in Fisher and Thurman 1989.
188 Neuberger 1977.
189 Tilly 1982, 1986.
190 Lampe 1972.
191 Borchardt 1973, p. 149.
192 Jörberg 1973, p. 409.

Banking in France became highly developed, indeed developed ahead of industry, and in so doing became distanced from it.[193] The lower level of commitment by banks to industry in France may have owed something to bankers' suspicions of industry, but probably more to lack of demand from industry itself, for fear of loss of control. Similar anxieties led French firms to rely mainly on bonds to raise capital, as compared with greater use of shares in Britain and Germany.[194] In practice, French joint-stock banks like the Crédit Mobilier did not aim at concentrated control of trade or manufactures.[195] However, in Germany and Austria there can be little doubt that banks sought to monopolize firms' financial arrangements and exercise direct influence over their manufacturing strategies. After 1870, German corporate law prescribed a dual board structure of supervisory board (for strategic decisions) and executive board, so for instance the Deutsche Bank found itself represented on 186 other companies' supervisory boards by 1914. Bank representation increased firms' attention to financial and commercial considerations, and especially encouraged the formation of large firms, mergers and cartels, though again more in a supporting than leading role.[196] Marshall[197] noted claims 'that their intimate association with large industrial movements keeps them alert: that they earn a higher rate of interest on their advances and can pay higher interest to their depositors than they otherwise could; and that they can in some cases undertake the flotation of new securities at lower charges than would be required by English financial houses'.

However, in the case of the largest German firms, it is difficult to say whether industry or banking was the dominant partner in their relationships. To the extent that banks had a large say, they tended to support expansion at the time of flotation, but subsequently to urge caution. On the other side, the Deutsche Bank was in fact set up by Georg von Siemens and others in 1870. Industrial firms like Krupp or AEG were too big for the bank representatives on their boards to control, and after about 1900 there were many industrial firms that were large enough on this criterion; moreover, the relative power of the executive boards increased.[198] The 'finance capital' argument needs to be tempered.

---

193 Chesnais, in Nelson 1993, p. 196.

194 Gille 1973, p. 263. The legal reforms mentioned above failed to quell this anxiety (Kemp 1971, p. 191).

195 Marshall 1919, p. 341.

196 Kocka 1980.

197 Marshall 1919, p. 342.

198 Gerschenkron 1962, p. 21; Milward and Saul 1977, p. 48; Kocka 1980.

VI: MARKETING AND DEMAND

A. Marketing

Despite the emergence of marketing strategies in retailing, e.g. in the French department stores (essentially world innovators), their importance to large manufacturing firms was long underestimated in Continental Europe. Markets controlled by governments or cartels were a more common occurrence than in Britain. European manufacturing firms placed greater stress on the technology and production sides of their businesses – according to Lévy-Leboyer (1980) the shift of emphasis from production and technology to organization and marketing was delayed until around the 1930s in France. Typical of the contrast with Britain was the German brewing industry, which forsook investment in pubs and retailing for technical developments.[199] Lack of focus on marketing may have contributed to capitulation to the American MNCs by some of the German light industries later in the 19th century.[200]

Marketing played a more potent role in the German heavy machinery industry, producing specialized goods through extensive design, credit and servicing contacts with clients.[201] Its importance in the 'science-based' industry of chemicals has been referred to – at Hoechst, there were as many commercial staff as chemists in the late 1870s, but twice as many by 1912. 'Success in the organic chemical industry depended on well-worn factors; the ability to respond to and manipulate the market'.[202] Many of these salesmen were, however, technically trained; hence (as at BASF) technical strengths also tended to dominate marketing.[203]

B. Competition

Imperfectly or monopolistically competitive industries can often be more aggressively competitive than perfect competition, as in the analysis of oligopoly given in Chapter 3 above. Even so, it seems reasonable to deduce that competition among large firms in countries like Germany was not intent on mutual destruction. Cartels in some activities and the pooling of patents and/or profits in some others suggest this. It seems hard to avoid the conclusion that long-term vision was encouraged by the weakness of aggressive competition. Although consumers may not have gained from this

---

199 Chandler 1990, p. 433.
200 *Ibid.*, p. 423.
201 *Ibid.*, p. 457.
202 Goodman and Honeyman 1988, p. 187.
203 Hohenberg 1967, p. 129.

in the short run, in the long term they may have benefited through rising employment and the dynamic advantages of science-based industry. There seems general agreement that people in Continental Europe placed less faith in the efficacy of competition than they did in Britain or later America.

C. Income Distribution and Tastes

The major role of income distribution in relation to differing macroeconomic growth patterns was noted in Section I above, along with the role of product differentiation in countries like France for competing against the more standardized products produced so cheaply on British machinery. In France, 'Rich and discriminating purchasers evoked the fine and delicate sensitiveness, and the best power of individual initiative from artisans, shopkeepers and merchants; while the absence of a strong middle class and the poverty of the working classes, except in Paris and a few other places, prevented the growth of large and profitable businesses'.[204] French culture also tended to set the standards for dress etc. in the rest of Europe.[205] The French lead in retailing was at the up-market end in Paris, in contrast to British leadership in selling to the working classes.[206] Marshall also stressed the role of schools of design and of copyright on designs in France, and indeed the whole emphasis placed on the design function: 'In France a single manufacturer would have several designers at work on his premises, while in England a single designer would work for several manufacturers'.[207] What struck him particularly was that the French governments had poured money into certain industries, to little productive effect, while virtually ignoring the funding of design, which had been so successful.[208]

Countries where domestic demand was weaker encountered greater difficulties, as with the Austrian cotton industry, which through concentration on low textile qualities for domestic markets failed to develop an export base. Germany may have suffered from a classically Marxist squeeze in which the forces of production outran the powers of consumption, resulting in a rather unsuccessful drive for compensatory colonial markets, and ultimately war.[209]

---

204 Marshall 1919, p. 111. Such inequalities led to political conflict, like the Paris Commune in 1871.

205 Steuart 1767/1966, pp. 249–50.

206 Palmade 1972, p. 23.

207 Marshall 1919, p. 116.

208 *Ibid.*, p. 120.

209 For the endorsement of an anti-Marxist, see Veblen 1915/1964, p. 200.

VII: INDUSTRIAL POLICIES

A. S&T Policy

Continental governments played a somewhat greater role than in Britain in supporting technological advances. In France, Colbert established the Académie Royale des Sciences in 1666 in imitation of Britain's Royal Society of 1662, and oriented it more to practical applications. Specific technologies such as the development of the important Leblanc process for making soda (1780s) were partially funded by the French state, and the equally innovative Girard method of flax spinning (1810) and Appert food-preserving process (1804) won prizes in government-funded competitions. The considerable popularity of industrial exhibitions in 19th-century Europe promoted quality, perhaps at the expense of process efficiency.[210] Imitation and diffusion were seen as major government functions for catching up – even before the French Revolution, French governments had helped finance the introduction of the flying shuttle, the mule-jenny, coke-smelting, etc. This continued through setting up conservatoires (1794) and industrial associations (1810) aimed at dissemination, also sponsoring industrial exhibitions. The judges at the Paris Exhibition in 1806 perceived, correctly according to my interpretation, that the French response should be to use modern methods to produce traditional high-quality products:

> In summary, the 1806 exposition's emphasis on mechanical processes and commercial viability stimulated the beginnings of modern light industry in France. The judges tried to encourage the invention of machines that would enable a few to produce what had required the energy of many craftsmen in the Old Regime. They rewarded inventors for devices that added speed, precision and simplicity to the manufacturing process.[211]

These perceptions were right even if the implementations were tardier.

The main contributions, however, came indirectly through educational and IPR policies. The role of formal education has been heavily stressed in all accounts of European industrialization. England and Belgium in fact developed earliest on the basis of poor educational systems, so that education at this stage was no bar, although the continuing lack probably contributed to the relative industrial decline of both countries later in the 19th century. Some late developers like Italy also had weak educational systems. Relative literacy in 1850 was poorly related to relative income levels at the time – for example, Sweden was highest in literacy but among

---

210 Mokyr 1976, p. 131.
211 Hafter 1984, p. 334.

the lowest in p.c. incomes – but strikingly correlated with growth a century later.[212] The French public education system expanded from the 1830s but remained somewhat elitist[213] – at the top, the École Polytechnique shifted slowly from scientists to engineers through the century, but there was a gap for the training of middle management.[214] Nevertheless, there was a close association within France between regions with better educational records and those with earlier industrialization, though which was cause and which effect is ambiguous.[215] For newer industries of the kinds described in Section II above, education probably mattered more, although older industries were also becoming more science-based by 1900. The governments of Prussia (with compulsory primary education in 1763) and later German states placed heavy emphasis on providing models of equipment to be imitated and diffused, as with the British machinery put on continuous display at the Gewerbe Institut (1821) in Berlin. The stress on education was itself no doubt partly caused by sensing the need to catch up in industry.[216] This may be seen as embodying the 'reactive nationalism' of Rostow's politics model in the take-off (cf. p. 69 above).

Policies towards intellectual property rights (IPRs), such as patents and copyrights, have been noted on several occasions already.[217] Prussian patent law was introduced in 1810 and, like the early English practice, at first encouraged imitation of foreign advances.[218] Imitation was sometimes accelerated by the *absence* of patent rights – suggested examples have included the Dutch electrical engineering industry (Philips), the Swiss dyestuffs industry, and some German imitation before 1877 when its patent law was at last unified. French industry was probably weakened in regard to innovation by having patent law which protected products more than processes, whereas German law took the reverse view. The contrast between favouring products in France and processes in Germany is strikingly similar to their respective technological heuristics.

B. Industrial and Competition Policies

Continental governments, at least from the time of their industrialization spurts, tended to be more pro-business than the British. Paternalist policies

---

212 Sandberg 1979, 1982.

213 Chesnais, in Nelson 1993, pp. 197–9.

214 Cameron 1961, ch. 3; Hohenberg 1967, pp. 67–71; Caron 1979, p. 47.

215 Fohlen 1973, pp. 22–5.

216 Kemp 1969, p. 101; Lilley 1973, p. 247. However, countries like Russia long remained suspicious that an educated labour force might lead to sedition.

217 Cf. North 1981.

218 Fischer 1963.

of firms were generally endorsed by their governments, and indeed often complemented them. Attitudes to trusts and cartels were particularly important. In France, trusts were actually forbidden under the Napoleonic Penal Code until 1884, and governments (especially from the 1870s) tended to favour SMFs. In Germany, cartels were made legal in 1897, and thus enforceable in court. This contrasted especially strongly with American policy (see Chapter 6).

From the time of Colbert's policies in the later 17th century (which included setting up the St-Gobain glassworks), French governments faced a tradition of direct government involvement in industry. Peter the Great shortly afterwards established a similar tradition in Russia. But in the 19th century the role was generally restricted to providing some set-up capital, and perhaps a few officials to manage, and then withdrawing fairly rapidly.[219] Pollard concludes that the role of the state has been overrated: 'It was the direct support for certain manufactures that has frequently been claimed as the main contribution of governments to industrialization but in retrospect it turned out to have been the least useful'.[220] One should not, however, underestimate the assistance from low-key 'encouragement to industry';[221] nor should one draw the conclusion that no intervention was the optimal policy.[222] French economists, even those favouring market solutions, saw a prime need for the state in raising quality of manufactures.[223] A more positive contribution was that to the construction of infrastructure, but even here political interference often led to railways being built at the wrong times or in the wrong places (e.g. the French *lignes électorales*). Building railways ahead of demand failed to induce growth.

The role of government demand, particularly for military procurement, also has been accorded considerable stress in the literature.[224] The opportunity cost of directing demand into areas like military spending, i.e. the sacrifice from ignoring other activities, unfortunately has not been properly assessed for any country. Thus one cannot know whether this on balance accelerated or retarded industrial growth. Perhaps the most extensive use of government demand to overcome deficiencies of private demand occurred in Russia from the 1880s. However, commitment to economic orthodoxy limited the macroeconomic, as opposed to sectoral, impact. Lack of resources from tax yields etc. prevented most governments

---

219 Milward and Saul 1973, p. 417.

220 Pollard 1981, p. 161; also Supple 1973, pp. 311–13; Tipton 1981.

221 Fischer 1963.

222 See Thomson 1991 on calico printing.

223 E.g. Say 1821, bk. III, ch. 4.

224 Minchinton 1973, pp. 104–8; Trebilcock 1973; Headrick 1981; Goodman and Honeyman 1988, pp. 99–102.

acting in Gerschenkronian fashion to take greater and greater roles in development as time went on.[225] Successful government policies probably followed as much as caused industrialization, as in early 19th-century Belgium.[226]

C. Free Trade

Most discussion, however, centred on trade policies, including the List case for 'infant industry' protection during early industrialization. As noted earlier, a common initial objective was to seek free internal mobility for goods, while maintaining external tariff barriers. The 'positive mercantilism' of Napoleon framed government thinking in France until the 1850s, though the tariffs were more defensive and protective than an infant industry strategy might have advised[227] – many tariffs were simply to raise revenue for their governments. The 'infant industry' contribution thus remains in doubt. The same could be said in Germany itself, which after setting up the *Zollverein* had comparatively low tariffs, and even under Bismarck did not, for instance, protect its very successful dyestuffs industry.[228] List's most direct influence was perhaps on Count Witte, Russian Minister of Finance 1891–1903, who is usually credited with giving Russian industrialization its initial momentum, though at the cost of storing up problems of social unrest from the consequent bias towards industry and unbalanced growth. Gerschenkron may, however, have mistaken rhetoric for reality in the Russian case.[229] His model for the dominant role of the state in late industrialization perhaps leans too heavily on this one questionable example – he admits[230] the ineptitude of direct government action in the coterminous case of Italy, not least in tariff policy. A more recent assessment sees this latter as too harsh, and believes that a Listian policy of 'infant industry' protection for certain sectors in Italy allowed the technological heuristics relevant to industries of high technological opportunity to take hold, through large firms.[231]

The British model was more extensively copied by shifts towards free trade in most Continental countries in the 1850s or 1860s, beginning in the trade-dependent smaller countries. Oddly enough, in France free trade was

---

225 Milward and Saul 1977, p. 463.

226 Mokyr 1976, p. 228.

227 Milward and Saul 1973, pp. 268–9.

228 Haber 1958, p. 222; for a more positive view of the impact on the steel industry, see Webb 1980.

229 Gregory, in Sylla and Toniolo 1991; cf. p. 71 above.

230 Gerschenkron 1962, pp. 79–83, 116–17.

231 Sapelli, in Dosi *et al.* 1992; but cf. Sylla and Toniolo 1991, ch. 10.

implemented by a St-Simonian (Chevalier). As we have already seen, free trade too did not always bring the expected positive results, and generated little structural change – it may have helped underdevelopment in southern Europe to persist longer.[232] Facing agricultural price declines and American competition in grain, many countries drifted back towards protectionism from the late 1870s. By 1914 only Switzerland, Belgium and the Netherlands had reasonably free trade, in addition to Britain. Neither Smithian policies of free trade nor Listian policies of aggressive protectionism seemed to have had the impact their proponents argued for. Perhaps the greatest contribution of governments was that which Adam Smith in fact made much of – providing internal peace and external security.[233] The loss of these benefits in the 20th century severely disrupted industrial progress, without bringing it to a complete halt. This story is taken further in Chapter 7 below.

---

232 E.g. Zamagni 1993, pp. 110–17.

233 Say 1821, bk. I, p. 307; Kemp 1971, ch. 8; Supple 1973, pp. 314–17; Pollard 1981, p. 159.

6. Industrialization in the USA, 1870–1930

I: INDUSTRIAL GROWTH AND CHANGE

According to the chronology of Kondratiev, revised by Schumpeter in his book *Business Cycles* (1939), the first two Kondratiev waves have now been covered. The 'Second Kondratiev' of early–mid-Victorian Britain did not appear to involve dramatic changes in any of the 'exogenous' conditions of growth.[1] Though there were some substantial advances in technology that certainly qualify as 'new combinations' in Schumpeter's sense, above all the coming of the railway, these are best seen as further working out the technological paradigms of the 'First Kondratiev' (e.g. the railways as the application of steam power to transportation, etc.). Nevertheless, it was in this era that growth accelerated and productivity began to rise in more sustained fashion. The diffusion of the new technological paradigms (mechanization, inanimate energy, etc.) and the new organizational paradigms (especially the factory system) within the leading countries took place not just horizontally but also 'vertically'. It may be recalled from Chapter 1 that vertical linkages cover both upstream/downstream links and forward/backward links, with the former referring strictly to process links (equipment, components, etc.) and the latter to product links (material flows, etc.). The importance of this contrast will emerge in this chapter, but for the moment we need only conclude that the result was a *macroeconomic* expansion to build upon the techno-economic paradigms created in the early Industrial Revolution.

The 'Third Kondratiev' from the late 19th century was a different story, involving fundamental differences in all spheres (technological, organizational, financial, product markets), plus a change in leadership at the country level. In the Schumpeterian chronology it covers the period from the 1890s to the 1940s, but the story should be taken back another

1 Von Tunzelmann 1994.

twenty years or so to study how it came into being, i.e. to the preceding 'recessionary' phase of the long wave.

A. The 'Decline' of Britain

In Schumpeterian terms, the entrepreneurship unleashed in new regions such as the USA had to be matched by 'Creative Destruction' in older regions, which in this case meant Britain. Britain's decline was relative to the growth of its new rivals rather than absolute: indeed in absolute terms it accelerated somewhat in the middle of the 20th century,[2] although there were considerable intervals such as in the early years of the 20th century when there was little or no growth. It has been perhaps the most-studied aspect of all British economic history, and can be summarized only superficially here.

1. Science and technology

Britain's long experience with 'practical tinkering' to advance technology left it behind in the development of organized industrial R&D.[3] However, many of the crucial scientific breakthroughs associated with the new industries such as steel and electricity were made in the UK, and budding inventor-entrepreneurs like Marconi in radio still migrated to Britain to work on their technologies. British science continued to perform respectably well into the 20th century, e.g. in the number of Nobel Prizes earned. Even British R&D levels have recent defenders.[4] The weakness in disseminating this information into production is another matter. Yet the manufacturing industries in which British firms remain world powers are typically 'science-based' in the Pavitt (1984) taxonomy, most notably pharmaceuticals. The carry-through into production was less successful in engineering-based industries, where R&D needed to be much more Development than Research.

2. Organization

The British tradition of the 'representative firm' (SMF) ran headlong into the developing business empires of rival countries in the late 19th century, and took many years to come to terms with them. British business organization thus proved hardly able to adapt to the large scale and high capital intensity of modern industry,[5] including the lack of development of

---

2 Matthews *et al.*, 1982.
3 Cf. Chapter 5 and below.
4 Edgerton and Horrocks 1994.
5 Hannah 1974, 1976.

organized R&D as implied in the previous paragraph.[6] The failure to introduce modern managerial systems of the kinds outlined later in this chapter might have played a part in British 'decline', although perhaps a lesser role than some recent opinion suggests.[7] Entrusting process control to foremen and trade unions restricted the possibilities for speeding up production sufficiently in Britain to compete with new rivals.[8] Although such 'craft control' might be beneficial in certain circumstances, in Britain it reflected a wider lack of inter-connection between production, engineering and management within firms,[9] and often between firms.[10] This has been attributed to inadequate education in managerial abilities,[11] but such education is subject to passing fads – the real deficiency was a lack of familiarity with or desire to learn about one another's responsibilities.

3. Finance

The British financial system expanded apace with the rise of the stock market for financing infrastructural investment, most conspicuously in the railway manias such as that of the mid-1840s.[12] But instead of turning to domestic manufacturing when the infrastructural booms expired, the British financial system turned overseas, to financing similar infrastructural developments in other countries, particularly railway construction. This was linked to the 'scramble' for empire, both formal and informal, in the late 19th century, with Britain competing for global annexations against the countries of Continental Europe, as in the Leninist thesis.[13] Thus British finance could have deprived domestic manufacturing of some funding at the same time as it helped build the infrastructure for the industrialization of some of its rivals.[14] The basic problem was not, however, any substantial discrimination against British industry by finance – rather it was a complete breach between the two in terms of the ways in which they interacted. To the present day, British industry blames British finance for failing to understand its needs, and vice versa.[15]

---

6 Mowery 1984.
7 Lazonick 1981b, 1983; Elbaum and Lazonick 1986; Chandler 1990, part III.
8 Lewchuk 1984; Elbaum and Lazonick 1986; Lazonick 1990, 1991.
9 E.g. Locke 1984, ch. 3.
10 Lazonick 1990, ch. 5.
11 Dintenfass 1992.
12 Mitchell 1964; Hawke 1970, ch. 14.
13 Lenin's thesis concerns the *re*-partition of the Third World. The precise costs are a matter of dispute; cf. Davis and Huttenback 1986; Offer 1993.
14 Marshall 1919; Kennedy 1987.
15 CIMA 1992.

4. Demand

With inadequate domestic growth of demand, British industry sought growth from the expansion of exports of goods and services, to some extent aligned with the export of capital as in the last paragraph. Expansion of Empire and similar markets arose mainly in low-quality goods, for which British technology was less well suited. Increasingly British goods encountered rising competition in these quarters from the exporters of the newer countries, though Britain longer retained some lead in services. Reliance on services exports continued to boost demand in the UK, though much of the gain was 'recycled' by way of further capital exports. However, such invisible exports gave only a limited amount of assistance to domestic *supply* factors e.g. in manufacturing, other than in areas like shipping/shipbuilding. Again, one was the world of finance and the other was the quite separate world of industry. British manufactured exports appeared to become trapped in a vicious circle of slow export growth and low investment at home.[16] With slow growth of demand, competitiveness was sought through cutting costs rather than raising output, and all too often this meant cutting wages rather than innovating.[17]

Behind the techno-economic problems therefore lie issues of social and economic stratification. No account of British successes and failures makes much sense without bringing in social class. Occupations and industries were implicitly divided into the respectable (like the case of auctioneering, discussed by Porter,[18] or more recently the case of pharmaceuticals) and the less respectable; and the individuals attached to them, even at senior levels, were divided into 'gentlemen' and 'players'.[19] Social distance ('them and us') disfigured finance/industry relations, labour relations, educational systems, demand structures, and so on. Elitist educational systems served some of the science-based industries reasonably well, but were made to serve activities where the rest of the world had passed by – in scale-intensive and specialized-supplier industries, 19th-century training methods were relied upon far into the 20th century.[20] Even ostensibly similar social strata were divided by a gulf in misunderstanding. Many of the individual elements making for advance seemed strong, but they failed to interact with one another.[21] If any one factor can be blamed for relative British decline, in my opinion it would have to be the distancing that came about as a result of

16 Matthews 1973.
17 Lazonick 1990, ch. 5; von Tunzelmann 1992a.
18 Porter 1990, ch. 6.
19 Coleman 1973; Coleman and MacLeod 1986.
20 Aldcroft 1992.
21 Walker, in Nelson 1993, pp. 178–82, includes a lucid assessment of this point.

complex social and economic divisions. Against these have to be weighed the strengths as well as the weaknesses of British economic performance.

B. The New 'Techno-Economic Paradigm'

Freeman (1989) considers the 'Third Kondratiev' to have been led in technological terms successively by steel, heavy engineering and, later, electricity supply. Its technological contributions did not end even there, as it also saw the basic technological achievements of industries such as chemicals and motor vehicles that were to become more dominant in the 'Fourth Kondratiev' from the late 1930s.

Partly as a result of the encumbrance of older industries and technologies, Britain reacted more slowly to the new opportunities that were to come with the 'Third Kondratiev' – this has popularly been described as 'the penalty of an early start'.[22] Specific problems arose where questions of technological 'interrelatedness' were critical;[23] for example, the dimensions of British railway tracks and tunnels limited the extent to which freight trains could be enlarged. Larger problems arose, however, in the context of shifting to a newer industrial base. Extensive studies by economic historians have indicated that British businessmen lost comparatively little from clinging to older technological styles in traditional industries – not enough, anyway, to explain Britain's relative decline.[24] Where they seemed to fall further behind was in their degree of commitment to wholly new industries and activities: as this new commitment was considerable in the case of S&T (see above), it must have owed most to overhangs from the past in the organizational, managerial and financial spheres.

Although the USA inherited much of Britain's technological tradition (see Section II below), it was left free to develop its own styles in these other spheres. I shall argue that it was here that lay the seeds of success, and in due course they permitted the sprouting of new industries like automobiles.

C. American Industrial Supremacy

The US economy before its Civil War (1861–65) was characterized by regional specialization in functions.[25] The slave-based economy of the southern states provided the export base in terms of raw cotton production, akin to Adam Smith's 'vent for surplus', but not the forward downstream linkages with marketing, nor linkages into the technologies of processing.

22 Cf. Veblen 1915/1964, pp. 130–32; Saul 1969.
23 Frankel 1955; David 1975.
24 E.g. McCloskey 1981; Allen 1979.
25 North 1961.

The war and defeat of the Confederacy brought a political and ideological framework permitting structural change and regional integration.

Exactly when the USA can be said to have overtaken the UK as the world's leading industrial power is contentious, partly because the macroeconomic growth and productivity statistics themselves are open to dispute. Recent estimates of Total Factor Productivity (TFP) levels suggest that the USA was only a little below the UK as early as 1880 and not far ahead sixty years later, with the actual overtaking occurring in the early years of the 20th century.[26] These results, especially for the interwar period, appear somewhat implausible, and are perhaps in need of further revision. At the micro level, there are indications from individual industries such as steel that the USA did not surpass Britain in TFP until the early years of the 20th century (though somewhat earlier in labour productivity), but then the two diverged considerably.[27] It was not that US productivity growth in steel surged ahead especially rapidly at this time – it was more the case that British productivity simply stagnated.

To the extent that the aggregate TFP figures and comparisons are valid, what they indicate is that the USA grew faster in output terms more because of rapid growth in inputs than because of productivity growth and its underlying determinants such as technical progress. The labour force grew rapidly, particularly because of the massive inflow of immigrants from Europe (originally from North-west Europe such as Ireland and Germany, and towards the end of the century from South and East Europe). Over 40 million immigrants flooded into the USA from Europe between 1815 and 1914 (around 60 million to the Americas as a whole), the greatest mass migration of all time. Nevertheless, after the ending of the Civil War in 1865, the growth of capital was even more rapid.[28] According to Kuznets's data, gross capital formation in the last three decades of the 19th century ran at over 30 per cent of GNP, its highest sustained level in the country's history. Notwithstanding the mass immigration of labour, the capital stock per member of the labour force almost doubled between 1870 and 1900 – growing at 1 per cent to 1.2 per cent p.a. 1880–1920, after which it seems to have stopped growing. In addition, that capital stock was shifting in its composition away from construction expenditures (especially plant, transport facilities, utilities and office buildings) and towards producer durables such as machinery. One way of interpreting this is as a 'traverse'

26 Maddison 1982; Wolff 1994.

27 McCloskey 1973a, ch. 7; Allen 1979.

28 Jeffrey Williamson (1974) attributes this epochal rise in capital formation partly to rising private savings rates (owing most, in his view, to the ending of 'crowding out' by Federal government expenditures, especially those of the Civil War itself), and partly to a falling relative price of investment goods (probably from reduced tariffs).

from initial rises in construction outlays to subsequent rises in utilization outlays (in the spirit of the work of Hicks, as described in Chapter 3 above). The main point for us, however, is the very rapid increase of capital intensity (capital/labour ratio) from the last third of the 19th century.

II: TECHNOLOGY: AMERICANS AS BORROWERS

Historians such as Nathan Rosenberg[29] have emphasized that the USA, by and large, did not initiate the major new technologies of the 'Third Kondratiev', though as we shall see in Chapter 7 they played the major role in technological development in the following 'Fourth Kondratiev'. In the former period, the major technological breakthroughs in steel were made in Britain, and in chemicals and the internal combustion engine in Germany, with much of the underlying science also developed in these two countries. The same could be said, though less adamantly, for electricity and electronics.[30] However, it was the USA, not these, that was to become the world's industrial powerhouse for most of the 20th century, and I shall thus argue that this did not result from a particular technological edge.[31] The USA did, however, lead – even if it was not alone – in the development of new technology *systems*, such as the electricity supply network, and therefore one could say in the *organization* of new technologies. As will be shown below, it was in organizational and marketing factors that US supremacy became most evident. This dominance of the latter over technology probably reached right back to the beginnings of American industrialization in the 18th century.[32]

A. Demand Factors

1. Composition of demand

Even for the technologies that the Americans 'borrowed', they were faced with a structure of demand that differed from that in the UK. The US population halfway through the 19th century was already somewhat wealthier than Britain's (real wages were around 20–40 per cent higher). More important still was the structure of that demand. The upper-class tier of Great Britain was almost entirely absent (apart from a limited number of plantation owners, who disappeared with the American Civil War), and

29 Rosenberg 1972, ch. 3; 1977.

30 Freeman 1982, ch. 4.

31 See the disparaging remarks of visiting German professors, quoted by Locke 1984, p. 96.

32 Rosenberg 1994, p. 110.

played no significant part in determining demand patterns until the rise of a new financial/industrial elite at the end of the century. The demand structure of the second half of the 19th century was dominated instead by large numbers of rural households owning modest amounts of land, 'relatively prosperous by European standards, with a strong preference for moderately priced household furnishings, durable goods and equipment – cooking equipment, stoves, sewing machines (with which clothing for women and children were manufactured in the home), cabinet furniture, carpets and a wide range of coarse textile fabrics, clocks and watches, china, glassware, etc.'.[33] Employment in the primary sector was not overtaken by secondary industry until early in the 20th century.

This had substantial effects not only on marketing (see below, Section V), but also on production. Whereas many British items were customized for wealthy purchasers, Americans concentrated on cheaper, more standardized items for the whole community – an example much referred to in the mid-19th century was guns, where (military purposes aside) the British concentrated on sporting pieces for the aristocracy while the Americans produced rifles and later pistols in large quantities for the small farmers and cowboys. Thus American demand sought, or at least appeared satisfied with, homogeneous goods for undifferentiated and extensive markets (mass consumption), which made it relatively straightforward to move towards mass production. Standardization was the key to American industrialization, including the standardization of units of weights and measures.[34] Even items that might be expected to be individually tailored were vastly more standardized in the USA, such as boots and shoes.[35]

2. Demand and innovation

In a well-known study, Jacob Schmookler went further and argued, from evidence on patenting, that fluctuations of demand led innovative activity in the late 19th century. Schmookler accepted that science could precede invention, but believed that the lags were likely to be very long: 'Hence, even when the idea for the invention is suggested by scientific discovery, the commitment to make it is generally an investment decision'.[36] In terms of the circular flow diagram (Figure 2.1, p. 25), the main causation thus ran from the bottom of the diagram (investment) to the top, rather than the conventional view that it flowed from the top (innovation) to the bottom.[37] Schmookler showed that economic activity (investment patterns, etc.)

33 Rosenberg 1972, p. 48.
34 Veblen 1904, ch. 2; Marshall 1919, *passim.*
35 *Ibid.*, p. 233.
36 Schmookler 1966, p. 69.
37 See also Scott 1989, ch. 5.

preceded patent fluctuations over the business cycle. Analysis of leads and lags in cyclical fluctuations is notoriously hazardous, and perhaps not too much should be made of this result, which in any case depends on assuming that patents average out as being of roughly equal value. Key breakthroughs (some of them imported) get rather lost amid the large numbers of patents of minor improvements. Schmookler[38] used data on important inventions in certain fields to rebut this criticism, and Khan and Sokoloff show that even the more dramatic inventions seem to have been demand-led between 1790 and 1865.[39] Moreover, Schmookler also shows that patents in related *product* fields all tended to move up and down together, even though they had no necessary *technological* connection with one another – for example, in railroads, there were synchronous fluctuations of patents in the locomotives, the rolling stock, the wheels and axles, and the steel track, even though these came from quite distinct industries (heavy engineering, wood products, metal-working, iron and steel). He did, though, accept that this may in part have been due to the way in which he reassigned the technology/process based patents data to product categories – with a technological rather than product classification, one might equally show the converse.[40] More inventions are likely to be made in expanding technological fields, whatever the end use.[41] These results, which suggested to Schmookler a flexible multi-purpose knowledge base, conform with my technology/product interpretation.

Schmookler's results point to important *systemic* interconnections between product-related areas. Rosenberg in several studies has drawn attention to imbalances in production processes ('bottlenecks'), which acted as a focus for innovation; for instance, the Westinghouse air brake for trains was the outcome of concern about stopping the larger and faster trains that could travel on the new steel rails. Similar imbalances arose with the development of high-speed steels early in the 20th century, which created a whole range of knock-on effects in user industries as well as within the machine-tool industry. The historian of technology, T.P. Hughes (1983), instead uses the military metaphor of 'reverse salients': some areas become conspicuous as resisting advance, and begin to block movement along the whole front, so these become the new focuses for innovation, as Hughes found in examining the early electricity networks.

As was found in the previous chapter, demand influences of this kind were not independent of existing supply factors. In this case, the demand exerted by speed-up (etc.) to meet expanding markets ran into the obstacle

---

38 Schmookler 1966, ch. 4.
39 Khan and Sokoloff 1993; also Sokoloff 1988; Sokoloff and Khan 1990.
40 Schmookler 1966, pp. 164–6.
41 *Ibid.*, p. 173.

of more stubborn supply in the bottleneck stage. The existing resources were inadequate to meet the goals aspired to, hence leading to 'reverse salients'.[42] The growth of demand thus interacted with the lack of growth of supply, and it is to the latter that I next turn.

B. Supply Factors

Even if the technologies were borrowed or copied from abroad, they had to be adapted to the different context of supply conditions in the USA. Out of this adaptation arose a pattern of production processes that was substantially different from those employed in Britain or the rest of industrializing Europe. That is to say, that the *paradigms* for technological innovation in manufacturing – though not elsewhere – were substantially the same as in Britain, and as will emerge below the *heuristics* for improving technologies were similar to those in Britain as outlined in Chapter 4, but the precise *trajectories* for technical advance were rather different. Just how different they were, and to what extent the countries had gone separate ways, is a matter of controversy. The trajectory, it may be recalled, represents the result of interaction between the technology and its immediate economic and social environment, so that we can look to what differed in American socio-economic conditions to establish in what ways the trajectories or paradigms differed. The most common assertion is that American techniques were more capital-intensive, based on the especially rapid growth of capital discussed above. Americans thus did not simply borrow English technology – Marshall[43] claimed that they reinvented it, through improving upon what would now be called 'reverse engineering'.

1. Differences in natural resources

The US techno-economic system in the 19th century was dominated by the availability of abundant supplies of land, obtained with varying degrees of subterfuge from the native population. These huge tracts of land were settled by small–medium farmers, allocated land in regular sizes under such provisions as the Homestead Act (1862), which generally granted 160 acres to the homesteader. The effects on demand have already been mentioned. On the supply side, the availability of more or less unlimited land at the frontier at low cost (mainly the cost of clearing it), meant that the classical model of Chapters 2 and 4, with its emphasis on fixed land supply, was quite inappropriate. For agriculture, the technology evolved not so as to raise land productivity as in Great Britain, but to allow the rather limited

---

42 Hughes, in Dosi *et al.* 1992, ch. 3. The 'goals' Hughes discusses are similar to my heuristics.

43 Marshall 1919, p. 774.

labour supplies to work more land.[44] Thus the abiding circumstance in American agriculture became like that in British *manufacturing*, but primarily for reasons of inadequate supply rather than expanding demand.[45] This quest to speed up the output of the scarcer inputs (labour and capital) meant adopting the machinery paradigm in US agriculture. The Americans thus effectively led the world from the 1830s in the mechanization of agriculture, through reaping machines, etc.[46]

Cheap land inputs also went with cheap timber and water inputs. The cheap timber meant widespread use of wood rather than iron, e.g. in construction, and use of wood rather than coal as a fuel, e.g. in steamboats or locomotives. It also promoted the role of wood-turning and related industries, for the production of wooden items such as furniture, gun-stocks, etc. Water availability meant use of water rather than steam as a major form of motive power – the energy supplied by steam engines did not exceed that from water power in the USA until the last third of the 19th century, and even afterwards the role of water partially returned in the form of hydro-electricity. It also meant the use of inland water rather than roads for transportation. However, all of these required adaptation from British or European standards, because in agriculture and related activities, topography varied so greatly. Steamboats had to be designed quite differently to suit the shallow waters of rivers like the Mississippi, evolving into the famous paddle-boats, with low draught and top-heavy superstructure.[47]

A further implication of abundant land was the need for cheap mass transportation. Steamboats became cheap but were slow – for links between the Midwest and the East, and later for opening up the broad, flat prairies, canals and waterways were superseded by railroads. Schumpeter argued that infrastructural development could lead economic growth by 'building ahead of demand', and considered that railroad construction could be regarded as such a case; with entrepreneurs seizing opportunities to 'Go West' and build railroads into sparsely populated territories, in the expectation that settlers would follow and justify the construction. Some of the transcontinental and other major lines were built with government subsidies,[48] but the conclusion of intensive research is that most railroads were built between already existing centres of demand, and that the subsidized railroads built into new areas rarely ever paid off financially, not

44 Hayami and Ruttan 1971; also Marx 1887/1965, p. 505.

45 Sporadic bursts of overseas demand did, however, play a subsidiary part, cf. David 1966.

46 *Ibid.*; also Olmstead 1975.

47 Hunter 1949; Rosenberg 1972, pp. 67–71.

48 Fogel 1960.

even after many years of operation.[49] The culmination of demand for mass transportation was the automobile, and such matters of geography partly account for America's rapid rise to ascendancy in this industry.

To an extent often not appreciated, US economic strengths resulted directly from the availability of land and natural resources. Cheap and abundant land meant that agricultural goods were relatively cheap, and a considerable portion of early mass production was devoted to food processing, such as the 'meat packing' industry in the Chicago area. US export patterns were (and to some extent still are) powerfully influenced by cheap land and materials,[50] as much as by industrial prowess in advanced labour-saving technologies.

However, as Rosenberg[51] has stressed, the causation here ran in both directions. Materials such as minerals could not be properly classified as resources until there was the technology available to extract and utilize them. Thus technology shaped resources just as much as resources shaped technology. This could involve shifts in the location of industry. For example, in the iron industry, there were greater gains to be made at first in reducing the consumption of coke as the fuel input than for reducing the iron ore. Initially several tons of coke were required per ton of ore consumed, so the furnaces were located around Pittsburgh, close to the source of the good coking coal. Eventually fuel economy was improved so far that less than one ton of coke was required per ton of ore, so the furnaces shifted west to the Michigan area, to be located nearer to the ore fields.[52] Thus to analyse the relationship between resources and technology we need a properly 'evolutionary' model.

2. Labour and capital

Both at the time and subsequently, attempts have been made to define the direction of technical change in 19th-century USA as 'labour saving'. Habakkuk's seminal study[53] attributed the high rate of labour-saving mechanization in the USA to the relative scarcity of labour, and especially to the inelasticity of the labour supply, which stemmed in his view from the competition for employment on those small–medium owner-occupied farms. There is little doubt that, by the standards of older countries, there was a scarcity of labour relative to land in the 19th-century USA, as reflected in the mass immigration throughout the period. As already noted,

49 Fishlow 1965, ch. 4.
50 North 1961, 1963; Wright 1990; Porter 1990, pp. 508–10.
51 Rosenberg 1972, p. 19.
52 Isard 1948.
53 Habakkuk 1962.

the land/labour disproportion in agriculture readily explains the adoption of the mechanization paradigm in that sector.

The problems really arise when one turns to manufacturing. Can we be sure that the shortages were just of labour? Like labour, capital flowed in massive quantities across the Atlantic.[54] The main difference was simply that the labour source was increasingly South and East Europe, whereas the capital source remained principally the UK – this was a major part of the export of capital referred to in relation to British industrial 'decline'. The flow of inputs thus points just as strongly to an incentive to capital saving as to labour saving, and the evidence we have on input prices, etc. also points to just as serious an initial shortage in capital as in labour,[55] a point made considerably earlier by Adam Smith and Alexander Hamilton.[56] Yet to explain mechanization in manufacturing it would appear necessary to posit a greater scarcity of labour than of capital.

The problems have been seriously compounded by the fact that mainstream economics has not been able to provide an agreed and plausible explanation for a bias towards labour-saving (or indeed capital-saving) innovation, as pointed out in Chapter 3 above. Yet studies within a neoclassical framework indicate that technical change in this era was biased towards labour saving, and not simply factor substitution.[57] Such problems have not reduced attempts to rescue the labour-saving hypothesis in many directions. For example, it is argued that a high land/labour ratio in agriculture might be sufficient to account for a high capital/labour ratio in manufacturing if industry also uses many agricultural inputs,[58] which as noted above it undoubtedly did do. A related argument is that the resource-intensive technologies used in American manufacturing, e.g. the woodworking in gun-making, also involved high capital-intensity and thus labour saving,[59] although as yet there is no very obvious logical explanation for this empirical observation. Technologies may have been aimed at reducing dependency on craft skills, either because of a link to resource use[60] or for deskilling.[61]

Although, therefore, there may be some validity in all these points, it seems more straightforward to step outside the apparatus of equilibrium-oriented neoclassical economics, and try to account for labour saving using

54 Williamson 1964.

55 Field 1983.

56 Smith 1776/1976, p. 109; Hamilton 1791/1964, pp. 142–9.

57 Cain and Paterson 1981, 1986.

58 Fogel 1967; Temin 1971.

59 Ames and Rosenberg 1967; David 1975.

60 James and Skinner 1985.

61 Brown and Philips 1986; though other evidence contradicts the deskilling notion (e.g. Nickless 1979 for cotton).

a different approach to the economics of innovation. Habakkuk himself[62] suggested that technological 'opportunities' were greater at this time at the labour-saving end of the technological spectrum. Thus the paradigm of machinery and mechanization made it easier, for the same amount of innovative effort, to come up with a labour-saving rather than a capital-saving advance. This requires extended consideration of concepts such as technological opportunity, which are more frequently encountered in the non-neoclassical literature (especially in evolutionary theory). At present the empirical support for this seemingly plausible notion is lacking and the issue of what determined the observed bias towards labour-saving innovation in the USA therefore remains inconclusive. My belief is that it can be explained by forces similar to those driving Britain towards mechanization during its industrialization phase, i.e. technological factors pushing for the saving of time. Outside of the manufacturing processes themselves, broader innovations in business organization and infrastructure were capital saving.[63] It will be suggested in the discussion of organizational factors below that such time pressures were even more intense in the USA than in Britain. To repeat what was said earlier, the paradigm and its heuristics for manufacturing industry differed from Britain not in kind but in degree. The resulting trajectories from confrontation with economic circumstances did, however, differ considerably.

C. New Technology Systems

The USA in many areas lagged behind Britain in the introduction of what were considered more modern technologies, and long persisted with techniques such as water power or charcoal smelting that in Britain were regarded almost as pre-industrial. However, I shall argue here that it led in terms of reorganizing technological *systems*.

Detailed studies of the delayed introduction of new technologies in the 19th-century USA indicate that, at least in the cases studied so intensively, both demand and supply factors seemed to be operating. Walsh (1975) re-analysed one of the best-known innovations of the mid-19th century, the change in fuel of the Pennsylvania iron industry from charcoal to coke (imitating the similar but earlier fuel shift for the British industry noted in Chapter 4). Using econometric methods to clarify causation patterns, Walsh found that there was some support for *all* of the extant hypotheses claiming to explain this fuel shift:

62 Habakkuk 1962, p.163.
63 Field 1987, 1992.

i the supply-side resource-exhaustion argument that charcoal persisted longer than in England because of the greater abundance and accessibility of timber in the USA;[64]

ii the quality-of-demand argument that, with a shift in relative use towards railroads, the inherent inferiority of coke pig iron mattered less than it had previously done, e.g. when used for making agricultural implements;[65]

iii the quality-of-supply argument that the opening up of new coalfields further west in the 1850s allowed higher quality coke and thus less inferior coke-smelted iron.[66]

Walsh found that major innovations were adopted as a package deal – developments to powerful blowing equipment depended on advances in steam power, and both came in with a shift of fuel in the plant to coke or anthracite coal. There was no observable gain in efficiency from introducing them sequentially; thus the case of American iron appears to support the importance of the role for 'systemic co-ordination'.

Such problems with introducing new technologies were amplified by shifts in technology paradigms. Electricity was widely in use for communications by the 1870s,[67] and had been commercialized for lighting following the work of Edison and Westinghouse by the end of the 1870s. The characteristic of electricity was that, in principle, its generation was subject to considerable economies of scale and could thus be centralized, so long as it could be networked to users sufficiently cheaply. The scale economies in generation were contingent on technological advances, especially the adoption of the steam turbine, invented by the Englishman Parsons and licensed for production in the USA by Westinghouse for use in large generating plants. Cheap networking, however, required agreement on *standards*, especially in the battle between direct current (DC) as favoured by Edison and alternating current (AC) as urged by Westinghouse. Edison capitulated from the late 1880s and his company was reorganized to emerge as General Electric in 1892. According to David (1992) the main factors behind the retreat of Edison were technological, particularly the invention of the polyphase AC motor and the associated 'rotary converter', which allowed DC generators to supply high-voltage AC transmission lines and thus acted as a gateway between the rival standards.[68]

---

64 Swank 1892.

65 Hunter 1929.

66 Temin 1964.

67 Morse's telegraph in 1837, followed by Bell's telephone in 1876.

68 The spread of the electricity networks in cities has been studied in detail by Hughes (1983).

The adoption of electricity as motive power was much more drawn out. In 1900 electricity was supplying only 4 per cent of the power used in manufacturing, whereas by the early 1920s it was supplying over half. This diffusion rested partly on hooking up to large central generating stations[69] and on rapid price declines.[70] However, it also rested on major reorganizations of the factories using the power and the technologies utilized for power transmission.[71] The greatest potential benefit of electricity was not its cheapness but its ability to supply 'fractionalized' power – power available at the flick of a switch exactly where it was needed.[72] But to do this, the organizational paradigm had to move away from the 19th-century notion of one large steam engine supplying the whole factory. 'Systemic co-ordination' had previously been attained by using the engine to control the machinery in a hierarchical way. This had to be dismantled in favour of a factory system in which individual machines patterned the system as a whole. The elaborate shafting and belting used to channel power from the engine to the many machines on different floors was replaced first by 'group drive' from a number of electric motors (separate for each floor or different machine clusters) and later by 'unit drive', with each machine redesigned to have its own electric motor. The elegant analysis of Devine (1983) shows just how complex this process was. In the pulp and paper industry, the corroborative but independent analysis of Cohen (1984) shows that the main object of introducing separate electric motors was again one of increasing speeds of operation.

Thus electrification helped solve problems of size associated with large firms in heavy industries.[73] Effectively the 'machine co-ordination' now regulated the 'systemic co-ordination' rather than the other way around, although as we shall see in later chapters this did not carry over into managerial structures and decision-making, which remained top-down and hierarchical.

Electricity was therefore not just a new technology, it was a new technological *system*, and ultimately it led to a new techno-organizational *paradigm*, based on centralization of energy generation but decentralization of energy application.

---

69 Average output per generating station rose from 0.7m kilowatt-hours in 1902 to 24.7m by 1929.

70 The price of electricity halved in this period while other prices more than doubled.

71 Hunter and Bryant 1991.

72 Du Boff 1967.

73 Marshall 1919, pp. 228–9, 789.

D. Research and Development

The orientation towards machines and mechanization, even more pronounced in the USA than in Great Britain, 'involved the solution of problems which required mechanical skill, ingenuity and versatility but not, typically, a recourse to scientific knowledge or elaborate experimental methods'.[74] Even in new products like steel, the level of scientific knowledge long remained low, and development continued to take place mainly through trial and error in production. Sir Henry Bessemer's work on steel, which paved the way for the modern steel industry, was announced in a paper to the Royal Society in London in 1856; but despite this scientific audience Bessemer understood little about chemistry, and the world for some time remained unaware that the Bessemer process would work only with iron ores of low phosphoric content. Other processes, which came to supersede the Bessemer converter, had to be developed for use on the more plentiful ores of higher phosphorus. In this respect, technology continued to lead science in the field of metallurgy until well into the 20th century – major product advances like high-speed steel (1898) and sintered tungsten carbide (1920s) preceded rather than followed the ultimately important development of crystallography.[75]

R&D of a more formal kind thus first developed in the USA for comparatively simple purposes, as the major advancing sectors like metallurgy, food processing and construction required better information about the quality of inputs; particularly as the range of potential materials widened, and also as the amount of processing increased (e.g. bacteria counts for the canning of food). Laboratories were involved in largely routine tasks, e.g. grading and testing materials, assaying minerals, controlling quality, writing specifications. In wheat, it was found that the chemical composition of the grain (protein and gluten composition, etc.) was much more important for its processing capabilities than its outward appearance (like colour), which had been the traditional basis for grading wheat. In 1902 the American Society for Testing Materials was founded, and acted to set standards and help codify the hitherto tacit knowledge concerning properties of metals. But the emphasis in all activities in the 19th century, even in the chemical industries, continued to be on 'old science', especially the properties of substances, rather than on the newer predictive forms of science usually associated with the Scientific Revolution.[76] Edison used his famous laboratory at Menlo Park, New

---

74 Rosenberg 1972, p. 54.

75 Mowery and Rosenberg 1989, on whom this section is based.

76 To be fair, even in the supposedly high-tech pharmaceuticals industry of today, most of the R&D is still more or less of this kind.

Jersey, mainly to push trial and error as far as was necessary for commercialization.[77]

The rise of large firms around the turn of the century was associated with the establishment of some new R&D laboratories in a number of these big firms, larger in size than their predecessors and entrusted with greater responsibilities. There was greater use of *experimental* science, and the nature of the science base also shifted, from a concentration on chemistry-based research towards more physics-based (electricity, transportation, instruments). Some companies specialized in conducting contract research for a wide variety of customers – firms like Arthur D. Little and Battelle – and these provided some access to R&D for SMFs that would otherwise have found their own R&D too expensive. But increasingly this contract research was limited to the more routine functions, like testing materials. The larger firms, especially, found it increasingly important to carry out R&D in-house. 'In-house research was better able to combine the heterogeneous inputs necessary for commercially successful innovation, to use and increase the stock of firm-specific knowledge learned from marketing and production personnel, and to exploit the close link between manufacturing and the acquisition of certain forms of technical knowledge.'[78] Thus R&D came to have 'two faces',[79] with the in-house advance and the externally acquired technology being complementary to each other. For most US companies in the early 20th century, even in industries like chemicals, the main emphasis, however, lay on product development rather than product innovation. 'After a product division had become a successful member of a new oligopoly, the purpose of its research units was to maintain plants at close to minimum efficient scale by developing new products that used much the same processes of production.'[80] For this it was not necessary to have a central R&D laboratory, as the facilities could be provided in separate product divisions.

One implication was that Schumpeter was partly right and partly misleading about increased routinization of R&D in large firms – right in calling attention to the unambitious objectives of most such R&D; yet the really routine operations were delegated to the contract research companies, while the large manufacturing firms themselves were required to put a much wider range of scientific disciplines together in 'new combinations' that uniquely benefited their own production systems and products. Studies of these early R&D laboratories show continuing tension among their scientists between conducting pure science and the patenting needs of the

---

77 Reich 1987.
78 Mowery and Rosenberg 1989, p. 71.
79 Cohen and Levinthal 1989.
80 Chandler 1990, p. 190.

companies that employed them.[81] Eventually General Electric Labs won two Nobel Prizes and the Bell Labs of AT&T (where special circumstances admittedly applied) as many as eight. The most successful laboratory managers carefully balanced basic and applied research.

These advances presaged the growing importance of in-house R&D later in the century. It should, however, be emphasized that until after the First World War, such activities were restricted to a minority of even the very large firms.[82] The dominance that these firms were already exerting in global competition came from other spheres.

III: ORGANIZATION AND MANAGEMENT: AMERICANS AS INITIATORS

A. Processes: The 'American System Of Manufactures'

What first attracted British attention to the fact that they had a major new industrial rival was not American technologies or even products, but American processes of manufacture. The very idea of assembly of components was so alien to the British observers in the 1850s – who coined the phrase, the 'American system of manufactures' – that whenever it was mentioned in their reports it was placed in inverted commas thus: 'assemble'.[83] What permitted such routine assembly in turn was the development of interchangeable parts, dating back to inventors such as Eli Whitney and Simeon North at the beginning of the 19th century. In their turn, interchangeable parts required a high degree of standardization and precision manufacture of the components. As noted previously, this was associated with the homogeneity of American demand, and also with the 'extent of the market' in Smith's sense, i.e. production for mass markets.

Interchangeable parts brought these advantages.

- i An obvious benefit to supply chains, in the ability to replace any defective part with another equally usable – and also subsequently to consumers (such as armies) in permitting cheap replacements, cannibalizing of equipment, etc.
- ii Dispensing with expensive and time-consuming handicraft labour, particularly the 'fitters' with chisels and files, etc., who typified British production in guns and other products. This highly labour-intensive set of tasks was not appropriate to the

81 Wise 1985; Reich 1985; Hounshell and Smith 1988.

82 Chandler 1990, pp. 47–8, 84, 604.

83 Rosenberg 1969; 1972, p. 94.

American situation of skilled labour scarcities. As Henry Ford (1926), or at least his scribe, remarked in the *Encyclopaedia Britannica*, based on his unique experience with automobile assembly lines, 'in mass production, there are no fitters'.

iii Dispensing with one-off designs through standardization, including the replacement of the British 'consulting engineer' with engineers' routines, implying also a shift from product concerns to process concerns.[84]

iv Dynamic advantages of further developing the machines and tools, effectively creating the machine tool industry, allowing the supersession of handicrafts work through specialization, in the manner forecast by Adam Smith.

v These machines in turn helped bring about a dramatic increase in speeds of 'throughput', i.e. the rate of processing, as the British parliamentary committees expressly observed.

The products of interchangeability became household brandnames – McCormick reapers, Colt revolvers, Yale locks, Singer sewing machines, Remington typewriters, etc. But the definitive study of the American System of Manufactures, by Hounshell (1984), shows that interchangeability developed quite slowly and sometimes painfully, nor did it guarantee commercial success. Singer took much longer than its two main rivals to apply interchangeability to sewing machines, but in the long run (and even in the short run) proved much more successful in business than they, mainly through predominance in marketing.[85] Unless the gains to consumers were substantial, much depended on realizing the full benefits of production, notably speed-up, and these did not come automatically.

Ultimately, interchangeable parts could lead in two main directions.

(a) To the assembly line and continuous processing, as introduced in automobiles (though with more primitive antecedents in other industries) by Ford in Detroit after 1909. On such huge, dedicated production lines, the components flowed successively to each worker, who stayed in the same place, thus minimizing the static loss which Smith had described from workers having to move between jobs, and maximizing throughput and 'scale'.[86] This

84 *Ibid.*, p. 47.

85 Hounshell 1984, ch. 2.

86 Williams *et al.* (1993) argue that Ford's first main plant at Highland Park obtained most of its cost savings not by the moving assembly line but by vertical process integration (making rather than buying machines and components), and by 'repetitive manufacture', i.e. Smith's first rather than second advantage of the division of labour. At the later Rouge plant the moving assembly line was more important.

'Fordist' paradigm of organization, involving close managerial control, will be studied in Chapter 7.

(b) Alternatively, to using the large amounts of fixed equipment much more flexibly, by re-programming its precision operations when required to produce different products. Throughput also rises rapidly from this strategy, but it is directed more at 'scope' than 'scale', i.e. at permitting a wider variety of products to be produced continuously. This is the basis of the Japanese system of manufacture, studied further in Chapter 10.

B. The Strategic Role of Machine Tools

The machines to make machines, i.e. Marx's 'machinofacture', crucially involved the development of machine tools, as Rosenberg (1963) showed in a seminal study. Machine tools were originally developed in the user industries, i.e. 'downstream', but then the machine-making industry began to split off from the machine-using sectors below them, and in due course the machine-tool industry split off from the machine-makers. It should be emphasized that this 'vertical disintegration', or separation, was in relation to *processes*, not to *products*. The distinct machine-tool industry dates from around the middle of the 19th century, and by 1914 Rosenberg believes that there were about 600 machine-tool firms in existence in the USA. The value of their output was not particularly large in financial terms, but they played a disproportionate technological role through their upstream command of processes.

Alongside such vertical disintegration of processes went a roughly synchronous trend towards 'technological convergence'. Across the whole range of industrial activities, the problems that machine tools were called on to tackle were similar – transmission, control, friction and heat resistance being among the most significant. The number of particular processes that the tools carried out was then equally limited – turning, drilling, planing, grinding, etc. (about seven in all) – irrespective of the industry concerned. Hence once the basic design breakthroughs had been made, the same principles could, with some extra effort, be applied across the board. The progression – 'learning by doing' – thus consisted of solving problems in technically advanced and technically demanding industries, then rapidly diffusing the principles to other industries that utilized the same types of tools. Following such observations, Marshall remarked: 'most of the operatives in a watch factory [in America] would find machines very similar to those with which they were familiar, if they strayed into a gun-making factory or sewing-machine factory, or a factory for making textile machinery'.[87] Rosenberg drew particular attention to two new kinds of machine tool, the milling machine and the turret lathe, which were adopted in many if not most industries.

Downstream, industries took it in turn to act as the carrier of technical progress. In the mid-19th century the firearms industry was the breeding ground for the early advances, whence they were to be spun off elsewhere. Sewing machine manufacture, having borrowed the milling machines and turret lathes from gun-making, then became a key carrier industry. Towards the end of the 19th century, bicycles took up the leading role, but were soon eclipsed by the automobile industry. 'Technological convergence' of similar kinds could also take place in the downstream industries themselves, for example the sewing machine was applied not only to producing ready-made clothing, but to tents and sailmaking, boot and shoe production, rubber and elastic goods, bookbinding, etc. The range of modernizing industries was steadily broadening.

Such 'learning by using' in the downstream industries fed back up to the machine-makers, who were encouraged to extend their sets of principles to new industries. In this they would draw upon their existing range of skills and competences, for instance the major early US locomotive builders came from a background in textile machinery. Thus learning by using and learning by doing were more fully integrated into 'learning by interacting'.

C. Vertical Integration

Technological learning thus appeared to be maximized in Smithian fashion by vertical disintegration of *processes*, and building on the dynamics of specialization. However, in regard to products, the opposite tendencies were sometimes at work. Along the 'value chain' from raw materials to finished products, there were pressures in late 19th-century America towards greater degrees of vertical integration. By failing to see that both forces were at work, Stigler in a well-known paper (1951) drew misleading historical conclusions concerning the links between the division of labour and the extent of the market.

One explanation for such vertical integration in products involves *external* scale economies of the Marshallian kind – the ability to utilize benefits from being located on the same site as other stages of processing, e.g. the additional savings possible from making use of the waste heat from the furnace in other process stages.[88]

Internal static scale economies underlay the more frequent explanation, in which the object of the integration was to exercise control. The static scale

87 Marshall 1890/1961, pp. 258–9.

88 The 'hot process' noted above in Chapter 5; cf. Marshall 1919, p. 220.

economies decided which stage possessed the greatest economic power and would therefore be the proactive element in any integration. But the intention was less one of reaping similar scale economies at the other stages than to control *quality* of inputs or products and to control their *rate of flow*. The speed-up conditions that fostered the latter will be described shortly. Thus in the taxonomy used in this book (Figure 4.1, p. 102), the causes were expressed through the quality and workflow dimensions of the organizational sphere.

In the iron industry, Temin[89] showed that the 'minimum efficient scale' (MES) in different branches of the industry varied considerably – the MES being the smallest output at which the plant could operate reasonably economically. In the mid-19th century, the most advanced rolling mills ('three-high mills'), used for rolling rails, required the combined output of three to four blast furnaces to supply them with pig iron, i.e. the MES in rail-rolling was 3–4 times that in smelting. Rolling mills thus looked to control inputs from these multiple blast furnaces, and integrated 'backwards' to help ensure their supply. With the advent of the Bessemer steel process, and steel rails, the disparity was reversed – one Bessemer mill fed ten rolling mills. Impetus for control therefore swung to the converter stage, with direct ownership being sought backwards and/or forwards.

Vertical integration occurred most frequently in activities for processing those raw materials whose supply was capable of being disrupted. Desire for security of supply of inputs meant that, in a range of minerals industries, the most powerful firms sought to control raw materials by direct ownership – at first within the country, and later through overseas acquisitions of semi-colonialist kinds. These operations mainly affected industries where there was some restriction (inelasticity) on the supply of inputs, and was most often defensive. Livesay and Porter (1969) found in the sample they investigated that forward integration into distribution and marketing was actually more common, and usually undertaken for offensive rather than defensive reasons.[90]

D. Horizontal Integration

Integration horizontally, i.e. linking to or acquiring other firms involved in the same stage of processing, was undertaken partly to reap internal economies of scale on the supply side, but more often perhaps for trying to gain control over *markets* on the demand side.[91] We saw in Chapter 5 that Marshall argued that most *technical* scale economies in his time could be

89 Temin 1964, ch. 5.
90 See also Williamson 1985, pp. 107–14.
91 Marshall 1919, p. 507.

reaped by medium-sized businesses, and that the driving force in the recent increases he observed came instead from the side of marketing.[92] Scale economies in production seem not to explain the great merger movement at the end of the 19th century, because the period of rapid factory growth had come about two decades earlier.[93] In many activities – meat-packing was one example – the process began from the marketing end of the companies and then worked 'backwards', often enhanced by combining the horizontal integration with a greater measure of vertical integration, as in the formation of the gargantuan US Steel (a merger of mergers) from 1901. Such a combination of vertical and horizontal integration was bred of a desire to internalize monopoly profits, rather than leave them to be bargained between suppliers and users, which might leave both worse off.[94] The quest for market control turned into the rise of Big Business, because that control was directed at a moving target: the rivals too were getting bigger.[95] This creation of giant firms has been studied most extensively by the eminent Harvard business historian, Alfred Chandler,[96] and his approach will be adopted here.

1. Mass distribution

As in Smith's model, it was extension of the market which normally came first, with the rise of 'mass distribution',[97] through the spread of transportation and communication networks (telegraphy and later telephony for the latter). Merchants and local 'general stores' were replaced by mass marketers, including large-scale wholesalers and later mass retailers (department stores, chain stores and mail-order houses). The families associated with these developments became some of the wealthiest in the country – Woolworths, Gimbels, Filenes, Wanamakers, etc. But generally there was no dramatic change of managerial structure, as the family-based owners remained in managerial control, and were often slow to develop modern accountancy, sales forecasting, etc. The major benefit from mass distribution alone, according to Chandler, was in speed rather than in size – in this case, expressed in high volumes of 'stockturn'.[98] Retailers and other distributors facing rapidly changing demands were often found to be leading the strategies of labour-intensive manufacturing industries (like

92 *Ibid.*, pp. 509, 513, 515.
93 O'Brien 1988; also James 1983.
94 Temin 1964, ch. 8.
95 Best 1990, ch. 2.
96 Chandler 1962, 1977, 1990.
97 Chandler 1977, ch. 7.
98 *Ibid.*, p. 236; 1990, p. 29.

clothing), where smaller firm sizes continued.[99] Marshall,[100] basing his evidence partly on Wanamaker, argued that 'the economies in time and trouble' for the customer as well as the retailer should not be underestimated either. In distribution, transaction costs were therefore reduced for both buyers and sellers through such organizational innovations. In our terms, mass distribution met the needs of consumers for diversity of *products*.

2. Mass production

Mass production placed much greater demands on technology than did mass distribution (for innovation in materials, power sources, machinery, etc.). The economies of scale which resulted, in Chandler's view[101] again related not so much to sheer size as once more to speed, in this case expressed as production throughput (intensity of use of processes). To achieve such throughput, mechanization now meant much more than just applying machinery to particular processes – it meant technical and organizational integration and synchronization throughout the factory. In the terminology of Chapter 4, 'systemic co-ordination' between the machines was *internalized* within the plant, through the coupling of technological changes by appropriate organizational innovations.[102] This reorganization of 'capital process' based on throughput had its counterpart in labour process in displacing worker skills through the kinds of processing methods utilized and through the concerted attack on craft unionism.[103] Work became machine-paced, sometimes to the point of dehumanization.[104] Learning, and control of production, were concentrated in the upper to lower managerial strata, largely to the exclusion of the workforce.[105]

Mass production came soonest in industries involved in processing liquids or semi-liquids (petroleum, etc.), for two reasons: (i) the scientific knowledge – chiefly chemistry – was more advanced, and therefore the technology was also advanced; (ii) the flow of materials was much more self-evident, so that fewer reorganizations had to be undertaken to augment the throughput. Of the industries that eventually moved to mass production in this era, the metal-working and metal-making industries came last, because their processes were least fluent between one stage and the next; but because the organizational readjustments therefore had to be more

99 *Ibid.*, pp. 45–6.
100 Marshall 1919, p. 297n.
101 Chandler 1977, p. 281.
102 Best 1990, pp. 53–4.
103 Lazonick 1990, ch. 7.
104 Braverman 1974.
105 Lazonick 1991, ch. 1.

radical, the outcomes were the most spectacular. Mass production thus met the need of producers for diversity of *processes*.

3. Big business

Chandler[106] defines big business as the integration of mass production with mass distribution within single business firms. The economies of speed were thus maximized, combining high volume throughput with high stockturn, and in this way generating a plentiful cash-flow. To run such enterprises required substantial management and corporate bureaucracies. These Chandler describes as the 'visible hand', contrasting with Smith's invisible hand based on competitive small firms. With some justification, Chandler evidently regards this creation of the 'visible hand' as the greatest industrial feat of its time.

This began in railroad companies, simply because in the mid-19th century they were much the largest businesses in the country in terms of turnover, and even more importantly because, as they integrated into the cross-country 'trunk-lines', they became responsible for operations over a very widespread geographical area.[107] Consequently they first developed the 'line and staff' system of hierarchical responsibility, delegating each hundred miles or so of country (each 'division') to managers (line executives), who were in turn responsible for all the functions appertaining to their particular territory (for which functions they employed 'staff'). Such a 'divisional' system differed from a 'departmental' one in which individuals responsible for each particular function at the local level were answerable to a superior in charge of that function at HQ. The departmental structure was therefore subdivided according to *function*, whereas the divisional system divided according to *product* and/or *region* (of course in practice these boundaries were often blurred). Sitting over all the division managers was a powerful if often small central office, responsible for the major strategic operations of the enterprise, such as which new lines to buy; but this came in only after the Civil War. Thus American firms led managerial reorganization partly because of the vast size of the country, i.e. because of space.[108]

Manufacturing industry developed similar structures about two decades after the railroads. Up to about 1860 the USA was characterized, like Britain, by single-function firms. Two decades or so later, the process of geographical expansion had created firms with several plants (multi-plant firms), but still carrying out one main function. The late years of the 19th century saw not just multi-plant enterprises but increasingly those that

---

106 Chandler 1977, p. 285.
107 Chandler 1965; 1977, chs 3–5; 1990, pp. 54–8.
108 *Ibid.*, pp. 51–3.

performed several functions as important parts of their operations, e.g. the industrial producer developing marketing (usually wholesaling), or transportation, or sourcing of materials. Such expansion was built on investment rather than on innovation.[109] However, until the 20th century most firms remained single-product firms, and it was only in the present century that multi-product firms became especially common, most notably in the new industries.[110]

4. Oligopolies and pools

The industrial structure which first emerged in the railroad business was not one of 'pure monopoly', with one seller dominating the market. Instead there were typically somewhere around four major competitors. A similar situation of 'oligopoly' also arose in several branches of manufacturing late in the century, with the average number of producers usually slightly higher than for railroads.

It was noted in Chapter 3 above that oligopoly, left to market forces, is typified theoretically by periods of stability followed by periods of extreme instability. For the railroads, the decade of greatest instability was the 1870s, when several cross-country trunk-lines had formed to give a variety of routes from the Midwest to the East Coast. Each was competing for *market share* – to do so, one might cut prices, but then to retain their own market share all others would do likewise, and consequently there would be a brief but highly unstable period of price wars, benefiting customers but of little collective benefit to the producers.

To cope with such potentially ruinous price wars, businessmen resorted sometimes to 'gentlemen's agreements', all of which proved ineffective and for obvious reasons ('none of them were gentlemen', 'they lasted as long as it took to get to the telephone outside'). An alternative was to cut prices secretly, and in rail shipments, secret rail rebates did last for surprisingly long periods, but had obvious limitations – you had to make the price cuts known to your major customers but not to your rapacious rival producers. It is not surprising that this practice should have been attempted, but it is astonishing that the system should have placed so much reliance upon it. Because of the evident limitations, the agreements were replaced with 'pools', organized more formally, and responsible for setting 'administered prices' and for allocating quotas of market shares to those firms in the pool. Most of the quotas seem to have been ineffective also, but the administered

---

109 *Ibid.*, pp. 62–3.

110 Chandler and Redlich 1961.

prices lasted for some spans of years before another price war came about.[111]

The effect of the oligopolies and pools on technical progress is a matter of serious dispute in the economics of innovation. Kamien and Schwartz[112] have shown that much depends on whether one is talking here about firms of large size or firms with large market shares, and that much of the literature has failed to clarify this distinction.[113] Firms of large size are contenders for recouping economies of scale, which may or may not be associated with technical progress. Firms with some degree of monopoly power might, however, be expected to rest on their laurels. It would appear that, in practice, the stabilization of products directed entrepreneurs towards searching for process innovations to cut costs, thus raising profitability in conditions of product price stability. The price wars might have occasionally accelerated this pattern, and in addition technical progress may sometimes have set them off. But, as the cliché has it, 'the jury is still out' on whether the oligopolies hastened or slowed technological change.

IV: FINANCE

A. Trusts

With the ascendancy of the 'visible hand', ownership became divorced from management. An internal solution to the problem of divided control came via the establishment of trusts, the first in industry being John D. Rockefeller's Standard Oil (today's Exxon). The shareholders or owners of the various operating companies traded in their equity holdings for certificates registering their share in the trusts – in effect, any voice in the running of the companies was handed over to the board of trustees, which in this case meant Rockefeller and his nine associates. When corporations were allowed to hold stocks of another corporation, as was legalized by the state of New Jersey in 1889, the way was paved to the 'holding company', of which the largest example at this time was US Steel, holding shares in no less than 785 operating plants. Thus the trust operated as a kind of internalized capital market.

---

111 MacAvoy 1965. The transaction cost approach ought to predict a quite different outcome, cf. Williamson 1985, p. 278.

112 Kamien and Schwartz 1975, 1982.

113 Schumpeter's analysis studied in Chapter 3 falls into this category of lack of clarity.

B. Investment Banking and Finance Capitalism

Ownership of trusts fell increasingly into the hands of the financial sector, which in the US case meant large investment bankers like J. Pierpont Morgan. Morgan began by taking over railroads in the later 1870s and moved into industrial securities in a massive way in the final few years of the 19th century. The bankers thus followed rather than led the developments in management, but after 1897 their role became more potent. Because of the financial security involved, and the financial profits obtainable from promotion, these bankers had come to support mergers at almost any cost – big was beautiful. Big in this sense meant centralization of financial control – the relationship with centralization of production was less consistent. The climax of such financial involvement was the aforesaid formation of US Steel from 1901 – the 'merger of mergers' in which industrial magnates like Andrew Carnegie (who had once declared, 'I manufacture steel, not securities') sold out to Morgan and the bankers.

Banks in the USA did not interpenetrate or dominate industry to the extent found in some European countries.[114] Marshall[115] concluded that, 'American industrialists for the present control finance, perhaps as much as they are controlled by it'.

The above discussion therefore follows the business history tradition of placing greater emphasis on trends in management than on trends in finance, and interprets the period as one of 'managed capitalism'. Lenin and the others were partly right that the separation of ownership and management was a fundamental characteristic of the period, and brought a source of tension and instability into the system, as was later to be demonstrated in the Wall Street Crash of 1929. But ownership (as distinct from management), remained largely in the hands of wealthy individuals and families up to the Second World War – it was the postwar dissolution of this pattern which contributed to the US 'retardation' from the 1960s.[116]

V: PRODUCTS

The preceding discussion has covered the major points relating to the product/demand side. To recapitulate:

(a) In terms of consumption, American demand traditionally favoured standardized items suited to mass consumption by

---

114 As discussed in Chapter 5, cf. Lenin 1917.

115 Marshall 1919, p. 566; also Ford 1922, chs 2, 11.

116 Chandler 1990, p. 625.

households of moderate wealth. Demand grew rapidly, partly because of the rapidity of growth of population able to find abundant land.[117]

(b) Consumer requirements for a range of products were met by retailers and by the emergence of 'mass distribution'.

(c) In terms of production, such demand was initially met by producers undertaking the assembly of components into a single product, as was to culminate in Henry Ford's assembly line for the Model T Ford, and 'mass production'.

(d) But the rise of oligopolistic competition meant that rival producers had to persuade consumers that their products were different, even if the real differences were small. Competition for single-product firms like Ford was to arise from multi-product rivals such as General Motors. This helped to shift the emphasis of producers from obsession with the organization of production to the organization of products and selling. The fusion of mass production and mass distribution is described as 'big business'.

With prices partly fixed by the nature of oligopolistic competition and the fear of ruinous price wars, competition increasingly took on non-price forms. In retailing the most obvious indicator was the growing sophistication of advertising and marketing, especially in aiming to cultivate brand names in order to retain customer loyalty even when rivals undercut prices. How much such advertising genuinely improved (or reflected) the quality of product is more debatable – Marshall considered that 'much of the modern expenditure on advertising is not constructive, but combative. ... The chief influence of such advertising is exerted, not through the reason, but through the blind force of habit'.[118] Its effect in his opinion, perhaps mistaken, was to keep distribution costs higher in the USA than in Europe, notwithstanding cost advantages arising elsewhere out of large scale, standardization, etc. The outcome of this focus on marketing and advertising was the cult of Madison Avenue, the New York centre for advertising companies, and 'The Man in the Grey Flannel Suit'. By the early 20th century, the USA led the world as much in marketing as in management.

Indeed, the two were connected. The new consumer goods from the 1880s, like meat packing (the Swift and the Armour companies), launched the path towards consolidation and centralization for the manufacturing sector, by first creating elaborate marketing organizations and purchasing departments, then steadily bringing the whole structure together in

---

117 Malthus, following the American statesman Benjamin Franklin, referred to this as availability of 'room'.

118 Marshall 1919, pp. 304, 306; also Veblen 1921/1954, pp. 109–14.

verticalized fashion.[119] And not only did marketing lead managerial organization, but it also could lead technology. In describing the sewing machine industry – the main 'carrier' industry for manufacturing technology around the 1860s – Thomson (1987) aptly refers to 'learning by selling'. Paradoxically, the fact that consumers wanted goods that were so similar probably intensified the quest for minor product differentiation to capture major market shares.

Consumers gained more obvious cost savings from the reduction in middlemen.[120] Lastly, it is worth repeating Marshall's reference[121] to the saving of time and trouble to *consumers* as well as salesmen from mass distribution, especially in the context of selling goods over such huge geographical areas.

American manufactures were launched on to world markets in the final years of the 19th century. However, the new capital-intensive technologies did not by themselves guarantee lower total costs than foreign rivals. Moreover, techniques such as the sewing machine were rapidly diffused even in 'cheap labour' countries, which thus maintained cost leadership through relative wage levels.[122] Where the USA forged far ahead was in the products of newer industries, especially those derived from mass production for its homogeneous domestic markets.

VI: GOVERNMENT POLICY

The structure of US households and firms was reflected in the policies adopted by government, and their not infrequent inconsistencies. According to Veblen,[123] America took farthest the classical economic doctrine of natural 'pecuniary' liberty, in which individual freedom was circumscribed by the sacredness and inviolability of property rights: 'America is the natural habitat of the self-made man',[124] and this was enshrined constitutionally in 'freedom of contract', but he went on to point out that it was increasingly threatened in practice by the concentration of power in big business. Yet though governments were often regarded as pro-capitalist in their sympathies, there was also widespread support for the 'small man' and the sporadic outbreak of quite powerful populist movements.[125] Popular

---

119 Chandler 1977, see p. 208 above.
120 Marshall 1919, p. 299.
121 *Ibid.*, p. 297n.
122 Milward and Saul 1973, pp. 175–6; cf. p. 161 above.
123 Veblen 1904, ch. 8.
124 *Ibid.*, p. 273.
125 Galambos 1968.

distrust of anything monolithic extended to distrust of governments, and the Constitution drawn up after Independence in the 18th century instituted the system of checks and balances. An important aspect of this system was the separation between state and federal governments, and the desire to maintain as much power as possible at the local and/or state level. We see this exemplified in every set of policies except the external (international) below; it also extended to areas such as banking policy.

A. Educational Policy

The rise to predominance of American industry has long been assumed to have been related to having a well-educated and well-trained population. Such a relationship was stressed by the same British parliamentary reports which drew attention to the 'American System of Manufactures'. This strength in education derived from moves from as early as the 1840s towards *public* provision of universal primary education.[126] The object of such locally based trends was probably not vocational – the evidence suggests that the main motive was 'social control'[127] – but the outcome was indeed the formation of human capital. The Federal government assumed no powers for maintaining the public schools, either at elementary or secondary level – they were charges on the individual states and local communities.[128] The Federal government did, however, make provision for the development of colleges (higher education), leading the way with the Morrill Act (1862), granting revenues from land sales towards setting up colleges, and the Hatch Act (1887) for agricultural extension services. Nor should the extraordinary benefactions of entrepreneurs like Carnegie and Rockefeller be overlooked.[129] Until about 1880 the colleges also existed primarily for social and consumption purposes, but thereafter they developed strong traditions in practical fields such as agriculture and engineering. Nelson (1990a, 1990b) considers that the extent of higher education and its orientation towards practical applications were the main source of American industrial supremacy in the 20th century (see Chapter 7).

---

126 Though delayed until well after the Civil War in the southern states, cf. Landes and Solmon 1972.
127 Field 1979.
128 Fishlow 1966.
129 Wren 1983.

B. Antitrust Policy

Since individual consumers were weak in relation to the rising corporations, control of the latter was sought through the legal system. In the USA, unlike say Germany, pools and cartels were not legally enforceable – US law descended from English common law, which for centuries had made agreements in restraint of trade illegal.[130] Such broadbrush opposition to anti-competitive measures was added to more directly by the passing of laws to regulate the large 'trusts' in some states in the 1880s, followed at the Federal level by the Sherman Antitrust Act of 1890. The latter made restraint of trade a criminal offence, though later legal judgments limited it as a Federal law only to trading across state boundaries. Supplemented by the Clayton Act of 1914, which clarified which kinds of behaviour could be defined as restraints of trade, this has remained the backbone of antitrust legislation and sentiment in the USA until relatively recently.

However, Federal governments found themselves caught between the interests of consumers as exerted through antitrust laws and those of big business. The ambiguities have been nicely caricatured by Cochran and Miller: 'Thus free competition became the keystone of the triumphal arch of American business philosophy, while monopolistic tendencies were ignored; science and mechanization became the grand avenues of progress while patent pools and social regimentation were obscured; thrift remained the first commandment in the decalogue of the new business society though conspicuous consumption was its sign of grace'.[131] Mergers were in part an evasive response to antitrust legislation, in order to internalize the pressures for collusion. Large firms were also able to 'capture' government regulatory agencies in sectors like railroads and telecommunications.[132] The Republican party, especially, fell under the dictates of big business. By the 1920s, governments could be heard voicing opinions such as that of President Calvin Coolidge: 'The business of the government is business'. The scope for conflict, often reflected in the contrasting policies of different government departments, has persisted up to the present day. The Supreme Court also argued that decisions on infringements of the law were its business, not that of government departments like the Federal Trade Commission, and in the interwar period the Supreme Court readily reversed the FTC's decisions. Moreover, as early as 1918, the FTC recognized that it might have to advocate collaboration in American export industries to counter organized foreign rivals such as the German cartels, notwithstanding its primary objective of promulgating domestic

---

130 Marshall 1919, p. 511; Davis and North 1971, p. 173.

131 Cochran and Miller 1942/1960, p. 123; also Best 1990, ch. 3.

132 MacAvoy 1965; Brock 1981.

competition.[133] Nor were these ambiguities limited to politicians – according to Veblen,[134] leading economic theorists were unable to resolve similar dilemmas when they turned to policy recommendations.

C. External Trade

In 1791 Alexander Hamilton, the first Secretary of the Treasury for the USA, who had already introduced a patent system (1790), argued that, as a latecomer to industrialization by comparison with Britain, the USA should establish tariff protection and subsidies to replace imports of manufactures. His arguments were various, including the proposition that manufactures were subject to decreasing costs (increasing returns).[135] Economic war with Britain from 1807 recruited popular support to this cause. Beginning in a substantial way in 1816, the 'lobbies' that characterized voting support in the US Congress succeeded in rigging tariffs according to their vested interests,[136] most notoriously in the 'tariff of abominations' 1828–33. Most of the nascent American industries thus obtained protective tariffs, though in industries like iron the tariffs were not always able to exclude competitive imports from Britain.[137] Paul David[138] has argued that the learning behaviour of the cotton textiles industry, though important in itself, was unrelated to the tariff protection, so that the 'infant industry' case for such protection was weak; moreover, it may never have overcome its competitive disadvantage.[139] But reducing tariffs did not necessarily promote competitiveness: the 'deluge' of American products on to world markets, which came in the 1890s, followed a modest resurgence rather than a weakening of protectionism.[140] Externally, the USA sought formal empire less actively than did some of its European rivals, but under Teddy Roosevelt in the early 20th century adopted the 'Big Stick' attitude to limiting European involvement in Central and South America. Up to the present day, American trade policy has been schizophrenic, arguing for free trade in products in which it dominates world markets and for high protectionism in products where it feels weaker. However, it is by no means the only country that has attempted to pursue such inconsistent policies.

---

133 Marshall 1919, pp. 613–14.
134 Veblen 1919/1961, p. 229.
135 Hamilton 1791/1964, p. 158.
136 Pincus 1977.
137 Fogel and Engerman 1969, 1971.
138 David 1970.
139 Bils 1984.
140 Hawke 1975.

7. Industrialization in the West, 1930s to the 1970s

I: GROWTH 1930–1970

A. Long-Run Growth Patterns

We have seen in Chapter 6 that, by the beginning of the 20th century, the USA was overtaking Britain in terms of industrial productivity, i.e. in total factor productivity (TFP) – with its greater labour-saving orientation it had already surpassed the UK in terms of labour productivity. Coupled with its greater size, in this way the USA was coming to act as the pace-setter for long-term growth and industrialization. Germany, too, was beginning to catch Britain, but because of its more limited resources as well as the effects of wars and extremist politics, Germany did not dominate the industrial world to the same extent as the USA. Up until the late 1920s, the gap between the USA and other industrial countries widened; although it began to narrow again first with the Slump in the 1930s and then by the phenomenon of industrial 'convergence' after the Second World War, as briefly noted in Chapter 3.[1]

The analysis of the prewar USA, as set out in Chapter 6, showed that its leadership was based primarily on managerial capacity, oriented on the one side to competences in the organization of production and on the other to competences in marketing. Its advantages in other dimensions were initially less secure. But that leadership was to be strengthened by the two world wars, fought offshore, such that one can classify its sources of postwar strength (following Abramovitz 1986) as:

i market size – the sheer extent and scale of the internal US market, eight times as large in economic terms as the next largest;

1 For simplicity, I shall refer throughout this book to the period up to 1914 as 'prewar', to the years 1918–39 as 'interwar', and to post-1945 as 'postwar'.

ii wealth – making a major contribution to that aggregate economic size, in terms of both high per-capita incomes and relatively egalitarian wealth distribution;

iii skills – a relatively well-educated and trained labour force;

iv technology – particular advantages in the commercialization of products and the ability to produce 'robust' product designs, e.g. in commercial aircraft;[2]

v management – attracting many of the most able individuals and drawing them into organized managerial structures.

The USA remained an internally-focused economy, with a very low ratio of exports or imports to GNP, and able to depend on its immense domestic resource base. But as its absolute size grew, its external operations, though relatively small in significance for its own economy, became increasingly important for the rest of the world. Its postwar strength enabled the USA to take the dominant role in reconstructing the world economy, including the provision of major stopgap measures like the Marshall Plan (1948). This gave the USA considerable power to open the markets of the war-stricken countries to trade, and to impose some of the norms of capitalist America on the recipient countries and on global trade and payments systems. At the same time, the 'Iron Curtain' came down and divided West and East (the 'First World' and the 'Second World'), with recovery in the East being promoted instead by central planning in socialist economies (see Chapter 9). 'Third World' experience in the Less-Industrialized Countries (LICs) was more variable, depending to a degree on First World demand for imports of foodstuffs and raw materials, but growing increasingly frustrated at the inadequacies of such dependence for sustained growth and catch-up.

B. Demand and Supply

Several economists pointed to a strongly positive relationship between output growth and (labour) productivity growth – this is commonly known as 'Verdoorn's Law'. Some denied that this had much significance because productivity growth equals output growth minus input growth (or growth of the labour force, for labour productivity). Others set about trying to explain the relationship, but explanations were divided between those stressing supply-side causes, who saw the process beginning with productivity growth (reducing costs and prices and hence encouraging output expansion[3]) and those stressing the demand side, who instead saw the process as beginning with output growth (allowing economies of scale,

2 Rothwell and Gardiner 1990.

3 E.g. Salter 1966.

intensification of work, etc.[4]). One sensible way of interpreting Verdoorn's 'Law' would be to regard it as a projection to the macro level of the learning curve, relating productivity to experience.[5]

Most explanations of growth can therefore be classified as cost-oriented or demand-oriented. Orthodox neoclassical economics, deriving ultimately from Say's Law that 'supply creates its own demand',[6] would tend to emphasize supply (cost) causes, such as technological or organizational change. For much of the postwar boom, i.e. from around 1950 to the late 1960s or early 1970s, however, the less orthodox demand-oriented economics (or the so-called 'neoclassical synthesis' combining the two views) was in the ascendancy, following the reconstitution of macroeconomics by Keynes in the 1930s.[7] Here, aggregate demand factors like the demand for investment would determine the level and growth of economic activity. The argument presumed that supply factors, e.g. supplies of raw materials or labour, were not a major constraint holding back growth, and this largely applied in the 1950s and 1960s, with (a) cheap oil from the Middle East and cheap food or materials from countries of the 'South'; and (b) adequate labour supplies from (i) the interwar unemployed, (ii) later, new labour pools, especially married women, (iii) outflows from poorer agricultural districts, and later (iv) migrant flows into the European countries, e.g. the German and Swiss *gastarbeiter*.[8]

However, cheap labour by itself would not have provided adequate *demand*. According to the 'Régulation school' of French post-Marxist scholars, wages were kept up by (a) the development of stronger trade unions, and (b) state intervention to stabilize wage bargaining. There could be some tension between keeping wages down to benefit the supply side (reduce wage costs) and keeping them up to boost consumer demand – if labour productivity were sufficiently increased, this could achieve both objectives at once.

C. Sectoral Growth

The correlation between productivity growth and output growth at the national (macroeconomic) level broke down at the sectoral level. Some industries grew relatively fast and others, especially older industries like leather or traditional textiles, grew quite slowly, with the relative rates being fairly similar across most of the AICs (Advanced Industrial

4 E.g. Kaldor 1966.
5 Corsi 1991, ch. 5; cf. p. 73 above.
6 See p. 46.
7 Cf. pp. 85–6 above.
8 Von Tunzelmann 1992b.

Countries). However, some of the industries whose output was growing relatively slowly were also experiencing quite high productivity growth, because they were releasing labour and other resources. Salter (1966) tried to show that this inter-sectoral movement of labour from industries of slow growth to industries of fast growth accounted for a substantial proportion of the aggregate industrial growth, but later research does not appear to support this finding.[9] On the other side, demand-oriented scholars like Kaldor (1966) argued that the pace was set by leading manufacturing sectors, with other activities like the services sectors adjusting their output and employment accordingly.

D. Fluctuations

The postwar boom of the 1950s and 1960s, on which this chapter will concentrate, has to be seen in the context of the even longer period of instability and insecurity that preceded it. The mass unemployment of the 1930s provided the immediate context for the reorientation of Keynesian economics towards the demand side and towards macroeconomic management. One of the most depressive aspects of the Great Slump of the 1930s had been the erection of tariff barriers as each country tried vainly to protect its farmers and industrialists from the effects of slumps in other countries. This simply had the result of reinforcing the downward spiral. Keynes's own greatest efforts were expended at a monetary conference at Bretton Woods in 1944, which conceived the World Bank and the International Monetary Fund, and thus effectively the postwar 'dollar standard' of quasi-fixed exchange rates revolving around the stability of the dollar as the key currency. The problem of tariff barriers and other obstacles to international trade were attacked by setting up GATT in 1947/8, and that of co-ordination of growth and macroeconomic policies by the founding the OEEC (later the OECD) in 1948, following a direction suggested by the Marshall Plan. Thus postwar growth tried to take a more expansionary and forward-looking perspective, and above all to stress international co-ordination in place of the interwar 'beggar thy neighbour'. However, it seems probable that explanations of postwar growth which attribute stability to the monetary and trade systems have things back to front, in the same way and for the same reasons as the attribution of growth before the First World War to the Gold Standard and Free Trade. Causality ran the other way – in both cases economies in strong trading positions (Britain before 1914, the USA from the late 1940s to the late 1960s) were prepared

9 Von Tunzelmann 1982, 1992b.

to act as 'drivers' to the vehicle representing the international economic system.[10]

E. Long Waves

As well as these changes in analysis and policy on the demand side, some long-wave scholars have drawn particular attention to the role of the 1930s in promulgating a new wave of technological change on the supply side.[11] Some, like Mensch (1979), place particular stress on the so-called 'depression trigger' along the lines of Schumpeter's 'creative destruction', that severe slump signals the irretrievable end of old paradigms and encourages the discovery of radical breakthroughs. Others, like Freeman,[12] instead argue that scientific advances are randomly distributed in time, but are likely to become commercialized innovations in times of upswing, so placing greater emphasis on the revival of the later 1930s (it will be recalled that Schumpeter himself thought that the 1930s Slump was too 'destructive' to be at all 'creative'). The issue remains open.

It was noted in Chapter 3 that long-wave theories could be classified according to the perception of the major dynamic factor, variously as innovation-led, investment-led, labour-oriented or materials-oriented.[13] Depending on which of these one pursues, it is possible to suggest quite different chronologies for the 20th-century long waves. None of these alone is able to account adequately for the long postwar boom – the obvious next step is to combine elements from each of them. Freeman's recent emphasis on 'new technology systems', which stresses the diffusion of innovations as much as their discovery, seems one appropriate way to do this.[14] The remainder of this chapter will examine the 'new system' in the postwar upswing, while the next chapter looks at how it appeared to fall apart in the downswing.

II: TECHNOLOGY

A. Product and Process Innovation

The product cycle models noted in Chapter 1 argue that product innovations come earliest in the lifecycle of new industries, with process innovations

---

10 Kindleberger 1973.
11 Cf. p. 99 above.
12 In Freeman *et al.* 1982.
13 Delbeke 1981.
14 Freeman and Perez 1988.

appearing in greater numbers once the basic designs and types of goods become standardized. The long-wave literature has attempted to distinguish product from process innovations in similar manner, although the definitions of what is a major innovation have to be rather arbitrary. Kleinknecht (1981) argues that evidence on major innovations supports a surge of product innovations in the 1930s, when demand was 'latent' and beginning to rise, that improvement and process innovations were at their strongest in the 1950s, while further upstream scientific instruments peaked in the 1960s. This indeed appears to confirm the product cycle model and suggests that it can help explain the pattern of the long wave (products to processes, thence to basic science), but the quality of the evidence remains controversial. Individual studies instead stress the great complementarity between product and process innovations, e.g. in the development of semiconductors (the main process innovation following the invention of the transistor in 1947 being the search for pure silicon). The relationship of product to process innovation, and of both to wider techno-economic trends, needs further research.

Analyses of growth since the 1930s have emphasized a range of 'new industries', such as motor vehicles, chemicals, artificial fibres and household durables. These have been subject to the same type of debate as that over innovation, i.e. whether they were the result of 'creative destruction' in the Slump or rising prosperity afterwards. Yet they do not represent quite the same phenomenon, because their growth rested on technological breakthroughs that were for the most part 30-60 years old by this stage;[15] in other words, they were the fruition of the major advances of the previous 'Kondratiev'. It would seem that the commercialization of innovations to the point of making a major contribution to national economies takes a full long wave to take effect, as already suggested in Chapter 3. Most of the technological breakthroughs of the 1930s, like television or jet engines, were not commercialized until after the Second World War.

B. Role of R&D

Whatever the precise pattern of innovation, there seems little doubt about the importance of organized research. As formal R&D grew in importance, the role of individual inventors waned – 78 per cent of US patents went to individuals in 1906, but this had fallen to 40 per cent by 1957. Thus industrial research became professionalized. Mowery and Rosenberg show that research intensity was correlated with the survival and growth of

---

15 Von Tunzelmann 1982.

individual firms.[16] As noted in Chapter 6, these authors demonstrated the complementarity between contracted-out research, increasingly for routine investigation in the interwar USA but more importantly for standardization, and in-house research, which had to tackle the rising complexity and idiosyncrasy of technology for particular firms. R&D departments broke away from mainstream production, partly because of the need to take much longer-term perspectives. Carl Bosch, director of R&D and later chairman of I.G. Farben, the giant interwar German chemicals combine, argued that a great research project took ten years to produce, gave ten years of substantial returns, then another ten years of sagging returns. 'It is not here to give big profits to its shareholders. Our guide and our duty is to work for those who come after us to establish the processes on which they will work.'[17] So R&D departments and laboratories developed their own momentum and dynamics.[18]

There were at least two other reasons that became increasingly pertinent to conducting R&D in-house. One was that, in order to benefit from 'spillovers' from R&D conducted in other firms (or other countries), one had to have a degree of 'absorptive capacity',[19] which came most readily from conducting one's own research in the area. The second was that it became common in a number of oligopolistic industries to 'pool' patents. In industries such as chemicals this was even done on an international basis, which to some extent obviated the need to conduct one's own R&D in other countries. But in order to have credibility in sharing in the patent pool, one had to be able to deliver to it patents of one's own. Even in supposedly individualistic capitalistic economies, sharing of such kinds is so common that it is almost the norm, but it will be offered only if there is some expectation of reciprocity.[20]

Studies in both the USA and UK showed the overwhelming importance of manufacturing for generating measured innovations,[21] confirming the central role ascribed to manufacturing in the unbalanced demand models of growth such as that of Kaldor (1966). Innovation fanned out from a smallish group of key innovating sectors – hence we can apply Rostow's leading sector concept to technology, or alternatively Sraffa's concept of 'basic' goods.[22] Such leading technology sectors were typically characterized by higher than average R&D though some of them (like

16 Mowery and Rosenberg 1989, ch. 4.
17 Hayes 1987, pp. 355–6.
18 Freeman 1982, ch. 3.
19 Cohen and Levinthal 1989.
20 Von Hippel 1989.
21 Scherer 1982; Robson *et al.* 1988; OECD 1992, ch. 2.
22 Sraffa 1960; Corsi 1991, ch. 5.

machinery) were more design-intensive than R&D-intensive. The main point was that the payoff to any such R&D has to be seen in the light of the interaction with users, who sometimes gained more of the benefit than did the innovation producers themselves.

The successful development of catalytic cracking in the 1930s, studied for its organizational impact below, was the world's largest single R&D project before the atomic bomb at the end of the Second World War, and evolved into a consortium headed by Standard Oil of New Jersey which included Shell, Anglo-Iranian (BP), Texaco, I.G. Farben and Kellogg for the construction.[23] Thus with the growing complexity of advance in technological systems, even the largest firms pooled their resources.

The rising scale on which R&D appeared to be needed could have provided an obstacle for SMFs. One solution was 'co-operative research', which on a formal basis developed first in the UK through 'Research Associations' (RAs) set up in many industries after the First World War. These were intended to be most active in industries characterized by a prevalence of SMFs, which in fact covered many industries in the UK. Their work has been rated as satisfactory, and large firms soon joined some of the RAs, mainly to share complementary research they were conducting in-house with the Associations.[24] The Research Association idea was copied in due course by France, Germany and (much later, but possibly more successfully) Japan. But in the UK (at least) they were unable to remedy the basic deficiency, which was the lack of an equivalent 'receiving mechanism' of in-house R&D in the firms. Studies in a number of countries have confirmed that in-house and externally performed R&D are not substitutes but complements, along the lines of the 'two faces' argument noted above and in Chapter 6. Moreover, the scale of R&D operations remained too small and diffused to wreak great changes.

The USA dominated early postwar R&D, with aggregate formal expenditures on R&D still three times those of the whole of Western Europe as late as the early 1960s.[25] Especially important was the Federal government, which at its maximum in the early 1960s funded two-thirds of formal US R&D, mostly through the Department of Defense (DoD), Atomic Energy Commission (AEC), and the National Aeronautics and Space Agency (NASA).[26] Much of this federally-funded research had modest civilian spillover. Thus 57 per cent of the huge American R&D expenditure of the early 1960s went on defence, nuclear energy and space, and only 31 per cent represented industrial research proper, which narrowed

23 Freeman 1982, ch. 2.

24 Federation of British Industries 1961; Mowery 1984.

25 Freeman and Young 1965, p. 73.

26 Mowery and Rosenberg 1989, ch. 6.

the advantage over Western Europe in the latter. Nevertheless much of the Federal funding was well targeted, through often employing the laboratories of private firms, or universities in the case of basic research, to perform the actual R&D.

C. Role of Science

The rise of industrially relevant science from the latter 19th century was referred to in Chapters 5 and 6. The areas in which science and technology directly overlapped, however, long remained somewhat limited,[27] with chemicals the main connection, as in the German chemicals industry. The strongest links involved the *coupling* of science-push or technology-push with demand-pull;[28] for example, in the early computer industry, IBM – though a late entrant and lacking many of the specific technological capabilities – quickly took over the lead from earlier and more technologically qualified entrants such as General Electric or RCA, because of its much longer dominance in the key markets of office equipment and business data-processing.

Science remained somewhat hit-and-miss in its ability to predict behaviour that was most 'needed' by industry. Freeman notes that one of the major objectives of the early R&D labs in German chemicals firms like BASF and Hoechst was the attempt from around 1880 to produce synthetic indigo dyes.[29] Commercialization failed for about a decade and a half, when finally a research worker's thermometer broke inside the reactor vessel and spilled mercury into the mixture, which then crystallized. Similar 'accidents' accounted for the discovery of penicillin by Fleming – allegedly the result of working in a filthy lab – and, a little less fortuitously, the discovery of polyethylene at ICI in the early 1930s – originally a dirty residue found at the bottom of the test-tube. As Price (1965) stressed, the dynamics (or our paradigms) of science and technology continued to remain rather distinct, as did their motives; but science had an important role to play in the education of technologists, especially in raising questions and suggesting procedures (like the test-tube) for solving puzzles.

D. National Differences

Little of the USA's early technological lead came from science, indeed many of the leading industries and management consultants of the early 20th-century USA were averse to science, e.g. F.W. Taylor. The importance

---

27 Price 1965.

28 Freeman 1982, chs 5, 10.

29 *Ibid.*, p. 31.

to American industry of having a well-educated and well-trained population, based on the early moves towards a public system of universal primary education has been referred to in Chapter 6. However, the American record in *secondary* education until the interwar years was little better than the British or French and well behind the German one. Porter considers that it still falters at this level.[30] Nelson (1990a) puts the main emphasis on widespread *higher* education in the USA, and especially its focus on practical education. The Federal land grant provision for founding colleges (1862) played an especially important role in this emphasis on practicality – Cornell and the Massachusetts Institute of Technology (MIT) being examples of land-grant colleges which became distinguished in engineering. US engineering education from the 1920s became especially oriented to the needs of big business.[31]

With the huge expansion of Federal research funding during and after the Second World War, universities and colleges moved into the lead in high-tech American industries, pushed by sponsors such as Vannevar Bush and his Office of Scientific Research and Development in 1945. Bush's book, *Science: the Endless Frontier* (1945), helped re-create the notion of a frontier to which the aspiring young American could 'Go West' (or in this case, often East) – an intellectual rather than a geographical 'frontier'. This was not just limited to native Americans: the result of the war also led to an influx of top scientific talent (including German scientists) into the USA. When the Russians launched the Sputnik satellite in 1957, there was a renewed attempt to push ahead American science, but to some extent at the cost of technology.

With such postwar expansion, American innovation came to lead the world, but to a lesser extent in the industries that had represented the advanced technologies of the first half of the 20th century (chemicals, metal-working, synthetics, plastics), where Germany and some other European countries retained some parity. Instead, the USA dominated in new sectors, most conspicuously electronics; again partly inspired by the demands of the military and space agencies during and after the Second World War, where the coupling to the expanded science base and to the advanced engineering skills bred in universities like MIT was strongest. America also led more broadly in the rate of commercialization of new technologies and products, owing considerably to its longer dominance in managerial and marketing skills.

The process of catching up with the USA, which began in Western Europe in the early 1950s, and which is at the heart of the alleged 'convergence' hypothesis (cf. Chapter 3), was thus not just a simple process of borrowing

30 Porter 1990, p. 520.
31 Lazonick 1990, pp. 231–2.

US technology: it required major indigenous efforts. In the early 1960s, gross expenditure on R&D in the USA was about four times as high in absolute terms and twice as high in relative terms as in five leading West European countries – two decades later the latter had caught up in research intensity, despite a slowdown in the UK.[32] Each country to an extent built on its own specific pattern of interactions with resources and capabilities, so the result was as much a question of parallel as of convergent technological paths. Labour productivity data for various manufacturing sectors show no catch-up pattern *within* each sector.[33] This notion of separate paths constitutes one of the basic propositions of the recent emphasis on distinct 'national systems of innovation'. The combination of the ways in which S&T was organized, firms and industries were structured, and markets were developed, conspired to keep many countries in tracks with which they were familiar.[34] Major changes of direction required some break-up of the existing 'national system of production', as happened in postwar France, when the state took a proactive role in altering the whole basis of French industry.[35] More often the activities of the state towards new directions were simply an addition to the existing structure, which continued to thrive in its more traditional ways, often much more successfully than the state managed to achieve.[36] However, countries which failed to put all the pieces together in either existing or new activities, notably Britain, fell by the wayside: still excelling in science, but with weak industrial commitment except in a few sectors such as pharmaceuticals.

E. Economic Characteristics

The obvious inference to be drawn from the patterns of organizational change in the preceding period, as set out in the last chapter – i.e. trends towards giant firms and plants and towards the 'deskilling' of labour on assembly lines – would be that the bias of technological change was strongly labour-saving. This view would be expected to take on even greater force after the Second World War, when growth rates of capital were vastly higher than in the insecure interwar period.

However, specific empirical studies failed to find quite as clear-cut an association as might have been expected. Keynes (1937) thought that innovation was becoming less capital-intensive, because of a shift towards services. In some celebrated studies, Leontief found that US exports were

---

32 Freeman 1987, pp. 7–13.

33 Broadberry 1993.

34 E.g. Keck (in Nelson 1993) for Germany.

35 Chesnais, in Nelson 1993.

36 E.g. in Italy, cf. Malerba in *ibid.*

on balance labour-intensive rather than labour-saving,[37] despite the fact that the country had the world's highest real wage levels. This contradicted any simple Ricardian or neoclassical notion of substituting capital for labour when the price of labour was high. Leontief argued instead that US export goods were research-intensive or knowledge-intensive, so that the apparent labour intensity was a mask for human capital intensity, i.e. knowledge 'embodied' in the workforce. Moreover, where there seemed to be a greater amount of true labour-saving, the labour saved was mainly unskilled, so reinforcing the tendency towards human capital intensity and contradicting the notion of a bias towards 'deskilling'.

The long-wave model of Freeman provides an alternative perspective, by drawing on his notion that the expansionary phases of the long wave are characterized by putting more labour to work, while the contractionary 'rationalization' phases involving cutting labour costs and employment.[38] As with many of the long-wave hypotheses, we really need a greater run of time series (perhaps more than can possibly be got) to test this proposition adequately.

Tendencies towards greater capital intensity that might have been expected from the organizational changes were offset, in part by the selfsame technical changes; for example, electricity permitted the establishment of small as well as large factories (see below), and new materials like plastics substituted for steel. As these examples suggest, the technologies utilized, especially in the USA, did appear to be energy-intensive (based on cheap oil and electricity) and materials-intensive. However, the bias towards capital-intensity was less potent than often imagined, partly because of the capital-saving advances such as have just been noted.

F. Technological Trajectories

According to the definitions employed in this book, technological trajectories represent the confrontation between 'natural' technological heuristics and the economic and social environments. Thus economic factors such as cheap fuels, abundant and often new materials, and rising human capital in terms of highly educated people, plus social factors including attitudes towards skills and sizes of firms, interacted with the logic of scientific and technological development as described above. Crucial science-based technologies like chemicals and later electronics became embedded in a widening range of user industries and their products.

---

37 Leontief 1953, 1956.

38 See p. 98 above.

Rather than a single dominant paradigm in manufacturing, this activity led to the rise of several technological paradigms. However, it by and large remained the case that these paradigms did not greatly compete with one another. There existed a range of sectors where the chemicals-related paradigm operated (e.g. synthetic materials and plastics, petroleum, pharmaceuticals), another set of sectors where the electrical–electronic paradigm operated, etc. Although chemicals-related sectors obviously used a certain amount of machinery or electrical equipment, the mode of problem-solving continued to be dominated by heuristics relevant to chemicals, and the same in other cases. In the electricals-related fields, the paradigm continued to be one of electrical operation (components, etc.) driven on machine principles – the so-called 'electromechanical' paradigm, with the switch to a fully digitalized 'electronics' paradigm beginning to intrude only very late in this period (and still far from completed today). Although there were overlaps, this kind of problem-solving, with a one-to-one relationship between the type of problem and the area of technological search, contrasts with the type of 'hyperchoice' of recent years, described in the next chapter.

For the great majority of manufacturing sectors – those which were not 'science-based' in the sectoral taxonomy of Pavitt (1984) – the relationship between machinery and motive power continued to lie at the heart of the choices of techniques. Whereas in the 19th century there was parallel development of energy *centralization* (through steam engines, etc.) and machinery *decentralization*, in the 20th century one could say that the reverse occurred. As already mentioned, the rise of electricity and the internal combustion engine allowed 'fractionalized' power, viable even in very small user sizes. The generation of the electricity, however, became increasingly centralized in massive generating plants – it was the networking of electricity through regional or national grids which permitted its broad dispersion. Thus production of energy in the form of electrification was increasingly centralized while its use was increasingly decentralized.

In the individual factory or plant, the use of this networked power allowed the further development of a kind of division of labour in the machinery, based on the specialization according to process which got under way during the Industrial Revolution – what is described in this book as 'capital process'. As previously noted, the early 20th century witnessed the installation of flow and assembly lines, e.g. in motor vehicles. It is not surprising that many see 'automation', especially in conjunction with mass production, as the techno-organizational paradigm of the 20th century. However, some recent writers have emphasized that automation has come slowly and incompletely. Martin Bell (1972) argued that automation involves three aspects – transformation, transfer and control – each with several levels of degree. Mechanized *transformation* was a predominant characteristic of 19th-century industry, as shown in earlier chapters, while at the other extreme, mechanized *control* is only recently becoming well established (through computer control, etc.). It follows that the major advance of the earlier part of the 20th century was in the mechanization of *transfer*, as represented for example by the 'Fordist' assembly line. Mechanization of control was possible only to a limited degree, in conditions of producing single products on dedicated assembly lines.[39]

Thus machinery became integrated not at the level of individual machines or functions, where the division of labour principle continued to dominate, but in terms of combining the various machines into a factory *system*. In the 19th century the motive power acted as a unit for the whole system, and a stoppage to one machine could stop the entire factory. The 'unit production' system that gradually emerged in the early 20th century[40] allowed the motive power plus machine to operate individually. With the steps taken towards interrelating the machines through mechanization of transfer, automation brought about a machine-based rather than an energy-based factory system.

III: ORGANIZATION

A. Capital Process

In the advanced industries of the early 20th century, batch production was replaced by flow production, as previously seen for some liquids and semi-liquids in the late 19th century. The development of fluid catalytic cracking in oil refineries from the 1930s, as an example of the shift to flow production was facilitated by six major developments:[41]

- i an enormous growth in the market for basic chemicals (soda, ammonia, chlorine, ethylene, propylene, etc.), i.e. in Smith's 'extent of the market';
- ii a switch in the basic feedstock materials from coal derivatives to oil and natural gas;
- iii increasing availability of electricity, and the development of electro-thermal and electrolytic processes;
- iv improved equipment and components (pumps, filters, valves, etc.);

39 Blackburn *et al.* 1985, chs 2–3.

40 Devine 1983; see Chapter 6 above.

41 Freeman 1982, ch. 2.

v new instruments for monitoring and controlling flows, also for testing;

vi application of basic scientific knowledge to production, especially the development of chemical engineering.

While these may have varied in individual importance for the evolution of the new system, it is apparent that they run the gamut of demand and supply influences (growth of market opportunity, shift in natural resources, electrification paradigm, further development of mechanical paradigm, standardization, increased science base). The consortium approach to reorganizing the system hastened the breakthrough in this case (see p. 226 above); in other industries the evolution of the new system could take much longer.

Development of flow processing thus involved speeding-up, assisted by electrification and by a host of minor innovations such as high-grade materials (steel, etc.), faster machinery, improved lubrication and use of ball and roller bearings. Time was saved via reduced downtime, faster throughput and better machine co-ordination. One example of a major innovation which achieved all three was found in coal-mining, where the Anderton shearer-loader allowed all three daily shifts in the mine to work on cutting, instead of using the second for loading and the third for setting-up.[42] As implied in Bell's analysis, the bottleneck or 'reverse salient' in manufacturing shifted from mechanization of transformation, now well advanced with its heuristics basically understood, to mechanization of the flow between operations (transfer), in similar vein to Smith's second advantage of the division of labour. Production was organized on a serial basis. As Marshall pointed out, scale economies came from applying the Babbage principle concerning skilled labour to machinery.[43]

The archetype of mass production was of course the automobile assembly line, pioneered by Henry Ford or others for the Model T in 1909–13.[44] On the assembly line, the downtime between consecutive jobs was minimized by bringing the partially assembled product to the worker along the line, rather than getting the worker to move to the product. Ford evaluated the success of the moving assembly line by the reduction of labour time per chassis (etc.).[45] Labour saving occurred *as a result*.[46] The assembly line involved the setting up of a dedicated line of extremely inflexible machinery, and to pay itself off required huge production runs of highly standardized products. The minimum efficient scale (MES) for the basic

42 Townsend 1976; Ashworth 1986.

43 Marshall 1890/1961, p. 265; cf. p. 36 above.

44 Ford 1922, ch. 5; Hounshell 1984, ch. 6.

45 Ford 1922, pp. 82–9.

46 *Ibid.*, p. 90.

elements, e.g. chassis, body and engine, typically required sales for several years, militating against frequent changes in these components.

Mass production in the 20th century has thus often been loosely described as 'Fordist', although in my view Fordism remained an extreme case rather than being typical of all manufacturing. European car manufacturers tried imitating the assembly line shortly after Ford, but as noted in Chapter 5, often to little avail. They thus faced severe American competition after the First World War, when European countries lacked the scale and motivation to match American process innovations like the assembly line. The assembly line in the USA was intended primarily to raise labour productivity, whereas in Europe it was seen as raising capital productivity.[47] French adopters of the assembly line concentrated first on issues of space and machinery, and only later turned their attention to issues of saving time.[48] Firms like Fiat avoided excessive installations of dedicated machinery in favour of greater product flexibility.[49] The European industry was more technology-led than process-led; for example, in regard to the crucial question of the car's power–weight ratio, Ford in the USA reduced the weight while Renault in France improved the power.[50] Demand factors were, however, as significant as supply in differentiating the European vehicles industry (see below, p. 242).

B. Labour Process

Though usually regarded as highly labour-saving, the kinds of labour saved by the assembly line were typically unskilled and often transient labour, as in the tyre industry.[51] The evidence suggests that the object was to speed up work rather than workers, i.e. directed at time-saving rather than labour-saving or labour-diluting. That the workers were often overworked is, however, difficult to deny (see p. 208). The Braverman (1974) interpretation of the assembly line as deskilling therefore remains controversial, not least because of the continued role of the workforce itself and its unions in job control. Perhaps too much has rested on the experience of Ford himself, who boasted that 43 per cent of his automotive workers could be trained in one day and another 36 per cent in one week.[52]

Problems such as altered skill structures, intense pressure of workpace and severe employment fluctuations, led workers to seek new forms of

47 Fridenson 1978.
48 Lewchuk 1984; Tolliday and Zeitlin 1986, ch. 2.
49 *Ibid.*, p. 86.
50 Milward and Saul 1973, p. 219.
51 D. Nelson 1987.
52 Ford 1922, p. 110; Granick 1967, p. 85.

combination to resolve them. The typical solution attempted was to replace traditional craft-based unions with industrial unions, which would co-ordinate disputes with management across the whole automobile or similar industry. Such unions emerged in countries like the USA and France in the later 1930s, but for the most part remained squeezed between governmental or managerial hostility from above and shop-floor conflicts over goals and procedures from below.[53]

So far as management's role in labour process was concerned, the equivalent paradigm to Fordism was 'scientific management', which became known as 'Taylorism' after the publication of F.W. Taylor's short but influential work, *The Principles of Scientific Management* (1911). Taylor argued that the needs of employers and employees could be reconciled through combining high wages with low labour costs, and the way to do this was to get employees to work at the fastest possible pace consistent with productive efficiency.[54] Significantly, he had been one of the discoverers of high-speed steel. While Ford wanted maximum throughput from machines, Taylor wanted it from workers, typically in bureaucratic organizations.[55] A task like shovelling or bricklaying could be reduced to a 'science' to determine the maximum speed for the task (determined by 'speed' and 'feed') and the optimum speed for the worker.[56] Though Taylor spoke of shared responsibilities and shared benefits, in practice managers employing scientific management organized while workers simply performed.[57] Taylor thus espoused such principles as tight supervision, effort-related payment systems (differential piece rates etc.), bureaucratic task allocation, and work-planning methods, like the notorious 'time and motion' studies.[58]

Though Taylorism derived from Taylor's own practical experience in engineering, it is often regarded as a logical development of Babbage's fourth advantage of the division of labour,[59] in which jobs are allocated on the basis of individual human capabilities for hard physical or mental work. By considering the 'carrot' as well as the 'stick', Taylor hoped to resolve the conflict which Marx had described concerning the 'social relations of production'. Even with fully machine-paced work, as on assembly lines, scientific management could still be used for the large numbers of

53 Tolliday and Zeitlin 1986, pp. 7–11.
54 Taylor 1911, ch. 1.
55 Littler 1982; Hounshell 1984, pp. 251–3.
56 Taylor 1911, ch. 2.
57 Braverman 1974, pp. 112–21; Lazonick 1990, p. 214.
58 For a comparatively balanced assessment, see Marshall 1919, bk. II, chs 11–12; Marx (1887/1965, p. 554), opposed systems in which the labourers effectively exploited themselves.
59 Babbage 1832, pp. 137–8.

employees who were not actively machine-paced, e.g. in metal-working, maintenance, supervisory roles, etc. In practice, in industry it became directed at foremen and gang bosses rather than at Babbage's notion of skilled workers. According to the 'Régulation School', it became embodied in specialized equipment and thus subverted into capital process and Fordism.

Following the principle of Weber that the crux of managerial capitalism was 'rational capital accounting',[60] American engineers in industry focused first on cost accounting and consequently on cost reduction.[61] By contrast, German engineers had a much stronger role as technicians (see Chapter 5 above). Thus American MNCs in their *European* factories, despite using American machine tools, were said to produce 10 per cent to 30 per cent less than in the USA; probably reflecting the lower emphasis on cost reduction in Europe.[62] European firms did, however, find Taylorism and piecework more appropriate to their needs than Fordism and high wages.[63]

C. Managerial Control

The pressure for standardized products under Fordism went alongside a hierarchical and centralized form of management. For single-product firms this was a logical enough association, but firms were increasingly multi-product. Companies rivalling Ford, especially General Motors after the First World War, aimed to market a whole range of cars satisfying different market segments.[64] The most straightforward development of linear management was the 'U-form' (Unitary form), in which central HQ contained middle-management strata responsible for co-ordinating, supervising and allocating resources to the different *functional* tasks (R&D, production, marketing, etc.), and with lower management answerable to the relevant functional manager at this middle level for each particular line of product. Top management was supposed to carry out strategic planning. The U-form proved unsatisfactory in practice: the functional units could not be adequately co-ordinated with one another when each had responsibility for a wide range of product lines, and in its turn, top management had to step in too often and take over too many non-strategic responsibilities. The consequence, pioneered by chairmen such as Alfred P. Sloan at General Motors, was the 'M-form' (Multidivisional form), with its antecedents in the 19th-century railroad companies as described in Chapter 6. In the M-

60 Weber 1927, chs 22, 30.
61 Clark 1923; Locke 1984, ch. 3.
62 Litterer 1961.
63 Tolliday and Zeitlin 1986, ch. 1; Kogut 1993, pp. 184–7.
64 Chandler 1962, ch. 3.

form company, each major *product* or *regional* line ('line of business') becomes a separate division, and carries out all relevant functions (R&D, production, etc.). Central office overviews all of them and ultimately allocates financial resources among them, typically using a 'profit centre' approach, i.e. using indicators like the ROI (return on investment) to flag the most profitable divisions. The M-form company had some similarities with the holding company structure being evolved by financial interests, but differed especially in the role of central HQ (the HQ of a holding company exists only to hold shares in subsidiaries). In effect, as Oliver Williamson[65] argues, the central office of an M-form company became a mini-internal capital market, responsible for allocating funds to the different divisions. This reflected a shift in balance of emphasis of what was required of the businessman from technology towards finance, not least because financial owners often withdrew from active management though not from control.[66]

The essence of success in an M-form company has, however, often been overlooked in a too-common functionalist notion of how the bureaucratic division of labour should be carried out. Its success in practice came from the extent to which line-and-staff specialists of the kind noted in Chapter 6 were converted into generalists with some knowledge of processes on the shopfloor, and with effective powers of decision-making about transforming technological into product knowledge.[67] Paradoxically, the success of the M-form company seemed to owe as much to 'mere management' as to 'entrepreneurship'. The work of Chandler on multidivisional companies has been understandably obsessed with entrepreneurs like Sloan and Pierre du Pont – without the likes of whom the experiment could not have got off the ground – rather than the middle management whom I see as the catalysts in the reaction.

Though the M-form structure in the USA developed rapidly in the years 1945–60, other countries followed the USA into M-form structures only with a considerable lag.[68] The UK continued to be dominated by 'family capitalism', resisting the encroachment of professional management.[69] France also pursued family capitalism, but allied to finance to a greater degree than was the case in Britain. A few German companies were relatively quick to espouse modern management – Siemens even had a multidivisional structure before the First World War, i.e. before many Americans – but within a more co-operative and less competitive capitalist

65 Williamson 1975, chs 8–9; 1985, ch. 11.

66 Veblen 1921; and see Chapter 8 below.

67 Lazonick, in Dosi *et al.* 1992, pp. 134–7.

68 Kogut 1993, pp. 191–7.

69 Only two British companies were M-form by 1939, according to Hannah 1976.

framework than operated in the USA.[70] The *Mittelstand* of SMFs was much more typical in Germany, however. European companies moved towards M-form structures after the Second World War, prompted partly by the arrival of many American MNCs in newer industries. The Japanese caught up rapidly in management techniques in the 1950s and 1960s, but the structure of Japanese companies is too different to assess in this way (see Chapter 10).

The national differences do not represent just leads and lags in organizational behaviour, contrary to the impression given in some of the literature (Chandler's earlier work is a serious offender). The nature of production organization is constrained by the 'institutions' or 'ideology' within which it is located in particular countries (see Figure 2.2). It thus depends in part on the legal and political environment, which can take varying views about the rightness or wrongness of big business and its manifestations.[71] Hostile corporate takeovers are normally regarded as legitimate in the USA but rarely so in Germany and still less in Japan. Thus to see the M-form as the acme of organizational perfection is misleading – rather it should be seen as a form which was well suited to its particular institutional and technological environment but perhaps not to others. Since the 1970s the American companies have been out-performed by those from countries with different ideologies (see Chapters 8 and 10); moreover, in countries like Britain, a number of family-based and similar firms have out-performed the managerialist ones in this period.

D. Multinational Companies

Many large companies became internationalized more or less at the time they became large, especially in the final years of the 19th century. The notion that they are recent phenomena is quite mistaken. In the case of European multinationals, the dominant firms today are much the same as they were at the turn of the century,[72] allowing of course for the rise of some new industries. However, the MNCs have changed in form and focus since the Second World War.

(a) As some giant firms moved to M-form or similar structures after the First World War, so their international operations frequently became a new division, or different divisions for the different regions in which they operated. This cut across the line of business as the determinant of the divisional basis and weakened its logic.

70 Chandler 1990, part IV.
71 E.g. Davis and North 1971.
72 Franko 1976; Hertner and Jones 1986; Keck (in Nelson 1993).

(b) Until the 1960s, the general pattern was to shift only certain functions abroad, with marketing typically being the first function to emigrate. Such production as was moved went normally to the next-wealthiest countries, following consumption, i.e. for demand-side reasons.[73] But most of the core and learning functions stayed at home.

From the 1960s, production was sometimes shifted ('offshore') to lower-wage countries, mainly to achieve cost savings in labour-intensive activities. The implications will be developed further in Chapter 11 below, but it may be noted here that the assumed savings in labour costs often failed to materialize – hourly wage rates in Volkswagen's Mexico plant were one-fifth of those in Germany, but total costs per vehicle remained stubbornly higher.[74] Low labour costs per unit of time require time-saving process improvements to translate into low labour costs per unit of output. Ohmae argues that direct labour costs in assembly operations have fallen from around 25 per cent of product costs to just 5–10 per cent,[75] so the payoff to lower hourly wage rates has dropped sharply. MNCs have found only limited breathing space from cheap offshore labour.

IV: FINANCE

A. Size of Firms

Fordism involved the establishment of large plants, in order to have viable throughput on the dedicated assembly lines. It would seem that this had an obvious link with the growth of large firms. Yet the link may not be as obvious as appears at first sight. Work done by Prais for the UK between 1930 and 1968 showed that, in looking at the *share* of large plants and large firms in total UK manufacturing, that of large *firms* increased considerably over this period but that of large *plants* scarcely increased at all. This appears to contradict the economies of scale argument for the growth of large firms, since as Prais points out, one would expect such economies to be exhibited at the plant as well as the firm level.[76] The lack of any noteworthy rise in share of the large plants does not, however, prove that there were no economies of scale: merely that such scale economies in production cannot account for the growing share of large firms in manufacturing. The sources of growth of large firms must therefore be

73 Vernon 1966.
74 Tolliday and Zeitlin 1986, pp. 249–50.
75 Ohmae 1985, p. 3.
76 Prais 1976, ch. 3; see also Morroni 1992, ch. 11.

sought elsewhere, as I do below. The robustness of Prais's findings for other countries is unknown.[77]

The substantial post-Schumpeterian literature on the relationship between firm size and innovation has at least clarified the issues, if not as yet reached any general empirically validated conclusions. Studies divide in two ways:

i use of measures of innovation input (usually R&D employment or expenditure) vs. measures of innovation output (usually patents, sometimes leading innovations);

ii correlation of innovation with firm size vs. correlation with market power (the degree of concentration of an industry).

The correlation of innovation with market power has been referred to in Chapter 6; the consensus goes no further than that it all depends on the countries and/or industries concerned.[78] In regard to firm size rather than market power, many studies conducted on US data appear to find that medium-sized firms achieve relatively most in terms of innovation,[79] so giving some support to the attempted break-ups of very large firms through antitrust legislation, etc. However, in the UK, SPRU studies[80] seem to find the opposite – that both small and large firms were very significant for innovation, but the medium-sized less so. The issue clearly needs to be explored much further.

B. External Funding

The separation that opened up between ownership and management in the corporation in the late 19th century created possibilities for the aggressive introduction of financial empires into the ownership of industry, as has already been seen happening in the USA from ca. 1897. The outcome was the typical holding company structure and 'leverage', i.e. control through a slight majority holding (usually 51 per cent). In such a way, a tycoon like Samuel Insull in the electricity supply industry of the USA in the 1920s could, by just $1 of investment in his holding company, control $1750 in a distribution company at the bottom of his pyramid, such as the Georgia Light and Power Co. Such leverage had disastrous effects when external demand conditions deteriorated, as in the 1929 crash.[81] In the USA, the Glass–Steagall Act of 1933 severely limited the opportunities for banks and similar financial institutions to deal in industrial shares.

77 Though see Marshall 1919, App. N, for earlier US data.
78 For a lucid survey see Freeman 1982, ch. 6.
79 See the summaries in Kamien and Schwartz 1975, 1982.
80 E.g. Pavitt *et al.* 1987.
81 Galbraith 1955.

In the postwar period, ownership of industrial stocks and shares, especially in the USA and UK, has moved towards large financial pools; notably insurance companies, pension funds and mutual associations. For reasons given in Chapter 6, such financial interests tend to equate size and centralization with stability, and in his work on the UK economy described above, Prais concluded that involvement of the financial sector in ownership in this manner was the principal explanation for the relative growth of large firms in the UK.[82]

Banking systems have evolved very differently across countries, as writers like Gerschenkron stressed. The market-oriented banking systems of the USA and UK have concentrated on providing only working capital for industry – in the USA because of the Glass–Steagall Act, in the UK because that had been customary practice since the Industrial Revolution. In the interwar period, bank intervention in industry in the UK was required mainly for industrial restructuring in the light of prevailing depression, and the lead was taken centrally by the Bank of England.[83] When some demand for capital for new firms in new industries arose at the end of the 1930s, new institutions had to be created.[84] These have evolved into venture capital markets, with the most spectacular example being the Silicon Valley phenomenon in California in the 1970s (see Chapter 8). Schumpeter believed that the reason US industry grew so fast in the early 20th century was precisely because its banking system was so bad!

V: PRODUCTS

A. Marketing

The combination of large firms using assembly-line process technology and oligopolistic market structures discouraged competition based on pricing, because of the risk that under-cutting of prices would lead to a price war. These did indeed occur sporadically, mainly to try to force rivals out of business and thus increase one's market share, but were generally found ruinous for the producers as a whole and thus for the most part avoided. Competition thus became based on 'quality' differences, real or alleged. Containing as it did many of the world's leading oligopolistic firms, the USA continued to lead the way in mass marketing, for example by introducing commercial television twelve years before any other country.[85]

---

82 Prais 1976, ch. 5.
83 Sayers 1976, vol. 1, ch. 14.
84 Thomas 1982, ch. 5.
85 Porter 1990, p. 300.

The problem this raised lay on the side of production. It has been shown that, in automobile production, the economics of the assembly line required that the basic elements like the body-pressing and engine required runs of several years before recouping their costs of being set up, and therefore could not be changed in any significant way over this period. Henry Ford's dictum of 1909 that, 'Any customer can have a car painted any colour that he wants so long as it is black',[86] has entered the language. For the product-differentiated markets found in Europe,[87] this raised considerable difficulties. The attempts by Ford to dominate the British market in the 1920s with the Model T petered out, as the company tried to rely on its American strategies and products.[88] The different demand structure prevailing in Europe required the development of small cars.[89] The European solution to the conflict between mass production and differentiated consumption was to embellish the semi-finished product (motor car) with a host of minor frills which could be changed annually without reconfiguring the basic design.[90] A characteristic of the motor industry became the annual unveiling of new models, which the major producers undertook at the same time, e.g. at a Motor Show. Such new models generally differed only in inessentials from those of the previous year.

To persuade customers that these differences, between models of different years and models of different producers, were of significance was the role of the advertising industry. Through association with such mass-produced products, advertising and distribution reaped their own economies of scale, and Prais considers this as a further reason for the relative growth of large firms[91] – perhaps less important than the financial causes but more important than technological economies of scale. The primacy of marketing benefited American industry from its early dominance in the field, and encouraged its postwar success in world markets.

Since rival producers were producing fairly similar products, the speed with which they could expand sales of the new models was crucial to their market performance. US firms in the early postwar world appeared to have an absolute advantage in the rate at which they commercialized new products, including products deriving from innovation. 'Speed to market' meant more than just the advertising campaign.

---

86 Ford 1922, p. 72.
87 Cf. Chapter 5 above.
88 Lewchuk 1984; Tolliday and Zeitlin 1986, ch. 1.
89 Altshuler *et al.* 1985, ch. 2; Tolliday and Zeitlin 1986, pp. 3–4.
90 Maxcy and Silberston 1959, chs 5–7.
91 Prais 1976, ch. 4.

To the extent that prices were kept fairly rigid, profits depended partly on thus expanding sales and raising market share, and partly on reducing costs. Technologies and production processes were therefore directed to producing cheaper rather than better products, and relying on the advertising to maintain market presence. Ford himself asserted: 'Our policy is to reduce the price, extend the operations, and improve the article. You will notice that the reduction of price comes first'.[92] The shift to low-wage countries for production in the 1960s, pointed out above, represented a further stage in this search for cost-cutting. Consumers may not have obtained better products but certainly benefited from the downward trend in prices, enabling many to purchase such goods for the first time. For long stretches of time, prices fell almost as fast as output rose, so that the total value of sales rose only slowly. This reinforced the oligopolistic style of rivalry based on market share.

B. Finance and Distribution

To boost sales, oligopolistic producers of the new range of consumer durables (cars, household electrical appliances, etc.) tried to support consumption, through innovative financial and distributional practices.[93] Henry Ford pioneered both in the provision of generous customer credit towards the purchase of his vehicles, and in establishing networks of dealerships for locating sales close to the customers. The system of franchised dealers was increasingly adopted from the 1920s in order to cope with the proliferation of individual customer requirements.[94] In the UK, 'hire purchase' became a standard means for acquiring such consumer durables. By the 1950s, hire purchase was so rampant that it had become a significant macroeconomic issue, and in the annual Budget, the Chancellor of the Exchequer often altered the terms (interest rates, etc.) on which hire purchase could be conducted.

C. Demand

The counterpart of mass production was mass consumption. As already implied, the focus of growth was on consumer durables, i.e. items like motor cars or household appliances, which typically catered for income levels well above the minimum. Where was the *expansion* of this demand going to come from? Given the logic of the production process (assembly line) towards producing standardized products, the most obvious target was

92 Ford 1922, p. 146.
93 Olney 1989.
94 T.G. Marx 1985.

the 'affluent worker'. However, at the micro level, the pressures for cutting costs and towards labour-saving technological change were inappropriate for creating a class of affluent workers. Henry Ford led the way with his $5 a day paid to assembly-line workers,[95] representing a doubling of the usual pay-packet of the time, but even he was unable to sustain high wages under cost-cutting pressures in the 1920s. The 'Régulation School' thus emphasizes the degree of mismatch, particularly in the 1930s, between new 'régimes of accumulation' (new technologies and industries, Taylorism, M-form control, oligopolistic product markets) on the one side and the wider socio-political 'mode of regulation' on the other.[96] The latter includes wage payment systems and labour process, hence the interpretation has similarities with the Freeman–Perez view of structural conflicts (cf. Chapter 3), which also focused on the extent of mismatch during the 1930s. The solutions were found partly in war and partly in a macroeconomic revolution (see below), as the micro level proved unable to reconcile these mismatches.

As citizens became more affluent, they had less desire for the standardized goods which best suited the conditions of mass production, and increasingly sought status goods ('merit goods' or 'positional goods'), such as smart but not ostentatious motor cars. Orthodox Fordism proved unable to cope with such product heterogeneity, although the assembly-line lifetime could be extended by the addition of minor fripperies in the way described above. Ford in the USA therefore succumbed to the pressure from General Motors in the later 1920s, which targeted what its CEO, Alfred P. Sloan, called the 'mass-class market'.[97] The M-form organization which Sloan introduced at GM was better designed to adjust for such variations in products, but what was ultimately called for was increased process flexibility, as the next chapter shows. Though there was some move in this direction at the time in GM, particularly through increasing interchangeability of parts, the company in fact relied mainly on shifting the burden of product changes and fluctuations on to the workers, via lay-offs or similar. Competition moved away from innovation and into the kinds of minor styling and marketing efforts noted above.[98]

In Britain and Continental Europe, a considerable number of producers continued to aim at luxury markets, as for instance in cars; though producing very small quantities. Production process was here virtually immaterial, and costs very high, but some technological leadership was offered from segments like sports cars, racing cars and engines. Though

95 Ford 1922, chs 8–9.
96 Boyer, in Dosi *et al.* 1988; see also Piore and Sabel 1984, ch. 4.
97 *Ibid.*, pp. 60–63; Best 1990, pp. 67–9, 79.
98 Tolliday and Zeitlin 1986, p. 5.

most of these specialist firms disappeared or were swallowed up, some were able to establish market niches after the Second World War which held up better than their larger Fordist rivals.[99]

VI: GOVERNMENT POLICY

A. Technology – Science and Technology Policy

War was a major catalyst for direct government sponsoring of R&D and science. In the Second World War, the British discovered that they had lagged behind the Germans in the prewar years in what had come to be the high-tech areas related to military objectives – specifically depending on German suppliers for such things as optical glass (for binoculars), synthetic dyes (for uniforms, e.g. khaki) and even explosives. This proved a profound stimulus to catch up, although limited to military purposes.[100] The British government co-opted universities to work on relevant science, and in 1916 set up the DSIR (Department of Scientific and Industrial Research) to help co-ordinate useful applications of science. This had considerable civilian spillover in the interwar period, e.g. helping to create some of the foundations of the resurgent British chemicals industry and making the British aero-engine industry the world's technological leader by 1918 – both fields in which the UK has maintained considerable international strength up to the present day. But after the First World War, the interest of the British government in R&D largely dissipated.

The Second World War had a radical effect on American Federal government funding of R&D. The emphasis lay on government funding but the actual R&D often being carried out in the private sector. With the atomic bomb (Manhattan) project during this war and the impetus of the Cold War shortly after, Federal agencies concentrated their funding on 'Big Science' and projects oriented towards national security,[101] channelled through lavishly funded departments such as the DoD (Department of Defense) and NASA. Ergas (1987) in a critical assessment of government R&D policy in the USA and UK, describes this as 'mission-oriented'. He contrasts it with the 'diffusion-oriented' approach to government-funded R&D in countries like postwar Germany, Scandinavia, etc., where the primary emphasis has been on accessibility and dissemination, including a more important role for 'Little Science' and for SMFs. In his view, this

99 *Ibid.*, ch. 11; also Chapter 8 below.
100 Sanderson 1972, ch. 8.
101 Freeman 1982, ch. 9.

strategy has been far more successful in the long run. However, as Mowery and Rosenberg (1989) stress, one should take a broader view of science policy than simply the innovation effects, and include the significant impact on creating a scientific milieu or ideology, and not least the training of many would-be scientists.

In the USA, wartime military demands in ballistics led to the development of the computer; in the early 1950s the nuclear submarine programme shaped the technology of nuclear reactors; while in the late 1950s the space programme fostered the drive to miniaturization that led to the integrated circuit (all American ICs and half of its semiconductors went to meet military or space demands in the early 1960s).[102] Thus the military-based programmes had major civilian spin-off, especially in terms of establishing the technological heuristics. They were less successful in terms of the demand side, i.e. for promoting mass consumption. The difficulty with military-oriented production was twofold.

(a) In an obvious sense, much was wasted in terms of possible alternative products that might have better suited popular tastes, also military competition deflected brain-power and R&D expenditure away from more socially acceptable goods. Weaponry is self-evidently an area where technological progress may not serve society's best interests. Studies at the macroeconomic level show that the postwar growth rates of countries that had relatively high military expenditures were slower than those where they were low.[103]

(b) Military products are 'baroque', in Mary Kaldor's (1982) terminology, for two reasons. They tend to be backward-looking, in providing further and further refinements to the military technology actually tested in the previous war (by the mid-1960s this was a long gap). Second, they tend to be evaluated by technocratic criteria rather than by commercial standards, leading to expensive 'gold-plating' through over-elaboration.

However, these adverse effects took some time to show their full effect, and in the early postwar period the positive impact of the military on aggregate demand probably outweighed the negative impacts of 'crowding out' civilian spending or producing uncommercial products.

B. Organization – Competition Policy

Antitrust legislation came early in the rise of American big business, as recounted in Chapter 6. Its precise impact is debatable, but undoubtedly it helped frame an ideology in which merger activity beyond certain levels

---

102 Mowery and Rosenberg 1989, p. 147.

103 Fagerberg 1988.

was discouraged, and covert collaboration (pooling, cartels, etc.) was distinctly discouraged. Such legislation may inadvertently have encouraged the rise of conglomerates, by not preventing diversification into unrelated businesses. British policy under its postwar Labour government moved half-heartedly in the same direction, setting up the Monopolies and Mergers Commission (1948), etc., fostered by the same underlying set of legal attitudes opposing restraint of fair trade as in the USA.

These forms of competition policy had to grapple with tendencies towards large-scale organization that came on the one side from process changes such as automation, and on the other from international competition. Countries with different legal traditions, including many of the countries of Continental Europe, also had such conflicts but tended to opt for solutions that favoured large-scale enterprise and collaboration rather than competition. Such differences remain to this day a potent area for international trade wars, with the Americans and British insisting on international competition on 'level playing fields', i.e. their type of playing field. In an era of global competition the role of national competition policy is unclear, to say the least.

In countries like Great Britain, the government was in any case creating its own agencies for big business. Direct government intervention in production was imposed in the UK by the world wars, but the interwar ethos remained vigorously opposed to direct intervention. Britain, however, moved some way in the interwar period to setting up public corporations like the British Broadcasting Corporation (BBC) and Electricity Grid, while the postwar Labour government nationalized some of the 'commanding heights' of industry, e.g. steel and coal. Ownership thus fell into the government's hands, although it wished the management to be largely independent, subject to meeting certain goals deemed to be in the wider interests of society. The original intention of 'National Socialism' in Germany in the early 1930s was the reverse – to leave ownership in private hands but nationalize management. This, however, never proceeded very far in practice under the Nazis. In other countries like France, nationalization also resulted directly from the Second World War (e.g. Renault), but in most countries the technological and organizational impacts were fairly short-lived and the industries began to wallow in bureaucracy. The imposition of central planning in Eastern Europe, on the other side of the Iron Curtain, of course had a quite different cause.

C. Demand – Macroeconomic Policy

Mass consumption was ultimately raised by the adoption of demand management policies at the macroeconomic level. These are referred to here for convenience as 'Keynesian' policies, although some like F.D. Roosevelt's 'New Deal' of 1934 preceded the publication of Keynes's theoretical work (1936). The package of government measures intended to bring the economies out of severe depression in the mid-1930s concentrated on public works projects and co-ordinated marketing of agricultural goods. In the UK, rearmament from 1934 brought similar results, with, however, the wasteful effects on production that people like Keynes had feared.[104] After the Second World War, European governments, including the UK, concentrated primarily on constructing the Welfare State, permitting access to the kind of 'affluent society' that Galbraith[105] talked about for the whole population. Wartime realignments of income and wealth (including the levelling effects of wartime taxation) helped equalize patterns of income distribution, especially in the war-devastated countries of Japan and Germany. In the USA, any income levelling was more dependent on market forces, though bolstered by measures such as racial discrimination laws from the 1960s. To varying degrees, the matching of mass consumption with mass production was thus met at the macro rather than the micro level after the Second World War.

104 Howson 1975, ch. 6.
105 Galbraith 1958, ch. 8.

8. Western Industrialization, 1970s to the 1990s

Competition is at once the god and the devil
(Penrose 1959/1980, p. 265)

I: GROWTH

A. Patterns

American GNP per employee was about double that in Western Europe and about five times that in Japan in the 1950s, but these three major industrial regions (the 'Triad' of debate in the 1980s) were approaching equality of incomes by the later 1980s.[1]

The 'locomotive' role that the USA played in the world economy from the Second World War until the late 1960s became increasingly dependent on huge budget deficits and balance of payments deficits incurred by the USA, brought about partly by external events such as the Vietnam War, and partly by internal factors as discussed below. Eventually world currency markets could not stand the strain, and the Bretton Woods scheme of quasi-fixed exchange rates had to be abandoned in the early 1970s, in favour of fluctuating exchange rates. This brought even greater instability into the changing global economic system. The USA became less and less a net exporter of capital (foreign direct investment) to the rest of the world, and in the 1980s a substantial net importer of capital, especially from Europe. The post-1970 period came to take on some of the characteristics that Kindleberger (1973) associated with turbulence in the interwar period, in

1 Note that all figures comparing countries and regions are very sensitive to the exchange rates used to convert incomes from one currency basis to another – therefore contradictory conclusions have sometimes been reached, and only rather general impressions are really robust. The most reliable data is that produced under the auspices of the World Bank by Summers and Heston (1988, 1991), measured in 'International Dollars', but even these figures have their quirks.

which no one country was both strong enough and willing enough to 'drive' the world economy.

The US share in high-tech industries largely persisted, with losses, however, in certain areas like instruments, telecommunications and especially consumer electronics. Elsewhere the Japanese are claimed to have replaced the falling share of Europe;[2] though this view of 'Eurosclerosis', i.e. a hardening of the economic and technological 'arteries' in Europe, is more contentious. Data on patenting in the USA show both Europe and Japan doing considerably better than the USA in the most scientifically-based sectors.[3] In my own data on the electronics industry alone, I find that much depends on whether the UK is included with 'Europe' or not: geographically and administratively, the UK is of course part of Europe in this period, but politically and economically it has more in common with the USA. Without the UK, the European performance from the late 1960s is considerably improved, at least until recent years.

The overall trend towards 'convergence' in the major Triad regions (North America / Western Europe / East Asia) may be accounted for:

- i by reductions in barriers to trade and other impediments, having the effect of equalizing 'effective' market sizes (most obviously within Europe with the EEC);
- ii by greater efforts in technology especially in the countries trying to catch up (see the figures on R&D intensity in Figure 8.1 and on patenting in the USA in Figure 8.2);
- iii by the higher costs of 'unproductive' expenditures and employment in the older leader countries, especially those for military purposes in the USA and UK.

Broad regional trends towards 'convergence' disguise a number of different patterns at the national or sub-regional level in different AICs, partly from the varying impact of the above factors on particular countries, but also from differing growth capabilities as described below. It has been noted in the previous chapter that the scope for growth from 'spillovers' of technological information, etc. was probably weaker than often portrayed,[4] and countries had to invest in their own technological and economic growth paths. Abramovitz's notion of 'social capabilities' is perhaps more helpful for discriminating between countries on the lines of their growth achievements (see Chapter 3 above). Growth was rather uneven in pattern from district to district within countries, as well as between countries.[5] For

2 Nelson and Wright 1992.
3 Patel and Pavitt 1987.
4 Cf. Baumol 1986.
5 Dunford 1992.

Figure 8.1: R&D intensity in the leading AICs, 1969–74 to 1985–90

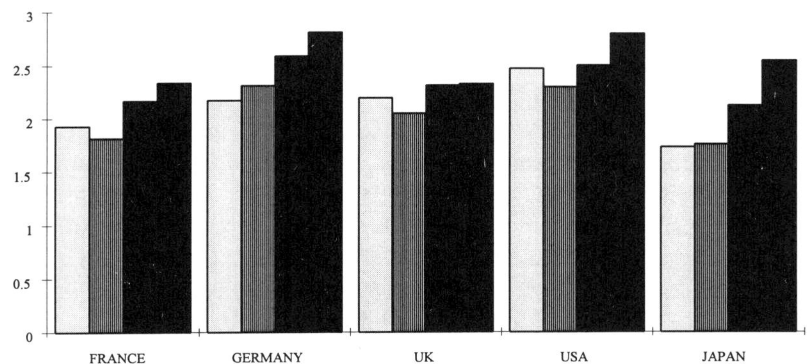

Source: Author's database, largely from OECD data.
Key:
Left-hand (lightest)bars refer to 1969–74
Second bars refer to 1975–79
Third bars refer to 1980–84
Final bars (darkest) refer to 1985–90
Note: R&D intensity = ratio of total R&D to GDP.

Figure 8.2: Source of annual patents in USA, 1950–1988

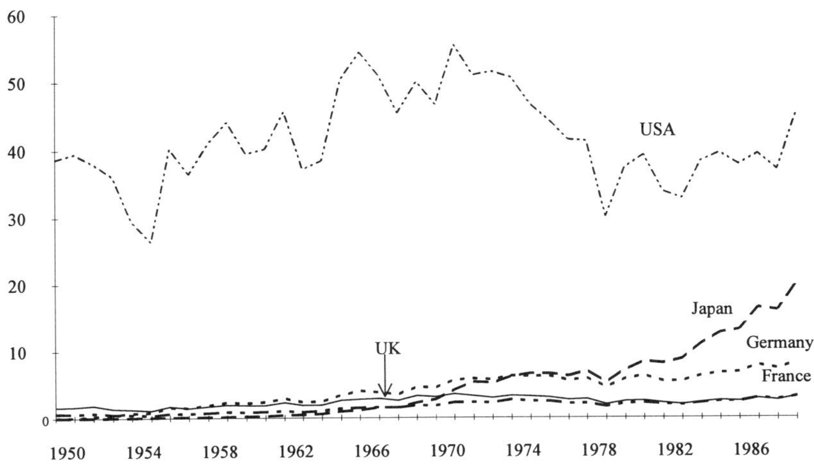

Source: OTAF database.
Note: 1979 figure excludes 13 weeks' observations.

the individual European countries and sub-regions, Abramovitz's[6] title of 'Catching up, forging ahead, and falling behind' is a more accurate picture of postwar developments than is simple 'convergence'.

Per-capita income growth in the USA slowed considerably in this period as compared with that during the long postwar boom. In the follower countries the impact upon growth rates was less marked, but there was unquestionably a growing sense of insecurity and instability, alongside rising indicators of economic malaise such as unemployment and inflation rates. The main task of this chapter will be to establish the factors involved in the retardation, and how they affected various countries to differing degrees.

B. Immediate Causes of Fluctuation and Relative 'Decline'

Some of the causes that have been proffered for the slowdown are better established in terms of quantitative evidence than others. Many of these have been regarded as not just immediate causes of the shift from expansion to retardation, but as basic causes of the continued retardation, though I shall expand later on those that seem to play a more enduring role.

1. Weakening demand

Macroeconomic policies of aggregate demand management no longer seemed able to deliver the kind of boom conditions experienced in the 1950s and 1960s. Two main reasons can be suggested for this.

(a) National economies had become increasingly interlinked by trade and payments ties, and so were less and less able to manage their domestic economies without having the effects spill abroad, or to manage them without reference to international influences; at the same time, international economic management was weakening as shown above.

(b) The Keynesian assumption of 'elastic' supply conditions for inputs, especially labour and raw materials, ceased to hold (see next point). As a result, the early 1970s were characterized by 'stagflation', combining the worst of both worlds with simultaneous stagnation in growth and inflation in prices.

There is thus good reason to believe that macroeconomic demand considerations helped trigger retardation, and as we shall see below, these were compounded by errors of policy in subsequent years which helped to prolong the recessionary phase. However, they should not be seen as independent of the changing (micro) environment to which they were

---

6 Abramovitz 1986; von Tunzelmann 1992b.

addressed. More precisely, it was this change in the economic environment which brought the problems out into the open, since for the time being the macro policies were essentially unchanged.

At the micro level, some believed that product markets had become saturated, as the more affluent societies had already absorbed the major new products, including the consumer durables like automobiles. Product diversification lagged behind the trend in growth of incomes. This 'satiation' was similar to Malthus's anxiety, and was seen as an element in the 'stalemate' between demand and supply.[7] Others, however, believed that it was unlikely that a wide enough range of product markets could stagnate at about the same time for this to have been a major factor in retardation. There was certainly no indication of declining aggregate demand within national economies, as the share of wages in national incomes continued to rise until the early 1970s; that is, there was no build-up of underconsumption, which some had blamed for the Slump in the 1930s. Later in this chapter I shall suggest a somewhat different interpretation of product diversification and the demand side, not rejecting their role but tracing the shortcomings to technological/organizational questions on the supply side.

2. Rising costs

In supply terms, the postwar boom was shown in the previous chapter to depend upon (a) elastic – though not necessarily cheap – supplies of labour, (b) rising investment, and (c) cheap and abundant energy and materials resources. Technical progress was biased towards extensive use of the latter, to a degree that was thought wasteful with hindsight. By the late 1960s the assumptions of elasticity of supply and abundance of resources were looking vulnerable.

(a) Labour costs as a proportion of total costs rose during the 1960s.[8] By the late 1960s there were mounting political battles between capital and labour, most conspicuously the *événements* in France in 1968, but also at about the same time in Italy, the UK, etc. Scholars of both the post-Marxian left and the right interpreted this as a squeeze on profits (or Marxian surplus values), depressing capital accumulation.[9]

(b) A popular argument in the USA was that the cost of capital was rising by the early 1970s, essentially for macroeconomic reasons associated with low rates of savings.

---

7 E.g. Mensch 1979; cf. p. 47 above.

8 See von Tunzelmann 1992b, Figure 2.19.

9 E.g. Mazier 1982; Lindbeck 1983; and cf. Marx 1857/1973, pp. 414–17.

(c) More apparent in the early 1970s was evidence of actual or prospective shortages of fuels and materials, relative to assumed future population growth. The hitherto wasteful use of these materials was also linked to growing anxieties about pollution and the ecosystem. Mathematical modelling approaches which called themselves 'systems dynamics', based mainly on simulation studies carried out at Harvard University and MIT, aimed to show that the world's economic-ecological-demographic system would in due course collapse.[10] Cole *et al.* (1974) argued that the underlying evidence was not strong enough to support such prognostications, and that alternative assumptions, e.g. about technological responses, could yield more optimistic long-term scenarios.[11] But by the time such critiques had appeared, the world was engulfed by the first 'oil crisis' and a quadrupling of crude oil prices, which lent considerable credibility to the systems dynamics views.

However, it remains to establish whether any of these factors bore a direct causal relationship to retardation. There is no doubt that energy growth slowed markedly after 1973, but measurements to date of the impact on slowdown or convergence between countries indicate that it has been a minor factor.[12] Nor is there much in the way of convincing evidence for a direct impact on overall TFP growth, though indirect impacts via demand shocks and the like may have been significant.[13] The issue has been studied most extensively in the USA, which experienced a 'productivity slowdown' from around 1966. Kendrick[14] does not rule out an overall impact of the oil crises on aggregate industrial growth, but argues that, at the *sectoral* level, there appears to be no relationship between the extent of energy consumption and the rate of slowdown. Moreover, the return of cheap fuel in the 1980s did not bring a sustained return to prosperity, although it may have had a positive shorter-term effect on industrial growth. In similar manner, there is no apparent relationship between sectoral slowdown and weaknesses in substituting capital for labour or in capital accumulation.[15]

---

10 The principal works were Forrester 1971 and Meadows *et al.* 1972, sponsored by the 'Club of Rome'. This brought a critique from SPRU in an interdisciplinary work, *Thinking About the Future: a critique of 'The Limits to Growth'* (Cole *et al.* 1974), which styled the systems dynamics approaches as 'Malthusian' – the French edition was actually entitled *Anti-Malthus* (though Malthus's own views would have had more in common with the previous point about demand satiation than with resource exhaustion).

11 See also Beckerman 1974; Rostow 1978b/1979, chs 1, 6.

12 E.g. Scott 1989, pp. 485–6; Maddison 1991, pp. 153–64.

13 OECD 1992, pp. 175–6.

14 Kendrick 1983, p. 48.

15 *Ibid.*, pp. 40–41; Dertouzos *et al.* 1989, p. 37.

Thus these cost factors are probably best seen as triggering decline rather than perpetuating it.

3. Declining innovation

The supply-side counterpart of the market saturation hypothesis in the 'technology stalemate' perspective was a belief that innovations had shifted from involving fundamental changes to more limited improvements, a view derived partly from product lifecycle concepts. However, it is by no means easy to judge how radical such recent innovations have been, and with a greater elapse of time we might now regard some of the changes of the early–mid-1970s as quite fundamental, e.g. the development of the personal computer in the IT industry, or of recombinant DNA in biotechnology. Alternatively, any decline in innovativeness might be regarded as a return to normalcy, with the preceding period representing abnormality, e.g. because of recovery from the Second World War.[16]

Figures for patenting do suggest a 'climacteric' in patenting by US inventors in the USA around 1970 (see Figure 8.2). However, this was partly offset by rising numbers of patents from the catching-up countries, most obviously Japan.

The role of innovation has been appraised at the sectoral level as well as at the technological level, most thoroughly for the USA, with its 'productivity slowdown'. It has been argued, on the one hand, that technological factors are likely to have been significant at the sectoral level in the USA, since R&D intensity was fairly strongly correlated with differences in sectoral productivity growth rates from 1948 to 1979.[17] Others have contended that technological factors are unlikely to have been the only causes of slowdown, since the latter extended across almost all sectors irrespective of technological leadership.[18]

To account for the persistence of retardation, it may be more appropriate to emphasize the slowness of diffusion rather than declining incidence of innovation in newer fields. It has also been argued that spillovers from military R&D slowed down in this period.[19] Such questions are considered in greater detail in the Technology section below. Even if the argument is substantiated, one still has to judge whether any such limits to diffusion originated in problems on the demand side or on the supply side. Though the evidence is limited, the indications are that the principal reasons for slow diffusion were not narrowly technological nor inadequacies of demand, but organizational weaknesses in coupling technology to adoption.

16 Rostow 1985.
17 Kendrick 1983, p. 45.
18 Baily and Chakrabarti 1985.
19 E.g. Mowery and Rosenberg 1993, p. 47.

4. Managerial/financial problems

The high growth of the 1950s and 1960s had established a 'virtuous circle' in which that high growth gave rise to high profits, which in turn permitted high rates of investment and thus further high rates of growth. One interpretation could thus be that the virtuous circle was turned into a vicious circle when profit rates collapsed (low investment, low growth, low profits, low investment, etc.). Such a view is consistent with arguments such as those about rising labour costs as described above. However, for the USA, Hayes and Wheelwright[20] argue that rates of return on industrial equity were little if any lower during the 1970s than in the boom years of the 1950s. Their view instead is that, as compared with the boom period, shareholder *dividends* paid out were one-third higher, i.e. less of the profit was being 'ploughed back' into industry for its growth.[21] Conceivably this was linked to the rising involvement of financial pools in industrial ownership as noted in the previous chapter (p. 240).

Nelson (1990a) argues that the largest US declines came in 'mid-tech' industries (automobiles, steel, etc.) rather than 'low-tech' ones, and these were industries characterized by highly capital-intensive plants and sprawling managerial bureaucracies. The case for managerial inflexibility and organizational rigidity therefore seems to be supported at the sectoral level. But here the impact may instead have been longer term, and will thus be taken up below.

II: TECHNOLOGY

A. R&D and Weakening Growth

In the USA as leader country, the R&D intensity (i.e. the ratio of R&D to GNP) failed to rise greatly and for a period actually declined. That in the UK also showed little growth from the 1970s, but in Germany and France the R&D intensity was maintained or slightly increased. By 1975 the total R&D expenditure of the USA was about half of that of the combined Western European countries, as compared with the situation 15 years earlier when it had been around three times as great. The overall R&D intensity thus appears to correlate fairly closely with relative growth trends in this period, and still more so when one observes the rapid increase of R&D in Japan. However, it can be argued that, like profits and capital investment,

---

20 Hayes and Wheelwright 1984, p. 6.

21 Akio Morita, the celebrated former head of Sony, remarked that the president of Sony's US subsidiary earned more than he did himself; quoted in Johnson 1982, p. 314.

the level of investment in R&D is as much a consequence as a cause of growth. The possibilities for a vicious or virtuous circle (low growth enforcing low R&D, leading to continued low growth, etc.) are equally evident here.

In any case, it has been argued that much of the decline in R&D was in the government-financed aspect. In the USA, virtually all of the declines were in Federal funding,[22] while in the eleven leading AICs including the US, *private* R&D expenditures rose a healthy 30 per cent between 1967 and 1975. Given the general belief that much of the government-funded R&D was by this stage having only a limited growth impact,[23] e.g. because of declining military/civilian spillovers, and that private R&D is likely to have more significant economic effects anyway, it is not clear that the correlation between R&D expenditures and slowdown is especially strong.

An alternative possibility is thus that the capabilities of particular levels of R&D expenditure to produce gains in output were declining – in other words, that the 'productivity' of R&D was falling. There is some scattered evidence for rising costs of R&D relative to the ultimate economic payoffs in projects characterized by technological complexity. This will be elaborated upon below, but at this stage one can point to the most obvious 'mission-oriented' projects like space, nuclear power and telecommunications, where each succeeding generation of products appeared to involve a doubling or more of R&D without proportionate improvement in the products. Formal calculations of the returns to R&D are, however, notoriously suspect. Nevertheless, there is some consensus that the uncertain business conditions from the early 1970s induced a shift from long-term exploratory research to shorter-term payoffs and minor improvements.[24] There was also a certain amount of R&D 'wasted' on long-term projects directed at the short-term causes of the retardation, e.g. searching for alternative oil sources.

If one looks at catching-up countries, these showed increases in R&D that were not necessarily matched by expansion of technology-based output. Malerba[25] shows that R&D growth in Italy in the 1980s was insufficient when what was wanted was more general development of technological capabilities. More generally, Scott (1989) gives strong theoretical and empirical reasons why R&D should be considered as only part of the very much broader class of expenditures to change the production environment.

---

22 Griliches 1986.

23 A point Griliches attempts to verify for the case of the USA.

24 E.g. Nelson 1990b.

25 In Dosi *et al.* 1992.

B. New Areas of Innovation

Some of the above arguments accord with Perez's long-wave hypothesis concerning the 'exhaustion of technological styles' in the later phases of the long wave (cf. p. 99). At the same time, there were, however, considerable advances in innovation in new sectors. Information and communication technologies (ICTs) were making possible a radically different pattern of advance. IT developed by making use of the heuristic of 'miniaturization': whereas many technologies evolved by scaling 'up', IT reversed this and scaled 'down'.[26] The drive towards miniaturization was spurred by the NASA space programme, with the need to save weight and volume as well as increase efficiency in the satellites. Thus the shift from valves to transistors in the 1950s and from transistors to integrated circuits (ICs) in the 1960s, followed by successive waves of large-scale integration (LSI, VLSI, etc.) from the 1970s, can be interpreted in these terms. Swann (1986) shows that, in microprocessors, the saving of size (increased density) had other positive effects, e.g. conserving power requirements and reducing heat dissipation. As there was thus every advantage to be gained from decreasing size (miniaturizing) so long as the costs did not rise excessively, the rate of sustained technical progress in electronic components (chips) was unprecedented by historical standards. For most technologies there were technical trade-offs to be reconciled with the underlying trajectory; but in the case of semiconductors the heuristic of miniaturization appeared to achieve virtually all the technical objectives simultaneously, and simply became a question of knowhow and cost. Growth of each successive generation of chips proceeded in mini-waves which I have described as 'dynamic diminishing returns',[27] with a switch to the next generation when the cost reductions attainable from the existing generation began to give out.

The productivity 'paradox' is then to explain why aggregate productivity (GDP per employee, etc.) failed to grow in response. Several causes have been suggested, but the most obvious is that diffusion of ICTs remained limited across sectors of the economy. In the last chapter, the upswing from the 1930s/1940s was seen as being led by industries whose fundamental innovations dated back about half a century to the previous Kondratiev. These were not necessarily the fastest-growing industries (synthetic materials showed very rapid expansion from the 1940s), but their impact on GNP was more substantial simply because they had grown to significant size. By the same token, the industries like electronics that were based on more recent fundamental breakthroughs were perhaps not yet sufficiently

26 Sahal 1981.
27 Von Tunzelmann 1989.

large in absolute size to offset weaknesses elsewhere. On the analogy with the Second and Fourth Kondratiev waves (steam, electrification, etc.), their full impact will come when they became 'pervasive' in their adoption across a wide range of user industries.

What their early development has already demonstrated is the consolidation of links between technology and scientific activity. In ICTs this was evident not just in areas like solid-state physics for the semiconductors, but in new disciplines such as 'computer science'. The still newer fields such as biotechnology and advanced materials owe virtually all of their development to science, much of it self-created in similar fashion (biotechnology as a new academic discipline, etc.). Even now after about twenty years they have yet to become commercialized on any appreciable scale, much less be detectable at a macroeconomic level. It seems likely that, for a considerable time to come, there will be high R&D costs and only limited economic payoffs in such areas, though the long-term payoffs are prospectively massive. It remains to be seen how adequate the existing institutions (e.g. finance) will be in accommodating these science-led developments.

C. Technological Trajectories and Economic Influences

The consequence of a rising science base was an increase in the 'knowledge-intensity' of advanced industries and economies.[28] Although this involved greater R&D-intensity by way of the augmented overhead costs of R&D just noted, it did not necessarily involve greater capital intensity in high-tech industries.

(a) The shift from mechanical and electro-mechanical to electronic-based systems, via miniaturization, permitted substantial capital savings in many cases, e.g. in Numerically Controlled Machine Tools (NCMTs) and transfer lines.[29] Although there was much reference to robots in production processes, robotization did not progress very fast, and much of the labour displaced was unskilled – requirements for skilled labour often rose.[30]

(b) Software became increasingly important in ICT systems, with software typically representing three-quarters or more of the total costs of, say, an advanced telecommunications switch. Software remained almost totally labour-intensive, despite attempts to automate software development by 'software engineering'.

---

28 Abramovitz 1993.

29 Carlsson 1984, 1989b.

30 Tidd 1990.

Hence, if there was any tendency towards labour 'rationalization' and redundancies during this downswing phase of the long wave, as argued by Freeman,[31] then it was not brought about by technological factors in the design or production of the high-tech equipment itself. It was a different matter in industries that were *users* of ICTs (computerization, telecoms operators, etc.). Here the impact on the productive factors such as labour depended on the way in which ICTs were actually implemented. If they were utilized in *decentralized* fashion to upgrade the quality of the labour force and its learning potential, as the logic of computerization increasingly warranted, then there was no good reason to save labour in greater degree than any other inputs. However, bureaucratic management was often driven by the logic of earlier hierarchically organized computer systems, typically built around an IBM mainframe, to use computers for increased centralization and control over the production process, including labour process. In such circumstances, the adoption of advanced technologies in user industries could indeed take on a labour-saving guise – not because of technological tendencies in the advanced technologies themselves, which in fact were moving in the opposite direction, but through managerial and organizational influences in particular sets of conditions. The issues were clouded by contradictory influences in regard to skilled labour,[32] and these were further clouded by gender issues.[33]

It therefore seems likely that the economic impact of high-tech industries depended not on technological imperatives, nor greatly on economic circumstances such as the relative price of labour (though there were some evident responses to the oil crises), but primarily on managerial-organizational determinants which are conditioned by 'ideological and institutional' influences (cf. Figure 2.2).[34] Proof of this will require more cross-country comparative studies than are at present available, but the studies we do have for individual countries appear to give some confirmation. In Britain, technical progress was quite inappropriately aimed at reducing labour per unit of output rather than expanding output.[35] Europe as a whole experienced 'jobless growth' of the kind that Freeman deplored, whereas the United States, with an ostensibly more labour-saving commitment to its technology, did much better in terms of creating employment, though almost entirely in new regions such as the southern

31 In Freeman *et al.* 1982.

32 E.g. increased manpower requirements in the computer or information systems departments of firms vs. deskilling of labour, cf. Vivarelli 1991.

33 E.g. employing cheap part-time female labour vs. male-biased reskilling, cf. Faulkner and Arnold 1985.

34 Morroni 1992, pp. 188–9.

35 McIntosh 1986.

'sunbelt',[36] and much of it in unskilled labour. Although this difference has widely been blamed on excessive labour costs in Europe, the jobless expansion in this region came in a period when the share of labour costs (including employer contributions) was declining.[37]

In Japan, much greater attention was paid to improving the quality of the labour force, and using ICTs in decentralized fashion. The very different managerial structures in Japan are described in Chapter 10. In that country, the ultimate incentives to adopt microelectronics were seen by the industrial leaders such as Kobayashi at NEC to save *time* and *space*.[38] Rising energy and materials costs also brought pressure on the Japanese to save on these resource inputs, but the radical solutions suggested had not become commercialized before the relevant economic conditions changed sharply in the 1980s.

For such reasons, we must also consider the organizational aspects in order to understand the techno-economic evolution.

III: ORGANIZATION

A. Automation

The progression of automation was described briefly in Chapter 7. In the period now considered, the reliance on interchangeable parts alone was becoming too cumbersome, and producers were looking to adapt existing machines and tools, e.g. by reprogramming. The stage was shifting from automation of 'transfer' to that of 'control'.[39] Numerically Controlled Machine Tools (NCMTs) held out greater prospects of integration into larger systems via Computer Numerical Control (CNC) or Direct Numerical Control (DNC), essentially aiming to forge a new 'systemic co-ordination' out of computer control. However, experience suggested that the organizational structure had to be got right at the same time – in the manner described in the previous sub-section, early DNC systems mimicked hierarchical management by their centralized structure, built around traditional mainframe computers, while more flexible 'open systems' of networked computers (workstations, etc.) required parallel managerial developments. There was also more than a whiff of the 'technical fix' about computerizing process control – South Korean firms eschewed computerization in their hunt for process improvements on such grounds,

36 Norton 1986.
37 Von Tunzelmann 1992b.
38 Kobayashi 1986; see Chapter 10 (p. 324) below.
39 Cf. Bell 1972, chs 18–20.

and relied on intensive manual methods.[40] Where they appeared, the computerized process systems like Flexible Manufacturing Systems (FMS) or the ultimate hope of Computer-Integrated Manufacturing (CIM) had major repercussions for both labour and capital process.

(a) In the labour process literature, this shift became known as 'NeoFordism', although associated with the automation of control and thus (like classical Fordism) more closely related to capital process. Human resource strategies were implemented, aiming to integrate 'teams' of shopfloor workers. Management attempted some 'recomposition of tasks', with job enrichment or job rotation, to increase worker commitment and broaden experience.[41] The trade unions which had been reconstituted on an industry base under Fordism were seen as inappropriate to this company-based teamwork and learning. In some countries like the USA and UK, their power was effectively destroyed through political and macroeconomic forces during the 1970s and 1980s; in others they were replaced by 'company unions' with attempts to foster corporate spirit and greater egalitarianism, along the lines of Japanese companies.

(b) On the side of capital process, these changes implied the possibility of extending automation from the long product runs of classical Fordism to small-batch production, which still accounted for perhaps 80 per cent of production in fields such as mechanical engineering.[42] This was referred to as 'flexible automation'. Rapid computer-controlled changes of dies and tools meant that even one-off products could potentially be produced via automated methods. Under traditional hierarchical management this could be seen as an opportunity to wrest control from the shopfloor, as a further step towards machine-paced work. In practice, the equipment still fell far short of the levels of automaticity that would have been required, and the successful strategies (as just mentioned in regard to labour process) involved stepping up labour involvement rather than the opposite, especially for skilled labour.[43]

The most successful implementations were often those that saved a great deal of time, for example the roller kilns that were introduced into SMFs in the Italian ceramic tile industry in the mid-1970s, which cut the cycle time for single-firing from 16–20 hours to 50–55 minutes.[44] While Taylorism

40 Amsden 1989, ch. 11.

41 Aglietta 1979, pp. 128–30; Piore and Sabel 1984, ch. 5; Lazonick 1990, ch. 9; Kern and Schumann, in Kogut 1993.

42 Blackburn *et al.* 1985, p. 54.

43 Ferraz *et al.* 1992, ch. 8.

44 Porter 1990, p. 217.

was directed at saving throughput time in a given environment, flexible automation was generally aimed at reducing lead time, set-up time and downtime in a *changing* environment.[45] Technological fixes alone were rarely able to achieve the kind of 'systemic co-ordination' noted in Chapter 4 above. Thus the rate of implementation of advanced process systems which permitted full flexibility in both process and product, like FMS, and beyond that CIM, was quite slow. This delay stemmed from the need for integration of the complete system extending from design, through organization and administration, to marketing.[46] Historical precedents suggest that such systemic change may be a full Kondratiev wave in the making.

B. Flexible Specialization

Whereas 'flexible automation' generally refers to *process* technologies, the booming literature on 'flexible specialization' mostly describes flexibility in *products*, including product innovation.[47] Moreover, flexible specialization generally considers the relationships among firms, as distinct from flexible automation within firms. It has been compared with the models of 'proto-industrialization' discussed in Chapters 4 and 5 above, for its focus on craft industry. The typical models for flexible specialization have been the American 'Silicon Valley phenomenon', the Japanese industrial groups (*keiretsu*) or the small firms of the 'Third Italy'. Here I shall concentrate on the latter,[48] as the former two are examined below and in Chapter 10.

While the Japanese model involves a 'hub' of a large firm central to the group, is commonly found in high-tech areas, and is backed up by central government legislation and agencies, the Italian model ostensibly involves dynamic regionally-based small firms with independent design capability in fairly traditional sectors such as clothing, ceramics or furniture. In the case of Baden-Württemberg in Germany, a postwar hub type has been superimposed on an older decentralized SMF network.[49] The contrast can be overdrawn, as in practice many of the Italian small firms undertake subcontract work for larger firms, while in Germany there has been a partial blending of the two.

Flexibility comes from the alleged ability to redesign products very rapidly in response to perceived market forces, without negotiating tiers of

45 Ferraz *et al.* 1992, pp. 16, 161.

46 'Systemation', in the phrase of Kaplinsky 1984.

47 For alternative meanings of the term 'flexibility', see Morroni 1992, ch. 12; and for a fuller description see Ferraz *et al.* 1992, ch. 1.

48 Cf. Piore and Sabel 1984, ch. 9; Best 1990, chs 7–8; Porter 1990, chs 4, 7.

49 Herrigel, in Kogut 1993.

managerial hierarchies. The relatively 'low-tech' character of the industries implies that technology is no great barrier to such product flexibility. Within the small firms there has to be flexibility in functions, as opposed to the Taylorist notion of compartmentalizing jobs. Specialization thus takes place between firms, with each possessing capabilities in rapid redesign. Overall purpose and direction comes from combining this decentralization of production capability (often family-based) through social integration, given by the sense of local community.[50] In towns such as Modena in the Emilia-Romagna region of Italy, the latter was provided by local government (the 'communist' party in this case), setting up local industrial parks through land expropriation and covenanted building programmes, installing practices of peer review and loan guarantees in place of formal banking practice for finance, and offering communal marketing and other services to share overheads. The greatest degree of specialization took place at the district level, with the small family firms in the district adopting individual designs via both competition and collaboration. The district as a whole has to go beyond Marshall's notions of external economics and be 'collectively entrepreneurial'.[51] In Baden-Württemberg, the regional government was noteworthy, but so also were educational establishments, trade associations, banks, etc.[52]

More recent research[53] suggests that, for the 'Third Italy', such small-firm dynamics may be limited to the lower-tech sectors, and especially the sectors which Pavitt (1984) labels 'supplier-dominated'. This supplier dominance of the Italian model more closely resembles the Japanese or other systems – even in Italy, the hub is often explicit, as instanced by firms like Benetton in clothing.[54] The hub could also be process-related rather than product-related; so, for instance, Porter[55] notes that the Modena region was also the home of companies celebrated for high technical and design sophistication, like Ferrari, Maserati and Lamborghini. Significant process advances could thus be involved in this product-based system, like the speedily responsive IT system employed by Benetton, or the faster production technologies adopted in Italian ceramic tiles (tunnel kilns and later roller kilns). In sectors where demand led through fashion and style, Italian

50 Best, *loc. cit.* Porter (1990, p. 443) considers that Italy is as much a collection of towns and localities as it is a nation, probably because of the long historical tradition of city-states.

51 Best 1990, p. 234.

52 Herrigel, *loc. cit.*

53 E.g. Belussi 1992.

54 Belussi 1987; Sapelli, in Dosi *et al.* 1992; Malerba, in Nelson 1993, pp. 236, 241, 255–6.

55 Porter 1990, p. 212.

machinery producers developed strong specialized competitiveness.[56] By contrast with this predominance of lower-tech industries, the American model described in the next sub-section has been limited to frontier high-tech sectors, as for Silicon Valley and Bug Valley in California or Route 128 in Massachusetts. Thus the sectoral scope for flexible specialization appears rather specific, while the regional scope also appears specific. The evidence now available suggests that it has derived from particular ownership and control patterns in specific regions and/or sectors, rather than being the 'Second Industrial Divide' as a viable alternative to mass production in the AICs, as originally portrayed by Piore and Sabel (1984). At the time of writing, there are anxieties that momentum has been lost, and this may be partly reflected in the changing political situation in Italy.

Despite this specificity, there are general lessons to be learnt from flexible specialization, through the organizational dynamics (learning, etc.) and the attention to product as well as process flexibility. Product flexibility could be gained through 'modularization', i.e. robust product or process designs which permitted a large degree of interchangeability between alternatives.[57] It is clear that this is one step further up from the notion of 19th-century interchangeability discussed in Chapter 6 above, which considered components. In medium-tech sectors, such as were experiencing the greatest problems in countries like the United States, the lesson lay in trying to marry product innovation and process innovation, which too few yet managed.[58]

C. Networks

These horizontal firm linkages of flexible specialization represent one aspect of a more general tendency that many have detected towards the use of networks in industry. In the cases described above, for lower-tech industries, the networks are a response to shortening product lifecycles and a shift to quality-based competition. In high-tech industries, these factors remain but are complemented by those of increasing R&D costs and technological complexity, as previously noted. Thus producers face the possibility of ever longer and costlier development stages for ever shorter product markets. Networks, both formal and informal, are therefore proposed as ways of climbing out of this two-edged trap.[59] US and UK industrialists found this environment harder to adjust to, being accustomed to arm's-length dealings – the USA had built many industrial complexes

56 *Ibid.*, p. 441.
57 *Ibid.*, p. 63.
58 E.g. Graves 1991 for automobiles.
59 OECD 1992, chs 3–4.

after the Second World War, but they were not closely interrelated within.[60] Both also seemed to suffer from a surfeit of the 'NIH syndrome' (Not Invented Here), as exemplified in the USA by what in contrast to 19th-century attitudes had become an obsession with originality and *individual* creativity.[61]

1. Formal networks

Strategic alliances among firms represent a formal means of networking, e.g. via joint ventures (JVs). Although formal alliances are by no means new, it is believed that they have changed in focus since the 1970s. Before then, they were typically 'one-directional', e.g. American firms with high-tech knowledge seeking market access in Europe, using local European firms as their market entry point. With the greater equalization of technological abilities among the 'Triad' regions (North America, Western Europe, East Asia), they have become increasingly 'bi-directional', involving mutual exchanges of both knowhow and markets, seeking complementarities. Second, they have been associated with a shift from the kinds of innovations that were 'internal' to industries in the 1950s and 1960s (e.g. containerization of transport) to the more pervasive technologies 'externalized' across industries in the 1980s and 1990s (e.g. information and communication technologies).[62]

A static argument in favour of such collaborations is to avoid research duplication by rival oligopolistic firms, where without collaboration they might be expected to be chasing similar targets. Some formal US collaborations in the 1980s such as the MCC (Microelectronics and Computer Technologies Corporation) saw this as their main function.[63] In practice, however, the motives have stressed strategic rather than static cost-reducing or even cost-sharing goals,[64] such as shortening lead times or permitting greater technological complexity. This accords with the 'dynamic transaction-costs' approach of Langlois (1992), noted in Chapter 1 above. But formal collaborations have probably been greatest in industries like aerospace where the R&D costs are especially high and the number of final products quite small but complex (e.g. aircraft, satellites).

2. Informal networks

Informal networks developed on the basis of (i) knowledge spillovers and (ii) relationships with suppliers. These too have a long history, like the

60 Porter 1990, p. 303.
61 Dertouzos *et al.* 1989, pp. 51, 79; Rosenberg 1994, p. 122.
62 Freeman 1994.
63 Peck 1986.
64 Hagedoorn and Schakenraad 1992.

Lancashire cotton district of the 19th century analysed by Alfred Marshall.[65] In high-tech industries, districts like Silicon Valley evolved on the basis of knowledge spillovers, including links to universities (Stanford, etc.). With knowledge being embodied in people and organizations in ways discussed earlier in this book, the spillovers were greatest where people migrated freely between organizations (like firms), and here the USA continued well ahead of most rivals. Many of these technologies (like software) were 'labour-embodied' rather than the traditional 'capital-embodied' of economic theory. The NTBFs (New Technology-Based Firms, see below) were secured not just by brash young graduates like Steve Jobs at Apple or Bill Gates at Microsoft, but by supportive outflows from established organizations like IBM or Bell Labs. After a period of decline in the early 1980s when Silicon Valley was eclipsed commercially and technologically by large firms, it is claimed that it is now reviving on the alternative basis of supplier and customer relationships.[66] Financial links (venture capital) were also critical to the evolution of Silicon Valley, based on close links to the lenders. As in the Japanese and Italian flexible specialization models, the supplier relationships aim to replace arm's-length market links with closer personal or community relationships. However, the links remain weaker than in the strategic alliance model – which some of their advocates see as a strength rather than a weakness, inasmuch as it gives greater flexibility. Saxenian draws a sharp contrast between Silicon Valley, based on regional networks, and the other well-known US high-tech region around Route 128 in Massachusetts: 'Silicon Valley continues to reinvent itself as its specialized producers learn collectively and adjust to one another's needs through shifting patterns of competition and collaboration. The separate and self-sufficient organizational structures of Route 128, in contrast, *hinder adaptation by isolating the process of technological change within corporate boundaries*.'[67]

3. Advantages and disadvantages

Both formal and informal links share some advantages and disadvantages, although to varying degrees. Both aim to reduce costs per product for individual firms belonging to the network, although the product gains as well as the costs will more obviously be shared among the members of formal alliances. Both can permit some 'unbundling' of technical knowhow, as a means to specialization within complex technologies, although these may perhaps be carried further in formal vertical links (user–producer). Both permit greater exchange of significant tacit

65 See p. 81 above.
66 Saxenian 1991, 1994.
67 *Ibid.*, p. 161, my italics.

knowledge; though allegedly some JVs are used by prospective rivals to *limit* the amount of information exchanged, using the JV on the principle of 'Chinese walls'. Formal alliances also allow large companies to access foreign national or supranational programmes, as for the attempts by IBM to enter EC programmes during the 1980s. Informal alliances obviously permit each partner to behave autonomously and perhaps pursue new alliances.

In terms of disadvantages, both suffer from their own high 'transaction costs', in the guise of costs of establishing and running the network. This is probably the greatest single obstacle to the wider use of networks. While they are often intended for the time-saving function of speeding up change, the transaction elements may mean that they actually slow it down. In formal alliances, there are managerial problems directly related to the JV, e.g. conflict between partners' interests, imbalances of contributions, or difficulties with cost control (as in some of the aerospace programmes). On the other side, informal networks involve 'soft governance' (absence of formal management structures) but thus rely heavily on trust.[68] There are fears that partners will be less committed to joint projects than their own, because of the sharing of the gains – this was Adam Smith's objection to shared production.[69] On the other hand, it is easy to give examples where unintegrated co-operative development has been more successful than in-house development, e.g. IBM and Microsoft for the joint development of computer-operating systems, contrasting with IBM's serious internal failures in the late 1980s.[70] In the USA fears have been voiced – though probably exaggerated – concerning the outflow of information to rival countries, and the possible creation of 'hollow corporations' which do not undertake actual production but leave it to the overseas partners. There are also anxieties about alliances being transformed into cliques or even cartels, and thus acting against consumer interests.

There is considerable debate about whether networks represent another transition phase or instead a genuinely new pattern of organization. The fact that networks have existed in one form of another for years (dating back well before industrialization) suggests the former. However, it seems unlikely that the underlying causal factors such as rising technological complexity and shortened product lifecycles will subside within the next few years, in which case the networks may be here to stay for the foreseeable future. My personal view is that the current period of 'fast history'[71] in technology may in due course abate, as it did following the first

68 Dodgson 1993.
69 Smith 1776/1976, p. 390.
70 Fransman 1994.
71 Klein 1977.

and third Kondratievs, in which case the main function of networks will have been as a restructuring device. In the mean time, they therefore act to reconcile firm-based technological cumulativeness with multiplying (and partially science-based) technological complexity. It may be that they give way to a spate of mergers and acquisitions or divestments, though there is considerable evidence that for some time to come they are likely to proliferate and become 'polycentric',[72] with the evolution of overlapping and multifunction networks. At present there is some evidence that the networks are 'lengthening',[73] although in the fullness of time it may prove more efficient to 'shorten' them (link final consumers closer to primary producers). Moves towards globalization enhance the necessity for inter-firm co-operation, e.g. in setting standards.[74] Networks are thus an avenue for establishing the 'new combinations' which Schumpeter saw as characterizing the Kondratiev upswing.

D. Management

Growing pressures to develop more integrative working relationships within companies (referred to above as 'NeoFordism'), and more extended and complicated sets of relationships outside (networks, etc.), greatly intensified the onus on management in this period.

1. Internal considerations

The freely mobile labour markets for skilled and administrative labour encouraged the diffusion of new technologies. The problem was that such labour markets acted equally as a disincentive to generate adequate supplies of skilled labour in the first place – firms trained less because they feared that their trainees would leave shortly afterwards, probably to rivals.[75] But the vitality of the American NSI came to depend considerably on new firm creation through such labour mobility, in good Schumpeterian fashion. In this respect, the US industrial structure had few serious rivals, owing to (i) the use of research establishments, often federally funded, as 'incubators', (ii) comparatively abundant venture capital, (iii) demand support from the military sector, (iv) liberal IPR attitudes, and (v) perhaps also the effects of antitrust legislation.[76]

---

72 Callon *et al.* 1992.

73 *Ibid.*

74 E.g. Philips, Sony and Matsushita now effectively act together to set worldwide standards in consumer electronics, while continuing to compete in the product marketplace.

75 Dertouzos *et al.* 1989, p. 21.

76 Mowery and Rosenberg 1993, pp. 48–9.

Within the large corporations, the situation seemed rather different; American managers, and others following in their footsteps, being severely criticized by a new generation of scholars mainly from the Harvard Business School.[77] According to their findings, corporate managers had only themselves to blame for weaknesses, instead of blaming governments or trade unions, as had been their wont. Management had become 'pseudo-professionalized' in their words (not least through the culture of Harvard MBA degrees, although they do not point this out!); top management in US companies shifted from those with manufacturing or engineering expertise and with hands-on experience of their line of business, to those with general financial, accountancy or legal backgrounds, who believed that they could step into almost any company regardless of what it produced and set it to rights. 'Fast-track' managerial career paths promoted short-termist attitudes to the companies being managed. Much of the time of top management was in practice being devoted either to making acquisitions and divestments or to fighting off takeover bids, with great status significance but often of little or no economic return to their corporations. Managerial short-termism lowered company loyalty through 'job-hopping' – the celebrated advocate of quality control, W. Edwards Deming, thought that the 'American system' was becoming 'interchangeable managers' rather than interchangeable parts.[78] This also encouraged a stultifying duplication of products among rivals ('me-toos') rather than genuine product differentiation, as the companies were perceived to be more or less interchangeable. Tough competition, e.g. with foreign rivals, was ducked because of the fear of eating into comfortable management bonuses.[79] As for most countries, internal US attitudes to its managers veered between excessive self-criticism and excessive complacency.[80]

With their financial backgrounds and short-term perspectives, top management evaluated projects according to the financial 'bottom line', typically the rate of return on investment (ROI). The quickest way to raise the ROI was to reduce the denominator, i.e. the investment, instead of raising the numerator, i.e. profits; so managers delayed replacements of equipment, lowered R&D and reduced training, all of which appeared to boost the ROI in the short term (for the next quarter's return) while undermining the viability of the company in the long term. In general, accountancy measures were given far too much credence.[81] The kind of

77 Abernathy and Hayes 1980; Hayes and Wheelwright 1984; Porter 1990, ch. 9; Lazonick 1991, ch. 1.

78 Quoted by Best 1990, p. 160; cf. Chapter 10 below.

79 Porter 1990, p. 530.

80 Compare lead stories in *Business Week* for 27.4.87 and for 16.5.94.

81 Best, *loc. cit.*

'product champion' necessary to develop radical change was heavily discouraged in this climate. M-form (multidivisional) companies were often in the worst position, as the ROI was used to allocate funding and support between the divisions and their distinct lines of business, and at the divisional level the figures could be massaged in all sorts of deleterious ways. Even the older generation at the Harvard Business School, above all Chandler, the prime advocate of the attractions of the M-form company, now argues that use of the ROI has been taken seriously astray in recent years, through being relied on for short-term allocation rather than longer-term strategic thinking.[82] Others point to the distancing between divisions encouraged by financially-based internal competition, heavily discouraging synergies and information flows among the various divisions.

Such financial developments if anything entrenched hierarchical management, making it still more aloof from the needs of shopfloor integration at a time when processes should have been changing drastically ('flexible automation'). Lazonick[83] claims plausibly that exploitative management, oriented to increasing its own payoffs, encourages workers to adopt conflictual behaviour by way of response. Adversarial labour relations proved counter-productive in the short term and destructive in the longer term. Nor were they the ideal basis for launching new technologies – dynamic learning gains were held back by leaving too little autonomy to the production workers.[84] In a major empirical and theoretical study, Kagono *et al.* (1985) contrast the 'group dynamics' of the typical large Japanese firm with what they rather kindly describe as the 'bureaucratic dynamics' of the all too typical US firm, where the latter serve mainly to create ever greater managerial bureaucracies. The characteristics of the Japanese model of management will be defined in Chapter 10, but it is pertinent here to look ahead and note their conclusion that successful management in both Japan and the USA was 'evolutionary' (in their phrase), in being able to adapt to rapid changes that were taking place in the external environment.

2. External factors

This brings us to the external aspects of management. There, the requirement of a flexible response to product market conditions and the development of a profusion of formal and informal networks added to the difficulties of management and again needed cutting through to prevent further and further tiers being added to the managerial structure. The weaker response was to continue with market-based relationships ('arm's length'), rather than cultivating links with suppliers or customers. Networks

82 Chandler 1992; also Galambos 1988; Dertouzos *et al.* 1989, ch. 4.

83 Lazonick 1990, p. 352.

84 Mowery and Rosenberg 1993, p. 32.

arising out of technological or product complexity, as described above, are problematic for traditional management, because they combine elements of both markets and hierarchies.[85] American companies seemed much less extensively involved in such 'organized markets';[86] though by no means absent from them either, as the work of von Hippel (1988) shows.

The geographical expansion of companies through multinationalism into other AICs also added to managerial problems in similar ways – through prospectively adding more divisions to cope with the overseas activities, and through encountering differing managerial and economic environments in other countries. A common attempted solution was to adopt 'matrix' forms of management, with individuals being responsible to both product divisions and regional divisions; but this can easily lead to an escalation of bureaucracy, since for each function one might have to be answerable to nearly all regions, and conversely for each region be answerable for nearly all functions. Tensions between large regions were reaching crisis level in many large corporations by the later 1980s, e.g. in computer companies like IBM and Digital.

The only real solution was to take management in a quite different direction, and Chapter 10 describes the Japanese system aiming at 'lean production', which had its counterpart in lean management. Large firms in most AICs were compelled to move away from traditional hierarchical control.

IV: FINANCE

A. Firm Size

The increasing diversity of technologies and products, noted above and discussed further in Section V, combined with the problems being encountered by traditional management, were widely considered to have shifted the balance of advantage from large firms (LFs) to small and medium-sized firms (SMFs). In the engineering industry, Carlsson (1989b) found that both plant and company size were falling in most AICs from the early 1970s. Theories of 'bureaucratic failure' to explain the problems of LFs were in vogue.[87] New decentralized technologies such as ICT networks continued the impetus previously provided by electricity to underpin the SMFs. In new fields like biotechnology there was a Schumpeterian

85 Lundvall *et al.* 1992, ch. 3; see p. 11 above.
86 Dertouzos *et al.* 1989, ch. 7.
87 E.g. Ouchi 1981.

'swarming' of new small firms, collectively referred to as New Technology-Based Firms (NTBFs), especially in the USA.[88] A major advantage of such 'flexible specialization' in high-tech industries was seen to be the hit-and-run lead time over the bureaucratic LFs, e.g. for advancing the technological frontier or for rapid changes in product quality. In Italy, the firms associated with the 'Third Italy' of flexible specialization were often very small indeed – in discussing the highly successful postwar ceramic tile industry in Sassuolo (Emilia-Romagna), Porter[89] quotes the local joke: 'With four people you can play cards. With three you can start a tile company'.

Others, however, stressed the great variability of SMFs across industrial sectors or regions. Even in the newest sectors, their dominance may have been relatively short-lived, as many were founded in the expectation of ultimately selling out to LFs (through selling their technology and marketing rights), while LFs were always likely to retain the upper hand during the scaling-up of production and mass marketing. In Japan, LFs thus undertook much of the creation of new activities; while in the USA, European firms were to be found among the acquirers of NTBFs (e.g. of the biotechnology firm Genentech by Hoffmann–LaRoche), partly through having apparently longer time horizons than their American rivals. Through reorganization to internalize economies of scope (i.e. synergies across product or other divisions) and appropriation (e.g. through trademarks), LFs were often able to reassert their dominant role. The adoption of ICTs greatly reduced the potentiality for conflict between such economies of scope and their more traditional economies of scale.[90]

B. External Funding

Ownership of many large US firms had remained concentrated in the hands of wealthy individuals or families as late as the Second World War, and even if in institutional investors like insurance companies, the stockholdings were generally understood as being retained for long-term growth. After the war, this concentration of ownership broke up, and new accumulations arose among institutional investors, especially pension and mutual funds.[91] These were necessarily committed to short-term buying and selling for immediate capital gains in the interests of their own investors – in this way patterns of ownership drove the changes in management observed above.

88 Daly 1985; Kenney 1986.
89 Porter 1990, p. 212.
90 Morroni 1992, p. 184.
91 Chandler 1990, p. 625; cf. p. 240 above.

The outcome was 'an institutionalized market for corporate control',[92] in which break-ups, takeovers and financial deals brought instability in place of long-termism. Industry lacked any 'financial commitment'.[93] Similar changes overtook the UK capital market.[94] Reports by City financiers on high-tech industries such as electronics concerned themselves solely with whether the companies were 'in play', i.e. accessible to takeover.

It is therefore usually argued that this type of financial involvement has been on balance harmful for industrial development. The standard argument goes that such short-termism is incompatible with the kind of long-run perspective needed for orderly industrial growth and particularly for innovation, where, as Carl Bosch at I.G. Farben had noted, the payoffs are almost invariably long term. Some financial economists, however, argue that the incentive in profit-making in an active capital market will produce the best long-term results in the best firms. Comparison with financial systems in some other countries would on balance seem to support the conventional view.

By contrast with the USA and UK, the financial systems of Continental Europe and Japan were more oriented to specific users and were involved from early days in long-term lending to industry. The amount of participation by banks as members of industrial executive boards was greater in such conditions. Even though the power of bankers to alter industrial strategies can be exaggerated,[95] what was most important was the very existence of such links. Recent findings have reinforced the traditional view that, although these capital markets are less 'perfect' in the economist's sense, contrary to orthodox economists' intuitions they have provided cheaper lending to industry than have financial institutions in the USA and UK.[96]

Conglomerates that had been put together essentially for financial integration from the 1950s had failed to achieve integration of the other functions, and often broke up in the 1970s and 1980s. Their role was logically limited mainly to industries with slow rates of learning and limited technological opportunities.[97] The long development times for high-tech industries required something different. The growth of networks in high-tech industries in countries like the USA was heavily dependent on financial innovation or risk-bearing, especially through the provision of 'venture capital'. New institutions set up to provide venture capital,

92 Manne 1965.
93 Lazonick 1991, p. 54.
94 Minns 1980; Ingham 1984.
95 See pp. 176–7 above.
96 Mayer 1992; Lundvall 1992 ch. 8.
97 Dosi *et al.* 1992, p. 203.

however, needed to be closely associated with the activities to which they were lending, which reinforced the advantages of localization in districts like Silicon Valley.

Successful finance involved 'learning' on both sides of the fence – by industry about finance and by financial institutions about industry and technological accumulation. Venture capital was necessarily somewhat hazardous in financial terms, and could easily be rendered unstable by changes in financial or technological environments. Without interactive learning, even supposedly venture capital firms pulled out of high-tech involvement, as happened in the UK. LFs were often important in providing successful venture capital, thus reinforcing hub-type networks. In other environments, e.g. Emilia-Romagna in the 'Third Italy', local governments or trade associations provided many of the assurances and intermediation between finance and industry.[98] The more formal collaborative arrangements which became popular in the USA after 1984 (when President Reagan altered antitrust law to permit the establishment of structures like the MCC) again tended to be funded by LFs or with government support (as in the US semiconductor programme, Sematech). In Japan, the industrial group structure internalized finance using the group's own banks (see Chapter 10). In rapidly deindustrializing countries like the UK, banking tended to remain at arm's length from manufacturing, with no interactive learning and the predominance of short-termism as discussed above in Chapter 6.[99] Financial services themselves grew rapidly.

C. Financial Globalization

Financial markets attained a very high level of internationalization, arguably in many cases to levels at which they were more attuned to financial markets of other countries than of their internal hinterland. The causes lay in both technological factors, like the development of high-speed ICTs, and organizational factors, like financial deregulation. The consequences for undermining national autonomy in terms of public finance (Keynesian demand management) have already been noted. As financial arbitrage became highly globalized, investment began to move much more freely across national and regional borders. Foreign direct investment (FDI) expanded much more rapidly than trade during the 1980s, and on balance followed a Myrdalian pattern of flowing much faster to the world's financial centres than to the needier parts of the world. As noted above, the

98 Best 1990, ch. 7.

99 For a discussion of financial systems in leading countries see Zysman 1983.

USA was the major beneficiary of net inflows of capital during that decade.[100]

V: PRODUCTS

A. Dynamic Competition

Kuznets had shown how manufacturing first rose, at the expense of agriculture, and then declined, in favour of services, in the course of long-run economic growth. According to Maddison's figures, employment in services in 16 AICs rose from 24.3 per cent in 1870 to 63.5 per cent by 1987.[101] However, the distinctions between manufacturing and services were less acute than they once had been, and many of the new industries (especially) took on certain characteristics of both – for example, both telecommunications and computers had areas in which the dividing line between manufacturing and services was almost artificial. On the side of manufacturing, the role of software had become so important in the product that it could dominate and even direct the production process; while on the side of services, the new technologies allowed services to be 'stored and forwarded', e.g. through recordings, instead of being consumed at the moment of production, as services had traditionally been defined.[102] In general, it seems more helpful to think in terms of product differentiation based on broadening ranges of technological inputs and blurring boundaries between types of output, rather than through the older sectoral classifications.

In place of the 'static' competition based on prices and costs, characteristic of much of the relatively stable postwar boom era, competition in the ensuing years has become more 'dynamic', based on product differentiation, with quality (relative to price) as the main issue. This is related to the shift of consumer tastes towards 'positional goods' as noted in Chapter 7. This 'dynamic competition' is manifested in (i) expanding product ranges and (ii) shortening product lifecycles, in which lead times are the most crucial source of appropriability.[103] By the 1970s, standard car lines like the Toyota Crown or equivalent American models

---

100 OECD 1992, ch. 10; see p. 249 above.
101 Maddison 1991, p. 73.
102 Soete 1987.
103 Cf. Levin *et al.* 1987.

were typically orderable in over 100,000 individual varieties, a world apart from Henry Ford's Model T.[104]

The former issue of expanding product diversity is examined in the next sub-section. The diversity of products was also fostered by the second issue, that of shortened product cycles. For instance, in telecommunications equipment, the technology of central switches had endured largely unchanged for around half a century from the 1910s to the 1960s (using electromechanical means); but the new generations of digital switches of the 1980s were not expected to last more than about a decade, while at the same time development times were lengthening and development costs spiralling. As already implied, this placed a high premium on 'flexibility', including the development of equipment and procedures to speed up design and commercialization, such as CAD/CAM systems. The problems were exacerbated by externally-conditioned changes in consumer tastes, especially shifts to more environmentally friendly products in the wake of the energy and materials crises, such as the 'downsizing' of motor cars.

The pace in 'dynamic competition' was set by the Japanese, who entered western markets in items like power tools or colour television sets by selling medium–high quality goods at medium–low prices.[105] Quality control moved from being essentially a defensive practice by companies to being used aggressively to capture markets. In this manner, the Japanese success, as we shall see in Chapter 10, was interpreted – not least by the Japanese themselves – as being based on the replacement of 'comparative advantage' (based on costs) with 'competitive advantage' (based on strategic foresight, and technology and product positioning). Organizational changes which permitted success in dynamic competition, like flexible automation, flexible (product) specialization, and dynamic networks, were major ingredients of 'competitive advantage', but dynamic management was necessary to bring them about.

B. Diversification

What was happening in the convergence of services and manufacturing was one aspect of an increasing complexity and interrelatedness of the structure of industries. As argued above in Chapter 1, industries can be thought of as associations of technologies and products, i.e. subsets of the whole range of available technologies *associated with* subsets of the whole range of products. Firms, in my micro taxonomy, are responsible for developing production processes and administrative structures in order to link particular

---

104 Asanuma, in Aoki and Dore 1994. However, Ford's Model T was not as unchanging as it is sometimes regarded, cf. Hounshell 1984, ch. 7.

105 Walker and Gardiner 1980.

technologies to particular products. In this period there was increasing diversity of products and technologies. For example, new advances in computing in the later 1980s involved not only solid-state physics (semiconductors) by way of science/technology background, but computer science (software), optical communications (fibre optics), optoelectronics (displays), molecular electronics, neural biology (neural networks), and so on. Applicable science itself was becoming far more interdisciplinary,[106] with biotechnology being one of the best-known examples. Thus the scientific and technological complexity of each individual product was rising. At the same time, 'pervasive' technologies, most obviously microchips, were being installed in an ever-widening range of products. Even older products were 'dematuring' and drawing on this broadening range of technologies. Moreover, production of top-end, high-quality items, such as certain brands of motor car, necessitated commitment to technology as well as design, as hinted by the Audi slogan, 'Vorsprung durch Technik'. The situation was thus as portrayed in Figure 8.3. This can be thought of as the equivalent for capital and processes of Alfred Marshall's motto for his book, *Industry and Trade* (1919), intended to explain human resources: 'The many in the one, the one in the many'.

The managerial implications were intensely complicated. Some firms sought to specialize in particular products but increasingly found their grasp of technologies inadequate, while others (or even the same firm at a later date) sought to specialize in particular technologies, but then found themselves losing product markets. The least effective strategy for most western companies was trying to persevere with the whole rapidly extending range of both technologies and products in a particular industry (the Dutch company, Philips, in the late 1980s was a good example of the problems this raised). The contrary advice often given was thus 'sticking to the knitting', but this did not solve the basic question of whether the technologies or the products – or some combination of the two – constituted the 'knitting'.[107] My presumption is that firms were most likely to survive by developing what Penrose[108] calls an 'impregnable base' out of specific sets of interlinkages between technologies and products. Diversification was inevitable if the companies were to continue to grow, but that diversification just as inevitably imposed rising costs, at least in the short term. As the core technological paradigm shifted towards ICTs, firms acquired, divested or exchanged particular 'businesses' (company divisions) as often as whole companies.[109]

---

106 Rosenberg 1994, ch. 8.
107 Dosi, Teece and Winter, in Dosi *et al.* 1992, ch. 6.
108 Penrose 1959/1980, p. 137.
109 *Ibid.*, ch. 8.

Figure 8.3: The entrepreneurial problem of scope and scale in the late 20th Century

1. Many more technologies to produce a single product

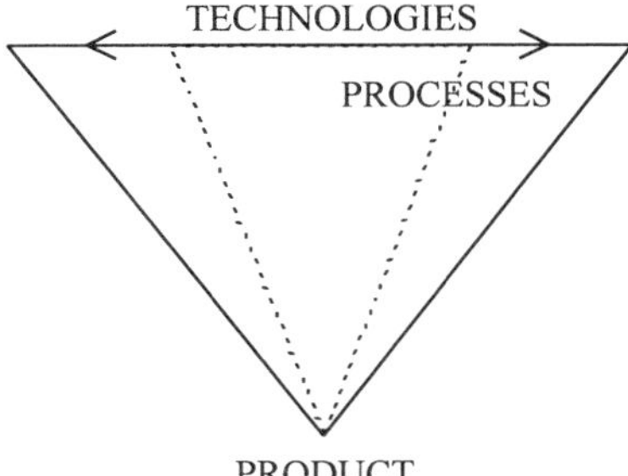

2. Many more products produced from a given technology

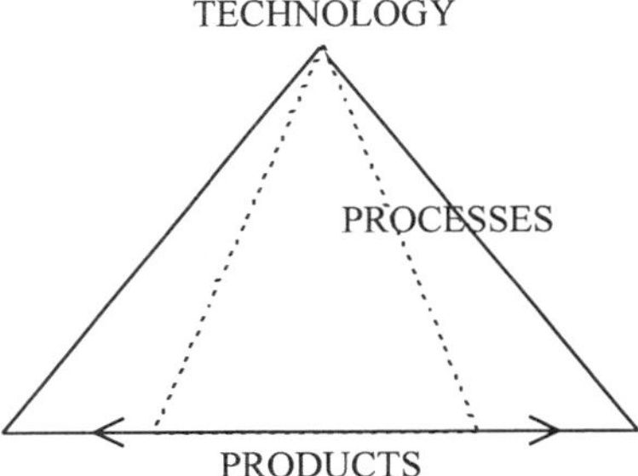

In most cases, it did not prove possible to track all the technologies plus all the products in-house, even after the reshuffling of company boundaries through mergers, etc. This helps explain the growing importance of formal and informal networks demonstrated above – the mapping of relationships between technologies and products was becoming hugely complicated in many cases, and traditional firm and even industry boundaries were losing their rationale. The obvious need and most difficult accomplishment was to develop heuristics for 'systemic co-ordination' to realize economies of scale, in the context of an ever-moving target.

Much of the economics and management literature emphasized lead times and the advantages of being a 'first mover'. This assumes a high degree of appropriability of the new technology/product structure. But such innovation often carried with it high costs in developing either the technologies or the product markets. In practice, the reduction in costs of imitation as compared with innovation often tilted the balance of advantage towards the 'fast second' strategy, of entering a market once the first movers had established its initial conditions. To do this successfully required additional incremental innovation to produce cheaper or better new products, but if this succeeded – in circumstances where the first movers were not able to capture all the gains – it could prove highly profitable, as shown by companies like Matsushita in consumer electronics. With the greater complexity of technologies, products and processes, the advantage fell to firms displaying maximum organizational flexibility.[110]

C. Product Globalization

The rapid diversification of products was also accentuated by the 'globalization' of product competition. As writers like Ohmae[111] have emphasized, this does not mean a convergence of world product types to the extent of selling the same goods in the same way in all world markets. Attempts by large motor vehicle companies to create a 'world car' in the 1970s failed, mainly because of the very differing natures of major markets,[112] though further attempts are going ahead in the 1990s. Instead the object of companies like Sony is to tailor their products to the needs of specific markets, while retaining as great a degree of technological and organizational synergy as possible. The slogan of ABB (Asea Brown Boveri), the Swiss–Swedish electrical engineering company, which has some reasonable pretensions to being one of the world's first truly globalized companies, captures this point: 'The art of being local worldwide'.

As implied in the previous chapter, globalization still has a long way to go outside of marketing, and most evidently so in the development of technology. The term 'glocalization' has been coined as an allegedly more accurate description of the current situation.[113] Patel (1995), basing himself on patents data, has suggested that the technology of particular firms has become more internationalized in *product* markets which are most *differentiated* from country to country, be it in high-tech products like pharmaceuticals or lower-tech products like building materials. This comes from the need to adapt the product in question to local needs in the manner suggested in the previous paragraph; for example, tailoring drugs to local

---

110 Morroni 1992, p. 42.

111 Ohmae 1985, 1992.

112 Altshuler *et al.* 1985, ch. 8.

113 E.g. van Tulder and Ruigrok 1993.

regulatory practices, health-care behaviour, and consumer tastes relating to drug delivery methods, etc.

Political scientists like Zysman (1993) stress that even the most 'globalized' (or 'glocalized') companies are still predominantly regionally based, notably in the 'Triad' division between North American, European and East Asian companies.[114]

VI: GOVERNMENT POLICIES

A. Macroeconomic Policy

The weakening of national macroeconomic policies demonstrated through 'stagflation' from the early 1970s, and of international policies by the flagging role of the USA (arising mainly out of domestic macroeconomic problems like budget deficits), has been noted above. With upward pressures on costs, i.e. supply limitations, helping to induce a quasi-permanent situation of inflation, attention of governments (sometimes boosted by international agencies such as the International Monetary Fund (IMF) for Britain in 1976) shifted to policies to contain inflation. 'Supply-side economics' thus aimed to restrain price or cost increases. However, this replacement of Keynesian orthodoxy, instead of examining the conditions of production at large as was warranted by the situation, became fixated on just one aspect – the supply of *money*. It would be difficult to find a sharper illustration of Marx's notion of 'fetishism'. Economists at the University of Chicago, led first by Milton Friedman (the 'monetarists'), believed that monetary policy was sufficient to contain inflation, and the containment of inflation would in turn squeeze out cost pressures. This fundamentalism became government policy under 'neoliberal' administrations such as that of Reagan in the USA and Thatcher in the UK in the 1980s. It was believed that if governments were restricted to imposing 'rules' for monetary behaviour, they would be prevented from interfering arbitrarily with the inherent supremacy of the 'invisible hand'. In practice, setting rules made it ridiculously easy for the public to out-think them and defeat their purpose – this became known as 'Goodhart's law'. The assumptions made by monetarists about learning behaviour were exceptionally naive.[115]

---

114 For a compact but comprehensive survey of trends towards 'globalization', see OECD 1992, ch. 10.

115 Lucas 1986.

In practice, policy measures in the West frequently took a somewhat different direction from that advocated by the monetarists. The McCracken Report of the OECD (1977) set out an agenda which aimed to curb public expenditure, i.e. reduce excess *demand.* The supposition underlying this policy was that excessive government expenditure was 'crowding out' private investment (which was assumed to be considerably more productive), either directly because of limitations on the supply of savings and capital funds, or indirectly through raising interest rates and thus choking off potentially deserving projects that would otherwise have been forthcoming from the private sector. Convincing evidence that a rise in government spending would bring a fall in private investment was never provided. In the event, the attempts to cut back government spending probably did more harm than good, by restricting demand expansion and thus output-inspired productivity growth (Verdoorn growth). The effects on technology, via demand-pull, etc., were never seriously thought through.

B. Liberalization

Under the neoliberal governments of the 1980s, the macroeconomic changes just described – which had in fact begun earlier, during the 1970s – became attached to the gospel of the 'free market'. It was argued that stagnation had come about through excessive government regulation and through trade-union obstructionism. These then became major targets of the 'New Right' governments. In Britain there seems little doubt that the labyrinthine structure of trade unionism that had evolved up to the 1970s was serving as a critical obstacle to rapid technological and process change – a view shared by some writers from the left[116] as well as most on the right wing. Studies appear to support the view that changes to trade-union law helped to bring about some recovery of growth in the UK in the mid-1980s, though their contribution may have been small.[117] The changes were, however, accomplished only at quite a high social cost, and more significantly may have led in precisely the wrong direction – the main impact was, and was intended to be, shifting power from labour to management, at a time when the Japanese system indicated that it would have been more productive to augment the power of (reorganized) labour.

Attacks on government regulation were even more indiscriminate. Industrial management proclaimed that excessive environmental or safety standards were stultifying growth, assisted by economists of the 'new right' claiming to demonstrate that regulations had perverse effects.[118] In fact,

116 E.g. Pollard 1982.

117 Metcalf, in Barrell 1994.

118 E.g. Peltzman 1974.

empirical studies in the USA showed no correlation between either unionism or levels of government regulation and the extent of productivity slowdown or subsequent recovery.[119] Failure to enforce adequate environmental standards probably worsened rather than improved the competitiveness of individual countries' industries in the long term, contrary to the declarations of their management, by avoiding the necessity to meet changing consumer tastes.[120]

In the UK and some other countries, liberalization became associated in the government's mind with 'privatization', i.e. the sale of ownership rights in industries nationalized since the Second World War to private investors. In practice, the old public (state) monopolies normally became private monopolies or duopolies, which because of their incentive and power to exploit consumer interests had to be regulated even more strongly than before, through the creation of governmental regulatory agencies (such as Oftel for telecoms and Ofwat for water in the UK). Thus privatization led not to deregulation so much as to 're-regulation'.[121] To confuse privatization with liberalization, as such governments themselves did, was a fundamental misunderstanding.[122]

The attitude that the market would govern industry and that free markets were thus the desideratum ignored the obvious point that markets, like any other economic institutions, are man-made and developed, and not divinely ordained. 'Supply-side economics', as implemented (if only partially) through monetarism, upheld the belief that all potentially profitable industrial opportunities would be seized on by rational entrepreneurs in free markets. Through adherence to an inappropriate economic model based on neoclassical competition, governments in the USA and UK undermined the productive bases of their economies in the belief that the effect would be greater stability[123] – in reality, such stability was more likely to come from enhancing production. Little heed was paid to the rapid changes occurring in the industries of AIC countries, or more disastrously to the need to *establish* relevant institutions in East European countries after 1989 when they sought to replace communism. There is evidence that this perspective is now being challenged, e.g. under the Clinton administration in the USA and with the resort to more pragmatic economics in parts of Eastern Europe (see Chapter 9).

---

119 Kendrick 1983. Kendrick's work was published by the American Enterprise Institute, generally regarded as a right-wing think-tank.

120 E.g. Graves 1990 for automobiles.

121 Melody 1986.

122 Kay and Thompson 1986.

123 Best 1990, pp. 200–201.

Liberalization was also attempted at the international level, particularly with the various GATT 'rounds' to liberalize trade, most recently the Uruguay Round. These encountered the problem already noted for the USA alone in Chapter 6, that countries proclaimed the desirability of universal free trade in products for which they had powerful world market positions, but the desirability of protection in areas where they were weak. The lengthy negotiations (seven years) over the Uruguay Round suggest that such liberalization is lagging behind changes in the industrial structure.

C. Regional and Sectoral Policies

Even so, in one respect the progress towards multinational liberalization was conspicuously more successful in these years, and that was towards enlarged *regional* free trade agreements. This may be regarded as an upgrading of List's original suggestion of creating Germany by way of a customs union (see Chapter 2 above). The process began in Western Europe, following from the Treaty of Rome in 1957, which led in this period to the progressive enlargement of the European Economic Community (EEC) and to the signing of the Single European Act at the end of 1992. By way of 'countervailing power', the USA with Canada and Mexico set up NAFTA (the North American Free Trade Agreement) and Japan and the Far East set up APEC (the Asia–Pacific Economic Co-operation). Essentially these represented a step-up of the 'Triad' and of global oligopolies.

Despite the attention naturally given to these developments, it was arguably at the local level that the determinants of industrial success were being forged. As seen above, it was in districts with robust local communities and identities, often with relatively strong and stable local governments (e.g. Emilia-Romagna in Italy, Baden-Württemberg in West Germany, Jutland in Denmark, Rhône-Alpes in France, Catalunya and Valencia in Spain), that industrial networks grew most successfully. The local government frequently acted as a catalyst for regional development, typically providing some of the collaborative requirements (information centres, advice, etc.) without detracting too much from competitive incentives – for example, providing assistance to industries rather than to particular firms.[124] According to Porter,[125] it is the combination of local and national (or regional) factors which most promotes 'competitive advantage', as the latter dictate broader policy and environment frameworks. It does not follow that such locally-oriented strategies can be implemented in just any industrial district, because the 'climate of opinion' and basic infrastructure

124 *Ibid.*, ch. 7.

125 Porter 1990, ch. 4.

have to be in place – several attempts to create industrial districts anew have brought about instability rather than growth.

At the sectoral level, the new policy orientation that appears to be emerging in some countries in the 1990s takes a different perspective from that of traditional industrial policy. In the productivity slowdowns and economic crises from the late 1960s, industrial policy had come to be associated mainly with rescuing 'lame duck' industries, primarily to limit the social damage. It is not difficult to see why this should have fallen into disrepute under neoliberal governments in the 1980s. However, simply leaving everything to 'market forces' did little to stave off recurrent industrial and economic problems, since the object was obviously to *change* the markets. The new ethos would instead imply a positive role for boosting potentially dynamic industries, even if they happened to be producing relatively mature products.

Even in the most passionately neoliberal countries of the 1980s there were some governmental programmes for high-tech sectors, e.g. Sematech in the USA and the Alvey Programme in the UK. These were often responses to perceived threats from competitors, e.g. from Japan's Fifth-Generation project (ICOT) in computing. But objections to interfering with market-based competition prevented these from developing 'downstream' towards commercialization, and their provenance of being limited to precommercial research often curtailed their eventual success. In many cases they were 'left hanging out to dry'.

The role of 'Vision' which Schumpeter attributed to the heroic entrepreneur was appropriated to a considerable degree by the state in Japan, and to some extent by local governments in Continental Europe. In the neoliberal countries this perspective remained anathema, at least until very recently, since industrial success was equated with competition rather than with the evolving blend of collaboration and competition that elsewhere appeared to characterize 'dynamic competition'.

9. Industrialization in the USSR

The conventional view today, in the Former Soviet Union (FSU) as well as in the West, is that the downfall of the communist system represents the inevitable supremacy of market-based systems over command economies. In that respect, it would appear to provide the clinching evidence in favour of privatization, liberalization and deregulation, along the lines being pursued a little more decorously in western nations in the 1980s. Without gainsaying for a moment the necessity of liberalizing the old repressive Soviet system, I argue in this chapter that one can focus too much on the differences between that system and capitalism in the West. Rather I wish to make more of the opposite perspective – that communism crumbled as much because its problems were *so similar* to those in western capitalism as described in the previous chapter, as because they were so different. Collapse came because the problems had become so much more acute. Schumpeter was proved right that top-heaviness of routines would cause the system eventually to fall apart, but it was socialism that expired in the face of capitalism rather than the converse he had predicted.

In this chapter I shall be focusing on the Soviet system as in its heyday. An alternative point of view is that the USSR was at bottom Russian, and many believe that the USSR represented the continuation of the Russian Empire by other means. Such arguments no doubt lie behind Gerschenkron's view that Russian industrialization even in the Soviet period can be taken as a late extension of the European model of industrialization (cf. p. 183 above). Unquestionably there were many similarities between the Soviets and their Russian predecessors (such as Witte in the late 19th century and even Peter the Great in the early 18th century) in the problems faced and some of the strategies pursued. However, in the schema I am utilizing (Figures 2.2 and 4.1), the Soviet system has to be seen as a major shift of balance towards a new pattern in which production was intended to act as the driving force.

In this respect it built more upon the American model of Fordism and Taylorism than on European models (hence some of the similarities to western problems). It failed through being a rigid, centralized, top-down, politically-based system. With the disintegration of the Soviet system in the late 1980s and early 1990s, the FSU has not yet been able to develop an adequate new driving force, and was perhaps fundamentally mistaken in trying to implement a kind of idealized Anglo-American capitalism rather than the Japanese version described in the next chapter which in my view would have served it better.

I: GROWTH

The guiding force of the USSR economy from its early days was the objective of 'catching and surpassing' the West, as enunciated in a speech by Stalin in 1928. This was most evident in the political and military spheres, where it established super-power status and a considerable degree of parity with its main rival, the United States, in military technology and production. It was also expressed throughout civilian industry, but with much less success in terms of the outcomes. Many of the failings of the civilian sector to overtake the West can be laid at the door of the primary commitment to political–military achievement, which evidently undermined the economic ability to sustain the non-military sectors in what was still a rather poor if geographically large economy. In this chapter, however, I intend to devote greater attention to the shortcomings of the civilian sectors themselves, in terms of their technologies, organizations, managements, etc.

A. Socialism in One Country

The twists and turns of Soviet strategy from late 1917 until the end of the 1920s form a fascinating story, but the detailed events of those years must be passed over, and left to the excellent histories such as that of Nove.[1] The main topic of this chapter is concerned with the uniquely Soviet contribution of central planning and the 'command economy', beginning with the First Five-Year Plan of 1928–29. After the death of Lenin, the rise to supremacy of Stalin in the late 1920s was associated with bringing about 'socialism in one country'. At this stage, it did not appear to him feasible to rely on outbreaks of socialist revolution in other countries for a 'big push' into capital-intensive industrialization.

The notion of a broader socialist base became a reality with the defeat of Nazi Germany in 1945. Having decided not to participate in the Marshall Plan, from which the USSR would almost certainly have been excluded anyway, Stalin struck credit agreements with East European allies and then drew up the Council of Mutual Economic Assistance (CMEA or Comecon) in 1949. As an agency for trade, however, it remained largely inactive for

1 Nove 1969, chs 2–6.

many years, with most eastern bloc trade being conducted bilaterally. Even so, it is difficult to avoid the conclusion that the USSR had sucked dry the resources of its satellite nations of Eastern Europe during the Iron Curtain period. As Nove[2] put it, 'to some extent Stalin really was engaged in building up the industrial base of a war economy in peacetime'. This involved imposing both the Soviet notion of central planning and the older Russian notion of empire on the Second World.

B. Planning, Prices and Markets

The most conspicuous feature of the centrally planned economy (CPE), to the eyes of a western economist, was the supersession of the market-based price system by the command economy. Planning shifted from being general guidance to being legally binding on enterprises under the Five-Year Plans (FYPs). Drafting and implementing the FYPs, together with their annual counterparts, was the main responsibility of the central planning apparatus. The planners, as at Gosplan, imposed target directives of increasing complexity, to be fulfilled by the various commissariats or ministries under them, which branched out down to the level of individual enterprises. The huge 'bounded rationality' problem – that central planners could have only a tiny fraction of knowledge of what was happening on the shopfloor, etc.[3] – limited their abilities to oversee radical change, and meant that in practice much was increased incrementally from one year to the next as a 'ratchet effect'. Sometimes targets were actually set in volume terms (tons of steel, etc.), but for the most part the goods produced were too heterogeneous to describe in this way, and the targets were thus simplified into a 'value' measure. This led to continuing and widespread abuses from the inability to specify product mixes accurately, epitomized by the cartoon in the underground magazine, *Krokodil*, ca. 1960, of a plant with a single enormous nail outside as large as the plant itself, and the manager proudly boasting, 'We fulfilled our target!'. For the enterprise, fulfilment of the plan was indeed always the overriding consideration. The central planners for their part had the job of equating supplies with demand, which was accomplished chiefly through the calculation of 'material balances' (basically input–output).

In the Soviet economy, prices were imposed, supposedly to meet the requirements of Marx's labour theory of value, as set out in Chapter 2 above – thus they were meant to reflect the 'socially necessary labour-time' for the production of the item in question. Since it was impracticable to assess exactly how much time was socially necessary, the inevitable

---

2 *Ibid.*, p. 378.

3 Nove 1977, ch. 4.

solution in most cases was to impose 'cost-plus' prices, with the 'plus' element representing the margin that needed to be added on to the sales revenues as a kind of 'profit'. In order to prevent values accumulating to non-existent capitalists, the rate of interest was set at zero for reckoning costs (until 1965 when its distortive effects were becoming increasingly evident).

Whatever the case, the objective was to set prices or values in the light of supply (cost) determinants, and to avoid prices that indicated what Marx termed 'use-values', i.e. demand-driven prices. Prices were set for the most part below what market-equilibrating forces would have led to, so creating quasi-permanent 'sellers' markets' in which *ex-ante* aggregate demand in the Keynesian sense outstripped aggregate supply. Kornai,[4] the eminent Hungarian economist, therefore characterized the CPE as a 'shortage economy', maintained as such by 'taut planning'. Planning had to be taut to maximize inducements to growth of output. Because of the obvious computational problems – there were around ten million prices to determine in the mid-1970s – prices tended to be left unchanged for long tracts of time. Even in the USSR some areas were left open to a measure of market influence (more so in most of its postwar communist allies in Eastern Europe). In consumer goods, for instance, it was generally left to the consumers to decide how much they wished to purchase at the imposed prices – formal rationing was resorted to at times during the early FYPs, but for the most part was reserved as in the West to wartime circumstances. With the 'sellers' market' and 'shortage economy', of course, there was extensive informal rationing through queues, etc., as well as the rise of black markets.

The most important, perhaps, of the market-based systems was the labour market, in which enterprises were expected to hire whatever workers they required to fulfil their plan, while conversely workers were required to find jobs for themselves if they needed them. Given the extremely high turnover of labour, at both manual and managerial levels, such mechanisms were often called into account. Stalin in 1931 declared that equality was a petty bourgeois concept, and opened the door to wide discrepancies in earnings even at the plant level.[5] However, in the context of the 'sellers' market' there was usually excess demand for labour, so unemployment remained low and urban income inequalities (except for the Party apparatchiks) did not usually become intolerable – they were narrowed as a matter of policy after Stalin's death. To quell disquiet and help ensure the plans approached fulfilment, there was always the threat of the secret police (successively Cheka, OGPU, NKVD and KGB) and/or the gulags.

---

4 Kornai 1980.

5 Lampert 1979, p. 141.

C. Output and Investment

Work by Bergson (1963), based on Total Factor Productivity (TFP) indicated that the 'static efficiency' of the USSR was low relative to the AICs, but 'dynamic efficiency' as measured by the growth rate of this indicator was high. Bergson attributed this primarily to (i) high rates of investment, with capital per head rising about eight times from 1928 to 1967,[6] (ii) rising labour skills, and (iii) borrowing advanced technologies, as in the catch-up model (see Chapter 3 above). Such views were largely supported in subsequent studies at the macroeconomic level but just as largely rejected by those at the micro level who believe organizational factors were more important.[7] Later macro estimates by Bergson and others indicated a tendency towards slowing down in the growth rate of TFP in more recent times, approaching zero by the 1980s.[8] To some degree this can be attributed to the 'just-in-case' hoarding of resource inputs like labour.[9] Other critics pointed to the severe difficulties with using a TFP assessment for an economy with administered rather than market-based prices.[10] Nove,[11] who rarely flinches from contention, reaches the point of despair and concludes that valid calculations of Soviet growth rates are unattainable – the rapid downward revisions of East European GNPs since 1989 regrettably support him. There seems some agreement nowadays that the probably high growth rates of the 1930s to the 1960s owed more to Lewis-like (classical) mechanisms of the transfer of labour from agriculture to industry and from unproductive to productive employment than to especially rapid change within industry.[12]

Similar pricing problems beset attempts to compare R&D expenditures with those of western countries – most estimates place the share of such expenditures in GDP as somewhat higher in the USSR.[13] Some part of this can be explained by high military-related R&D, which used to be supposed to be over half the Soviet total, though post-Soviet re-estimates put the military share as high as three-quarters. By western standards, there was also a disproportionately high share of Research rather than Development.

---

6 Grossman 1973, p. 515.

7 Granick 1967, pp. 7–8, 265; Amann *et al.* 1977, ch. 1.

8 Bergson 1978, ch. 9; Desai 1987, ch. 3; Hanson and Pavitt 1987, pp. 66–8; Dyker 1992.

9 *Ibid.*; and see below, p. 334.

10 E.g. Amann *et al.* 1977, pp. 11–12.

11 Nove 1969, App.

12 *Ibid.*, p. 267; Bergson 1978, ch. 2; Dyker 1992; cf. ch. 3 above.

13 Hanson and Pavitt 1987, p. 54; but see Gokhberg and Mindely, in Glaziev and Schneider 1993.

There appears to have been considerable decline in total innovational output in the late years of the USSR, especially in the 1980s.[14]

High levels of investment in plant and also R&D, leading to high capital-intensity, thus encountered low rates of profitability on the supply side and severe problems of 'realization' on the demand side. Like Schumpeter, Marx's prognosis seems to have been right for the wrong sort of economy.

II: TECHNOLOGY

A. Sectors and the Soviet Industrialization Debate

The sectoral basis for industrialization lay at the heart of the intellectual debates of the mid-1920s, because it raised the crucial political as well as economic issues at their starkest. The Bolsheviks had come somewhat unexpectedly to power in the October Revolution of 1917 through a rather unlikely tactical alliance (*smychka*) between industrial workers and non-socialist peasants. This was sporadically threatened by economic and political disturbances through the early 1920s, and raised the question of how industrialization could then proceed.

In sectoral terms, three main positions were staked out by the intellectual leaders, following Lenin's death.[15] On the 'far right' was a small group, represented by Shanin at the State Bank, advocating the tactical need to rely in the mean time on comparative advantage, which meant investing in labour-intensive agriculture to expand primary exports – these could be used to import equipment, etc. as a foundation for manufacturing, with trade acting as an 'engine' of growth. The problem here – apart from the political one of depending on the peasantry – was the static nature of the argument.[16] In the middle (though soon to be denounced as 'right-wing deviationists'), Bukharin and others objected to the implicit support this would have offered to anti-socialist forces in agriculture, and especially the better-off peasantry (kulaks). They instead advocated industrialization via light industry, thus following the pattern of Britain and many Continental countries, essentially on grounds of conserving the USSR's limited capital and skill resources. Any technological stagnation that might seem to be equated with this choice could be offset by 'rationalization' (speed-up, etc.) and electrification.[17] The capital requirements of the construction phase – the problem Hicks was later to identify – would be kept down by this

14 Hanson and Pavitt 1987, pp. 60–62; Gokhberg and Mindely, *loc. cit.*

15 Erlich 1960; Nove 1969, ch. 5.

16 Erlich 1960, pp. 132–5.

17 *Ibid.*, p. 67.

strategy. Trade here acted more as a 'handmaiden' to growth.[18] On the 'left wing' were such as Preobrazhensky, who considered that both of these positions consigned the country to slow growth of capacity, and who thus supported the immediate resort to heavy industry and to 'socialist protectionism'. In contrast to the 'balanced growth' of those advancing the cases of investment in agriculture or light industry, this was therefore a plea for 'unbalanced growth', stressing the forward-linkage effects of massive investment in basic industries and infrastructure (cf. pp. 86–7 above).

B. Capital Intensity and Imported Technology

Where would the huge requirements of capital for such an unbalanced growth programme come from? Distantly echoing Marx (see Table 2.1 above), Preobrazhensky looked for 'primitive socialist accumulation' to forced savings from the peasantry (obtained through manipulating prices) and foreign borrowing. Stalin rejected international assistance as improbable (something the onset of Slump made even more plausible) and solved the conundrum by the enforced collectivization of agriculture, to 'liquidate the kulaks as a class' and squeeze the maximum surplus out of the remaining peasantry. Ellman (1975) shows that the brunt of the burden was in fact borne by the workers themselves, through massive declines in real wages, in other words through a kind of draconian Ricardian strategy. Similar sources also probably paid for much of the Soviet effort in the Second World War.

The right-wing position in the industrialization debate originally advocated capital-saving, labour-using techniques, essentially on the same grounds as were 20 years later to be advanced by Lewis in his model.[19] By 1926 most, however, had rejected this path as the route to long-run stagnation. The logical argument for favouring capital intensity and heavy industry was put forward in the economic model of Fel'dman in 1928[20] – which looked backwards to Marx's model of 'extended reproduction' but was also a precursor of the Harrod–Domar model as Domar[21] himself acknowledged. The first FYP therefore assumed that fast growth entailed moving as rapidly as possible to the technological frontier, and importing or copying best-practice techniques in the AICs. The latter were generally identified with the USA, and in view of the technological biases adopted in that country, the implication was that the USSR would install capital-intensive processes as well as products, even though these were

18 *Ibid.*, p. 140.
19 Nove 1969, pp. 130–31; cf. pp. 63–4 above.
20 *Ibid.*, pp. 132–3.
21 Domar 1957, ch. 9.

'inappropriate' for its existing resource endowments. The central planners from early years placed heavy emphasis on introducing imitated technologies, via capital goods imports and often turnkey plants.[22]

What exactly they gained from their strategy is more debatable – the pattern that emerged was more dualistic, with areas of both high and low capital intensity depending on the sector, and large segments of labour intensity in auxiliary operations like fitting and handling within large plants.[23] For the specific case of the metal-fabricating industries in the 1930s, Granick (1967) concludes that both the resort to capital-intensive processes and the associated importation of unadapted western technologies were at best counterproductive and at worst disastrous. On balance, the evidence he marshals suggests that they set back the rate of growth instead of bringing about a leapfrog. He does, however, emphasize that he is considering only the *intra*-sectoral impact within the particular sector he studies, and not the sectoral changes outlined above. In the next chapter, it is seen that postwar Japan made a similar set of choices in favour of heavy industry, capital intensity and advanced technologies, contrary to the then-existing pattern of factor endowments; and that by general consent this strategy there proved highly successful for leapfrogging. Aside from the obvious differences in political context, this suggests that it is the implementation of the strategy that is crucial, rather than its inherent rightness or wrongness.

The achievements soon came to be criticized for technological conservatism, whatever the intentions may have been. Old methods like coal rather than oil, or steam rather than diesel locomotives, or traditional building materials, or the neglect of chemicals, were being thought by the mid-1950s to have persisted too long; a decade later, Kosygin as prime minister pointed to unacceptable lags in the take-up of transistors, polypropylene, etc.[24] Even with the advantage of imitation, lead-times in development and assimilation in new industries were substantially longer than in the USA,[25] and steadily lengthening. Lead-times were also inordinately long in diffusing specific technologies licensed from the West[26] – one suggested reason was that Soviet government negotiators received bonuses for securing the licences at lower prices, even if this meant further delays in completing the deal.[27] There were bigger obstacles, however – enormous political barriers to visits by industrialists to western plants

22 Grossman 1973, p. 514; Berliner 1976, p. 3; Lewis 1979, p. 116.
23 Granick 1967; Dyker 1992.
24 Zaleski *et al.* 1969, pp. 394, 398.
25 *Ibid.*, pp. 400–401; Amann and Cooper 1982, pp. 17, 37, 447.
26 Hanson and Pavitt 1987, p. 84.
27 Amann and Cooper 1982, pp. 437–43.

severely restricted the spillovers of production knowhow.[28] Overall, there is some indication that industries in which the Soviets were most dependent on imported western technology were those in which it was farthest behind (e.g. computers, semiconductors, chemicals). Although some of this may be put down to American prohibitions on high-tech exports to the Comecon bloc, as through COCOM, the general view appears to be that the technological gap was in any case too large for such prohibitions to have bitten very hard. The deficiencies were in knowledge rather than information. The Soviet economy seemed much more successful in scaling up existing methods than in rapidly diffusing new methods, even when the latter could be imitated from the AICs. A recent estimate (by the then Russian Minister for Foreign Economic Relations) put the average technological gap with the West in major industries at 10–15 years in the mid-50s, rising to 20–30 years by the mid-80s, with the greatest retardation in high-tech sectors.[29] As technological complexity intensified in the West, and the technological paradigms began to shift – in ways illustrated in the previous chapter – the USSR fell further and further behind.

C. Process vs. Product Innovation

The basic weakness of the Soviet economy was that it was never able to sustain a high enough rate of *productive* innovation to succeed in its aim of overtaking the capitalist West, other than in a few sectors like defence where special considerations applied. The emphasis is on ‘productive’ innovation because there were considerable incentives towards differentiating products. Each research institute or design bureau was likely to come up with hosts of ‘new’ products, which for the most part were incompatible with their predecessors, and a large part of the time in no obvious way superior to the rival products of other institutes and bureaux. Nevertheless, the institute in question would fulfil its plan by delivering them. Design bureaux were judged for planning purposes by the number of designs they produced, in complete contravention of the objective of reducing duplication. Only 17 per cent of designs in the control and instrumentation industry were actually utilized.[30] Much the same went for specialist project-technical institutes intended specifically for designing new production processes, and capital project organizations for new plant. Product lifecycles in practice were thus long extended, with the intention of maximizing learning-curve effects, but actually minimizing the learning

28 Berliner 1976, p. 515.
29 Glaziev and Schneider 1993, p. 238.
30 Cf. Amann and Cooper 1982, pp. 14, 46.

that comes from new models.[31] Organizations had no responsibility for delivery on time, and it is no accident that the demand side was referred to as 'distribution', not 'marketing'.[32]

While the problems of product innovation had to do mainly with the lack of economic incentives from the demand side, for process innovation the main problems were organizational.[33] In a context of exacting production targets, process technologies were required to meet the objectives of reduced downtime, fast throughput, machine co-ordination and systemic co-ordination discussed in Chapter 4 above. Early attempts to augment throughput focused on labour process, best known via the 'Stakhanovite' movement in 1935, whereby employment was reorganized in Babbage-like fashion to attain very high output per shift. This was interpreted by Soviet scholars as a Marxian reduction of the socially necessary labour time, and can be regarded as time saving in our sense, in that output increased per unit of time from an undiminished labour force – though later there did arise some concern over technological unemployment.[34] The second phase of Stakhanovism in 1939 instead concentrated on machine productivity, i.e. 'capital process', again time saving but in relation to equipment.[35] Despite their high propaganda value, neither phase took hold in a permanent way. Only to a limited extent were they directed at innovation, as distinct from speeding up existing technology.[36] Engineering solutions were developed to solve problems of capital process, such as 'group technology',[37] but their diffusion was disappointing.

There were frequently voiced complaints about lags in delivery times for new equipment orders – the annual planning process meant that each stage in turn had usually to be planned for the following year, without any cross-consultation, so that delivery might take several years longer than necessary simply because of the bureaucratic delays arising out of planning. Downtimes were high because of low labour skills, poor quality components, and lack of supplies at vital times. The problem of distancing between innovation producer and user raised the added complication that often the equipment supplied was incompatible with what was already in place – thus systemic co-ordination was weak. If fast throughput was attained, it was regarded as being achieved by sacrificing product quality, all too often to an unacceptable degree.

31 Berliner 1976, pp. 197–8.
32 *Ibid.*, ch. 7.
33 Amann and Cooper 1982, pp. 18, 249.
34 Berliner 1976, pp. 158–69.
35 Granick 1954, p. 86.
36 *Ibid.*, pp. 247–8.
37 Amann and Cooper 1982, ch. 3.

D. R&D and Learning – Segmentation

The roots of such inadequacies lie further back, in the segregation of science from industry in Tsarist Russia, caused by official suspicion of the intelligentsia on the one side, and the large degree of control of modern industry by foreign capital on the other.[38] Its basis lay in a strictly 'linear' notion of the process of technological accumulation, i.e. one in which science develops basic research, R&D laboratories and the like apply this research to practical industrial problems, and then firms take up the applied results and diffuse them across the face of industry. As indicated elsewhere in this book, governments in the West often pursued similar notions of the R&D process, even though most technological advance in practice came about in quite different ways. In the USSR, the division of R&D labour was associated with a vertical segmentation of the R&D process. At the top, in basic research, came the USSR Academy of Sciences (supported in later years by the Academies of the larger republics), with full responsibility for basic research. Below it came a range of research establishments, especially the numerous research institutes, mainly responsible for applied research. Initially it was intended that these would deliver the information about technologies to the user firms with which they were organizationally linked. This structure made some sense in the early industrialization spurt, when technologies were mostly imported.[39] But as time went on, and there were greater calls for indigenous development, it became evident that the information passed on by the research institutes was often barely usable by firms, so a lower tier of design bureaux was added, aiming at Development rather than Research. Manufacturing enterprises were construed as largely passive users of technologies, not their producers.

This hierarchical, linear procedure for generating new technologies proved grossly inadequate, essentially because of the lack of learning and especially interactive learning between research and production.[40] Research institutes and the other tiers fulfilled their plans when delivering the target values of new techniques, with the values appraised usually by the labour costs of their production. They were widely criticized for 'ivory tower' attitudes to industry.[41] The technologies they produced frequently showed little awareness of the technological heuristics being pursued by industry, e.g. towards saving capital.[42] It was hard luck for the user firms if all sorts

38 Lewis 1979, p. 3; Lampert 1979, chs 1–3; Amann and Cooper 1982, p. 131; Glaziev and Schneider 1993, pp. 129–31.

39 Berliner 1976, pp. 196–7; Amann and Cooper 1982, p. 19.

40 Zaleski *et al.* 1969, p. 425.

41 Lewis 1979, pp. 130–32; Amann and Cooper 1982, p. 16.

42 Granick 1967, p. 198.

of adaptations were required to get the techniques to work in practice – worse than that, any diversion of the enterprise's activities to getting the defective technique up and running threatened its own ability to fulfil exacting annual output targets. Discovery of faults in new designs typically came long after their commercialization.[43] Thus enterprises were discouraged by their own (imposed) short-term horizons from adopting new technologies, and particularly any radical technical changes, which might severely interrupt normal production. This was the first way in which the Soviets' problem echoed that in the West, with the difference being that short-termism was imposed by diktat rather than by financial imperatives.

The downstream knock-on effects of R&D shortcomings were exacerbated by the fact that the percentages of fulfilment of Science and New Technology plans were well below those of production plans.[44] However, the most serious problem was the lack of in-house R&D within manufacturing enterprises, the source of strength in the more dynamic capitalist firms as seen in Chapter 6 – though many had 'laboratories', their primary function was usually routine testing of precisely the kind that, as we saw, American firms tended to contract out.[45] Wage differentials also strongly favoured employment in research institutes rather than factory-based R&D, as did provision of instrumentation and equipment.[46]

From 1960 there were attempts to replace the cost-based system with a concept of 'economic return' to successful applied research, but evaluating the various costs and benefits proved predictably taxing.[47] The meaning of the benefits was dubious in a situation in which planners determined the size of the market. There was in any case considerable opposition to a more market-based system, quite apart from any ideological reservations. One was that it would make output and investment planning more difficult for the central planners. A second, and more profound, was that technology development in the USSR was based on the assumption that technology was 'information' – the production of new technology could be costed in terms of the labour values but it then ought to be provided free of charge to users, in order to maximize its diffusion and hence the industrial rate of growth. A compromise was sought from the mid-1960s in arguments for considering a 'research-production cycle' in which longer time horizons and interactions would be given explicit attention.[48] These bore some fruit in the form of the

---

43 Amann and Cooper 1982, p. 87.

44 Zaleski *et al.* 1969, p. 90.

45 *Ibid.*, p. 410; Berliner 1976, pp. 32–3, 105; Lewis 1979, chs 3, 8; Amann and Cooper 1982, p. 165.

46 *Ibid.*, pp. 412, 427.

47 Zaleski *et al.* 1969, pp. 43–4.

48 *Ibid.*, pp. 40–42.

'science-production associations' set up after 1968, aimed at institutionally bringing R&D and production together, which did claim to reduce lead times, although failing to escape the long arm of output targets or problems of divided loyalties.[49]

Contract research was introduced on a limited scale after 1932 and again from the mid-1950s in an effort to get the various upper tiers in the R&D process to produce technologies that better met the needs of downstream users.[50] Though this enjoyed some popularity, it did not go far enough towards filling the research–production gap, for two main reasons. One was that it still involved the vertical segmentation, effectively continuing to treat technologies as information rather than as knowledge. One slightly absurd consequence of this was that industrial espionage undertaken by Soviets in the West was entrusted to apparatchiks and professional spies rather than to the scientists or industrialists who might have actually learnt something from it. Second, there was another kind of segmentation, which chopped the process into still more unconnected pieces. This was the structure of sectoral/industrial divisions, or 'branches', inaugurated in the many commissariats of the interwar and wartime periods, and continued under ministries postwar. Each branch ran its own set of research institutes and design bureaux, as well as enterprises. Although introduced to combat the wasteful duplication of R&D facilities which Soviet critics levelled at western firms, the result was precisely the opposite, of leading to a vast amount of duplication among branches which did not communicate with one another.[51] There was therefore little or no 'technological convergence' of Rosenberg's kind in the upstream process sectors (capital goods).[52] Branches like machine tools produced narrow product ranges in large factories using low-skilled labour, as contrasted with western emphasis on small firms and high skills.[53] Above all, the integration of multiple technologies into products of the complex kind described in the last chapter proved practically out of the question.

The result of these vertical and horizontal stratifications was that, by world standards, basic research was more advanced than applied research, applied research more so than development, development more so than commercialization of innovation, while diffusion of innovation was the most backward of all.[54] The long lead-times for establishing new industries were mentioned above in regard to imported methods, and more generally

49 Berliner 1976, pp. 136–47; Amann and Cooper 1982, pp. 32, 199, 241, and ch. 10.
50 Zaleski *et al.* 1969, pp. 452–4, 465–9; Lewis 1979, ch. 7.
51 Berliner 1976, p. 124; Nove (1977, ch. 3) described this as 'centralized pluralism'.
52 Berliner 1976, p. 112.
53 Amann and Cooper 1982, p. 41.
54 Amann *et al.* 1977, ch. 2.

there is strong empirical evidence that lead-times for indigenous innovation were unduly long and growing.[55] Some of this had to do with unduly slow rates of scrapping obsolescent plant and equipment, the result of the predominance of plan fulfilment targets and the 'ratchet effect', plus problems of accurately valuing capital – thus inducing a negative commitment to older technologies and processes. Some of it had to do with the over-engineering of capital goods.[56] But there was also a lack of positive commitment on the demand side to newer methods, for reasons already adduced.

The above description naturally varied in detail from one branch to another, and there were a number of exceptions. One branch that was much more successful in its R&D was defence (including military-related areas like nuclear power). Three reasons can be given for this. One was that technologies for the defence sector in the West as well as the USSR are organized according to the linear model of vertical segmentation. The second was the topmost priority and attention given to the defence sector at the highest political levels – here Russian imperialism and Soviet theory joined hands.[57] But the most interesting reason for us is the third: that in this field, many of the evident gaps in the civilian sectors were explicitly filled – there was extensive user–producer interaction, knowledge sharing, project-based work, emphasis on Development in users rather than Research, focus on simplicity of design, use of interchangeable parts and sub-assemblies, and so on. Innovation was frequently based around project teams led by highly talented 'first circle' designers, for example the likes of Tupolev, Yakovlev, Mikoyan and Sukhoi in aviation – often in direct competition.[58] Granted that a 'mission-oriented' approach would have been less satisfactory in many other fields, it was the failure to develop a similarly complex structure for the rest of industry that was at the heart of the failure of Soviet technological accumulation, and it would appear that that has to be blamed primarily on political and organizational rather than economic factors.

55 Amann and Cooper 1982, p. 84; Hanson and Pavitt 1987, p. 31; Dyker 1992.
56 Berliner 1976, ch. 12.
57 Amann and Cooper 1982, p. 279.
58 Amann *et al.* 1977, chs 9–10; Lewis 1979, ch. 9; Amann and Cooper 1982, chs 7–8.

III: ORGANIZATION

A. Hierarchies and Bureaucracies

The above discussion of central planning has given some idea of the ways in which rigidly hierarchical systems operated in the Soviet Union, not least in the area of new technologies. The vertical top-to-bottom scale was divided horizontally into commissariats (later ministries) with responsibility for a particular branch of industry. This fostered primary allegiances to branches ('branch patriotism') rather than to the broader goals of overtaking the West, etc.[59] Branches, and the R&D establishments attached to them, sought mainly to amass resources and power, rather than effect major savings.[60] Such problems were never resolved. The problems from multiple decision-making did not rest there, however. As implied in regard to technology, each function was also separated, up to the highest levels. At the top, the central planning agency (Gosplan, etc.) and other central committees, the various ministries, the Ministry of Finance, the State Bank and other banks, all had their separate views on where the economy was to go, and lower echelons might receive demands from all of these.[61] These functional schisms further added to the confusion and to the difficulties of achieving any particular set of targets – the problem was known in Russian as *funktsionalka*.[62] In an economy where prices were mostly imposed by authority (or authorities), the conflicts had to be met by pushing vast amounts of paper and documentation around the system. Thus arose unwieldy bureaucracies, which further served to slow down procedures which they were originally intended to accelerate. Though the Soviets ostensibly regarded bureaucracies as evil, they succeeded only in proliferating them, and blamed individuals when things went wrong.[63] The USSR after 1934 can be thought of as a kind of giant M-form company, but unable ever to overcome the potential weaknesses of the M-form structure.[64]

The Communist Party was assigned the role of trying to repair and re-integrate these functional schisms, at all levels from the factory floor up to the Politburo.[65] Though sometimes committed Party members proved able

59 Berliner 1976, p. 69; Glaziev and Schneider 1993, pp. 26–7.
60 *Ibid.*, p. 44.
61 Berliner 1976, pp. 33–8; Lewis 1979, ch. 4.
62 Nove 1969, p. 213.
63 Granick 1954, ch. 14.
64 Before 1934 the structure was more like U-form, with a functional partitioning, cf. *ibid.*, p. 31.
65 *Ibid.*, ch. 12.

to do this, the general outcome was all too predictable, being one of adding yet another layer of confusion to the system, from top to bottom.

B. Scale and Scope

One of the less emphasized issues in the great industrialization debate of the 1920s, but just as important, was that over the organization of industry. The choice was seen as coming down clearly between a German pattern, based as in Chapter 5 above on skills, moderate throughput, and SMFs, and an American pattern, as in Chapter 6 above, replacing skills, building large plants, and achieving high throughput from advanced process technologies and Fordist–Taylorist working practices. The West European model was accepted to be more appropriate to the existing industrial situation, and the problems associated with the rigidity of the American mass production model were equally accepted.[66] Nevertheless, the Soviets plumped unhesitatingly for the latter, partly because of fears that the USSR lacked a skilled labour force, and partly on the positive grounds that this – like capital intensity – was seen as the route to fast catch-up. From virtually zero in 1929, the proportion of machine tools working on large lots by 1932 had risen to 21 per cent and the same for continuous-flow production, whilst in low-skill areas alone the ratios had become 39 per cent and 44 per cent.[67] This emphasis on new construction and giant plants remained: thus heavy chemical plants in the 1970s were typically 60–70 per cent larger than their US counterparts.[68]

It was assumed that scale economies would be maximized by building plants as big as total output (regional or national) required.[69] Whether giant plants really did achieve static, much less dynamic, cost reductions when set against counteracting forces such as managerial diseconomies of scale is more dubious (recollect Marshall's findings about technological economies of scale being maximized in medium rather than very large firms). There were at least three negative consequences which could offset any such scale economies, and which led to the giant enterprises often being denounced as 'gigantomania'.

(a) Dynamic scale economies from repeated construction of more or less standardized factory layouts failed to emerge, as a consequence of putting all the eggs in one basket, i.e. one very large plant, as happened in setting up the tractor industry.[70] In other

66 Granick 1967, pp. 24–5.
67 *Ibid.*, pp. 25–6.
68 Amann and Cooper 1982, p. 128.
69 Rosenberg 1992.
70 Granick 1967, pp. 117–19.

activities, the importation of a turnkey plant often failed to lead to any capability to replicate it domestically.[71]

(b) Monopolization was strongly encouraged, hence adding to the difficulties of Soviet production as viewed from the demand (product) side.[72] Between one-half and two-thirds of industrial products were produced by just one or two enterprises.[73] As the system began to fall apart in the later 1980s, de-monopolization was seen as one of the most pressing of needs for reconstruction.[74]

(c) Plants – even large plants – were encouraged to produce a very narrow range of goods, again in the expectation that such was the way to maximize the economies of scale.[75] In conjunction with monopolization, this served consumers very badly, but it also implied a deficiency in reaping economies of scope on the supply side. When allied with an equally restricted range of upstream suppliers, it tended to imply a very limited range of operation for learning by using.

There was a case for new plant construction to achieve catch-up in the early years of the 'command economy', though its success in practice was muted. Once indigenous development became predominant, any such dynamism flagged.[76] On the other side, there was no real effort to imitate the core of the 'American system of manufactures', which was the provision of interchangeable parts and sub-assemblies. This owed partly to the lack of a large enough market, but also to the lack of development of complementary inputs – leapfrogs like this needed to be grounded in much greater accumulation of knowledge.[77] The Soviets instead believed Henry Ford that workers could be trained rapidly on the job (see p. 234 above). Peasant youths and untrained women were preferred as employees to recruiting artisans from SMFs.[78] Continuous-flow production ebbed away as a result of such deficiencies.[79]

C. Vertical Integration

This lack of standardization also owed much to the peculiarly Soviet structure of verticalized branches of industry. The most serious problem a

71 Amann and Cooper 1982, p. 444.
72 Berliner 1976, p. 529.
73 Glaziev and Schneider 1993, p. 239.
74 *Ibid.*, p. 46.
75 Granick 1967, pp. 36, 40.
76 Hanson and Pavitt 1987, p. 33.
77 Granick 1967, pp. 44–7.
78 *Ibid.*, pp. 92–3.
79 *Ibid.*, pp. 112–15.

manager of an enterprise regularly encountered in trying to meet his or her output target was not distribution or the demand side, since the central planners were supposed to take care of that. The most common problem in the context of the 'shortage economy' was instead the inflow of supplies. If there was an interruption in the supplies of materials, etc., not only would his production fall, but more than likely he would be blamed for it, or be compelled to blame himself through 'self criticism'.[80] Nor could he necessarily build up a rapport with suppliers that might overcome the immediate problem, because the planners (ministries or sub-branches) were wont to change the supplier source at will from one year to the next. Apart from the quantity of supplies, quality was also highly unreliable, for reasons discussed above.[81] There were efforts to introduce 'zero defects' practices, the 'Saratov system',[82] but in the absence of strong user–producer relationships these achieved little.

Managers, confronted by such problems – as they often were – might well resort to attempted bartering with suppliers or to the black market. Greater assurance was, however, found by producing the supplies, typically including equipment and machinery, in-house. These enterprises were pressured to create vertically integrated structures, in which both process and product chains became vertically linked. Minor components were produced in their own 'dwarf workshops'.[83] All this ran wholly counter to the intentions of top authorities to maximize the division of labour and gains from specialization.[84] 'Taut planning' perversely generated offsetting searches for slack wherever it could be found, and vertical integration was one means towards it.[85] The integration also went far further than the experience of rival capitalist countries, where the product chains sometimes became vertically integrated, but dynamic gains proved more efficient when the process chains were kept largely separated. In the Soviet Union such dynamic gains from sideways spillover were rarely available – a survey in the early 1980s showed that over 80 per cent of innovations produced by supplier firms were used in just one or two downstream plants.[86]

80 Granick 1954, chs 7–8; 1967, ch. 5.
81 Amann and Cooper 1982, p. 93.
82 Cf. Berliner 1976, p. 111.
83 Dyker 1976, p. 47.
84 Granick 1967, p. 143.
85 *Ibid.*, 1967, p. 224.
86 Glaziev and Schneider 1993, p. 47.

IV: MANAGEMENT

A. One-Man Management

Given the rigidly hierarchical and linear structure of organizations and decision-making, it might well be thought that the director of an enterprise had little autonomy to act in managerial fashion. Indeed, it is not really appropriate to talk about 'firms' in the Soviet context,[87] and better to use the word 'enterprise'. With the economy, or at least a branch of the economy, being thought of as a kind of overgrown multidivisional company, the enterprise more resembled a division or department of an analogous western firm, and its director a divisional head. The enterprise itself was only part-way down the hierarchy – within the enterprise there were likely to be several shops devoted to particular products or processes, and often enough within each shop several 'brigades' that were process and product specific. Thus one can readily imagine a one-way traffic in decisions all the way down the hierarchy.

In practice, it did not work out like that, and it was perhaps at the enterprise manager (director) level that the flow was most interrupted.[88] For one thing, the plans of the central authorities would become merely fantastical (as they often did in earlier years) without a reverse flow of more realistic forecasts from enterprises back up to them. For this reason, the final form of the FYP was often not agreed and accepted until after it was actually in operation. A second reason was that no centrally determined plan could possibly take into account all factors that would crop up in a year, much less five years – hence there were countless individual decisions that still needed to be taken at the enterprise level. A third and arguably most important explanation for the importance of the plant or enterprise manager was dealing with the multiplicity of decision channels, functionally specialized in the manner already described. Reconciling conflicting targets and priorities was his or her job, if only implicitly through the actual outcomes attained.

The directors of enterprises therefore were by no means necessarily cyphers. It is true that they faced a more powerful political counterweight than did their equivalents in a capitalist firm, in the form of the local Communist Party membership – by the mid-1930s most industrial managers belonged to the Party, though no doubt often for tactical as much as ideological reasons, and unquestionably without ending the feuding

87 The Russian word for firm (*firma*) was a specialized term meaning a merger of several very small enterprises into a small–medium one.

88 Granick 1954, *passim*; Berliner 1976, p. 15.

between the two.[89] But even allowing for that, they – rather than (as intended) the Party stalwarts – probably played the decisive role in most cases in successfully or unsuccessfully implementing the plan. In this sense, their contribution matched that of their western counterparts, and especially the middle management of American firms as described in Chapter 6.

From the early days of War Communism after 1917, Lenin was repudiating the 'syndicalism' implied by worker-managed enterprises[90] and asserting the primacy of 'one-man management', meaning that – so long as the directives handed down from above were observed as fully as possible – the director could be expected to hold sway in his enterprise. Lenin was extremely impressed by the potentialities of Taylorism, and argued that, 'We must organise in Russia the study and teaching of the Taylor system and systematically try it out and adapt it to our ends'.[91] The term 'one-man management' constantly resurfaced during the launching of the command economy in the late 1920s and early 1930s, with Stalin's backing.[92] In this respect, the key role of plant management was paid at least lip-service, and often much more than that, at the highest political levels. The limitation of the system was therefore not so much internally within plants, but externally in relationships with other enterprises and organizations.[93]

B. Managerial Incentives

It was recognized to be the counterpart of that attitude to 'one-man management' that carrots as well as sticks needed to be offered to secure the quality of managerial effort required. Bonuses were thus constructed to favour the specific kinds of achievement which higher authority wished to see prioritized. As implied in the preceding discussion, bonuses – as well as wage increases – tended to be greatest for fulfilling the outputs stipulated in the annual plan. The director's role was to achieve this in Fordist fashion, by means of high throughput. On average, bonuses made up 11 per cent of managerial earnings in 1940 and over one-third in 1970.[94] Managerial behaviour could be understood in terms of efforts to maximize their bonuses, since they had a comparatively high degree of control over the factors by which such premia were gauged.[95] Short-termist behaviour to

89 Granick 1954, ch. 3; Lampert 1979, ch. 6.

90 Nove 1969, p. 41.

91 Quoted by Braverman 1974, p. 12.

92 Granick 1954, ch. 2; Nove 1969, p. 212; Lampert 1979, chs 5–6.

93 Berliner 1976, p. 523. It is also worth pointing out that the enterprise managers have become the crux of any emergence of entrepreneurship in the FSU since *perestroika*, cf. Kuznetsov 1993.

94 Granick 1954, p. 193; Berliner 1976, p. 478.

95 *Ibid.*, p. 405; Dyker 1976, ch. 3.

meet the current year's plan and associated bonuses was thereby fostered. In this way, Soviet management behaved much like the western managers of the last chapter who sought to maximize their pay-packets, sometimes to the longer-term detriment of the corporations they were running.

Bonuses arose not just for fulfilling the output plan, though this was always regarded as the most important determinant, but also for such achievements as cost reduction, product-mix attainment and innovation in products or processes – by the 1970s there were nine criteria for setting the managerial bonus.[96] These have been listed in roughly descending order of average importance, measured in monetary terms to the manager. Nor did it help that over-fulfilment of the plan earned bonuses. The supplementary bonuses can be regarded as stopgap efforts to try to remedy the most evident deficiencies of central planning, and undoubtedly had some positive impact in the way intended, but for the most part were never large enough to tempt managers decisively away from the short-termist inducements offered by the main incentives.[97]

This can be seen in regard to incentives supposedly favouring innovation. Product innovation was to be encouraged by permitting higher prices to be charged for new products. This led to endless discussions about how much higher they needed to be to reward the producer for implementing them, and of course the higher they were, the more users were discouraged from purchasing them. Berliner concluded that the resulting compromises usually discouraged innovation, while 'temporary' high prices to offset this usually brought cost inflation.[98] More complicated and fairer pricing schemes were later developed, but at high administrative cost.[99] In general, the incentives offered were too small and the potential losses too large: 'The point is that the avoidance of innovation is a device for minimizing uncertainty over supply'.[100] The array of requirements diverted a vast amount of 'entrepreneurship' into opportunistic distortion of results, objectives, etc.[101]

C. Business Accounting

Although the cost-based, output-oriented targets remained primary, there grew up a secondary structure for assessing performance at the enterprise level. This was known as *khozraschet*, and was translated as 'business

96 Berliner 1976, p. 42.

97 Granick 1954, ch. 9; Berliner 1976, chs 14, 16; Amann and Cooper 1982, pp. 68, 255, 495–8.

98 Berliner 1976, pp. 250–54 and ch. 10.

99 *Ibid.*, ch. 11.

100 *Ibid.*, p. 73; Nove 1977, pp. 168–9.

101 Glaziev and Schneider 1993, p. 54.

accounting' or 'economic accounting'. It was intended to be a more financial rather than volume measure of attainment, and in effect generally meant 'profits'. Talk of profits ran into obvious ideological difficulties of tainting with capitalism, so the role played by *khozraschet* throughout remained secondary. Nevertheless, it too was paid attention at the highest levels from early Soviet days. Since the planners dictated what was to be produced, *khozraschet* was mainly intended to economize upon resource use.[102] After the Second World War, it became increasingly obvious as time passed that some measure of profitability was going to have to be admitted into the planning calculus to maintain productivity growth and the momentum for catch-up. So long as profitability was defined merely as the difference between real (labour) costs and *imposed* prices, it did not take the motivation very much further. And while socialism adhered to the centralized Soviet model, the emphasis on profitability could never be more than half-hearted – even so, it was a leading characteristic of the attempted major reforms of the planning system after the death of Stalin in 1953, and especially of the post-Khrushchev era. It did not inspire managers that much of the benefit from any cost savings went straight back to the state budgets.[103]

Algebraic formulae were developed by theoreticians to measure the 'economic effectiveness' of innovation, in 'codes' agreed from 1962 onwards. These estimates of potential costs and benefits were subject to countless errors and omissions; moreover, the formulae assumed that the benefits came from cost savings rather than better quality, etc.[104] Economic accounting seemed only to heighten the scope for opportunism.[105] As ever, the more the criteria were refined, the more the confusion that was created. Paradoxically, the effort to develop incentives to encourage innovation had the opposite result, of institutionalizing conservatism.[106]

The combination of organizational and managerial weaknesses meant that 'economies of speed' in the systemic sense were seriously deficient. Lilja *et al.* (1989) compared two paper mills in the *perestroika* period (late 1980s), one in Finland and one just over the border in the USSR, with virtually identical plant and equipment. They found that machine output per minute in the Finnish mill was twice that in the Soviet mill, expected shutdowns in the Soviet mill were three to five times those in the Finnish mill, and yet

[102] Nove 1969, p. 265.

[103] Profitability did not raise such severe ideological issues in the kinds of 'market socialism' experimented with in some other East European countries from the 1960s, cf. Vanek 1970.

[104] Zaleski 1969, pp. 461–4.

[105] Lewis 1979, pp. 98–9.

[106] Amann and Cooper 1982, p. 210.

first-quality paper represented 97 per cent of the Finnish output as compared with 65 per cent of the Soviet. Thus the key heuristic of time-saving was ignored in the Soviet Union in favour of large production units and central control.

V: FINANCE

A. Problems of Funding Innovation

The Soviet system of course solved the issue of ownership very simply, by enforcing the collective ownership of the means of production. Mild exceptions were allowed for garden plots and the like in agriculture, and other East European economies often allowed more than this, but in principle the situation in industry was quite straightforward.

Capital support from other enterprises or trusts was abolished in 1930, in favour of direct bank credits through the State Bank.[107] Financial authority thereafter rested mainly with the State Bank, which was under the control of the planning authorities and concentrated mostly on large enterprises, but was still able to exercise some autonomous powers over plan fulfilment and cost reduction. However, its role was mainly supervisory.[108] Growth of commercial banking had to await the *perestroika* years of the second half of the 1980s. Until then, most investment and R&D remained state-financed.

Investment expenditures were to be met mainly by (i) budgetary subsidies, (ii) enterprises' own resources, and (iii) bank credits. In relation to new technologies, all were criticized regularly by the enterprises for inadequate scale of funding, misdirection of what funding there was, and excessive 'red tape' in raising and using them.[109] Specialized funds were set up trying to patch up the most evident weaknesses in the organizational arrangements for innovation. A Fund for the Assimilation of New Technology was set up in 1965 and a Fund for Current Regulation of Prices in 1968, both aimed at offsetting disincentives to implementing new processes and products; there were also various surcharges and special funds. The quantity of funds made available was, however, usually tiny, and they were often misused, for a variety of administrative reasons.[110] Where validly used, they were employed mainly for incremental rather than radical changes. No such special funding, it appeared, could be steered in the right direction without overburdening the complexities of their administrative details and

---

107 Nove 1969, p. 214.
108 Granick 1954, p. 173.
109 Zaleski *et al.* 1969, pp. 115–24; Berliner 1976, pp. 182–6.
110 Zaleski *et al.* 1969, pp. 107–15, 478–9.

enforcement. Whatever decentralization of financing there was, was not matched by decentralization of decision-making, which might have given it some teeth.[111]

B. Soft Budgets

From outside, criticism was especially directed at the notion that Soviet enterprises faced 'soft' budgetary constraints.[112] In western capitalist countries, firms which failed to make profits would before long either be taken over or go bankrupt. In the eastern socialist countries, they were likely instead to appeal up the hierarchy to be bailed out. About 10 per cent of state enterprises at any one time were thought to be making losses and requiring subsidies.[113] Although provision was made in 1954 for insolvency, Berliner reported that up to the time he was writing there were no known cases![114] – though Granick[115] claims insolvency was 'far from rare' in the period he studied (1934–41). It is evident from what has already been said in this and the preceding chapters, that this is too strong to serve as a simple dividing line between West and East: there were shades of grey as much as black and white (for example, many western public-sector enterprises have traditionally faced soft budget constraints). Nevertheless, there are good reasons – many of them already noted – to believe that Soviet industrial firms able to fall back on soft budget constraints faced less constant pressure to innovate.[116] For example, in the CPE penalties for failing to scrap outdated processes and products were much too weak.[117] Similarly, R&D establishments were largely freed from market tests, and, scattered as they were across ministries, allowed to carry on churning out minor advances; though again much the same was often the case in the West. One gets the impression that it was not the softness of the budget *per se*, but the organizational framework within which these soft budgets were couched, that was the basic problem – though Kornai subsequently argued that the two were necessarily linked.[118]

---

111 *Idem.*
112 Kornai 1980.
113 Berliner 1976, p. 244.
114 *Ibid.*, p. 531.
115 Granick 1954, pp. 166–8.
116 Hanson and Pavitt 1987, pp. 8–12.
117 Zaleski *et al.* 1969, p. 401.
118 Kornai 1992, pp. 100–105; but cf. Gomulka 1990, p. 102.

VI: DISINTEGRATION OF THE SOVIET TECHNOLOGY SYSTEM

A. An Impossibility Theorem?

Arrow – elsewhere the author of a celebrated 'impossibility theorem' in welfare economics – declared that the 'socially managed economy' appeared to solve the problem of technological innovation and diffusion in a way that capitalist economies had seemed unable to do.[119] He specifically drew attention to the Soviet Union, which had based its diffusion strategy on the premise of making technology freely available to all users, hence in principle maximizing the rate of diffusion by pricing technology at zero. To solve the problem of producing innovations, the USSR had instead resorted to awarding prizes, like the Lenin Prizes, paid for quite independently out of state budgets.[120] Thus the 'socially managed economy' appeared to resolve Arrow's paradox of information by disconnecting the payments for supply from the payments for demand, and thereby allowed – at least in theory – the maximization of both production and use of technology.

We have seen that the outcome in reality fell far short of this theoretical ideal. Other than in military-related areas, one has to conclude that there was nothing very remarkable about Soviet technological performance, except in the sense that so much was spent to achieve so little. The basic problem with Arrow's formulation in practice is the one emphasized throughout this book – that technology is not just information.[121] The disconnection between production of technology and its use did indeed generate a large amount of technological information, but at the same time it tended to minimize the generation of practical knowledge required for implementing that information. Learning by interacting, as seen above, was virtually non-existent. The boundaries between manufacturing and services, which have become blurred in western economies in recent years (see p. 276), remained rigidly separated in the Soviet Union. The Soviet model seemed to show the serious shortcomings of hierarchies for innovation.[122]

So long as the basic Soviet organizational structure remained in place, this seems to me to have been an inevitable outcome. The process of

---

119 Arrow 1962a.

120 Zaleski *et al.* 1969, pp. 473–6; Berliner 1976, ch. 15; Hanson and Pavitt 1987, p. 30.

121 *Ibid.*, p. 42.

122 *Ibid.*, pp. 12–15. It is true that the brunt of innovation in western capitalist firms came in-house within hierarchies (firms), but this segmentation of knowledge can also be one of the most damaging aspects of a purely 'arm's-length' market-based transactional system, so the implications for the transaction-costs approach of Williamson are ambiguous.

technological accumulation is not a linear one. Science first has to be transformed into technology, but this generally involves a *new combination* of several scientific disciplines, or perhaps the emergence of new 'transfer sciences'.[123] Second, it was bad enough having the vertical segmentation of the linear-model kind, but even worse was the horizontal segmentation into branches of industry, with little or no cross-fertilization. This greatly limited the possibilities for new combinations among technologies. Thus machine tools in general performed much better than Numerically Controlled Machine Tools before 1965, because the latter required combining with the instrumentation industry.[124] Third, and most serious, were the problems of transforming technologies into products, which this book assigns to firms. With the growing complexity of both technologies and products, and especially of their interactions, the linear-based and compartmentalized Soviet system became increasingly unable to cope. Once again, engineering fixes like 'automated management systems' were sought as inadequate solutions to bigger problems.[125] Western firms had trouble enough with the rising complexity of interactions between technologies and products (see Figure 8.3), and as I have shown tried – often none too successfully – to meet the problem through 'matrix management', 'flexible specialization', and so on. The Soviet branch-based organizational structure found it well-nigh impossible to meet – no system in which production decisions were made by self-contained branches and functionally specialized bodies could handle *both* technologies *and* products as these became increasingly differentiated in their interactions. This was the problem of the M-form company writ large. Much has been made of the extent to which the Soviet economy rejected Adam Smith on the 'invisible hand', but much less has been made of how far it went in embracing Smith on the division of labour. At rock bottom, insisting on a static interpretation of the division of labour will simply not succeed in a dynamic context – and the fact that Smith in the same breath emphasized pluralism in sources of innovation and learning shows that he was fully aware of this. The indications have to be that specialization of *functions* from the very top down is inherently misguided.

Geographical diversity also caused severe problems for the centralized structures, just as it did for the western MNCs organized on a multidivisional basis as seen in Chapter 8. In a country as huge in expanse and diversified in culture as the Soviet Union, such problems were acute. There was constant pressure from the republics to be permitted greater regional autonomy, for example to allow better integration of research and production, instead of being physically far removed from the R&D nuclei

---

123 See OECD 1992, ch. 1; and Chapter 8 above.

124 Amann and Cooper 1982, p. 63.

125 *Ibid.*, ch. 5.

around Moscow and Leningrad. Attempts to decentralize the system, as under Khrushchev (1957–65), had, however, foundered on the inherent contradiction with maintaining overall centralization.[126] For all the problems of 'bounded rationality', etc., the Soviet system achieved more when centralized than when decentralized.

Under Gorbachev's *perestroika,* which basically implied decentralization, the 'marketization' of R&D began with a decree of September 1987 abolishing ministry organizations and monopolies in R&D, and liberalizing R&D prices. From this time, there was a mushrooming of horizontally-oriented research organizations, particularly contract-based co-operatives, based on the proposition that the *project* at the end of the day was a more compelling objective than the technology halfway through the day. Problems with capital funding were obviated by concentrating on labour-intensive new technologies such as software production. The emphasis lay on lower prices for R&D services, and more rapid completion times. The means were self-organization in relatively small units, through the semi-legal privatization of R&D.[127] In 1988 alone, contract research rose from 30 per cent to 70 per cent of the total, and real output of industrial R&D rose 43 per cent.[128]

B. A Disequilibrium Spiral

The brief boom which lasted until 1989 then reversed. Demand at the macroeconomic level dropped precipitously, as Gorbachev dealt better with immediate rather than underlying issues.[129] Gorbachev was of course also undermined by geographical diversity, as seen in the growing desire for autonomy in the republics and the rise of Yeltsin in Russia, with Yeltsin emerging as the most powerful individual in the FSU after the aborted coup of 1991.

This stopgap nature of change was also evident in the field of technological accumulation. The new semi-privatized R&D units preceded equivalent reforms in the economy at large, but when the economy cracked after 1989, the demand impact on R&D was devastating.[130] As profitability collapsed, the economic opportunity to re-equip collapsed with it. New freedoms, democracy and competitive markets were in principle beneficial for R&D, but the latter also required organization, management and

---

126 Nove 1969, pp. 343–4, 358–9.

127 Glaziev and Schneider 1993, p. 33.

128 *Ibid.*, p. 242.

129 Dyker 1992.

130 OECD 1994, p. 16.

finance, which lagged well behind.[131] For instance, there was little move towards in-house R&D in manufacturing firms, in such a hostile economic climate. In fields like software where other factors seemed favourable, the continuing detachment of developers from sales remained a serious weakness.[132] Large-scale projects were maintained but in-house and interlinked R&D fell sharply.[133] As in other East European countries, R&D declined drastically, and became attenuated between the surviving (if depleted) Academy-based basic research and the downstream growth of near-market development activities.[134] The already vulnerable 'transfer sciences' were hit especially hard. Lacking strong 'network entrepreneurs', emerging firms turned to becoming subcontractors for western firms.[135]

Managers were given all the rights of private entrepreneurs but without the associated responsibilities, like the need to invest in R&D.[136] Privatization all too often acted simply to divert state enterprise revenues into private pockets.[137] Serious deficiencies could not be met without serious expenditures, especially on equipment – a survey in 1989 showed an average of one computer per 50 Russian scientists, and many of those were obsolete; nor was it helpful that computer prices were reckoned to be 30 or more times world prices.[138] Networking with foreign S&T was severely restricted by lack of funds for information sources.[139] In the absence of major restructuring of R&D, the transition to a market seemed to have led only to higher prices and lower production.[140] By the early 1990s it was feared that the destruction of accumulated R&D (e.g. through illegally selling off the state IPRs) and similar resources, whatever their earlier shortcomings, had gone so far as to threaten any possible recovery.[141] Among the neglected essentials was a need to shift from obsession with frontier science to an emphasis on diffusion and on technological accumulation.[142] The country needed to build upon the more viable existing structures rather than just tear them down, and some middle way had yet to be found between the dead hand of ministerial bureaucracies and the

131 Glaziev and Schneider 1993, p. 37.
132 *Ibid.*, p. 142.
133 *Ibid.*, p. 247.
134 Radosevic 1994.
135 Kuznetsov 1993; OECD 1994, pp. 69–71.
136 Glaziev and Schneider 1993, p. 240.
137 *Ibid.*, p. 245.
138 *Ibid.*, pp. 8–10, 68.
139 OECD 1994, p. 66.
140 Glaziev and Schneider 1993, pp. 249–50.
141 *Ibid.*, pp. vii–viii, 38, 247–9.
142 OECD 1994, pp. 62, 85.

crassness of economic 'liberalism'.[143] The passion of some East Europeans and their western advisers for the latter meant replacing the system that failed so badly in the East for one like that described in Chapter 8 which was failing in the West.[144]

143 *Ibid.*, p. 12.
144 I owe this point to Keith Pavitt.

10. Industrialization in Japan

I: GROWTH OF THE JAPANESE ECONOMY

A. Long-Term Trends

Though the 'Japanese miracle' has commanded attention only in comparatively recent times, the evidence available suggests that growth has accumulated over many years. Conventionally the 'turning point' has been dated to the Meiji Restoration in 1868, indicating a growth pattern lasting for a century and a quarter, but some advances had come even earlier, during the preceding Tokugawa regime. Most, however, now place the turning point a little later. Rostow tentatively put the start of the Japanese 'take-off' in the second half of the 1870s,[1] and similarly Kuznets (1971) dated the onset of 'Modern Economic Growth' to the same years, though Rostow subsequently pushed the dates a little later. Minami (1986) presents more recent evidence for a take-off from the 1880s, followed by MEG proper early in the 20th century, while Lockwood's earlier authoritative study (1954) stressed the 1890s. Thereafter the trend has been persistently upward, although there have been disruptions to this sustained growth pattern, most evidently the impact of the Second World War. As well as setbacks there were major growth spurts well before the 1950s.[2] Thus in looking to the sources of the 'Japanese miracle', we need to back-track considerably. For such reasons, the Japanese model may have only limited applicability to late-developing countries.

Not only was growth a long-term phenomenon, so was structural change. Manufacturing throughout enjoyed the highest rates of growth. Its growth rate was about twice the estimated world average for manufacturing between the 1870s and 1930s.[3] The output of producer durables (capital goods) rose from under 18 per cent of Gross Domestic Fixed Capital Formation in the 1880s to 60 per cent before the Second World War,[4]

1 Rostow 1960/1971, p. 38.
2 Ohkawa and Rosovsky 1973, p. 3 and ch. 2.
3 Lockwood 1954, p. 117.
4 Macpherson 1987, p. 71.

including substantial shifts towards heavy industry in the interwar years; so industrialization in depth as well as breadth has a long history in Japan.

The composition of Japanese GNP shows a remarkably high level of savings undertaken by each major segment of the Japanese economy, personal as well as corporate;[5] high not only relative to those of most other countries, which they were, but high even at modest levels of income. Even in periods of very rapid growth, such as the 1960s, the supply of savings in the economy often exceeded the levels of fixed capital formation and rarely fell far short. In consequence, interest rates normally remained at low levels, and cheap finance provided a crucial input into growth.

Thus growth of the Japanese economy can fairly be said to have been savings- and investment-led, built on this high internal propensity to save.[6] Although government and military investment were rising in the early growth period during the second half of the 19th century and continued to be significant in total expenditure until the end of the Second World War, subsequently the picture has been dominated by private investment.[7] The increase in private investment from around 20 per cent of Gross National Expenditure at the start of the 1950s to around 40 per cent by the end of the 1960s has been considered as perhaps the largest ever obtained in a market (non-communist) economy in peacetime.[8]

B. External Trends

The Japanese had taken a cautious and somewhat suspicious view of foreigners from the time the Europeans first began arriving in numbers in the Far East, around the 16th century. Rather than opening doors as the Chinese often did, the Japanese aimed to restrict the admission of Europeans and their cultures as far as possible, confining them to a small number of locations. Direct inflows of products and resources were tightly controlled by the Japanese state. This isolationism was breached by the arrival of Commodore Perry and his fleet of black ships in Yokohama Harbour in 1853. The effect on Japanese morale was profound – even a century later, in the 1960s, some Japanese viewed any liberalization of foreign capital inflows as like the Perry 'invasion',[9] notwithstanding the rather more serious foreign invasions that had occurred in the meantime.

---

5 *Ibid.*, ch. 8.

6 Lockwood 1954, ch. 5; Ohkawa and Rosovsky 1973, *passim*.

7 For much of the period, moderate inflation helped to raise investment by diverting resources to the capitalists. Yet the amount of 'forced savings' obtained through taxation and inflation was comparatively modest; cf. Lockwood, *loc. cit*.

8 Patrick and Rosovsky 1976, p. 18.

9 Lockwood 1965, p. 492; Vestal 1993, p. 53.

The more immediate effect, in the Meiji period from 1868, was to produce what Rostow called 'xenophobic nationalism', or desire for Japan to grow in power indigenously in order to keep foreign intrusions to a minimum. Some scholars see this as the original motivating force impelling Japanese development.[10]

Exports in the second half of the 19th century were led by primary products, including silk, but their share steadily declined, to be replaced first by textiles and other light industrialization, and then from the time of the 1930s Slump by exports of heavy manufactures. This change in pattern thus came about well before Second World War. The pattern of import shares was the equal and opposite of that for export shares. Textile imports fell away as textile exports were rising in the late 19th century; similarly, heavy manufactures fell as a proportion of total imports in the interwar period, just at the time they were expanding rapidly on the export front. Spurts of economic growth were closely associated with spurts in import substitution.[11] The rising dependence on imports of basic items such as foodstuffs led to feelings of external insecurity and to demands for colonialist acquisition – Formosa (Taiwan) after the war with China in 1894–95 and Korea after that with Russia in 1905 (formally annexed 1910), primarily to act as a source of supply for rice.

The reverse symmetry between exports and imports, together with their rapid joint expansion after 1868, has led some to describe Japanese growth as 'export-led' – a view taken, for example, by Rostow (1960). However, imports usually exceeded exports, and together with more detailed evidence, this suggests instead that exports were led by imports or domestic growth rather than vice versa.[12] It was true that exports served as a key entry point for imported technologies, not least because early exports concentrated on standardized items.[13] But most goods first expanded in the domestic market before their exports surged, and the export surges owed much to price declines from this earlier internal expansion.[14] Furthermore, development was characterized by recurring balance-of-payments crises.[15] Only in recent years there is more convincing evidence to support the notion of growth being export-led for Japan.[16]

---

10 E.g. Rostow 1960/1971, pp. 27–9.
11 Ohkawa and Rosovsky 1973, p. 189.
12 E.g. Lockwood 1954, chs 6, 7; Ohkawa and Rosovsky 1973, ch. 7; Johnson 1982, p. 16; Minami 1986, ch. 7; Macpherson 1987, p. 48.
13 Lockwood 1954, *loc. cit.*
14 Ohkawa and Rosovsky 1973, *loc. cit.*
15 Ohkawa and Rosovsky, in Lockwood 1965; Patrick, in *ibid.*
16 See the discussion of export demand in Section V below.

C. Uneven Growth

Aside from foreign trade, there were imbalances within the Japanese economy which could have threatened the continuity of growth, though in the Japanese case often seemed to act as a kind of spur to growth. Disparities between regions of the country, and especially the different economic standing of the various main islands of the Japanese archipelago, have long formed a subject of government anxiety.[17]

In sectoral terms Japan, like virtually all developing countries, was initially characterized by an agricultural sector that employed a large share of the population, but at comparatively low levels of productivity. Again like most developing countries, this 'surplus' labour from agriculture constituted a source of cheap labour for potential industrial development. Yet the pace of economic growth in the later 19th century was so sustained that the major part of the labour 'surplus', strictly defined, had probably gone by the interwar period, according to one influential estimate,[18] leaving only pockets in the most disadvantaged regions. Moreover, population growth was fairly slow even in pre-industrial times, because of the lack of 'room', though it accelerated with early modernization. In this strict sense, the 'dualistic economy' of orthodox development economics may have largely disappeared at a relatively early stage of industrialization.[19]

However, dualism did not really disappear. Dualism was maintained additionally by differences within secondary industry, between large firms and small and medium-sized firms (SMFs). The historical antecedents of this gap are debated, but it seemed to widen in the 1920s.[20] It has been attributed some of the blame for militarism in the 1930s, though the precise links are unclear. Morishima[21] thus describes this as 'a chronic illness of the Japanese economy'. The most obvious indicator of such dualism was the wage gap between large firms and SMFs, which, even in comparatively modern times, was estimated to be of the order of 100:60, compared with around 100:80 or 85 in the western AICs, and if anything rising through time, at least until the 1960s.[22] Absolute numbers in the unincorporated sectors continued to rise until recently.[23] The services sectors, too, have remained somewhat underutilized, though there seems to have been some

17 Okita, in Lockwood 1965.

18 Fei and Ranis 1964, p. 148; this requires defining the marginal productivity of labourers as being close to zero.

19 For other views, see Macpherson 1987, p. 65; also Minami 1986, ch. 9.

20 *Idem.*; Ohkawa and Rosovsky, in Lockwood 1965; Levine, in *ibid.*

21 Morishima 1982, p. 110.

22 Dore 1986, p. 49; also Ohkawa and Rosovsky 1973, p. 198.

23 *Ibid.*, p. 91.

convergence between the primary, secondary and tertiary sectors since the 1960s.

Nevertheless, despite the wage gaps, income in Japan is relatively equally distributed by international standards, certainly more so than in the major western AICs after the Second World War.[24] Equalization was aided by the abolition of the traditional social class system following the Meiji Restoration,[25] and was furthered by postwar land reform. This comparative equality has been the most probable cause of the perpetually high levels of demand and especially savings in the Japanese economy, which drove its industrialization in the manner already noted. The celebrated degree of Japanese consensus for rapid growth emerged only in the 1950s, when all segments shared fairly equitably in it.[26] Japanese society, while relatively egalitarian over income, wealth and power, has been considered inegalitarian over social prestige, although not to the extent of loss of 'togetherness'.[27]

II: TECHNOLOGY

A. Technology Borrowing and Catch-Up

The tradition of keeping foreigners at bay, while selectively borrowing and learning from what they had to offer, has been traced back at least as far as the 7th century. Direct western involvement was excluded from the time that the Portuguese arrived in the 16th century, while at the same time many Japanese were trying to adopt some of the technology.[28] The 'reactive nationalism' exhibited during the Meiji era after 1868, responding to the arrival of the US warships in 1853, was characterized by a combination of attempted isolationism coupled with a degree of imitation that was often parodied as being slavish.

While the first efforts were thus aimed at indiscriminate copying, there were sustained efforts thereafter to indigenize the technology, in order to limit the external dependence. This was bolstered by the militaristic orientation of early government involvement, which naturally sought technological strengths based on Japanese industry rather than imports. Internal technological spillovers from military pursuits were substantial,

---

24 Macpherson 1987, p. 50; also Chapter 11 below.

25 Rosovsky 1966.

26 Johnson 1982, p. 239.

27 Dore, in Aoki and Dore 1994.

28 Morishima 1982, ch. 2. The policy of seclusion and closing the country (*sakoku*) was formally adopted in 1637.

especially during the enforced demilitarization after the Second World War.[29] The tradition was equally maintained in the civilian sector. Japanese technology borrowing in the 20th century, up to the present day, has often limited the import component to the first plant only of each generation of the technology, requiring domestic industry to construct subsequent plants. Thus 'reverse engineering' and similar strategies have loomed large. About one-third of Japanese R&D in the modern era is considered as being spent on 'processing' foreign technologies.[30]

Japan obtained some short-cuts ('leapfrogging') by being a later developer than the UK or USA. Perhaps most crucial among these was in coming virtually straight to electrification, rather than having to convert from older energy sources such as steam power.[31] This had important ramifications for the structure of industry, as discussed below.

One should not overlook the many failures that were incurred in attempts at technology imports, especially in the earlier years of modernization.[32] In some cases there was no adaptation to Japanese conditions, and this could cause problems – for example, eastern Japan borrowed German electricity technology and adopted as standard 50-cycle AC, whereas western Japan borrowed American technology and still has 60-cycle AC.[33] Indigenization proceeded much faster where it could build upon existing domestic technologies and technical expertise. The experience of textile spinning, where foreign technologies were totally different from the traditional Japanese ones, and indigenization took many decades, contrasted sharply with textile weaving, where foreign power looms could be gradually imitated by upgrading traditional hand-looms, and indigenization was relatively rapid, though output growth was slower.[34]

The sustained efforts to catch up rapidly, accentuated by defeat in the Second World War (which brought the lag behind western technology home to many Japanese), meant on the one hand a major commitment to 'technological scanning' in both public and private sectors, to detect the nature and characteristics of significant overseas developments. However, this involved a redoubling of domestic commitment to R&D, rather than an alternative to it. Imports of technology were regarded as complements to domestic advances, rather than as substitutes for them. Links to industrial R&D laboratories and to universities were maintained continuously.[35]

29 Ohkawa and Rosovsky 1973, pp. 92–3; Nelson 1992.
30 Mansfield 1988a.
31 Minami 1986, ch. 5.
32 *Ibid.*, p. 418.
33 *Ibid.*, p. 140.
34 Sugiura 1994.
35 Freeman 1987, chs 2–3.

Diffusion of technological practices was assisted by the creation of regional R&D institutions (prefecture labs).

The converse implication was the limited role from the very beginning in Japanese economic development played by Foreign Direct Investment (FDI) and by private external funding generally, as a way of maintaining the independence from outside influence. Foreign MNCs arrived in greater numbers after the 1890s, but usually were limited to minority or joint ownership of Japanese equivalents. Such trends in the private sector were supported by government policy, on the grounds that foreigners were less likely to be influenced by government advice and 'guidance'.[36] Governments thus undertook most of the foreign borrowing themselves – whether the proceeds were used wisely is another question.

B. Technological Trajectories

The Japanese archipelago is similar in size to the British Isles, but the cultivable land area is very much smaller and the endowments of natural resources far less abundant. Thus, even more than Britain, the Japanese sought innovations for agriculture which 'saved' land, at least in the form of higher yields per acre[37] – this included silkworm cultivation, which did not greatly compete for land with rice, etc., plus the kinds of biological–chemical innovations already indicated for the UK. Savings on space became critical in industry as well, with the population becoming increasingly urbanized. Savings on mineral and energy resources have also remained a fixation of Japanese technological trajectories. Much of Japan's 'improvement engineering' has been in these directions.

Greater controversy surrounds the role of labour savings. As reflected in the pattern of import substitution and export promotion noted above, early Japanese industrialization was based on labour-intensive textiles and light consumer goods (toys, footwear, etc.). This early sectoral focus on light industry was built in part on the static comparative advantage of 'cheap labour', i.e. labour paid low hourly wage rates. The silk industry was based in the countryside, but for cotton spinning (where the units of production were considerably larger) the labour supply was drawn from the daughters of rural peasants, housed together in dormitories and overseen in a very paternalistic fashion.[38] Difficulties, however, arose in regard to growing shortages of adequate skilled labour. Moreover, there were arguments over whether, in productivity terms, the labour was really all that 'cheap' – after

36 Lockwood 1965, p. 490.

37 Lockwood 1954, chs 4, 5; Sawada, in Lockwood 1965; Hayami and Ruttan 1971, ch. 6; Ohkawa and Rosovsky 1973, ch. 4; Macpherson 1987, ch. 6.

38 Lockwood 1954, p. 30; Allen 1946/1962, p. 78; Saxonhouse 1976.

allowing for costs of recruitment, training, etc., the cost of labour per unit of output was not seen as particularly low.[39] A British investigation by Hubbard argued that Japan's success in taking much of the Asian textile market from the British in the prewar and early interwar periods owed little to low-cost labour (once composition of the labour force was allowed for), and most to a range of industrial, technological, vocational, transportation and marketing advantages.[40]

As in the earlier industrialization of Britain, it may be said that labour saving occurred mainly as a result of technologies directed towards saving time. Around 1900, cotton output per spindle was two or three times as large as in western countries, whereas the Japanese spinning and weaving mills required about four times the labour of American equivalents.[41] Landes[42] notes that modern equipment was adopted in certain fields, but the Japanese 'adapted them to the pattern of relative factor costs by running the equipment for longer periods and at higher speeds'. Minami[43] claims that daily output per loom in cotton weaving rose nine times as a result of mechanization plus electrification in the early 20th century, though these technologies also permitted a substantial rise in the number of looms each weaver could manage. Because of capital scarcities, much effort in areas like textiles went into developing technologies that aimed at saving capital rather than labour.[44] Similarly, infrastructural capital goods, especially those related to construction and civil engineering, were created using traditional labour-intensive technologies from Meiji times.[45]

Nevertheless, support for the strategy of building industrial expansion in the recovery from the Second World War on the alleged cost advantages of 'abundant' labour and light industries came from advisers of the American Occupation and later traditional 'monetarist' sources within Japan. As late as 1950, the Governor of the Bank of Japan declared that it was absurd for the country to build motor cars, because in the postwar age of the international division of labour, they should be imported from the USA.[46] However, the newly-formed Ministry of International Trade and Industry (MITI) repudiated such static cost-based arguments, and instead advocated an explicit policy of *capital-intensive* advance in heavy industries. MITI argued that a commitment to *heavy* industry represented Japan's 'dynamic

39 Macpherson 1987, ch. 7.
40 Hubbard 1935, chs 1–2; Amsden 1989, pp. 59–61; also Lockwood 1954, p. 173.
41 Lockwood 1954, p. 30.
42 In Lockwood 1965, p. 117.
43 Minami 1986, p. 128.
44 Lockwood 1954, p. 198.
45 Ohkawa and Rosovsky 1973, p. 17.
46 Tolliday and Zeitlin 1986, p. 169.

comparative advantage'. Such dynamism was expected to come partly from a belief that future technological progress was likely to be faster in suchc heavy sectors,[47] and even more from the anticipated linkage effects to other sectors that were suppliers to or users of the products of such heavy industries. Although MITI faced much opposition in many of its other policies, as shown below in Section VI, it was generally successful in its attempt to reject the orthodox economic argument for static advantage, and to shift the orientation of Japanese sectoral development towards heavy industries.

Although this implied substantial requirements for capital and for foreign exchange, which as the banking opposition pointed out were in scarce supply, it was assumed that, dynamically, the accumulation of profits in these rapidly advancing sectors would generate the resources for the higher level of capital-intensity. Thus over time the high investment demand would 'create' its own supply of investible funds via profits, as a kind of sectoral Keynesianism. The extraordinarily high savings (corporate as well as household) and investment achievements of the Japanese economy reflect their optimism. Encouragement was given to 'mitigation techniques' to make the imported or capital-intensive technologies less 'inappropriate' to the available factor endowments,[48] such as using multiple shifts, importing second-hand machinery, or using cheap, small electric motors.

The industries first prioritized by MITI were typically materials in short supply, such as steel or coal; later there was a shift to assembly-line manufacturing industries such as automobiles. But by the later 1960s, despite all the 'mitigation techniques', the resource-intensity (heavy materials requirements) and despoiling nature of such heavy manufactures were beginning to pose threats to the industrial strategy, and indeed to the quality of life generally. In 1971 there was thus a decision by MITI to switch the orientation of industrial policy. This took the following forms:

(i) moves to offset the environmental degradation resulting from heavy industries such as chemicals, as shown for example by the ninefold increase in expenditure on pollution control in the years 1968–74[49] – note that this preceded the alarms raised by the 'Club of Rome' in the West;

(ii) moves to reduce dependence on (mainly imported) materials and energy sources, redoubled after the first oil crisis in 1973, which had traumatic effects on Japan;

(iii) an aim to stave off labour shortages by continuing labour-saving advance;

---

47 Akin to the Habakkuk argument noted on pp. 197–8 above for the USA.

48 Ohkawa and Rosovsky 1973, p. 90.

49 Dore 1987, p. 14; the Japanese word *kogai* means 'public wound'.

(iv) above all, a shift towards 'knowledge-intensive' industries, especially the incoming information and communication technologies (ICTs).

Labour saving was in practice limited to situations where there were evident physical shortages of labour. This might seem inconsistent with the relatively high rate of introduction of industrial robots in Japan, but most Japanese robots were of simpler ('pick and place') rather than more complex kinds.[50] Porter remarks that the 'Direct cost savings were often not the most important benefit',[51] and shows that the trajectories of the robots themselves were towards reduced downtime ('mean time between failures' or MTBF) and higher operating speeds, etc.,[52] i.e. time saving. Japanese unions co-operated with their introduction.[53]

The objectives of the shift to knowledge-intensive industries were twofold. The most obvious was the continuation of the strategy of pursuing 'dynamic comparative advantage', by way of the industries perceived to be undergoing the most rapid rates of technological progress (the boundaries of knowledge-intensive industries were drawn very widely, for example they included the fashion industry). The second linked to this, in that these new sectors were more 'appropriate' to Japanese conditions than were the older heavy industries, which in any case were showing signs of technological 'stalemate'. Porter[54] describes the Japanese motivation towards products that were 'light, thin, short, small' *(kei-haku-tan-sho)*. The sectors and products were more appropriate inasmuch as they were seen as bringing benefits primarily in the form of saving (i) space (e.g. portable televisions and miniaturization generally, or compact cars) – overcrowding was the most evident detraction from the quality of life in the Japan of this period – and (ii) time (e.g. the speed-up resulting from ICTs).[55] These were similar motivations to those which earlier in the century had led to the rapid diffusion of electric power, even in small factories.[56] The *quid pro quo* was a stepping up of demands for human capital to supply the basic input requirements of the knowledge-intensive industries.

---

50 Mansfield 1988b; Tidd 1990.

51 Porter 1990, p. 226.

52 *Ibid.*, pp. 227–9.

53 Aoki 1988, pp. 46–8.

54 Porter 1990, pp. 89–90, 403.

55 Cf. Kobayashi 1986, pp. 48–9 – Kobayashi was for many years Chairman or President of the electronics company, NEC.

56 Minami 1986, p. 129.

C. Technological Capabilities

From Tokugawa times, there was a strong tradition of *diffusion* of newer technologies, both those imported from the West in the restricted manner described, and those that evolved in Japanese towns and cities, with particular impact upon many rural areas.[57] Diffusion rested to a considerable degree on the circulation of experts around the country, including in Meiji times the circulation of foreigners teaching their techniques. It also rested on having a relatively educated group of potential adopters.[58] The largest contributions to early MEG came from traditional sectors and indigenous impulses.

The creation of Indigenous Technological Capabilities (ITCs, cf. Chapter 11 below) depended heavily – as in many countries – on the establishment of a viable capital goods sector, especially for producing machinery. The Tokugawa period was characterized by a rising importance of machine engineering, known as *karakuri* because of the basic moving mechanism which was applied variously to machines, tools, clocks, toys, etc.[59] *Karakuri* masters were much involved in the indigenization of imported technologies such as electrical equipment in the Meiji era; one such being S. Toyoda, the inventor of an automatic loom and founder of the Toyoda (Toyota) company.[60] In Meiji times, the textile machinery sector split off from textiles producers, imitating the American pattern described in Chapter 6, and indeed making some use of American advisers early in the 20th century. The major difficulties were organizational, in shifting Japanese machine-building from a craft-based to a factory-based production system,[61] and the effort was initially confined to a small number of advanced producers such as Toyoda Loom.

'The advance of productivity in Japanese agriculture, in many services, and even in a large share of manufacturing industry proceeded mainly by the cumulative spread of such modest innovations through millions of small establishments.'[62] Exports also sprang largely from SMFs until after the Second World War.[63] With a tradition of technological borrowing and improving, the national system of innovation (NSI) in Japan could only slowly move towards the development of radically new technologies. In

57 Macpherson 1987, p. 28.
58 Nakamura 1981; see next sub-section.
59 Odagiri and Goto 1993, p. 78.
60 The self-stopping mechanism which he developed for weaving proved to be the link to the Toyotan assembly line and distinctive 'Japanese system of manufactures' described below.
61 Sugiura 1994.
62 Lockwood 1954, p. 192.
63 *Ibid.*, p. 371.

lieu of many major technological breakthroughs, advance took the form of creating new industries through Schumpeterian 'new combinations'. The most apparent form this took in modern times were the policies favouring 'technological fusion', extensively studied by Kodama.[64] Examples of such technological fusion were the emergence of 'mechatronics' (1975), as a fusion of machine tools and electronics at the *production* level, or optoelectronics, which represented a fusion of optical and electronic properties, but instead at the *scientific* level.[65]

As in Schumpeter, the new combinations were not simply at the technological level, and came about more readily in Japan than elsewhere because of the high degree of networking (user–producer relationships, etc.) and horizontal decision-making associated with Japanese industry (see below). Miyazaki (1995) shows that optoelectronics by and large polarized around the existing core lines of business of the particular companies, some primarily in communications and others in consumer electronics. On a few occasions, and after long-term developmental effort, some companies like NEC were able to cross over into the other main line of business by capitalizing on the technological linkages which arose out of strength in developing the technologies of key components, such as semiconductor lasers or liquid crystal displays. In similar fashion, Canon developed laser printers out of its strength in photocopiers. There are parallels here with the combination of technological convergence and vertical disintegration which Rosenberg (1963) found in 19th-century machine tools. But such economies of scope were won only by unremitting developmental work.

The crystallizing of such new combinations is aided by having R&D in Japan organized according to the structure of industries, whereas in the USA it more often reflects the structure of academic disciplines.[66] Japanese R&D functions were thus closely integrated with manufacturing. Its lagging science base has long been a source of disquiet, though opinions differ on the extent to which it will hamper Japanese industry now that it has reached the technological frontier in many lines of business.

D. Education System

As implied above, the Japanese industrial success was built more on utilizing labour and its skills than on giving priority to capital and the asset structure, as in 'Anglo-Saxon capitalism'.[67]

---

64 Kodama 1991.
65 Miyazaki 1995.
66 Westney, in Kogut 1993.
67 Cf. Albert 1993.

In the pre-Meiji times of the Tokugawa dynasty, Japanese society had already reached relatively literate standards, based on a largely private educational system.[68] The Meiji regime went further and aimed at universal primary education – by the end of the 19th century, it was estimated that about 90 per cent of children had had some primary education. Drop-out rates were, however, high until after 1900,[69] and secondary schooling was considerably less adequate in this period.[70] Dissatisfied with the training received in state schools, the large firms decided to build their own Industrial Schools and Workers' Schools for vocational training, as for instance at the Mitsubishi Nagasaki shipyard, the nation's largest private shipyard at the beginning of the 20th century.[71] Secondary education and its 'hothouse' academic nature have remained controversial in Japan up to the present day.

In higher education, the major thrust of early effort went into the sciences and engineering, because it was in the years that these were becoming at last well established in the West that the Japanese higher education system was effectively founded. Unlike the older-established western universities, their Japanese counterparts could make them the centrepiece of tertiary education from the start. The newly created Polytechnic in 1873 imported a principal from the West, a Scotsman called Dyer, who was primarily responsible for initiating the pattern of Japanese higher education out of the eclectic mix of German-style polytechnics (stressing practical training), French-style *grandes écoles* (stressing theory), and the Scottish system from which Dyer had come. Among other things, there was early incorporation of compulsory two-year placements in government factories or mines, and this has been regarded as crucial in breaking down the distance between Qualified Scientists and Engineers (QSEs) and the workplace.[72] This Polytechnic became the Engineering Department of what was to become the University of Tokyo in 1886, and many of its graduates went on to found major Japanese companies. Thus, on the one hand there was less of a divide between the arts and the sciences than in, say, the UK, and indeed a pre-eminent role for engineering in higher education; while on the other side there was greater familiarity of university-trained or polytechnic-trained engineers with the realities of the shopfloor.[73] Technology continued to impart greater dynamism in Japanese corporations than science.

---

68 Dore 1965; Rosovsky 1966; Minami 1986, p. 18; Odagiri and Goto 1993, p. 78.

69 Ohkawa and Rosovsky 1973, p. 57.

70 Lockwood 1954, p. 511; Landes, in Lockwood 1965; Fukasaku 1991.

71 Fukasaku 1992.

72 Morikawa 1991.

73 From the side of industrial demand, the emphasis has been laid on hiring generalists rather than specialists, in the belief that specific knowledge is better accumulated

This use of qualified western experts to found schemes of higher instruction was fairly common in the early Meiji period. Other examples included the staffing of schools of navigation and marine engineering after 1875 with British experts,[74] and more famously the recruitment of American experts in industrial quality control after the Second World War (e.g. W. Edwards Deming and Joseph Juran). Thus formal learning could utilize world frontier teachers, whilst not abandoning any Japanese control at the production or enterprise level (and as quickly as possible, the trained Japanese stepped into their shoes). The coupling of intensive secondary and higher education with enterprise-level training has continued to characterize the Japanese educational system to the present day.[75]

III: ORGANIZATION

A. Employment System

On the shopfloor evolved a very distinctive pattern of labour process, typifying social relations of production in Japan and to an extent in other parts of East Asia later. This has been attributed by some well-known scholars to 'Confucianism'.[76] Alleged characteristics of Japanese society include discipline, acceptance of authority, deference to seniors, and especially subjection to the group (first households and later companies).[77] But Confucianism was interpretable in many ways – indeed its strength in Japan, like that of the also powerful Buddhism and especially Japan's own imperial religion of Shintoism, probably lay in the vague and flexible 'broad-church' way in which it could variously be applied. Moreover, the current labour process system appears to have arisen mostly in the aftermath of the First World War and particularly the Second World War,[78] so it was not the historical relic it is often assumed to be.

The basic tenets of this Japanese labour process were:

(i) the seniority (age-related) principle for the promotion of workers within a company *(nenko joretsu)*;

---

within firms. There is thus strong resistance to employing workers with doctorates, cf. Westney, in Kogut 1993.

74 Allen 1946/1962, p. 90; see also Lockwood 1954, p. 328; Macpherson 1987, p. 36.

75 Freeman 1987.

76 E.g. Dore 1987; Morishima 1982, *passim.*

77 *Ibid.*, Macpherson 1987, p. 12.

78 Levine, in Lockwood 1965; Johnson 1982, p. 14; Abegglen and Stalk 1985, p. 209; Tolliday and Zeitlin 1986, ch. 7, on Toyota; Macpherson 1987, p. 68; Aoki 1988, pp. 51, 186–90; Lincoln, in Kogut 1993.

(ii) 'lifetime' employment contracts with the company – in practice limited mainly to adult males in large companies only;
(iii) trade unions based on the company ('company unions'), and spanning all groups of workers, including younger echelons of management, thus minimizing rivalries within the company;
(iv) collective decision-making, based on the above principles.

These tenets took hold after the two world wars to meet immediate problems of scarcities of skilled labour and reconstruction needs, *faute de mieux*. They constituted the basic institutional conditions around which the remainder of the distinctively Japanese organizational system outlined below came to develop. They also framed the technological trajectories as described above – with lifetime employment, companies chose to adopt technologies which maximized the productivity of their existing labour force, often through a high degree of automation. The employees with their employment guaranteed also gained maximally from the productivity advance by way of ensuing increase in wages.[79] Employment patterns for women had quite different origins, in the highly paternalistic dormitory system described above, and this resulted in large gender gaps.

B. Horizontal Information Flows

In contrast with the typical American style of hierarchical control and 'vertical' decision-making (from top to bottom of the managerial/worker pyramid), as in M-form organizational structures for example, the Japanese companies evolved styles of decision-making that were typically 'horizontal'.[80] This meant that there was direct interchange of the information relevant to production along, say, a production line. Companies like Toyota introduced deliberate policies of 'lending a hand', in contrast to the rigid demarcations of western companies.[81] To do all this necessarily required a well-educated and well-trained workforce, and this the companies obtained in exchange for granting semi-tenured ('lifetime') employment. Conversely, the 'lifetime' commitment of Japanese workers to their company meant that they would not take the benefits of their training to any rival, so that companies had the incentive to train their employees to the utmost (although stories circulated about Japanese workers 'moonlighting' to rivals at weekends, in later years to South Korea). The even more obvious implication for labour process was for relatively egalitarian social relations, and Japanese firms indeed became celebrated for abolition of intra-company class distinctions, creation of team spirit and

79 Porter 1990, p. 399.
80 Aoki 1986; 1988, ch. 2.
81 Tolliday and Zeitlin 1986, p. 239.

a unified company ethos. Effectively, large Japanese companies upgraded blue-collar male workers to white-collar status rather than the reverse.

The horizontal decision-making attained most of the gains of 'time saving' discussed in Chapter 4 above. It proved much more flexible than hierarchies in saving downtime when emergencies arose, since shopfloor workers could usually take the necessary corrective action.[82] 'Systemic co-ordination' advanced using the knowledge that workers obtained about a variety of machines.[83] Smith's kind of time saving from reduced sauntering between operations was achieved by reorganizing several machines semi-circularly around each worker.[84] It has been shown by theoretical and simulation analysis that such horizontal flows of information are superior to vertical flows for bringing efficiency in production when there are a large enough number of sequential stages of production amongst which the information is required to flow.[85] In the typical complex process, for products in which the Japanese developed world market leadership from the 1970s, there could be hundreds and even thousands of such stages.[86] The main gain is, however, intuitively obvious under conditions of dynamic competition, namely that of enlarging the number of participants in learning to the greatest possible extent. By contrast, the pure hierarchy reduces learning to just the topmost levels of management, who whatever their talents must succumb both to 'bounded rationality', i.e. inability to think through more than a small part of the information with which they are bombarded, and to implications of 'asymmetric information', e.g. not being fully informed of what is happening on the shopfloor. Moreover, the employment guarantee helps co-opt workers into the organization's learning process, since, as pointed out above, labourers will not lose their jobs from any labour-saving change and are quite likely to improve their working conditions. The key to the development of the 'Japanese system of manufactures' in the early postwar years, in companies like Toyota Automobile Works, lay in convincing their workers that they would actually benefit from it.[87]

The increased flow of information within companies could have been offset by reduced flows to and from other companies. Duplication of efforts to accumulate knowledge in different plants could obviously prove wasteful. Apart from government efforts to raise such information flows among companies, the in-house strategy adopted seemed even more

82 Aoki 1988, p. 13.
83 *Ibid.*, p. 15.
84 *Ibid.*, p. 14.
85 Marengo 1991.
86 Abegglen and Stalk 1985, pp. 61–3; Rosenberg 1994, ch. 7.
87 Carmichael and MacLeod 1993.

wasteful than this, as it consisted of setting up rival R&D units within each company. For example, in the early 1970s Matsushita set three teams to work in competition with one another (and Sony ten!) to develop a video recorder that would satisfy certain customer criteria – as it happened, one of them, JVC, came up with a format (VHS) that proved all-conquering, but naturally much of the remaining effort (in other companies as well) was at least partially 'wasted'.

Such non-hierarchical information flows in companies are partially offset by hierarchical rankings relating to the seniority system of promotion, aimed at enhancing 'contextual skills'.[88] Although most are retained in employment by the company because of the lifetime 'contract', wage gaps between workers of different abilities open up in their middle age. The higher wage increments go, however, to those with the greatest accumulation of expertise, rather than as in some western countries to those with higher social class status or with greater strength from the 'voice' they utter in trade-union activity on the shopfloor. Thus the system of *incentives* is typically hierarchical, while it is the *co-ordination* that is non-hierarchical. In contrast to western notions of performance-related pay, though, the rewards are based on *long-term* performance.[89]

Such accumulation of expertise was augmented by job rotation, i.e. by periodically moving employees to different stages of production, so that they could eventually build up their knowledge of all the production activities in which the enterprise was engaged. In this way, their knowledge would be of maximum benefit to the company, not only in enlarging their own personal knowledge bases, but in showing them what would be most beneficial to pass on elsewhere. Multiskilling of Japanese workers and its benefits to their company have been much commented upon[90] – Koike argues that multiple skills of individuals are more significant than teamwork in the usual sense, as here the machines represent the 'team'.[91] The foundation nevertheless lay in knowledge sharing rather than skill specialization – a good analogy may be drawn with a leading baseball or rugby team, in which both individual skills and teamwork must be of high order.[92] In this way, the excesses of the American-style M-form company, in which each division competed with the others and thus kept the maximum amount of information to itself, were directly overcome. Learning could be said to be taking place in the organization as a whole,

---

88 Aoki 1986; 1988, ch. 3.

89 Itoh, in Aoki and Dore 1994, ch. 9.

90 E.g. Dore 1973; Aoki 1986; Carmichael and MacLeod 1993.

91 In Aoki and Dore 1994; in other words, the issue is capital process, not labour process.

92 Best 1990, pp. 154, 156.

and not just its individual parts.[93] Horizontal integration in Japanese companies was soon extended to cover not just the production stages but the whole operating system, including R&D, design and marketing.[94] Employees circulating at various times of their long company association among virtually every phase of company activity would thus magnify the possibilities for interaction and feedback.

The price was paid in terms of reducing what was potentially available in Smithian terms from economies of specialization. However, it will be recalled that Smith himself later pointed out the diminishing returns obtainable from specialization when boredom began to set in, and that Arrow and other students of learning behaviour drew similar conclusions. Job rotation, apart from enriching the personal experience of the employees, may also have counteracted the onset of such diminishing returns. Moreover, the cost of American specialization was high in terms of managerial co-ordination between the various specializations. Aoki[95] shows formally why the hierarchical American system, which Williamson (1975) argued would be adopted to minimize transaction costs, in practice achieved the opposite. Williamson implicitly assumed that the main gains would come from traditional static economies of size, whereas in actuality the dynamic gains came in the other ways noted above.[96]

C. Management

Instituting bottom-up and 'horizontal' decision-making had the effect of freeing top management for long-term strategic thinking. This took two major and interrelated forms. One was the consideration given to the firm's external links, and especially to the networks that evolved around supply–demand chains (see below). The second and broader aspect, which subsumed the first, was the emphasis on 'Vision' – the insistence that top management should act in Schumpeterian fashion and think through future scenarios for the firm and its environment. In contrast to the American firm discussed in some preceding chapters, where owners and managers controlled the firms, Japanese firms are best seen as coalitions between owners and workers, with management between them striking a balance.[97] This was based on a consensual approach to the establishment of 'visions', drawn upwards from the nature of horizontal decision-making within the company and outwards from association with industrial groups (*keiretsu*)

93 Cole, in Aoki and Dore 1994.
94 Westney, in *ibid.*
95 Aoki 1988, ch. 2.
96 *Ibid.*, pp. 29–30.
97 *Ibid.*, ch. 5.

and government policy-making. As shown in Section VI below, the government conversely adopted procedures for policy-making through 'vision', by developing consensual agreements with firms or with broader organizations like the Federation of Economic Organizations (*Keidanren*).

Not only did this lead to a clearer division of responsibility between top and lower management than found in many contemporary western firms – in certain respects returning to the original bases of the managerial division of labour in the latter – but with the growing hold of bottom-up decision-making for day-to-day matters, it also permitted the reduction or abolition of many intermediate tiers of management. The padding of 'line and staff' found in bureaucratic structures of many western corporations and undertakings is abruptly terminated by giving the intermediate 'staff' responsibilities to the shopfloor and by truncating the 'line' between top and bottom. Efficiency in Japanese firms thus has been oriented partly to creating 'lean' administrative systems, in sharp contrast to the attempts to introduce bureaucratic managerialism in western parastatal activities.

The sense of greater corporate than individual responsibility as compared with western firms seems to have helped in the evident acceptance of lower profit margins by Japanese than by American companies, as a result of which a larger number of admissible projects have gone ahead. This, allied to the emphasis on long-term strategic thinking, appears to have enlarged the ability to broaden the competence base of the firm and its potentiality for reaping economies of scope. According to my database on technologies of electronics MNCs, Japanese firms have been more successful than American or European firms since the 1970s at diversifying into related technologies and products. Nor is top management paid the kind of telephone-number salaries and bonuses all too often – and destructively – found in western corporations (for a start, there is no suggestion of outbidding a rival company for the services of top management). Corporate goals were often directed not to short-run profits so much as to the firm's market share, and especially the *growth* of that share – for it was out of an improvement in the market share that virtuous circles would be set in motion, and conversely out of a deterioration that a vicious circle, perhaps leading to the shame of bankruptcy, might set in.[98]

D. Processes and Production Engineering

With learning geared to the production system in its entirety, in place of a degree of internal competition between different divisions, the whole factory comes to act as a laboratory.[99] Companies based themselves on the

98 Abegglen and Stalk 1985, ch. 3.
99 Baba 1985.

doctrine of continuous improvement (*kaizen*). The typical Japanese procedure for introducing innovative technologies or products is to begin with a fairly lengthy set of discussions, both internal and external to the firm, in which the pros and cons for all stages of production and distribution are debated. Once consent is finally reached, there is then a very rapid implementation of the innovation, partly because all the foreseeable problems have been thought through in advance. The move to new generations of innovative technologies is accelerated by the overlapping rather than sequential phasing of design and product development – that is, the early discussions on the next generation begin as the product development phase of the current generation is being launched, and so on.[100] In such ways, the delays induced by the lengthy initial discussions are offset, and the lead times to *successful* commercialization are much reduced by comparison with western companies. The main achievement of the 'Japanese system of manufactures' was thus learning how to learn about *process* innovation. Products could be imitated, but in processes the Japanese were evolving something hitherto unique.[101] Mansfield (1988a) found that about two-thirds of Japanese R&D was process-oriented, whereas two-thirds of American company R&D was *product*-oriented.

The time saving accruing in new product development, arising out of consensual decision-making and lean administrative systems, is accentuated by time-saving arrangements in the organization of production.[102] In alignment with the pattern of horizontal decision-making, this is oriented towards creating 'lean production systems',[103] and it is these that western companies have struggled hardest to copy. Such lean production systems present the most immediately recognizable form of Japanese industrial superiority, not least from the results in terms of high physical productivity per unit of time to which they give rise (for example, the much lower number of man-hours required to produce an average motor car than in the USA).[104]

One of the most celebrated constituents of the lean production system is the adoption of 'Just-in-Time' (JIT) production scheduling. Components required for assembling a particular line of products are thus ordered to arrive at the moment they are needed for incorporation into the work in progress. This is in obvious contrast with the traditional western 'Just-in-Case' scheduling, where large stocks of each possible component are kept at hand, 'in case' they turn out to be needed when the product line is

100 The 'sandwich system', cf. Imai *et al.* 1985.

101 Rosenberg 1994, ch. 7.

102 Best 1990, p. 14.

103 Womack *et al.* 1990, *passim*.

104 Cf. *ibid.*, ch. 4.

altered. Indeed, in the West, JIT is often simply regarded as a better method of inventory (stock) control, cheapening the cost to the firm of holding inventories of such components. However, as Schonberger (1982) argues, the more significant impacts of JIT appear to be dynamic rather than static gains, especially in raising worker commitment and motivation as each is responsible for the ordering, etc. – equally, each had only himself or herself to blame if mistakes were made.[105] There are evident comparisons with the static vs. dynamic gains among Adam Smith's advantages of the division of labour. Changes were also required within the factory in capital process, including 'downsizing' of special-purpose machinery to reduce the MES,[106] and reduction of changeover times including methods for rapid tool change ('single-minute exchange of dies').[107]

The other well-known constituent of lean production is the adoption of 'Total Quality Control' (TQC). Paradoxically, notions of TQC came from ideas advanced by US advisers to Japanese industry in its period of reconstruction after the Second World War, especially Deming in 1950 and Juran in 1954. In Japan the implementation of higher product quality began with *ex-post* statistical sampling of product runs to detect any defective items, as also occurred in progressive western companies. From this, however, it steadily moved towards *ex-ante* reduction – and if possible elimination – of defects before the production process began, i.e. elimination of defectives at source. Thus, for instance, wastage arising out of half-building a car before the problem from a faulty component became recognized could be overcome – this was the policy of 'zero defects' as fully worked out. 'Quality circles' have been increasingly directed at identifying potential *future* problems. Quality control remained the responsibility of the shopfloor, in contrast with the USA where it was seen as a tool of management.[108]

The main dynamic gains came from the combination of these two concepts, given their overlapping nature. JIT production plus the scrapping of *ex-post* quality control not only reduced buffer inventories and induced fast feedback on defects, but in dynamic terms led to heightened awareness of problems and their causes, and thus on to their solutions.[109] For the firm as a whole, it led not only to static cost gains from lower material and labour inputs, having the effects of saving working capital and saving time, but also to faster market response, better forecasting and leaner

105 See also Tolliday and Zeitlin 1986, ch. 9.
106 *Ibid.*
107 Abegglen and Stalk 1985, ch. 5; Best 1990, pp. 150–53.
108 Lazonick 1990, p. 292.
109 Schonberger 1982, Figure 2–3.

administration.[110] In industries like automobiles, the Japanese found that there did not have to be a trade-off between throughput and quality – on the contrary, guaranteed component quality permitted an acceleration of throughput. JIT and TQC in combination fitted best into the Japanese style of management, based as they were on consensual approaches (as in the 'quality circles') plus bottom-up decision-making for routine operations (individual worker responsibility for orders, etc.). Because of this, they were often much less statically and dynamically efficient when introduced as management techniques in western companies.

Still more important, they were better suited than orthodox western management styles to the way in which global competition was evolving, based on rapid product diversification and quality upgrading – the elements of 'dynamic competition' as set out in Chapter 8. By 1978 Toyota was producing – efficiently – no less than 32,100 variants of car per quarter-year, and on average just 11 of each variant.[111] The number of basic product 'lines' or families, like the Toyota Crown to which these data pertain, was however kept small, in order to avoid the long changeover times and high costs associated with multiplying relatively unrelated lines.[112] It is thus no surprise that these factors are given such weight in accounting for Japanese success. On the other hand, the extent to which processes were improved incrementally in bottom-up fashion could prove limiting in circumstances where customized product demand necessitated radical process innovation. Thus in semiconductors, the Japanese have succeeded much better in memory chips (DRAMs, etc.) than in microprocessors,[113] while the balance of demand in recent years has switched from the former to the latter.

E. Networks

Just-in-Time relationships require close integration of the manufacturing (assembling) firms with the suppliers of components. Otherwise, all that happens when the assembly company reduces its inventories is that it pushes the burden of carrying such inventories upwards to the components suppliers, and in western companies which attempted to introduce JIT this occurred all too frequently. For JIT to benefit the production process at large, 'arm's-length' supplier–user relationships are not good enough – suppliers need to remain continuously well-informed about the prospective needs of their manufacturing customers.[114] Japanese manufacturers are thus

110 *Idem.*
111 Aoki 1988, p. 25; Asanuma, in Aoki and Dore 1994.
112 Abegglen and Stalk 1985, ch. 4; Best 1990, p. 142.
113 Okimoto and Nishi, in Aoki and Dore 1994.
114 Best 1990, p. 15.

painstaking in the attention they devote to a careful choice of suppliers, to guarantee both zero defects in the supplied components and forethought to future needs. The main issue in the connection is a basis in commitment to *quality and reliability* – price is much less significant than for suppliers based on market-only linkages, as in the usual western circumstances.

One possible solution is to integrate vertically, which as we saw in Chapter 6 was typically what happened in US industries where control of input quality was crucial. Much the same occurred in early Japanese industry, but more because of shortages of capital. In the Meiji period and up to the Second World War, modern industry was dominated by large vertically and horizontally integrated enterprises, known as the *zaibatsu* (literally 'money-cliques') – some indeed dated back well before Meiji times, and all had close connections with the government. They permitted what Lockwood[115] called 'combined investment', through simultaneously developing vertically and horizontally linked industries. Normally they were family-owned and controlled, though some (like Mitsui) were run by managers. Although by the interwar period the control of vast economic (and political) empires exerted within these *zaibatsu* attracted most attention, in their earlier days they are regarded by present-day scholars as having provided a necessary framework for group-based entrepreneurship in the first stages of economic development.[116] Generally the *zaibatsu* competed hotly with one another, but did not aim to drive one another out of the market, because strength in one market was often offset by relative weakness in others, where any aggressive action might encounter successful retaliation.[117] On some occasions they co-operated for militaristic or similar purposes. Conversely, despite the internal sharing of risk and finance, there could even be some competition between the units of one particular *zaibatsu*, e.g. between Kanegafuchi Spinning and Toyoda Loom in the Mitsui group.[118] Cartelization was not especially evident until given legal force by the state in 1931.[119] The semi-feudal and hierarchical *zaibatsu* were formally broken up by the Americans during the postwar Occupation, because of their powerful military origins or connections. Many were, however, to re-emerge in more muted form within a few years in order to meet American procurement requirements for the Korean War, but usually with new teams of managers, and with lessened family control.

Their postwar structure came more to resemble that of other industrial groups – the *keiretsu* – which became established around emerging large

115 Lockwood 1954, p. 227.
116 Imai 1989.
117 Lockwood 1954, p. 229.
118 Sugiura 1994.
119 Lockwood 1954, p. 230.

firms (the *kaisha*). The main differences from the *zaibatsu* lay in the central role of production rather than finance and the decentralization of decision-making and general weakening of interconnections.[120] Subcontracting was the typical basis of these relationships – instead of the formal vertical integration previously encountered, this has been described as 'quasi integration'.[121] Such new groups were particularly prominent in the second-wave manufacturing industries, like vehicles and electronics. The major industrial groupings (e.g. Dai-ichi, Fuji, Sanwa), were composed of many *kaisha*, each of which normally acted as a hub for networks of smaller suppliers. In this way, the dualistic divide between large and small firms was partially remedied. Within the group, the *kaisha* interlinked with one another, each being responsible for a principal line of business and with a strong emphasis on reciprocity. Thus there exists strong collaborative support vertically and laterally within each of the major groups, including R&D support.[122] However, between such groups (and sometimes between competing firms within them) there is intense competition. Thus there are about five major automobile manufacturers, each in a different group.[123] Each within the group draws benefit from links with components suppliers, firms in other major businesses, etc., but each competes aggressively with the other vehicle manufacturers, located in rival groups. In this way, Japanese industry manages to combine many of the possible benefits of collaboration *and* competition. Hence one can think in terms of an industrial structure of dynamic oligopolies – in a dynamic market process, 'markets and organizations interpenetrate each other'.[124] In the more fully developed network structures of recent times, bonds have become weaker and membership more fluid. This has assisted the development of the kinds of technological fusion described above, pushed by pressures from employment, finance, etc. to enter new product markets.

The picture is further complicated in that the firms in particular lines of business were often able to work collaboratively, as well as (and even at the same time as!) competitively. Writers like Porter[125] who argue that the 'single greatest determinant of Japanese success, based on our research, is the nature of domestic rivalry', miss a key point. The flow of ideas between companies has been central to their strategies, and much of the reason why

---

120 Minami 1986; Imai 1989 – the term *keiretsu* in Japanese is rather imprecise.

121 Aoki 1988, ch. 6.

122 Fruin and Nishiguchi, in Kogut 1993; Westney, in Aoki and Dore 1994.

123 The notion that each major group has at least one company in each industry is known in Japanese-English as 'one set-ism', although obviously each may have a different balance of interests.

124 Imai 1989, p. 123.

125 Porter 1990, p. 411.

'fast second' strategies have been particularly successful. Allegedly at Matsushita, the world's largest consumer electronics company and an acknowledged practitioner of the 'fast second' strategy, it is said that, 'We have the world's best laboratory. It's called Sony!'.[126] From a relatively early date, Engineering Research Associations were set up in particular fields, along the lines of the British models. According to Mowery and Rosenberg,[127] who have made the most intensive study of both, the Japanese were much more successful in deriving substantial results from privately-organized collaborative R&D. The locally-based prefectural labs, of which there are around 170, have also been quite successful in supporting SMFs in their district. Japanese governments also aimed to work collaboratively with the private sector in their larger research projects, with results that are assessed further in Section VI below.

IV: FINANCE

A. Size of Firms

As already mentioned, the Japanese industrial structure has long been characterized by a dualism between large and small firms.[128] Despite the wage gap between the two, the SMFs were by no means universally stagnant. Their survival rested on the very early adoption of electric power,[129] permitting the kind of fractionalization in small factories witnessed in Chapter 6 above for the USA. While the evolution of *keiretsu* networks was able to suck some of the smaller firms into the dynamic structure of large firms, for the most part the dualism continued after the Second World War. Policy oriented towards growth tended to favour the enlargement of firms, especially in secondary industry, while policy oriented towards employment tended to protect the smaller firms, especially in primary and tertiary sectors. SMFs were particularly significant for exports, producing 75 to 80 per cent of manufactured exports in 1909 and still 60 per cent in 1956.[130]

Though the number of major industrial groupings did not rise very much postwar, the number of significant hubs formed by major companies within each grouping did rise. The dynamic oligopolies described above were able

126 I owe this to Hidenori Oda.

127 Mowery and Rosenberg 1989, ch. 8.

128 For earlier data see Lockwood 1954, pp. 201–10.

129 Minami 1986, p. 126.

130 Rapp, in Patrick 1976; LFs are defined as those with over 500 employees. By 1970 the LF share of manufactured exports had risen to 75 per cent.

to reap many of the gains of scale economies in production through the network, but without excessive centralization in individual firms. In this way, the requirements for finance of individual firms were kept down.[131] Though flexible manufacturing methods gave particular stress to economies of scope, growth of individual companies was still warranted for attaining scale economies in technologies (R&D) at one end, or products (marketing) at the other end.

B. Equity Funding

The increased complexity within major groups led to increased shareholding by each company in others in the same group (cross-holdings). These were necessitated by the prevailing capital shortage after the Second World War. Such cross-holdings were made up of shareholders highly committed to the success of the companies whose shares they held, precisely because they were part of the same interrelated group. This gave a degree of security to equity holdings that was considerably higher than for equivalent independent western companies.[132]

The high rates of household saving, however, also meant a greater role for shareholdings by the public at large. Empirical evidence suggests that the Japanese public invested mainly in the expectation of future capital gains, i.e. for increases in the selling prices of the shares they held, rather than for yearly or quarterly dividends. This allowed Japanese companies to distribute lower proportions of their profits as dividends than did corresponding US companies, where (as seen in Chapter 8) there was upward pressure on dividend payouts, especially from the late 1960s. Moreover, dividends of Japanese companies were measured relative to par (historical) values, rather than to current values, so allowing them to keep dividend payouts low even while their share prices were rising. Furthermore, interest on bank loans was tax-deductible, whereas dividends had to be paid after tax, so the former were cheaper for the firms. Finally, debt:equity ratios were substantially higher on average than in the USA, so the exposure to dividend payouts (and to general insecurity) was proportionately reduced. Although in pure theory the Modigliani–Miller theorem claims that the debt:equity ratio should make no effective difference, under the distortions of the real world and in circumstances of imperfect information such as arise with technological advance, it can be shown that it does.[133] Debt was used aggressively to fund rapid growth[134] –

131 Aoki 1988, p. 109.

132 Sheard, in Aoki and Dore 1994.

133 E.g. Santarelli 1991.

134 Abegglen and Stalk 1985, ch. 7.

ploughback accounted for only about one-third of corporate finance ca. 1960 as private banks provided most of it.[135] A stock exchange for equity trading along American lines took many years to develop – its functions were usurped by the process of 'overloaning' described next. In recent years, stockholdings by financial institutions have grown more rapidly.[136] How far this trend has been to blame for the apparently increased instability of the Japanese economy is an open question (see below).

C. Role of the Private Banks

Particular attention thus fell on debt, and on the role of the banks. Corporate borrowing from banks ran at high levels, as the counterpart to the central bank's 'overloan' system: 'a group of enterprises borrows from a bank well beyond the individual companies' capacity to repay, or often beyond their net worth, and the bank in turn overborrows from the Bank of Japan'.[137] The imbalances were accentuated by coupling high lending to a deliberate policy of low interest rates for industry.[138] The *zaibatsu* had a long historical tradition of including major commercial banks in their structure, thereby establishing from Meiji or even earlier times patterns of interaction and mutual learning between such banks and the industrial activities of the group.[139] This contrasts with the growing separation of finance and industry in countries such as the UK, though outside the groups the large Japanese banks had less to offer. Small banks in towns did much less to finance industry, although Patrick argues that banks led industrialization in the early Meiji period, partly through government subsidies.[140] In banking as in industry, *keiretsu* partly succeeded the *zaibatsu* after the Second World War, with many similarities to the German system described in Chapter 5.[141]

The present-day pattern follows historical precedent in appointing a 'main bank', designated to oversee particular companies. Japanese law, as amended during the period of US Occupation, prevents banks from holding more than 5 per cent of the equity of a particular industrial company (the *keiretsu* cross-holdings are not covered by this law). Thus the 'main bank' may not own a great many of the shares of each individual designated

135 Lockwood 1965, p. 472.
136 Aoki 1988, ch. 4.
137 Johnson 1982, p. 203.
138 Minami 1986, p. 358.
139 Hirschmeier, in Lockwood 1965. A more static version of the same argument is that the Japanese system reduced 'informational asymmetries' between finance and industry, cf. Hoshi, in Aoki and Dore 1994.
140 Cameron *et al.* 1967, ch. 8.
141 Johnson 1982, p. 205.

company, but it would be expected to act as and when necessary. It was normally expected that even the 'main bank' would not be involved in routine executive decision-making, either at bottom or top levels. It might, however, step in if the company got itself into severe trading difficulties, such that a financial rescue seemed necessary. In extreme cases of this kind, the bank might ultimately take over the company, at least until its health began to be restored, but it was assumed that such occasions would be very rare.[142] Aoki has recently argued that, because Japanese main banks are prevented from underwriting corporate bonds, they took their funds elsewhere during the 1980s (often to real estate), and contributed to the speculative bubble of the late 1980s. Moreover, Sheard[143] has argued that the fall-back role of the main bank may encourage a 'soft-budget' attitude in companies, akin to that which raised such problems in Eastern Europe, though in the case of Japan the discipline exercised was generally too tough to permit huge excesses.

D. Public Banks

In addition to the private commercial banks, public banks were established from the 1870s. Under the influential Count Matsukata (allegedly a disciple of J.-B. Say) as Minister of Finance, a central banking system on the European pattern was inaugurated in 1881, quickly followed by setting up the Bank of Japan in 1882. Apart from control of domestic commercial business, Matsukata concentrated on mobilizing the savings of the poorer classes, handling foreign exchange, and providing long-term investment in industry and agriculture, with a system that owed most to the French one (p. 175 above). Among the special banks (state appointed, though not predominantly state-owned) were the Yokohama Specie Bank (1880, reorganized 1887) for foreign exchange; the Hypothec Bank (1896) for long-term loans to agriculture (modelled on the Crédit Foncier); Industrial Bank of Japan (IBJ, 1900, modelled on the Crédit Mobilier), again for long-term lending, at first mainly to large-scale firms and especially the *zaibatsu*.[144] Because of their associations with imperialism, most of the special banks were broken up or converted into commercial banks during the American Occupation, but following the IBJ tradition, the Japan Development Bank (JDB) was established in 1951. Like its predecessors, the JDB was deliberately aimed at segmenting the capital market, for instance in order to permit prioritization of particular industries by MITI.

---

142 Aoki 1990, and in Aoki and Dore 1994; Hoshi, in *ibid.*

143 In Aoki and Patrick forthcoming.

144 Allen 1946/1962, chs 3, 6; Lockwood 1954, ch. 10; Cameron *et al.* 1967, pp. 270–71.

However, its contribution to total bank lending amounted to only about 5 per cent of all industrial loans in the 1960s and 4 per cent in the 1970s,[145] and after the 1950s the commercial banks played an increasingly dominant role in industrial finance.

The short-loan market in Japan was much less developed[146] – all the focus lay on the longer term.

V: PRODUCTS AND DEMAND

A. Government Consumption

Government investment during the Meiji 'take-off' of the late 19th century generally exceeded private productive investment.[147] Government expenditures remained very prominent in activities relating to the military through the expansionist interwar period; with an especially pronounced orientation to modern industry.[148] Japan was compelled to disband its military organization after the defeat in the Second World War, and most accounts attribute at least a part of the high postwar rates of growth of the economy to the low commitment to military expenditure in those years.[149] However, procurement by the US military during the Korean War period from 1950 to 1953 appears to have been very important on the demand side in restoring Japanese industry, not least in demonstrating that much Japanese equipment was outdated,[150] so the role of the military even in Japan was not purely negative.[151] In their purchasing policies, Japanese governments seem to have been 'tough customers'.

Some leading scholars have thus given special emphasis to the role of government (investment as well as consumption) in raising demand;[152] though most authorities seem somewhat sceptical of this.[153] Ohkawa and Rosovsky[154] see government investment in the 20th century as larger during periods of sagging growth, while private investment led the growth spurts. Japanese governments, however, did relatively little in a Keynesian way to

145 Vestal 1993, ch. 8.
146 Allen 1946/1962, pp. 59, 107.
147 Ohkawa and Rosovsky 1973, p. 16.
148 Lockwood 1954, p. 188.
149 E.g. Fagerberg 1988.
150 Vestal 1993, p. 30.
151 Nelson 1992, and above.
152 E.g. Rosovsky 1961.
153 E.g. Minami 1986, p. 346, who elsewhere argues that Japan can be seen as an exemplar of 'cheap government' in Adam Smith's sense.
154 Ohkawa and Rosovsky 1973, p. 156.

boost demand e.g. via deficit finance and government borrowing – suppression of inflation was perceived to be too urgent a task to permit them such latitude.

Specific government procurement policies for high-tech industries may have had a more substantial effect. The Japanese Electronic Computer Company, set up by MITI in 1961 to buy computers built by Japanese companies in rivalry with IBM, has been seen as the cornerstone of the Japanese computer industry.[155]

B. Consumer Demand

The major part of the postwar boom was, however, led by *private* consumption. As income levels revived, there was a very inelastic response in terms of the demand for necessities like foodstuffs and housing, in that consumption of such items barely increased at all even though incomes were growing relatively rapidly.[156] Instead demand switched towards 'decencies', especially consumer durables – 'white goods' and 'brown goods', led in the first instance by refrigerators and radios. The relatively egalitarian income distribution after the Second World War permitted mass consumption of such 'decencies' and thus mass production. Conversely, the marginal propensity to consume luxuries out of high incomes (e.g. *zaibatsu* families) was very low.[157] Japanese manufacturers aimed at offering a wide selection of particular product characteristics, e.g. in cars, so far as was compatible with the production facilities.[158] Partly for space-saving reasons, the increased expenditure on 'little items' like household appliances was proportionately much greater in the postwar era than that on 'big items' like cars and houses.[159]

Japanese consumers themselves showed a nationalistic desire for consuming Japanese-made products, instead of expending their enlarged incomes on imports; seemingly believing – and probably correctly – that it was in their own long-term best interests to boost domestic industry. Japanese governments reinforced this home-produced bias. Imports had little destructive effect on traditional or new manufactures – their strongest impact was to spur indigenous production.[160] The 'commercialization point' at which commodities like consumer electronics began to achieve

155 Anchordoguy 1989.

156 Nurkse 1953, p. 75; Lockwood 1954, pp. 74, 147; Macpherson 1987, p. 51; for earlier data see Gleason, in Lockwood 1965.

157 Lockwood 1954, p. 284; see *ibid.*, ch. 8, for detail on earlier consumption patterns.

158 Tolliday and Zeitlin 1986, p. 227.

159 Ohkawa and Rosovsky 1973, p. 158.

160 Lockwood 1954, ch. 6.

widespread market acceptance was attained very rapidly, and subsequent market penetration and saturation followed closely thereafter. Emphasis on product quality encouraged consumption of home-made goods.

Wages were generally kept in line with productivity growth, to maintain the expansion of demand without generating undue inflation, through the annual 'Spring Offensive', in which unions bargained with government and industrial leaders for a fair overall wage increase. Stagnation of consumption in the early 1980s has been blamed on unions seeking too low an average wage increase![161]

C. Investment Demand

Despite the consumption boom, Japanese households and corporations maintained the spectacularly high levels of savings remarked on above, and even increased them in the postwar expansion. Corporate savings by themselves, though rising in trend, were inadequate to fund the high rate of business expansion[162] – for this, private savings had to be extensively tapped, using a broad range of financial means. Investment demand was geared towards a sectoral emphasis on 'sunrise' industries, fostered by consensual government policy-making, and a technological emphasis on machine tools and 'machinofacture'. The object was to obtain as substantial a set of dynamic links as possible, e.g. through technologies such as CNC machine tools. Thus the role of the machinery sector was seen not only in terms of the demand for investment in a sectoral sense but as a supplier of technologies to user industries. Japanese policy-making in a sectoral dimension placed great emphasis on 'development blocs'[163] or what the French call *filières*, i.e. industrial webs.

D. Export Demand

Initially, the import/export function was in the hands of large foreign merchants (in 1885 only 9 per cent of the Japanese export trade was in Japanese hands), but under the aegis of the *zaibatsu* the marketing and distribution aspects were steadily taken over by Japanese general trading companies (*sogo shosha*), most of them with close links to the major industrial groups or indeed a part of them (like Mitsui Bussan in 1876), and with close familiarity with world trading and market conditions.

The Japanese export 'invasion' of world markets began in high-volume markets for fairly standardized goods. In such areas, especially noteworthy

161 Vestal 1993, p. 181.
162 Ohkawa and Rosovsky 1973, p. 168.
163 Dahmén 1955.

in the 1930s and 1950s, the Japanese were donning the mantle traditional for catching-up late developers, of chasing 'segment retreat' by the advanced high-income producers in North America and Western Europe. These were products of relatively low quality sold at low prices, in which the low hourly wage rates and other costs of the late developers enabled them to undercut the earlier industrializers. Efforts were made through a law passed in 1925 to set up guilds to raise product quality standards of manufactures and exports, but they were long regarded as ineffective.[164] Japanese exports maintained their reputation for cheapness and shoddiness in the early postwar period,[165] but overcame this liability through the demands of tough domestic customers. The main thrust of Japanese export growth from the mid-1960s was, however, to come in medium-to-high quality products, where the Japanese outcompeted the incumbent advanced nations by setting medium-to-low prices. Typical examples were power tools[166] or Sony's Trinitron colour TV tube – products whose rather high quality was evident to most consumers abroad, sold at prices only a few notches above the standard item. Such prices were attainable because of this focus of process improvement on medium-performance products. At times, Japan was accused by other countries of 'quality dumping', i.e. selling higher-quality steel (etc.) products at average-quality prices.[167] Whether valid or not, the fears led to imposition of 'voluntary' restraints on imports from Japan into western industrial countries.

It has been remarked in Section I above that, for the most part, Japanese growth was not truly 'export-led', in that domestic expansion – sometimes fostered by import substitution – came first. Export surges came at times when world trade was not expanding especially fast, suggesting that domestic supply factors were the driving force.[168] Moreover, the bulk of Japanese industrial exports before the Second World War were to Asian countries with even lower per-capita incomes than Japan.[169] If there was any 'dumping', it would reinforce the view that exports tailed after. Even so, one of the requirements of the export-led model soon came to be met – balance of payments crises were moderated by the strength of exports, assisted by occasional devaluation (e.g. 1931), so that expansion could be sustained. The export-led model proper required exports to outrun imports persistently, with pressures on the balance of payments for *revaluation* of

164 Allen 1946/1962, p. 130.
165 Porter 1990, p. 410.
166 Walker and Gardiner 1980.
167 Amsden 1989, p. 310.
168 Ohkawa and Rosovsky 1973, ch. 7. There were briefer periods when export drives did compensate for sagging internal growth (*ibid.*, pp. 145, 177).
169 Lockwood 1954, p. 442.

the yen. This came only around the mid-1960s, and was led from internal sources through the massive improvements in processes and products already described.

VI: GOVERNMENT INDUSTRIAL POLICIES

Analyses of the policies of Japanese governments, especially by western economists, have generally tried to appraise them in a framework drawn from the equilibrium-oriented 'neoclassical synthesis', and in doing so fail to appreciate the main point: that postwar Japanese policy-making has sought the active promotion of disequilibrium in the economic arena. 'Policy towards exchange rates and interest rates showed a conscious intent to prevent markets from clearing'.[170] Conversely, economic policy at the same time sought *social* stability, e.g. through trying to minimize unemployment, or in later years seeking to improve the quality of life. Brief comments have been made above about the state's role in aggregate demand policies, financial policies, etc. This summary will consider only 'industrial policy', although its effects are often difficult to disentangle from those of other policies, and indeed from the workings of the private sector in industry. It cannot be over-emphasized from the outset that the role of the Japanese state has been in no way monolithic.

A. State Control

Government industrial policy in the Meiji period was shaped by military considerations and by the desire for domestic production of military or related *matériel* and undertakings. As a result, it was especially prominent in building infrastructure (shipyards, railways) and related capital goods industries (e.g. iron and steel), which were seen as crucial to political as well as industrial strength. However, the governments were unable to expand the system efficiently and for the most part quit other activities in which they had become involved from the 1880s, such as the early model factories; not because of a belief in laissez-faire but because state control was found to be highly inefficient and a drain on the state's financial resources.[171] Thus the lesson learned by the Japanese was that governments might help fund capital-intensive projects, but that they were best developed and run by companies, whether state-owned or privately owned. By 1912 only 12 per cent of factory workers were employed in government

---

170 Vestal 1993, p. 10.
171 Landes, in Lockwood 1965.

establishments, mostly iron and steel;[172] by 1933 this had fallen to 8 per cent.[173] Some part of the postwar disaffection from state control was also a reaction to the intrusion of the state and the military in the later 1930s and during the war.

The resulting government function was entrusted in large part to particular ministries staffed by elites, the first important one being the Ministry of Commerce and Industry in 1925. This became the Ministry of Munitions in the Second World War, but was reformed postwar first by reverting to the Ministry of Commerce and Industry and then in 1949 as the Ministry of International Trade and Industry (MITI), which was to play an especially conspicuous role in the postwar shaping of the Japanese industrial structure.

The government in the 1930s entrusted business to 'self-control'; in the 1940s the pendulum swung to 'state control'. Both failed. Thus the postwar government role was exercised by 'orchestration', particularly through MITI.[174] Johnson (1982) concludes that Japan can best be described as a *developmental state*, a role contrasting with the primarily *regulatory* role of the state in a country like the USA. Relatively low levels of state-run entrepreneurship and of government spending were part of this developmental co-operative role, and in the following sub-sections further implications are drawn. However, Johnson's view has been thought by many to exaggerate the cohesion of Japanese policy-making.

B. Large and Small Firms

At the time it was founded in 1925, the Ministry of Commerce and Industry began with the role of trying to subsidize SMFs against the *zaibatsu* – a strategy frequently attempted up to the present day by various ministries but just as often regarded as being oppositional to industrial expansion. By the later 1920s this Ministry was turning to more general pro-industrial attempts to foster quality, co-operation, and especially 'rationalization' (through cartels, etc.), based mainly on the German model. After the Second World War the Ministry (which had become MITI in 1949, as mentioned) subscribed to the view that SMFs had been responsible for economic stagnation in the interwar period, and thus put greater emphasis still on large firms. Though pure monopolization was rare, cartelization was legalized by a series of laws beginning in 1952. As in the 1930s, much attention was paid by government to the problem described as 'excessive competition' (*kato kyoso*). Although western scholars from the 1960s onwards placed heavy emphasis on the role of MITI, both their western

---

172 Allen 1946/1962, p. 127.
173 Lockwood 1954, p. 110.
174 Nelson, in Dosi *et al.* 1988.

successors and Japanese scholars have more recently argued against the view of industry expansion led from the front by MITI, and in favour of the view that pro-competitive agencies, especially the Fair Trade Commission (FTC, 1947), also had a major role to play, and one that was often directly opposed to MITI's. Nevertheless, MITI weakened the FTC's tough Anti-Monopoly Law in 1953, by measures which recognized recession cartels and rationalization cartels, allowed cross-shareholdings, allowed manufacturers the right to set prices, and abolished provisions against industrial associations. For lengthy periods, antitrust seemed to 'fall asleep'.[175] However, government continued to play an active part in promulgating SMFs, if only for employment and social reasons, e.g. through making available low-interest loans through the JDB and in 1953 the Smaller Business Finance Corporation. In the 1960s, policies towards SMFs became less defensive and more forward-looking, e.g. in the Basic Law for SMFs of 1963.

MITI generally did not protect particular firms so much as particular industries or technologies. Thus the foreign technology licensed (monopolistically) by MITI was made accessible as soon as practicable to a number of firms (though one might be singled out at the very beginning), and technology diffusion strongly encouraged. In this way, internal competition could be preserved.[176]

C. Networks

Government regulation was important from the early days of industrialization for bringing firms together and establishing networks – for example, by licensing plants for egg-raising or filature, it brought together user–producer relationships among SMFs in the otherwise highly fragmented silk industry, which in Allen's view[177] allowed it to out-compete and eventually crush the Chinese silk industry (which had no such regulatory framework). Trade associations (*kumiai*) were encouraged first by a law of 1884, aimed at co-operation in areas such as standards, quality, bulk purchase and the like, and also acted as a useful avenue for official control, especially of SMFs.[178]

MITI in the postwar period also aided wider exchange of leading-edge ideas through co-operative research, by sponsoring government laboratories to work on advanced technologies. The programmes have met with mixed success, partly because of the unwillingness of the *kaisha* to work too

---

175 Johnson 1982, p. 226.
176 Vestal 1993, p. 42.
177 Allen 1946/1962, p. 69.
178 *Ibid.*, pp. 131, 153; Lockwood 1954, pp. 569–70.

closely with their rivals. The most extensive study, by Fransman, shows that much depended on the method of organizing relationships between the government laboratories and the generally much more important corporate laboratories.[179] In general, one can agree with Porter[180] that government-sponsored co-operative research existed mainly to flag new areas that were likely to receive state blessing. More recently, a 'third sector' lying between the public and private laboratories has been attempted, e.g. for advanced ceramics.[181]

MITI's degree of success was also furthered by 'old boy' networks, which extended into links with many large firms.[182] These helped form a base for the development of industrial consensus.

D. Consensus and 'Visions'

State-led planning during the postwar American Occupation, based on dictating sectoral priorities, effectively ended in 1949 with the setting up of the committee-based Industrial Rationalization Council, shortly after MITI replaced the Ministry of Commerce and Industry – this formally introduced a broad industrial base and accentuated the 'corporatist' ethos in the policy-making process. MITI's approach moved further away from direct interventionism over time, towards developing 'visions' in concert with the industrial sector; typically choosing around 400 leaders of industry to produce a 'vision' based on Delphi methods, which would then be diffused to the whole of the rest of industry. The object was to reduce uncertainty, by informing the industrial sector and economy as a whole of where the government hoped they were going, so that mutually consistent plans could be laid by the private sector. The government's own plans did not usually specify targets, but gave as much information as possible on the general direction it wanted industry to go.

Within its consent-oriented perspective, MITI opted generally for indirect means of stimulating growth in the 'right' sectors and technologies, rather than planning them itself. Thus, after 1962, MITI spoke of 'administrative guidance' rather than direct intervention, a role which had its antecedents in the cartelization phase during the 1930s. Freeman[183] places particular emphasis on the 1952 Law to Promote the Rationalization of Firms that permitted the use of government subsidies for experimental installations,

---

179 Fransman 1990. The government funded only 21 per cent of R&D in 1987, according to Porter 1990, p. 398.

180 *Idem.*

181 Lastres 1992.

182 Johnson 1982, p. 253.

183 Freeman 1987, p. 35.

tax subsidies, accelerated depreciation, and the building of infrastructure. MITI was quickly given considerable powers to allocate scarce foreign imports, including technology imports. The latter were decoupled from imports of capital goods in 1950, and MITI given substantial power to bargain in unified and centralized fashion with foreign corporations for licensing their technology. In 1952 it was given power over the foreign exchange budget, effectively granting it control over all imports. The most stringent controls, such as that over import allocation, were lost in the 1960s.

MITI relied mostly on direct physical controls during the 1950s, at a time when physical scarcities prevailed in many areas, especially strategic materials. Sectoral policy was thus oriented towards industries like coal and steel, where the shortages seemed greatest while at the same time needs of the rest of the industrial sector were the most extensive. With the shortages mostly overcome, policy tools in the 1960s moved towards indirect means, such as general macroeconomic policies. In the 1970s and 1980s, and especially following the *débâcle* of the first oil crisis in 1973–74, policy returned somewhat towards a sectoral focus. However, the notion of 'picking winners' became more oriented towards new *technologies* rather than to new *industries.*[184] It was the task of the private corporations and groups to convert these new technologies into viable industries, abetted by strategic visions for the sectors planned in conjunction with MITI.

E. Declining Industries

MITI also had to meet the problems of 'sunset' as well as 'sunrise' industries, especially as industrialization gathered pace. The consensual approach permitted a more restrained and socially acceptable process for assisting the decline of the sunset industries. MITI initially propped up employment, but later gave greater emphasis to retraining employees and restructuring industries. The main weapon to be used, at least in the earlier years, was reduction of competition. At times MITI sought directly to reduce the number of competitors, as it did in automobiles and computers, but it was generally unsuccessful at the level of the larger firms. It was equally unsuccessful in restricting the size of plants, as for instance it attempted to do at the giant Kawasaki integrated steel mill. When success did come, it was mainly because MITI and other government agencies or ministries were able to give the impression that any relief would be short-lived, and that competition loomed ahead.[185]

---

[184] Vestal 1993.

[185] Best 1990, p. 266; Vestal 1993.

Rationalization by the mid-1950s had come to be interpreted at three levels: at the inter-industry level, of selecting winners and losers (this policy was, as we have seen, later amended); at the intra-industry level, of enlarging firm sizes; and at the firm level, of sponsoring new technologies and management.[186] MITI by the 1970s was working in Schumpeterian fashion to try to assist declining sectors to evolve into expanding ones by controlled diversification, e.g. encouraging steel firms to move into electronics.[187]

F. Competitive Advantage

As shown by the rivalry with the FTC, the view that there was a more 'dialectical' evolution of policy-making than the 'mighty MITI' interpretation allowed for seems well taken.[188] The dialectics can be simplified into a debate between German (occasionally Soviet) and American models in a Japanese context. Other ministries, such as Finance, Agriculture, Transport and Construction, also had major roles to play in formulating and executing industrial policy. What does seem valid is the view that it was precisely this diversity in bureaucratic decision-making (which as stated above extended well outside the civil service) – indeed a degree of contestability and competition in policy-making – which helped bring a satisfactory outcome. The common 'Japan Inc.' view of Japanese success pays insufficient attention to this pluralism. Government–business relations have been interwoven rather than pyramidal – 'a web with no spider'.[189] The pattern of decision-making has reflected that of Japanese corporations in being typically 'bottom-up', in lieu of the 'top-down' structure of some corporatist European states.[190]

Moreover, a high degree of liberalization was partly enforced by external pressures. The Tokugawa government was forced under international pressure to sign the Unequal Treaties agreement with the major western powers in 1858, not revised until 1911; hence infant industry tariffs could not play any major role. Quantitative controls, also, were little used before 1933.[191] In more recent times such external pressure has continued to be exerted, e.g with the USA's deployment of its 'Section 301' provisions, and through international agencies such as the IMF, OECD and GATT, especially as rising Japanese trade success encountered foreign criticism.

---

186 *Ibid.*, p. 31.
187 Best 1990, pp. 192–3.
188 Lockwood 1965; Best 1990, ch. 6.
189 Lockwood 1965, p. 503.
190 Aoki 1988, ch. 7.
191 Lockwood 1954, pp. 532, 539ff.

After the completion of GATT's Tokyo Round in 1979, Japan's average tariffs were estimated to be lower than the nominally free-trader countries like the USA and UK.

One should not, however, dismiss the positive effects that interventionism or 'guidance' achieved. MITI led the early rejection of 'comparative advantage', and determined the sectoral priority pattern on dynamic (long-term industrial benefit or 'competitive advantage') rather than static comparative advantage. Its main contribution can fairly be summed up as a long-term vision as to the ends combined with pragmatism about the means.[192] Competitive advantage meant basing the country's industrial strength on groups of competitive firms. In this sense, although MITI referred to 'market forces' it did not imply 'market discipline' as in some western countries. Markets were there to be made, through the strength of the firms and their groups. How successful this strategy would continue to be once Japan reached the world's technological frontier was a more contentious matter, debated as hotly inside Japan as outside. We have yet to see.

---

192 Freeman 1987, ch. 2.

11. The Newly Industrializing Countries

This survey of the Newly Industrializing Countries (NICs) compares East Asian and Latin American experience. Most attention is paid to just two countries in each of these regions, namely South Korea and Taiwan in East Asia and Brazil and Argentina in Latin America. As the National System of Innovation (NSI) and much other literature emphasize, each country is different, and there are quite evident problems with generalizing from these case studies to the situations of East Asia or Latin America as a whole. Some of the major intra-regional differences are referred to, but this does not pretend to be a comprehensive analysis. Moreover, as some of the earlier chapters showed, there may even be considerable differences between districts within these particular countries, especially the large Latin American ones.

For reasons that should become clearer as the chapter progresses, East Asia will be taken as a case of relative 'success' and Latin America as relative 'failure'; thus using the two regions as a pairwise set of comparisons of success and failure. These should be judged only against one another – by historical standards, the East Asian performance probably merits the common description of an 'East Asian Miracle',[1] and thus registers as 'super-success'. Similarly, the Latin American performance, while overshadowed by East Asia, has been tolerable by comparison with the economic disasters in many countries of Africa, and hence might better be termed 'partial-success'. Much of the literature on Latin America, and not least that written by Latin American scholars themselves, has been unduly pessimistic. My discussion necessarily reflects the Latin American pessimism vs. East Asian optimism of most of the literature.

In this respect, it is noteworthy that sometimes a particular factor argued as contributing to Latin American 'failure' was equally argued by other scholars as a cause of East Asian 'success'. The pairwise comparisons yield many points of contrast, but it seems certain that the list of causes of the differences is 'over-determined' – that is, we can produce too many rather than too few causes for success vs. failure. It seems highly probable that not all of the items mentioned below were individually that important. However, it is the systems as a whole that are really being contrasted, and in

1 E.g. World Bank 1993.

that sense the ways in which the macro and micro results come together is the main issue of analysis.

I: GROWTH OF THE NICs

A. Relative Position in the Early Postwar Years

1. East Asia

The chosen countries, South Korea and Taiwan, had a long history of some growth in output, and manufacturing output in particular. For Korea, the equivalent to Japan's fleet of American ships in 1853 was the coercion by Japan to trade in 1876.[2] According to Wade,[3] both Korea and Taiwan had higher growth rates of GDP than Japan in the interwar period (1911–38), and Taiwanese manufacturing grew at the rate of 6 per cent p.a. 1912–40. But both countries had been prostrated by the Second World War, together with postwar inflation and political conflict (the beginnings of the Korean War in 1950 dividing North and South Korea, the separation of Taiwan from China after the Communist Revolution in the latter in 1949). High levels of aid from the USA of course greatly assisted recovery, yet Wade's figures for GNP per capita in 1962, some years after these problems had been encountered and indeed after some rapid growth in the later 1950s, show them still comparable with some African countries and falling into the 'least-developed' bracket of countries, with seemingly unattractive growth prospects.[4] However, they ranked much more highly in terms of wider 'sociopolitical' criteria.[5]

2. Latin America

National income figures for a similar period put the large Latin American countries in the middle-income bracket, and at this stage (ca. 1960) nearer to the AICs in many respects than to the less-developed countries proper (which of course included South Korea and Taiwan). Both Brazil and Argentina had had a long history of reasonably high per-capita incomes and, especially since the 1930s, had had a considerable expansion in manufacturing (see below).

---

2 Amsden 1989, ch. 2.
3 Wade 1990, p. 74.
4 *Ibid.*, p. 35.
5 *Ibid.*, p. 307.

B. Subsequent Growth Performance

1. East Asia

Growth rates of the 'Four Tigers' (including Hong Kong and Singapore) were typically 7 to 10 per cent p.a. throughout the period from the early 1960s to the late 1980s. These went with very high growth rates of manufacturing output, and especially manufactured exports. In Taiwan, manufacturing grew at the rate of 12 per cent p.a. 1952–58, to represent 22 per cent of its GDP by 1960, a proportion comparable with Brazil at that time.[6] By 1977, manufactures represented 37 per cent of GDP, a ratio equal to Argentina's, at the head of the middle-income countries.[7] South Korea followed a similar path but lagged some years behind Taiwan. Korean export growth averaged 40 per cent p.a. 1962–71 and 28 per cent p.a. 1972–79.[8] For technological accumulation, high growth of investment mattered even more than exports.[9] The East Asian countries replicated the Japanese compositional shift in production and trade patterns (cf. Chapter 10), but brought about in an even shorter time interval.

2. Latin America

These countries saw rapid growth beginning in the late 1960s, allowing them to qualify as Newly Industrializing Countries despite their older manufacturing history. However, in Brazil the 'miracle' lasted only six years, from 1968 to 1974, and was followed by stagnation, which by and large has persisted up to the present day. Between 1980 and 1990, GDP per capita in Brazil *fell* by some 6 per cent.[10] Argentinian output per head was 20 per cent *lower* in absolute terms in the late 1980s than in the mid-1970s.[11] The growth period of the late 1960s and early 1970s saw some rise in manufactured exports, as befitting the 'NIC' status, but the rise was followed by a plateau and then a decline.

The contrasting experience of the two regions, in terms of their initial (low vs. medium) income endowments as compared with their ensuing (high vs. low) growth performance, might seem to support to 'convergence' notion introduced in Chapter 3. Comparison with the AICs, however, indicates that the regions belong to different 'clubs', in the terminology of Baumol.[12]

---

6 *Ibid.*, p. 77.
7 *Ibid.*, p. 88.
8 Amsden 1989, p. 55.
9 Enos and Park 1988, p. 30.
10 Ferraz *et al.* 1992, p. 56.
11 Katz and Bercovich 1993.
12 Baumol 1986; De Long 1988.

C. Incentives for Industrialization

1. East Asia

Korea, especially, and Taiwan were both reacting against colonization by the Japanese, which was of course ended by Japanese defeat in the world war in 1945. The Japanese as colonial powers are often considered to have been less opposed to industrial development than most western colonialists, partly because of Japan's own domestic shortages and import needs. However, as implied in Chapter 10, Japan's main quest – certainly in Korea – was for a 'rice basket', and moreover indigenous Koreans were excluded from any managerial posts in larger industrial firms in their own country under Japanese rule.[13] Like Japan, but even intensified because of their smaller sizes, South Korea and Taiwan both sought self-sufficiency partially for strategic reasons.

2. Latin America

The vulnerability of dependence on a limited range of primary exports, together with political fluctuations, had led to some early industrialization in countries such as Argentina and Brazil, relying considerably on tariff protection.[14] Pressures for industrialization in the larger South American countries really began during the Great Slump of the 1930s, when prices of primary products collapsed, and inelasticities in the supplies of such exports met highly inelastic world demands. Flights of capital out of these countries exacerbated their problems of indebtedness, and manufacturing industry (in lieu of heavy imports of manufactures) came to be advocated by way of economic relief.[15] These pressures were accentuated in the Second World War by being cut off from trade with the AICs, especially Europe. Shortly after the war there emerged the 'ECLA school' from the UN Economic Commission for Latin America, headed by economists such as Raúl Prebisch. This school distinguished the 'centre' and the 'periphery', and used historical evidence on the terms of trade between manufactured goods and primary products, to argue that there was a long-term bias against the latter, so that industrialization of the periphery would reap greater rewards in the long run.[16] This evidence has long been contested, and does indeed appear to show different patterns at different times;[17] but a recent econometric investigation does support the notion of a long-run downward

13 Amsden 1989, p. 33.
14 Díaz–Alejandro 1970; Leff 1982.
15 Furtado 1970, chs 9, 11.
16 Prebisch 1950; Singer 1950.
17 Spraos 1980.

trend,[18] though the adequacy of the price indices must remain in dispute. Whether such a downward trend is sufficiently pronounced to justify overturning the apparent comparative advantage in primary products is also unanswered by this evidence. However, this book is broadly sympathetic to the notion of 'dynamic comparative advantage' based on the accumulation of technological competences, which may be at variance with static comparative advantage, as seen in the previous chapter for postwar Japan. The appraisal of European economic development in Chapter 5 suggested that the real issue is trade defined by goods with high technology content or potential, against those with low technology content or potential, in the spirit of the 'technology gap' interpretation of international trade. Manufacturing has provided heuristics for more sustained technological accumulation, but some countries have instead benefited from high-tech agriculture.

D. Exports vs. Import Substitution Strategies

1. East Asia

Shortages of foreign exchange and persistently overvalued exchange rates encouraged these countries to begin with 'Import-Substituting Industrialization' (ISI) in the 1950s. Both Taiwan and South Korea, however, moved quite rapidly to an export-promotion strategy, e.g. in the latter under General Park Chung Hee (1961–79). Exports rose from under 5 per cent of Korean GNP in the 1950s to around 35 per cent in the 1980s,[19] a remarkably high ratio for a country with a population around the 40 million mark. Exports were regarded as being preferable to simple import substitution because:

(a) the comparatively limited size of their domestic markets implied few scale economies;

(b) exports would encourage their industries to be competitive in world markets;

(c) exports could act as a funnel for foreign technology imports.[20]

However Wade,[21] basing himself on Taiwan's experience, argues that there were subsequent bursts of ISI as industrialization deepened, and provisionally concludes that perhaps ISI is always required as a forerunner to successful export promotion. Similarly, South Korea expanded into new fields partly through ISI policies, e.g. into electronics after the Electronics

18 Ardeni and Wright 1992.
19 Amsden 1989, p. 70.
20 L. Kim 1993, p. 364.
21 Wade 1990, p. 84.

Industry Promotion Law of 1969.[22] There, the lag of exports behind ISI varied from near zero (e.g. in steel and ships) to two decades (e.g. in automobiles).[23] These observations suggest that Porter's view that ISI policies are likely to obstruct the process of development is incorrect.[24]

2. Latin America

From the 1930s, the Latin American countries adopted ISI, but they were never really successful – except perhaps during the brief 'miracles' – at moving up a notch into export development in these new industries. Instead, ISI was extended upstream in the process dimension, beginning with consumer goods before shifting into intermediate and capital goods. For reasons advanced below, it can be argued that ISI was less a choice than a virtual necessity.[25] The effects were:

(a) the larger markets of the two principal countries allowed some prospective gain of economies of scale, but these were rarely attained in practice;

(b) their industries thus never became internationally competitive other than in a few restricted areas, and rank inefficiency of domestic industry too often became the norm;

(c) foreign technologies had to be purchased directly in 'embodied' form (such as the 'turnkey' systems described below), leading to *increased* foreign dependency.

Although there was a limited amount of subsequent exportation, mainly to other Latin American countries, ISI ran the danger of becoming self-perpetuating, and in the Latin American case this is normally what happened. ISI in the postwar period was ineffective in bringing about structural change.[26] The problem appears not to be the existence of ISI *per se*, but whether the processes as well as the products become indigenized, and local learning takes hold (the precise form of the ISI policies may of course matter). Some have blamed the lack of development in Latin America primarily on the neglect of export activity following the adoption of ISI policies[27] – a view which Prebisch himself appeared to share[28] – but also convincing is Furtado's point that the deficiencies of technological

22 Amsden 1989, ch. 4.

23 *Ibid.*, p. 155.

24 Porter 1990, pp. 548, 677. For an attempted formal comparison of ISI and export-oriented policies, see Chenery *et al.* 1986.

25 Furtado 1970.

26 *Ibid.*, p. 113.

27 E.g. Díaz–Alejandro 1970, ch. 2, for Argentina, blaming faulty domestic policies under Perón, etc. postwar; also Leff 1982, p. 185.

28 Rostow 1990, p. 405.

dynamism in domestic industry were equally important.[29] We must look to the microeconomic level to understand why there was such limited dynamism in domestic industrial development, and why it failed to turn outwards.

II: TECHNOLOGIES AND PROCESSES

A. Borrowing Strategies

1. East Asia

Foreign borrowing in Taiwan and South Korea was conducted mainly by governments, usually on a portfolio basis (i.e. as non-specific loans to governments). Little use was made of Foreign Direct Investment (FDI) in manufacturing, i.e. specifically directed foreign lending, and what little there was was mainly utilized for export promotion in the specific industry in the receiving country. Foreign funds were primarily for the acquisition of capital goods, rather than for equity holdings.[30] However, Singapore relied heavily on inward investment by MNCs, to a degree which Porter[31] considers might seriously retard development. A centrepiece of all these countries' strategies for rapid industrialization was the high ratio of imports of capital goods, with such capital goods imports being used to provide kick-starts to export-oriented industries. Later, once they had been successfully implanted, ISI could be extended to these upstream activities. Only later still, when domestic manufacturing capabilities were reasonably advanced, was greater use made of foreign licensing (FL) as a means of acquiring new technologies. Amsden (1977) thus claims that the Taiwan machine tool industry used FL generally when sufficiently strong to be able to judge which foreign designs had the greatest growth potential in a Taiwanese setting. However, critics contend that the continuing high level of capital goods imports demonstrates a lack of adequate indigenization, especially because of shortcomings in the development of design capabilities.[32]

Initially design capability was 'bought' on world markets. A salutary example was provided by Hyundai Heavy Industries (HHI), the world's largest shipbuilder, when it came to build its first 260,000 DWT supertankers after 1972. The designs were commissioned from a Scottish firm (Scotlithgow) which had only enough capacity to build half a ship at a

29 Furtado 1970, pp. 144–5.
30 Enos and Park 1988, p. 35.
31 Porter 1990, p. 679.
32 S.R. Kim 1993.

time. 'But when HHI put the two halves together, *they didn't fit*'.[33] HHI thus first developed capability in design modification, and in due course basic design. As late as 1986, it was calculated that in-house basic design cost 50 per cent more than purchasing it, but it was nevertheless considered to be ultimately cheaper, in order to avoid the delivery delays and penalties incurred by going outside.[34] Excessive diversification by sprawling giant firms in Korea has elsewhere limited the attainment of a necessary degree of specialization required for design capability, e.g. in machine tools.[35]

2. Latin America

The large Latin American countries put very high stress on FDI from the beginning. In the early stages of development from the late 19th century onwards (and indeed during the earlier contact with Europe), FDI concentrated on extraction of raw materials and supporting infrastructure.[36] This became criticized for leading to the development of 'export enclaves', with few spillover effects other than a limited amount of employment on the domestic economies,[37] and even that not great because of the utilization of imported labour-saving technologies.[38] Around the Second World War, the focus for FDI in Latin America shifted towards manufacturing industry.[39] The overseas ownership of many plants, firms and indeed industries limited the degree of control that could be exerted over the industrial activities taking place within their borders. As ISI strategies moved quickly towards trying to replace imported capital goods with equivalents domestically produced, the import ratios for capital goods were very low. In practice, the occasional surges of industrialization, like that of the late 1960s, were met by an immediate flood of capital goods imports, paid for by foreign credits (i.e. foreign debts). This temporary import dependency was exacerbated by imports of intermediate goods, such as oil during the oil crises. Thus the low average levels of capital goods imports largely reflected low industrial growth in the longer term.

Foreign licensing (FL) was used as a major incentive for attracting the high levels of FDI, in effect giving monopolistic control in exchange for the construction of the plants. FL costs in Latin America are believed to be

33 Amsden 1989, pp. 276–8.

34 *Ibid.*, p. 279.

35 S. R. Kim 1993.

36 Ford 1962; Furtado 1970.

37 Nurkse 1953.

38 Furtado 1970, ch. 17. Such enclaves did not develop in countries like Taiwan, because the exports came from the peasantry rather than from a specialized plantation sector (Fei *et al.* 1979, p. 25), although they developed similarly to Latin America in many South Asian countries (Myint 1964).

39 Díaz-Alejandro 1970, pp. 265–6.

quite high, though much of the data is secret.[40] With no domestic rivals of substance, foreign licensers aimed to perpetuate the dependency upon themselves, through obtaining further extensions of licences and contracts. Thus FL often implied the survival of older generations of technology. Even more frequently, imported technologies were accused of being 'inappropriate', for example 'turnkey' projects biased towards large scale and capital intensity (see below).

B. Product vs. Process Innovation

1. East Asia

The East Asian countries established new industries predominantly on the basis of product designs imported unchanged from the relevant AICs, such as the 'cloning' of personal computers. Production was often undertaken on the type of relationship known as 'OEM' (Original Equipment Manufacturer), i.e. fabrication and assembly to the designs of American, European or Japanese corporations, which then 'badged' the product and sold it under their own brand-names. The input of Taiwanese and South Korean firms consisted of low-cost processing, based on their low hourly labour costs and capabilities in production engineering. They are still today well behind the most advanced Japanese companies in terms of process capability, but comparable with many firms of the western AICs. Korea has been more successful in building own brand-names in the 1980s (e.g. Hyundai, Samsung, Goldstar), because of the greater use of large firms (*chaebol*, see Section III below). The generally smaller Taiwanese firms, however, still rely mainly on OEM production.

2. Latin America

Behind the protective barriers, the range of products mushroomed. In indigenous firms, there was excessive *product* diversification, relative to the size of the industrial plants, on the one side; and only limited *process* change, because of the lack of international linkages and the weak domestic knowhow base, on the other side. Subsidiaries of MNCs were more influential in introducing process change, but were severely constrained in their product choices, and the spillovers to domestically-based industry were restricted, especially as many had been granted quasi-monopolistic status and thus had few indigenous counterparts. Katz[41] divides incremental technical advance into (i) product design engineering, (ii) production

---

40 Teitel 1993, pp. 149–52. Colombia, however, had some success in imitating MITI by establishing an agency in the late 1960s to bargain down licensing costs (*ibid.*, p 157).

41 Katz 1985, 1987.

process engineering, and (iii) production planning and organization ('industrial engineering'), and considers the third of these largely absent in Latin America.

C. Indigenous Technological Capabilities (ITCs)

Countries can successively develop the competences: first to be able to *operate* plants and equipment that others had built within them; second to be able to *invest* in and install new plants and equipment of their own; third to be able to *innovate* new designs of plant and equipment.[42] ITCs may represent such capabilities at any one or more of these levels. The key issue in industrial development is the upgrading from one level to the next.

1. East Asia

Development of ITCs was the cornerstone of industrial advance, with the aims of minimizing foreign control as quickly as possible and generating export competitiveness, including that among SMFs. Operation of the early petrochemical plants was expected to be absorbed within the first year in Korea.[43] Beyond the operation stage, 'imitator' strategies based on reverse engineering, using very close copying, were more common in the earliest years; but later there was a shift to 'apprenticeship' strategies, with adaptations carried out as the imports were duplicated.[44] 'Turnkey' projects, i.e. importing the whole plant in a state ready to be switched on, were restricted as much as possible to the scale-intensive process industries like petrochemicals, and even there were progressively indigenized in later plants. Foreign engineers had been completely supplanted by Koreans in the first petrochemical plant (Hanyang) within four years.[45] Production capability and investment capability were achieved at practically the same time, and innovation capability followed within a handful of years – twenty years after the giant Korean steel firm, POSCO, was founded, it was exporting its technology to the USA.[46] Formal R&D expenditures were not very large, as the main emphasis lay on importing and indigenizing foreign technologies.[47]

---

42 Katz 1985; Westphal *et al.* 1985.

43 Enos and Park 1988, p. 69.

44 Amsden 1989, ch. 9.

45 Enos and Park 1988, pp. 103–9.

46 Amsden 1989, ch. 12; Wade 1990, p. 319.

47 Enos and Park 1988, pp. 43–7.

2. Latin America

In Latin America, light industries like textiles, themselves developed partly through ISI policies, proved unable to transmute into dynamic technological capabilities,[48] as such industries seemed to have done in countries like Switzerland and Japan. Instead, dynamic ITCs were attempted through extending the ISI programmes. Typical procedures involved 'unpackaging' imported system technologies and trying to copy the more amenable sub-branches or elements of the larger system.[49] By doing so, the ability to integrate the production system into an efficiently functioning whole was impaired and even lost. Turnkey projects were the alternative, i.e. making no attempt at all to indigenize. In Latin America these were frequently used in close association with FDI, including a high reliance on overseas systems contractors and architects, so that capabilities in domestic *investment* were not accumulated either.[50] The lack of eventual success in ITC through the ISI/FDI route can be attributed to a combination of weak domestic efforts and incentives and of lack of access to better standards of imported technologies.[51] A survey in Brazil by Ferraz *et al.*[52] revealed that legal problems with imports plus high price of equipment were by far the dominant reasons for not proceeding with flexible automation. An older survey of manufacturers in the less-industrialized countries (LICs), including African as well as Latin American countries, by Teitel (1978), showed that tie-ins to suppliers were rated as the most crippling restrictive practice in regard to inward transfer of technology (far ahead of price factors, IPR problems, etc.), and the supplying of technology as a package was the greatest obstacle to local adaptation of such technology transfer (far ahead of local deficiencies e.g. skills).[53]

D. 'Appropriateness' of Technology

In the 1970s (especially) there was much concern over the 'appropriateness' of technology, and in particular a belief that 'inappropriate' technology was being transferred from First-World to Third-World countries.[54] This inappropriateness was accentuated by the vehicles for technology transfer, which often consisted of MNC subsidiaries or else aid packages administered from the AICs. 'Inappropriate' technology most often meant

48 Furtado 1970, ch. 11.
49 Freeman 1993.
50 *Ibid.*
51 Dahlman and Frischtak 1993.
52 Ferraz *et al.* 1992, p. 113.
53 See also Teitel 1993, pp. 183–4.
54 E.g. Stewart 1977, chs 3–4; Carr 1985.

capital-intensive, highly mechanized technology, e.g. sending tractors rather than simple implements for agriculture; though the criteria for appropriateness were often left vague.[55]

1. East Asia

The East Asian countries being studied here instead followed the trajectories of postwar Japan, in shifting rapidly from light to heavy industry. Low wages represented practically the only source of competitive advantage in the early days of exporting light manufactures, but as Amsden[56] points out, they were 'an ambiguous blessing. They helped a learner like Korea to enter world markets, but they went hand in hand with backwardness. Backwardness, moreover, imposed heavy costs in the form of low domestic purchasing power, low productivity, an almost total reliance on imports for inputs, low savings, and high interest rates. These costs made it harder both to enter world markets in the first instance and to progress up the ladder of technological complexity.' Because of the lower productivity, unit labour costs for textile exports were no lower than Japan's in the 1960s.[57] Wages in any case rose very rapidly, especially for production workers, mainly because of relying heavily on workers for learning processes in more advanced industries, in Smithian fashion: 'workers were paid relatively high wages not because of a shortage of particular skills but in order to induce them to exercise their intelligence and make imported technology work'.[58] This reflected the emphasis on *process* change, which required especially adaptable workers. In many such industries, the modes of learning were uncodified, which accentuated the reliance on worker responsibility, as compared with 'supplier-dominated' industries like textiles, where the changes were to a large extent embodied in capital goods.[59] Within heavier industries such as machinery, it was, however, found that simpler and less capital-intensive techniques were easier to imitate.[60] Following Japan, a major objective was seeking technological changes that saved time, especially through reducing downtime.[61] A second significant objective was to upgrade quality, e.g. through introducing quality circles.

---

55 E.g. Stewart 1977, ch. 4; Teitel 1993, ch. 8.
56 Amsden 1989, p. 63.
57 *Ibid.*, p. 68.
58 *Ibid.*, p. 190.
59 *Ibid.*, p. 265.
60 Enos and Park 1988, pp. 172–3.
61 Amsden 1989, ch. 7, also p. 253 for textiles, p. 272 for shipbuilding, p. 305 for steel; cf. Porter 1990, p. 465, as quoted below.

As in Japan, the purpose of shifting towards heavy industry was one of pursuing 'dynamic comparative advantage', i.e. the greater possibilities for investment and especially innovation in heavy industries, rather than the static comparative advantages implied by labour-intensive low-wage light industries. In this sense, these East Asian countries would appear to have selected 'inappropriate' technology quite deliberately. While Taiwan utilized labour-intensive products, mostly produced in SMFs, as the basis for its export drive from 1951, the state built up heavy industry from the late 1950s – mostly for domestic consumption in the first instance. By 1965 heavy and chemical industries comprised half the industrial output of Taiwan.[62] In South Korea in the 1950s there was a debate between US aid advisers recommending 'appropriate' investment in light industries and infrastructure, and Korea's own military favouring heavy industry,[63] mirroring the equivalent debate in Japan a few years earlier. In the Korean case, the debate was resolved by General Park's accession to power in 1961. Heavy manufactures rose to 14 per cent of merchandise exports in 1971 and no less than 60 per cent by 1984, while over the same period, light industry fell from 60 per cent of manufacturing output to 38 per cent.[64] Profit rates alone would have encouraged persisting with light industry, and re-direction thus required a push from government.[65] Amsden[66] stresses that the firms involved in heavy industry were necessarily different from those responsible for light industry, implying a deliberate discontinuity in industrialization. The shift to heavy industry was much less pronounced in Hong Kong where the government played a much smaller role in industrial policy.[67]

As in Japan, savings rates rose alongside the expansion of capital-intensive industry. By 1987 Korea and Taiwan had the world's highest savings rates, although real interest rates remained very high, suggesting that investment outstripped them.[68] Equally like Japan, all of the Tigers turned increasingly and successfully towards new knowledge-intensive industries (ICTs) from the later 1960s – electricals and electronics had become Taiwan's second biggest export industry (after textiles) as early as 1968, and the biggest by 1984.

---

62 Wade 1990, p. 45.
63 Amsden 1989, ch. 2.
64 *Ibid.*, pp. 55, 58.
65 *Ibid.*, pp. 85–9.
66 *Ibid.*, p. 20.
67 Though see Wade 1990, pp. 331–3.
68 Porter 1990, p. 467.

2. Latin America

The larger Latin American countries also pursued a track towards heavy industry in the 1960s, but the forms of heavy industry involved were resource-intensive – often making little use of the kinds of natural resources locally available but instead using imports – and built partly on military thinking and influence. Capabilities were accumulated in older technologies (those of the AICs of the pre-1970 years), but Latin American countries were relatively unsuccessful in leaping into 'Fifth-Kondratiev' technologies such as ICTs, because of the deficiencies in their knowledge bases. In Brazil the state aimed to develop domestic computer and other electronic industries through 'market reserve' policies of protectionism – such policies had some justification in the particular circumstances,[69] but the industries failed to develop 'depth'.[70] Attempts were made to establish a Brazilian software industry, on the argument that the software industry is highly labour-intensive and thus superficially 'appropriate'; but the attempt failed for a number of reasons, including the lack of local skills.[71]

In his book, *The Strategy of Economic Development*, Hirschman (1958/1961) advocated the adoption of machine-paced methods in LICs (here thinking primarily of the Latin American countries), on the grounds that such countries were particularly deficient in skills, and hence the Fordist type of machine-pacing would be better for redressing the productivity differential behind the AICs through reducing skill requirements, even though such methods might be capital-intensive. The argument here is similar to that used in the USSR in the 1930s (see p. 302 above). Positive correlations between capital intensity and productivity measures modestly support Hirschman's argument; but when mechanization rather than capital intensity is used as the relevant variable, the argument is rejected on the grounds that the more mechanized industries generally involved higher rather than lower degrees of skill.[72] However, there were a few plants that maintained rapid technical change in continuous-process industries in Latin America;[73] which suggests that dynamic comparative advantages might well have been achieved had the Hirschman strategy been pursued further than it was. Export performance in practice tended to correlate with abundance of natural resources or labour, i.e. with static comparative advantage.[74]

---

69 Schmitz and Cassiolato 1992, chs 2, 5.
70 Dahlman and Frischtak 1993.
71 Gaio 1990, also in Schmitz and Cassiolato 1992, ch. 4.
72 Teitel 1993, ch. 4; cf. also Chapters 6 and 7 above.
73 Maxwell 1981; Katz 1987.
74 Teitel, *loc. cit.*

Though these examples show the potentiality for development, in general it seems reasonable to conclude that Latin American and other LICs fared badly in terms of the criteria that this book has particularly emphasized, especially economies in time (space was admittedly less critical in Latin America than in East Asia or Japan).[75] Machine throughput was low and downtime especially high, leading to the much remarked-upon underutilization of capacity, notwithstanding the alleged shortage of capital in these countries. This excess capacity was justified at times by arguing that levels of demand were low, but this did not prevent much greater rates of expansion by the somewhat smaller economies of East Asia.[76] Inappropriateness thus came from excessive product diversification, unduly large or complicated plant, inadequate maintenance of equipment, lack of export development in manufactures, and the like, all serving to counteract gains from time saving either on the demand side or on the supply side. In neoclassical analysis, the problems have been blamed on 'abundance' of labour and thus the lack of development of labour-saving technologies. Díaz-Alejandro (1965), however, found a modest correlation between the labour intensity of a particular Argentine industry and its productivity gap *vis-à-vis* the USA – in other words, there was a comparative *disadvantage* in labour-intensive sectors. Indeed, the countries we are studying were little different in terms of factor endowments from North America in the late 19th century – they too had very high land/labour ratios and encouraged European immigration to undertake agricultural cash crops and also industry.[77] The response in terms of mechanization nevertheless failed to eventuate in Latin America, most probably because of extreme inequalities in the distribution of landed wealth and especially the lack of middle-range landholders equivalent to the US homesteaders, noted in Chapter 6 above.[78]

In the end, the key factor endowment indeed proved to be human capital (knowledge) – the East Asian countries accumulated it and successfully underwent structural change, while the Latin American countries were far less successful in both respects. In a dynamic sense, the issue was shown to be not one of choosing 'appropriate' technologies to fit the existing factor endowments, but how quickly the endowments themselves could be augmented in the interests of long-run industrial advantage.

---

75 The presence of inflation encouraged a certain amount of technological speed-up, such as single-day cheque clearance systems, but too often diverted attention to financial speculation; see Cassiolato, in Schmitz and Cassiolato 1992, ch. 3.

76 As shown below Korea, etc. also suffered from excess capacity, but through over-building supply rather than under-providing demand, which duly generated growth rather than stagnation.

77 Furtado 1970, chs 5, 14.

78 *Ibid.*, ch. 7; Díaz-Alejandro 1970, ch. 4.

E. Educational Systems

1. East Asia

By Third-World standards, literacy was relatively high in the early postwar period. This owed a certain amount to the preceding era of Japanese colonial rule, which had brought the Japanese tradition of widespread primary education, and had also acquainted businessmen with the Japanese language. The illiteracy rate in Korea was still 78 per cent, however, when Japanese colonial rule ended.[79] Literacy rates in Taiwan were estimated at already 54 per cent in 1960, and had risen sharply to 82 per cent by 1977.[80] Primary education in that country had been compulsory and free since 1950, and secondary school enrolment reached 80 per cent by 1980, but tertiary (higher) education stood at only 14 per cent for men and 12 per cent for women as late as 1985. Although this implied a weak commitment to advancing frontier research in Taiwan, it has to be set against the fact that the main impetus in higher education in the country after 1966 went into vocational rather than academic training. Linsu Kim[81] also believes that higher education was inadequately developed in South Korea (although some of the deficiency was alleviated by sending graduates to be trained abroad), and that this was beginning to affect the performance of the advanced sectors by the late 1980s; although a range of specialized government-funded research institutes were being developed to help meet industry requirements, like KAIST (Korean Advanced Institute of Science and Technology).

Despite these reservations about higher education, in the light of comparable overseas standards one ought to stress the expansion of education in these countries at all levels. According to Porter, the high average level of education had direct implications for production: 'In industries such as shipbuilding and construction, for example, the quality of the labor force translates into uniquely fast building times and deliveries often ahead of schedule'.[82] Governments played some part in this, for example in Korea education rose from 2.5 per cent of the government budget in 1951 to 22 per cent by the 1980s, but two-thirds of educational expenditures were borne privately.[83] Korean companies above a certain size are legally obliged to provide training for their employees.[84] Particular

79 L. Kim 1993, p. 358.
80 Wade 1990, p. 64.
81 L. Kim 1993, p. 371.
82 Porter 1990, p. 465; he considers the Korean commitment to education 'the strongest I observed in any nation we studied'.
83 L. Kim 1993, p. 358.
84 Porter 1990, p. 466.

stress within higher education was placed upon engineering, imitating the Japanese bias – Taiwan by 1980 had 50 per cent more qualified engineers per head of population than the USA. Amsden (1977) shows that the three successive stages in ITC – capabilities first in operating equipment, later in investing in new plant and equipment, and finally in innovating – corresponded with capabilities successively in production engineering, systems engineering and finally design engineering. Thus ITCs were built upon expansion in the number and ability of engineers and technicians – considerable use also being made of training opportunities in the USA. South Korea, however, followed Japan in undervaluing female employment, having one of the developed world's highest gender wage gaps.[85]

A claim can therefore be made that, in a quasi-Schumpeterian sense, the East Asian Tigers were 'building education ahead of demand'. This is suggested by the unduly high expenditures on education relative to average per-capita incomes through time.[86] However, the claim is strongly disputed by Amsden,[87] who argues that the *quality* of education, especially in the vocational field, was by no means high enough to initiate growth. Mass education was instituted mainly for 'social control',[88] a proposition we have also found to have held in the 19th-century USA. Nevertheless, the more general evidence considered in this book suggests that, whatever the merits or demerits of 'social control', the provision of a *generalized* (non-vocational) primary and secondary educational system represents a key contribution to development, in providing 'training for training'.[89] At the same time, one can hardly disagree with Porter[90] that there have to be complementary investments by firms and industries in specialized training and education.

2. Latin America

By contrast, educational levels and achievements were probably much lower in Latin America than in East Asia. Around 1950, about 66 per cent of Argentinian 5 to 14 year-olds and only 26 per cent of Brazilians were said to be enrolled in primary school,[91] though the amount of effective education was probably lower than these ratios suggest. Even nowadays, substantial proportions of the population do not complete even primary

85 Amsden 1989, pp. 203–4.
86 L. Kim 1993, p. 359.
87 Amsden 1989, ch. 9.
88 *Ibid.*, p. 219.
89 L. Kim 1993.
90 Porter 1990, ch. 12.
91 Furtado 1970, p. 48, based on ECLA data.

school. Adult literacy in Brazil was reckoned at 78 per cent in 1989, as compared with 95 per cent in Korea.[92] In higher education, there was believed to be considerable under-production of Qualified Scientists and Engineers (QSEs), although the official UNESCO statistics suggest a higher share of QSEs in the workforce than in East Asia. Indeed, there is a contrary view that too large a share of the educational resources was directed to the university sector.[93] According to Katz and Bercovich (1993) excessive attention within universities was devoted to non-applicable basic research.[94] In a series of papers, Katz and others[95] have shown how the progression of ITCs from operation to investment and finally innovation was halted at the first stage in Latin America, partly through the lack of educational or training provision, and partly also from the lack of systems-oriented thinking. Admittedly, in countries like Argentina, military repression drastically restricted the opportunities for universities, although there was also continuing enmity between government and students in South Korea. Overall, the proportion of the central government's budget allocated to education in Argentina fell from around 20 per cent in 1972 to just 6 per cent by 1987, partly squeezed out by the debt crises,[96] and coinciding with the period of substantial absolute decline in real per-capita GNP.

III: ORGANIZATION

A. Local vs. Foreign Ownership

1. East Asia

The medium-sized East Asian countries made little use of MNC subsidiaries, although the city-state Tigers (Hong Kong and Singapore) did so to a greater extent. This may seem surprising, in view of the fact that patterns of organization in the AIC countries were importantly shaped by the 'offshore' movement of assembly operations (cf. Chapters 7 and 8), beginning with investments by the US company, Fairchild, and the Dutch company, Philips, in Taiwan in 1961. So, indeed, a limited number of these 'screwdriver' assembly plants were tolerated, but the main emphasis was still placed on indigenization. Foreign ownership was particularly controlled in the largest of the Tigers, South Korea, though Hong Kong for

92 Ferraz *et al.* 1992, p. 62.
93 *Ibid.*, p. 63.
94 Though L. Kim in his contribution to the same book believes that South Korea *under*-invested in basic research.
95 E.g. Katz 1987.
96 OECD 1992, p. 267.

one adopted a more laissez-faire stance towards foreign investment and ownership. This may partly explain why Hong Kong was much slower than the other Tigers to develop ITCs.[97]

A high degree of process capability was attained, even from unpromising origins in screwdriver assembly. Allegedly, the leading American microprocessor company Intel had to re-import production methods into the USA from its plant in Taiwan in the later 1980s, having lost such capability at home!

2. Latin America

High reliance was placed in Latin America on setting up MNC subsidiaries, as a way of obtaining investment and some innovation through 'buying' them rather than 'making' them.[98] At best, the subsidiaries might develop local capability for product innovation while at the same time fulfilling a role as supplier of components to the firm at large, as Volkswagen pursued in Brazil and Mexico.[99] But even in these cases, supplies for the local market tended to be segmented from those for export markets, and used obsolete labour-intensive production methods.[100] Some of the consequences of the overseas dependence, especially towards its self-perpetuation, have been noted above. The exposure that this gave all such Latin American countries was reflected in the rather sudden departure of many MNCs and closure of their plants during the unstable times of the 1980s, notwithstanding their often favoured position within the particular country. Although more prominent in newer than older industries, MNCs rarely undertook any serious R&D in these subsidiaries, so there was little or no impact on ITCs.[101] Older industries remained largely in the hands of family enterprises.[102]

B. Large vs. Small Firms: Scale and Scope

1. East Asia

Patterns varied widely. South Korea's 'giantism', partly inspired by the military, was evident at the plant level, the firm level and the industry level. By the end of the 1970s it had the world's largest plant in textiles, in plywood, in shipyards, in cement and in heavy machinery.[103] Substantial

---

97 Hobday 1994, p. 357.
98 Furtado 1970, ch. 18.
99 Tolliday and Zeitlin 1986, p. 245.
100 *Ibid.*, p. 248.
101 Ferraz *et al.* 1992, p. 68; Teitel 1993, p. 156.
102 Furtado 1970, p. 176.
103 L. Kim 1993, p. 367.

excess capacity – i.e. greater installations of production plant and equipment than warranted by the flows of output – prevailed throughout much of South Korea's development of heavy industry; though such 'unbalanced growth' seemed to sustain itself, unlike in most western countries. At the firm level, the country relied extensively on the large *chaebol* (very diversified firms) to develop new and heavy industries from the 1970s. Diversification came not through Schumpeterian 'New Men' or 'New Firms', but through product-linked changes within existing *chaebol*.[104] Ownership remained family-based, contradicting the common US opinion that this would restrict rapid expansion. In just a decade, from 1974 to 1984, the combined sales of the top ten *chaebol* rose from being equivalent to 15.1 per cent of Korean GNP to 67.4 per cent.[105] Amsden asks why there should have been greater diversification in Korea (or Japan) than in American M-form companies, and concludes that the former was more *product*-related (overcoming small market sizes, supplier deficiencies, etc.) while the latter was more *technology*-related (synergies in technical expertise, etc.).[106] Entry into new product areas by Korean firms was led by highly committed internal task forces, known as 'technosections'.[107]

Finally, at the industry level, there was emphasis on cartels and oligopolies – even the cotton textile industry, which bore the brunt of industrial expansion in the 1960s, was a cartelized oligopoly.[108] This made it easier for the government to direct its export-subsidizing strategy.[109] However, Taiwan used larger firms (which in any case were themselves really only medium-sized by Korean standards) mainly for domestically-oriented heavy industries, while exports continued to come overwhelmingly from SMFs, a pattern which replicated Japan's earlier experience but to an even greater degree.[110] In Korea, SMFs were unimportant for initiating growth but 'pivotal' for diffusing growth, mainly via subcontracting; their role was primarily to serve the domestic market.[111]

---

104 Amsden 1989, ch. 10; Amsden and Hikino 1994.

105 Amsden 1989, p. 116; also L. Kim 1993; but note that these figures may not be strictly comparable.

106 Amsden 1989, ch. 5.

107 *Ibid.*, p. 128.

108 *Ibid.*, p. 65.

109 *Ibid.*, p. 68.

110 Cf. Johnson 1982, p. 98.

111 Amsden 1989, ch. 7. Note that all figures on the contribution or productivity of SMFs are dubious, because of the existence of a probably large 'informal' sector inadequately covered by the statistics (*ibid.*, p. 163.)

2. Latin America

Plant sizes were usually small even in the advanced industrial sectors of Latin American economies, typically between 1 per cent and 10 per cent of the size of an equivalent plant in the AICs. Even the MNC subsidiaries, though often large relative to domestic firms, were normally small relative to their parents in the AICs. Thus Argentina in the 1960s had ten automobile producers – subsidiaries of European as well as American companies – while in the USA at the time, a market 40 times as large, there were just four.[112] As previously noted, there was excessive product diversification from these small-sized plants, both domestic and foreign-owned, and changeovers between each product meant long downtimes (there was little 'flexibility') and low accumulation of learning by specializing. Economies of scale and even scope were thus limited. Firms – the larger of them with many scattered plants – often had monopoly rights based on licence privileges, and over time industries tended to become more vertically integrated (see the discussion of networks below), which increased their power but often also their paralysis.

C. Management Framework

1. East Asia

Partly because of earlier Japanese colonial influences, and partly because of simple geography, these East Asian countries tended to pattern their management to a greater degree on Japanese systems, nowhere more so than in South Korea. Ironically the Koreans initially imitated Japanese management out of strong nationalistic desires to outstrip the Japanese (join them to beat them). The resulting similarity included a discouragement of excessive layers of management in the firm, and a preference for internal promotion, especially of engineers.[113] Internal networks, and dependence on 'bottom-up' information flows, were established in the large firms from an early stage.[114] As in the USA, wage increases were used to raise labour productivity, but the greater gains came from giving that workforce responsibility.[115] Taiwan was considerably more dependent upon American linkages, including having a sizeable number of young professional managers educated in the USA, and hence adopted managerial styles midway between the American and Japanese.[116] Both adopted Japanese

---

112 Teitel 1993, p. 142 – Brazil had a similar number of producers and Mexico and Chile even more!

113 Amsden 1989, ch. 7.

114 *Ibid.*, ch. 8.

115 *Ibid.*, p. 213.

116 Amsden 1977.

'workaholic' traditions, with South Korea having much the longest average working week in industry of any country (53.8 hours a week in manufacturing in 1985[117]).

2. Latin America

The Latin American countries were instead tied by both geography and FDI/MNC links to American management practices, not least through their tendency to employ US management consultants. Often these trapped the Latin American firms in rigid Fordist practices more appropriate for labour-saving mass production industries than for new-generation technologies such as ICTs.[118] As has recently been shown by Ricardo Semler (a Harvard Business School graduate!) in his machinery company in São Paulo, there is nothing in the Latin American environment which inherently disfavours more democratic and flexible management structures.[119]

D. Networks

1. East Asia

Less use is made of subcontracting in the Tigers than is the case in Japan. Links have been fostered horizontally by governments, e.g. the Electronic Research and Service Organization (ERSO) for the electronics industry in Taiwan.[120] The Korean *chaebol* have often been criticized for having weak network links within the country, with particular deficiencies in supplier networks, and these have curtailed their attempts to develop managerial practices along Japanese lines and hampered flexibility.[121] Subcontracting has been carried along by the expansion of the *chaebol*, but lagged well in arrears.[122] Nevertheless, user needs have acted as the major impulse to upstream development – for instance, the development of the machine tools industry in South Korea, which is now a considerable force in world markets, depended on the prior development of the main user industry, automobiles.[123] Moreover, forward linkages into marketing were promulgated in both South Korea and (especially) Taiwan, and this included foreign marketing (see below).

Joint Ventures (JVs) in Taiwan began with a technology agreement between the local firm Tatung and a Japanese firm in 1953, although most

117 L. Kim 1993, p. 360; see also Amsden 1989, pp. 205–6.
118 Freeman 1993.
119 Semler 1993.
120 Wade 1990, pp. 103–8.
121 L. Kim 1993; S.R. Kim 1993.
122 Amsden 1989, ch. 7.
123 Lee 1993.

agreements struck before the 1980s were 'one-way', for importing foreign technology (as for example by Samsung when it intended to set up electronics manufacturing in South Korea). In the 1980s they became more commonly 'two-way', with reciprocal exchanges of technology, as ITCs have been improved in high-tech industries. The MERIT databank of Jon Hagedoorn shows East Asia as the only significant area outside of the AICs proper where formal foreign links were growing during the 1980s, at a time when the rapid growth of these links among the AICs themselves signalled a rapid process of change.

2. Latin America

The Latin American countries have been severely criticized in the NSI literature for the weakness of their domestic supplier networks, preventing anything like a Japanese-style hub network.[124] Vertical integration of the kind noted above came about partly because links to other companies were so weak, and in turn restricted any further development of networks, consequently rigidifying the industrial structure and limiting flexibility in new industries. If any one major cause needs to be ascribed to the retardation of the Latin American economies, then perhaps it should be the weakness of functional links of the kind embodied in my schema (Figure 2.2): the links, say, between R&D and production, or production and marketing. In a very different economic and political climate, the fundamental problems thus had some parallels with those in the command economies such as the Soviet Union (cf. Chapter 9).

IV: FINANCE

A. Domestic Funding

1. East Asia

Internal financing by firms in South Korea was very low by international standards, contributing only about 20 per cent of total financing 1963–73 (compared to 65 per cent in the USA 1947–63) and allegedly less than 10 per cent in 1983[125] – the remainder was highly subsidized by government. Governments thus dominated the provision of capital, owning and controlling most commercial banks in the early years of industrialization. Under international pressure, South Korea denationalized commercial banks in the 1970s then 'liberalized' them in the 1980s, but unwittingly allowed

---

124 E.g. OECD 1992, p. 266.
125 Amsden 1989, p. 85.

them to fall into the hands of the *chaebol*, thus accentuating the concentration of financial/industrial power.[126] Korean governments provided direct R&D subsidies in the 1980s, but much the most important assistance to technology was indirect, via preferential loans (see below). Nationalized banks were mostly responsible for administering preferential loans in Taiwan also, but here small firms were more catered for by the semilegal and private 'curb' (street) market, relying mainly on the postdated cheque as its instrument.[127]

2. Latin America

Traditional Latin American industry was rarely able to call upon the organized capital market for funds, which came mainly from kinship groups, etc.[128] Hence banks were set up specifically to cater for industrialization, e.g. the National Bank for Economic Development (BNDE, 1954; subsequently BNDES) in Brazil, which expanded lending after 1974. Regrettably, their distance from industrial firms limited the extent to which they could change policies once retardation set in. In Brazil, the Agency for Financing Studies and Projects (FINEP) aimed to subsidize loans and share risks from 1973, but suffered from bureaucratic encumbrances and did relatively little for NTBFs.

B. International Funding

1. East Asia

The larger East Asian Tigers relied quite heavily on foreign borrowing, but as already shown this was mostly undertaken via their governments in order to limit the amount of FDI and foreign control by MNCs. Thus foreign borrowing reinforced the power of the state over allocations to development, with all foreign investments having to be scrutinized by government. The South Korean government had little compunction about foreign borrowing in order to escape from short-term economic problems, despite being sporadically called to account for it by the IMF; and over a longer period, foreign debt rose from 4 per cent of GNP in 1963 to 40 per cent in 1975 and 53 per cent by 1982–4.[129]

2. Latin America

Despite the relative wealth of the upper strata of the population, there was under-funding of manufacturing in countries like Argentina from the late

---

126 L. Kim 1993, p. 368.
127 Wade 1990, ch. 6.
128 Haber 1991.
129 Amsden 1989, pp. 94–6.

19th century, mainly because of a political divide between the wealthy agricultural landlords and industry[130] – foreign capital poured in not to create 'dependency' (*dependencia*) in the first instance but to plug a domestic gap. In the postwar years, mounting external debts from ISI efforts and costs of servicing those debts characterized developmental efforts in the larger Latin American countries. In Brazil this situation has been described as 'debt-led growth' from the 1960s, fostered by heavy and often wasteful state investments from the 1950s, plus floating exchange rates in the 1970s which had the effect of increasing the real burden of the foreign debt. By the early 1980s, additionally encumbered by oil crises and 'dependency', the Latin American debt burden became one of the major features of global finance, undermining world monetary systems. The full explanation of why mounting foreign debts caused so much greater difficulties in Latin America than East Asia is beyond the scope of this survey, but it would seem that the entrapment within ISI policies and the inadequacy of response by merchandise exports had something to do with it.

V: PRODUCTS

A. Foreign vs. Domestic Consumers

1. East Asia

The above-mentioned export orientation necessarily geared the countries to foreign markets. The lack of marketing expertise abroad was compensated by the considerable use of large foreign buyers, such as American retailers (Sears Roebuck, etc.), or Japanese *sogo shosha* (e.g. C. Itoh). Taiwan has found 'learning to market' more difficult than 'learning to produce', although its medium-sized firms are currently developing 'ODM' (own design and manufacture) strategies as an attempt to replace the initial OEM (original equipment manufacturer) ones.[131] As already noted, the South Korean *chaebol* were able to use their greater size and technological capabilities to develop some brand-name images in the 1980s. Korean exports have seemingly been more successful on moving up-market in quality terms, while Taiwan has targeted speed to market.[132] The smaller Tigers, Hong Kong and Singapore, throughout placed greater emphasis on commercialization than production.

---

130 Guy 1984.
131 Hobday 1994, pp. 351–2.
132 Wade 1990, p. 320.

2. Latin America

In Brazil, the 'market reserve' policies adopted in certain new industries like some of the ICTs had the effect of protecting producers rather than aiding customers and consumption. They probably bolstered innovation but were not so well suited to the ensuing phase of *diffusion* of technologies.[133] For this and other reasons, domestic consumers preferred imported to domestically produced goods, i.e. the opposite of, say, the Japanese situation. Methods geared to raising quality, such as quality circles, have made virtually no impact.[134] Foreign consumers of course tended to find the high prices and indifferent quality of such manufactured exports unattractive, although there was some success in niche markets built on the lower wage costs.

B. The Structure of Domestic Demand

1. East Asia

In South Korea and Taiwan, land reforms, begun by the Japanese in their colonialist years and substantially extended by the occupying American forces postwar, destroyed much of the old aristocracy and created a relatively egalitarian wealth and income distribution pattern. Although the figures have been challenged as being of dubious validity,[135] even the critics accept that the countries could plausibly claim 'equality of opportunity' in the aftermath of the land reforms.[136] Allowing for such data deficiencies, Taiwan emerged as having the most equal income distribution in a 16-country study in the late 1960s – more so than Japan or South Korea, which were also relatively egalitarian by western standards.[137] Its postwar industrialization seems to have omitted the Kuznets phase of initial deterioration of income distribution for the whole economy, although it experienced this at first within industry.[138] The recent World Bank study (1993) has computed for 40 countries the ratio of income share of the top fifth to the poorest fifth, as a rough measure of inequality, and ranks Taiwan just behind Japan as the countries with least inequality; the study finds a strong negative correlation between growth rates (1965–90) and inequality, and comments that all of the high-growth/low-inequality countries are to be found in South-east Asia. This apparently egalitarian wealth and income structure partly compensated on the demand side for the low average wage

133 Schmitz and Cassiolato 1992, ch. 5.

134 Ferraz *et al.* 1992, p. 134.

135 Amsden 1989, p. 16n.

136 *Ibid.*, p. 38.

137 Wade 1990, p. 38.

138 Fei *et al.* 1979, pp. 2, 103.

levels, which continued in Taiwan. It boosted demand for the household durables and decencies which the industries of these countries proved so competent at producing. South Korea also stands quite high in terms of income equality, although (like Japan) it has a very high degree of dispersion of wages within manufacturing, plus also the gender gap mentioned above.[139]

2. Latin America

In virtually all Latin American countries, the structure of wealth remained highly unequal, typified in many of the medium-sized countries by the economic and political dominance of the first forty or so families. Agricultural power remained substantially in the hands of *latifundios* (large farmers) and similar large farmers producing cash crops for export markets. Land reforms like that in Mexico early in the 20th century (creating the *ejidos*) commanded much political attention but less economic success.[140] The same World Bank report (1993) just mentioned found that all of the Latin American countries it included had above-average degrees of inequality, and all of them were congregated in the low-growth quadrant as well. Thus these countries matched South-east Asia in reverse, by coupling low growth and high inequality. Brazil had one of the highest computed inequality levels (exceeded only by Botswana and Zambia in these data, and then not by much), but it did have the highest growth rate for 1965–90 of the included Latin American countries, although it will be recalled that virtually all of this growth took place in the early years of that period. Though the World Bank study suggested a reasonable decline in the numbers below the official poverty line in Brazil from 1960 to 1980, there is a widespread feeling that income distribution in that country has worsened since the mid-1960s. In the mid-1980s, the top 10 per cent of the population in Brazil earned 47.7 per cent of total income, as compared with 27.5 per cent in South Korea and just 22.4 per cent in Japan.[141] Between 1981 and 1989, during the 'lost decade' of declining growth and social conditions, the share of the top percentiles in Brazil rose sharply – for the richest 10 per cent, from 46.6 per cent to 53.2 per cent.[142] The high Latin American inequality polarized demand between highly-differentiated luxury goods and the cheap, low-quality end of the market. Policies adopted by the various governments tended for the most part to accentuate rather than offset this concentration of wealth, through the particular policies

---

139 Amsden 1989, ch. 8.
140 Furtado 1970, ch. 23.
141 Ferraz *et al.* 1992, p. 62.
142 *Ibid.*, p. 63.

implemented for taxation, education, etc.[143] ISI policies protected the existing home markets, based on such unequal income distributions, and thus encouraged the extreme proliferation of products produced by relatively backward processes.[144] ISI itself was also undermined by the demands of high-income groups for luxury imports.

The congregation of demand at the lower end of the income distribution was accentuated by relatively rapid population growth, itself partly the product of the comparative emptiness of South America in the early 19th century.[145] By contrast, the East Asian countries of this study were relatively crowded from the beginning, and population growth rates fell more sharply – in Malthus's language (1798), there was less 'room' for population growth in East Asia.

C. Role of the Government and Military

1. East Asia

Because of their own military situations, both South Korea and Taiwan have had very high levels of military spending – defence represents about 6 per cent of South Korean GDP – and both have been dominated for much of the time by military-oriented governments. Korean industrialization in its early years was heavily dependent on American military contracts, e.g. in construction, plywood and tyres. According to conventional wisdom, this military orientation should have retarded growth, but plainly any such effect was not enough to offset their dramatic growth performances. A possible explanation is that the military component seems to have been relatively insulated from the civilian economy except in terms of supplying heavy machinery. Haggard (1988) believes that the military-led view of Korean industrialization is overstated, and that reliance by the military on civilian entrepreneurs was substantial. The subject is evidently in need of further analysis.

2. Latin America

In somewhat parallel fashion, military regimes have dominated industrialization programmes in Latin America, dating back for Argentina to 1930 and for Brazil to 1964. The external threats did not match the East Asian context – the Falkland Islands can scarcely be mentioned in the same breath as, say, North Korea. Perhaps by way of perverse result, the involvement of the military in the civilian economy was probably higher. Arms exports have formed an important component of such expansion of

143 Furtado 1970, p. 67.
144 *Ibid.*, pp. 147–8.
145 *Ibid.*

exports as there has been. Other than the military production itself, the military influence dictated high levels of R&D (out of a low overall total) in areas like nuclear energy and space, with apparently little or no economic payoff (the Argentinian nuclear power industry has been completely undercut by gas). These countries were notorious for political corruption, but so also was – for instance – South Korea; the biggest problem was perhaps the extent of bureaucratic delay and obfuscation in Latin America. This can be readily identified in the implementation of the government policies studied in the next section.

VI: GOVERNMENT POLICIES

A. Governments and Firms

1. East Asia

Despite often having military allegiances, the governments of the chosen East Asian countries appeared from the 1960s to be acting most of the time in the general interest (at least as they perceived it) rather than their own. In this sense, both South Korea and Taiwan can be described as successors to the Japanese 'developmental state' as illustrated in a qualified fashion in the preceding chapter.[146] As for Japan, there are dangers in overstating the extent of a monolithic state.[147] According to Haggard (1988), the Korean government forged a political link with big business not because of political will (its roots lay in the peasantry, small firms and labour) but because of *realpolitik* – whatever its inclinations, only the large firms constituted an effective power base. 'Economic democratization' was attempted in the 1970s and 1980s in South Korea to diffuse power away from the *chaebol*, but they continued to grow, as figures quoted above reveal.[148] Despite their expansion, the government placed great emphasis on rewarding the *chaebol* which performed well and penalizing the poor ones. In this way, the *chaebol* were put under continuous pressure to perform, especially in regard to exports, in order not to lose their favoured status – in practice there was a quite rapid turnover among the list of the ten largest *chaebol*.[149] As in Japan, there was intense competition between the *chaebol*, with rewards not just in profits but in prizes awarded by government.[150] Such competition

---

146 Wade 1990.
147 Chu 1989; S.R. Kim 1993.
148 L. Kim 1993, p. 367.
149 *Ibid.*, p. 363.
150 Amsden 1989, p. 129.

tended to be in forms other than prices: the best foreign licences, the biggest state subsidies, etc.[151]

'Where Korea differs from most other late industrializing countries is in the discipline its state exercises over private firms.'[152] Free entry of firms into new industries was discouraged, but in most industries at least two firms were supported, to ensure some internal competition. In the case of the giant integrated steel mill set up by the Pohang Iron and Steel Company (POSCO) after 1968, there was little possibility of internal competition, so the state has continued to own the plant, with no evident loss of competitiveness.[153] Every major shift in industrial diversification was instigated by the state – entrepreneurship for the firm centrally involved working in some way with government.[154] The implication was that planning was much more top-down in Korea than in Japan, and there was little public discussion.[155] This centralized state was, however, dominated by technocrats, who were likely to favour a development orientation.[156] But with moves towards 'liberalization' in Korea (supported by the World Bank) after the assassination of General Park in 1979, the power of the government over the *chaebol* waned, and the latter found greater opportunities for indulging in antisocial behaviour.[157] Perversely, 'liberalization, therefore, contributed to a rise, not to a decline, in economic concentration'.[158] Amsden plausibly concludes that competition 'tends to be a consequence of growth, not a cause of it'.[159]

Taiwan has a reputation for a low degree of direct government intervention, but in fact it has been one of the highest in the non-communist world, as measured by the share of public enterprises in GDP.[160] This intervention was heavily concentrated in upstream activities.[161] Outside of direct intervention, the government's agencies paid particular attention to making information extensively and cheaply available.[162] Rostow's *Stages of Economic Growth* (1960) was allegedly an important stimulus to Taiwanese industrial policy, based on a sectoral strategy of 'making

151 *Ibid.*, p. 152.
152 *Ibid.*, p. 14.
153 *Ibid.*, pp. 292–5.
154 *Ibid.*, p. 80.
155 *Ibid.*, pp. 84–5.
156 Haggard 1988.
157 Amsden 1989, ch. 5.
158 *Ibid.*, p. 136.
159 *Ibid.*, p. 150.
160 Wade 1990, ch. 6.
161 *Ibid.*, pp. 179–80.
162 *Ibid.*, p. 146.

winners'![163] As in Korea, the state acted in much more authoritarian fashion than in the consensual Japanese case.[164]

The types of government operating in these countries cover almost the whole spectrum of political possibilities – liberal democratic in Japan and Hong Kong, authoritarian anti-communist in Singapore, Taiwan and South Korea, communist in the emerging South China. Seemingly, rapid growth is compatible with virtually any kind of political system, so long as growth is its primary concern.[165]

2. Latin America

In the absence of a strong co-ordinative organization among firms in the private sector, the state was called upon to play a major role in linking locally-owned and foreign-based firms into the productive structure – this has been termed 'associated capitalism'.[166] Nevertheless, growth was not the primary concern of most Latin American governments, despite the lip-service paid to it – control was the main objective. This has been traced back to the patterns of conquest and colonization by the Spanish and Portuguese from the 16th century.[167] Growth ran the risk of disrupting such control, much as innovation can do within a firm. In industry, monopolies and privileges remained, and the firms acted as if they would remain for ever. Statist participation persisted in sectors that were deemed to be strategic, like steel, petrochemicals and heavy capital goods, and private entry was restricted. Again, control rather than growth was the intention and the main outcome. Paradoxically, as shown further below, the quest for control without first securing growth was to prove self-destructive. Policy was characterized by extreme instability and confusion.[168]

B. Liberalization vs. Protectionism

1. East Asia

There is considerable debate over the extent to which the state controlled industrialization in Taiwan and South Korea, but the present evidence in my view leans sharply towards the conception of these economies as being 'Government-Managed'. Certainly this is the opinion of the most thorough

---

163 *Ibid.*, p. 188.
164 *Ibid.*, ch. 9.
165 Tylecote 1992.
166 Ferraz *et al.* 1992, p. 53.
167 E.g. Furtado 1970.
168 Ferraz *et al.* 1992, pp. 57–9.

recent surveys of Wade for Taiwan and Amsden for South Korea.[169] Few reading Wade's account of its foreign trade and investment policies could see Taiwan as taking a hands-off attitude, in terms of the range of instruments employed to alter production and export patterns.[170] Governments controlled or channelled most of the developmental requirements, and tried to hold off 'liberalization' as long as possible until the ITCs were adequately established. There were subsidies for credit, for technology inputs, and for users. In South Korea the government helped to subsidize the foundation of particular *chaebol* and, once established, used them as their agents; but as just pointed out, would drop them if they failed to deliver the required performances. Direct support, usually linked to export performance, included R&D subsidies, preferential financing and tax incentives.[171] Preferential loans were much the most important of these, representing 94.3 per cent of government assistance and 64 per cent of total manufacturing R&D expenditure in 1987.[172] These were directed overwhelmingly towards the *chaebol*, and SMFs suffered from having to pay much higher interest rates in unofficial capital markets, although the Bank of Korea has tried to redress this imbalance since 1983.[173] The Korean government was the main agent in the crucial role of negotiating terms with initial foreign suppliers.[174]

As in Japan, the government in the 1980s moved somewhat away from protecting industries to protecting technologies.[175] In Taiwan, the government itself built many of the first plants of new industries (for example in plastics), then handed over to private entrepreneurs. The widespread impression that growth in East Asia rested on rampant private capitalism has, perhaps, some applicability to Hong Kong (which benefited hugely from its *entrepôt* role) but to little else in the region. So far from being paeans to the virtues of the free market, Amsden[176] has argued – convincingly in my opinion – that their success has derived more from 'getting the prices wrong', through adroit government actions, including negative real interest rates for favoured firms, and deliberately distorted

169 Amsden 1989; Wade 1990. See World Bank 1993 for a contrary view, though one with little micro-level evidence – one of its signatories, Joseph Stiglitz (1994), now appears to subscribe to Wade's term, 'governing the market'.

170 Wade 1990, ch. 6.

171 L. Kim 1993, pp. 372–4.

172 *Ibid.*, p. 373.

173 S.R. Kim 1993.

174 Enos and Park 1988, p. 248.

175 L. Kim 1993, p. 369.

176 Amsden 1989, ch. 6.

exchange rates. Liberalization of exports proceeded far faster than liberalization of imports.[177]

2. Latin America

The Latin American countries also leaned towards protection, but in most interpretations the regimes were over-protectionist – a stifling form of protectionism which allowed inefficiencies and anti-social behaviour to perpetuate. Reasons for this have been given above. Protectionism was oriented to *products*, i.e. markets, rather than to technologies/processes, as was more the case in East Asia. Governmental competence to discriminate among potential technology imports was undeveloped, and the strategy of protecting technologies was thus not usually adopted.[178] While East Asian governments also tried to protect domestic markets, this policy was coupled with other policies (e.g. in regard to credit) that were *firm*-specific. As for East Asia, these Latin American countries faced international pressures from the 1970s to deregulate and reduce protectionism, but the effects were adverse, raising real interest rates and worsening income distributions. The protectionist measures often differed little on paper from those used in East Asia, but the outcomes were quite different – for this, we should particularly blame the unwillingness or inability to impose performance standards on beneficiary firms, along with the absence of contestability in the guise of serious threat of competitive entry.

C. Public vs. Private Funding of Technology

1. East Asia

The East Asian countries adopted some direct support for R&D and research institutions, though more often at an infrastructural level, for instance by establishing Hsinchu Industrial Park in Taiwan, or through specific technology development, for instance Korea's VLSI project in the 1980s. State-conducted research was not particularly successful in South Korea; more, perhaps, was achieved by the incentives offered to the private sector to set up their own laboratories, using instruments of the kinds already noted. The pattern of R&D funding and execution in South Korea mimics that of Japan, with an overwhelming proportion of R&D both funded and performed privately by industry. However, it can be argued that it was too slow in reorienting from traditional policy instruments such as preferential loans to those more suited to high-tech industries, such as state-

---

177 Wade 1990, p. 336.
178 Teitel 1993, p. 155.

led R&D.[179] More use is made of public R&D facilities like ERSO in Taiwan,[180] no doubt partly because of the smaller size of progressive firms.

2. Latin America

In Latin America, by contrast, the major role was played by central government agencies – examples being CNPq and CAPES in Brazil, or CONICET in Argentina. Large proportions of R&D are both funded and performed by government. In this they compare with a comparatively unsuccessful South Asian country, namely India. In Argentina, R&D collapsed almost entirely with economic and political instability in the early 1980s.

D. Macroeconomic and International Policies

1. East Asia

These countries pursued relatively 'orthodox' monetary and fiscal policies, partly through the impact of US advisers in the early postwar years, and it is no doubt for this reason that macro-focused studies like that of the World Bank (1993) can conclude that their governments were less interventionist. As shown above, this fails to give due weight to the interactions with the private sectors. Even at the macroeconomic level, the governments permitted a certain amount of inflation, and never allowed control of inflation to impede industrialization seriously[181] – in this way acting again like Japan but unlike some western countries. 'If the lesson that the United States learned from the Korean [postwar] upheavals was the need for stability before growth, then the military [who ran Korea from 1961] learned that causality ran in the opposite direction, from growth to stability.'[182]

2. Latin America

Central banks were set up in Latin American countries during the heyday of the interwar Gold Exchange Standard. From the beginning, however, they felt it necessary to meet the special conditions of their countries, dependent on exports of a range of primary products and encountering unstable markets. Conservative monetary policies then involved more or less permanent depression of the domestic economy, and there was little attempt

179 S.R. Kim 1993.
180 Wade 1990, p. 321.
181 Amsden 1989, pp. 100–101.
182 *Ibid.*, p. 49.

to make the cure of inflation a matter of top priority.[183] Inflation was claimed to originate in 'structural' causes, including:

i inelastic supply of agricultural products, especially for home markets;
ii inadequate infrastructure;
iii inadequate labour skills;
iv inadequate fiscal systems;
v increased financial commitments, including those for imported equipment.[184]

These were aggravated by inappropriate government policies and circumstantial factors.[185] Thus, in the reverse of the East Asian situation, lack of growth induced instability. In the postwar period, the return to 'structural inflation' from the 1960s may have been difficult to prevent, because of feedback mechanisms which made escape hugely costly in the short run, but led to instability, short-termism, capital flights in the 1980s and the debt crises. Apart from the disastrous impacts on growth, these further reduced the autonomy of governments in industrial policies, as international banks and agencies required budget cuts, liberalization, etc. High reliance on FDI to solve their difficulties, as repeatedly advocated by the World Bank, may have proved counterproductive.[186] But Katz and Bercovich (1993), as leading domestic critics, argue that domestic factors were more important than international ones in bringing decline, and it is these which have been our major concern above.

183 Instead, the financial systems innovated in other ways, cf. Furtado 1970, ch. 9.
184 *Ibid.*, ch. 12.
185 *Idem.* The monetary system acted as a propagation mechanism for such inflation, rather than its underlying cause, cf. *ibid.*, p. 101.
186 Hobday 1994.

12. Conclusions

> No nation can simply import the Industrial Revolution from abroad, uncrate it like a piece of machinery, and set it in motion. (Lockwood)[1]

Technology and industrialization can be approached from a variety of angles. In this book I have chosen to dwell mainly on the role of firms and nations. Although individual firms have not been examined in any detail, the discussion of countries has been located at the firm level, because it is there that the managerial role of integration of functions (which have been notionally separated into four kinds) and the entrepreneurial role of strategic change are expressed. These are taken to be the empirical micro-foundations of growth and structural change at the macro level. The national level is equally important, in that it is here that the context of each function is primarily decided. For simplicity, the structure of the national system of innovation, the national mode of regulation, the national financial system and the national level and composition of demand, are taken as exogenous to the individual firm; though of course it is the cumulative impact of all the country's firms which helps change these circumstances, as well as being changed by them. The resulting overall 'national system of production', embracing techniques, production processes, products, and administrative and financial organizations, is seen as changing through a secular process often described as 'modernization', by way of industrialization. It should scarcely be necessary to reiterate the point made at the very beginning that the analysis is positive rather than normative – I do not mean to imply that modernization or any of its characteristics is necessarily and always 'a good thing'.

The book has particularly focused upon the respective periods in which each major industrializing nation shifted decisively towards industrialization. Three main phases of industrialization are assessed – the first launched in Britain during the 18th century, the second in the USA in the late 19th century and the third in Japan in the latter part of the 20th century. These have close affinities with Lazonick's three phases of capitalism, which he describes as 'proprietary capitalism' (for Britain in the

---

1 Lockwood 1954, p. 499.

First Industrial Revolution), 'managerial capitalism' (for the USA in the Second Industrial Revolution), and 'collective capitalism' (for Japan in what might turn out to be the Third Industrial Revolution).[2] These phases constitute the basic ideological frameworks and the contexts for production organization (see Figure 12.1, which is a compound of Figures 2.2 and 4.1). However, the present book has concentrated on the technology phases, and on the interaction between technology and organization (Marx's forces of production and relations of production). Over time the impact has shifted from the micro to the macro level as technologies, organizational structures and the rest are diffused across the economy – in Figure 12.1, this appears as a shift of emphasis from the spheres seen as endogenous to the individual firm (the rectangles) to those which for simplicity are taken to be exogenous (the circles).

It scarcely needs adding that, besides the industrialization spurts on which the book has concentrated, there were other periods when the impetus abated, and even the secular processes were called into question. The book errs on the side of optimism about technology, as the price paid for its focus. In practice, changes in the national systems of production have come about more hesitantly over the 'long wave' or Kondratiev cycle, brought about in Freeman–Perez fashion by tensions between the major spheres,[3] i.e. between the areas nominated as exogenous to the individual firm in Figure 12.1. Rifts brought about by the logic of development (heuristics) within each sphere express themselves through the feedback loops (reverse arrows) at the national level. In the context of competitive threats from new, very different 'national systems of production' in emerging countries, relative industrial retardation can set in. Whether the tensions lead to quasi-permanent retardation (as in Britain after 1870) or to restructuring (as is being claimed nowadays for the USA) remains a moot point.

I: SUMMARY OF EMPIRICAL FINDINGS: COUNTRIES

In answer to the question, why was science backward in the Middle Ages, Postan (1951) replied that, 'Mediaeval technology and mediaeval science each kept to their carefully circumscribed spheres'.[4] The answer to the more commonly posed questions of why modernization should have taken place, and why in Britain, goes beyond the inference that Rostow, Kuznets and others drew, that technology came to be influenced by modern science.

2 Lazonick 1991, ch. 1; also Dosi *et al.* 1992, ch. 4; though one may dispute Lazonick's term as a description of the Japanese case.

3 See below, pp. 412–13.

4 Quoted by Rostow 1975, p. 26.

Figure 12.1: A Completed Micro-level Taxonomy for Production in the Firm

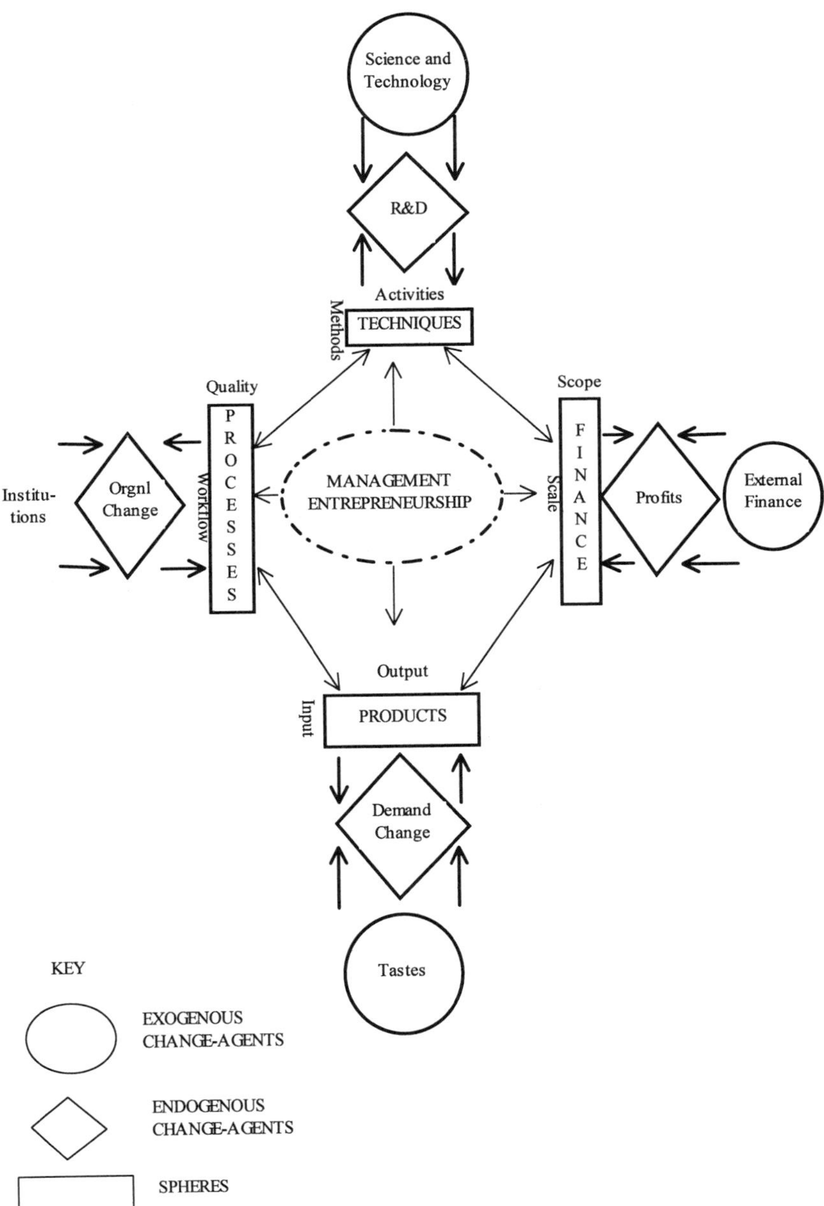

Here it is suggested that it was in 18th-century Britain that all the main pieces in the jigsaw began to fit together: scientific method, capitalist ideology, commerce, finance and availability of factor inputs (see Chapter 4). The relatively simple nature of the technology and the markets permitted this to happen relatively informally – even the most technologically complex machine of the time, the steam engine, was produced by a partnership between a man gifted in technology (Watt) and another in marketing (Boulton). This does not mean that a complete set of 'necessary preconditions' had to be in place for industrialization. One could instead support Gerschenkron's argument that other countries could find acceptable substitutes, with the problems and solutions always changing through time.[5] The basic argument is rather that successful industrialization involved a degree of coherence and interaction among all the spheres (technology, processes, finance, etc.).

Development along all the necessary fronts was far from symmetrical, with progress often coming from tensions and bottlenecks. The experiences of the three or four main types of industrialization instead show contrasts in what might be termed the 'leading sphere', which played the role of a 'binding agent' in the words of Hirschman.[6] Here the 'binding agent' in the First Industrial Revolution in Britain is seen in the expansion of markets and especially in the active role of merchants. But as scholars like Rostow have emphasized, expansion of the market is not a sufficient condition for industrialization – the technology, organization and finance had to sustain industry's response. The leading contemporary economists (Hume, Steuart, Smith, etc.) recognized that the merchant supplied not only marketing but finance. Chapter 4 above takes a broader view and stresses the advent of the machine as a paradigm for technology and the factory as a paradigm for organization in manufacturing industry, as providing a continued solution to the problems encountered. These solutions of machine technology and factory organization could potentially be stretched further and further, so long as they met the objectives, of which the most important was defined as the need to save time. This therefore established the heuristics for manufacturing development. It came through a shift from product to process innovation, which developed steadily through the 18th century. Though writers have variously attributed this to technological or organizational causes, the nature of that process innovation indicates that those who instead claim the primary role for market growth can equally be supported – the orientation of the process technologies towards saving time was largely a consequence of having to meet expanding markets. This leadership from the expansion of markets was even more evident where

5 Pollard 1981, pp. 187–90, 213, also in Dosi *et al.* 1992, pp. 47–9.
6 Hirschman 1958, p. 7.

product innovations were directly linked to process change, as in the pottery industry.[7]

The British lead started to be called into question when the close linkages between commerce (marketing) and manufacturing (technology) began to break up. On the one side, manufacturing became embroiled in a class divide between workers and owner-managers (capitalists), brought about through the technological and organizational changes of machinery and factory, in ways indicated by Marx. On the other side, commerce drifted into the arms of finance, which developed independently to provide infrastructure (railways, etc.). British science continued to fare reasonably well, but failed to integrate with technology to the same degree as in Britain's emerging rivals. Without adequate financial backing, and no doubt also out of personal preference, industrial organization and management were not sufficiently revamped to suit the new needs of 'big business'. Thus British industrial 'decline' (relative of course, rather than absolute) came mainly from the growing separation of functions.

Traditional comparisons between British and Continental industrialization concentrated on slower (France) or later growth spurts in the latter. Recent studies have instead emphasized that there was less difference in the rates of growth than in the precise patterns.[8] The power and the vigour of the British merchant was less in evidence in Continental Europe. Gerschenkron thus found 'substitutes' in the role of banking in Central Europe (from north to south), and in the role of the state in Eastern Europe. As shown in Chapter 5, current thinking gives moderate support to Gerschenkron and earlier writers for the characterization of banking in this region, but generally sees its role as that of following rather than leading industrialization. This permitted the growth of large-scale organization, such as suited some of the new activities like chemicals and electricity generation. But it means that we have to look elsewhere for the driving forces of Continental industry. In the case of France, where the role of banking in industry was in any event weaker, the most apparent difference from Britain lay in the importance of *differentiated* demand for products. Industry served to meet markets where the British absolute advantage in costs mattered least, in customized demand for semi-luxury goods and services. The consequence for technology was a lessened importance of the role of throughput, and hence of the emphasis on machinery and factory encountered in Britain. On the other side, the French pattern required particular attention to the roles of design and skills. Thus whereas British industrialization had been characterized by a shift from product-based to process-based learning, that in France continued to pursue product-based learning, with a modicum of

7 Rosenberg and Birdzell 1986, p 162.

8 E.g. O'Brien and Keyder 1978; Crafts 1984; Cameron 1985; O'Brien 1986.

process change. Coherence was maintained by the predominance of family dynasties which proved able to diversify without losing direction. The slower technological track than for the British heuristics, and the limitations on supply of finance, etc. for smallish, family-based firms, implied a slower rate of total industrial growth than for the UK. However, given the range of circumstances beyond the control of individual firms, it does not follow that French industry would have grown faster using British (or for that matter German) heuristics, in view of both the French strengths and the competitive pressures the country faced.

Since the Second World War especially, the design-intensive, family-oriented SMF has shown not just resilience but considerable dynamism in countries following what might be called the French track (e.g. Italy). To achieve this has required overcoming its inherent limitations of being too inward-looking, and instead interacting closely with its external environment, on the side of both demand (customers) and supply (equipment suppliers and fellow-producers). Information has flowed freely around local communities, which have provided supporting finance and marketing. Such networks are encountered in several slightly different forms in a number of countries – Italy has taken over the lead in this 'flexible specialization', though its base is essentially regional. The 'external economies' which Marshall perceived could be obtained in industrial districts integrated the various functions, assisted by localized 'collective invention' of the kind described by Allen (1983).

In contrast to the French educational system, which tended to emphasize elite values and high quality, the German system, moulded out of states like Prussia, from early days stressed dissemination and breadth. The characteristic most frequently commented upon was the focus on technical training. German industrialization thus placed increasing emphasis on engineering and the role of technology. Again, speed of process was often sacrificed, but in this case for the pursuit of *technical* (as distinct from product) quality. With the accommodating nature of German banking and its liaison with big business, German industry developed competitive advantage in R&D-intensive activities such as chemicals. Thus the leader role among the functions was played by the technology sphere. To the present day, the greatest anxiety about the state of German industry still concerns the lack of attention to *process*. The kinds of engineering in which the Germans have excelled – electrical, mechanical, etc. – are relevant to strength in technologies but less often include those most relevant to production processes, viz. production engineering. In sectoral terms, leadership therefore came from the capital goods industries.

Thus the spread of industrialization across the face of Europe was not just a matter of finding substitutes, in the manner suggested by Gerschenkron, since the role of leading function (binding agent) changed from one case to the next. This went alongside a change in the leader role in terms of country, principally from Britain to Germany, with later industrializers trying to replace imports of *German* equipment and knowhow in their efforts to catch up. The implications are witnessed even more strikingly in the Communist economies of Eastern Europe in the 20th century. For Gerschenkron and Rostow, Soviet Russia was at heart a later version of the European pattern of industrialization, with the state replacing the role of the German banker. Here I see a very different story unfolding. The absence of a role for demand and markets and their replacement by planning and the role of the military are of course obvious, but perhaps just as important was the almost complete separation between technology and production. Though this had pre-revolutionary roots, for example in Imperial Russia's heavy reliance on capital inflows, the functions remained almost totally divorced under the Soviet system. Confronted by a choice between a German-style machinery sector based on skills and an American-style sector based on mass production, the Soviets chose the latter, ill-advisedly if the detailed study of Granick (1967) is to be accepted. By accentuating (mass) production, the central planners supposed that technology and products would develop through complementarity – in practice, the rigid hierarchical planning system meant that production bore most of the weight while technology languished elsewhere and products were largely neglected. Integration was supposed to be vouchsafed by political means (the role of the Communist Party), but this was more successful for 'labour process' such as employee relations than for 'capital process', especially in inter-enterprise and inter-industry relationships. Ironically, the USSR was least successful among the industrializaing countries for resolving the Marxian contradiction between the forces of production (modern technology) and the relations of production (here planning and control).[9] Such fundamental shortcomings of technological dynamism in Communism Soviet-style came to a head in the later 1980s.

American technology also originally spun off from the British, and remained tied more closely to its parent than was true of some of the Continental European countries. The USA thus long remained a borrower in technologies, but proved adept in modifying those technologies to suit the very different demand and supply characteristics of the American economy. It was processes that were unique to the USA in the mid-19th century: the 'American System of Manufactures' based on interchangeable parts. Its 20th-century command of technologies began to emerge from indigenous development of complex technological systems in a range of newer

9 Nove 1977, p. 20.

activities. Rosenberg draws attention to the importance of 'systems engineering'.[10] The ingredients for success here appear to have come more broadly from American supremacy in the link between administration and marketing, with the integrating role being played by middle management in hierarchically controlled large-scale firms. Analyses of American technology have concentrated on its labour-saving characteristics, which were undoubtedly part of the story, but here rather more stress is given to the accentuation of time saving that came from mass production and mass distribution. The 'visible hand', rightly lauded by Alfred Chandler in his seminal studies, could be extended in the 20th century to diversified activities, without great loss of processing efficiency, through the mechanism of the multidivisional company. The American model externally achieved a potency which would-be imitators found daunting[11] when new technologies like electronics were internally developed and linked by way of these highly structured administrative systems to new products like computers.

Like the British economy of the late 19th century, the US economy in the later 20th century, however, began to drift in a way that seemed to presage industrial decline. Management became too closely affiliated to financial imperatives and to its own rent-seeking behaviour. Learning in hierarchical organizations was too centralized and insufficiently responsive to new consumer demands, including those imposed by broader economic circumstances such as reflected in the 'energy crises'. High-tech companies like IBM witnessed a fossilization of their bureaucratic administrative systems. R&D and production were typically much less well integrated than in equivalent Japanese companies.[12] At the time of writing, there is nevertheless a growing view that US manufacturing has overcome some of its worst deficiencies, and if so, this will of course represent a quite different outcome than earlier for Britain, where the problems simply rigidified.[13] The outcome will also depend on the extent to which the rival East Asian industrial model is able to override some of its own weaknesses.

The rise of Japan after the Second World War exposed the deficiencies of American process systems such as Fordism. It was precisely there that the Japanese exhibited their distinctive national system of production. The Soviets had placed primary emphasis on production processes but failed to regard them as the link between evolving technologies and evolving products – in the Japanese system, processes played the role of the driving force. Such strengths were built on a commitment to production

---

10 In Dosi *et al.* 1992, ch. 2.

11 E.g. Servan-Schreiber 1968.

12 Rosenberg 1994, ch. 7.

13 Elbaum and Lazonick 1986.

engineering, and to constant improvement in production processes stemming from broadly-based learning; involving interaction within the firm between managers and employees, interaction between firms in industrial groups, and interaction with government through 'administrative guidance' and consultation. Both speed and quality were stressed in the principles espoused by Japanese companies. These were achieved by placing as much responsibility for decision-making as possible on the factory floor, and giving incentives for continuous improvement. The types of process improvements introduced required the sharing of knowledge between producers and users, and this was most often sought through networks of the hub kind (the *keiretsu*), including integration of finance within the industrial groups. The methods served them well in producing diversified goods that met changing consumer needs. Aoki (1988) demonstrates that the Japanese system of bottom-up decision-making is less advantageous when the technological environment is extremely stable (since incremental innovations are not of consequence) or highly unstable (since the shopfloor is not a good starting-point for radical innovation). The Japanese thus fared less well in goods where high-tech, laboratory-based techniques on the one hand, or a high degree of product customization on the other, were required. One can only speculate on whether these challenges may eventually be overcome, something which an historian can leave to others to do.

East Asian countries, led by South Korea and Taiwan, typically aimed to imitate the Japanese system and its emphasis on process. The wider systems built around this leader function, however, differed considerably from country to country, for example the contrast in competitive structure between the large *chaebol* in Korea and the SMFs in Taiwan. All, nevertheless, focused on indigenization of technological knowledge and capability. Latin American countries found technological indigenization much less attainable, partly through the high reliance on turnkey projects and operations of multinational subsidiaries. Though many of the specific policies were similar to those implemented in East Asia, the outcomes proved much inferior. Beneath the surface of the policies lay deeper-seated problems – perhaps including what Hirschman describes as the ego-focused rather than group-focused or co-operative nature of industrial society in Latin America (lack of networks, etc.).[14] On the demand side, income inequalities inherited from their colonial past imposed a burden experienced in only a few East Asian countries.

Thus all four spheres have in one country and context or another acted in the leader function (binding agent) role – to quote again examples,

14 Hirschman 1958, pp. 11–16; but see p. 375 above.

marketing (merchants) in Britain during its Industrial Revolution, technology in Germany, administration in the United States and processes in Japan. In successful industrializations, these acted in concert with the other functions, and usually required some independent initiative from at least one of those other functions – for instance, from technology in industrializing Britain, finance in Germany, marketing in the USA and government in Japan (again the examples are easy to multiply).[15] In unsuccessful cases the spheres went their separate ways, and pulled apart rather than together. We ought, therefore, to reject the case for a rigid stage model of development. But we should also reject the view, which slips into the writings of even such careful historians as Chandler, that there is a uniquely better way of running firms and industry. When British companies try to bolt on Japanese methods such as Just-in-Time or quality circles, the results are often unsatisfactory, since there is no attempt to modify British hierarchical decision-making, etc.[16] Different 'national systems of production' vary in their productiveness and developmental impact, but to have any sustained success need to be reasonably cohesive. Such cohesion ought to be dynamic, as pursued through learning processes which allow the functions to evolve in acceptable and comprehensible – as well as supportive – ways. This is based on adequately integrating operations at the micro level of individual firms.

II: SUMMARY OF EMPIRICAL FINDINGS: FIRMS

My object has been to link these more macro-level findings to detailed consideration of firm behaviour at the micro level. To avoid undue repetition, the micro aspects will be discussed in the form of a series of open issues (information versus knowledge, etc.), before coming back to the macro implications for growth and for policy. The basic argument of the book is that firms are required to transmute knowledge, in taking knowledge relating to technology (which they might generate themselves, or bring in from scientific or other research) and seeing – and overseeing – how to transform it into knowledge relating to products and markets, by way of the processes they employ. Failure to transform adequately was at the heart of the weakness of the USSR and its allies in many non-defence-related sectors.

---

15 Chandler (1990) now stresses a 'three-pronged investment' in manufacturing, marketing and management, but says surprisingly little about technology, even for the technology-led case of Germany.

16 See more generally Dosi and Kogut, in Kogut 1993, and the considerable literature on Japanese 'transplants' in the UK and USA.

A. Information vs. Knowledge

The study has placed much heavier emphasis on knowledge than on information. There is strong evidence that information about innovation spreads rapidly. Implementation of that information in production can sometimes be held up by legal means such as patents, but the indications are that, save for a few industries such as pharmaceuticals where the nature of the products makes the IPRs especially restrictive, the hold-up to a determined follower is short-lived. Lead times rather than secrecy or patenting are the major source of competitive advantage for most fields of both product and process innovation.[17] Industries of the kind Pavitt (1984) calls 'supplier-dominated' can and do start up in follower countries on the basis of imported equipment, but the indications are that they become self-sustaining only when local equipment suppliers themselves become self-sustaining (compare Switzerland's success and Norway's failure in textiles in the 19th century). For industry to become self-sustaining, much more than information is required. Knowledge has to be accumulated first to undertake 'technological scanning', i.e. to perceive what machines will be most suited to the follower country's needs; thus knowledge shapes a coherent choice of information. Second, knowledge is required to interpret what there is to learn from 'reverse engineering', i.e. analysing the imported equipment. Third, the bulk of the knowledge in such fields is 'tacit' and uncodified, and hence cannot be learnt from simply reading trade journals, patent specifications, and the like. Follower countries were thus often compelled to hire and train skilled workers, as well as purchase the equipment. Fourth, the progress from operation to investment and innovation required higher orders of knowledge accumulation.

The nature of such accumulation of knowledge is therefore a crucial focus of the book. The three-way division of learning into learning by using, learning by doing and formal learning was adopted by Adam Smith, though the terms themselves are more recent. Upstream processes (machinery, energy source, etc.) were advanced mainly by learning by using in their early years, once the initial breakthroughs had come, and often from the efforts of skilled workers operating the equipment. As Smith recognized, these processes could be reconstituted as separate industries, in the course of which they developed more structured learning procedures of their own. Practical engineering (mechanical, electrical, chemical, etc.) became a necessary if hardly sufficient condition for dynamism at these levels. Learning by using was still, however, required to complement such learning by doing in terms of modifying the equipment for continued incremental

17 Levin *et al.* 1987.

improvement. Countries varied considerably in the ways in which engineering became formalized – some like France treated it as highly academic, and benefited from doing so in the early development of radical change such as the motor car; but it was those like Germany, the USA and Japan, where practical experience was emphasized, who ultimately sustained competitive advantage in their chosen fields. R&D in Japan has been structured in a way more closely related to the pattern of industrial organization than is true in the USA, where scientific disciplines still dominate the ways in which R&D is organized.[18]

B. Paradigms, Heuristics and Trajectories

The formalization (often partial) of engineering into distinct fields reflected, and in due course promoted, the ways in which technological paradigms unfolded. The concept of technological paradigm is used in this book to refer to the bounds to codified or uncodified knowledge within which solutions to technical problems are sought. Procedures for searching for the next steps to take are called 'heuristics' here. The use of deductive science is an obvious way in which next steps might be taken, though in practice rules of thumb and serendipity continue to exercise a powerful influence. The early bases of mechanics for manufacturing and energy for mining were shaped almost entirely by techniques rather than by science, and indeed brought about radical changes in the relevant sciences (e.g. the laws of thermodynamics).[19] As is well known, the balance here has altered with each successive paradigmatic shift (chemicals, electronics, biology, etc.), though industries that have been largely science-driven, like nuclear energy, have not yet lived up to expectations. The heuristics that have mattered have continued to be for the most part engineering-based, and it is for this reason that such emphasis has been placed here on knowledge acquisition via engineering. Their nature has been one of coupling the broadest constraints imposed on human life on this planet – above all, saving time and space – with the practicalities of engineering procedures. Thus machines in the British Industrial Revolution, drawn from the mechanical paradigm, incorporated means such as rotary motion to speed up production; while nowadays ICTs, based on the electronics paradigm, are used to speed the flow of information to all parts of the globe, through space- and time-saving methods such as digitalization. Note that the same

18 Westney, in Kogut 1993.

19 Since it was engineering rather than science which long provided the dominant set of technological heuristics, I would here reject the view of North (1981) that the major turning point dates only from the fusion of science and technology in the late 19th century.

heuristics can apply to quite different paradigms. Detailed assessment of these heuristics will have to await future work aimed more directly at the technologies themselves.

Paradigms have differed considerably from sector to sector, but in my view have followed broadly similar patterns from country to country. The precise 'trajectories' of technological change depend upon the interaction of such heuristics with the specific economic circumstances of each country or region, and these are likely to vary substantially across countries. Similar technical problems could lead to a range of solutions, of differing impact on the countries' levels of productivity. Generally, technical progress will save some of each input per unit of output, but to describe the outcome as 'labour saving' is often to miss the point of what has been happening. To begin with, it is helpful to divide innovations into those aimed at expanding output from given levels of resources, and those aimed at reducing the levels of resources to produce a given level of output. Because both increase productivity, conventional economic analysis treats them identically, and of course in practice elements of both are often involved. But the distinction makes it easier to divide influences into those from the demand side – Smith's 'extent of the market' – and those drawn more conventionally from factor-saving and the supply side. In regard to computers, Cave remarks that: 'The main justification for computers in management may not be that they enable an organisation to do more cheaply what it did before, but that they enable the organisation to do things which were previously impossible'.[20]

Marx interpreted the factor-savings as coming from the savings of 'necessary labour-time', but left open the issue of whether this was more likely to come from saving labour (fewer employees to produce the given output in a given time) or from saving time (same number of employees producing the given output more quickly). He also considered the possibility of saving materials (as part of 'constant capital') in manufacturing, though believed this was less common. The savings in time, however, opened up the possibility that fixed capital might be saved per unit of output, for example in the development of what Smith called 'cheaper and simpler machinery'.[21]

---

20 In Amann and Cooper 1982, p. 236; based on the deduction of Stoneman 1975 that labour savings from computers were limited and long delayed.

21 It should be emphasized that the savings of time are with respect to production, not consumption. Producing more television sets in a given time in a consumer electronics factory, or using computer controls to speed up tool changes in a machine-making factory, are time saving in this way. This would not preclude consumers using the products to 'waste time' instead of saving it, e.g. in watching television at home, or playing arcade games on computers. This distinction between

The obvious problem with saving labour in this sense was that it could lead to unemployment. So long as macroeconomic conditions allowed, countries normally leaned towards solutions that expanded output rather than reducing the labour input. There were two problems that this raised. The first was where the demand expansion was to come from, a point discussed in regard to policy below. The second, pursued here, was that decisions about innovations were generally made at the level of the firm, not of the country. Many individual innovations were originally developed to expand output and preserve employment, but firms as administrative units in general took the line of least resistance. As individual firms they might find it difficult to reduce factor prices (cut wages, etc.) without a fight, but often it proved possible to pick off individual employees and cut employment. The types of employment taken on to work the machinery often differed from what they replaced, in terms of age, sex and skill composition. Some of the Marxist literature has suggested a close link between time-saving technical change (speed-up) and 'deskilling',[22] though in practice it appears that much of the labour 'saved' by automation was unskilled, even in the case of the USA. The most concerted efforts to reduce skilled labour seem, paradoxically enough, to have arisen in the USSR. At the other extreme lay the strategy of large Japanese firms, of converting unskilled into skilled workers *en masse*.

For all of these considerations, the present study argues that the role of labour saving has been exaggerated. At the macro level, Rostow appears more convincing than Marx, in arguing that fixed capital formation would build up to a plateau rather than propelling itself ever further upwards into a capitalist crisis. At the micro level, firms would not always find it particularly easy even to cut employment, and did fear fomenting the kinds of unrest and revolution which Marx saw as lying in store for them. Success was allied with *dynamic* efficiency. This meant that capital-intensive techniques were often adopted even in low-wage economies, such as Japan after the Second World War or South Korea later, because they were regarded as having greater long-term growth and competitive potential. The key issue here was the capability for learning in particular types of techniques – a Schumpeterian rather than a neoclassical notion of efficiency.[23] Given the particular types of technologies involved, these were directed at raising the growth of output, through speed-up, etc., rather than

savings in production and those in consumption has been a source of much unwitting confusion in the literature.

22 Braverman 1974.

23 To be sure, the neoclassical armoury includes the notion of the 'efficiency wage', i.e. the wage adjusted for productivity, but such 'efficiency' should be seen as the consequence rather than the cause of innovation.

minimizing costs. Again, capital intensity alone was not necessarily desirable and could prove wasteful: it was the potential for longer-term learning that was the objective.

The outcomes looked different across countries because of the different economic contexts. A potentially serious obstacle to raising output through faster production was maintaining or enhancing quality. A number of Continental European countries, led by France, achieved less spectacular growth rates than Britain had spearheaded, but preserved market niches and specialist competitive advantages by stressing quality. Other countries, like Germany, found shortages of materials most disabling, and sought to bypass the problems, e.g. through developing synthetic substitutes. The particular 'development blocs', forged out of specific combinations of technologies (for energy, machinery, transportation, materials, etc.), thus evolved in distinctive sectoral patterns. Industrial take-off has been more aligned with the emergence of coherent technological systems than with the appearance of specific advanced technologies. The degree of complexity has risen through time, to the point where industrial structures are highly differentiated among firms and countries (Chapter 8). But without some degree of coupling between process change and product evolution, there was likely to be relative stagnation, as in the less successful industrializing countries of the late 20th century.

This growing complexity has been a major factor behind the rising importance of human capital formation, which in turn becomes a key source for continued innovation, not least because of the difficulty of codifying production knowhow. On one side, it is the *continuity* of technological change which has been the distinguishing feature of the industrial era. On the other, the stress on education in the East Asian countries is too potent to neglect. Even supposedly labour-intensive technologies like software are extremely demanding in terms of human capital requirements, which undoubtedly goes far to explain why countries like India and Brazil, which have been acting concertedly to build on their labour cost advantages to develop world-class software industries, have had only moderate success to date. Hence one can readily agree with Porter (1990) that it is not generally appropriate to think in terms of factor 'endowments' – it is factor enhancements which have been crucial.

C. Make or Buy?

All industrializing countries – even Britain at the beginning – relied extensively on imported technologies and knowhow in their early years of advance. It has been the commercialization of technologies, rather than their original development, which has correlated with economic success. Import-

Substituting Industrialization (ISI) has therefore almost invariably had a key role to play, and little deserves the opprobrium meted out to it by many economists. However, they are right to believe that the basic question is how rapidly the distortive aspects of ISI can be overcome, and the country be able to stand on its own productive feet. Success in developing Indigenous Technological Capabilities (ITCs) logically would begin in operating plants and industries, then proceed towards capabilities to undertake investments, and in time to innovate in these activities. The complex nature of modern technology necessitates a certain amount of 'turnkey' investment, where the alternative of copying is likely to prove expensive and any delays may have serious downstream effects. Elsewhere, reliance on Foreign Direct Investment (FDI) is likely to perpetuate dependency on imported and often inappropriate technologies, e.g. through the plants of subsidiaries of multinational companies.

At the same time, the 'unpackaging' of imported items, as for instance by 'reverse engineering', runs the risk that the systemic aspects of production will be neglected. Some importation of leading-sector technologies thus seems required, but linkages forward and backward or upstream and downstream are in large part the responsibility of the country concerned. Domestic accumulation was a necessity and not an option if the development was to take hold – its importance had to be increased as foreign licensing (FL) rose. In this way, the 'development blocs' are built up, beginning at the micro level of supplier networks. In the USSR on the one hand or Latin America on the other, such co-ordination often seems to have been lost. At the same time, the upstream development of capital goods industries has to be carefully handled. The technological convergences which in the past encouraged the disengagement of capital goods like machine-makers from user industries also mean that selective imports of capital goods should continue, otherwise indigenization diffuses inefficiency.[24]

D. Processes vs. Products

The historical evidence indicates that substitution of imported by home-produced *products* may be at first necessary but is rarely sufficient. It is the command of *processes* which lies at the heart of ITC, and a commitment to process and production engineering has proved decisive, though the forms this has taken have varied widely. While some of this has to be learnt by doing, the advance of such production engineering needs to be accelerated

24 This can be thought of as a 'Sraffarian' argument for emphasizing capital (basic) goods (cf. Sraffa 1960), but here depends more on their technological than their economic characteristics.

in the early stages, in order to speed up indigenization and ingenuity. Even the notorious 'screwdriver industries' can act as a vehicle for indigenization, if control of the processes is obtained quickly enough, and if domestic efforts to develop capabilities are adequately sustained.

Product lifecycle models of the kind surveyed in Chapter 1 suppose a shift over time from product to process innovation. While there is some support for this at the level of particular manufactured products, the situation at the national level was different. Each case of successful catching-up detailed above began with a focus on processes. The products often amounted to little more than standardized versions of existing goods produced by more advanced rivals – production could begin, for example, on an OEM (Original Equipment Manufacturer) basis in this manner. In similar vein, downstream user industries even in advanced countries often followed a 'reverse product cycle'.[25] While the cycles can be staggered to a certain extent, in the last analysis it is the meshing of product and process innovation which has become critical in many fields.

While process innovation in the British Industrial Revolution was directed at some high-quality as well as some standard-quality products, US industrialization focused largely on the latter. Process technologies like interchangeable parts and assembly lines were linked to organizational structures for mass production and big business, at some cost in flexibility. American industry has thus proved vulnerable in more recent years to competition from areas like Japan and East Asia in industries where process innovation has been carried far enough to permit relatively cheap production of higher-quality items. Under the pressure of shortening product lifecycles, the Japanese offered a profusion of variants on a basically robust product design. Bottom-up decision-making encouraged continuous improvement in processes needed for higher product qualities, in contrast to the tendency in western companies to add further bureaucratic tiers in order to manage quality. In this fashion, the Japanese made fewer sacrifices of throughput on the process side in the quest for market acceptability on the product side. Simple product diversification without attention to process implications again perpetuated inefficiency, and tended to characterize the less successful industrial activities in the USSR or Latin America, with excessive changeover times and little learning from specialization.

---

25 Barras 1986, 1990.

E. Demand vs. Supply

A crude initial hypothesis would run that product innovation was driven by demand factors and process innovation by supply factors.[26] Certainly it has been found that the composition of demand has frequently had a leading role in determining the quality structure of products, as witnessed by the link between the homogeneous and fairly well-to-do domestic market and the standardized pattern of products in the 19th-century USA. Across countries, income equality has been closely correlated with industrial success in the late 20th century, no doubt working mainly through the demand side, although the precise links with industrialization here remain somewhat obscure. On the supply side, one might have expected to find the opposite result, with low wages being associated with a boost to low-cost production, and there is some evidence supporting this for periods in which industry was just about taking hold, but in the longer term the benefits of low wages seemed much more ambiguous. If factor prices or quantities are too flexible, the line of least resistance will avoid undertaking any innovation, as exemplified by 'sliding scales' for wages in British coal-mining in the late 19th century[27] and by the elasticity of labour supplies in many LICs.[28] The only conclusion that seems clear enough is that, to the extent that they are pulling in contrary directions, demand and supply factors both need to be considered.

The analysis, however, has gone further than the crude hypothesis, in demonstrating a more direct link between demand factors and process change. This arose through time saving of the kind referred to above, with larger demands compelling more output per unit of time. Specifically, the time savings came through four avenues: reduced downtime, increased throughput, better machine co-ordination and better systemic co-ordination, and of course through various combinations of these. These gains operate on a ratchet principle – there is no corresponding innovation to slow things down when demand flattens out or declines, though of course the firm may choose to shut down production for longer periods. Cost minimization, with or without innovation, is therefore likely to be sought when demand falls back (quality upgrading is a possible alternative). Unfortunately, this argument leaves the source of the demand increases unexplained, and on present evidence it is not possible to go much further than Adam Smith's original notion that there may be some external source of demand growth, e.g. increased trade, which then sets up interactive demand-and-supply determinants of innovation. At favourable times, trade may thus have acted

26 See p. 13.
27 Von Tunzelmann 1992a.
28 Furtado 1970, p. 84.

as an 'engine of growth',[29] but the main orientation of this study has been to regard trade as a 'handmaiden' of growth,[30] complementing internal efforts. Through a combination of demand and supply, the 'spread effects' of growth in leader countries spilling over to followers could be raised and the 'backwash effects' of undermining the followers reduced.[31] The supply side is as important in this story as the demand side. Over time, the supply side in the follower country can take on a momentum of its own, as happened with the German organic chemicals industry, through the fostering of formal means of technological progress, i.e. R&D.

F. Technology vs. Organization

Technologies aimed at speeding up production had to be matched by organizational advances, particularly when automation moved beyond the level of 'transformation' (machine co-ordination) to 'transfer' etc. (systemic co-ordination). In the British Industrial Revolution, systems were handled externally via production networks, which also figured in some recent developments, as described under the next heading. In late 19th-century USA, system co-ordination was instead handled through internalizing speeded-up production systems within large firms. Organizational advances thus took the form of bureaucratic administrative structures aimed at controlling and promoting the pace of work, most obviously on the assembly line. The implication of Chandler's work on the 'visible hand' is that speed-up was most effectively achieved by designing and implementing managerial bureaucracies.[32]

Even within such bureaucracies, there were substantial differences across countries in the roles of marketing, finance, technology and processes, as summarized for the countries above. Under the postwar Japanese system, led from the side of processes, speed-up came up from the shopfloor, rather than being imposed upon it. The implications went much wider than the precise processes (like Just-in-Time) utilized, to include the replacement of bureaucratic management – much of it 'unproductive' in the classical sense – with 'lean' administrative systems, and to change the whole 'mode of regulation' and balance of power and decision-making in industry. The consequences were thus markedly different from Marx's inferences about 'intensification of labour', although Japanese factories could be very demanding to work in.

29 Nurkse 1961, ch. 11.

30 Cf. Kravis 1970.

31 This is by no means intended to excuse the kinds of policies referred to by Kuznets, adopted by AICs to the direct detriment of LICs

32 E.g. Chandler 1977, 1990.

The study thus supports the perspective of Elbaum and Lazonick (1986) that production systems varied in the extent to which bureaucratic management on the one side or shopfloor on the other side effectively controlled the processes ('management-operated' vs. 'labour-operated' production processes).[33] However, I depart from that perspective when it appears to imply that management-led systems, like those of US corporations, were necessarily more efficient. 'Capital process' needs to be considered alongside 'labour process', as Marx did himself. These two points are interconnected through the growing needs for flexibility in the equipment, hence the merits of management-operated vs. labour-operated processes will depend on the precise circumstances.[34] Hierarchical management may have contributed to the problems of industry since the 1970s by seeking solutions in technical, administrative or financial fixes rather than in systemic analysis.[35] Management which has little knowledge of production would appear to be the worst of all worlds. However, for 'complex products' of the kind mentioned in Chapter 1, the production decisions might be better taken by management rather than by labour, so long as that management was sufficiently knowledgeable or willing to learn about the processes involved. Even within the same industry, the advantages in one or other organizational framework could alter over time, as exemplified by the European motor car industry, where the early German lead based on technology passed to the French when cars were purchased as differentiated luxury goods, then back to the Germans in the mid-20th century when standardization for mass markets and quality became more important.

Evidently the issue is at heart one of 'institutions and ideology' in the schema of Figure 12.1, but it would be premature to discard the view that the technological and economic environment played a part. Organizational structures as we have seen were the chief source of American industrial leadership from the late 19th century, and were the main vehicle for implementing labour-saving and time-saving technical change. Yet it is striking that the same process paradigm of the assembly line was aimed at saving labour in US automobiles but saving capital in European automobiles in the early 20th century (see p. 234). It seems barely conceivable that the patterns could have been uninfluenced by differences in resource endowments (the USA being comparatively deficient in supplies of labour). Thus organization as well as technology can be described in

---

33 This should not be equated with 'capital-managed' vs. 'labour-managed' enterprises, which refer to the sphere of administration rather than processes.

34 Marengo 1991.

35 The transaction-cost school of analysis has not adequately examined the paradox that hierarchies introduced to reduce opportunism may end up doing the opposite.

terms of paradigms and heuristics (the factory, the corporation, etc.), and it is the interaction of these heuristics together with their equivalents in the remaining spheres which finally shape the industrial trajectories.[36] The 'coupled dynamics' of technological plus institutional change further limit the extent to which countries can imitate one another, since they require a two-dimensional adaptation.[37] If political issues are left to one side, the main objective of organization considered in this work is its efficacy in transforming knowledge about technologies into knowledge about products. Existing large firms aimed to meet radical changes in technology by incrementally adjusting their organizations and processes, and sometimes found themselves outflanked by new start-up companies or by small firms in their networks. Again, the key issue was one of dynamic efficiency, and by the late 20th century concepts such as 'flexible automation', in which change was assumed to be the norm, were beginning to reveal the inadequacies of a static Taylorist interpretation of the division of labour.

G. Centralization vs. Decentralization

Technology and organization did not necessarily pull in the same direction. Sometimes the conflict was so abrupt as to be damaging, as in the adoption of Fordist management and labour-saving technologies in MNC subsidiaries in Latin America. In such situations, where organizations were in essence imposed from outside, 'enclaves' were likely to ensue and development fail to take hold, as for instance occurred at the sectoral level in manufacturing in the antebellum US South, or in mineral exploitation in more recent LICs.

Less disruptive, and much less widely noticed, was the curious disparity at the firm level between the growing decentralization of technology (machinery, IT, etc.) and the growing centralization of management, which was a characteristic of industrialization in the USA from the time of the 'Second Industrial Revolution'. Perhaps it was the case that bureaucratic centralization was required to compensate for a tendency towards fragmentation in production. The more recent trends away from managerial centralization, however, suggest that Schumpeter was right, and that the best was not being got out of the technology. At the very least, it would again appear that the 'visible hand' often arose in the way it did for reasons of ideology and control rather than for compelling technological reasons.

In accounting for the size (scale and scope) of firms, Alfred Marshall opined that technological factors might explain medium-sized firms but were exhausted before one got to very large firms. He therefore stressed marketing causes for the existence of large firms, while subsequent studies

---

36 Sapelli, in Dosi *et al.* 1992; Nelson 1994; Zysman 1994.
37 Dosi *et al.* 1992, pp. 20–21.

have given greater weight to financial factors. Over time, there were a number of technological system trends permitting the survival of smaller as well as larger firms, for instance the development of electric power and synthetics in the energy and materials fields. The evidence here indicates that in practice it was not necessarily an either/or question, but often one of a combination of these determinants. Economies of scale flowed not just from sheer size of operation, but from the number of processes and the speed of throughput (see Chapter 1), which in turn reflected a balance of demand factors like market size and supply considerations. Thus 'thresholds' for the minimum efficient scale of operations were the outcome of the composite of factors including demand as well as supply, as indeed the literature on the diffusion of innovations has argued.[38]

In vertical integration, scale economies helped dictate which firms acted as driving forces towards integration. Their intention was less one of reaping similar scale economies at the other stages of production than of controlling *quality* of inputs or products and controlling their *rate of flow*.[39] These causes were therefore directly obtained through the quality and workflow dimensions of the organizational sphere (Figure 12.1).

The size and integration of firms was profoundly affected by the accumulation of knowledge. 'Scope', in the sense of diversity of products produced by the firm, might at first sight appear to be gained only at some cost in scale and the economies of specialization. But since scale was basically a characteristic of processes and scope of products, there need not be a serious trade-off. The Japanese production of a multitude of 'variants' was to satisfy as broad a range of market demands as possible, without the high cost of multiplying processes on the supply side. In practice the matter often seemed to come down to a trade-off between accumulating knowledge within firms and accumulating knowledge between firms. I have demonstrated that vertical integration was much more common in the product chain than in the process chain. Suppliers of equipment etc. remained independent of their users because the scope of their knowledge could be extended at relatively low cost across a much wider range of users, as Rosenberg (1963) showed for the case of machine tools. Any gains in knowledge generation from integrating with one particular kind of user were heavily outweighed by the gains actually achieved by the 'technological convergence' among their products. Users could accept this situation so long as they were not in thrall to one particular supplier. But as the complexity of knowledge requirements escalated, networks were utilized as a substitute for vertical integration.

---

38 David 1975.

39 See Chapter 6; also Langlois and Robertson 1989.

The main determinant of long-term success or failure was the extent to which knowledge in the various fields could be made to pull together rather than pulling in different directions. Some cohesive force is usually required to achieve this, in the manner of Hirschman's 'binding agent', perhaps supplied by particularly influential groups of individuals, like the merchants in the early British Industrial Revolution or Schumpeterian entrepreneurs blessed with vision, or through local communities as in the case of the 'Third Italy', or through the hub of powerful firms. The separation between ownership (and finance) and management under 'finance capitalism' has proved especially problematic for such cohesion, particularly when financiers came to lead instead of just following.[40] As ownership shifted towards institutional investors obsessed with short-term capital gains, able to sell out at any moment, the long-term interests of the firm and its other stakeholders, including the employees, were sacrificed. For the same reasons, family ownership, while obviously limiting in many ways, was perhaps less disastrous than often maintained.[41]

Just as efforts to balance specialization against diversification usually ended in some kind of compromise, preferably one that got as much as possible of the benefits of both, so and for similar reasons did efforts to balance centralization against decentralization. Decentralization to subdivide problems has often increased rather than decreased the difficulties that institutions face – examples being some UK and US M-form companies at the micro level, or Soviet planning under Khrushchev at the macro level. In our context the basic reason is evident – that problems are not one-dimensional. To develop both technologies and products in a production system requires a complex intermeshing of information spillovers and knowledge sharing, as pointed out in Chapter 8. In hierarchical (micro or macro) systems the result is likely either to fall between all stools or to become a bureaucratic nightmare. It is hard to escape the conclusion that, to date at least, the Japanese system of manufactures has coped best with the inherent difficulties, by decentralizing as much responsibility as possible to the shopfloor level while maintaining through collaboration and discussion an overall sense of purpose.

H. Growth vs. Fluctuations

Thus the problems at the micro level become magnified to the macro level. The summary of national systems at the start of this chapter showed how

---

40 Agency theory sees the problem as one in which the 'agents' – here managers – fail to act in the best interests of 'principals' – here the owners (Rees 1985). From a production perspective, the problem was if anything the opposite.

41 Church 1993.

different spheres acted as the driving force for industrial progress in different countries or regions. The different national systems which took it in turn to act as driving forces for the international economy at large – Britain in the mid 19th-century, the USA in the mid-20th century, and perhaps East Asia (including China) in the mid-21st century – each acted on the demand side to spur exports and investment in follower countries, and (more to our point) on the supply side as role models for technologies, processes and organizations. The 'new growth theory' outlined in Chapter 3 has again drawn attention to the possibilities for technological spillover, to which the remaining spheres like organization can be added as contenders for spillover. At the regional level, especially, there are clear indications of 'trickle-back' or 'trickle-up' along the supply chains for products and processes, as follower countries within the region began development by supplying materials or parts for the regional leaders.[42] Within regions it is not just the technologies but the wider institutional/ideological aspects which tend to resemble one another – when the whole techno-organizational paradigms are essentially the same, imitation of individual bits is much more straightforward. This combination of supply and demand spillovers concentrated at the regional level gives credence to the notion of growth 'clubs'.[43]

The main focus of the book has, however, placed three major qualifications against these spillover notions. The first is that national or regional systems of innovation have shown little convergence with one another. The heuristics which described, say, German industry in the late 19th century still tell us more about German industry today than does the ensuing rise of US industry to world leadership – the latter has at most deflected rather than reoriented the pattern of German industrialization. The same goes for the other major species of industrialization studied in this book: they have not stood still (some alas have regressed), but they have changed in ways that are driven at least as much by internal-dependency as by external influences.

The second reservation, linked to the first, is that industrialization appears to have depended far more upon internal than external efforts – certainly no country achieved much without a huge commitment to pulling itself up. This applies not least in technological development – just as R&D has 'two faces' at the level of the firm,[44] so it does at the macro level of the country. In the light of the dominant heuristics portrayed in this study, it is worth

42 For the impact of Japan on East Asia, see e.g. Gregory 1985/1986, ch. 10; Abegglen 1994.

43 Baumol 1986, etc.

44 Cohen and Levinthal 1989.

pointing out that catching-up is in many respects a race against time.[45] The USSR failed in this race, except to a degree in defence industries. R&D should be thought of more broadly here as efforts towards technological accumulation of all kinds, expanding the 'absorptive capacity' for being able to borrow knowhow from abroad. The loci of such accumulation of organizational as well as technological knowledge have substantially influenced the respective growth performances: compare the concentration of learning and decision-making at the level of the social elite in the UK, the ideological elite in the USSR, the broader managerial elite in the USA, and the even broader large-firm elite in Japan.

The third problem is that co-ordination between technology, processes, products and finance is even weaker at an international than at a national level. Different parts of the system 'globalized' at different times, and this often limited the extent to which industrialization could spin off to the recipients. The widening separation between finance and industry, already problematic within some of the leading industrial countries, often became acute in international dealings, and accentuated the adverse 'backwash' effects of international economic linkages (cross-country 'vicious circles').

Interactions between finance and industry could lead to 'virtuous circles', e.g. through better technology improving profits, which in turn allowed greater ploughback into R&D, or alternatively to 'vicious circles' where both worsened interactively. 'Virtuous circles' may also be expected to arise internally through interaction between technologies and products, and conversely 'vicious circles' exacerbate decline when one or the other is neglected. Though no detailed analysis of cyclical fluctuations has been made in this book, the evidence it surveys is consistent with a view that such virtuous and vicious circles may account for instances of growth or retardation. Macroeconomic studies have noted a correspondence between growth of output and growth of productivity, though analyses have differed in whether they ascribe this correlation to demand (output) or supply (productivity). Conceivably the causal pattern may alternate over time, to generate long swings or long waves through expansion and contraction.

The discussion has had somewhat more to say about the long Kondratiev waves. My suggestion is that observed 50-year cycles (or thereabouts) are in fact a composite of century-long revolutions at the micro level, which through lengthy internal diffusion processes are taken up at the macro level with a lag of about half a century.[46] This could account for the lack of success in identifying Kondratiev waves in economic data – more work is needed here on relating technological to economic indicators. New

45 Gerschenkron 1962, p. 137.

46 This is consistent with my earlier findings on the steam engine, for example (von Tunzelmann 1978).

activities are launched for reasons which seem to have come originally from micro demand factors like speed-up, and which get taken up in the form of radical innovations. These become incorporated by way of organizational and associated changes, and eventually become isolated as new industries, being new in regard to consumer demand as well as supply characteristics. This is roughly speaking the chronology of the so-called new industries of the interwar period, which harked back to radical innovations in the late 19th century. Plausibly the macro-level impact was associated with a secondary wave of innovations of the Schumpeterian kind. In the 1990s it seems likely that we have still to see the fruition at the macroeconomic level of the diffusion of the radical innovations of the postwar era. The nature of this argument supports the Freeman–Perez case for structural 'mismatches', especially between technologies and organizations. To the Kondratiev time pattern they observe one can also add a cross-national dimension, for instance the clash between British technology and German ethos in imperial Germany, to which Veblen (1915) drew attention.

The need here to consider technologies as well as products (sectors) has led to an emphasis on 'leading technologies' alongside Rostow's notion of 'leading sectors'. These stem from the 'methods' as compared with the 'activities' dimension of the technology sphere in Figure 12.1. It is success in the embodiment of technologies into products, enabled by firms as the essence of their existence, which is likely to be at the heart of national competitiveness.

I. Implications for Public Policy

Many of the issues just covered are highly relevant to governmental concerns over industrial policy-making, particularly the roles of technological accumulation and knowledge accumulation more generally, though too often they have been ignored.[47]

Governments have sought to sponsor the expansion of 'sunrise' industries in a variety of ways, including various protective measures that have been bundled together here under the label of ISI. The main theme of this book urges that technologies for industries need to be considered separately from the products which they occasion, and the implication is that the sponsoring of technologies merits special attention. For industrialization to take hold, the evidence here lies heavily on the side of the significance of production processes, though beyond that also emphasizes the importance of interlinkages between process and product innovation (or imitation). There is a close correlation at the country level between rates of growth and

47 An excellent survey of policy in a theoretical context similar to that of this book is given in OECD 1992.

degrees of exploitation of the prevailing heuristics in capital goods industries such as mechanization.[48] Most state intervention in practice has by these standards been misdirected. Policies of selective technological importation followed by concerted efforts to bring about *efficient* indigenous production seem to have worked best, though too rarely attempted. This has to be balanced against over-protection of domestic suppliers of capital goods. Thus one should think more in terms of 'infant technologies' than 'infant industries', and leave some role for competition especially in regard to products. The studies of individual countries show very clearly that simply establishing infant-industry protection on the one hand, or free trade on the other, by itself does little to change things – successful policies of either kind have been those which were backed up by trenchant government efforts to indigenize technologies and/or promote exports. To avoid fragmentation between new technologies and new products, such as proved so deleterious in the Soviet Union, the government needs to relate its sponsorship of technologies to success by the firms in product development.

Comparative advantage of the Ricardian kind as a basis for industry has the disadvantage of locking the country into existing technological bases, whereas a dynamic approach clearly requires consideration of the potential for future technological change. Thus, as noted in relation to trajectories above, countries like Japan bypassed existing labour-intensive activities and sought dynamic comparative advantage at first through capital intensity and eventually through knowledge intensity. This implies an active role for government: the divinity which many economists of the 1980s ascribed to free-market competition is absurd. As Zysman points out,[49] markets and political systems are not antitheses but inextricably entwined. One has to strip aside mythology here, because in reality the 1980s appear to have been a decade of 're-regulation', as well as deregulation (see Chapter 8). That apart, the Pareto principle shows that, at best, competitive markets drive to equilibrium at the pre-existing level of income distribution – in other words, unreservedly freeing a market can reinforce the power structure ('social relations of production') already in existence. In this way, privatization in countries like the UK ran the risk of converting public monopolies into greedier private monopolies. It was to prevent the worst excesses of rapacity that the 're-regulation' occurred, but the evidence at hand suggests that it has not been adequate to the task. A thoroughgoing reorganization of the productive structure was really required if the public good was to be properly served. The policy of 'getting the prices right' to promote development founders on precisely the same Pareto principle – the object of

48 De Long and Summers 1991.
49 Zysman 1983.

innovation policy should be to change behaviour, not to reinforce it. The study echoes the belief that competition is or ought to be as much a consequence as a cause of industrialization.[50] The most disastrous practical consequences to date of unguardedly introducing unrestrained competition have been observed in the eastern European countries after 1989.

Support for free market policies has come indirectly from observing the strong outward-orientation of the East Asian 'Tigers' in recent debates. On the one side, this may exaggerate the extent of their outward-orientation. Second, the cross-country evidence that outward-orientation is correlated with strong economic performance is much less convincing than often assumed.[51] Third, and most important, is that an export-orientation does not necessarily imply free trade: Korea, the country rating highest in terms of outward-orientation on World Bank scales, has as high trade controls, price distortions, etc., as many strongly inward-oriented countries.[52] The present study shows that espousal of free trade has been mere rhetoric for many AICs.

The analysis highlights two kinds of reasons, leaving aside the Pareto questions, why free markets may prove inadequate. The experience of the Soviet Union certainly provides ammunition for the argument of Hayek (1945, etc.) that systems which try to plan in terms of quantities rather than prices will overlook the economies in information obtainable from prices, and quickly exceed their 'bounded rationality'. The more complex products became, the more relevant this deficiency became. However, that increasing complexity was associated with increasingly fine quality distinctions. If the number of prices has to be multiplied to match the multiplication of qualities, then the economizing on information from using prices will be largely lost. This study points to an even deeper problem – quality differences apart, prices collapse the information too far, for example because we have to consider demands and supplies for both technologies and products (cf. Chapter 1 above). Prices set high to encourage technology creation may equally discourage technology diffusion; in parallel fashion, prices set high to encourage product producers may discourage consumers. With the several dimensions, there can be no simple assurance which prices will be 'optimal'.

For related reasons, governments have generally not fared very well in attempting to favour firms as opposed to industries and/or technologies. Governments at best can draw on only a tiny fraction of the knowledge of

50 Amsden 1989. The Structure–Conduct–Performance school of industrial economists such as Porter fails at this point.

51 Wade 1990, pp. 16–18.

52 *Ibid.*, pp. 18–21.

the communities they govern.[53] Direct government production in non-socialist countries has often been necessitated for reasons of 'market failure', but failure within firms is a much more serious problem for most economies than failure between firms in markets. Bureaucratic demarcations are a major cause of organizational failure within firms, and government-run firms are particularly prone to these – here the most apparent examples arose in Eastern Europe *before* 1989. To reiterate, the basic rationale for firms is seen here as amalgamating knowledge about technologies, processes, products and finance, not compartmentalizing it. In regard to private firms, governments have variously sponsored large firms, medium firms and small firms. Each of these seems to have had a measure of success (and failure), which suggests that for industrial policy the strategy for firm size may not matter too much. Support for particular firms is likely to be against the public good, unless (as in South Korea) the decision as to which firms to sponsor is 'contestable'. The implications of firm size are likely to be considerably greater for employment policy, where excessive concentration on large firms may involve a cost in unemployment. The conclusion appears to be that governments should pay attention to the structure of industries as a whole, and particularly to the networks of interconnections between firms of different sizes.

Policies directed specifically at raising human capital formation appear, as might be predicted, to have had a substantial impact on long-term development. Countries have sometimes had to wait a very long time indeed for any payoff, as the case of Sweden shows. Whether educational systems can be 'built ahead of demand', as has been argued for East Asia, remains an open question. There is a clear association between the breadth or narrowness of the educational system and the breadth or narrowness of the learning and decision-making structure in industry. Causality here is probably mutually reinforcing, as the primary determinant of educational structures in most countries has been 'social control', even in East Asia. This has not necessarily prevented mass education from becoming the basis for 'learning to learn' or 'training for training' in industry. Enlarged 'social capabilities' have, however, been as much a consequence as a cause of growth, via greater resources for education, widened markets, higher savings ratios, etc.[54]

So far as direct policies for R&D are concerned, the main issues seem to have been: (i) who performs it, as opposed to who funds it; (ii) how successfully its benefits are diffused. The USA has had a powerful and enviable track record in getting (Federal or other) government to fund R&D carried out in private firms, and thus to some extent getting the best of both

53 Mill 1848/1909, p. 947.
54 Ohkawa and Rosovsky 1973, p. 212.

worlds. Even so, this was of only limited benefit if the government funding freed private firms from having to control the costs of developing the technologies or products concerned. R&D carried out by governments can too easily become 'mission-oriented', pursuing enormously expensive projects of dubious economic merit, for political muscle rather than public benefit.[55] Those policies of the USSR that were successful were almost exclusively of this kind, with consequences that are now all too obvious. To avoid excessive overlap and impart some push, it may prove necessary for central government to take direct action; but it is essential that these efforts are matched, and more than matched, by the other side of the R&D face in entrepreneurial firms. It is doubtful whether these objectives are being met by, say, the current emphasis on limiting government support to pre-commercial technologies.[56] To harp again on my main theme, technological information is of limited benefit until it is embedded as knowledge in firms and transmuted into production knowledge permitting the emergence of commercial products. Specific policies by governments to boost R&D in private firms, such as R&D tax credits, are controversial – at the time of writing, the consensus appears to be that such policies have had a moderately beneficial impact. Policies to foster intellectual property rights (IPRs) have been much touted by the 'property rights' school of economists,[57] but it has to be recalled that catching-up countries need to imitate and indigenize rather than innovate, and restrictive IPRs can prove a significant obstacle. Even leader countries like Britain in the Industrial Revolution probably benefited from having imperfect patent systems.[58] Some later countries imitated rapidly by eschewing patent rights, but more generally the practice in recent years has been negotiating realistic licence fees. As shown in Chapters 10 and 11, foreign licensing (FL) should generally follow rather than precede the first steps towards technological learning. More broadly, it may be remarked that tautly drawn property rights may rigidify underdevelopment[59] – the object has to be creating opportunities for the entrepreneurially inclined to exercise their abilities.

Governments in both leader and follower countries have tended to interpret their role here as one of cutting costs through reducing duplication of R&D effort. Comparative-static neoclassical analysis inadvertently overplays this problem,[60] and the results have distorted policy conclusions.

55 Ergas 1987.
56 Rosenberg 1994, pp. 51–2.
57 E.g. North 1981.
58 Mokyr 1990, p. 252.
59 A good example was French rural society under the *Code Napoléon*, cf. Fohlen 1973, p. 30.
60 E.g. Dasgupta and Stiglitz 1980.

The difficulty here is the evolutionary one – that eliminating alternatives reduces the possibilities for advance through dynamic Schumpeterian competition between species. The argument emphasised in this book that there is no one-to-one relationship between technologies and saleable products helps indicate why market-based solutions are not sufficient, and why plurality is to be desired. It is conceivable that institutional arrangements mistakenly directed at eliminating waste (like Sematech in the USA) may triumph in other ways, but there is no proof as yet.

Macroeconomic policies that have favoured moderate expansion have been consistently the most successful for industrial progress. Again this may seem somewhat predictable, but economic policies may have to perpetuate a modest amount of disequilibrium, as compared with the textbook notion of attaining equilibrium. Growth in demand is required for much of the kinds of time-saving technical change described throughout this book, namely that arising out of expanded output; but the scope for Keynesian policies of unbalanced budgets has been circumscribed by globalization and adverse supply-side trends, and indeed East Asian countries have made little use of them. Moderate inflation has nevertheless usually proved a price worth paying as against the shock therapy of severe deflation; though inflation can easily become a soft option (line of least resistance), and hence postpone instead of promote technical advance through lack of cost-side (supply) incentives. Shock therapy may, however, be required at some stage for the structure of demand, given the evidently strong relationship between income equality and growth.

In parallel fashion to private firms, the position of the government or at least its departments ought itself to be 'contestable' – both growth and decline have been accelerated by governments of every imaginable political hue,[61] but the most persistent failures have occurred in autocracies with power bases in anti-industrial minorities (reactionary landlords, the military, etc.). Over-centralization in government, whether it be in the USSR under Stalin or less spectacularly in the UK under Mrs Thatcher, suffers from the same deficiencies as excessive centralization in bureaucratic firms. Once an acceptable social basis has been attained, governments like those of Japan – through industrial policies such as firm size, employment policies, and so on – have aimed to balance economic disequilibrium against social stability. The experiences of various countries related in this book support the view that, properly controlled, growth has been the most successful way of achieving social stability.

61 In similar fashion, Gerschenkron 1962, p. 86, noted the great variety of ideologies which seemed to serve development more or less equally well.

III: SUMMARY OF THEORETICAL FINDINGS

The most evident conflict between the empirical findings at the level of both country and firm described so far, and the theoretical models old and new outlined in Chapters 2 and 3 above, is the lack of multiple dimensionality in the latter. Economists' models, even of microeconomic behaviour, tend to lump together technologies, processes, and products, as if they were virtually synonymous. This brought some advantage in trying to formalize the micro level of production behaviour, but at the cost of losing sight of the essence of what is happening, and indeed of why institutions such as firms exist. Most of the functions have been treated satisfactorily at one time or another – the most overlooked, that of production processes, was central to Adam Smith's famous opening pages – but their integration into a comprehensive picture has been especially deficient. Empirical writers have not done very much better – the diversity of functions is better recognized, but too often the approach has been through just 'one pair of eyes'. The balance between greater accuracy and undue complexity is to some extent a matter of personal preference, and few may be persuaded by the compromise which I have tried to strike. My belief remains that minimally the degree of disaggregation to the four functions of my schema is essential for understanding industrial development, but no doubt historians on the other side will still consider these categories too aggregated and oversimplified.

The main economic justification for adopting such levels is that it remains possible, as in Figure 12.1, to parameterize each level and in principle identify its characteristics over space and time, of course at the cost of adding third and fourth dimensions. The approach, though in origin taxonomic, thus provides the potential framework for an evolutionary model, inasmuch as it: (i) has demonstrable time patterns, (ii) can be differentiated according to particular context, (iii) is holistic, in having a whole which is more than the sum of the individual parts.

The major theoretical conclusions can be summarized as follows:

(a) that technology and process have to be treated as issues in their own right, and are not simply derived from product characteristics and dimensions;

(b) that there is an associated need for trying to understand the nature of process innovation, and particularly its technological determinants;

(c) that the latter, contrary to what might be imagined, help to shift the emphasis from traditional supply (cost) determinants towards demand-side factors, once the demand influences and their pathways are properly understood;

(d) that attention ought to be drawn to the crucial role of learning, and to a distinction between information and knowledge, with most knowledge having to be accumulated internally within firms or through networks involving close contacts;

(e) that firms exist as institutions to transform technological knowledge into product knowledge, making use of processes and of administrative and financial structures;

(f) that dynamic efficiency is the main test of success of a productive system, and this can be gauged by the rate at which the constituent firms accumulate and generate productive knowledge, be they hierarchical, (dis-)integrated, networked, or whatever;

(g) that (underlying the above) it is from the micro-level behaviour of firms that macro-level growth and structural change arise, though causation runs in both directions, since output growth feeds back into investment and innovation through time-saving changes.

My original intention was to reassess theories of growth and structural change in the light of the empirical findings. I have subsequently decided against this, for two sorts of reasons. One is that the discussions in Chapters 2 and 3 were in any event partially directed towards these conclusions, through rather selective use of older and newer economic theories of growth and structural change. A blow-by-blow account of the strengths and weaknesses of each approach in the light of the findings could only be repetitive and tiresome. Most of them contain elements of insight that I have utilized at one stage or another, and are thus constructive contributions. A more fundamental reason is that given by Kuhn (1962) – approaches such as the neoclassical, the institutional economic and the evolutionary economic represent different scientific paradigms, and cannot be accepted or rejected just on the basis of observed data. By making the appropriate ad-hoc assumptions any outcome can be regarded as support for each paradigm. The all-or-nothing attitudes to intellectual supremacy which have permeated these and other approaches are the stuff of academic politics but of questionable benefit in seeking to understand industrialization. The evolutionary approach has been adopted (though not to exclusion) in this book because it puts *change* at the very core of the debate. The disadvantage of evolutionary approaches – and the plural is appropriate here – is that almost anything except time running backwards becomes logically possible, and the formal analysis thus may become intractable. In this book I have tried to show how history selected among the many analytically feasible outcomes, and hence defined what precisely was the role of technology in industrial progress.

References

Abegglen, J.C., and Stalk, G., jr. (1985), *Kaisha: the Japanese corporation*, Basic Books, New York.

Abegglen, J.C. (1994), *Sea Change: Pacific Asia as the new world industrial center*, Free Press, New York.

Abernathy, W.J., and Utterback, J.M. (1978), 'Patterns of industrial innovation', *Technology Review* **80**, pp. 40–7.

Abramovitz, M. (1956), 'Resource and output trends in the United States since 1870', *American Economic Review* **46**, pp. 5–23; repr. in Rosenberg (1971), *op. cit.*, pp. 320–43.

Abramovitz, M. (1961), 'The nature and significance of Kuznets cycles', *Economic Development and Cultural Change* **9**, pp. 225–48.

Abramovitz, M. (1968), 'The passing of the Kuznets cycle', *Economica* **35**, pp. 349–67.

Abramovitz, M. (1986), 'Catching up, forging ahead, and falling behind', *Journal of Economic History* **46**, pp. 385–406.

Abramovitz, M. (1993), 'The search for the sources of economic growth: areas of ignorance, old and new', *Journal of Economic History* **53,** pp. 217–43.

Abramovitz, M. (1994), 'The origins of the postwar catch-up and convergence boom', in Fagerberg *et al.* (1994), *op. cit.*, pp. 21–52.

Aglietta, M. (1979), *A Theory of Capitalist Regulation: the US experience* (transl. D. Fernbach) New Left Books, London; original French edn., Calmann–Lévy, 1976.

Aitken, H.G.J. (1976), *Syntony and Spark: the origins of radio*, John Wiley, New York.

Albert, M. (1993), *Capitalism against Capitalism* (transl. P. Haviland), Whurr Publrs., London; original French edn., Edns. du Seuil, 1991.

Alchian, A., and Demsetz, H. (1972), 'Production, information costs, and economic organization', *American Economic Review* **62,** pp. 777–95.

Aldcroft, D.H. (1992), *Education, Training and Economic Performance, 1944 to 1990*, Manchester University Press, Manchester.

Allen, G.C. (1946), *A Short Economic History of Modern Japan, 1867–1937*, Allen and Unwin, London; revised edn., 1962.

Allen, R.C. (1979), 'International competition in iron and steel, 1850–1913', *Journal of Economic History* **39,** pp. 889–910.

Allen, R.C. (1983), 'Collective invention', *Journal of Economic Behavior and Organization* **4**, pp. 1–24.

Altshuler, A., Anderson, M., Jones, D., Roos, D., and Womack, J. (1985), *The Future of the Automobile: the report of the MIT's international automobile program*, MIT Press, Cambridge MA.

Amann, R., Cooper J., and Davies, R.W. (eds.) (1977), *The Technological Level of Soviet Industry*, Yale University Press, New Haven and London.

Amann, R, and Cooper, J. (eds.) (1982), *Industrial Innovation in the Soviet Union*, Yale University Press, New Haven and London.

Amendola, M. and Gaffard, J.-L. (1988), *The Innovative Choice: an economic analysis of the dynamics of technology*, Blackwell, Oxford and New York.

Ames, E., and Rosenberg, N. (1968), 'The Enfield Arsenal in theory and history', *Economic Journal* **78**, pp. 827–42.

Amsden, A.H. (1977), 'The division of labor is limited by the type of market: the Taiwanese machine tool industry', *World Development* **5**, pp. 217–33.

Amsden, A.H. (1989), *Asia's Next Giant: South Korea and late industrialization*, Oxford University Press, New York and Oxford.

Amsden, A.H., and Hikino, T. (1994), 'Project execution capability, organizational know-how and conglomerate corporate growth in late industrialization', *Industrial and Corporate Change* **3**, pp. 111–48.

Anchordoguy, M. (1989), *Computers Inc.: Japan's challenge to IBM*, Harvard University Press, Cambridge MA.

Andersen, E.S. (1991), 'Techno-economic paradigms as typical interfaces between producers and users', *Journal of Evolutionary Economics* **1**, pp. 119–44.

Aoki, M. (1986), 'Horizontal vs. vertical information structure of the firm', *American Economic Review* **76**, pp. 971–83.

Aoki, M. (1988), *Information, Incentives, and Bargaining in the Japanese Economy*, Cambridge University Press, Cambridge; p/b edn., 1989.

Aoki, M. (1990), 'Towards an economic model of the Japanese firm', *Journal of Economic Literature* **28**, pp. 1–27.

Aoki, M. and Dore R. (eds.) (1994), *The Japanese Firm: sources of competitive strength*, Clarendon Press, Oxford.

Aoki, M., and Patrick, H. (eds.) (1995), *The Japanese Main Bank System: its relevance for developing and transforming economies*, Clarendon Press, Oxford (forthcoming).

Ardeni, P.G., and Wright, B. (1992), 'The Prebisch–Singer hypothesis: a reappraisal independent of stationarity hypotheses', *Economic Journal* **102**, pp. 803–12.

Arrow, K.J. (1962a), 'Economic welfare and the allocation of resources of invention', in R.R. Nelson (ed.), *The Rate and Direction of Inventive Activity: economic and social factors*, Universities – NBER/Princeton University Press, Princeton NJ, pp. 609–25; repr. in Rosenberg (1971), *op. cit.*, pp. 164–81.

Arrow, K.J. (1962b), 'The economic implications of learning by doing', *Review of Economic Studies* **29**, pp. 155–73.

Ashton, T.S. (1955), *An Economic History of England: the 18th century*, Methuen, London.

Ashworth, W. (1986), *The History of the British Coal Industry, vol. 5, 1946–1982: the nationalized industry*, Clarendon Press, Oxford.

Baba, Y. (1985), 'Japanese colour TV firms: decision–making from the 1950s to the 1980s – oligopolistic corporate strategy in the age of micro-electronics', D.Phil. thesis, SPRU, University of Sussex.

Babbage, C. (1832), *On the Economy of Machinery and Manufactures*, Knight, London; repr. Augustus M. Kelley, New York, 1963.

Baily, M.W., and Chakrabarti, A.K. (1985), 'Innovation and productivity in US industry', *Brookings Papers in Economic Activity* **2,** pp. 609–32.

Bairoch, P. (1976), 'Europe's Gross National Product: 1800–1975', *Journal of European Economic History* **5,** pp. 273–340.

Bairoch, P. (1982), 'International industrialization levels from 1750 to 1980', *Journal of European Economic History* **11,** pp. 269–333.

Barras, R. (1986), 'Towards a theory of innovation in services', *Research Policy* **15,** pp. 161–74.

Barras, R. (1990), 'Interactive innovation in financial and business services: the vanguard of the service revolution', *Research Policy* **19,** pp. 215–38.

Barrell, R. (ed.) (1994), *The UK Labour Market: comparative aspects and institutional developments*, NIESR/Cambridge University Press, Cambridge.

Barro, R.J. (1991), 'Economic growth in a cross-section of countries', *Quarterly Journal of Economics* **106,** pp. 407–43.

Baumol, W.J. (1986), 'Productivity growth, convergence, and welfare: what the long-run data show', *American Economic Review* **76,** pp. 1072–85.

Baumol, W.J., Panzar, J., and Willig, R. (1982), *Contestable Markets and the Theory of Industrial Structure*, Harcourt Brace Jovanovich, New York.

Beckerman, W. (1974), *In Defence of Economic Growth*, Cape, London.

Bell, R.M. (1972), *Changing Technology and Manpower Requirements in the Engineering Industry*, Engineering Industry Training Board/Sussex University Press, Brighton.

Bell, M., and Pavitt, K. (1993) 'Technological accumulation and industrial growth: contrasts between developed and developing countries', *Industrial and Corporate Change* **2,** pp. 157–210.

Bell, R.M., and Scott–Kemmis, D. (1985), 'Who learned what by doing what?: a re-examination of "learning by doing" in the airframe and shipbuilding industries', mimeo, SPRU, University of Sussex; forthcoming in *Industrial and Corporate Change*.

Belussi, F. (1987), 'Benetton: the innovation potential of traditional sectors', SPRU Occasional Paper, No. 25.

Belussi, F. (1992), 'Industrial innovation and firm development in Italy: the Veneto case', D.Phil. thesis, SPRU, University of Sussex.

Beniger, J.R. (1986), *The Control Revolution: technological and economic origins of the information society*, Harvard University Press, Cambridge MA.

Berend, I.T., and Ránki, G. (1974), *Economic Development in East–Central Europe in the 19th and 20th Centuries* (transl. R. Rocker), Columbia University Press, New York and London; Hungarian edn. 1969.

Berg, M. (1985), *The Age of Manufactures: industry, innovation and work in Britain, 1700–1820*, Fontana Press, London.

Berg, M. (ed.) (1991), *Markets and Manufacture in Early Industrial Europe*, Routledge, London and New York.

Bergson, A. (1963), 'National income', in A. Bergson and S. Kuznets (eds.), *Economic Trends in the Soviet Union*, Harvard University Press, Cambridge MA, pp. 1–37.

Bergson, A. (1978), *Productivity and the Social System – the USSR and the West*, Harvard University Press, Cambridge MA and London.

Berliner, J.S. (1976), *The Innovation Decision in Soviet Industry*, MIT Press, Cambridge MA and London.

Best, M.H. (1990), *The New Competition: institutions of industrial restructuring*, Polity Press, Cambridge.

Bils, M. (1984), 'Tariff protection and production in the early US cotton textile industry', *Journal of Economic History* **44,** pp. 1033–46.

Biucchi, B.M. (1973), 'Switzerland 1700–1914' (transl. M. Grindod) in Cipolla (1973b), *op. cit.*, pp. 628–55.

Blackburn, P., Coombs, R., and Green, K. (1985), *Technology, Economic Growth and the Labour Process*, Macmillan, London.

Blaug, M. (1962), *Economic Theory in Retrospect*, Irwin; quoted from Heinemann edn., London (1964).

Borchardt, K. (1973) 'Germany 1700–1914' (transl. G. Hammersley), in Cipolla (1973b), *op. cit.*, pp. 76–160.

Braun, E., and Senker, P. (1982), *New Technology and Employment*, Manpower Services Commission, London.

Braverman, H. (1974), *Labor and Monopoly Capital: the degradation of work in the twentieth century*, Monthly Review Press, New York and London.

Broadberry, S.N. (1993), 'Manufacturing and the convergence hypothesis: what the long-run data show', *Journal of Economic History* **53,** pp. 772–95.

Brock, G.W. (1981), *The Telecommunications Industry: the dynamics of market structure*, Harvard University Press, Cambridge MA and London.

Brown, M., and Philips, P. (1986), 'Craft labor and mechanization in 19th-century American canning', *Journal of Economic History* **46,** pp. 743–56.

Bruland, T. (1982), 'Industrial conflict as a source of technical innovation: three cases', *Economy and Society* **11,** pp. 91–121.

Bruland, K. (1989), *British Technology and European Industrialization: the Norwegian textile industry in the mid nineteenth century*, Cambridge University Press, Cambridge.

Bruland, K. (ed.) (1991), *Technology Transfer and Scandinavian Industrialisation*, Berg, New York and Oxford.

Bush, V. (1945), *Science: the Endless Frontier*, National Science Foundation, Washington.

Business Week (1987), 'Can America compete?', 27 April 1987, pp. 40–65.

Business Week (1994), 'America's new growth economy', 16 May 1994, pp. 42–8.

Cafagna, L. (1973), 'Italy 1830–1914' (transl. M. Grindod), in Cipolla (1973b), *op. cit.*, pp. 279–328.

Cain, L.P., and Paterson, D.G. (1981), 'Factor biases and technical change in manufacturing: the American system, 1850–1919', *Journal of Economic History* **41,** pp. 341–60.

Cain, L.P., and Paterson, D.G. (1986), 'Biased technical change, scale, and factor substitution in American industry, 1850–1919', *Journal of Economic History* **46,** pp. 153–64.

Callon, M., Laredo, P., Rabeharisoa, V., Gonard, T., and Leroy, T. (1992), 'The management and evaluation of technological programs and the dynamics of techno-economic networks: the case of the AFME', *Research Policy* **21**, pp. 215–36.

Cameron, R. (1961), *France and the Economic Development of Europe 1800–1914: conquests of peace and seeds of war*, Princeton University Press, Princeton NJ.

Cameron, R. (ed.) (1972), *Banking and Economic Development: some lessons of history*, Oxford University Press, New York.

Cameron, R. (1985), 'A new view of European industrialization', *Economic History Review* **38,** pp. 1–23.

Cameron, R., with Crisp, O., Patrick, H.T., and Tilly, R. (1967), *Banking in the Early Stages of Industrialization: a study in comparative economic history*, Oxford University Press, New York.

Cannadine, D. (1984), 'The past and the present in the English Industrial Revolution 1880–1980', *Past and Present* **103,** pp. 131–72.

Carlsson, B. (1984), 'The development and use of machine tools in historical perspective', *Journal of Economic Behavior and Organization* **5**, pp. 91–114.

Carlsson, B. (1989a), *Industrial Dynamics: technological, organizational, and structural changes in industries and firms*, Kluwer Academic Press, Boston.

Carlsson, B. (1989b), 'The evolution of manufacturing technology and its impact on industrial structure', *Small Business Economics* **1**, pp. 21–37.

Carmichael, H.L., and MacLeod, W.B. (1993), 'Multiskilling, technical change and the Japanese firm', *Economic Journal* **103,** pp. 142–60.

Caron, F. (1979), *An Economic History of Modern France* (transl. B. Bray), Methuen, London.

Carr, M.N. (ed.) (1985), *The A.T. Reader: theory and practice in appropriate technology*, Intermediate Technology Publicns., London.

Catling, H. (1970), *The Spinning Mule*, David and Charles, Newton Abbot.

Chandler, A.D. jr. (1962), *Strategy and Structure: chapters in the history of the American industrial enterprise*, MIT Press, Cambridge MA and London; p/b edn., 1969.

Chandler, A.D. jr. (1965), 'The railroads: pioneers in modern corporate management', *Business History Review* **39,** pp. 16–40.

Chandler, A.D. jr. (1977), *The Visible Hand: the managerial revolution in American business*, Belknap Press, Cambridge MA and London.

Chandler, A.D. jr. (1990), *Scale and Scope: the dynamics of industrial capitalism*, Belknap Press, Cambridge MA and London.

Chandler, A.D. jr. (1992), 'Corporate strategy, structure and control methods in the United States during the 20th century', *Industrial and Corporate Change* **1,** pp. 263–84.

Chandler, A.D. jr., and Daems, H. (1980), *Managerial Hierarchies: comparative perspectives on the rise of the modern industrial enterprise*, Harvard University Press, Cambridge MA and London.

Chandler, A.D. jr., and Redlich, F. (1961), 'Recent developments in American business administration and their conceptualization',

Weltwirtschaftliches Archiv **86,** pp. 103–30; repr. in *Business History Review* **35**, 1961, pp. 1–27.

Chapman, S.D. (1972), *The Cotton Industry in the Industrial Revolution*, Macmillan, London and Basingstoke.

Chenery, H.B., Robinson, S., and Syrquin, M. (eds.) (1986), *Industrialisation and growth: a comparative study*, Oxford University Press/World Bank, New York.

Chu, Y.-H. (1989), 'State structure and economic adjustment of the East Asian Newly Industrializing Countries', *International Organization* **43,** pp. 647–71.

Church, R. (1993), 'The family firm in industrial capitalism: international perspectives on hypotheses and history', *Business History* **35,** pp. 17–43.

CIMA (1992), 'Performance measurement in the manufacturing sector: a pilot study', mimeo, CIMA, London.

Cipolla, C.M. (1973a), *The Fontana Economic History of Europe, vol. 3: The Industrial Revolution*, Collins/Fontana, London.

Cipolla, C.M. (1973b), *The Fontana Economic History of Europe, vol. 4: The Emergence of Industrial Societies*, Collins/Fontana, London, 2 vols.

Clark, C.A. (1940), *The Conditions of Economic Progress*, Macmillan, London; 3rd edn., 1960.

Clark, G. (1994), 'Factory discipline', *Journal of Economic History* **54,** pp. 128–63.

Clark, J.M. (1923), *Studies in the Economics of Overhead Costs*, University of Chicago Press, Chicago.

Clarkson, L.A. (1985), *Proto-industrialization: the first phase of industrialization?* Macmillan, London and Basingstoke.

Coase R.H. (1937), 'The nature of the firm', *Economica* n.s. **4,** pp. 386–405; repr. in Williamson and Winter (1993), *op. cit.*, pp. 18–33.

Cochran, T.C. and Miller, W.. (1942), *The Age of Enterprise: a social history of industrial America*, Macmillan, New York; quoted from the 1960 edn.

Cohen, A.J. (1984), 'Technological change as a historical process: the case of the US pulp and paper industry, 1915–1940', *Journal of Economic History* **44,** pp. 775–99.

Cohen, W.M., and Levinthal, D.A. (1989), 'Innovation and learning: the two faces of R&D', *Economic Journal* **99,** pp. 569–96.

Cole, H.S.D., Freeman, C., Jahoda, M., and Pavitt, K.L.R. (eds.) (1973), *Thinking About the Future: a critique of 'The Limits to Growth'*, Chatto and Windus, London.

Coleman, D.C. (1973), 'Gentlemen and Players', *Economic History Review* **26,** pp. 92–116.

Coleman, D.C. (1983), 'Proto-industrialization: a concept too many?', *Economic History Review* **36,** pp. 435–48.

Coleman, D.C. and MacLeod, C. (1986), 'Attitudes to new techniques: British businessmen, 1800–1950', *Economic History Review* **39,** pp. 588–611.

Constant, E.W. (1983), 'Scientific theory and technological testability: science, dynamometers and water turbines in the nineteenth century', *Technology and Culture* **24,** pp. 183–98.

Corsi, M. (1991), *Division of Labour, Technical Change and Economic Growth*, Avebury/Gower, Aldershot/Brookfield VT.

Crafts, N.F.R. (1983), 'Gross National Product in Europe, 1879–1910: some new estimates', *Explorations in Economic History* **20,** pp. 387–401.

Crafts, N.F.R. (1984), 'Economic growth in France and Britain, 1830–1910: a review of the evidence', *Journal of Economic History* **44,** pp. 49–68.

Crafts, N.F.R. (1985), *British Economic Growth during the Industrial Revolution*, Clarendon Press, Oxford.

Crafts, N.F.R. and Harley, C.K. (1992), 'Output growth and the Industrial Revolution: a restatement of the Crafts–Harley view', *Economic History Review* **45,** pp. 703–30.

Crouzet, F. (1972), 'Editor's Introduction', in F. Crouzet (ed.), *Capital Formation in the Industrial Revolution*, Methuen, London, 1972, pp. 1–69.

Crouzet, F. (1985), *The First Industrialists: a problem of origins*, Cambridge University Press, Cambridge.

Dahlman, C.J., and Frischtak, C.R. (1993), 'National systems supporting technical advance in industry: the Brazilian experience', in Nelson (1993), *op. cit.*, pp. 414–50.

Dahmén, E. (1955), 'Technology, innovations, and international industrial transformation', in L.H. Dupriez (ed.), *Economic Progress*, Institut de Recherches Economiques et Sociales, Louvain, pp. 293–306.

Daly, P. (1985), *The Biotechnology Business: a strategic analysis*, Pinter, London.

Dasgupta, P. and David, P.A. (1987), 'Information disclosure and the economics of science and technology', in G. Feiwel (ed.), *Arrow and the Ascent of Modern Economic Theory*, Macmillan, London.

Dasgupta, P.D., and Stiglitz, J.E. (1980), 'Industrial structure and the nature of innovative activity', *Economic Journal* **90,** pp. 266–93.

David, P.A. (1966), 'The mechanization of reaping in the ante-bellum Midwest', in H. Rosovsky (ed.), *Industrialization in Two Systems: essays in honor of Alexander Gerschenkron*, Wiley, New York, pp. 3–39; repr. in Rosenberg (1971), *op. cit.*, pp. 229–73; also in David (1975), *op. cit.*, pp. 195–232.

David, P.A. (1970), 'Learning by doing and tariff protection: a reconsideration of the case of the ante-bellum United States cotton textile industry', *Journal of Economic History* **30,** pp. 521–601; repr. in David (1975), *op. cit.*, pp. 95–173.

David, P.A. (1975), *Technical Choice, Innovation and Economic Growth: essays on American and British experience in the nineteenth century*, Cambridge University Press, London and New York.

David, P.A. (1992), 'Heroes, herds and hysteresis in technological history: Thomas Edison and "the battle of the systems" reconsidered', *Industrial and Corporate Change* **1,** pp. 129–80.

Davies, S.W. (1979), *The Diffusion of Process Innovations*, Cambridge University Press, Cambridge.

Davis, L.E., and Huttenback, R.A. (1986), *Mammon and the Pursuit of Empire: the political economy of British imperialism, 1860–1912*, Cambridge University Press, Cambridge.

Davis, L.E., and North, D.C. (1971), *Institutional Change and American Economic Growth*, Cambridge University Press, Cambridge.

Delbeke, J. (1981), 'Recent long-wave theories: a critical survey', *Futures* **13**, pp. 246–57; repr. in Freeman 1984, *op. cit.*, pp. 1–12.

De Long, J.B. (1988), 'Productivity, convergence, and welfare: a comment', *American Economic Review* **78,** pp. 1138–54.

De Long, J.B. (1992), 'Productivity growth and machinery investment: a long-run look', *Journal of Economic History* **52,** pp. 307–24.

De Long, J.B., and Summers, L.H. (1991), 'Equipment investment and economic growth', *Quarterly Journal of Economics* **106,** pp. 445–502.

Deming, W.E. (1986), *Out of the Crisis: quality, productivity and competitive position*, Cambridge University Press, Cambridge; 1st edn. 1982.

Denison, E.F. (1962), *The Sources of Economic Growth in the United States, and the alternatives before us*, Committee for Economic Development, New York.

Denison, E.F., and Poullier, J.P. (1967), *Why Growth Rates Differ*, Brookings Institution, Washington.

Dertouzos, M.L., Lester, R.K., and Solow, R.M. (eds.) (1989), *Made in America: regaining the productive edge* (The MIT Commission on Industrial Productivity), MIT Press, Cambridge MA.

Desai, M. (1974), *Marxian Economic Theory*, Gray–Mills, London.

Desai, P. (1987), *The Soviet Economy: problems and prospects*, Blackwell, Oxford.

Devine, W.D. jr. (1983), 'From shafts to wires: historical perspectives on electrification', *Journal of Economic History* **43,** pp. 347–72.

Dhondt, J. and Bruwier, M. (1973), 'The Low Countries 1700–1914' (transl. A.J. Pomerans), in Cipolla (1973b), *op. cit.*, pp. 329–66.

Díaz-Alejandro, C.F. (1965), 'Industrialization and labor productivity differentials', *Review of Economics and Statistics* **47,** pp. 207–14.

Díaz-Alejandro, C.F. (1970), *Essays on the Economic History of the Argentine Republic*, Yale University Press, New Haven and London.

Dintenfass, M. (1992), *The Decline of Industrial Britain 1870–1980*, Routledge, London and New York.

Dodgson, M. (1993), *Technological Collaboration in Industry: strategy, policy and internationalization in innovation*, Routledge, London and New York.

Dollar, D. (1986), 'Technological innovation, capital mobility, and the product cycle in North–South trade', *American Economic Review* **76,** pp. 177–90.

Domar, E.D. (1946), 'Capital expansion, rate of growth and employment', *Econometrica* **14,** pp. 137–47; repr. in Sen (1970), *op. cit.*, pp. 65–77.

Domar, E.D. (1957), *Essays in the Theory of Economic Growth*, Oxford University Press, New York.

Dore, R.P. (1965), *Education in Tokugawa Japan*, Routledge, London.

Dore, R.P. (1973), *British Factory: Japanese Factory: the origins of national diversity in industrial relations*, Allen and Unwin, London.

Dore, R.P. (1986), *Flexible Rigidities: industrial policy and structural adjustment in the Japanese economy, 1970–1980*, Athlone Press, London.

Dore, R.P. (1987), *Taking Japan Seriously: a Confucian perspective on leading economic issues*, Athlone Press, London.

Dornbusch, R. (1976), 'Expectations and exchange rate dynamics', *Journal of Political Economy* **84,** pp. 1161–76.

Dornseifer, B., and Kocka, J. (1993), 'The impact of the preindustrial heritage: reconsiderations on the German pattern of corporate development in the late 19th and early 20th centuries', *Industrial and Corporate Change* **2,** pp. 233–48.

Dosi, G. (1982), 'Technological paradigms and technological trajectories: the determinants and directions of technical change and the transformation of the economy', *Research Policy* **11,** pp. 147–62; repr. in Freeman 1984, *op. cit.*, pp. 78–101.

Dosi, G. (1984), *Technical Change and Industrial Transformation: the theory and an application to the semiconductor industry*, Macmillan, London.

Dosi, G. (1988), 'Sources, procedures, and microeconomic effects of innovation', *Journal of Economic Literature* **26,** pp. 1120–71; repr. in Freeman (1990), *op. cit.*, pp. 107–60.

Dosi, G., Freeman, C., Nelson, R., Silverberg, G., and Soete, L. (eds.) (1988), *Technical Change and Economic Theory*, Pinter, London.

Dosi, G., Giannetti, R., and Toninelli, P.A. (eds.) (1992), *Technology and Enterprise in a Historical Perspective*, Clarendon Press, Oxford.

Dosi, G., Pavitt, K., and Soete, L. (1990), *The Economics of Technical Change and International Trade*, Harvester/Wheatsheaf,

Dowrick, S. (1992), 'Technological catch-up and diverging incomes: patterns of economic growth 1960–88', *Economic Journal* **102,** pp. 600–10.

Dowrick, S. and Nguyen, D.T. (1989), 'OECD comparative economic growth 1950–85: catch-up and convergence', *American Economic Review* **79,** pp. 1010–30.

Du Boff, R. (1967), 'The introduction of electric power in American manufacturing', *Economic History Review* **20,** pp. 509–18.

Dunford, M. (1992), 'Socio-economic trajectories, European integration and regional development in the EC', in D. Dyker (ed.), *The European Economy*, Longman, London and New York, pp. 155–81.

Dutton, H.I. (1984), *The Patent System and Inventive Activity during the Industrial Revolution, 1750–1852*, Manchester University Press, Manchester and Dover NH.

Dutton, H.I., and Jones, S.R.H. (1983), 'Invention and innovation in the British pin industry, 1790–1850', *Business History Review* **57,** pp. 175–93.

Dyker, D.A. (1976), *The Soviet Economy*, Crosby Lockwood Staples, London.

Dyker, D.A. (1992), 'Soviet Union', in D.A. Dyker (ed.), *The National Economies of Europe*, Longman, London and New York, pp. 301–26.

Easterlin, R.A. (1968), *Population, Labor Force, and Long Swings in Economic Growth*, Columbia University Press/NBER, New York.

Edgerton, D.E.H., and Horrocks, S.M. (1994), 'British industrial research and development before 1945', *Economic History Review* **47,** pp. 213–38.

Elbaum, B., and Lazonick, W. (eds.) (1986), *The Decline of the British Economy*, Clarendon Press, Oxford.

Ellman, M.J. (1975), 'Did the agricultural surplus provide the resources for the increase in investment in the USSR during the First Five Year Plan?', *Economic Journal* **85**, pp. 844–63.

Elster, J. (1985), *Making Sense of Marx*, Cambridge University Press, Cambridge.

Enos, J.L., and Park, W.-H. (1988), *The Adoption and Diffusion of Imported Technology: the case of Korea*, Croom Helm, London.

Ergas, H. (1987), 'The importance of technology policy', in P. Dasgupta and P. Stoneman (eds.), *Economic Policy and Technological Performance*, CEPR/Cambridge University Press, Cambridge, pp. 51–96.

Erlich, A. (1960), *The Soviet Industrialization Debate, 1924–1928*, 2nd edn., Harvard University Press, Cambridge MA, 1967.

Esposto, A.G. (1992), 'Italian industrialization and the Gerschenkronian "great spurt": a regional analysis', *Journal of Economic History* **52,** pp. 353–62.

Fagerberg, J. (1988), 'International competitiveness', *Economic Journal* **98,** pp. 355–74.

Fagerberg, J., Verspagen, B., and von Tunzelmann, N. (eds.) (1994), *The Dynamics of Technology, Trade, and Growth*, Edward Elgar, Aldershot.

Faulkner, W., and Arnold, E. (eds) (1985), *Smothered by Invention: technology in women's lives*, Pluto Press, London and Sydney.

Federation of British Industries (1961), *Industrial Research in Manufacturing Industry: 1959–60*, FBI, London.

Fei, J.C.H., and Ranis, G. (1964), *Development of the Labor Surplus Economy: theory and policy*, Irwin, Homewood IL.

Fei, J.C.H., Ranis, G., and Kuo, S.W.Y. (1979), *Growth with Equity: the Taiwan case*, Oxford University Press/World Bank, New York/Washington.

Feinstein, C.H. (1978), 'Capital formation in Great Britain', in P. Mathias and M. Postan (eds.), *The Cambridge Economic History of Europe: vol. VII, part I*, Cambridge University Press, Cambridge, pp. 28–96.

Fellner, W. (1961), 'Two propositions in the theory of induced innovation', *Economic Journal* **71,** pp. 305–8; repr. in Rosenberg (1971), *op. cit.*, pp. 203–8.

Ferraz, J.C., Rush, H., and Miles, I. (1992), *Development, Technology and Flexibility: Brazil faces the industrial divide*, Routledge, London and New York.

Field, A.J. (1979), 'Economic and demographic determinants of educational commitment: Massachusetts, 1855', *Journal of Economic History* **39,** pp. 439–59.

Field, A.J. (1983), 'Land abundance, interest/profit rates, and nineteenth-century American and British technology', *Journal of Economic History* **43,** pp. 405–31.

Field, A.J. (1987), 'Modern business enterprise as a capital-saving innovation', *Journal of Economic History* **47,** pp. 473–85.

Field, A.J. (1992), 'The magnetic telegraph, price and quantity data, and the new management of capital', *Journal of Economic History* **52,** pp. 401–14.

Fischer, W. (1963), 'Government activity and industrialization in Germany (1815–70)', in Rostow (1963), *op. cit.*, pp. 83–94.

Fisher, D., and Thurman, W.N. (1989), 'Sweden's financial sophistication in the nineteenth century: an appraisal', *Journal of Economic History* **49,** pp. 621–34.

Fisher, F.M., and Temin, P. (1973), 'Returns to scale in research and development: what does the Schumpeterian hypothesis imply?', *Journal of Political Economy* **81,** pp. 56–70.

Fishlow, A. (1965), *American Railroads and the Transformation of the Ante-Bellum Economy*, Harvard University Press, Cambridge MA.

Fishlow, A. (1966), 'Levels of nineteenth-century American investment in education', *Journal of Economic History* **26,** pp. 418–36.

Flinn, M.W. (1984), *The History of the British Coal Industry, vol. 2: 1700–1830 : the Industrial Revolution*, Clarendon Press, Oxford.

Floud, R., and McCloskey, D. (eds.) (1994), *The Economic History of Britain since 1700*, 2nd edn., vol. 1: 1700–1860, Cambridge University Press, Cambridge.

Fogel, R.W. (1960), *The Union Pacific Railroad: a case in premature enterprise*, Johns Hopkins University Press, Baltimore.

Fogel, R.W. (1967), 'The specification problem in economic history', *Journal of Economic History* **27,** pp. 283–308.

Fogel, R.W., and Engerman, S.L. (1969), 'A model for the explanation of industrial expansion during the nineteenth century: with an application to the American iron industry', *Journal of Political Economy* **77,** pp. 306–28.

Fogel, R.W., and Engerman, S.L. (eds.) (1971), *The Reinterpretation of American Economic History*, Harper and Row, New York.

Fohlen, C. (1973), 'France 1700–1914' (transl. R. Swann), in Cipolla (1973b), *op. cit.*, pp. 7–75.

Foley, D.K. (1986), *Understanding Capital: Marx's economic theory*, Harvard University Press, Cambridge MA and London.

Ford, A.G. (1962), *The Gold Standard, 1880–1914: Britain and Argentina*, Clarendon Press, Oxford.

Ford, H. (1922), *My Life and Work*, with S. Crowther, Heinemann, London; quoted from 1924 edn.

Ford, H. (1926), 'Mass production', *Encyclopedia Britannica*, 13th edn., Supp. vol. 2, Chicago, pp. 821–3 (written by W.J. Cameron).

Forrester, J.W. (1971) *World Dynamics*, Wright–Allen Press, Cambridge MA, 2nd edn., 1973.

Frankel, M. (1955), 'Obsolescence and technological change in a maturing economy', *American Economic Review* **45,** pp. 296–319.

Franko, L.G. (1976), *The European Multinationals: a renewed challenge to American and British big business*, Harper and Row, London.

Fransman, M. (1985), 'Conceptualising technical change in the Third World in the 1980s: an interpretive survey', *Journal of Development Studies* **21,** pp. 572–652.

Fransman, M. (1990), *The Market and Beyond: cooperation and competition in information technology in the Japanese system*, Cambridge University Press, Cambridge.

Fransman, M. (1994). 'Information, knowledge, vision, and theories of the firm', *Industrial and Corporate Change* **3**, pp. 713–58.

Freeman, C. (1982), *The Economics of Industrial Innovation*, 2nd revised edn., Pinter, London; 1st edn. Penguin Books, Harmondsworth Middx., 1974.

Freeman, C. (ed.) (1984), *Long Waves in the World Economy*, Pinter, London and Dover NH.

Freeman, C. (1987), *Technology Policy and Economic Performance: lessons from Japan*, Pinter, London and New York.

Freeman, C. (1989), 'The third Kondratieff wave: age of steel, electrification and imperialism', mimeo, SPRU/MERIT, Sussex/Maastricht.

Freeman, C. (ed.) (1990), *The Economics of Innovation*, Elgar Reference, Aldershot and Brookfield VT.

Freeman, C. (1993), 'Interdependence of technological change with growth of trade and GNP', in M. Nissanka and A. Hewitt (eds.), *Economic Crisis in Developing Countries*, Pinter, London and New York, pp. 157–77.

Freeman, C. (1994), 'Technological revolutions and catching-up: ICT and the NICs', in Fagerberg *et al.* (1994), *op. cit.*, pp. 198–221.

Freeman, C., Clark, J.A., and Soete, L. (1982), *Unemployment and Technical Innovation: a study of long waves and economic development*, Pinter, London.

Freeman, C. and Perez, C. (1988), 'Structural crises of adjustment: business cycles and investment behaviour', in Dosi *et al.* (1988), *op. cit.*, pp. 38–66.

Freeman, C. and Young, A. (1965), *The Research and Development Effort: in Western Europe, North America and the Soviet Union*, OECD, Paris.

Fridenson, P. (1978), 'The coming of the assembly line to Europe', in Krohn *et al.* (1978), *op. cit.*, pp. 159–76.

Fukasaku, Y. (1991), 'In-firm training at Mitsubishi Nagasaki Shipyard, 1884–1934', in H.F. Gospel (ed.), *Industrial Training and Technological Innovation*, Routledge, London and New York, pp. 148–71.

Fukasaku, Y. (1992), *Technology and Industrial Development in Pre-war Japan: Mitsubishi Nagasaki Shipyard 1884–1934*, Routledge, London and New York.

Furtado, C. (1970), *Economic Development of Latin America: a survey from colonial times to the Cuban Revolution*, Cambridge University Press, Cambridge.

Gaio, F.J. (1990), 'The development of computer software technological capabilities in developing countries: a case study of Brazil', D.Phil. thesis, SPRU, University of Sussex.

Galambos, L. (1968), 'The agrarian image of the large corporation, 1879–1920: a study in social accommodation', *Journal of Economic History* **28,** pp. 341–62.

Galambos, L. (1988), 'What have CEOs been doing?', *Journal of Economic History* **48,** pp. 243–58.

Galbraith, J.K. (1952), *American Capitalism: the concept of countervailing power*, Houghton Mifflin, Boston; 2nd edn., Blackwell, Oxford, 1980.

Galbraith, J.K. (1955), *The Great Crash, 1929*, Hamish Hamilton, London.

Galbraith, J.K. (1958), *The Affluent Society*, Houghton Mifflin, Boston; 4th edn., Andre Deutsch, London, 1985.

Gatrell, V.A.C. (1977), 'Labour, power, and the size of firms in Lancashire cotton in the second quarter of the nineteenth century', *Economic History Review* **30,** pp. 95–139.

Gerschenkron, A. (1952), 'Economic backwardness in historical perspective', in B. Hoselitz (ed.), *The Progress of Underdeveloped Areas*, Chicago University Press, Chicago, pp. 3–29.

Gerschenkron, A. (1962), *Economic Backwardness in Historical Perspective: a book of essays*, Belknap Press, Cambridge MA.

Gerschenkron, A. (1963), 'The early phases of industrialization in Russia: afterthoughts and counterthoughts', in Rostow (1963), *op. cit.*, pp. 151–69.

Gerschenkron, A. (1968), *Continuity in History, and other essays*, Belknap Press, Cambridge MA.

Gibbons, M., and Johnston, R. (1974), 'The roles of science in technological innovation', *Research Policy* **3,** pp. 220–42.

Gille, B. (1973), 'Banking and industrialisation in Europe, 1730–1914' (transl. R. Greaves), in Cipolla (1973a), *op. cit.*, pp. 255–300.

Glaziev, S., and Schneider, C.M. (eds) (1993), *Research and Development Management in the Transition to a Market Economy*, IIASA, Laxenburg.

Goldfrank, W.L. (ed.) (1979), *The World-System of Capitalism: past and present*, Sage Publicns., Beverly Hills and London.

Gomulka, S. (1990), *The Theory of Technological Change and Economic Growth*, Routledge, London and New York.

Goodman, J., and Honeyman, K. (1988), *Gainful Pursuits: the making of industrial Europe 1600–1914*, Edward Arnold, London.

Granick, D. (1954), *Management of the Industrial Firm in the USSR: a study in Soviet economic planning*, Columbia University Press, New York.

Granick, D. (1967), *Soviet Metal-Fabricating and Economic Development: practice versus policy*, University of Wisconsin Press, Madison WI and London.

Granstrand, Ö., Håkanson, L., and Sjölander, S. (eds.) (1992), *Technology Management and International Business: internationalization of R&D and technology*, Wiley, Chichester.

Graves, A. (1990), 'Environmental issues and European collaboration in automotive R&D – Prometheus', mimeo, SPRU.

Graves, A. (1991), 'International competitiveness in technology development in the world automobile industry', D.Phil. thesis, SPRU, University of Sussex.

Gregory, G. (1985), *Japanese Electronics Technology: enterprise and innovation*, Wiley, New York; 2nd edn., 1986.

Griffiths, T., Hunt, P.A., and O'Brien, P.K. (1992), 'Inventive activity in the British textile industry, 1700–1800', *Journal of Economic History* **52,** pp. 881–906.

Griliches, Z. (1986), 'Productivity, R&D, and basic research at the firm level in the 1970's', *American Economic Review* **76**, pp. 141–154.

Gross, N.T. (1973), 'The Habsburg Monarchy 1750–1914', in Cipolla (1973b), *op. cit.*, pp. 228–78.

Grossman, G. (1973), 'Russia and the Soviet Union', in Cipolla (1973b), *op. cit.*, pp. 486–531.

Guy, D.J. (1984), 'Dependency, the credit market, and Argentine industrialization, 1860–1940', *Business History Review* **58,** pp. 532–61.

Habakkuk, H.J. (1962), *American and British Technology in the Nineteenth Century: the search for labour-saving inventions*, Cambridge University Press, Cambridge.

Haber, L.F. (1958), *The Chemical Industry during the Nineteenth Century: a study of the economic aspect of applied chemistry in Europe and North America*, Clarendon Press, Oxford.

Haber, S.H. (1991), 'Industrial concentration and the capital markets: a comparative study of Brazil, Mexico and the United States, 1830–1930', *Journal of Economic History* **51,** pp. 559–80.

Hafter, D.M. (1984), 'The business of invention in the Paris industrial exposition of 1806', *Business History Review* **58,** pp. 317–35.

Hagedoorn, J. (1989), *The Dynamic Analysis of Innovation and Diffusion*, Pinter, London.

Hagedoorn, J., and Schakenraad, J. (1992), 'Leading companies and networks of strategic alliances in information technologies', *Research Policy* **21**, pp. 163–90.

Haggard, S. (1988), 'The politics of industrialization in the Republic of Korea and Taiwan', in H. Hughes (ed.), *Achieving Industrialization in East Asia*, Cambridge University Press, Cambridge, pp. 260–82.

Hahn, F., and Matthews, R.C.O. (1964), 'The theory of economic growth: a survey', *Economic Journal* **74,** pp. 779–902.

Hamilton, A. (1791), 'Report on Manufactures', repr. in J.E. Cooke (ed.), *The Reports of Alexander Hamilton*, Harper Torchbooks, New York, 1964, pp. 115–205.

Hannah, L. (1974), 'Managerial innovation and the rise of the large-scale company in interwar Britain', *Economic History Review* **27,** pp. 252–70.

Hannah, L. (1976), *The Rise of the Corporate Economy*, Methuen, London.

Hanson, P., and Pavitt, K. (1987), *The Comparative Economics of Research Development and Innovation in East and West: a survey*, Harwood Academic, Chur.

Harley, C.K. (1993), 'Reassessing the Industrial Revolution: a macro view', in Mokyr (1993), *op. cit.*, pp. 171–226.

Harris, J.R. (1988), *The British Iron Industry, 1750–1850*, Macmillan, Basingstoke.

Harrison, J. (1983), 'Heavy industry, the state, and economic development in the Basque region, 1876–1936', *Economic History Review* **36,** pp. 535–51.

Harrod, R.F. (1939), 'An essay in dynamic theory', *Economic Journal* **49,** pp. 14–33; repr. in Sen (1970), *op. cit.*, pp. 43–64.

Hatton, T.J., Lyons, J.S., and Satchell, S.E. (1983), 'Eighteenth-century British trade: homespun or empire-made?', *Explorations in Economic History* **20,** pp. 163–82.

Hawke, G.R. (1970), *Railways and Economic Growth in England and Wales 1840–1870*, Clarendon Press, Oxford.

Hawke, G.R. (1975), 'The United States tariff and industrial protection in the late nineteenth century', *Economic History Review* **28,** pp. 84–99.

Hayami, Y., and Ruttan, V.W. (1971), *Agricultural Development: an international perspective*, Johns Hopkins Press, Baltimore and London.

Hayek, F.A. von (1945), 'The use of knowledge in society', *American Economic Review* **35,** pp. 519–30.

Hayes, P. (1987), 'Carl Bosch and Carl Krausch: chemistry and the political economy of Germany, 1925–1945', *Journal of Economic History* **47,** pp. 353–63.

Hayes, R. and Abernathy, W.J. (1980), 'Managing our way to economic decline', *Harvard Business Review* **58,** pp. 67–77.

Hayes, R.H., and Wheelwright, S.C. (1984), *Restoring our Competitive Edge: competing through manufacturing*, Wiley, New York.

Headrick, D. (1981), *The Tools of Empire: technology and European imperialism in the nineteenth century*, Oxford University Press, New York and Oxford.

Hertner, P., and Jones, G. (eds.) (1986), *Multinationals: theory and history*, Gower/European Science Foundation, Aldershot and Brookfield VT.

Hicks, J.R. (1965), *Capital and Growth*, Clarendon Press, Oxford.

Hicks, J. (1969), *A Theory of Economic History*, Clarendon Press, Oxford.

Hicks, J.R. (1973), *Capital and Time: a neo-Austrian theory*, Clarendon Press, Oxford.

Hilferding, R. (1981), *Finance Capital: a study of the latest phase of capitalist development* (transl. M. Watnick and S. Gordon, ed. T. Bottomore), Routledge, London; 1st German edn., Wiener Volksbuchhandlung, Vienna, 1910.

Himmelfarb, G. (1984), *The Idea of Poverty: England in the early industrial age*, Faber, London.

Hirschman, A.O. (1957), 'Investment policies and 'dualism' in underdeveloped countries', *American Economic Review* **47**, pp. 550–70.

Hirschman, A.O. (1958), *The Strategy of Economic Development*, Yale University Press, New Haven and London; p/b edn. 1961.

Hobday, M. (1994), 'Export–led technology development in the Four Tigers: the case of electronics', *Development and Change* **25**, pp. 333–61.

Hohenberg, P.M. (1967), *Chemicals in Western Europe, 1850–1914: an economic study of technical change*, Rand McNally, Chicago, and North-Holland, Amsterdam.

Honeyman, K. (1982), *Origins of Enterprise: business leadership in the Industrial Revolution*, Manchester University Press, Manchester.

Hounshell, D.A. (1984), *From the American System to Mass Production, 1800–1932: the development of manufacturing technology in the United States*, Johns Hopkins University Press, Baltimore and London.

Hounshell, D.A., and Smith, J.K. (1988), *Science and Corporate Strategy: Du Pont R&D, 1902–80*, Cambridge University Press, New York.

Houston, R., and Snell, K.D.M. (1984), 'Proto-industrialization: cottage industry, social change and the Industrial Revolution', *Historical Journal* **27**, pp. 473–92.

Howard, M.C., and King, J.E. (1985), *The Political Economy of Marx*, Longman, London and New York, 2nd edn.; 1st edn. 1975.

Howson, S. (1975), *Domestic Monetary Management in Britain, 1919–38*, University of Cambridge DAE Occasional Paper 48, Cambridge University Press, Cambridge.

Hubbard, G.E. (1935), *Eastern Industrialization and its Effect on the West: with special reference to Great Britain and Japan*, Oxford University Press/Royal Institute of International Affairs, London.

Hughes, T.P. (1983), *Networks of Power: electrification in western society, 1800–1930*, Johns Hopkins University Press, Baltimore.

Hume, D. (1955), *Writings on Economics* (ed. E. Rotwein), Nelson, Edinburgh; based on *Political Discourses*, 1st edn., Edinburgh 1752, and *Essays and Treatises on Several Subjects*, 1758 edn., London.

Hunter, L.C. (1929), 'The influence of the market upon techniques in the iron industry in Western Pennsylvania up to 1860', *Journal of Economic and Business History* **1,** pp. 241–81.

Hunter, L.C. (1949), *Steamboats on Western Rivers: an economic and technological history*, Harvard University Press, Cambridge MA.

Hunter, L.C., and Bryant, L. (1991), *A History of Industrial Power in the United States, 1780–1930, vol. 3: the transmission of power*, MIT Press, Cambridge MA and London.

Hyde, C.K. (1977), *Technological Change and the British Iron Industry, 1700–1870*, Princeton University Press, Princeton NJ.

Imai, K. (1989), 'Evolution of Japan's corporate and industrial networks', in Carlsson (1989a), *op. cit.*, pp. 123–56.

Imai, K., Nonaka, I., and Takeuchi, H. (1985), 'Managing the new product development process: how Japanese companies learn and unlearn', in K.B. Clark, R.H. Hayes and C. Lorenz (eds.), *The Uneasy Alliance: managing the productivity–technology dilemma*, Harvard Business School Press, Boston, pp. 337–82.

Ingham, G. (1984), *Capitalism Divided?: the city and industry in British social development*, Macmillan, Basingstoke and London.

Isard, W. (1948), 'Some locational factors in the iron and steel industry since the early nineteenth century', *Journal of Political Economy* **56,** pp. 203–17.

James, J.A. (1983), 'Structural change in American manufacturing, 1850–1890', *Journal of Economic History* **43,** pp. 433–60.

James, J.A., and Skinner, J.S. (1985), 'The resolution of the labor-scarcity paradox', *Journal of Economic History* **45,** pp. 513–40.

Johnson, C. (1982), *MITI and the Japanese Miracle: the growth of industrial policy, 1925–1975*, Stanford University Press, Stanford CA.

Jones, E.L. (1965), 'Agriculture and economic growth in England, 1660–1750: agricultural change', *Journal of Economic History* **25,** pp. 1–18.

Jones, E.L. (1988), *Growth Recurring: economic change in world history*, Clarendon Press, Oxford.

Jörberg, L. (1973), 'The Nordic countries 1850–1914' (transl. P.B. Austin), in Cipolla (1973b), *op. cit.*, pp. 375–485.

Jorgenson, D.W., and Griliches, Z. (1967), 'The explanation of productivity change', *Review of Economic Studies* **34,** pp. 249–83; repr. in Sen (1970), *op. cit.*, pp. 420–73.

Kagono, T., Nonaka, Y., Sakakibara, K., and Okumura, A. (1985), *Strategic vs. Evolutionary Management: a US–Japan comparison of strategy and organization*, North-Holland, Amsterdam.

Kaldor, M. (1982), *The Baroque Arsenal*, Deutsch, London.

Kaldor, N. (1966), *Causes of the Slow Rate of Economic Growth in the United Kingdom*, Cambridge University Press, Cambridge.

Kamien, M.I., and Schwartz, N.L. (1975), 'Market structure and innovative activity: a survey', *Journal of Economic Literature* **13,** pp. 1–37.

Kamien, M.I., and Schwartz, N.L. (1982), *Market Structure and Innovation*, Cambridge University Press, Cambridge.

Kaplinsky, R. (1984), *Automation: the technology and society*, Longman, Harlow.

Katz, J. (1985), 'Domestic technological innovations and dynamic comparative advantages: further reflections on a comparative case-study programme', in Rosenberg and Frischtak (1985), *op. cit.*, pp. 127–66.

Katz, J.M. (ed.) (1987), *Technology Generation in Latin American Manufacturing Industries*, Macmillan, London and Basingstoke.

Katz, J.M., and Bercovich, N.A. (1993), 'National systems of innovation supporting technical advance in industry: the case of Argentina', in Nelson (1993), *op. cit.*, pp. 451–75.

Kay, J.A., and Thompson, D.J. (1986), 'Privatisation: a policy in search of a rationale', *Economic Journal* **96,** pp. 18–32.

Keck, O. (1993), 'The national system for technical innovation in Germany', in Nelson (1993), *op. cit.*, pp. 115–57.

Kemp, T. (1969), *Industrialization in Nineteenth-century Europe*, Longmans, London and Harlow.

Kemp, T. (1971), *Economic Forces in French History: an essay on the development of the French economy, 1760–1914*, Dennis Dobson, London.

Kendrick, J.W. (1983), *Interindustry Differences in Productivity Growth*, American Enterprise Institute, Washington.

Kennedy, C. (1964), 'Induced bias in innovation and the theory of distribution', *Economic Journal* **74,** pp. 541–7.

Kennedy, W. (1987), *Industrial Structure, Capital Markets, and the Origins of British Industrial Decline*, Cambridge University Press, Cambridge.

Kenney, M. (1986), 'Schumpeterian innovation and entrepreneurs in capitalism: a case study of the US biotechnology industry', *Research Policy* **15,** pp. 21–32.

Kenwood, A.G., and Lougheed, A.L. (1982), *Technological Diffusion and Industrialisation before 1914*, Croom Helm/St Martin's Press, London and Canberra/New York.

Keynes, J.M. (1930), *A Treatise on Money, vol. II*, repr. as *The Collected Writings of John Maynard Keynes, Vol. VI*, Macmillan/Royal Economic Society, London and Basingstoke, 1971.

Keynes, J.M. (1933), *Essays in Biography*, repr. as *The Collected Writings of John Maynard Keynes, vol. X*, Macmillan/Royal Economic Society, London and Basingstoke, 1973.

Keynes, J.M. (1936), *The General Theory of Employment, Interest and Money*, repr. as *The Collected Writings of John Maynard Keynes, vol. VII*, Macmillan/Royal Economic Society, London and Basingstoke, 1973.

Keynes, J.M. (1937), 'Some economic consequences of a declining population', *Eugenics Review* **29,** pp. 13–17; repr. in *The Collected Writings of John Maynard Keynes, vol. XIV*, Macmillan/Royal Economic Society, London and Basingstoke, 1973, pp. 124–33.

Khan, B.Z. and Sokoloff, K.L. (1993), '"Schemes of practical utility": entrepreneurship and innovation among "great inventors" in the United States, 1790–1865', *Journal of Economic History* **53,** pp. 289–307.

Kim, L. (1993), 'National system of innovation: dynamics of capability building in Korea', in Nelson (1993), *op. cit.*, pp. 357–83.

Kim, S.R. (1993), 'Beyond state and market – the role of the state in Korean industrial development: the case of machine tools', mimeo, Wissenschaftszentrum Berlin für Sozialforschung.

Kindleberger, C.P. (1964), *Economic Growth in France and Britain: 1851–1950*, Simon and Schuster, New York; p/b edn., 1969.

Kindleberger, C.P. (1967), *Europe's Postwar Growth: the role of labor supply*, Harvard University Press/Oxford University Press, Cambridge MA/London.

Kindleberger, C.P. (1973), *The World in Depression, 1929–1939*, Allen Lane, London.

Klein, B. (1977), *Dynamic Economics*, Harvard University Press, Cambridge MA.

Kleinknecht, A. (1981), 'Observations on the Schumpeterian swarming of innovations', *Futures* **13**, pp. 293–307; repr. in Freeman 1984, *op. cit.*, pp. 48–62.

Kobayashi, K. (1986), *Computers and Communications: a vision of C&C*, MIT Press, Cambridge MA.

Kocka, J. (1980), 'The rise of the modern industrial enterprise in Germany', in Chandler and Daems (1980), *op. cit.*, pp. 77–116.

Kocka, J. (1981), 'Capitalism and bureaucracy in German industrialization before 1914', *Economic History Review* **34,** pp. 453–68.

Kodama, F. (1991), *Analysing Japanese High Technologies*, Pinter, London.

Kœrgård, N. (1990), 'The industrial development of Denmark, 1840–1914', *Journal of European Economic History* **19,** pp. 271–92.

Kogut, B. (ed.) (1993), *Country Competitiveness: technology and the organizing of work*, Oxford University Press, New York and Oxford.

Kondratieff, N. (1984), *The Long Wave Cycle* (transl. G. Daniels), Richardson and Snyder, New York.

Kornai, J. (1980), *The Economics of Shortage*, North-Holland, Amsterdam.

Kornai, J. (1992), *The Socialist System: the political economy of communism*, Clarendon Press, Oxford.

Kravis, I.B. (1970), 'Trade as a handmaiden of growth', *Economic Journal* **80**, pp. 850–72.

Kriedte, P., Medick H., and Schlumbohm, J. (1981), *Industrialization before Industrialization: rural industry in the genesis of capitalism* (transl. B. Schempp), Cambridge University Press, Cambridge; original German edn. 1977.

Krohn, W., Layton, E.T. jr., and Weingart, P. (1978), *The Dynamics of Science and Technology: social values, technical norms and scientific criteria in the development of knowledge*, Reidel, Dordrecht and Boston.

Krugman, P. (1979), 'A model of innovation, technology transfer, and the world distribution of income', *Journal of Political Economy* **87,** pp. 253–66.

Krugman, P.R. (ed.) (1986), *Strategic Trade Policy and the New International Economics*, MIT Press, Cambridge MA.

Krugman, P.R. (1990), *Rethinking International Trade*, MIT Press, Cambridge MA and London.

Kuhn, T.S. (1962), *The Structure of Scientific Revolutions*, University of Chicago Press, Chicago and London; 2nd enlarged edn.,1970.

Kuznets, S. (1930), *Secular Movements in Production and Prices: their nature and their bearing upon cyclical fluctuations*, Houghton Mifflin, Boston and New York; repr. Kelley, New York, 1967.

Kuznets, S. (1940), 'Schumpeter's business cycles', *American Economic Review* **30**, pp. 257–71.

Kuznets, S. (1959), *Six Lectures on Economic Growth*, Free Press of Glencoe, New York.

Kuznets, S. (1964), *Postwar Economic Growth: four lectures*, Belknap Press, Cambridge MA.

Kuznets, S. (1965), *Economic Growth and Structure: selected essays*, Norton, New York.

Kuznets, S. (1966), *Modern Economic Growth: rate, structure, and spread*, Yale University Press, New Haven and London.

Kuznets, S. (1971), *Economic Growth of Nations: total output and production structure*, Belknap Press, Cambridge MA.

Kuznets, S. (1973), 'Modern economic growth: findings and reflections', *American Economic Review* **63,** pp. 247–58.

Kuznets, S. (1974), *Population, Capital, and Growth: selected essays*, Heinemann, London; American edn., Norton, New York, 1973.

Kuznets, S. (1979), *Growth, Population, and Income Distribution: selected essays*, Norton, New York and London.

Kuznets, S. (1989), *Economic Development, the Family, and Income Distribution: selected essays*, Cambridge University Press, Cambridge.

Kuznetsov, Y. (1993), 'Development of firm-level organizational capabilities to enhance manufacturing exports: lessons from the Commonwealth of Independent States', mimeo, ICRET, Moscow.

Lakatos, I. (1987), *The Methodology of Scientific Research Programmes: philosophical papers vol. 1* (ed. J. Worrall and G. Currie), Cambridge University Press, Cambridge.

Lampe, J.R. (1972), 'Serbia, 1878–1912', in Cameron (1972), *op. cit.*, pp. 122–67.

Lampert, N. (1979), *The Technical Intelligentsia and the Soviet State: a study of Soviet managers and technicians 1928–1935*, CREES/Macmillan, Birmingham/London and Basingstoke.

Landes, D.S. (1969), *The Unbound Prometheus: technological change and industrial development in Western Europe from 1750 to the present*, Cambridge University Press, Cambridge.

Landes, D.S. (1983), *Revolution in Time: clocks and the making of the modern world*, Harvard University Press, Cambridge MA.

Landes, D.S. (1986), 'What do bosses really do?', *Journal of Economic History* **46,** pp. 585–624.

Landes, D.S. (1993), 'The fable of the dead horse; or, the Industrial Revolution revisited', in Mokyr (1993), *op. cit.*, pp. 132–70.

Landes, W.M., and Solmon, L.C. (1972), 'Compulsory schooling legislation: an economic analysis of law and social change in the nineteenth century', *Journal of Economic History* **32,** pp. 54–97.

Langlois, R.N. (1986), 'Science, technology and public policy: lessons from the classicals', mimeo, University of Connecticut (Storrs).

Langlois, R. (1992), 'Transaction-cost economics in real time', *Industrial and Corporate Change* **1,** pp. 99–128.

Langlois, R.N., and Robertson, P.L. (1989), 'Explaining vertical integration: lessons from the American automobile industry', *Journal of Economic History* **49,** pp. 361–75.

Lastres, H.M.M. (1992), 'Advanced materials and the Japanese National System of Innovation', D.Phil. thesis, SPRU, University of Sussex.

Latsis, S.J. (ed.) (1976), *Method and Appraisal in Economics*, Cambridge University Press, Cambridge.

Lazonick, W. (1979), 'Industrial relations and technical change: the case of the self-acting mule', *Cambridge Journal of Economics* **3,** pp. 231–62.

Lazonick, W. (1981a), 'Factor costs and the diffusion of ring spinning in Britain prior to World War I', *Quarterly Journal of Economics* **96,** pp. 89–109; repr. in Lazonick 1992, *op. cit.*, pp. 20–40.

Lazonick, W. (1981b), 'Competition, specialization, and industrial decline', *Journal of Economic History* **31,** pp. 31–8.

Lazonick, W. (1983), 'Industrial organization and technological change: the decline of the British cotton industry', *Business History Review* **57,** pp. 195–236; repr. in Lazonick 1992, *op. cit.*, pp. 41–82.

Lazonick, W. (1990), *Competitive Advantage on the Shop Floor*, Harvard University Press, Cambridge MA and London.

Lazonick, W. (1991), *Business Organization and the Myth of the Market Economy*, Cambridge University Press, Cambridge.

Lazonick, W. (1992), *Organization and Technology in Capitalist Development*, Edward Elgar, Aldershot and Brookfield VT.

Lee, K.-R. (1993), 'The role of user firms in industrial innovation: the case of machine tools in Japan and Korea', D.Phil. thesis, SPRU, University of Sussex.

Lee, W.R. (1988), 'Economic development and the state in 19th-century Germany', *Economic History Review* **41,** pp. 346–67.

Leff, N.H. (1982), *Underdevelopment and Development in Brazil, vol. I: economic structure and change, 1822–1947*, Allen and Unwin, London.

Leijonhufvud, A. (1968), *On Keynesian Economics and the Economics of Keynes*, Oxford University Press, New York.

Lenin, V.I. (1917), *Imperialism: The Highest Stage of Capitalism: a popular outline*, Petrograd; repr. International Publishers, New York, 1977.

Leontief, W. (1953), 'Domestic production and foreign trade: the American capital position re-examined', *Proceedings of the American Philosophical Society* **97**; repr. in *Economia Internazionale* 7 (1954).

Lévy–Leboyer, M. (1980), 'The Large Corporation in Modern France', in Chandler and Daems (1980), *op. cit.*, pp. 117–60.

Levin, R.C., Klevorick, A.K., Nelson, R.R., and Winter, S.G. (1987), 'Appropriating the returns from industrial research and development', *Brookings Papers on Economic Activity* **1987:3,** pp. 783–831.

Lewchuk, W.A. (1984), 'The role of the British government in the spread of scientific management and Fordism in the interwar years', *Journal of Economic History* **44,** pp. 355–61.

Lewchuk, W.A. (1987), *American Technology and the British Vehicle Industry*, Cambridge University Press, Cambridge.

Lewis, G. (1991), 'The constraints of a proto-industrial society on the development of heavy industry: the case of coal-mining in the south-east of France, 1773–1791', in P. Mathias and J.A. Davis (eds.), *Innovation and Technology in Europe: from the eighteenth century to the present day*, Blackwell, Oxford and Cambridge MA, pp. 65–82.

Lewis, R. (1979), *Science and Industrialisation in the USSR: industrial research and development, 1917–1940*, CREES/Macmillan, Birmingham/London and Basingstoke.

Lewis, W.A. (1954), 'Economic development with unlimited supplies of labour', *Manchester School of Economic and Social Studies* **22,** pp. 139–91.

Lewis, W.A. (1955), *The Theory of Economic Growth*, Allen and Unwin, London.

Lewis, W.A. (1958), 'Unlimited labour: further notes', *Manchester School of Economic and Social Studies* **26,** pp. 1–32.

Lewis, W.A. (1978), *Growth and Fluctuations, 1870–1913*, Allen and Unwin, London.

Lewis, W.A. (1980), 'The slowing down of the engine of growth' (Nobel lecture), *American Economic Review* **70**, pp. 555–64.

Liebenau, J. (1987), *Medical Science and Medical Industry: the formation of the American pharmaceutical industry*, Macmillan, Basingstoke and London.

Lilja, K., Tainio, R., Gaskov, V., Tornqvist, S., and Lopponen, P. (1989), 'Adjusting to perestroika: the case of Svetogorsk mills', working paper, Helsinki School of Economics.

Lilley, S. (1973), 'Technological progress and the Industrial Revolution', in Cipolla (1973a), *op. cit.*, pp. 187–254.

Lindbeck, A. (1983), 'The recent slowdown of productivity growth', *Economic Journal* **93**, pp. 13–34.

List, F. (1844), *The National System of Political Economy* (transl. S.S. Lloyd), new edn (ed. J.S. Nicholson), Longmans, Green and Co., London, 1904.

Litterer, J.A. (1961), 'Systematic management: the search for order and integration', *Business History Review* **35,** pp. 461–76.

Littler, C.R. (1982), *The Development of the Labour Process in Capitalist Societies: a comparative study of the transformation of work organization in Britain, Japan and the USA*, Heinemann Educational, London.

Livesay, H.C., and Porter, P.G. (1969), 'Vertical integration in American manufacturing, 1899–1948', *Journal of Economic History* **29**, pp. 494–500.

Locke, R.R. (1984), *The End of the Practical Man: entrepreneurship and higher education in Germany, France, and Great Britain, 1880–1940*, JAI Press, Greenwich CT and London.

Lockwood, W.W. (1954), *The Economic Development of Japan: growth and structural change 1868–1938*, Princeton University Press, Princeton NJ, expanded edn. 1968.

Lockwood, W.W. (ed.) (1965), *The State and Economic Enterprise in Japan: essays in the political economy of growth*, Princeton University Press, Princeton NJ.

Lorenz, E.H. (1984), 'Two patterns of development: the labour process in the British and French shipbuilding industries 1880 to 1930', *Journal of European Economic History* **13**, pp. 599–634.

Lucas, R.E. jr. (1986), 'Adaptive behavior and economic theory', *Journal of Business* **59**, pp. S401–26.

Lucas, R.E. jr. (1988), 'On the mechanics of economic development', *Journal of Monetary Economics* **22**, p. 3–42.

Lundvall, B.-Å. (ed.) (1992), *National Systems of Innovation: towards a theory of innovation and interactive learning*, Pinter, London.

MacAvoy, P.W. (1965), *The Economic Effects of Regulation: the trunk line railroad cartels and the Interstate Commerce Commission before 1900*, MIT Press, Cambridge MA.

McCloskey, D.N. (1973a), *Economic Maturity and Entrepreneurial Decline: British iron and steel, 1870–1913*, Cambridge MA.

McCloskey, D.N. (1973b), 'New perspectives on the Old Poor Law', *Explorations in Economic History* **10**, pp. 419–36.

McCloskey, D.N. (1981), *Enterprise and Trade in Victorian Britain: essays in historical economics*, Allen and Unwin, London.

McCormick, W.W. and Franks, C.M. (1971), 'A self-generating model of long-swings for the American economy, 1860–1940', *Journal of Economic History* **31**, pp. 295–343.

McIntosh, J. (1986), 'Economic growth and technical change in Britain 1950–1978', *European Economic Review* **30**, pp. 117–28.

MacKenzie, D. (1984), 'Marx and the machine', *Technology and Culture* **25**, pp. 473–502.

MacLeod, C. (1988), *Inventing the Industrial Revolution: the English patent system, 1660–1800*, Cambridge University Press, Cambridge.

MacLeod, C. (1992), 'Strategies for innovation: the diffusion of new technology in nineteenth-century British industry', *Economic History Review* **45**, pp. 285–307.

Macpherson, W.J. (1987), *The Economic Development of Japan, c. 1868–1941*, Macmillan, Basingstoke and London.

Maddison, A. (1982), *Phases of Capitalist Development*, Oxford University Press, Oxford.

Maddison, A. (1983), 'A comparison of the levels of GDP per capita in developed and developing countries, 1700–1980', *Journal of Economic History* **43**, pp. 27–42.

Maddison, A. (1991), *Dynamic Forces in Capitalist Development: a long-run comparative view*, Oxford University Press, Oxford.

Malthus, T.R. (1798), *Essay on the Principle of Population ...*, J. Johnson, London; 2nd enlarged edn., J. Johnson, London, 1803; variorum edn. (ed. P. James), Cambridge University Press/Royal Economic Society, Cambridge, 1989.

Malthus, T.R. (1820), *Principles of Political Economy ...*, John Murray, London; repr. (with annotations by D. Ricardo), in P. Sraffa (ed.), *Works and Correspondence of David Ricardo, vol. II*, Cambridge University Press, Cambridge, 1951; 2nd revised edn., William Pickering, London, 1836; variorum edn. (ed. J. Pullen), Cambridge University Press/Royal Economic Society, Cambridge, 1989.

Mandel, E. (1975), *Late Capitalism* (transl. J. de Bres), Verso, London; German edn., 1972.

Mandeville, B. (1714), *The Fable of the Bees: or, Private Vices, Publick Benefits*, J. Roberts, London; revised edn., 1723; p/b edn. (ed. P. Harth), Penguin Books, Harmondsworth, Middx., 1970.

Manegold, K. (1978), 'Technology academised: education and training of the engineer in the 19th Century', in Krohn *et al.* (1978), *op. cit.*, pp. 137–58.

Manne, H.G. (1965), 'Mergers and the market for corporate control', *Journal of Political Economy* **73**, pp. 110–120.

Mansfield, E. (1988a), 'Industrial R&D in Japan and the United States: a comparative study', *American Economic Review, Papers and Proceedings* **78**, pp. 223–8.

Mansfield, E. (1988b), 'The diffusion of industrial robots in Japan and the United States', mimeo, University of Pennsylvania.

Marengo, L. (1991), 'Knowledge, coordination and learning in an adaptive model of the firm', D.Phil. thesis, SPRU, University of Sussex.

Marglin, S. (1974), 'What do bosses do?: the origins and functions of hierarchy in capitalist production', *Review of Radical Political Economics*

6, pp. 33–60; repr. in A. Gorz (ed.), *The Division of Labour*, Harvester Press, Hassocks Sx., 1978, pp. 13–54.

Marshall, A. (1890), *Principles of Economics*, ed. C.W. Guillebaud, 9th (variorum) edn., vol. 1, Macmillan/Royal Economic Society, London 1961.

Marshall, A. (1919), *Industry and Trade: a study of industrial technique and business organization ...* Macmillan, London.

Marx, K. (1857/8), *Grundrisse: foundations of the critique of political economy*, English edn., ed. N.I. Stone, Chicago 1904; (transl. M. Nicolaus), Penguin Books edn., Harmondsworth Middx., 1973.

Marx, K. (1859), *A Contribution to the Critique of Political Economy*, German edn., 1859; English edn. (transl. S.W. Ryazanskaya, ed. M. Dobb), Progress Publrs./Lawrence and Wishart, Moscow/London, 1971.

Marx, K. (1887), *Capital: a critical analysis of capitalist production, vol. I: Capitalist Production*, German edn., O. Meissner/L.W. Schmidt, Hamburg/New York, 1867; English edn. (transl. S. Moore and E. Aveling from 3rd German edn., ed. F. Engels, 1883); quoted from 1965 edn., Progress Publrs./Lawrence and Wishart, Moscow/London.

Marx, K. (1909), *Capital: a critique of political economy, vol. III: The Process of Capitalist Production as a Whole*, German edn. (ed. F. Engels, O. Meissner, Hamburg), 1894; English edn., Charles H. Kerr, Chicago, 1909; quoted from 1977 edn., Progress Publrs./Lawrence and Wishart, Moscow/London.

Marx, K. (1919), *Capital: a critique of political economy, vol. II: The Process of Circulation of Capital*, German edn. (ed. F. Engels, O. Meissner), Hamburg, 1885; English edn., Charles H. Kerr, Chicago, 1919; quoted from 1967 edn., Progress Publrs., Moscow.

Marx, K., and Engels, F. (1888), *The Communist Manifesto*, German edn., London, 1848; English p/b edn. (ed. A.J.P. Taylor), Penguin Books, Harmondsworth Middx., 1967.

Marx, T.G. (1985), 'The development of the franchise distribution system in the US automobile industry', *Business History Review* **59**, pp. 465–74.

Mathias, P. (1959), *The Brewing Industry in England, 1700–1830*, Cambridge University Press, Cambridge.

Matthews, R.C.O. (1954), *A Study in Trade-Cycle History: economic fluctuations in Great Britain, 1833–1842*, Cambridge University Press, Cambridge.

Matthews, R.C.O. (1973), 'Foreign trade and British economic growth', *Scottish Journal of Political Economy* **20**, pp. 195–209.

Matthews, R.C.O. (1986), 'The economics of institutions and the sources of growth', *Economic Journal* **96**, pp. 903–18.

Matthews, R.C.O., Feinstein, C.H., and Odling-Smee, J.C. (1982), *British Economic Growth 1856–1973*, Clarenden Press, Oxford.

Maxcy, G. and Silberston, A. (1950), *The Motor Industry*, Allen and Unwin, London.

Maxwell, P.I.L. (1981), 'Technology policy and firm learning effects in less-developed countries: a case-study of the experience of the Argentine steel firm, Acindar S.A.', D.Phil. thesis, SPRU, University of Sussex.

Mayer, C. (1992), 'The financing of innovation', in A. Bowen and M. Ricketts (eds.), *Stimulating Innovation in Industry*, Kogan Page, London, pp. 97–116.

Mazier, J. (1982), 'Growth and crisis – a Marxist interpretation' in A. Boltho (ed.), *The European Economy: growth and crisis*, Oxford University Press, Oxford, pp. 38–71.

Meadows, D.H., Meadows, D.L., Randers, J., and Behrens, W. (1972), *The Limits to Growth: a report for the Club of Rome's project on the predicament of mankind*, Earth Island, London.

Medick, H. (1976), 'The proto-industrial family economy', *Social History* **1**, pp. 291–315.

Melody, W.H. (1986), 'Telecommunication – policy directions for the technology and information services', *Oxford Surveys in Information Technology* **3**, pp. 77–106.

Mendels, F.F. (1972), 'Proto-industrialization: the first phase of the industrialization process', *Journal of Economic History* **32**, pp. 241–61.

Mensch, G. (1979), *Stalemate in Technology: innovations overcome the depression*, Ballinger, New York; original German edn., Umschau, Frankfurt, 1975.

Mill, J.S. (1844), *Essays on Some Unsettled Questions of Political Economy*, 2nd edn., Longmans, 1874; repr. Augustus M. Kelley, New York, 1968.

Mill, J.S. (1848), *Principles of Political Economy, with some of their applications to social philosophy*, Parker and Co.; (ed. W.J. Ashley), Longmans, Green and Co., London, etc., 1909.

Miller, R., Hobday, M., Leroux-Demers, T., and Olleros, X. (1995), 'Innovation in complex systems industries: the case of flight simulation', *Industrial and Corporate Change* **4**, pp. 363–400.

Milward, A.S., and Saul, S.B. (1973), *The Economic Development of Continental Europe, 1780–1870*, Allen and Unwin, London.

Milward, A.S., and Saul, S.B. (1977), *The Development of the Economies of Continental Europe, 1850–1914*, Allen and Unwin, London.

Minami, R. (1986), *The Economic Development of Japan: a quantitative study*, transl. R. Thompson and R. Minami, Macmillan, Basingstoke and London.

Minchinton, W. (1973), 'Patterns of demand, 1750–1914', in Cipolla (1973a), *op. cit.*, pp. 77–186.

Minns, R. (1980), *Pension Funds and British Capitalism: the ownership and control of shareholdings*, Heinemann, London.

Mirowski, P. (1989), *More Heat than Light: economics as social physics, physics as nature's economics*, Cambridge University Press, Cambridge.

Mitch, D. (1993), 'The role of human capital in the First Industrial Revolution', in Mokyr (1993), *op. cit.*, pp. 267–307.

Mitchell, B.R. (1964), 'The coming of the railway and United Kingdom economic growth', *Journal of Economic History* **24**, pp. 315–36.

Miyazaki, K. (1995), *Building Competences in the Firm: lessons from Japanese and European optoelectronics*, Macmillan, London.

Mokyr, J. (1976), *Industrialization in the Low Countries, 1795–1850*, Yale University Press, New Haven and London.

Mokyr, J. (1990), *The Lever of Riches: technological creativity and economic progress*, Oxford University Press, New York and Oxford.

Mokyr, J. (ed.) (1993), *The British Industrial Revolution: an economic perspective*, Westview Press, Boulder.

Mokyr, J. (1994), 'Technological change, 1700–1830', in Floud and McCloskey (1994), *op. cit.*, pp. 12–43.

Morgan, K. and Sayer, A. (1988), *Microcircuits of Capital: 'sunrise' industry and uneven development*, Polity Press, Cambridge.

Morikawa, H. (1991), 'The education of engineers in modern Japan: an historical perspective', in H.F. Gospel (ed.), *Industrial Training and Technological Innovation*, Routledge, London and New York, pp. 136–47.

Morishima, M. (1973), *Marx's Economics: a dual theory of value and growth*, Cambridge University Press, Cambridge.

Morishima, M. (1982), *Why Has Japan 'Succeeded'?: western technology and the Japanese ethos*, Cambridge University Press, Cambridge.

Morroni, M. (1992), *Production Process and Technical Change*, Cambridge University Press, Cambridge.

Mowery, D.C. (1984), 'Firm structure, government policy, and the organization of industrial research: Great Britain and the United States, 1900–1950', *Business History Review* **58**, pp. 504–31.

Mowery, D. (1992), 'Finance and corporate evolution in five industrial economies, 1900–1950', *Industrial and Corporate Change* **1**, pp. 1–36.

Mowery, D., and Rosenberg, N. (1979), 'The influence of market demand upon innovation: a critical review of some recent empirical studies', *Research Policy* **8**, pp. 103–53; repr. in Rosenberg (1982), *op. cit.*, pp. 193–244.

Mowery, D.C., and Rosenberg, N. (1989), *Technology and the Pursuit of Economic Growth*, Cambridge University Press, Cambridge.

Mowery, D.C., and Rosenberg, N. (1993), 'The US national innovation system', in Nelson (1993), *op. cit.*, pp. 29–75.

Musgrave, P.W. (1967), *Technical Change, the Labour Force and Education: a study of the British and German iron and steel industries, 1860–1964*, Pergamon, Oxford.

Myint, H. (1964), *The Economics of the Developing Countries*, Hutchinson, London.

Myrdal, G. (1956), *An International Economy: problems and prospects*, Routledge and Kegan Paul, London.

Myrdal, G. (1957), *Economic Theory and the Under-developed Regions*, Duckworth, London.

Nadal, J. (1973), 'Spain 1830–1914' (transl. J. Street), in Cipolla (1973b), *op. cit.*, pp. 532–627.

Nakamura, J.I. (1981), 'Human capital accumulation in premodern rural Japan', *Journal of Economic History* **41**, pp. 263–81.

Nelson, D. (1987), 'Mass production and the US tire industry', *Journal of Economic History* **47**, pp. 329–40.

Nelson, R.R. (1990a), 'US technological leadership: where did it come from and where did it go?', *Research Policy* **19**, pp. 117–32.

Nelson, R.R. (1990b), 'Capitalism as an engine of progress', *Research Policy* **19**, pp. 193–214.

Nelson, R.R. (1992), 'National innovation systems: a retrospective on a study', *Industrial and Corporate Change* **1**, pp. 347–74.

Nelson, R.R. (ed.) (1993), *National Innovation Systems: a comparative analysis*, Oxford University Press, New York and Oxford.

Nelson, R.R. (1994), 'The co-evolution of technology, industrial structure, and supporting institutions', *Industrial and Corporate Change* **3**, pp. 47–64.

Nelson, R.R., and Winter, S.G. (1974), 'Neoclassical vs evolutionary theories of economic growth: critique and prospectus', *Economic Journal* **84**, pp. 886–905; repr. in Freeman (1990), *op. cit.*, pp. 3–22.

Nelson, R.R., and Winter, S.G. (1977), 'In search of useful theory of innovation', *Research Policy* **6**, pp. 36–76.

Nelson, R.R., and Winter, S.G. (1982), *An Evolutionary Theory of Economic Change*, Belknap Press, Cambridge MA and London.

Nelson, R.R. and Wright, G. (1992), 'The rise and fall of American technological leadership: the postwar era in historical perspective', *Journal of Economic Literature* **30**, pp. 1931–64.

Neuberger, H. (1977), 'The industrial politics of the *Kreditbanken*, 1880–1914', *Business History Review* **51**, pp. 190–207.

Nickless, P.J. (1979), 'A new look at productivity in the New England cotton textile industry, 1830–1860', *Journal of Economic History* **39**, pp. 889–910.

Nooteboom, B. (1992), 'Towards a dynamic theory of transactions', *Journal of Evolutionary Economics* **2**, pp. 281–300.

North, D.C. (1961), *The Economic Growth of the United States, 1790–1860*, Prentice-Hall, Englewood Cliffs NJ; repr. Norton, New York, 1966.

North, D.C. (1963), 'Industrialization in the United States (1815–60)', in Rostow (1963), *op. cit.*, pp. 44–62.

North, D.C. (1968), 'Sources of productivity change in ocean shipping, 1600–1850', *Journal of Political Economy* **76**, pp. 953–70; repr. in Fogel and Engerman (1971), *op. cit.*, pp. 163–74.

North, D.C. (1981), *Structure and Change in Economic History*, Norton, New York and London.

North, D.C., and Weingast, B.R. (1989), 'Constitutions and commitment: the evolution of institutions governing public choice in 17th-century England', *Journal of Economic History* **49**, pp. 803–32.

Norton, R.D. (1986), 'Industrial policy and American renewal', *Journal of Economic Literature* **24**, pp. 1–40.

Nove, A. (1969), *An Economic History of the USSR*, Penguin Books, Harmondsworth Middx.; Pelican edn. 1972.

Nove, A. (1977), *The Soviet Economic System*, Allen and Unwin, London.

Nurkse, R. (1953), *Problems of Capital Formation in Underdeveloped Countries*, Blackwell, Oxford.

Nurkse, R. (1961), *Equilibrium and Growth in the World Economy: economic essays by Ragnar Nurkse* (ed. G. Haberler and R.M. Stern), Harvard University Press, Cambridge MA.

Nye, J.V. (1991), 'The myth of free-trade Britain and fortress France: tariffs and trade in the nineteenth century', *Journal of Economic History* **51**, pp. 23–46.

O'Brien, A.P. (1988), 'Factory size, economies of scale, and the great merger wave of 1898–1902', *Journal of Economic History* **48**, pp. 639–49.

O'Brien, P.K. (1982a), 'European economic development: the contribution of the periphery', *Economic History Review* **35**, pp. 1–18.

O'Brien, P. (ed.) (1982b), *Railways and the Economic Development of Western Europe, 1830–1914*, Macmillan, London.

O'Brien, P.K. (1986), 'Do we have a typology for the study of European industrialization in the XIXth century?', *Journal of European Economic History* **15**, pp. 291–333.

O'Brien, P.K., and Keyder, C. (1978), *Economic Growth in Britain and France, 1780–1914*, Allen and Unwin, London.

Oda, S.H. (1991), 'A theoretical study of non–proportionally growing economies with technical progress', D.Phil. thesis, SPRU, University of Sussex.

Odagiri, H., and Goto, A. (1993), 'The Japanese system of innovation: past, present, and future', in Nelson (1993), *op. cit.*, pp. 76–114.

O'Driscoll, G.P., jr., and Rizzo, M.J. (1985), *The Economics of Time and Ignorance*, Blackwell, Oxford and New York.

OECD (1977), *Towards Full Employment and Price Stability: a report ... by a group of independent experts*, (chairman: P.W. McCracken), OECD, Paris.

OECD, Technology/Economy Programme (1992), *Technology and the Economy: the key relationships*, OECD/HMSO, Paris/London.

OECD (1994), *Science, Technology and Innovation Policies: Federation of Russia, vol. 1: evaluation report*, OECD, Paris.

Offer, A. (1993), 'The British Empire, 1870–1914: a waste of money?', *Economic History Review* **46**, pp. 215–38.

Ohkawa, K., and Rosovsky, H. (1973), *Japanese Economic Growth: trend acceleration in the twentieth century*, Stanford University Press, Stanford CA, and Oxford University Press: London.

Ohmae, K. (1985), *Triad Power: the coming shape of global competition*, Free Press, New York.

Ohmae, K. (1992), *The Borderless World: power and strategy in the interlinked economy*, Fontana, London.

Olmstead, A.L. (1975), 'The mechanization of reaping and mowing in American agriculture, 1833–1870', *Journal of Economic History* **35**, pp. 327–52.

Olney, M.L. (1989), 'Credit as a production-smoothing device: the case of automobiles, 1913–1938', *Journal of Economic History* **49**, pp. 377–91.

Ouchi, W.G. (1981), *Theory Z: how American business can meet the Japanese challenge*, Addison-Wesley Press, Reading MA.

Palmade, G.P. (1972), *French Capitalism in the Nineteenth Century* (transl. G.M. Holmes), David and Charles, Newton Abbot; French edn., Librairie Armand Colin, Paris, 1961.

Patel, P. (1995), 'Localized production of technology for global markets', *Cambridge Journal of Economics* **19**, pp. 141–53.

Patel, P., and Pavitt, K. (1987), 'Is Western Europe losing the technological race?', *Research Policy* **16**, pp. 57–85.

Patel, P., and Pavitt, K. (1991), 'Large firms and the production of the world's technology: an important case of non-globalization', *Journal of International Business Studies* **22**, pp. 1–21.

Patrick, H. (ed.) (1976), *Japanese Industrialisation and its Social Consequences*, University of California Press, Berkeley.

Patrick, H.T. and Rosovsky, H. (eds) (1976), *Asia's New Giant: how the Japanese economy works*, Brookings Institution, Washington.

Pavitt, K. (1984), 'Sectoral patterns of technical change: towards a taxonomy and a theory', *Research Policy* **13**, pp. 343–74; repr. in Freeman (1990), *op. cit.*, pp. 249–79.

Pavitt, K. (1986), ''Chips' and 'trajectories': how does the semiconductor influence the sources and directions of technical change?', in R. MacLeod (ed.), *Technology and the Human Prospect*, Pinter, London and Wolfeboro NH, pp. 31–54.

Pavitt, K., and Patel, P. (1988), 'The international distribution and determinants of technological activities', *Oxford Review of Economic Policy* **4**, pp. 35–55.

Pavitt, K., Robson, M., and Townsend, J. (1987), 'The size distribution of innovating firms in the UK: 1945–83', *Journal of Industrial Economics* **35**, pp. 297–316.

Pearce, R.D. (1993), *The Growth and Evolution of Multinational Enterprise: patterns of geographical and industrial diversification*, Edward Elgar, Aldershot and Brookfield VT.

Peck, M.J. (1986), 'Joint R&D: the case of Microelectronics and Computer Technology Corporation', *Research Policy* **15**, pp. 219–31.

Peltzman, S. (1974), *Regulation of Pharmaceutical Innovation: the 1962 amendments*, American Enterprise Institute for Public Policy Research, Washington.

Penrose, E.T. (1959), *The Theory of the Growth of the Firm*, Blackwell, Oxford; 2nd edn. (ed. M. Slater), Blackwell, Oxford, 1980.

Perez, C. (1983), 'Structural change and the assimilation of new technologies in the economic and social system', *Futures* **15**, pp. 357–75.

Pincus, J.J. (1977), *Pressure Groups and Politics in Antebellum Tariffs*, Columbia University Press, New York.

Piore, M.J., and Sabel, C.F. (1984), *The Second Industrial Divide: possibilities for prosperity*, Basic Books, New York.

Pollard, S. (1964), 'Fixed capital in the Industrial Revolution', *Journal of Economic History* **24**, pp. 299–314.

Pollard, S. (1965), *The Genesis of Modern Management: a study of the Industrial Revolution in Great Britain*, Edward Arnold, London.

Pollard, S. (1973), 'Industrialization and the European economy', *Economic History Review* **26**, pp. 636–48.

Pollard, S. (1981), *Peaceful Conquest: the industrialization of Europe 1760–1970*, Oxford University Press, Oxford.

Pollard, S. (1982), *The Wasting of the British Economy: British economic policy 1945 to the present*, Croom Helm, London.

Pollard, S. (1991), ‘Regional markets and national development’, in Berg (1991), *op. cit.*, pp. 29–56.

Porter, M.E. (1990), *The Competitive Advantage of Nations*, Free Press, New York.

Postlethwayt, M. (1749), *A Dissertation on the Plan, Use, and Importance of the Universal Dictionary of Trade and Commerce ...*, J. and P. Knapton, London; repr. in *Malachy Postlethwayt, Selected Works, vol. I, 1745–1751*, Gregg International, Farnborough, 1968.

Postlethwayt, M. (1757), *Britain's Commercial Interest Explained and Improved...*, D. Browne, A. Millar, *et al.*, London; repr. Gregg International, Farnborough, 1968.

Pounds, N.J.G., and Parker, W.N. (1957), *Coal and Steel in Western Europe: the influence of resources and techniques on production*, Faber and Faber, London.

Prais, S.J. (1976), *The Evolution of Giant Firms in Britain: a study of the growth of concentration in manufacturing industry in Britain, 1909–70*, NIESR/Cambridge University Press, Cambridge.

Prebisch, R. (1950), *The Economic Development of Latin America and its Principal Problems*, United Nations, New York.

Pressnell, L.S. (1956), *Country Banking in the Industrial Revolution*, Clarendon Press, Oxford.

Price, D. de S. (1965), ‘Is technology historically independent of science?’, *Technology and Culture* **6**, pp. 553–68.

Price, D. de S. (1984), ‘The science/technology relationship, the craft of experimental science and policy for the improvement of high–technology innovation’, *Research Policy* **13**, pp. 3–20.

Price, J. (1989), ‘What did merchants do?: reflections on British overseas trade, 1660–1790’, *Journal of Economic History* **49**, pp. 267–84.

Radosevic, S. (1994), ‘Transfer of national systems of innovation in Central and Eastern Europe: between restructuring and erosion’, mimeo, SPRU.

Reader, W.J. (1970), *Imperial Chemical Industries: a history*, Oxford University Press, London.

Rees, R. (1985), ‘The theory of principal and agent’, *Bulletin of Economic Research* **37**, pp. 3–26 and 75–95.

Reich, L.S. (1985), *The Making of American Industrial Research: science and business at GE and Bell, 1876–1926*, Cambridge University Press, Cambridge.

Reich, L.S. (1987), ‘Edison, Coolidge, and Langmuir: evolving approaches to American industrial research’, *Journal of Economic History* **47**, pp. 341–51.

Reid, G.C. (1989), *Classical Economic Growth: an analysis in the tradition of Adam Smith*, Blackwell, Oxford.

Ricardo, D. (1817), *On the Principles of Political Economy and Taxation;* 3rd edn., 1821; repr. in P. Sraffa (ed.), *Works and Correspondence of David Ricardo, vol. I*, Cambridge University Press, Cambridge, 1951.

Rimmer, W.G. (1960), *Marshalls of Leeds: flax-spinners, 1788–1886*, Cambridge University Press,

Robbins, L. (1932), *An Essay on the Nature and Significance of Economic Science*, Macmillan, London; 2nd edn., Macmillan, London, 1935.

Robson, M., Townsend, J., and Pavitt, K. (1988), 'Sectoral patterns of production and use of innovations in the UK: 1945–1983', *Research Policy* **17**, pp. 1–14.

Roehl, R. (1976), 'French industrialization: a reconsideration', *Explorations in Economic History* **13**, pp. 233–82.

Roemer, J.E. (1981), *Analytical Foundations of Marxian Economic Theory*, Cambridge University Press, Cambridge.

Roemer, J.E. (1988), *Free to Lose: an introduction to Marxist economic philosophy*, Century Hutchinson, London.

Roll, E. (1930), *An Early Experiment in Industrial Organization: being a history of the firm of Boulton and Watt, 1775–1805*, Longmans, London; repr. Cass, London, 1968.

Rosenberg, N. (1963), 'Technological change in the machine tool industry, 1840–1910', *Journal of Economic History* **23**, pp. 414–46; repr. in Rosenberg (1976), *op. cit.*, pp. 9–31.

Rosenberg, N. (ed.) (1969), *The American System of Manufactures*, The University Press, Edinburgh.

Rosenberg, N. (1972), *Technology and American Economic Growth*, Harper and Row, New York.

Rosenberg, N. (1976), *Perspectives on Technology*, Cambridge University Press, Cambridge.

Rosenberg, N. (ed.) (1971), *The Economics of Technological Change: selected readings*, Penguin Books, Harmondsworth Middx.

Rosenberg, N. (1977), 'American technology: imported or indigenous?', *American Economic Review, Papers and Proceedings* **67**, pp. 21–6.

Rosenberg, N. (1982), *Inside the Black Box: technology and economics*, Cambridge University Press, Cambridge.

Rosenberg, N. (1992), 'Economic experiments', *Industrial and Corporate Change* **1**, pp. 181–203; repr. in Rosenberg (1994), *op. cit.*, pp. 87–108.

Rosenberg, N. (1994), *Exploring the Black Box: technology, economics, and history*, Cambridge University Press, Cambridge.

Rosenberg, N. and Birdzell, L.E. (1986), *How the West Grew Rich: the economic transformation of the industrial world*, I.B. Tauris, London.

Rosenberg, N. and Frischtak, C. (1984), 'Technological innovation and long waves', *Cambridge Journal of Economics* **8**, pp. 7–24; repr. in Rosenberg (1994), *op. cit.*, pp. 62–84.

Rosenberg, N. and Frischtak, C. (eds.) (1985), *International Technology Transfer: concepts, measures, and comparisons*, Praeger, New York.

Rosovsky, H. (1961), *Capital Formation in Japan, 1868–1940*, Free Press of Glencoe, New York.

Rosovsky, H. (1966), 'Japan's transition to Modern Economic Growth, 1868-1885', in H. Rosovsky (ed.), *Industrialization in Two Systems: essays in honor of Alexander Gerschenkron*, John Wiley, New York, pp. 91–139.

Rossi, N. and Toniolo, G. (1992), 'Catching up or falling behind?: Italy's economic growth, 1895–1947', *Economic History Review* **45**, pp. 537–63.

Rostow, W.W. (1953), *The Process of Economic Growth*, Clarendon Press, Oxford; 2nd enlarged edn., 1960.

Rostow, W.W. (1956), 'The take-off into self-sustained growth', *Economic Journal* **66**, pp. 25–48.

Rostow, W.W. (1960), *The Stages of Economic Growth: a non-Communist Manifesto*, Cambridge University Press, Cambridge; 2nd enlarged edn., 1971.

Rostow, W.W. (ed.) (1963), *The Economics of Take-off into Sustained Growth*, Macmillan, London.

Rostow, W.W. (1971), *Politics and the Stages of Growth*, Cambridge University Press, Cambridge.

Rostow, W.W. (1975), *How It All Began: origins of the modern economy*, Methuen, London.

Rostow, W.W. (1978), *The World Economy: history and prospect*, Macmillan, London and Basingstoke.

Rostow, W.W. (1978), *Getting from Here to There*, Macmillan, London and Basingstoke (British edn., 1979).

Rostow, W.W. (1980), *Why the Poor Get Richer and the Rich Slow Down: essays in the Marshallian long period*, Macmillan, London and Basingstoke.

Rostow, W.W. (1987), *Rich Countries and Poor Countries: reflections on the past, lessons for the future*, Westview Press, Boulder and London.

Rostow, W.W. (1990), *Theorists of Economic Growth from David Hume to the Present: with a perspective on the next century*, Oxford University Press, New York and Oxford.

Rothwell, R., and Gardiner, P. (1990), 'Robustness and product design families', in M. Oakley (ed.), *Design management: a handbook of issues and methods*, Blackwell, Oxford, pp. 279–92.

Sabel, C., and Zeitlin, J. (1985), 'Historical alternatives to mass production: politics, markets and technology in nineteenth-century industrialization', *Past and Present* **108**, pp. 133–76.

Sahal, D. (1981), *Patterns of Technological Innovation*, Addison-Wesley, Reading MA.

Sahal, D. (1985), 'Technological guideposts and innovation avenues', *Research Policy* **14**, pp. 61–82; repr. in Freeman (1990), *op. cit.*, pp. 442–63.

Salter, W.E.G. (1966), *Productivity and Technical Change*, 2nd edn. (ed. W.B. Reddaway), DAE Cambridge Monographs, Cambridge University Press, Cambridge; 1st. edn. 1960.

Samuelson, P.A. (1965), 'A theory of induced innovation along Kennedy–Weisäcker lines', *Review of Economics and Statistics* **47**, pp. 343–56.

Sandberg, L.G. (1979), 'The case of the impoverished sophisticate: human capital and Swedish economic growth before World War I', *Journal of Economic History* **39**, pp. 225–41.

Sandberg, L.G. (1982), 'Ignorance, poverty and economic backwardness in the early stages of European industrialization: variations on Alexander Gerschenkron's grand theme', *Journal of European Economic History* **11**, pp. 675–97.

Sanderson, M. (1972), *The Universities and British Industry, 1850–1970*, Routledge, London.

Santarelli, E. (1991), 'Asset specificity, R&D financing, and the signalling properties of the firm's financial structure', *Economics of Innovation and New Technology* **1**, pp. 279–94.

Santarelli, E., and Pesciarelli, E. (1990), 'The emergence of a vision: the development of Schumpeter's theory of entrepreneurship', *History of Political Economy* **22**, pp. 677–96.

Saul, S.B. (1969), *The Myth of the Great Depression, 1873–1896*, Macmillan, London and Basingstoke.

Saxenian, A. (1991), 'The origins and dynamics of production networks in Silicon Valley', *Research Policy* **20**, pp. 423–38.

Saxenian, A. (1994), *Regional Advantage: culture and competition in Silicon Valley and Route 128*, Harvard University Press, Cambridge MA and London.

Saxonhouse, G.R. (1976), 'Country girls and communication among corporations in the Japanese cotton-spinning industry', in Patrick (1976), *op. cit.*, pp. 97–125.

Say, J.-B. (1821), *A Treatise on Political Economy; or the production, distribution, and consumption of wealth* (transl. C.R. Prinsep, from 4th French edn.), Longman, London; 1st French edn., 1803.

Sayers, R.S. (1976), *The Bank of England 1891–1944*, Cambridge University Press, Cambridge.

Scazzieri, R. (1993), *A Theory of Production: tasks, processes, and technical practices*, Clarendon Press, Oxford.

Scherer, F.M. (1982), 'Inter-industry technology flows in the US', *Research Policy* **11**, pp. 227–46.

Schmitz, H., and Cassiolato, J. (eds) (1992), *Hi-tech for Industrial Development: lessons from the Brazilian experience in electronics and automation*, Routledge, London.

Schmookler, J. (1966), *Invention and Economic Growth*, Harvard University Press/Oxford University Press, Cambridge MA/London.

Schmookler, J. (1972), *Patents, Invention, and Economic Change: data and selected essays* (ed. Z. Griliches and L. Hurwicz), Harvard University Press, Cambridge MA.

Schonberger, R.J. (1982), *Japanese Manufacturing Techniques: nine hidden lessons in simplicity*, Free Press, New York.

Schumpeter, J.A. (1911) *Theory of Economic Development: an inquiry into profits, capital, credit, interest, and the business cycle* (transl. R. Opie), Harvard University Press, Cambridge MA, 1934; repr. Oxford University Press, London, 1961.

Schumpeter, J.A. (1928), 'The instability of capitalism', *Economic Journal* **38**, pp. 361–86; repr. in Rosenberg (1971), *op. cit.*, pp. 13–42.

Schumpeter, J.A. (1939), *Business Cycles: a theoretical, historical and statistical analysis of the capitalist process*, McGraw-Hill, New York and London.

Schumpeter, J.A. (1943) *Capitalism, Socialism and Democracy*, McGraw-Hill, New York.

Schumpeter, J.A. (1954), *History of Economic Analysis* (ed. E.B. Schumpeter), Allen and Unwin/Oxford University Press, London.

Scott, M.FG. (1989), *A New View of Economic Growth*, Clarendon Press, Oxford.

Segreto, L. (1985), 'More trouble than profit: Vickers' investments in Italy, 1905–39', *Business History* **27**, pp. 316–37.

Semler, R. (1993), *Maverick!: the success story behind the world's most unusual workplace*, Random House, London.

Sen, A.K. (1960), *Choice of Techniques: an aspect of the theory of planned economic development*, Blackwell, Oxford.

Sen, A.K. (ed.) (1970), *Growth Economics*, Penguin Books, Harmondsworth Middx.

Senior, N.W. (1836), *An Outline of the Science of Political Economy*, repr. Allen and Unwin, London, 1938.

Senker, J. (1995), 'Tacit knowledge and models of innovation', *Industrial and Corporate Change* **4**, pp. 425–48.

Servan-Schreiber, J.J. (1968), *The American Challenge* (transl. R. Steel), Hamish Hamilton, London; original French edn., Eds. Denoël, Paris, 1967.

Singer, H.W. (1950), 'Distribution of the gains between investing and borrowing countries', *American Economic Review, Papers and Proceedings* **40**, pp. 473–85.

Sloan, A.P., jr. (1965), *My Years with General Motors*, eds. J. McDonald and C. Stevens, Sidgwick and Jackson, London.

Smith, A. (1776) *An Inquiry into the Nature and Causes of the Wealth of Nations*, W. Strahan and T. Cadell, London; repr. (ed. E. Cannan, 1904), Methuen, London, 1961; bicentennial edn. (eds. R.H. Campbell, A.S. Skinner and W.B. Todd), Clarendon Press, Oxford, 1976.

Soete, L. (1987), 'The newly emerging information technology sector', in C. Freeman and L. Soete (eds.), *Technical Change and Full Employment*, Blackwell, Oxford and New York, pp. 189–220.

Sokoloff, K.L. (1988), 'Inventive activity in early industrial America: evidence from patent records, 1790–1846', *Journal of Economic History* **48**, pp. 813–50.

Sokoloff, K.L., and Khan, B.Z. (1990), 'The 'democratization' of invention during early industrialization: evidence from the United States, 1790–1846', *Journal of Economic History* **50**, pp. 363–78.

Solomou, S. (1987), *Phases of Economic Growth, 1850–1973*, Cambridge University Press, Cambridge.

Solow, R.M. (1957), 'Technical change and the aggregate production function', *Review of Economics and Statistics* **39**, pp. 312–20; repr. in Rosenberg (1971), *op. cit.*, pp. 344–62.

Soltow, L. (1989), 'The rich and the destitute in Sweden, 1805–1855: a test of Tocqueville's inequality hypothesis', *Economic History Review* **42**, pp. 43–63.

Spraos, J. (1980), 'The statistical debate on the net barter terms of trade between primary commodities and manufactures', *Economic Journal* **90**, pp. 107–28.

Sraffa, P. (1960), *Production of Commodities by Means of Commodities*, Cambridge University Press, Cambridge.

Steuart, J. (1767), *An Inquiry into the Principles of Political Oeconomy ...*, A. Millar and T. Cadell, London; (ed. and abridged A.S. Skinner), Oliver and Boyd, Edinburgh and London, 1966.

Stewart, F. (1977), *Technology and Underdevelopment*, Macmillan, London.

Stigler, G.J. (1951), 'The division of labor is limited by the extent of the market', *Journal of Political Economy* **59**, 185–93; repr. in G.J. Stigler, *The Organization of Industry*, Irwin, Homewood IL, 1968, pp. 129–41.

Stiglitz, J.E. (1994), 'Economic growth revisited', *Industrial and Corporate Change* **3**, pp. 65–110.

Stoneman, P. (1975), 'The effect of computers on the demand for labour', *Economic Journal* **85**, pp. 590–606.

Stoneman, P. (1983), *The Economic Analysis of Technological Change*, Oxford University Press, Oxford.

Sugiura, K. (1994), 'The technological role of machinery users in economic development: the case of textile machinery industry in Japan and Korea', D.Phil. thesis, SPRU, University of Sussex.

Summers, R., and Heston, A. (1988), 'A new set of international comparisons of real product and price levels: estimates for 130 countries, 1950–1985', *Review of Income and Wealth* **34**, pp. 1–25.

Summers, R. and Heston, A. (1991), 'The Penn world table (mark 5): an expanded set of international comparisons (1950–1988)', *Quarterly Journal of Economics* **106**, pp. 1–41.

Supple, B.E. (1973), 'The state and the Industrial Revolution, 1700–1914', in Cipolla (1973a), *op. cit.*, pp. 301–57.

Swank, J.M. (1892), *History of the Manufacture of Iron in All Ages, and particularly in the United States ...*, 2nd edn., American Iron and Steel Association, Philadelphia; 1st edn. 1884.

Swann, G.M.P. (1986), *Quality Innovation: an economic analysis of rapid improvements in microelectronic components*, Pinter, London.

Sweezy, P.M. (1939), 'Demand under conditions of oligopoly', *Journal of Political Economy* **47**, pp. 568–73.

Sylla, R. and Toniolo, G. (eds.) (1991), *Patterns of European Industrialization: the nineteenth century*, Routledge, London and New York; p/b edn., 1992.

Taylor, A.J. (1949), 'Concentration and specialisation in the Lancashire cotton industry, 1825–1850, *Economic History Review* 2nd ser. **1**, pp. 114–22.

Taylor, F.W. (1911), *The Principles of Scientific Management*, Harper, New York and London; repr. Norton, New York and London, 1967.

Teece, D.J. (1977), 'Technology transfer by multinational firms: the resource cost of transferring technological know–how', *Economic Journal* **87**, pp. 242–61.

Teece, D., Pisano, G., and Shuen, A. (1990), 'Firm capabilities, resources, and the concept of technology', CCC working paper, Center for Research in Management, Berkeley CA.

Teitel, S. (1978), 'On the concept of appropriate technology for less industrialized countries', *Technological Forecasting and Social Change* **11**, pp. 349–60.

Teitel, S. (1993), *Industrial and Technological Development*, Inter-American Development Bank, Washington.

Temin, P. (1964), *Iron and Steel in Nineteenth-Century America: an economic inquiry*, MIT Press, Cambridge MA.

Temin, P. (1971), 'Labor scarcity in America', *Journal of Interdisciplinary History* **1**, pp. 251–64.

Temin, P. (1988), 'Product quality and vertical integration in the early cotton textile industry', *Journal of Economic History* **48**, pp. 891–907.

Thomas, W.A. (1982), *The Financing of British Industry 1918–1976*, Methuen, London and New York.

Thompson, E.P. (1967), 'Time, work-discipline, and industrial capitalism', *Past and Present* **38**, pp. 56–97.

Thomson, J.K.J. (1991), 'State intervention in the Catalan calico-printing industry in the eighteenth century', in Berg (1991), *op. cit.*, pp. 57–89.

Thomson, R. (1987), 'Learning by selling and invention: the case of the sewing machine', *Journal of Economic History* **47**, pp. 433–45.

Tidd, J. (1990), *Flexible Manufacturing Technology and International Competitiveness*, Pinter, London.

Tilly, R.H. (1982), 'Mergers, external growth, and finance in the development of large-scale enterprise in Germany, 1880–1913', *Journal of Economic History* **42**, pp. 629–58.

Tilly, R.H. (1986), 'German banking, 1850–1914: development assistance for the strong', *Journal of European Economic History* **15**, pp. 113–52.

Tipton, F.B., jr. (1981), 'Government policy and economic development in Germany and Japan: a skeptical reevaluation', *Journal of Economic History* **41**, pp. 139–51.

Tocqueville, A. de (1835), *Democracy in America* (transl. H. Reeve), Saunders and Otley, London; repr. Knopf, New York, 1945; original French edn., Librairie de Charles Gosselin, Paris, 1835.

Tolliday, S., and Zeitlin, J. (eds) (1986), *The Automobile Industry and its Workers: between Fordism and flexibility*, Polity Press, Cambridge.

Tortella, G. (1972), 'Spain, 1829–1874', in Cameron (1972), *op. cit.*, pp. 91–121.

Trebilcock, C. (1973), 'British armaments and European industrialisation 1890–1914', *Economic History Review* **26**, pp. 254–72.

Townsend, J. (1976), 'Innovations in Coal-mining Machinery: the Anderton shearer-loader and the role of the NCB and supply industry in its development', SPRU Occnl. Paper 3, University of Sussex.

Tylecote, A. (1992), *A Long Wave in the World Economy: the current crisis in historical perspective*, Routledge, London.

Utterback, J.M. (1994), *Mastering the Dynamics of Innovation: how companies can seize opportunities in the face of technological change*, Harvard Business School Press, Boston.

Utterback, J.M., and Abernathy, W.J. (1975), 'A dynamic model of product and process innovation', *Omega* **3**, pp. 639–56; repr. in Freeman (1990), *op. cit.*, pp. 424–41.

van Duijn, J.J. (1983), *The Long Wave in Economic Life*, Allen and Unwin, London.

van Tulder, R., and Ruigrok, W. (1993), 'Regionalisation, globalisation, and glocalisation: the case of the world car industry', in M. Humbert (ed.), *The Impact of Globalisation on Europe's Firms and Industries*, Pinter, London and New York, pp. 22–33.

Vanek, J. (1970), *The General Theory of Labor-Managed Market Economies*, Cornell University Press, Ithaca and London.

Veblen, T. (1904), *The Theory of Business Enterprise*, repr. Augustus M. Kelley, New York, 1965.

Veblen, T. (1915), *Imperial Germany and the Industrial Revolution*, ed. J. Dorfman; repr. Augustus M. Kelley, New York, 1964.

Veblen, T. (1919), *The Place of Science in Modern Civilisation, and other essays*, B.W. Huebsch; repr. Russell and Russell, New York, 1961.

Veblen, T. (1921), *The Engineers and the Price System*, B.W. Huebsch; repr. Viking Press, New York, 1954.

Vernon, R. (1966), 'International investment and international trade in the product cycle', *Quarterly Journal of Economics* **80**, pp. 190–207; repr. in Rosenberg (1971), *op. cit.*, pp. 440–60.

Vestal, J.E. (1993), *Planning for Change: industrial policy and Japanese economic development, 1945–1990*, Clarendon Press, Oxford.

Ville, S. (1986), 'Total factor productivity in the English shipping industry: the north-east coal trade, 1700–1850', *Economic History Review* **39**, pp. 355–70.

Vivarelli, M. (1991), 'Technology and employment: the economic theory and the empirical evidence', D.Phil. thesis, SPRU, University of Sussex.

von Hippel, E. (1988), *The Sources of Innovation*, Oxford University Press, Oxford.

von Hippel, E. (1989), 'Cooperation between rivals: informal know-how trading', in Carlsson (1989a), *op. cit*, pp. 157–76.

von Tunzelmann, G.N. (1967), 'On a thesis by Matthews', *Economic History Review* **20**, pp. 548–54.

von Tunzelmann, G.N. (1978), *Steam Power and British Industrialization to 1860*, Clarendon Press, Oxford.

von Tunzelmann, G.N. (1981), 'Technical progress during the Industrial Revolution', in R. Floud and D. McCloskey (eds.), *The Economic History of Britain since 1700, vol. 1: 1700–1860*, 1st edn., Cambridge University Press, Cambridge, pp 143–63.

von Tunzelmann, G.N. (1982), 'Structural change and leading sectors in British manufacturing, 1907–1968', in C.P. Kindleberger and G. di Tella (eds.), *Economics in the Long View*, Vol. 3, Macmillan, London and Basingstoke, pp. 1–49.

von Tunzelmann, G.N. (1985), 'The standard of living debate and optimal economic growth', in J. Mokyr (ed.), *Economic History and the Industrial Revolution*, Rowman and Allanheld, Totowa NH, pp. 207–26.

von Tunzelmann, G.N. (1986), 'Malthus's Total Population System: a dynamic reinterpretation', in D. Coleman and R. Schofield (eds.), *The State of Population Theory: forward from Malthus*, Blackwell, Oxford, pp. 65–95.

von Tunzelmann, G.N. (1989), 'The supply side: technology and history', in Carlsson (1989a), *op. cit.*, pp. 55–84.

von Tunzelmann, N. (1991), 'Malthus's evolutionary model, expectations, and innovation', *Journal of Evolutionary Economics* **1**, pp. 273–91.

von Tunzelmann, N. (1992a), 'Exhaustibility of coal in long-run perspective', in J.E. Jacobsen and J.W. Firor (eds.), *Human Impact on the Environment*, Westview Press, Boulder, pp. 115–40.

von Tunzelmann, N. (1992b), 'The main trends of European economic history since the Second World War', in D.A. Dyker (ed.), *The European Economy*, Longman, London and New York, pp. 15–50.

von Tunzelmann, G.N. (1993), 'Technological and organizational change in industry during the Industrial Revolution', in P.K. O'Brien and R. Quinault (eds.), *The Industrial Revolution and British Society*, Cambridge University Press, Cambridge, pp. 254–82.

von Tunzelmann, N. (1994), 'Technology in the early nineteenth century', in Floud and McCloskey (1994), *op. cit.*, pp. 271–99.

von Tunzelmann, G.N. (1995), 'Time-saving technical change: the cotton industry in the English Industrial Revolution', *Explorations in Economic History* **32**, pp. 1–27.

von Weiszäcker, C.C. (1966), 'Tentative notes on a two-sector model with induced technical progress', *Review of Economic Studies* **33**, pp. 245–51.

Wade, R. (1990), *Governing the Market: economic theory and the role of government in East Asian industrialization*, Princeton University Press, Princeton NJ.

Walker, W., and Gardiner, J.P. (1980), 'Innovation and competitiveness in portable power tools', in K. Pavitt (ed.), *Technical Innovation and British*

Economic Performance, SPRU/Macmillan, London and Basingstoke, pp. 184–99.

Wallerstein, I. (1979), *The Capitalist World Economy: studies in modern capitalism*, Cambridge University Press, Cambridge.

Walsh, V. (1984), 'Invention and innovation in the chemical industry: demand pull or discovery push?', *Research Policy* **13**, pp. 211–34.

Walsh, W. (1975), *The Diffusion of Technological Change in the Pennsylvania Pig Iron Industry*, New York.

Webb, S.B. (1980), 'Tariffs, cartels, technology and growth in the German steel industry, 1879 to 1914', *Journal of Economic History* **40**, pp. 309–29.

Weber, M. (1927), *General Economic History* (transl. F.H. Knight), Greenberg, New York; ed. I.J. Cohen, Transaction Books, New Brunswick and London, 1981.

Westphal, L.E., Kim, L., and Dahlman, C.J. (1985), 'Reflections on the Republic of Korea's acquisition of technological capability', in Rosenberg and Frischtak (1985), *op. cit.*, pp. 167–221.

Williams, E.E. (1944), *Capitalism and Slavery*, North Carolina University Press, Chapel Hill NC.

Williams, K., Haslam, C., and Williams, J. (1993), 'The myth of the line: Ford's production of the Model T at Highland Park, 1909–16', *Business History* **35**, pp. 66–87.

Williamson, J.G. (1964), *American Growth and the Balance of Payments: a study of the long swing*, University of North Carolina Press, Chapel Hill.

Williamson, J.G. (1974), *Late 19th-Century American Development: a general equilibrium history*, Cambridge University Press,

Williamson, O.E. (1975), *Markets and Hierarchies: Analysis and Anti-trust Implications: a study in the economics of internal organization*, Free Press/Collier Macmillan, New York/London.

Williamson, O.E. (1985), *The Economic Institutions of Capitalism: firms, markets, relational contracting*, Free Press/Collier Macmillan, New York/London.

Williamson, O.E., and Winter, S.G. (eds.) (1993), *The Nature of the Firm: origins, evolution, and development*, Oxford University Press, New York and Oxford.

Wise, G. (1985), *Willis R. Whitney, General Electric, and the Origins of US Industrial Research*, Columbia University Press, New York.

Wolff, E. (1994), 'Technology, capital accumulation, and long-run growth', in Fagerberg *et al.* (1994), *op. cit.*, pp. 53–74.

Womack, J.P., Jones, D.T., and Roos, D. (1990), *The Machine that Changed the World: based on the MIT study of the future of the automobile*, Rawson, New York.

World Bank (1993), *The East Asian Miracle: economic growth and public policy*, World Bank, Washington.

Wren, D.A. (1983), 'American business philanthropy and higher education in the nineteenth century', *Business History Review* **57**, pp. 321–46.

Wright, G. (1990), 'The origins of American industrial success, 1879–1940', *American Economic Review* **80**, pp. 651–68.

Wrigley, E.A., and Schofield, R.S. (1981), *The Population History of England 1541–1871: a reconstruction*, Arnold, London.

Young, A. (1928), 'Increasing returns and economic progress', *Economic Journal* **38**, pp. 527–42.

Zaleski, E., Kozlowski, J.P., Wienert, H., Davies, R.W., Berry, M.J., and Amann, R. (1969), *Science Policy in the USSR*, OECD, Paris.

Zamagni, V. (1993), *The Economic History of Italy, 1860–1990* (transl. P. Barr), Clarendon Press, Oxford (Italian edn., Sta. Editrice Il Mulino, Bologna, 1990).

Zysman, J. (1983), *Governments, Markets, and Growth: financial systems and the politics of industrial change,* Cornell University Press/Martin Robertson, Oxford.

Zysman, J. (1993), 'Regional blocs, corporate strategies and government policies: the end of free trade?', in M. Humbert (ed.), *The Impact of Globalisation on Europe's Firms and Industries*, Pinter, London and New York, pp. 105–13.

Zysman, J. (1994), 'How institutions create historically rooted trajectories of growth', *Industrial and Corporate Change* **3**, pp. 243–83.

Index of Names

General notes: * = inventor or entrepreneur
** = company or organization
Footnote references are not separately distinguished.

Index of Places

Note: Major references are in bold type

Index of Subjects

Note: Specific innovations or products are indexed under the appropriate industries.